EFFECTIVE PUBLIC RELATIONS

SCOTT M. CUTLIP

Professor of Journalism
the University of Wisconsin

ALLEN H. CENTER

Vice President for Public Relations
Motorola, Inc.; Lecturer in Public Relations
Northwestern University

PRENTICE-HALL, INC., Englewood Cliffs, N.J.

EFFECTIVE PUBLIC RELATIONS

FOURTH EDITION

TO
ERNA
AND
NANCY

EFFECTIVE PUBLIC RELATIONS

SCOTT M. CUTLIP

ALLEN H. CENTER

FOURTH EDITION

© 1971, 1964, 1958, 1952 by Prentice-Hall, Inc. Englewood Cliffs, New Jersey

13–245027–5

Library of Congress Catalog No.: 76–141501

Printed in the United States of America

Current Printing:

10   9   8   7   6

PRENTICE-HALL INTERNATIONAL, INC., London

PRENTICE-HALL OF AUSTRALIA, PTY., LTD., Sydney

PRENTICE-HALL OF CANADA, LTD., Toronto

PRENTICE-HALL OF INDIA PRIVATE LIMITED, New Delhi

PRENTICE-HALL OF JAPAN, INC., Tokyo

Ivy Lee

Edward L. Bernays

AMONG THE PIONEERS

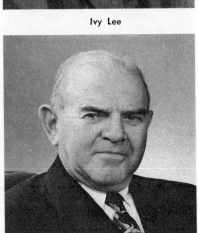

Carl Byoir

Paul Garrett

Arthur W. Page

John W. Hill

PREFACE

This launches the fourth edition of a book first published in 1952. In nineteen years this book has become the most widely used textbook in this field. It has been published in Italian, Korean, and Spanish editions and has been used around the world to introduce a generation of practitioners to this challenging and essential calling.

When the first edition appeared, the field of public relations was mushrooming; its function was not clearly defined, and its essentiality was not fully accepted. Today, the growth has slowed to a solid, steady gait. The function has diversified, yet it is more clearly defined and more widely understood. Today the essentiality of this function is seldom questioned in a time when the world suffers from conflicts in which confrontation all too often displaces communication. As society continues to become more massive, more impersonal, and more segmented, the need for public relations grows. The practitioners, individually and collectively, have made progress in improving their competence and in raising the ethical level of their work. This is reflected in the accreditation programs of the Public Relations Society of America and the Canadian Public Relations Society. The growing number of college and university teachers in public relations has had a major role in these advances. These two decades have brought much progress in public relations; there is need for more. The authors hope that their efforts continue to contribute to this progress.

Though the book has changed greatly over the years, our objective has remained constant. As stated in the first edition, it is:

> We have endeavored to be comprehensive in our approach, yet not to be trapped into an "umbrella" concept of the public relations function. The content focuses on the role of the practitioner as a specialist in communications, an analyst of public opinion, and a counselor to administrators in these areas. Behavioristic study of the function will demonstrate that these tasks comprise the responsibilities delegated to most practitioners. There is need to concentrate more on the matters in which the practitioner may lay justified claim as a specialist. There is ample challenge within this area for the best talent we can muster without ranging far afield for worlds to conquer. We have tried to point this up by dealing with two aspects generally neglected—the *ecology* and the *evolution* of this specialized administrative staff function.

The book has been thoroughly and carefully revised for this edition. Rapid-fire, far-reaching developments of recent years required nothing less in what proved to be a two-year project. We have tried to make it more relevant to the tasks confronting today's practitioner. Problems occasioned by technological advance, social unrest, and major shifts in public opinion are interwoven. We have emphasized the need for more effort in monitoring the public opinion environment and less on publicity-getting.

We have added chapters on Corporate Public and Urban Affairs and on Trade Associations, Professional Societies, and Labor Unions to reflect the growth of the practice in these areas. We have endeavored to reflect the maturity of the calling and to include the fruits of experience and research accumulated in this field over these two decades. The Case Problems, which many teachers have found useful, have been retained and revised. The supplementary readings, based on Scott Cutlip's continuing bibliographic research, have been updated. Fresh examples of the practice have been woven into the text to illustrate principles and procedures.

The rapid growth of public relations around the world during the past fifteen years is reflected in a chapter updated by the lecture trips the authors have made abroad in recent years. The increased public scrutiny of the impact of public relations on our society and the redoubled efforts of practitioners to police their ranks are given more adequate attention in this edition.

New developments, new tools, and new problems in the practice are also covered more thoroughly. Nonetheless, the basic organization and philosophic approach which characterized the earlier editions have been retained because of widespread endorsement by our fellow teachers and practitioners.

The authors know full well that no textbook can be more effective than those who translate it for students. We believe that those who teach public relations should be singled out, applauded, and encouraged. They have done much to shape this vocation and to advance its ethics and its competence. For these reasons we wish to salute the teachers who have provided us thoughtful suggestions for the book's improvement. Similarly, we owe a debt to the many students who have volunteered reactions to the book by letter or in conversations in many parts of the world.

The authors have incurred a heavy debt to many people for friendly encouragement, wise counsel, and information generously provided over these nineteen years. Some have been acknowledged in earlier editions; only a few new debts contracted in preparing this edition can be acknowledged here.

There are a number of individuals who have earned a public salute for important contributions to this Fourth Edition. Scott Cutlip wants to acknowledge with gratitude the help of: Alvo Albini of Loyola University,

Chicago; Anand Akerkar, Director Consilium International, Bombay, India; Robert J. Doyle, Wisconsin Universities system; Professor Wayne L. Hodges, Cornell University; George F. Hamel, Fairfax County Public Schools; Byron DeHaan, Caterpillar, Inc.; Professor Harish Jain, McMaster University; Olle Kellerman, Skandia Insurance, Stockholm; John W. Leslie, American College Public Relations Association; Roy J. Leffingwell of Honolulu and his associates in the International Public Relations Group; Professor Robert Lindsay, University of Minnesota; Lt. Col. Dan J. Maguire and Col. George Moranda, United States Army; Vice-President Michael Radock, University of Michigan; Irving L. Rimer, American Cancer Society; Rea Smith, PRSA; Shirley Smith, Association-Sterling Films; Professor Walter W. Seifert, Ohio State University; Professor Raymond Simon of Utica College, Syracuse University; Harold N. Weiner, National Public Relations Council for Health and Welfare Services; Miss Elma Williams of the National Education Association; Roy K. Wilson, National School Public Relations Association; and Bernard E. Ury, Chisago counselor. A special debt of gratitude is owed to a colleague and friend, Professor Douglas C. Jones of the University of Wisconsin, who helps at every bend in the road. Last but far from least is the debt owed Erna F. Cutlip who has worked faithfully in partnership on this enterprise since it was undertaken two decades ago.

Allen Center wishes to acknowledge the helpful contributions of time and information by John T. Geoghegan, Lawrence S. Waddell, and James Beall, American Gas Assn.; Robert L. McHale, American Trucking Assn.; Joseph W. LaBine, Continental Illinois Bank; James B. Watt, Bank Marketing Assn.; Carl F. Hawver, National Consumer Finance Assn.; J. Carroll Bateman, Insurance Information Institute; Theodore H. Pincus, The Financial Relations Board; Oscar Beveridge, Beveridge, Penney & Bennett; Professor Walter W. Seifert, Ohio State University; Albert J. Zack, American Federation of Labor-Congress of Industrial Organizations; and Robert W. Taft, Hill and Knowlton, Inc.

Both of us owe a special debt to Miss Mary Ann Yodelis, Ph.D. candidate at the University of Wisconsin, who painstakingly checked and corrected the completed manuscript. She saved us from many a mistake. We are also indebted to Professor Daniel Pliskin of Fairleigh Dickinson University for his constructive criticisms of this revision.

SCOTT M. CUTLIP
ALLEN H. CENTER

CONTENTS

ECOLOGY—
THE ENVIRONMENT   *97*

6

PERSUASION AND PUBLIC OPINION   *123*

7

THE FUNCTION'S PLACE AND PURPOSE   *154*

8

THE PROCESS:
FACT-FINDING AND FEEDBACK—
THE FIRST STEP   *185*

9

THE PROCESS:
PLANNING AND PROGRAMMING—
THE SECOND STEP 213

10

THE PROCESS:
ACTION AND COMMUNICATION—
THE THIRD STEP 236

11

THE PROCESS:
EVALUATION—
THE FOURTH STEP 263

12

THE TOOLS OF COMMUNICATION 280

18

THE PRACTICE:
PUBLIC RELATIONS FOR BUSINESS 429

19

THE PRACTICE:
CORPORATE PUBLIC AND URBAN AFFAIRS
—EMERGING FUNCTIONS 447

20

THE PRACTICE:
CORPORATE FINANCIAL RELATIONS 463

21

THE PRACTICE:
TRADE ASSOCIATIONS,
PROFESSIONAL SOCIETIES,
AND LABOR UNIONS   *486*

22

THE PRACTICE:
WELFARE AGENCIES, HOSPITALS, AND CHURCHES   *501*

23

THE PRACTICE:
GOVERNMENTS AND CITIZENS   *528*

24

THE PRACTICE:
PUBLIC SCHOOLS   *560*

25

THE PRACTICE:
HIGHER EDUCATION 585

26

THE PRACTICE:
THE ARMED FORCES 607

27

THE PRACTICE:
PUBLIC RELATIONS AROUND THE WORLD 634

28

TOWARD A PROFESSION 658

CHAPTER 1

CONTEMPORARY PUBLIC RELATIONS— AN INTRODUCTION

Public relations is the planned effort to influence opinion through socially responsible performance based on mutually satisfactory two-way communication.

Public relations, as a management concept and as a staff function, has grown rapidly over the past four decades. This rapid development comes as a result of the increasing complexity of modern society, increased power of public opinion, and the growing insights into what motivates individuals and groups. Gaining the support and cooperation of others through persuasion is part of the day-by-day work of every organization—government agencies, business firms, labor unions, universities, and welfare agencies. Public relations became a commonplace term in the language and thought of twentieth-century America. It is an important factor in contemporary decision making.

The essentiality of public relations is beyond debate in a world bound together by interdependence and swift communications yet split by recurring crises of change and confrontation. Even so, the term is not always precisely defined. Though the dimensions of the mature concept are clear, public relations is still defining itself. Its function varies from organization to organization. A wide variety of activities parades under the banner. There is still some difference between the function as defined in textbooks and the function as practiced. The literature and shoptalk of the craft are filled with an abundance of definitions. Some lack universality; others are too broad. Many define public relations as it ought to be, not as it often is. Nonetheless, the fundamentals of a mature, accepted concept are emerging.

It must be emphasized at the outset that public relations concepts and their implementation do not constitute a panacea for all problems; some conflicts will not yield to public relations solutions. On occasion the practice is held out as a cure-all for the ills and problems which confront organizations and individuals. Florida officials urge an oil company to launch a public relations program to overcome opposition to offshore drilling. Tavern owners are warned to "avoid mistakes in public relations or be voted out of business." Industrial executives are advised that "sound public relations is the only salvation of free enterprise." Union members are exhorted to improve their public relations if they are to stave off anti-union legislation. Conservationists are counseled that "wildlife management cannot function in America without public support achieved through public relations."

2

On the other hand, public relations is scorned by some as press-agentry or worse. An editor tells his readers: "If you want to get plausible disguises for unworthy causes, hire a public relations expert." Professor-author Mark Van Doren once said, "Public relations is the curse of our times. It could be a sign of a very deep disease." [1] A newspaper columnist wrote that "public relations is only an aristocratic term for publicity or press-agentry." A major U.S. newspaper called public relations "a parasite on the press." As recently as 1970 *Barron's* headlined an article: "Flack's Progress. Public Relations Has Improved Its Own Image on Wall Street." Such charges and terms are generally unfounded or outmoded. However, the exploits of the unscrupulous and the shortcomings of the incompetent tend to give such accusations validity. The unfavorable stereotype is reinforced when *Life* publicizes a counsel who says he can elect a person to office if he has "$60,000, an I.Q. of at least 120, and can keep his mouth shut." [2] A lawyer familiar with this field has observed: "The ethical public relations man must live with the image of the historic figure of the circus press agent on the one hand and with the reality of some high pressure charlatans on the other." [3]

Public relations thinking has served to deepen the sense of social responsibility in our public enterprises. It has contributed to public welfare. It has improved the communications required in our society. It has brought to public notice the ills and needs of our society. *Public relations thinking is a requirement for every successful administrator*. Discussing the requirements of the presidency, Peter Drucker asserts: "All our effective presidents were experts at public relations, untiring propagandists for themselves and their ideas." The power the president has acquired in this century illustrates the potential, the necessity, and the impact of contemporary practice. Today he sets the legislative agenda using leverage acquired through public support. The president is peculiarly dependent upon the news media for his power. The power of Lyndon B. Johnson in 1964 and his fall from power in 1968 make the point. Public relations' impact on society is seen in the shift in power in our government flowing from Presidential use of this expertise. [4]

Distortions and disfavor cloud the term *public relations,* as indicated in a study made by Blaine K. McKee. He found that in a random forty-eight news mentions of this field, thirty-four were neutral, eleven unfavorable in connotation, and only three favorable. To encourage a positive

---

[1] "The Arts and Uses of Public Relations," *Time Magazine* essay, July 7, 1967.

[2] Robert Wernick, "The Perfect Candidate," *Life*, Vol. 60, June 3, 1966, p. 41. Close-up of Hal Evry who dubs himself a "political counselor."

[3] Mark Richardson, *The Antitrust Bulletin*, Vol. 10, July–August, 1965, p. 511.

[4] For illuminating discussion of these points, see Elmer L. Cornwell, Jr., *Presidential Leadership of Public Opinion* (Bloomington: Indiana University Press, 1965).

view of this essential function, those in it must continue the advance toward professionalism and weed out the unethical and incompetent.[5] Only as the status of public relations is enhanced, can it recruit into its ranks the talented, ethical specialists today's society urgently requires. There is also need for a wider understanding that public relations does not constitute a handy umbrella to protect an institution against a storm of unfavorable public opinion and that it requires a high order of expertise. The hard fact is, despite its seventy years as an identifiable vocation, public relations remains a nasty word to some administrators, a confused concept to others. It is also an inescapable fact that the work of many practitioners is based on outmoded practices of the 1920s. Why this should remain so in a day of communication chasms that lead to conflict and confrontation is difficult to explain.

A PROBLEM OF SEMANTICS

That the term *public relations* is used in at least three different senses— and often interchangeably with *information, communications,* and *public affairs*—adds to the confusion. Holding that *public relations* is an artificial term, L.L.L. Golden suggests that the field would be better understood if the term, *relations with the public,* were used. "Then it would be seen clearly that the relations of the corporation or university or trade union or other organization to the public is what is meant. It would become clear that "public" means every group or segment with which the institution has relations . . . employees, customers, suppliers, stockholders, communities, governments, and academics." [6] The senses in which *public relations* is used are: (1) relationships with individuals or groups which compose an institution's publics; (2) the ways and means used to achieve favorable relationships with these sub-publics; (3) the quality or status of an institution's relationships. This one term, *public relations,* cannot be used to label both *means* and *ends* without creating confusion. The synonyms— *information, communications,* and *public affairs*—have come into increasing use in recent years as titles for this function. *Information* is used in government to describe the functions as a means of avoiding legislative criticism. *University relations* is a title often used in higher education. All embrace essentially the same function.

Clarity will replace confusion, in part, if the term is restricted to describing *the planned effort to influence opinion through socially responsible and acceptable performance, based on mutually satisfactory two-way*

[5] "Public Relations—Its Connotations in Newspaper Usage," *Public Relations Journal,* Vol. 24, July, 1968, p. 25.

[6] "The Difficult Years," *Saturday Review,* May 10, 1968, p. 79.

communication. Other needs for the term will be met if an institution's relations with various publics are labeled *public relationships.* Little is to be gained by creating artificial terms to describe this function. This text will use the term *public relations* to encompass the performance and communications used to build profitable *relationships with the public.* Incidentally, although the term *public relations* is plural, it is used in the singular.

CURRENT DEFINITIONS

What, then, are the current definitions? *Webster's New International Dictionary,* Third Edition, defines public relations as: [7]

1. The promotion of rapport and goodwill between a person, firm, or institution and other persons, special publics, or the community at large through the distribution of interpretative material, the development of neighborly interchange, and the assessment of public reaction.
2. (a) the degree of understanding and good will achieved between and individual, organization, or institution and the public. (b) the application of the techniques for achieving this relationship.
3. (a) the art or science of developing reciprocal understanding and goodwill. (b) the professional staff entrusted with this task.

Public relations is often confused with and used as a handy synonym for some of its functional parts, such as publicity, press-agentry, public affairs, propaganda, and institutional advertising. These may be parts of the whole of public relations, but none of the parts equals the whole. Reflection on these definitions will make it clear that, thus defined, publicity, press-agentry, propaganda, and advertising become tools or subfunctions of public relations, not its equivalent. For example, when someone in Indian headdress sends up the smoke signal "Give" on Michigan Avenue during a Red Cross fund campaign, this is not public relations. It is an act of press-agentry, although it may be part of a public relations program.

The International Public Relations Association defines the practice in this way:

> Public relations is a management function, of a continuing and planned character, through which public and private organizations and institutions seek to win and retain the understanding, sympathy and sup-

[7] By permission. From *Webster's Third New International Dictionary.* Copyright © 1966 by G. & C. Merriam Company, publishers of the Merriam-Webster dictionaries.

port of those with whom they are or may be concerned—by evaluating public opinion about themselves, in order to correlate, as far as possible, their own policies and procedures, to achieve by planned and widespread information more productive cooperation and more efficient fulfillment of their common interests.

The British Institute of Public Relations defines the function as: "The deliberate, planned and sustained effort to establish and maintain mutual understanding between an organization and its publics."

Implicit in these definitions is the threefold function of the professional practitioner (1) to ascertain and evaluate public opinion as it relates to his organization, (2) to counsel executives on ways of dealing with public opinion as it exists, and (3) to use communication to influence public opinion. Reduced to simple terms, the practitioner is the middleman in a continuously circulating pattern of communication.[8]

This function may be illustrated by the way a major public relations agency, Carl Byoir & Associates, describes its work: [9]

1. *Analysis* . . . of policies and objectives of the client . . . of relationships with various publics, including employees, customers, dealers, shareholders, the financial community, government and the press (with continuing research to keep the analysis up to date).
2. *Planning and Programming* . . . of specific undertakings and projects in which public relations techniques can be employed to help attain the objectives through effective communication between the client and its publics.
3. *Implementation* . . . of the programs and projects by maximum and effective use of all avenues of communication, internal and external, to create understanding and stimulate action.

Sound relationships with the public over time are compounded of *performance* that satisfies the public and communication of such satisfactory performance. This fundamental principle has been long expressed in public relations literature by using the formula:

X (the Deed) plus Y (the way the deed is interpreted) $=$ Public Attitudes.

This formula is grounded in the fundamental fact that we often are more influenced by the way an event is interpreted than we are by the

---

[8] For another concept see practitioner Robert O. Carlson's definition in "Public Relations," *International Encyclopedia of the Social Sciences* (New York: The Macmillan Company & The Free Press, 1968), pp. 208–217.

[9] For way large agencies work in serving clients, see T. A. Wise, "Hill and Knowlton's World of Images," *Fortune*, Vol. 76, September 1, 1967. A useful article though marred by some inaccuracies.

event itself. The act of a steel company's raising prices can be interpreted as a necessary move to insure adequate profits or it can be interpreted as a harmful act inducing inflation. The United States' war in Vietnam was defended by its spokesmen as a fight against Communism and damned by its critics as an unwarranted intervention in a nation's civil war. Much of the public relations practitioner's effort goes into putting the best possible interpretation on the acts and views of those identified with his institution —acts which these persons undertake in pursuit of the organization's mission.

Fundamentally, it is the performance of those identified with an organization—the army's soldiers, the university's students, the corporation's employees, *e.g.*—as they carry out the organization's objectives that eventually culminates in public attitudes toward the organization.[10] This is shown in the chart on this page. Events, coupled with their interpretation, move public opinion. For example: When the Chinese Communists attacked

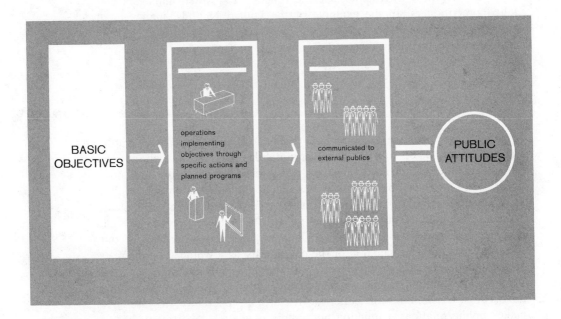

India on October 20, 1962, public opinion in India underwent a rapid and radical change toward the United States. Opinion in Delhi was sampled

10 For evidence, see study by Research Department, Batten, Barton, Durstine, & Osborn, Inc., *How Public Attitudes Influence Corporate Profits, 1969.* Study showed that if consumers think a company "cares about the public interest" they will willingly pay more for its products, pay a higher price for its stock, and that such companies enjoy a high price/earnings ratio.

for the U.S.I.A. one week before, and again five weeks after the Chinese attack. In this six-week period esteem for the United States rose from 34 to 89 per cent.[11] Landing men on the moon dramatically communicated to all on earth the courage of America's astronauts and the ability of her scientists.

Much of the confusion cited earlier will be cleared away if we understand the distinction between public relations as an *operating concept of management* and public relations as a *specialized staff function* serving management.

The first is a general operating principle or philosophy which guides administrators, to a greater or lesser degree. For example, the decision of the United Nations that "the activities of the Department of Public Information should be so organized and directed as to promote . . . an informed understanding of the work and purposes of the United Nations among the peoples of the world . . ." is *management policy*.

The second is a dynamic, specific function for which managers hire skilled practitioners. In the example of the United Nations, management policy is implemented by specialists who are "equipped to analyze trends," "provide all the services for the daily, weekly, and periodical press . . ." etc.

THE MANAGEMENT CONCEPT

In today's interdependent society, all institutions are vested with public responsibilities. They must accept accountability for all of their actions that affect others. Full acceptance by public enterprises—profit and non-profit alike—of their obligations to those sections of the public whom they serve or affect is far from realized. But the trend in this direction is clear. As one of the nation's business leaders put it: "We know perfectly well that business does not function by divine right but, like any other part of our society, exists with the sanction of the community as a whole. The interests of the community are in turn expressed through governments. . . . Today's public opinion, though it may appear as light as air, may become tomorrow's legislation—for better or for worse. Therefore, a wise firm makes public relations a function not simply of a staff department, but of top management—so that every major business decision is considered from the standpoint of its public impact." His words are dramatically illustrated

11 Thomas C. Sorensen, *The Word War* (New York: Harper & Row, 1968), p. 163. This is one of several books describing the work of the United States Information Agency, this nation's public relations agency to provide exchange of ideas and information with other peoples of the world.

by the successful advocacy of national automobile safety legislation by Ralph Nader.[12]

For the progress toward an increased sense of social responsibility in contemporary management, practitioners deserve much credit. This enlightened management concept has emerged slowly, unevenly, over the past several decades in response to the ability of our citizens to express themselves in the market place, in the polling booth, and through countervailing power blocs. Recognition of public as well as corporate or institutional responsibility is manifested in the adoption of a public relations point of view. This can best be termed *public relations thinking.*

Such thinking finds expression in this typical remark of a corporation executive: "At least half our time is taken up with discussing the repercussions of what we propose to do." Once embraced, the concept gathers strength as it goes. The more an organization woos the public, the more the public expects to be courted. And what one organization does, its competitors must match if they are to be successful in the spirited struggle for public favor. *Responsible performance on the part of a corporation, governmental agency, or nonprofit organization is the foundation of sound public relationships.* Public relationships, in these broad terms, are the responsibility of an organization's directing executives, not of its staff or line specialists. Nonetheless, the 1970's public relations man should be the catalyst for social programs, not merely the specialist who publicizes them; yet it must be firmly emphasized that the *specialist is employed to advise and assist management, not to manage.*

THE FUNCTIONAL CONCEPT

In the trend to conglomerate, farflung, impersonal organizations, American public enterprises have outgrown the directive capacities of any one man or small group of men. Today's administrator requires the assistance and counsel of a host of skilled specialists and consultants if he is to manage at all. The public relations officer or consultant is one of these. He is chosen by top management:

1. To facilitate and insure an inflow of representative opinions from an organization's several publics so that its policies and operations

---

[12] This landmark case study in public relations is discussed in two excellent articles: Dan Cordtz, "The Face in the Mirror at General Motors," *Fortune,* Vol. 78, August, 1966; Robert L. Bishop and Jane Kilburn, "Penny Whistle or Public's Advocate," *Public Relations Quarterly,* Vol. 12, Winter, 1968. For the book that shook an industry, see Nader's *Unsafe at Any Speed* (New York: Grossman Publishers, Inc., 1965).

may be kept compatible with the diverse needs and views of these publics.

2. To counsel management on ways and means of shaping an organization's policies and operations to gain maximum public acceptance.

3. To devise and implement programs that will gain wide and favorable interpretations of an organization's policies and operations.

America's growing need for men and women with the special talents to perform these tasks is being met in any one or a combination of three ways. We have (1) the fulltime staff official on the organization's payroll, who, with the aid of assistants, serves the employer exclusively; (2) the independent counselor, who maintains his own offices and staff to serve a number of clients with non-conflicting interests; (3) the advertising agency that provides counseling and service either through a subsection in the agency or through a subsidiary firm.

The internal staff department represents the dominant pattern. However, whether the service is supplied by staff on the organization's payroll, by outside counselors, or by a combination, the function is much the same.

IMPLICATIONS OF THE DEFINITION

The common purpose of all that is labeled public relations is to influence public opinion. There can be no escape in today's world from the grinding wheels of public attitudes. The increased power of public opinion, and recognition of that power, constitute one of the mainsprings propelling the function. This is the era of "The Public Be Pleased." More than ever, "the genius of the people must be consulted." No individual, no institution, can long prosper without public support or, at least, without public sufferance. Faith in the good sense of the people is the foundation of intelligent contemporary thinking and practice.

The practice of public relations is predicated on the belief that *only an informed public can be a wise public.* One of the basic precepts is: "People are essentially rational by nature; they respond to facts and want the truth; and they will ultimately find it and act upon it." There is abundant evidence in American history to sustain this faith.[13] Yet this precept is open to question.

Satisfying the public interest to the mutual advantage of all parties in conflict is a prerequisite to profitable public relationships. Arriving at mutual interests requires public-minded performance and satisfactory two-

---

[13] For this point of view, see William Lydgate, *What America Thinks* (New York: Thomas Y. Crowell Company, 1944). For opposite view, see Nicholas Samstag, *Persuasion for Profit* (Norman, Okla.: University of Oklahoma Press, 1957).

way communication. The basic problem is to adjust the institution to the climate of social change in a way that will serve both the public and private interests insofar as this is possible. The practitioner, in his role of communicator and interpreter, makes a vital contribution to this process. The practitioner is expected to counsel his institution on the social changes, coming now with breath-taking rapidity. He must creatively search for means of adapting to these changes. For example, ponder the problems posed for the nationwide store chain in adapting to an integrated way of life in the South, the problems created by the advent of television and its influence on our life style, or the psychological implications of automation; or consider the problems posed for federal and state governments by the mushrooming needs of education, poverty, urban renewal, health care, pollution abatement, transportation, worldwide starvation, and recreation.

A sure, sensitive reading of the changing environment can be the practitioner's most valuable service to his organization. Anticipating and preparing to meet problems before they explode in crisis is a prime responsibility. That some practitioners do not measure up to this responsibility was shown in the way institutions were caught flat-footed by the Civil Rights Revolution of the 1960s. Robert L. Bishop asserts, with validity, "most public relations offices are still publicity bureaus." To discern the trends and forces at work in society requires a broadly educated person. Public relations is not sailing with the winds of public opinion but rather navigating an institution through them. The practitioner is not the captain of the ship but rather the navigator who reads the stars, winds, and tides of public opinion for management. There is challenge and satisfaction for the practitioner who uses the channels of communication to eliminate conflict and build bridges of understanding so that a complex, enterprising nation can stay on its course as it approaches its 200th year and the Twenty-first Century.

THE DAY-BY-DAY PRACTICE

Daily practice consists of a multitude of little tasks and a few big tasks. It is the application of common sense, common courtesy, and common decency. It can be doing favors for others. It can be pleading a cause in the arena of public opinion. It can be entertaining a visitor. It can be preparing a speech or giving one. It can be a news conference or the dedication of a new building. It can be as important as providing counsel that leads management out of a tight strike situation. It can be helping a newsman get his story from a press-shy executive. It can be writing a letter to a hurt, irate parent whose son has been expelled from college. To show the immense variety, here are some actual examples.

To remind the nation of the progress and the increased costs in commercial aviation, Trans World Airlines marked the thirtieth anniversary of its all-air transcontinental passenger service by once again flying a Ford tri-motor airplane over the initial route. The ancient Ford plane lumbered along at 110 miles an hour, taking 36 hours to complete a trip made by today's jet in some four hours.

To dramatize the spirit of American Thanksgiving, the U.S. Ambassador to Ecuador invited 250 workers and their families to a Thanksgiving dinner at a Y.M.C.A. in a workers' district of Quito. Six hundred persons were served dinner by American Girl Scouts, Brownies, and Boy Scouts. The Ambassador read the President's proclamation and explained the meaning of Thanksgiving and America's desire to share its abundance with all peoples. The event, planned by the Ambassador's information officer, was recorded for rebroadcast over Ecuador's radio stations, the main channel of communications in a nation where illiteracy is common.

Allis Chalmers, a manufacturer of heavy equipment, dealt with problem drinkers among employees by trying to rehabilitate them rather than to weed them out. Communication was established in two ways. The company hired a psychologist, himself a rehabilitated alcoholic, to counsel those who sought help. Supervisors were taught to treat alcoholism as an illness and to coax victims toward the counselor. This dramatized the firm's concern for its employees.

When the Imperial Hotel in Tokyo, Japan, announced plans to raze its old structure, built in 1922 and designed by Frank Lloyd Wright, to make way for a new skyscraper hotel-office building, an unanticipated storm of protest arose in Japan and abroad. Groups organized to save the world-famous structure. The press was crowded with letters and editorials urging that destruction be stopped. The hotel corporation agreed to help finance rebuilding of the main entrance and part of the lobby at Meiji Village, a repository for Western structures built during the Meiji Era. This mollified the critics.

In 1963, the Swedish Parliament voted to change Sweden's traffic from left-hand to right-hand driving. This change was effected in September, 1967, with a minimum of difficulty and a reduction, not increase, in auto accidents. The successful switch was made possible because of the $5-million public relations and advertising campaign that paved the way for this drastic change in driving-walking habits. A research group prepared sixty reports and guiding memoranda. These were used as the basis of an imaginative, intensive educational effort that saturated every channel of communication and reached every person in Sweden.[14]

---

[14] For details, see A.R. Roalman, "How Sweden Won The Big Traffic Battle," *Public Relations Journal*, Vol. 24, February, 1968.

Reflecting America's belief in the open society, the United States National Aeronautics and Space Administration (N.A.S.A.) provides the world's news media with facts, pictures, and facilities—enabling newsmen to report fully and at first hand on America's manned space flights.

Concerned about students' negative attitudes toward business careers, the chairmen of Goodyear, Dow Chemical and Motorola engaged in spirited exchanges of letters with bright students. Both sides of the dialogue concerning the role of business in society were published during alternate weeks in forty-eight campus daily papers.

THE ORGANIZED PRACTICE

(1) PRESS-AGENTRY

There are no firm, fixed lines separating what are popularly termed press-agentry, product promotion, and product publicity. The emphasis, the objective, and the approach used largely determine how a particular publicity activity is classified. Press-agentry was born in the entertainment and political worlds of the nineteenth century. It still flourishes, though with less outright fakery than formerly. One of its commonest forms involves arranging for a person or product to be seen in association with celebrities—in a photograph with a motion-picture star, for example, or as a give-away prize on a television program. In the orchestra of public relations, press-agentry represents the brass section. Mae Lyons, former press agent for Ringling Bros. & Barnum & Bailey Combined Shows, Inc., says, however, "The circus drumbeater now plays all instruments in the public relations band." She adds, ". . . there is more to circus public relations than exaggerated fibbing. There is far more to it than a story and picture in the newspapers." [15] Jim Moran, another well-known press agent, says that "It is the fun part of the business."

The term and practice have become tainted. *The aim of the press agent is more to attract attention than to gain understanding.* Press-agentry is a necessary activity in the box-office worlds of circuses, theaters, movies, night clubs, resorts, hotels, and commercial sports. It adds drama but adds little stature and little value to the ultimate public relations aims. That many press agents, to achieve respectability, assume the title of "counselor" does not alter this fact. In the candid words of a Hollywood press agent: "We stoop to anything, but our stuff gets printed." A rock group's earning

---

[15] "Ringling's Public Relations Director 'Speaks' to Children of All Ages," *Public Relations Journal*, Vol. 19, April, 1963. For a candid look at the work of a Broadway press agent, see Richard Maney, *Fanfare* (New York: Harper & Row, 1957).

power may be more a tribute to the skill of its press agent than to its exceptional music ability.

Press-agentry might best be illustrated by the success of the late Steve Hannagan. He built monuments to his skill and to the power of press-agentry in making the Memorial Day auto races at Indianapolis a national event and in making Miami Beach and Sun Valley internationally known resorts.[16] Current examples of press-agentry are to be found in your daily newspaper under the datelines of Hollywood, Las Vegas, Miami Beach, and Monte Carlo. The many "beauty queens" are tools of press-agentry: Miss America, Miss Tuna Fish, Miss National Press Photog, Miss Rheingold, Miss Universe, and Miss Swim For Health.

(2) PRODUCT PROMOTION

Public relations staffs serve and support an organization's line and staff functions. In business, this includes support of marketing. Counselor Bernard Ury suggests: "If properly understood, organized, and budgeted by the marketing executive and applied by professionals, public relations techniques can make a direct and powerful contribution to better marketing." Marketing support is supplied mainly by product promotion, but in this day of articulate consumerism, marketers needs counsel on the public relations impact of their marketing techniques.

Today's practitioners in industry define product publicity as a going part of the job. In some cases, it becomes almost the whole job. Some businessmen will argue that the product-publicity task might be more effectively assigned to sales and marketing. The basic public relations function is to build confidence in the maker of the products, which will contribute to the sale of goods. Yet the proper publicizing of a product can contribute as helpfully to building a corporate image as other public relations methods.

Product publicity is an important aspect of today's product promotion. Because of the skills and the knowledge of news media required in this task, this work is usually assigned to the public relations department. The work of many counseling firms and advertising agency departments is mainly involved with getting a free ride for the products in the news media. This is a service which corporate staffs often provide to the marketing-sales staffs in the same way that they provide employee communications counsel

[16] For background on Hannagan, see "Steve Hannagan Is Dead in Africa," *New York Times,* February 6, 1953, p. 19; "Steve Hannagan," *Current Biography,* Vol. 5, August, 1944, pp. 29–31; "Prince of Press Agents," *Collier's,* Vol. 120, November 22, 1947, p. 75ff; and "For the Defense, Steve Hannagan," *Public Relations Journal,* Vol. 26, August, 1970.

to the industrial relations department or community relations counsel to plant management.

Product promotion is most heavily used in the fields of fashions, foods, home furnishings, cars, appliances and travel. One of the outstanding product promotions of this generation has been making "The Coffee Break" a fixed habit. Many other examples can be found in daily newspapers—articles promoting wall-to-wall carpeting in homes or, the opposite, open, waxed hardwood floors; articles suggesting a return to overhead lighting fixtures in the home; articles promoting the use of new synthetic fabrics in clothing or a revival of cotton.[17]

(3) PUBLICITY

Corporate nonproduct publicity and all the information output of governmental agencies, schools, nonprofit welfare agencies, and similar organizations are generally lumped under the elastic term *publicity*. Publicity to build a favorable image and understanding of a concern or agency is one of several tools. *It is not the whole of public relations.* Publicity takes the form of reporting an institution's or industry's day-by-day activities deemed newsworthy. This would include the earnings of a corporation, the progress of a Girl Scout fund drive, scientific findings from the nation's latest space flight by the National Aeronautics and Space Administration, and the return to duty of an ailing Congressman. Publicity also results from the staging of more or less newsworthy events, such as ground-breakings, dedications, anniversary celebrations, and seminars.

The confusion of the publicity tool with the broader practice of public relations is understandable. The practice, in part, has evolved from publicity. Much of contemporary practice is still concerned with publicity.[18] Many practitioners do little else. They are more accurately titled "information men" or "publicity men." There is a legitimate need for the publicist or information practitioner. This practitioner is most often found working in governmental agencies, the military forces, social agencies, and fund-raising campaigns.

(4) LOBBYING

The term lobbying has become an ugly word and is often inferred as the manipulation of government for selfish interests. Yet the right freely to

---

17 For examples, James E. Burke, "A Look at Product Public Relations," *Public Relations Journal*, Vol. 17, May, 1961.

18 For affirmation on this point, see Bishop-Kilburn article cited in fn. 11.

petition our government is a constitutional right of every citizen, every organization. Public relations, by definition and practice, often embraces lobbying. Washington, D.C., and the state capitals are centers of such activities. This phase may include: (1) getting information from government officials; (2) persuasively informing government officials; (3) promoting legislative or administrative action for an organization or against an adverse interest; (4) obtaining governmental cooperation or sponsorship, such as a governor's proclamation of Fire Prevention Week.

Every firm and organization today has a host of relationships with the proliferating number of governmental agencies and activities. These relationships require the skills of opinion analysis, mediation, and communication. Relationships with government once were almost wholly the work of lawyers. Today this task is being shared. The registered list of lobbyists in the nation's capital and in state capitals where such registration is required carries names of many well-known practitioners. When the practitioner is engaged exclusively in government relations, he will continue to be called "lobbyist" by popular usage, however distasteful the term.

Trade associations are major employers of public relations specialists. Much of the work for these interest groups involves lobbying. The railroads, airlines, and buslines all lobby to persuade lawmakers and voters that their mode of transportation deserves preferential consideration. Each will say, with logic and eloquence, that it serves the public interest first.[19]

Most practitioners are primarily engaged in the increasingly important task of building public support for issues and institutions in the voting precincts. Taking your case to the people, as Ivy Lee discerned long ago, is the most effective kind of lobbying. It is important that the practitioner know when he crosses the line from straight public relations into lobbying as defined by law. The Federal government and twenty-seven states require lobbyists to register and to report their activities and expenditures. Enforcement of the Federal act has been lax and many loopholes in it have been found; enforcement of state laws varies.[20]

---

[19] For discussion of this aspect of public relations, see Bert Goss, "PR Is Not Lobbying," *PR*, Vol. 1, July, 1956; Robert L. L. McCormick, "The Anatomy of Public Relations in Washington," *PR*, Vol. 2, January, 1957; Morris Victor Rosenbloom, "Effective Public Relations with Washington, D. C.," *Public Relations Quarterly*, Summer, 1967. For best documented case detailing use of public relations to influence legislation, see *Noerr Motor Freight, Inc., et al. v. Eastern Railroad Presidents Conference, et al.* in *Federal Supplement*, Vol. 155, December 23, 1957, pp. 768–841; 273 F. 2d 218 (1959); 81 *Supreme Court Reporter*, 523, February 20, 1961. For two long-term public relations-lobbying efforts to influence government, see two books by Richard Harris: *Silent Voice* details efforts of drug manufacturers to blunt regulation; *The Sacred Trust* recounts campaign of American Medical Association to block government health insurance.

[20] For discussion of legal aspects of lobbying, see Morton J. Simon, *Public Relations Law* (New York: Appleton-Century-Crofts, 1969), pp. 801–820.

(5) PUBLIC AFFAIRS

Lobbying, as such, is not to be confused with the Public Affairs function in industry though the two overlap, are coordinated, and both are frequently manned by lawyers. The Public Affairs function, a concept spreading in industry, is concerned with the total concept of corporate citizenship—political education for employees, civic service by employees and managers, the encouragement of voting and political party contributions, and urging greater civic, social, and political participation by business leaders in an effort to meet today's urgent problems.

(6) PUBLIC RELATIONS

Mature, full-blown practice is *empathic listening, counseling management, imaginative planning, and persuasive communication.* Breadth of knowledge, moral commitment, and a high sense of ethics are implicit. A wide variety of tasks is discharged. No two programs have precisely the same objectives, aim at the same publics, or embrace identical tasks. Nor should they. *A program, to be effective, must be tailored to the industry or institution it serves.* For example, there is little need for a formal, shareholder-relations program in a family business. And the program of a mental health association will differ markedly from that used by a trade association of florists. The principles of earning and getting public goodwill are constant, but the publics, tools, and emphases must vary considerably.

The content and emphasis in programs may be seen in this illustrative cataloging of publics for—

INDUSTRY	or a	UNIVERSITY
Employee relations		Student relations
Community relations		Faculty relations
Stockholder relations		Staff relations
Customer relations		Community relations
Governmental relations		Alumni relations
Educational relations		Donor relations
Dealer relations		Government relations
Press relations		Foundation relations
Public relations		Trustee relations
		News media relations

and in these media:

Formal public opinion polls
Informal opinion surveys
Questionnaires
Personal contacts
Correspondence
Company newspapers, magazines
News releases
Radio and TV programs
Exhibits, displays
Special events
Bulletin boards
Employee awards
Annual reports
Motion and slide films
Payroll inserts

Employee letters
Shareholder letters
Shareholder magazines
Speeches
Art shows
Booklets, brochures
Open house, plant tours
Materials for schools
Essay contests
Photographs
Suggestion systems
Visitors' parking
Recreational programs
Dividend inserts
Advertising

PATHWAYS TO PUBLIC FAVOR

By now, the destination toward which the practice and programs travel, whatever their nature, should be clear: *to gain and hold the favorable opinions of the publics of an institution or industry.* Agreement on this destination is general. Disagreement and divergence set in when the choice of route to this favorable environment is to be made. Practitioners are known by the routes they take, not by the ones they pretend to travel.

There are, in the main, four possible pathways. Two are deceptive detours, full of bumps and chuckholes. Another is an old, almost abandoned cow path, grown over with thorny underbrush. Only one, the fourth, is a cleared, graded, and open pathway, broad enough to carry the requisite two-way traffic. Even it is not paved. There is no easy road to public favor.

One detour has been beaten out by those who think publicity alone is the sure-fire answer to an organization's public relations problems. This is the pathway that leads simply to "getting publicity" without regard to its purpose or effectiveness. It is also taken by those who think that pretty words and pretty pictures can beautify the ugliest of institutions or situations. This detour has a road marker that reads:

THE FALLACY OF PUBLICITY

The other detour, on the opposite side of the main-traveled path, is taken by those who assume that good works and good motives, even though unheralded, will produce a favorable public-opinion environment. This idea has considerable merit and there is no question that an institution's works must move society toward its goals, but idealistic intent alone fails to reckon with the babble and bedlam of today's public opinion arena. This one is posted: *Virtue Earns Its Own Reward.*

The third, the old, overgrown cow path, is still taken by those who hold public opinion in contempt. This is the path originally cleared in this century by the robber barons. This old path, also a detour, is marked by the sign, *The Public Be Damned.* Those who take this route with the philosophy, "To hell with the public interest; let's get ours," may get to their destination. And then, they may not. Detours are usually the long way around. It is easy to get lost on them.

The fourth pathway, modern and in process of construction, is built to carry an increasing load of traffic. This pathway is chosen by those who recognize that sound public relationships are built on good works and sound communication practices. It is the safest, smoothest way. The road was cleared and graded by those who saw the importance of doing a good job and letting everybody know about it. More persons will probably take this route in the future. This signpost reads: *Good Performance Publicly Appreciated.*

ADDITIONAL READING

"Management's Self-Conscious Spokesmen," *Fortune,* Vol. 52, November, 1955.
"Public Relations Today," *Business Week,* July 2, 1960. A *Business Week* Special Report.
"The Arts & Uses of Public Relations," *Time Magazine* essay, July 7, 1967, pp. 40–41.
These three magazine articles trace over time the media's view of public relations.
BERTRAND R. CANFIELD, *Public Relations,* 5th ed., Homewood, Ill.: Irwin, 1969.
RICHARD W. DARROW, DAN J. FORRESTAL and AUBREY O. COOKMAN, *Public Relations Handbook,* Chicago: Dartnell Corporation, 1968. Comprehensive coverage of the practice.
PAUL GARRETT, "The Four Dimensions of Public Relations," *Printers' Ink,* Vol. 203, June 11, 1943; and his "A New Dimension in Public Relations," *Public Relations Journal,* Vol. 12, October, 1956.
These articles give philosophy of one who developed the large-scale General Motors program
RICHARD HARRIS, "Annals of Legislation: If You Love Your Guns," *The New Yorker,* April 20, 1967. Detailed account of National Rifle Association's lobbying-public relations campaign against effective gun controls.
ALAN HARRINGTON, *Life in the Crystal Palace.* New York: Knopf, 1959. Satire on public relations work in a large corporation.
ROBERT L. HEILBRONER, "Public Relations—The Invisible Sell," *Harper's* Magazine, Vol. 215, June, 1957. (Also available in Christenson and McWilliams, *Voice of the People,* pp. 426–37.)

PHILIP LESLY, ed., *Public Relations Handbook,* 3rd ed., Englewood Cliffs, N.J.: Prentice-Hall, Inc., 1968.

DAVID A. LOEHWING, "Uncertain Trumpet? Public Relations May Be Ill-Equipped for the Militant Seventies," *Barron's,* April 13, 1970.

JOHN MARSTON, *The Nature of Public Relations.* New York: McGraw Hill, Inc., 1963.

IRWIN ROSS, *The Image Merchants.* Garden City: Doubleday & Company, Inc., 1959. A candid look at "the fabulous world of public relations."

RAYMOND SIMON, ed., *Perspectives in Public Relations.* Norman: University of Oklahoma Press, 1966. A collection of readings.

CHAPTER 2

THE PRACTITIONERS— STAFF AND STATUS

The specialty of public relations will attain top professional
status at an accelerated speed, but the distance
to go is still substantial.
—DAN J. FORRESTAL

The lack of clear-cut parameters for the practice of public relations has thwarted efforts to tabulate the number of practitioners accurately. Public relations directors tend to be confused on occasion with subfunctions such as publicists, writers, or editors; counselors are confused with account executives; and public relations as a title is equated with public affairs. Dual listing in surveys is common. The use of neutral synonyms in the public service to shelter the function further complicates an accurate count. Thus, the figures vary widely.

The 1960 U.S. Census showed 31,141 men and women engaged in the practice, yet estimates from other sources run as high as 110,000. The 1970 Census also is of doubtful value because corporate practitioners were counted as part of their employer's industry. However incomplete, the 1960 census figures reflected a gain from 1950 of some 63.9 per cent in number of practitioners. Applying the growth rates used for the 1950–60 comparison, this would place the total in practice at 51,040 in 1970. Continued growth is seen for the 1970s. Irving L. Straus predicted in 1970 that the some $750 million in fees being paid counseling firms that year would reach the $3 billion mark by 1975. These figures exclude expenditures for internal corporate departments. The dimensions of the practice in non-profit institutions are growing at a corresponding rate.

Whatever the precise numbers, evidence of growth abounds. The Public Relations Society of America had 3,130 members entering 1960, 7,010 members in 1970, a growth of 123 per cent over the decade. A *Public Relations Quarterly* survey late in 1966 found that 70 per cent of 141 counselors responding had started their businesses in the 1960s, and 87 per cent of the counselors had started their firms since World War II. A survey made by Grey Public Relations, Inc., the same year found that corporate public relations budgets had doubled in a five-year period. The increase in students enrolled in university courses and known growth of department and counseling firm sizes would suggest that the 63.9 per cent growth projection used for the 1950–60 decade was conservative for the 1960–70 decade. For an understanding of the functional dimension, a total of "more than 50,000" is sufficiently accurate.[1] Of this number, the Labor

---

[1] "Occupational Outlook Report Series" Bulletin No. 1550-2, 1968. U.S. Department of Labor, Bureau of Labor Statistics.

Department estimates that one-fourth are women. A careful census of metropolitan New York found that there were about 4,500 practitioners at work in 1968 and that 20 per cent of these were women.[2]

THE SIZE OF PR STAFFS

From one man and a secretary, or a man and wife team, staffs in counseling range up to the hundreds of persons.

Table 2-1 shows the following ranking of the largest ten, including independents and advertising agency departments.[3]

TABLE 2-1

	1969 NET FEE INCOME	DOMESTIC EMPLOYEES	FOREIGN EMPLOYEES	TOTAL
1. Hill and Knowlton	$8,370,000			348
2. Ruder & Finn	$6,000,000+	271 [1]	57	328
3. Carl Byoir & Assocs.	——	265	20	285
4. J. Walter Thompson PR *	$5,575,000	140	195	335
5. Burson-Marsteller *	$4,400,000	195	65	260
6. Harshe-Rotman & Druck	$4,000,000+	185		
7. Public/Financial Rel. Board [2]	$2,800,000	137		
8. Selvage, Lee and Howard	$2,500,000	115		
9. Daniel J. Edelman	$2,000,000+	125	11	136
10. Ketchum, MacLeod & Grove * ..	$2,000,000+	85		

* Ad agency PR dept.

[1] Excludes 37 design and production people.

[2] FRB bills $1.8 million, PRB bills $1 million.

Among the industrial giants, budgets are guarded as competitive information. Size of professional staff, not counting secretarial or clerical in 1969, was revealed by General Motors as 220, Chrysler 75, U.S. Steel 65, Mobil Oil 29. Headcount or size of budget are influenced to a major degree by the nature and variety of functions defined as public relations from one organization to another.

A survey of several hundred subscribers to a professional newsletter, PR Reporter, in 1970 compiled averages and drew comparisons. The

[2] Lee Levitt, "Public Relations in New York City," *Public Relations Journal*, Vol. 25, March, 1969, p. 26.

[3] *Jack O'Dwyer's Newsletter*, Vol. 3, No. 5, February 4, 1970.

average age, years experience, median salary and median budget for public relations officials, and their departments [4] are shown in Table 2-2:

TABLE 2-2

	AVERAGE AGE	YRS. PR	MEDIAN SALARY	MEDIAN BUDGET
Consumer Products Companies	46	16	24,000	*200,000
Other Industrials	45	15	22,000	175,000
Associations	43	13	19,000	88,000
Government	45	16	18,000	126,000
Insurance and Banking	42	11	19,000	250,000
Colleges	42	13	17,000	75,000
Hospitals	42	13	14,000	70,000
Health and Welfare	46	17	19,000	90,000

* For the vast majority of respondents, budgets were reported increased modestly over previous years despite a lowered economy.

The profile of the "average" professional director or officer showed him to be 44, a graduate of a state university, entering the field 15 years ago from journalism. He has held his present job 7 years. He earns a little over $20,000 and administers a budget of around $110,000. His organization doesn't yet retain a counseling firm, but it won't be long before it does.

As a principal in a counseling firm, the average professional is 47, has been in the field since 1950. He belongs to PRSA, but is not accredited by the society. He earns $28,000 annually, and is a college graduate with an A.B. degree.

PRACTITIONERS' TASKS

Eight major job classifications of public relations work were developed in a vocational guidance survey conducted by the Education Committee of the Public Relations Society of America. These are:

1. *Writing*. Reports, news releases, booklet texts, radio and TV copy, speeches, film sequences, trade paper and magazine articles, product information, and technical material.

[4] *PR Reporter,* Vol. 13, April 13, 1970.

2. *Editing*. Employee publications, newsletters, shareholder reports, and other management communications directed to both organization personnel and external groups.

3. *Placement*. Contacts with the press, radio, and TV, as well as with magazine, Sunday supplement, and trade editors, with a view toward enlisting their interest in publishing an organization's or a client's news and features.

4. *Promotion*. Special events, such as press parties, convention exhibits, and special showings; open house, new facility, and anniversary celebrations; special day, week, or month observances; contests and award programs; guest relations; institutional movies; visual aids.

5. *Speaking*. Appearances before groups and the planning requisite to finding appropriate platforms. The preparation of speeches for others, organization of speakers' bureaus, and the delivery of speeches.

6. *Production*. Knowledge of art and layout for the development of brochures, booklets, special reports, photographic communications, and house periodicals as required.

7. *Programming*. The determination of need, definition of goals, and recommended steps in carrying out the project. This is the highest level job in public relations, one requiring maturity in counseling management.

8. *Institutional Advertising*. Advertising a company's name and reputation through purchased space or time. Close coordination with advertising departments is maintained and frequently the advertising-public relations responsibility is a dual one.

To this list must be added two others. One is *participation* on frequent occasions as the representative of an organization in projects related to civic, social, cultural, political, educational, and public affairs. The second is *opinion and historical research,* as a preface to engaging in the other tasks.

THE SCOPE OF THE FUNCTION

Narrowing the practice to industry, some 250 corporation chairmen and presidents responded as follows when asked to check those activities for which their public relations departments were responsible.[5]

[5] Robert W. Miller, *Corporate Policies and Public Attitudes* (Washington, D.C.: The American University, 1965), p. 24.

TABLE 2-3

Press Relations	87%
Community Relations	76
Annual Report Preparation	73
Speech Writing	73
Other Publications	68
Counseling Management on Public Attitudes	63
Public Affairs	57
Graphic Arts and Film	57
Stockholder Relations	56
Product Publicity	54
Internal Communications	54
Public Opinion Research	51
Policy Recommendations	49
Participating in All Major Policy Discussions	31
Customer Relations	27
Employee Relations	26
Supplier Relations	9

As for counseling firm functions, data collected by *Advertising Age* showed these "other services performed" beyond the clearly defined area of communications:

Legislative Work	Spot Assignments
Advertising Agencies Selection	Labor Relations
Institutional Advertising Planning	Stockholder Relations
Institutional Advertising Preparation	Trade Shows and Exhibits

The variety of services provided and the demand for them is reflected in a survey which elicited valid responses from 271 firms. Table 2-4 shows a breakdown of the number and percentage of firms offering the 30 specialized services listed in the questionnaire: [6]

TABLE 2-4

RANK	SERVICE	NO. OFFERING	%
1.	News Releases	264	97.4
2.	Speech Writing	245	90.4
3.	Policy Making	244	90.0
4.	Community Relations	233	86.0
5.	Product Publicity	227	83.8
6.	Special Events	226	83.4
7.	Miscellaneous Manuals & Leaflets	223	82.3

[6] Joan Zimmerman Garver, unpublished master's thesis, Ohio State University, 1966.

RANK	SERVICE	NO. OFFERING	%
8.	Annual Reports	221	81.5
9.	External Publications	214	79.0
10.	Customer Relations	204	75.3
11.	Employee Relations	200	73.8
12.	Stockholder Relations	195	72.0
13.	Investor Relations	188	69.4
14.	Employee Publications	179	66.0
15.	Institutional Advertising	176	64.9
16.	Trade Shows & Exhibits	172	63.5
17.	Still Photography	161	59.4
18.	Sales Promotion	148	54.6
19.	Slide Film Creation	147	54.2
20.	Direct Mail Campaigns	146	53.9
21.	Survey Research	140	51.7
22.	Motion Picture Production	119	43.9
23.	School Relations	103	38.0
24.	Fund-Raising Campaigns	98	36.1
25.	Product or Service Advertising	96	35.4
26.	Labor Relations	92	33.9
27.	Company Contributions	78	28.8
28.	Lobbying	66	24.4
29.	Training Programs	66	24.4
30.	Motion Picture Distribution	60	22.1

The titles by which practitioners are known tended in Professor Miller's study to confirm the variety, increasing scope and independent status of the function, as shown in Table 2-7.

TABLE 2-7
TITLE OF TOP PUBLIC RELATIONS EXECUTIVES

Vice President	50%
Director of Public Relations	32
Manager of Public Relations	11
Special Assistant for Public Relations	3
Treasurer	1
Outside Counsel Executive	1
General Manager	1
Assistant Vice President	1

It is noteworthy that public relations has become more and more distinguishable and separate from other staff functions, such as industrial relations, personnel, and advertising. However, a new note of confusion in the corporate practice has entered with the emergence of the public affairs function. This is covered in a separate chapter.

STATUS

Reporting relationships comprise a reliable guide to the stature attained for the functions. These are shown in Table 2-8, side by side for the Miller and *PR Reporter* studies, the latter reflecting to some degree a cross section of profit and non-profit employees.

TABLE 2-8

MILLER STUDY: PR Man Reports to		PR REPORTER: PR Director Reports to	
President-Chairman	78%	Chairman	10%
Senior Vice President	4	President	50
Vice President, Marketing	3	Exec. Vice President	20
Exec. or Group Vice President	4	Senior Vice President	9
Vice President, Finance	2	Vice President, Marketing	15
Vice President, Advertising	1	Others, such as General Man-	
Assistant to President	1	ager, Exec. Director, etc.	6
Manager, Corporate Personnel	1		
Vice President, Secretary	1		
Vice President, Operations	1		

The totals do not add to 100 per cent because of dual reporting relationships, no response, or the chief executive officer's having a title other than chairman or president.

Attesting to the recognition of the function and its value on the management or administrative staff, *Public Relations News* reported 794 promotions of practitioners in its 1968 issues. Four were named Chairman of the Board, 10 advanced to President, 11 to Executive Vice President or equivalent, 16 to Senior Vice President, 147 to Vice President and 12 were named to corporate directorships or nonprofit trusteeships.[7]

REMUNERATION

With the increased responsibility accorded practitioners has come improvement in earnings for both men and women that reflect more than cost of living adjustments.

This is illustrated in Table 2-9 by comparing as well as possible equivalents in surveys by the Chicago Publicity Club in 1961 and the *PR Reporter* in 1968.

[7] *Public Relations News, Vol. 25, January 27, 1969.*

TABLE 2-9

	AVERAGES	
Position	Publicity club 1961	PR reporter 1968
Public Relations Director	$15,500	$18–$21,000
Assistant Director	11,500	15– 20,000
Publicity Director	10,500	12– 18,000
Writer	9,500	10– 15,000
Account Executive	15,000	12– 18,000
Editor	10,000	
Radio-TV Manager	12,500	
Fund Raising	10,700	
Community Relations Director	8,000	
Beginner	7,500	

The Miller study showed the average salary of the corporate public relations executive to be $31,642, with 48 per cent above $25,000 and 4 per cent of those above $60,000. The *PR Reporter* commented that the $15,000 to $20,000 range accommodated assistant or associate directors and account or group supervisors. That survey found salaries of $35,000–$50,000 not uncommon for public relations directors, officers, and counseling firm owners and presidents. The ceiling with some exceptions was $75,000 on the counseling side and $100,000 on the corporate side. All studies, including one by Profs. Walter Seifert and William Moore in Columbus, Ohio, found geographical variations and salaries to women generally lower than to men.

A 1968 survey of the membership of the Public Relations Society of America based on a 91 per cent response of its members found their annual compensation to be as shown in Table 2-10: [8]

TABLE 2-10

Up to $15,000	35%
$16–20,000	25%
$21–25,000	19%
$26–35,000	13%
$36–50,000	5%
Over $50,000	3%

[8] Quentin L. Harvell, "New Statistical Picture of the Public Relations Field," *Public Relations Journal,* Vol. 24, November, 1968, p. 35.

A survey made the same year by the American College Public Relations Association, of 378 representative institutions of higher education, found: Salaries ranged beyond $30,000 for the managers of advancement programs and into the upper $20,000 range for chief fund raising officers and chief public relations officers. The median for seventeen persons managing the total program in their respective private universities was in the $25,000–$29,999 range. Their counterparts in state universities were a notch below, in the $20,000–$24,999 bracket. A comparison made with the salaries for the same positions in 1964–65 found "most of the medians for the chief officers jumped one salary bracket (i.e. $2,500) over the three-year span." [9]

COUNSELING FEES

The services of a counsel or counseling firm may be obtained for a specific finite project or for a continuing infinite service, reviewable and renewable at intervals.

Fees for continuing services are usually established in one of these three ways: [10]

A fixed monthly retainer fee.

A retainer plus monthly billing for actual staff time on an hourly or per diem basis.

A base fee, billed monthly, to which are added increments for services performed beyond the retainer.

Out-of-pocket expenses generally are billed at cost and are exclusive of the fee.

There are wide variables in the size of fees. One of the largest counseling firms, Hill and Knowlton, has had a minimum fee of $4,000 per month. Carl Byoir has charged a flat fee of $50,000 a year to corporate clients which gross over $30 million. At the other end of the scale, counseling firms may provide a limited service, such as writing occasional news releases, for as little as $100 a month, or $50 per news release.

Regardless of the variables, five elements are reflected in fees and over all charges.

[9] John W. Leslie, *Focus on Understanding and Support, a Study in College Management* (Washington, D.C.: American College Public Relations Association, 1969), p. 18.

[10] *Public Relations and Public Relations Counseling* (New York: The Counselors Section, Public Relations Society of America, 1966).

[11] Josh William Stailey, "Budgeting, Accounting and Pricing Policies of Selected Public Relations Counseling Firms in Central and Southwestern Ohio" (Master's thesis, Ohio State University, 1969), pp. 63–64.

1. Cost of the staff used on the project.
2. Executive time and supervision.
3. Overhead costs.
4. Out-of-pocket costs—for example telephone and travel.
5. A reasonable profit for doing the work.

Accounting practices also vary in computing costs. For example, there are different methods used for determining the hourly value of individuals working on accounts. Some firms use cost accounting, based on dollar salary cost per hour plus overhead and profit, determined by mathematical formulas; some firms guess at their approximate cost and then apply an arbitrary factor for all clients; others use different factors for different clients. There is equal variation in arriving at overhead costs. Some firms put time spent getting new business into overhead; others do not.

As indicated, agency billing practices vary widely, particularly among the smaller agencies. A survey of twelve firms in Ohio, for example, found that seven firms billed their services by the hour, three charged monthly, and two charged by more than one method, depending on the type of account and client's preference. Eight of these counselors charged on a fee plus expenses basis, two charged an all inclusive fee, and two others used a combination of these systems. Only seven kept timesheets. Two of the twelve charged commissions on out-of-pocket expenses. Public relations agencies, generally speaking, need better cost accounting procedures and more common agreement on methods of charging clients.[11]

THE WORKING OF A DEPARTMENT

Where there is no outside counseling, an internal department handles all four steps in the public relations process. Operating on a budget, the staff undertakes fact finding. It sets up public relations objectives and plans programs. The staff follows through with the necessary communications and events. Then it evaluates results. Many departments vary this pattern by hiring opinion research firms to measure public opinion and to evaluate results. Some employers hold that a staff would be subject to bias in evaluating the results of its work, thus turn to an outside research agency for this task.

The work of the staff will in all probability be segmented. Different persons might be designated to edit the house magazine, to handle the news service, to contact the press, to stage special events, to conduct the plant tours, or to prepare speeches.

The alternative to dividing the tasks among the staff is to establish a Jack-of-all-trades group, assigning projects on a "who's not busy now?" basis.

In both of these setups there may be the need to retain some outside services, because either time or talent is lacking internally. Typical outside services would be the layout, artwork, printing, binding, and mailing of a fiftieth-anniversary booklet. The internal staff might have planned the book, determined its content and distribution, and written its copy.

Other examples of outside services could be the catering of refreshments for an open house, monitoring press notices, cutting tapes for radio or film for TV broadcasts, providing a speaker for a nonprofit occasion, or mimeographing and mailing news releases.

THE DEPARTMENT'S ADVANTAGES

An internal staff practitioner has four factors working for him or her:

1. Team membership.
2. Knowledge of the organization.
3. Economy to the organization.
4. Availability to associates.

Team Membership is a great advantage. The confidence and support of team members go with it. This tends to overcome or to relegate into unimportance any antagonism toward the public relations function. At the same time, the close connection between the function, the department and the chief executive office of the organization provides *first team* membership rather than remote or insignificant membership.

Knowledge of the Organization means an intimate, participating knowledge that comes from being an insider. This is particularly important in a period of growth and change. The staff man or woman knows the relationships between individuals and their functions. He knows the undercurrents of influence, the key people, the conservatives, the harmful ones who put personal ambition and expedience ahead of the organization's interests, the articulate and the tongue-tied.

This kind of knowledge can be acquired by an outsider. But the insider is in a position to do most about it *continuously*. He or she can advise where needed, conciliate, and render services from within to induce attitudes and actions that will bring about harmonious relationships *inside* as well as outside.

Economy can result simply from residency in an organization and from integration in an organization. For example, the department's bills for rent, heat, and light in a large organization do not loom large. They are expressed generally as a small part of an over-all cost for many departments and offices.

Similarly, for an event like a 100th anniversary, the department's activity is not a single, separate cost. It is part of a celebration cost. Perhaps the only separate departmental tasks are to prepare a booklet and to place a giant cake with 100 candles on the front lawn. Concurrently during the year the advertising department may run special ads. The board of directors may establish a scholarship in memory of the founder. All employees may be given a holiday on the birth date. These activities, to the publics involved, would all be public relations. Only two, however, were in this instance charged or executed departmentally.

Availability of the staff practitioner has many facets. When things go wrong, he is not one minute from a face-to-face meeting with the organization's officials. As a deputy, he can be entrusted with delicate matters. When a senior executive resigns in a huff, the president wants a public relations man or woman on the spot, who knows the background, understands the dangers of mishandling the news, and has credibility with the press. In such a situation, the head of an organization would feel uneasy communicating through an outside person or agency.

Availability means that the staff is on call for all departments, divisions, decentralized units and emergencies. The staff man can slip into and out of committees and meetings. He *belongs*. He is handy for consultation. He has both acceptability and authority.

His availability to perform service functions involves him in a broad range of activities. He may be asked to handle a tour of facilities for some foreign visitors who do not speak English. He may represent his organization on a local civil rights or fund-raising committee. He may respond for the organization on receipt of a citation. Or, he may make the arrangements for the president's vacation or his daughter's wedding.

THE DEPARTMENT'S HANDICAPS

The staff practitioner's advantage of team membership and continuous availability are handicaps on occasion. *He loses objectivity*. In being supported by the team, he tends to be compromised in his views. He is in constant danger of becoming a "yes" man. Much of his time is diverted from long-range planning to daily errands of small import. These handicaps add up to *domination and subjectivity*. This can be a serious handicap, given the practitioner's important responsibility for providing his organization with feedback objectively from the various publics.

A biblical saying describes the occupational hazard of the staff man: "A prophet is not without honour save in his own country and in his own house." At a glance that seems in strange contradiction with the support and deference often rendered him by teammates. It bears closer inspection because the support tends to become possessive in the manner of a bear hug.

While the staff man may not be a prophet, he *is* in his own country. He *is* in his own house. He is contained by all the emotional elements of belonging in an organization. He is harnessed to an office a large part of the time. In that office are—a desk to catch the daily mail, a telephone to receive the daily calls, chairs to accommodate the daily visitors from down the hall. As a result, tending to details gets in the way of regular outside contacts for refreshing stale viewpoints. The people with whom he has lunch and with whom he exchanges opinions daily tend to look, to feel, and to talk the same as they did the day before. There is the daily necessity of making innumerable small decisions that push from his mind the challenge of grappling with larger or more remote matters.

Availability Exacts a Price

As a part of the restrictive influences, the staff practitioner's viewpoints on specific areas of communication trouble tend to be subordinate to the viewpoints of operating officials. The staff man must strive to hold to an objective viewpoint. This is never easy.

THE OUTSIDE COUNSELOR OR AGENCY

The 1,600 or more public relations counseling firms in the United States range widely in size and scope of service. A large number of advertising agencies also offer public relations services to some degree.

The majority of counseling firms are engaged in public relations work exclusively. A growing number, however, are offering advertising, graphic arts, trade association management, and sales promotion services as well. There is a discernible trend toward specialization among public relations firms; for example, in financial relations, employee communications, association management, and public affairs.

Most advertising agencies have found it difficult to determine what public relations services to offer, how to effectively organize the function, and how to sustain it apart from the advertising relationship where it derives its tonnage of dollar billings. N.W. Ayer pioneered in 1920, when it offered a publicity service for its advertising clients. In 1925, Albert Frank-Guenther Law took the next step when it expanded its operations to offer a full-fledged public relations and publicity service. In the next few years, J. Walter Thompson, Young and Rubicam, and Benton & Bowles followed suit. By the mid-1940's, seventy-five agencies were providing publicity service for clients, according to an *Advertising Age* survey. In 1953, *Advertising Age* made another survey and concluded: "The role of the public relations department in the advertising agency is a strange one.

Many topflight agencies billing over $5-million a year still do not have one. Many of those that do regard it purely as a service function."

Consequently the attitude of many ad agencies is one of ambivalence. One survey found that of 97 large agencies (billing over $5-million), only 39 said they actively seek public relations business; only 32 said they offer public relations because it is a profitable business for them. Another survey, this one of smaller agencies ($1-million to $5-million in billings), found that most of these agencies offer most public relations services, that the public relations department is usually headed by an agency principal, and that most of these departments provide up to 25 per cent of the agencies' total billing.[12] On the other hand many admen do not want to combine these services. David Ogilvy, in his *Confessions of an Advertising Man,* said bluntly: "We have no public relations department. I take the view that public relations should be handled by the manufacturer himself or by specialist counsel."

In 1956 Marion Harper of McCann-Erickson (now Interpublic), broke new ground by setting up that agency's public relations department as a wholly owned subsidiary corporation, Communication Counselors, Inc. Other agencies to follow suit included Benton & Bowles, Inc., with its General Public Relations, and Chirurg & Cairns, which set up Creative Public Relations. Harper ultimately folded CCI into Communications Affiliates, Inc. In 1970, Batten, Barten, Durstin, and Osborn, a major ad agency, closed its public relations division.

There are basically two kinds of advertising agencies—those offering some measure of public relations service and those who shun it. Most agencies service only advertising clients; a few take on non-advertising clients for public relations or publicity service. The pioneer ad agency, N. W. Ayer, relaxed its policy of serving only advertising clients in 1969 when it took on a few non-advertisers as public relations clients. Most public relations work in advertising agencies is product publicity. Few agencies are adequately equipped to offer broad-gauge public relations counseling. Irving Smith Kogan asserts that "in spite of its growth, PR in the advertising agency business has had spotty success."[13]

Executive Report, a Prentice-Hall publication for top management, has predicted after making a special study, that both public relations and advertising services will be taken over by agencies offering a complete communications service to industry by 1980. Marion Harper's Communications Affiliates was an effort to move in this direction. In a special report, *Executive Report* predicted that "the communications specialist will cut

---

12 Thomas L. Harris, "Public Relations in the Ad Agency," *Public Relations Journal,* Vol. 24, October, 1968, p. 35.

13 In "Public Relations: Agency Stepchild," *Madison Avenue,* June, 1962, pp. 14–15 and 30.

across artificial boundaries to solve the specific corporate problem most effectively." This publication predicted a need for an agency to which a client could take a total marketing or some other communication problem and have it handled under one roof, coordinated through one account executive. *Executive Report* concluded: "We don't get Public Relations 1980 until the entire communications structure is unified. In part, most public relations agencies handle a variety of communications services. But all, to date, stop short of total communications service . . ."[14]

A practitioner, William Safire, predicted the same thing in his *The Relations Explosion.* He thinks "relations services must change swiftly to meet the changing character of business." He predicts "A new type of communications method will develop. It will fuse together all the relations services to deal cohesively with the publics that any business has to serve."[15]

If Safire's predictions come true, the public relations, advertising, and marketing agencies undoubtedly will find the amalgamation painful. Safire joined President Nixon's White House staff in 1969 as a speech writer which suggests his concept didn't find a ready market.

Wherever public relations, advertising, and promotional services are mutually rendered, there is usually an effort to identify the firm as offering a "complete marketing service."

Separate from counseling firms that offer a range of services, there are some that offer services of a highly specialized nature. Some offer only research, employee communications advice, liaison in Washington, financial press contacts, or product promotion. Diversification within a single agency to offer clients specialized services also is taking place.

Quite often the client first seeks the counseling firm when he has an emergency situation. This was the case, for example, when medical research reports linked cigarette smoking to cancer. Entering an emergency situation, the counselor has no choice. He or she must immediately try to correct the existing misunderstandings. Later on he or she can investigate the sources of the communication or performance breakdown and suggest preventive measures for the future.

In normal circumstances, the counsel will begin the service to a new client by exploring the health of the relationships between the client and those publics on whom he depends. The initial exploration might take months. Whenever it is completed, one of three things can be expected to happen. The counselor tells the client that he finds no problem or threat of harm in communication of a magnitude to require outside assistance.

---

[14] Special study, "Inside Public Relations," issued by *Executive Report,* August, 1963. Published by Prentice-Hall, Inc.

[15] Published by the Macmillan Company, 1963, with subtitle: "The Coming Boom and Shakeout in Corporate Relations."

Or, he tells him that the problems disclosed by the research are in a realm other than that of his field. Or, he tells him that there are problems which can be solved through the application of public relations techniques.

In the last case, the counsel arranges to make a presentation of his findings. In this presentation are exposed: (a) the central core of the difficulty, (b) its current status in terms of harm to the organization, (c) related difficulties which must be considered, (d) ultimate alternatives to be faced, (e) desirable objectives, (f) a long range plan shaped toward the objectives, and (g) an immediate program of actions involving anything pertinent, even if it involves the removal of a senior officer.

Regarding presentations, a survey by *Public Relations Quarterly* found these mixed reactions by industrial executives: "Moderately effective 49%, General waste of time 28%, Highly effective 5%." [16]

Not all factors in a presentation are exposed invariably at one sitting. However, to establish a suitable working climate, the counselor must obtain an understanding over the full range before his firm's talents can be committed sincerely to the tasks.

The burden of proof for the effectiveness of advice and actions rests with the counsel. Many results are intangible or nebulous. Who can tell how many extra dollars for a charity drive came in because of the newspaper stories about the work of the charity during the year? Polls are helpful, but many of the common yardsticks are not appropriate. In oversimplified terms, the counsel submits reports of progress, holds periodic meetings with key people in the client's organization, and coordinates the program. As the counselor-client relationship matures, the shape of the client's enterprise most likely undergoes cloud-like variations. Communications programs are revamped, scrapped, or replaced. New ones are activated. Special devices are "imagineered" to deal with peculiar needs.

The counselor usually functions in one of three ways with clients:

1. Provides advice, leaving the execution of plans to others.
2. Provides advice and undertakes full execution of plans.
3. Provides advice and collaborates with the client's staff to execute the plans.

Burger lists six reasons why outside agencies are retained: [17]

1. Management has not previously conducted a formal public relations program and lacks experience in organizing one.

---

[16] Tom M. Hopkinson, "A Survey of Public Relations Counseling Today and Tomorrow," *Public Relations Quarterly*, Vol. 11, Winter, 1967, p. 8.

[17] "Why Haven't PR Agencies Grown?," *op. cit.*, pp. 18–19.

2. Headquarters may be located away from New York City, the communications and financial center of the nation.

3. A wide range of up-to-date contacts are maintained by an agency.

4. An outside agency can provide services of experienced executives who would be unwilling to move to other cities or whose salaries could not be afforded by a single firm.

5. An organization with its own PR department may be in need of highly specialized services, which it cannot afford on a permanent basis.

6. Crucial matters of over-all outside policy dictates need for the independent judgment of an outsider.

THE COUNSELOR'S ADVANTAGES

The greatest single advantage of the counselor to the client is the opportunity for *objectivity*. This is an advantage enjoyed over the staff people and the client in varying degree. The counselor need not be confused by the internal frictions of the organizations served; he or she need only be concerned with recognizing them and helping things run more smoothly. The fact that one vice president's wife snubs another vice president's wife is no cloud on the counselor's vision. He need not live with the day by day minutiae which plague clients. He can stand apart from the complaints that reach the top official's desk each day, complaints that keep him so busy patching up communication chinks in the organization that he has no time to think through plans for a major overhaul. The counselor can conceive the overhaul without wasting time on the chinks. He or she is, in a phrase, a relatively free agent.

A second advantage to the counselor is the *scope* of his operations and variety of skills. From an office in New York, Washington, or Chicago he can serve clients in Colorado, West Virginia, and Vermont. If that becomes impractical, he can open branch offices in major population centers. He can exchange services with firms in other cities and countries. In cases of need, he can install sandlot offices in Colorado, West Virginia, and Vermont. Reasonably intimate contact can be maintained through periodic meetings on the premises of clients. If that does not suffice, the counsel can help the client obtain a suitable staff director or he can lend someone from his own staff. At the same time, the counselor's central location in a metropolitan communications hub permits frequent and personal contact with the press, radio magazines, and TV—the main means of outward communication for all clients. His contacts embrace the press in New York, Washington, Chicago, San Francisco, and Hollywood. Several firms offer publicity services on a United States network basis and a few on an international basis.

The staffs of large counseling firms or advertising agency departments might include news writers, magazine writers, trade journal writers, and speech writers. There might be radio and TV programmers, trained researchers, home economists, educators, lawyers, sociologists, merchandisers, fund raisers, economists, engineers, political campaign experts, artists, and photographers.

Third in importance among the advantages accruing to a counselor is *flexibility*. In the course of any year, a counselor will be confronted with communication problems of varied natures. Typical would be a strike in a small town, a brutality case in a public institution, the introduction of a new product by a manufacturer, prospective legislation harmful to the interests of a trade association, and the inauguration of a new university president. The range of a successful counselor's services is wide. If the agency is a successful, substantial one, its range of experience is equally wide. In a sense, a public relations firm is a useful repository of living case histories. Each project adds to its fund of knowledge. Experience and versatility of staff make this synergy possible. The counselor approaches the situations bolstered by past familiarity with them and a knowledge of the success or failure that attended previous encounters.

As shown in Table 2-11, a survey by *Public Relations Quarterly* of 217 practitioners showed the following to be "the most important contribution to a corporation's or other organization's welfare that a capable agency can best perform." [18]

TABLE 2-11

1. Offer Objectivity	20%
2. Creativity	18
3. Broad Scope (Skills, experience)	7
4. Add Depth	5
5. Integration with internal staff	4

THE COUNSELOR'S HANDICAP

The foregoing may make it sound as though the task of the counselor was simply to arrive on the premises. In rendering a counseling service—and this applies to almost all consultants—there is, with rare exception, an area of opposition ranging from nonacceptance to antagonism. That is the counselor's handicap. The resistance of outsiders is a natural human trait. The old guard resists change as a threat to its security. That goes for the new idea, the new approach, the new look. This resistance is common. It is almost a certainty in organizations that have been static for

[18] Hopkinson, *op. cit.,* p. 3.

years and perhaps most need a new look in public relations. There is resistance—probably plenty of it. That does not mean that the idea is no good. It means that hostility comes naturally when changes of drastic or sudden nature are proposed.

The counselor, more often than not, is in the position of having to suggest changes designed to improve relationships. Whether the suggested changes involve policies, equipment, methods, or practices, the people responsible for them historically are alienated. Their realm is being "invaded." Their judgment is being "criticized." The offended ask, "What does *he* know about *our* business?"

Other handicaps for the counselor grow from this embryo. Insiders may attempt to discredit a counselor. He or she is labeled with the worst possible connotations of the term "outsider." A finger of accusation might be pointed at the *superficiality* of the counselor's grasp of the organization's unique problems, the local angles of the problems, the historical contributions to success made by the policies and methods now being maligned. A finger of criticism might be pointed at the costs entailed in retaining the counselor's services and carrying out the program he proposes—with no guarantee that there will be concrete results.

In the *Public Relations Quarterly* poll, public relations corporate executives were asked "Based on your own experience, what factors have caused serious problems in your relations with counseling firms?" In reply, "The agency did not deliver what they promised"—71%; "Lack of agency creative and original ideas"—59%; "The agency tended to be a 'yes' man and failed to fight for its convictions"—29%.

Counselors asked to describe their main problems in effective service said:

1. Being unable to hire the right number and kind of professional staffers 38%
2. Having to report to client contacts of unprofessional caliber. .35%
3. Lack of or poor direction from client 26%
4. Being denied suitable access to top management 15%
5. Failing to ascertain what the client really wanted and/or needed 13%
6. Personality conflicts 9%
7. Failing to deliver what we originally promised 2%

THE DIVISION OF RESPONSIBILITY

Regardless of variations in staff and scope, advantages and handicaps, all practitioners have the same philosophy of service. There are several natural questions. Is the counseling firm more or less effective than the department of the advertising agency? Than the internal staff? Are they all necessary? If so, in combination or separately?

Forces in society making public relations service essential are such that the question of relationships between the outside counsel and internal staff is not critical. It is a matter of each organization's working out a pattern of services suited to its particular needs. A small company in a Midwestern state may need to augment its internal staff for a period of six months to introduce a new product. In this case, it is simpler to retain outside counsel for this project. A large company or university may get caught in the crunch of crisis, find its internal department deficient, and consequently turn to outside counsel for guidance. A West Coast company will retain a public relations agency in New York so that it can have direct access to the national news media.

Whether a public relations agency or a public relations department within a larger advertising agency is best suited to serve the client is again a matter of variance. If the need is primarily product publicity to support the marketing function, then it may well be feasible to use the same agency for both advertising and publicity. Generally speaking, the advertising agency public relations departments or subsidiaries are not equipped to provide broad range public relations counseling. Howard Chase, a counselor who has served as a staff director in a corporation, as head of McCann-Erickson's subsidiary, and now as head of his own agency, rightly describes advertising and public relations as "unidentical twins." He has asserted:

"While the target of both advertising and public relations may be a share of the human mind, the scope of advertising is limited, and will be limited, by the availability of purchasable media. There are no limitations on the scope and range of public relations. . . . It is my impression that recognition of these functional differences will gain wide acceptance in the years ahead at high executive levels."

In the large entity, "there is plenty of room for everyone," as one counselor put it. Public relations reinforces marketing as it does employee recruiting. Advertising of products in corporations is a phase of marketing. Advertising of diversification or of unity in a conglomerate is a top management concern implemented by public relations or by advertising where the two are joined into a "communications" responsibility. The internationalizing of U. S. industry has added dimension to both public relations and advertising. The broadened aspects of "public affairs" and "identity" or "image" requirements have brought legal considerations and design considerations into the picture. Bigness and abuse have emphasized the need for better financial relations, concern with antitrust laws, handling of militants. This calls variously for public relations counseling and advertising.

THE TREND—A HARMONIOUS TEAM

An effective working combination is the trend. The corporate publicity or product function is but one segment of public relations work. Certainly no advertising agency has claimed superiority in employee communications or civic events. In fact, most shun public relations, except as a clearly identified advertising function such as that of the Advertising Council. Certainly, the matter of product promotion is not a major interest to the chairman of the Red Cross campaign, or to Columbia University. The division of responsibility would not concern a manufacturer of capital earth-moving equipment to the extent that it might interest the manufacturer of *consumer* garden tools.[19]

In practice, individual crusades must be less and less a part of the organizational concept. The team is the thing. It constitutes a logical trend in the specialization of industrial and institutional work. It is logical in the decentralization of industry, in the departmentalizing of government and the Armed Forces. Among corporations with products or services for mass consumption, complementing of counsel and staff is common. The same can be said of trade associations, trade unions, and welfare agencies, to name a few. Even universities and religious orders have retained counseling firms in recent years.

Exceptions are found among several very large corporate enterprises. In these instances—U. S. Steel is a case in point—there is no regular outside counseling, but the internal staff is of such depth that its top level can devote itself entirely to the counseling function. Other very large undertakings—Standard Oil Company of New Jersey, for example—are staffed internally in depth, yet retain outside counseling. Still a third setup provides for wide internal staff with outside counseling called in for special matters.

In organizations financed by public funds, the general practice excludes expenditures for outside counsel, although the Armed Forces use counsel for recruiting programs, and other special government programs employ counsel from time to time. For example, the Department of Health, Education and Welfare retained a New York agency on a short-term basis to assist with its saturation publicity campaign to get all eligible persons to sign for Medicare after that law was passed. The restraint in the use of

---

[19] For typical patterns of organization and their evolvement over the past several years, see: *National Industrial Conference Board Studies Public Relations in Industry* (New York: National Industrial Conference Board, 1956), No. 80, and *Advertising, Sales Promotion, and Public Relations—Organizational Alternatives, Experiences in Marketing Management* (New York: National Industrial Conference Board, 1968), No. 16.

counseling seems more a consideration of politic usage of tax monies than a decision based on evaluations of the most effective approach to communications problems. Also, specialized talent quite often is already located somewhere in the organization, needing only reassignment and integration of efforts.

Two team organizations are common and both have been successful. One is a combination of outside counsel, either public relations firm or ad agency, with a small internal staff to handle the localized problems. In the other organization, a large internal staff calls on counseling firms for advice in problems which need the outside viewpoint. In these two types of teams, each component aids the other. The outside counsel adds to the stature of the internal staff among the top-echelon people in the organization by reinforcing its recommendations. The internal staff aids the counselor by easing any antagonism.

There is no guaranteed combination. Public relations teams must be tailored for each organization. They cannot be removed from one organization and slipped into another without some alteration. *Adaption to the specific problems of each organization is a necessity.*

ADDITIONAL READING

ASSOCIATION OF NATIONAL ADVERTISERS, *How Public Relations and Advertising Are Working Together to Meet Company Objectives.* New York: The Association, 285 Madison Avenue, New York 10017.

CAROLINE BIRD and THOMAS D. YUTZY, "You Have to Manage Public Relations," *Harvard Business Review,* Vol. 35, November-December, 1957.

COUNSELORS' SECTION, PUBLIC RELATIONS SOCIETY OF AMERICA, *Public Relations and Public Relations Counseling.* New York: PRSA, 1962, 12 pages.

ROBERT GAINES, "The PR Girl," *Cosmopolitan* Magazine, February, 1967. A candid, perhaps exaggerated closeup of one kind of publicist.

BERT C. GOSS, "How Public Relations Counsel Works with Corporate Management," speech, February 6, 1956, and published by Hill & Knowlton, Inc.

WILLIAM J. LONG, "Inside or Out?", *Public Relations Journal,* Vol. 12, May, 1956.

ALFRED G. PAULSON, "Profit Control in a Personal Service Business," *The New York Certified Public Accountant,* Vol. 33, January, 1963.

"Budgeting in the Public Relations Agency," *Quarterly Review of Public Relations,* Vol. 6, Fall, 1961.

"Fee Billing: A Return for the Effort Spent," *ibid.,* Vol. 6, Winter, 1961.

REA W. SMITH, "Women In Public Relations," *Public Relations Journal,* Vol. 24, October, 1968.

IRWIN ROSS, *The Image Merchants,* New York: Doubleday & Company, Inc., 1959. Profiles leading New York counselors.

MORTON J. SIMON, *Public Relations Law,* New York: Appleton-Century-Crofts, 1969. See Chapter 2, "Legal Relationships and Liabilities of Public Relations Counsel," and Chapter 3, "Public Relations Counsel and Their Employees."

CHAPTER 3

HOW IT ALL BEGAN— THE FORERUNNERS

The way to get at the nature
of an institution, as of anything else
that is alive, is to see how it has grown.
—A. G. KELLER

Study of the origins of public relations provides a helpful insight into its functions, its strengths, and its weaknesses. The history is a fascinating story, but a comprehensive history remains to be written. Published histories have been telescoped and oversimplified. There has been an overemphasis on novelty and on a few of the many colorful personalities. Even a slight probing of history will quickly dull the sheen of novelty often given to public relations.

The effort to deal with the force of opinion and to communicate with others goes back to antiquity. Only the tools, degree of specialization, breadth of knowledge, and intensity of effort required today are relatively new. Increased specialization and emphasis give the delusion of newness.

The growth of the field has extended over many decades. The factors inducing its origin and development are many and complex. The turbulent stream of history rushes along in a manner that defies neat cataloguing. The history of public relations cannot be told by simply saying that it grew out of press-agentry. Nor can it be fully told in terms of the influential career of an Ivy Lee.

The power of public opinion to control human affairs has been recognized down through the centuries. Although the term *public opinion* was not coined until the eighteenth century, the force of people's opinions was demonstrated and recognized in ancient times. With recognition of the power of people's opinions, there came, in response, practices we now call public relations. They were of a most rudimentary sort, to be sure. Public opinion played a part in shaping events among the early Greeks and Romans, even though the publics were small in size and number, the channels of expression limited, and the communications crude.

The Greek theorists studied the importance of the public will, even though they did not specifically use the term *public opinion*. The urban culture of the later Roman Empire gave scope to the opinion process. Certain phrases and ideas in the political vocabulary of the Romans and in the writings of the medieval period are related to modern concepts of public opinion. The Romans inscribed upon their walls the slogan, "S.P.Q.R.— the Senate and the Roman People." Later, the Romans coined the expression *vox populi, vox Dei*—"the voice of the people is the voice of God." Machiavelli wrote, in his *Discoursi,* "Not without reason is the voice of the people compared to the voice of God." Machiavelli held that the people must be either caressed or annihilated.

Efforts to communicate information to influence viewpoints or actions likewise can be traced from the earliest civilizations. Archeologists found a farm bulletin in Iraq which told the farmers of 1800 B.C. how to sow their crops, how to irrigate, how to deal with field mice, and how to harvest their crops. This effort was not unlike today's distribution of farm bulletins by our United States Department of Agriculture. Much of what is known of ancient Egypt, Assyria, and Persia was recorded in efforts to publicize and glorify the rulers of that day. Much of the literature and art of antiquity was designed to build support for kings, priests, and other leaders. Virgil's *Georgics* represented a persuasive effort to get urban dwellers to move to the farms to produce food for the growing city. Demosthenes used publicity to oppose the imperialist schemes of Philip of Macedon. The walls of Pompeii were inscribed with election appeals. Caesar carefully prepared the Romans for his crossing of the Rubicon in 50 B.C. by sending reports to Rome on his epic achievements as governor of Gaul. Historians believe *The Commentaries* were written by Caesar as propaganda for Caesar.

Rudimentary elements of public relations can be found in the history of ancient India. In writings of the earliest times there is mention of the king's spies who did more than carry on espionage. Their functions included keeping the king in touch with public opinion. They also championed the king in public and spread rumors favorable to the government.[1] The employment of specialists by governments to report on its actions and accomplishments is not an invention of this century. As long ago as 1030 when St. Olaf, King of Norway, drew up his men in battle order, he arranged for his *skalds*—ancient Scandanavian bards—to be present on the field, within a shield fence of the strongest and boldest warriors, so that "ye shall remain here and see the events which may take place and then ye will not have to follow the reports of others in what ye afterwards tell or sing about it." The knight of old had his press agent in his *avant courier.*

Public relations was heralded many centuries ago in England, where the kings maintained Lords Chancellor as "Keepers of the King's Conscience." These functionaries surely offer a historical counterpart. Long before the complexities of communication, there was acknowledged need for a third party to facilitate communication and adjustment between the government and the people. So it was with the church, tradesmen, and craftsmen. The word *propaganda* was born in the seventeenth century, when the Catholic Church set up its College of Propaganda to propagate the faith.

In a still later day, Catherine the Great, able autocrat of all Russia,

---

[1] A. L. Basham, *The Wonder That Was India* (London: Sidgwick & Jackson, 1954), p. 122.

displayed a "genius for publicity." "She looked on publicity as an essential instrument in the art of government. Always she drafted her *ukazi* and manifestoes in the way to make the fullest appeal to her people, and often this was their main, if not their only, purpose. Likewise on every public occasion she was conscious of the impression she must make." [2] Today's practitioner has had many counterparts in history.

Close examination of history reveals the direct relationship between the growth of the practice and the periods of intense struggle for power among the competitive elements of society. Public relations, as a prime agent in public-opinion formation, has been developed to meet the needs of power groups for public support. The American beginnings of public relations are to be found in the American Revolution, which brought the struggle for power between the patrician-led patriots and the commercial, propertied Tories. It is evident in the conflict between the trade and property interests led by Hamilton against the planter-and-farmer bloc led by Jefferson; in the struggle between Jackson's agrarian frontiersmen and the financial forces of Nicholas Biddle; and in the nation's greatest internal conflict of all—the Civil War.

The later stages of development are directly tied to the power struggles evoked by the political reform movements of Theodore Roosevelt, Robert M. LaFollette, Woodrow Wilson, Franklin D. Roosevelt, Harry S. Truman, and John F. Kennedy. Their party programs, reflecting strong tides of protest against entrenched power groups, provided the catalytic agents for much of the growth. Contemporary practice has emerged from the political economy of the United States in the continuing struggle of political and economic groups for dominance and from the increasing necessity for each group to "have the public on its side." It has also emerged in response to the need to gain public acceptance and utilization of our swiftly advancing technology.

The history is meaningful only when it is related to these power conflicts and recurring crises of change. For example, it is not mere coincidence that large business interests in the past have taken public relations most seriously when their position of power was challenged or threatened by the forces of labor, the farmer, the small shopkeeper or a maturing generation. Nor is it a coincidence that labor's programs have been intensified when an adverse public reaction to labor was crystallizing in regulatory legislation. Similarly, the most intense developments within government have come in periods of crisis: World War I, the Depression, World War II, the Korean War, Vietnam, and the uneasy years with Russia and China.

The origins need to be examined in their natural social and historical

---

[2] Ian Grey, *Catherine the Great, Autocrat and Empress of All Russia* (Philadelphia: J. B. Lippincott Co., 1962), pp. 143–144.

setting. The threads that form the tapestry, when pulled out of the fabric and examined singly, leave a confused, raveled impression.

THE AMERICAN BEGINNINGS

Utilization of publicity to raise funds, promote causes, boost commercial ventures, sell land, and build box-office personalities in the United States is older than the nation itself. The American talent for promotion can be traced back to the first settlements on the East Coast in the sixeenth century. The exaggerated claims that often characterize publicity began with Sir Walter Raleigh's ill-fated effort to settle Roanoke Island off the Virginia coast. When Captain Arthur Barlowe returned to England in 1584 from that desolate, swampy area, he reported to Raleigh that: "The soile is the most plentiful, sweete, fruitfull and wholesome of all the worlds . . . they have those Okes that we have, but farre greater and better. . . ." He even described the Indians as "most gentle, loving, and faithfull, voide of all guile or treason."

Probably the first systematic effort to raise funds on this continent was that sponsored by Harvard College in 1641 when that infant institution sent a trio of preachers to England on a "begging mission." Once in England, these fund raisers found that they needed a fund-raising brochure—today a standard item in a fund drive—and relayed this need back to Harvard. In response to this request came *New England's First Fruits,* largely written in Massachusetts but printed in London in 1643, the first of countless billions of public relations pamphlets and brochures.[3] And perhaps it was Columbia University that first used the press release as a means of gaining public notice. News announcements of the first commencement at King's College, as Columbia was then called, June 21, 1758, ran in all of the New York City journals and all accounts were identical. Someone, his name lost to oblivion, sent the copy to the publishers with a June 26 release date. The handouts quaintly said: "Mr. Printer. Please to insert the following in your next paper." This first college commencement itself was perhaps the first in a long series of events publicly staged to gain public attention.

The tools and techniques of public relations have long been an important part of the weaponry in political warfare. The origins of sustained efforts to move and manipulate public opinion lead back to the Revolutionary War and the work of Samuel Adams and his cohorts, "Sam Adams owned no superior as a propagandist. No one in the colonies realized more

---

[3] Samuel Eliot Morison, *The Founding of Harvard College* (Cambridge, Mass.: Harvard University Press, 1935), p. 303.

fully than he the primary necessity of arousing public opinion, no one set about it more assiduously." [4] In the view of a contemporary practitioner, Adams' "classic campaign foreshadowed, in certain elements, some of the principles of persuasion which remain evident two centuries later." [5] Although the common people gave the Revolution its strength, it was a small group of men who organized and promoted the revolt. These militants— among them Adams, his cousin John Adams, Thomas Paine, Alexander Hamilton, Benjamin Franklin, John Dickinson, Dr. Joseph Warren, and Thomas Jefferson—brought about the birth of this nation.

The twenty-year struggle from 1763 to 1783 was sustained by this small band of revolutionaries who struggled uphill against great odds— against the strong pro-British loyalties of many influential citizens, against the apathy of most persons who were occupied with the hard tasks of life in a primitive country. These men were among the first to demonstrate the power of an organized, articulate minority carrying the day against the unorganized, apathetic majority—a lesson that has marched around the world and into this day. Davidson rightly states "the influence of the propagandists was out of all proportion to their number." John Adams would reflect: "The Revolution was indeed effected in the period from 1761 to 1775. I mean a complete revolution in the minds of the people. . . . All this was done and the principles all established and the system matured before the year 1775." [6] Then, as today, public opinion could be moved over time but the task took skill, time, persistence, and organization.

These propaganda efforts were given added power by the slow, feeble lines of communication to and from England. Then, as now, a vacuum of public concern would be filled by rumor and allegation if not first filled with authentic information. It would take from eight to ten weeks to get an act of Parliament published in the colonies. Even more time would elapse before the often angry reaction of the colonists would be fed back to the British authorities by the royal governors; quite often this feedback was distorted or sugar-coated. Recognizing this communications gulf, Edmund Burke observed ". . . the want of a speedy explanation of a single point is enough to defeat a whole system." Historian Arthur Schlesinger Sr.'s observation that "the London authorities were too far away and too immersed in their own concerns to give the situation more than offhand attention" can be applied to many executives today.

Sam Adams and his fellow revolutionaries understood the importance of public opinion and knew, intuitively, how to arouse and channel it to-

---

[4] Philip Davidson, *Propaganda and the American Revolution, 1763–1783* (Chapel Hill: University of North Carolina Press, 1941), p. 3. Now available in paperback.

[5] William H. Baldwin, Jr., "Bicentenary of a Classic Campaign," *Public Relations Quarterly*, Vol. 10, Spring, 1965, p. 9.

[6] Page Smith, *John Adams* (New York: Doubleday & Co., 1962), 2 vols., p. 1097.

ward their predetermined ends. To do this they used pen, platform, pulpit, staged events, symbols, the leak, and political organization—in a determined, imaginative, and unrelenting way. Adams worked tirelessly to first arouse and then organize public opinion, proceeding always on the assumption that "the bulk of mankind are more led by their senses than by their reason." Adams early discerned that public opinion resulted from the march of events and the way these events were seen by those active in public affairs. He once wrote Joseph Warren: ". . . it will be wise for us to be ready for all Events, that we may make the best improvement of them." Adams would create events to meet a need if none were at hand to serve his purpose.

In staging the Boston Tea Party, Sam Adams demonstrated the value of created events to dramatize a point of view or situation. From this carefully-planned protest came a new spirit of unity in colonial America.[7] An Adams biographer, John C. Miller, believes the Tea Party "was a headlong plunge toward a revolt which set free the forces, long gathering in America, that led to the war." The dumping of British tea in Boston harbor was effective because Adams and his colleagues got their side of the story to the public first. Paul Revere rode express to carry the patriots' version of the Tea Party to New York and Philadelphia. A broadside was published which appealed for support in the common cause, and letters were written by members of the committee of correspondence.

Similarly, Adams and his group had exploited the Boston Massacre and turned a skirmish between some British soldiers and a gang of toughs into an emotional symbol of brutality and oppression. On the night of March 5, 1770, a file of British regulars, after a sentry had been attacked near the Boston Customs House, fired into their tormentors. Five were killed, others hurt. The propagandists quickly labeled this the "Boston Massacre" and, in the words of Bruce Lancaster, "turned the dead port toughs into martyrs, orating and thundering how they had been shot down in cold blood by hireling troops." The Boston Town Meeting quickly issued a pamphlet giving its version of "the HORRID MASSACRE" and disseminated it to the English-speaking world. The date, under Adams' deft hand, became a hallowed anniversary in the colonies.

In the same fashion, these propagandists saw to it that the patriots' version of the clash at Lexington and Concord got to England ahead of the official account sent by General Gage to defend his actions. Carried by Captain John Darby of Salem, a skipper who knew how to crowd sail, the colonists' version was rushed to London where colonial propagandist, Arthur Lee, quickly circulated it among the not inconsiderable group of

---

[7] Benjamin Woods Labaree, *The Boston Tea Party* (New York: Oxford University Press, 1966), p. 168.

American supporters. Gage's account was anti-climactic when it got there eleven days later.[8]

From the founding of the *Independent Advertiser* in 1748, Adams, under a variety of pseudonyms, wrote hundreds of essays attacking England. Near the climax of the struggle, he filled the *Boston Gazette* and other colonial papers with emotion-laden articles, letters from other colonies, clippings from other newspapers—all designed to arouse hatred of the British and arouse demands for self-government. "No other pen in Boston was so busy as his," Royal Governor Bernard once wrote of Adams. "Every dip of his pen stung like a horned snake." Colonial newspapers bore the brunt of the anti-British campaign, and publication of these essays "emboldened patriots everywhere to speak their minds." "Press-agentry took on more of its modern form in the years leading up to and during the first war with England," writes Alfred McClung Lee. "Samuel Adams and his associates between 1748 and the Revolution centered a propaganda exchange about Rogers and Fowle's *The Independent Advertiser* (Boston) until 1750 and Edes & Gills' *The Boston Gazette* from 1775; that bureau had all the fundamentals of George Creel's organization of World War fame. . . ."[9]

Heavy reliance was also placed on the pamphlet, described by Bailyn as "the distinctive literature of the Revolution." More than 400 of these polemical, vituperative, passion-arousing pamphlets were published between 1750 and 1776, and by 1783, more than 1,500 had appeared. These were primarily political documents.[10]

To create a channel of communication that would solidify the thirteen scattered colonies, Adams organized the Committees of Correspondence to circulate information, a channel suited to the day of letter writing when stages and express couriers linked the main cities along the Atlantic Seaboard. Through these committees passed a constant flow of information and exhortation to concerted action against the British. Adams saw the committees as a means of building confidence in one another, in forming plans of opposition, and making clear to the British that the opposition came from all colonies. By August, 1774, the entire country was covered by this communications chain, made possible by the enlarged postroads system started by Benjamin Franklin in 1753. Communication was not easy in a colonial America without the telegraph, telephone, television, or a

[8] Arthur B. Tourtellot, *William Diamond's Drum* (New York: Doubleday & Co., 1959), pp. 236–241.

[9] *The Daily Newspaper in America* (New York: The Macmillan Company, 1937), p. 40. A useful book by America's pioneer public relations teacher.

[10] Bernard Bailyn, *The Idealogical Origins of the American Revolution* (Cambridge, Mass.: Harvard University Press, 1967).

national press. For example, it took six weeks for the news of Lexington and Concord to permeate the colonies.[11]

The revolutionaries made extensive and effective use of symbols— for example the Tree of Liberty in Boston's Hanover Square—, rallies of protest, parades, poetry, anniversary salutes, slogans, and songs to keep up their drumfire of protest. Without doubt, Adams "was a master of stage-craft, deeply versed in the art of swaying the popular mind." Miller records: [12] "The Sons of Liberty celebrated the repeal of the Stamp Act with 'such illuminations, bonfires, pyramids, obelisks, such grand exhibitions, and such fireworks as were never before seen in America.' Effigies of popular enemies were used to inflame the people's passion; cartoons exhibiting in easily understood form the wickedness of the Tories and mother country were passed from hand to hand; stirring phrases were coined and spread among the common people with greater effect than whole volumes of political reasoning (e.g. No taxation without representation); Whig newspapers carried the radicalism of the seaboard towns to every corner of the province." They even used slides to get across their message. Paul Revere fashioned a crude sort of slide by displaying oilpaper transparencies on a font in front of lighted candles. These, says Schlesinger, "lent color and drama to nocturnal Whig affairs." These slides usually depicted American magnanimity and British malignity side by side.

In weak contrast to the bold, effective ways of communication developed by the revolutionists, the Tories, supporters of King George and the British Empire, relied not so much on propaganda as on legal and military pressures—to no avail. Little wonder that an exuberant Sam Adams would exult when he heard the firing at Lexington, "Oh, what a glorious morning this is!" He and his fellow propagandists had done their work well.

The next skirmish in the continuing struggle for power in this new land came in the conflict of those brilliant protagonists, Hamilton and Jefferson. Without stretching the point, the *Federalist* papers can be called public relations documents. David Truman says, "The entire effort of which The *Federalist* was a part was one of the most skillful and important examples of pressure group activity in American history." Morrison and Commager hold that "unless the Federalists had been shrewd in manipulation as they were sound in theory, their arguments could not have prevailed."

Historian Allan Nevins extravagantly describes the propaganda efforts

[11] Frank Luther Mott, "Newspaper Coverage of Lexington and Concord," *New England Quarterly*, Vol. 17, December, 1944, pp. 489–505.

[12] John C. Miller, *Sam Adams, Pioneer in Propaganda* (Stanford, Calif.: Stanford University Press, 1960), p. 112.

of Alexander Hamilton, James Madison, and John Jay as "history's finest public relations job." He believes, "Obtaining national acceptance of the Constitution was essentially a public relations exercise, and Hamilton, with his keen instinct for public relations, took thought not only to the product but to the ready acquiescence of thoughtful people; and he imparted his views to others. . . . Once the Constitution came before the country, the rapidity with which Hamilton moved was a striking exemplification of good public relations. He knew that if a vacuum develops in popular opinion, ignorant and foolish views will fill it. No time must be lost in providing accurate facts and sound ideas." [13]

A Hamilton contemporary, James Wilson, saw the Federalist papers as "the frankest, baldest, and boldest propaganda ever penned." Robert Rutland in *The Ordeal of the Constitution* terms this effort to win ratification our "first national political campaign." Whatever its weight in the final decision may have been—and this is a matter of conjecture—Hamilton's shrewd and skilled publicity campaign set political propaganda patterns that lasted well into the Nineteenth Century. The opposing public relations effort was spearheaded by Richard Henry Lee of Virginia who chose the tactics of gentle persuasion in sharp contrast with the stridency of some Antifederalists.

Professor William Crosskey strongly dissents from the Nevins view, arguing that "the Federalist Papers were not widely read or copied hardly at all." "This fable," asserts Crosskey, "is repeated by writer after writer, with no apparent notion of the truth." [14] A more balanced view is expressed by Douglass Adair, who says, "The Federalist's propaganda value, as first published in the newspapers, should not be overrated; the essays probably influenced few votes among the general electorate." [15] Then, as now, it was hard to measure the impact of propaganda tracts. For certain, Hamilton never "neglected the cultivation of popular favor by fair and justifiable expedients."

The first clear beginnings of the public support-seeking Presidential campaign and of the presidential press secretary's function came in the era of Andrew Jackson and in the work of Amos Kendall. The late 1820s and early 1830s was the period in which the common man won the ballot and started the free public school. The literate public was greatly enlarged, and its political interests were stimulated by a burgeoning, strident party press as a new generation pushed to the fore. As the people gained political power, it became necessary to campaign for their support. No longer

---

[13] Allan Nevins, *The Constitution Makers and the Public, 1785–1790* (New York: Foundation for Public Relations Research and Education, 1962), p. 10.

[14] William Crosskey, *Politics and the Constitution* (Chicago: University of Chicago Press, 1953), 2 vols., p. 9.

[15] Douglass Adair, "The Authorship of the Disputed Federalist Papers," Part II, *William and Mary Quarterly*, Vol. 1, 1944, p. 236.

was government the exclusive concern of the patrician few. "The new Democracy was heavily weighted with what gentlemen were pleased to call the rabble." With the rise of democracy in America came increasing rights for, and power of, the individual.[16] The ensuing power struggle produced another unsung pioneer in public relations, Amos Kendall.

As the key member of President Jackson's "Kitchen Cabinet," Kendall, a former Kentucky newspaper editor, served Jackson as a pollster, counselor, ghost writer, and publicist. The "Kitchen Cabinet" was almost supreme in creating events to mold opinion. On all vital issues that arose, Jackson consulted these key advisers. Most of them were former newspapermen.

Jackson, an unlettered man inarticulate in political or social philosophy, could not get his ideas across with ease. He, like many a modern executive, needed Kendall, the specialist, to convey his ideas to Congress and the country. Jackson's political campaigns and his governmental policies clearly reveal the influence of Kendall's strategy, sense of public opinion, and skill as a communicator.

Although Samuel Adams had used the press, committees of correspondence, staged events, and other devices, his lasting influence on public relations is negligible. Once the Revolution was won, Adams turned to other things. Kendall, in contrast, more closely approached today's counselor in his concepts and practices. He closed out his life as a lobbyist. The role played by Kendall in Jackson's administration is quite comparable to that of James Hagerty in President Eisenhower's administration. Kendall worked at the top policy-making level and was always closely consulted on major issues while they were being shaped. He devised much of Jackson's strategy.

Amos Kendall wrote most of Jackson's speeches, many of his letters and reports. He organized and developed the administration's official mouthpiece, *The Globe,* which set a new pattern for the party press of that day. He wrote and sent out countless releases on a wide basis. By the time Jackson was elected President, the United States had more newspapers and more readers than any other country in the world. Kendall sensed the increased impact the press had on opinion. He possessed a sure sense of mass psychology and an ability to communicate complex ideas in the plain language of the frontier.

He also shrewdly polled public opinion. Kendall carefully analyzed newspaper comment and content and sensitively gauged the public temper. Jackson drew much of his strength from the people by offering ideas congenial to them. Kendall took care to find out what the people wanted. During the Bank fight with Nicholas Biddle, for example, Kendall made a

---

[16] T. Swann Harding, "Genesis of One 'Government Propaganda Mill,'" *Public Opinion Quarterly,* Vol. 11, Summer, 1947, pp. 227–35. History of public relations in Department of Agriculture.

trip to Baltimore, Philadelphia, New York, and Boston. He sounded out bankers and others on Jackson's plan to withdraw federal funds from the Second Bank of the United States and to place these deposits with state banks. Kendall made a favorable report upon his return, and the President withdrew the deposits. Kendall sought to keep open the lines of communication between Jackson and the people from whom he drew his support.

Nicholas Biddle and his associates also were fully alert to the ways of influencing public opinion. In fact, banks were the first business interests to use the press to try to influence opinion. The banks, by loans to editors and by placement of advertisements, influenced many newspapers and silenced others. John C. Calhoun asserted as early as 1816 that the banks had, "in great measure, control over the press." [17] Biddle's publicist, Mathew St. Clair Clarke, saturated the nation's press with press releases, reports, and pamphlets stating the bank's case. In 1830 it spent $7,000 for printing and distributing a bank report and pamphlet by Albert Gallatin. In March, 1831, the bank's board authorized Biddle "to cause to be prepared and circulated such documents and papers as may communicate to the people information in regard to the nature and operations of the bank." The pamphlets, the many articles planted in the press, the build-up of Davy Crockett, and the lobbying efforts by Biddle and his associates were unavailing against the forces of Jackson and Kendall.[18]

Like many of today's practitioners, Kendall operated from backstage and preferred anonymity. Most of his work for Jackson was performed while he served in the rather obscure post of fourth auditor of the treasury. Kendall could often be found late at night, sitting in his unpretentious office in the old treasury building, preparing messages, writing pamphlets, devising political war maps, or earnestly consulting Jackson's other advisers. On other nights he would be working in the White House. The President's White House bedroom was the scene of many night conferences, at which Kendall was the chief scribe. It was there that Jackson and Kendall planned strategy, fashioned their verbal thunderbolts, and prepared speeches and state papers. From this backstage position, the unkempt but shrewd Kendall contributed much to Jackson's success, to American history, and to the beginnings of public relations.[19]

---

[17] James L. Crouthamel, "Did the Second Bank of the United States Bribe the Press?" *Journalism Quarterly*, Vol. 36, 1959.

[18] See: Bray Hammond, *Banks and Politics in America* (Princeton: Princeton University Press, 1957) and Mathew St. Clair Clarke and D. A. Hall, *Legislative and Documentary History of the Bank of the United States* (Washington, D.C., 1832).

[19] For one example of Kendall's work, see Lynn Marshall, "The Authorship of Jackson's Bank Veto Message," *Mississippi Valley Historical Review*, Vol. L, December, 1963. For fuller view of Kendall's influence see Arthur M. Schlesinger, Jr.'s *The Age of Jackson* and other histories of this period. Also, *Autobiography of Amos Kendall* (Micro-Offset Books, 1949, reprinted). To compare Kendall's role with that of Hagerty, see "The White House: Authentic Voice," *Time*, Vol. 71, January 27, 1958.

THE STAGE IS SET BY 1900

The modern concept and terminology were little known in those days of young America. There were few coercions for the development of full-scale public relations in nineteenth century America. There were no means of mass communication on a national basis. Group relationships were relatively simple, and people, on the whole, were rather self-sufficient and independent. Large-scale development was to wait for the twentieth century, after our history had passed through the watershed of the 1890s. But many of the generating forces had their origins in the last century. Alan Raucher holds: [20] "Three major antecedents of twentieth-century publicity can be distinguished from their sometimes shady pasts. One of these was press-agentry. Another was advertising. A third antecedent for publicity, rather unexpectedly, came from business critics and reformers. By the first decade of the century, those three elements, largely unnoticed by contemporaries, fused into a new compound." Of the elements that formed this new compound, public relations, three of these—press-agentry, political campaigning, and business practices—merit a word. The roots of a practice so varied, a concept so diffused, are to be found in many places.

PRESS-AGENTRY

It is a gross oversimplification to state flatly that public relations has evolved from press-agentry. Such a statement, however, does have a degree of truth. Systematic efforts to attract or divert public attention are as old as efforts to persuade and propagandize. Much of what we define as public relations was labeled press-agentry when it was being used to promote land settlement in our unsettled West or to build up political heroes. For example, the legend of Daniel Boone, now woven deeply in the fabric of our culture, was the creation of a land owner promoting settlement in Kentucky.[21]

Elements of press-agentry are to be found in many public relations programs today but not as strongly as the critics of public relations assert. Mainly the press agents, beginning with Phineas T. Barnum and the theatrical press agents who followed, developed as an adjunct to show business and advertising. Box-office enterprises still are the prime employers of press agents.

Amos Kendall's time brought an effective demonstration of the "build-

---

[20] *Public Relations and Business, 1900–1929* (Baltimore, Md.: Johns Hopkins University Press, 1968). A history.

[21] John Walton, *John Filson of Kentucky* (Lexington: University of Kentucky Press, 1956). Filson created the Boone legend.

up" when Jackson's opponents created the myth of Davy Crockett in an effort to woo the frontier vote away from Old Hickory. Crockett's press agent was Mathew St. Clair Clarke. The Davy Crockett legend was given an intensive if short-lived revival in the 1950s, when Walt Disney featured that "yaller flower of the forest" in movies, TV programs, books, and records. Disney did not create the Crockett legend; he embellished it. Davy was a boorish boob, not a brave hero. The Whigs, stressing his eccentricities, humor, and lusty pioneer spirit, turned him into a vote-getting buffoon. Books were turned out in the name of this almost illiterate man. When he was defeated for Congress, Crockett told his constituents that they could go to hell, and went off to Texas to die at the Alamo. This put a dramatic finish to his life but not his colorful legend.[22]

But the master of them all was Phineas Taylor Barnum—and he knew it. Barnum was born in 1810 and died in 1891. His life span covered a period of great importance in the evolution of public relations. His influence lives today. Barnum's recent biographer, Irving Wallace, writes: "Barnum's showmanship was evident not only in a canny instinct that enabled him to give the masses what they wanted, but also in his ability to dictate to them a desire for what he thought they should want. . . . Every man has his star. Barnum's star was an exclamation mark." Promoter Barnum also employed a press agent—Richard F. "Tody" Hamilton. Dexter Fellows, a latter-day circus drumbeater, said that "Tody" Hamilton developed the art of exaggeration into a fine art. Fellows writes: "Chary as Barnum was of giving credit to anyone but himself, he has been quoted as saying that he owed more of his success to Tody Hamilton than to any other man." [23]

Barnum's most notable successes were in the build-up of Tom Thumb, the midget, the American tour of Jenny Lind, "The Swedish Nightingale," and the circus that long carried his name. When he died, he left an estate of more than $4-million. Barnum, a master showman, was fully aware of publicity and used it cleverly. He knew how to exploit the news values of controversy, the bizarre, the fantastic. He knew the box office appeal of pure notoriety. He bought yards of newspaper space to hawk his wonders. But he got much more through fakery and staged events.[24] It was an early

---

22 For accounts of Davy's build-up: James A. Shackford, *David Crockett, the Man and Legend* (Chapel Hill: University of North Carolina Press, 1956); Marshall Fishwick, *American Heroes*, pp. 70–71; and Vernon Parrington, *Main Currents in American Thought*, Vol. Two, pp. 173–178.

23 Dexter W. Fellows and Andrew A. Freeman, *This Way to the Big Show* (New York: Halcyon House, 1938), p. 193.

24 See: *The Life of P. T. Barnum, Written by Himself* (Redfield, 1855), pp. 154–174; Harvey W. Root, *The Unknown Barnum*; James S. Hamilton, *Barnum*; Waldo R. Browne, *Barnum's Own Story*; and the most recent and reliable biography, Irving Wallace, *The Fabulous Showman: Life and Times of P. T. Barnum.*

rival of Barnum's, Hackaliah Bailey, who first used paid advertising in 1815 to publicize the first elephant brought to America. A circus historian asserts: [25]

> It was clearly the circus which originated and developed newspaper display advertising. . . . It started with the very first traveling menagerie, Hackaliah Bailey's tour of 'Old Bet,' and grew with the industry. The first press agent; the first advertising agencies; first regular and specialized use of cuts and mats, press releases, free publicity . . . all came at the hands of the circus.

The earliest known use of the term *press agent* is found in the 1868 roster of John Robinson's Circus and Menagerie. This listed, as the circus's third top executive, "W. W. Duran, Press Agent." It can be presumed that Robinson's competitors used press agents, possibly before he did, and that they were fairly common even at that early date. Their number today is legion. The showman led the way and others followed in an ever-increasing number. Success begets imitators. During the two decades before 1900, the art infiltrated from the show business into closely related enterprises. In due time it was in almost every type of enterprise that needed to attract the public's attention. Book publishers, for example, found this new technique profitable in boosting book sales.

"Buffalo Bill" Cody is another American folklore hero who owes his place in history to the work of press agents. Marshall Fishwick writes: [26] "Cody's principal hero-makers were Ned Buntline, Prentiss Ingraham, and John Burke. Also helpful were Nate Salesbury, Texas Jack Omohundro, Dexter Fellows, Courtney Ryley Cooper, and Johnnie Baker. To them belongs credit for making Buffalo Bill the most highly publicized figure in Western history. What they did was not easy; no one should underestimate their endeavors. More spectacular men had to be outdistanced. Mountains had to be made out of molehills."

In 1911, Will Irwin, a shrewd and observing journalist, wrote: [27]

> But while the theatrical press agent declined, a hundred, a thousand other kinds of press agents arose, unperceived by the public. The theatrical managers had shown how easy it was to get free news space—more valuable, generally, than any amount of display advertising—by a little ingenuity and much inside knowledge of the newspaper game. They had

[25] Robert Parkinson, "The Circus and the Press," *Bandwagon*, Vol. 7 (1963), pp. 3–9.

[26] Fishwick, *American Heroes*, pp. 100–110. Also see Dixon Wecter's *The Hero in America* (Ann Arbor: University of Michigan, 1963), pp. 341–363.

[27] Will Irwin, "The Press Agent: His Rise and Decline," *Collier's*, Vol. 48, December 2, 1911, p. 24.

proved another thing—how smooth a good press agent can make the relations between a corporation or an institution and the prying, troublesome newspapers. Forthwith, there arose a new profession, numbering its
hundreds, its thousands, and finally its tens of thousands. "Half the population is trying to get into the newspapers and half to keep out"—that is
a maxim almost as old as the news era. But where the assault on the news
columns had been a straggling, guerilla fight, it became organized warfare, full of strategies so subtle that the keenest and most conscientious
news editor must be beaten in detail again and again.

As press agents grew in number and their exploits became more incredible—albeit successful more often than not—it was natural that they
would arouse the hostility and suspicion of editors. It was inevitable that
the practice and its practitioners would become tainted. This inherent suspicion remains as part of public relations' heritage.

POLITICAL CAMPAIGNING

Public relations has long been an essential part of the political party's
apparatus. Virginian John Beckley must rank among the first of a long line
of political propagandists and organizers who have made our political party
system work. He was a devoted aide of Thomas Jefferson in building what
was then known as the Republican Party but today is the Democratic
Party. He was Jefferson's eyes and ears and his propagandist, "one of the
leading party organizers of the 1790's." [28] However, development of modern political campaign methods and techniques, except insofar as these
have been modified by television, are largely rooted in the last decade of
the nineteenth century. Increasingly "the activities of the public relations
man have become a significant influence in processes crucial to democratic
government." [29] In the final two decades of the nineteenth century, techniques used by the political party managers changed with the changing
American environment, then rushing headlong toward industrialization and
urbanization. Between 1880 and 1900 the political campaign methods that
still prevail crystallized. The campaign methods originated by Kendall and
his fellow "Kitchen Cabinet" members had remained essentially unchanged
after the rise of democracy and enfranchisement of the people, save for a
few minor refinements.

The bitter, close race in the Tilden-Hayes presidential campaign
jarred both groups of party leaders. They began searching for new ways

[28] Noble E. Cunningham, Jr., "John Beckley: An Early American Party Manager," *William and Mary Quarterly*, Vol. 13, January 1956, pp. 40–52.

[29] Stanley Kelley, Jr., *Professional Public Relations and Political Power* (Baltimore: Johns Hopkins University Press, 1956). Provides more recent examples and discusses rise of public relations man in political parties.

to enlist the support of the rapidly growing host of voters in a population fed by high birth rates and immigration. The campaign of 1880 saw the introduction of campaign literature on a mass scale. This development stemmed, in part, from the growth of the press, improved printing presses, a more abundant supply of cheap paper, and the need to "educate" the new immigrants. This development, in turn, spurred the evolution of the party "literary bureau" into a real press bureau. *Munsey's Magazine* says that "campaign literature" was carefully prepared and read.[30]

> Expert and experienced political managers give their closest attention to this detail. Men who are learned as regard to the issues at stake, and who have that requisite of the successful politician which might be termed a knowledge of applied psychology, hold the blue pencil. Paragraphs, sentences, and words are weighed with reference to their effect on the mind of their reader. What will be of advantage to one part of the country may be useless or possibly harmful in other parts.

The hard-hitting Bryan-McKinley campaign of 1896 marked the first use of modern political campaigning methods. It set a pattern which served for sixty years. Both parties moved their campaign headquarters to Chicago for this epic struggle. From both headquarters there flowed a heavy stream of pamphlets, posters, press releases and other campaign propaganda, now a standard part of the American political campaign. The 1896 pattern of campaigning was, for the most part, repeated in 1900 and continued in subsequent campaigns, with slight modification, until the introduction of radio broadcasting in the mid-1920's.

In this precedent-setting 1896 campaign, the Republicans relied primarily on a costly publicity campaign and on GOP-financed pilgrimages of special groups to McKinley's front porch in Canton, Ohio. The penny-pinched Democrats relied mainly on the oratory of Bryan, carried across the country in the first campaign train. McKinley's Chicago headquarters spent nearly a half-million dollars for printing, and the publicity bureau, under Perry Heath, flooded the nation's press with releases, cartoons, and boiler plate and the nation's homes and stores with posters and pamphlets. A conservative estimate places the GOP campaign budget at $3.5-million. The Republicans even took a rudimentary public opinion poll, today a central instrument of political campaigns. The large-scale publicity bureau and the campaign train used in this contest became fixtures of national election campaigns in a nation whose electorate now stretched across a 3,000 mile continent.[31]

---

[30] Luther B. Little, "The Printing Press in Politics," *Munsey's Magazine*, Vol. 23, September 1900, pp. 740–744.

[31] For full account, see Stanley L. Jones, *The Presidential Election of 1896* (Madison, Wis.: University of Wisconsin Press, 1964).

Full-scale use of television in 1952 and 1956 marked the beginning of the end of this historic pattern. As the population grew, the voters became more and more out of reach of the stump-speaker. Indirect methods of communication were inevitably pushed to the fore. This trend started in the latter part of the nineteenth century. By 1900, the manager of the political press bureau, both national and state, had assumed most of the functions which characterize today's practitioner. Ivy Lee's first appearance on the national scene came as publicity man for Judge Alton B. Parker in the 1904 Presidential campaign.

THE BEGINNINGS IN BUSINESS

The last two decades of the nineteenth century brought discernible beginnings of today's public relations practice. It is here that we find the roots of a vocation that flowered in the seedbed years of 1900–1917. The fundamental force in setting the stage for public relations in the Twentieth Century was the wild, frenzied, and bold development of industry, railroads, and utilities in America's post-Civil-War years. In the twenty-five breathtaking years from 1875 to 1900, America doubled its population and jammed its people into cities; went into mass production and enthroned the machine; spanned the nation with rail and wire communications; developed the mass media of press and magazine; replaced the plantation baron with the prince of industry and finance; and replaced the versatile frontiersman with the specialized factory-hand. In all this was laid the foundation for the mightiest industrial machine the world has yet known. These were years of rapid change exceeded only by the acceleration since then.

The rise of powerful monopolies, concentration of wealth and power, and the roughshod tactics of the robber barons and their imitators were to bring a wave of protest and reform in the early 1900's. Contemporary public relations, as a practice and as philosophy, was to emerge out of the melee of the opposing forces in this period of the nation's rapid growth. Goldman observes, "Shouldering aside agriculture, large-scale commerce and industry became dominant over the life of the nation. Big business was committed to the doctrine that the less the public knew of its operations, the more efficient and profitable—even the more socially useful—the operations would be." [32] As the autocratic railroad magnate E. H. Harriman told Clarence J. Hicks, "I don't want anything on this railroad that I cannot control." Bold exploitation of the people and of the natural resources of this rich, young continent was bound to bring, ultimately, protest and

---

[32] Eric F. Goldman, *Two-Way Street* (Boston: Bellman Publishing Co., 1948). A sketchy history.

reform once the people became aroused. This was the era of "the public be damned."

Incidentally, there is considerable dispute about the origin of this often quoted remark. It frequently has been erroneously attributed to salty old Commodore Vanderbilt. If it was used at all, it was used by his son, William Henry Vanderbilt, in an interview with Chicago reporters aboard his private railroad car, October 8, 1882. When questioned about the public's interest in the removal of a fast New York Central train between New York and Chicago, young Vanderbilt was quoted as saying, "The public be damned. . . . I don't take any stock in this silly nonsense about working for anybody's good but our own because we are not. When we make a move we do it because it is in our interest to do so. . . ." A few days later, in an interview with a reporter from the *New York Tribune,* Vanderbilt denied using the phrase: "I never used it, and that is all there is about it." Whether or not Vanderbilt used the phrase mattered little. The quote stuck with him because it accurately symbolized the attitude of the business giants of that day, men whom Charles Francis Adams described as a "coarse, realistic, bargaining crowd."

The first strong protest movement came from the National Grange, an obscure secret order known at first as "Patrons of Husbandry." The Grange had a sudden and spectacular growth. This spearhead of the agrarian revolt was largely responsible for passage of the Interstate Commerce Act of 1887, first of the Granger regulatory laws designed to curb the excesses of the new industrial era. This Act subsequently was influential in inducing PR programs in public utilities and carriers. After this peak, the Grange slowly receded in influence. Its protest strength flowed into other groups, such as the Farmer's Alliance, the Greenbackers, and the Populist Party. The people were on the march against the excessive abuses of Big Business in what Parrington called "a huge buccaneering orgy."

The prevailing hard-bitten attitudes of businessmen toward people— be they employees, customers, or voters—in this era was epitomized in the brutal methods used by Henry Clay Frick to crush a labor union in the Carnegie-Frick Steel Company's Homestead, Pa., plant in 1892. Callous, tough Henry Frick directed the struggle while Carnegie indifferently viewed events from afar in his Scottish castle, seemingly unperturbed by the brutality and killings Frick ordered. The employees' strike was ultimately broken and the union destroyed by the use of Pennsylvania state militia. Coldblooded might won this battle. The employees would eventually win the war. Much of public relations history is woven into this unending struggle between employer and employee which today, fortunately, is fought with public relations men, not Pinkertons.[33]

---

[33] For concise account, see Leon Wolff, *Lockout* (New York: Harper and Row, 1965).

Big business's response to the swelling protests of an increasingly articulate public is reflected in the changing posture and tactics of John D. Rockefeller's Standard Oil Trust. In the 1880s and 1890s, Standard Oil came to stand before the bar of public opinion as the epitome of the evils of business. At first Rockefeller and his associates ignored their critics and gave the public no information, as they went about the business of getting a stranglehold on the petroleum industry. As criticism mounted, Standard Oil began to respond with apologia and with subsidies to organs of opinion. For example, it bought stock in Oil City, Pa., and Cleveland newspapers and paid George Gunton, an English-trained economist, to rebut the charges of the fiery Dr. Washington Gladden, a Congregational minister. Next, it turned to paid but unlabeled editorial readers placed in newspapers by the Malcolm Jennings News Bureau and Advertising Agency. None of these tactics proved effective in the long run.[34]

Historian Merle Curti observes, "Corporations gradually began to realize the importance of combating hostility and courting public favor. The expert in the field of public relations was an inevitable phenomenon in view of the need for the services he could provide. As early as the 1890's, George Harvey, a newspaper man and publisher, was engaging in public relations activities for Thomas Fortune Ryan and Harry Payne Whitney, well-known promoters and financiers." [35] Even before this, the Mutual Life Insurance Company had employed a man by the name of Charles J. Smith to manage a "species of literary bureau," in about 1888. According to one writer, "In ordinary times his (Smith's) activities have been general and rather unimportant, but in time of emergency they are enlarged; for instance, last September when the investigation began, he turned all his strength to preparing articles calculated to counteract the reports of the investigations sent out through regular news channels." [36]

In fact, there is evidence that these buccaneers of old utilized "press representatives" as early as 1869, when a congressional committee brought out that John Bigelow, editor of the *New York Times,* had dealt with James McHenry, a press representative of the notorious Fisk-Gould interests. In the latter half of the nineteenth century, the railroads were the intensive users of publicity men and promotional agents. Railroads developed the art of publicity to promote settlement along the iron rails reaching to the Pacific Ocean and to fend off rising tides of public criticism. In 1859 Charles Russell Lowell, a promoter for the Burlington Railroad,

---

[34] For details, see Ralph W. and Muriel E. Hidy, *History of the Standard Oil Company (New Jersey): Pioneering in Big Business, 1882–1911* (New York: Harper, 1955).

[35] Merle Curti, *The Growth of American Thought* (New York: Harper & Row, 1964), 3rd ed., p. 634.

[36] "Manufacturing Public Opinion," *McClure's Magazine,* Vol. 26, February, 1906, pp. 450–52.

wrote: "We are beginning to find that he who buildeth a railroad west of the Mississippi must also find a population and build up business. We wish to blow as loud a trumpet as the merits of our position warrant." [37] Ten years later the Burlington hired "Professor" J. D. Butler to promote Iowa and Nebraska lands through his "widely published entertaining and practical letters," and by means of "well-concocted circulars, posters, and a judicious amount of advertising," which Butler was certain would produce "a big stampede of immigrants for these favored lands." [38] In 1877 Jay Gould hired Robert Strahorn, traveler, promoter, and publicist, to create a literary bureau and advertising department for the Union Pacific Railroad for the same purpose.

Raucher holds that advertising is one of the antecedents of public relations. Though the two functions are fairly distinct in today's business enterprise, they have developed along parallel lines with overlapping of function, blurring of distinctions, and confusion in the public mind. Advertising evolved to meet the needs of business; public relations evolved partly for this reason, but mainly for other reasons. Advertising and product promotion, today intertwined and often confused, have their roots in the post-Civil War industrialization. With introduction of mass production methods, more and more businesses needed regional or national distribution of their soaps, foods, and other products. For example, "To break down consumer bias against eating meat that had been slaughtered weeks earlier and half a continent away, Swift turned to advertising." [39] By 1879, advertising revenue in newspapers totalled $21-million. Much of this early advertising promoted patent medicines. As James Harvey Young has written, "The well-greased engines of advertising and public relations that dominate Madison Avenue today had a humble beginning in the nineteenth century in the promotion of pills and potions guaranteed to cure everything from corns to senility."

What was probably the first corporate public relations department, in the contemporary meaning of this term, was established by George Westinghouse for his newly founded electric corporation in 1889. Westinghouse organized his firm in 1886 to promote his then revolutionary alternating current system of electricity. Thomas A. Edison's Edison General Electric Company was already established with its direct current system of distribution. The now famous battle of "the currents" ensued. Immediately Edison, aided by his right-hand man, the astute public relations-minded Samuel Insull, launched a scare campaign against the West-

---

[37] Richard C. Overton, *Burlington West* (Cambridge: Harvard University Press, 1941), pp. 158–163.

[38] *Ibid.*, pp. 298–303.

[39] Ray Ginger, *The Age of Excess* (New York: Macmillan, 1965), p. 25.

inghouse AC system. McDonald records: [40] "Edison General Electric attempted to prevent the development of alternating current by unscrupulous political action and by even less savory promotional tactics. . . . The promotional activity was a series of spectacular stunts aimed at dramatizing the deadliness of high voltage alternating current, the most sensational being the development and promotion of the electric chair as a means of executing criminals." The State of New York adopted electrocution in 1888. The next year Westinghouse realized he had to get his story to the public, and hired E. H. Heinrichs, a Pittsburgh newspaper man, for this purpose. Heinrichs served Westinghouse as his personal press representative until the latter's death in March, 1914. Heinrichs later indicated that he was not hired because of the "battle of the currents," but because Westinghouse, like today's executive, did not have time to deal with the press. Heinrichs was the company's main channel through which news about the company passed to the press and the one who received reporters. Within the Westinghouse companies, department heads passed news on to Heinrichs which he released to the Pittsburgh press by telephone or personal contact and to other publications by typed press releases. [41] Then, as now, it took specialized skill to gain a hearing in the public opinion arena and to deal with media demands.

OTHER THREADS

Still other threads in the fabric were first woven in the 1880s. The American fund-raising drive, an important task in PR today, was born in the Civil War. Jay Cooke, "the first to understand the psychology of mass salesmanship," conceived and executed the first American fund-raising drive. "A propagandist of truly heroic proportions," Cooke sold war bonds for the Union by first selling patriotism and building a militant public opinion. Many of his techniques reappeared in the bond drives of World Wars I and II. Also, by the time of the Civil War, the United States Marine Corps was using advertising on a regular basis to attract recruits. And in the Spanish-American War of 1898, the work of Cuban propagandists did much to arouse American sympathies for Cuba and to discredit Spain. This junta used press releases and mass meetings to raise funds and promote support for the Cuban cause from 1895 on.

Even professional groups were taking cognizance of public opinion more than a century ago. In 1855 the American Medical Association

---

[40] Forrest McDonald, *Insull* (Chicago: University of Chicago Press, 1962), pp. 44–45. Biography of utility magnate who blazed many pioneer trails in public relations before he crashed to his ruin.

[41] "America's First Press Agent a Well-Known Pittsburger," clipping in Westinghouse Company files, circa 1906.

passed a resolution "urging the secretary of the Association to offer every facility possible to the reporters of the public press to enable them to furnish full and accurate reports of the transactions." And in 1884 the A.M.A. launched the first of its many programs to counter the attacks of the antivivisectionists. Evidence that *public relations thinking* is not brand new is shown in the letter of Theodore N. Vail, rare for its time, reproduced here.

Subject, **re information as to service, rates &c.**

Wm. R. DRIVER, Treasurer.

W.H. FORBES, President.

THE AMERICAN BELL TELEPHONE CO.

THEO. N. VAIL, General Manager.

Nᵒ 95 MILK STREET.

P.O. DRAWER 2.

Personal

W. A. Leary, Esq.
Iowa Union Tel. & Tel. Co.
Davenport, Iowa.

Boston, Dec. 28th, 1883.

In reply to yours

No. 1

Dear Sir : -

    Now that the Telephone business has passed its experimental stage, I would like to get your opinion upon points given below. This opinion to be based upon our existing relations, and upon your own and your associates observation and experience in your particular field : -

    Is the Telephone service as it is now being furnished, satisfactory to the public.

    Are the prices satisfactory to the public, considering the facilities and service that is given.

    Would it be advantageous to furnish the same service now being furnished at any lower rate provided it could be done.

    Is it possible in view of the contingencies of storm, under ground legislation &c., to make any lower rate to the public for same classes of service.

    Is it desirable, and what would be the most practicable way, to provide a service at a rate which would be within the reach of families. etc,.

    Is it practicable to give different classes of service within the same Exchange.

    What has been the tendency of the relationship between the public and the local Co's., for the past year ie., are the relations between the public and the Co's. improving.

    Where there has been any conflict between the local Exchange and the public, what has been the cause of the difficulties, and what has been the result.

    A full and detailed reply from you by the 8th, of January, would be of great service to me. Trusting that I am not asking too much,

    I am,

    Very respectfully, &c.

    Theo.N.Vail

    The Association of American Railroads claims that it was the first business organization to use the term "public relations"—in 1897 in the *Year Book of Railway Literature*.

ADDITIONAL READING

STEWART BEACH, *Samuel Adams, the Fateful Years 1764–1776.* New York: Dodd, Mead and Co., 1965.

EDWARD L. BERNAYS, *Public Relations.* Norman, Okla.: University of Oklahoma Press, 1952. Part One: The Growth of Public Relations.

RAY ALLEN BILLINGTON, *Words That Won the West.* New York: Foundation for Public Relations Research and Education, 1964.

CHARLES P. CULLOP, *Confederate Propaganda in Europe: 1861–1865.* Coral Gables: University of Miami Press, 1969.

MERRILL JENSEN, ed. *Tracts of the American Revolution 1763–1776.* Indianapolis: Bobbs-Merrill, 1967.

For full history of Revolution see his definitive *The Founding of a Nation,* Oxford, 1968.

HUGH T. LEFLER, "Promotional Literature of the Southern Colonies," *Journal of Southern History,* Vol. 33 (1967), p. 24.

ROBERT LINDSAY, *This High Name: Public Relations and the U.S. Marine Corps.* Madison, Wis.: University of Wisconsin Press, 1956.

SIEGFRIED MICKELSON, "Promotional Activities of the Northern Pacific's Land Department," *Journalism Quarterly,* Vol. 17, December, 1940.

CHARLES L. MOWAT, "The First Campaign of Publicity for Florida," *Mississippi Valley Historical Review,* Vol. 30, December, 1943.

"What Mr. Vanderbilt Says," *Railroad Gazette,* Vol. 14, October 13, 1882. (See page 627 for account of interview, page 649 for denial.)

FRANK E. VANDIVER, *The First Public War, 1861–1865.* New York: Foundation for Public Relations Research and Education, 1962.

JAMES HARVEY YOUNG, *The Toadstool Millionaires.* Princeton, N.J.: Princeton University Press, 1961.

CHAPTER 4

FROM 1900 ON— THE BEGINNINGS

I believe in telling your story to the people. If you go
direct to the people and get them to agree with you . . .
everybody else must give way in your favor.

—IVY LEE

Although the roots of today's practice extend deeply into the sands of
time, the *definite beginnings* date from the early 1900s, when the United
States entered the wholly new, exciting, and eventful twentieth century.
The dividing lines may be blurred, but the growth can be traced through
five main periods of development:

1. 1900–1917—The era of muckraking journalism countered by defensive publicity, a period of far-reaching political reforms;
2. 1917–1919—World War I, which brought dramatic demonstrations
   of the power of organized promotion to kindle a fervent patriotism
   —to sell war bonds, and to raise millions for welfare work;
3. 1919–1933—This period saw the principles and practices of publicity learned in the war put to use promoting products, earning
   acceptance for changes wrought by the war-accelerated technology,
   winning political battles, and raising millions of dollars for charitable causes;
4. 1933–1945—The period of the Great Depression and World War
   II, events profound and far-reaching in their impact, which advanced the art and extended the practice of public relations;
5. 1945–present—The Mid-Twentieth Century era, which has brought
   a tremendous boom in public relations practice and a maturing
   concept.

The excesses of the large corporations, railroads, banks, utilities, and
other elements of the business world fed the fires of reform and protest,
as America moved into the twentieth century. The popular revolt against
business was inspired in large part by the astute political leadership of
Theodore Roosevelt, Robert M. LaFollette, and Woodrow Wilson. They
capitalized on public opinion aroused by the writings of David Graham
Phillips, Lincoln Steffens, Upton Sinclair, Ida Tarbell, and others. These
muckraking journalists effectively exploited the newly developed national
forums provided by the popular magazines, national press services, and
feature syndicates. Regier says, "Muckraking . . . was the inevitable result of decades of indifference to the illegalities and immoralities attendant

upon the industrial development of America." [1] The reform and protest period extended, roughly, from 1900 to 1912. The muckrakers took their case to the people and got action, a fact which shrewd observers fully noted. The agitation before 1900 had been primarily among farmers and laborers. Now the urban middle classes took up the cry against corruption in government and the abuses of Big Business. The little fish did not enjoy being swallowed by the big ones. These writers thundered out their denunciations in bold face in the popular magazines and metropolitan newspapers, which now had huge circulations. By 1900, there were at least fifty well-known national magazines, several with circulations of 100,000 or more. The *Ladies Home Journal,* founded only seventeen years before, was approaching a circulation of one-million. The impact of the growing mass media was beginning to be felt. [2]

The muckraker was a key figure in the Progressive movement, which found its strength in the journalism of exposure. "Before there could be action, there had to be information and exhortation. Grievances had to be given specific objects. These the muckraker supplied. It was muckraking that brought the diffuse malaise of the public into focus." [3] The work was dramatically begun by Thomas W. Lawson's *Frenzied Finance,* appearing as a series in *McClure's Magazine* in 1903. Parrington says that the success of the Lawson series "proved that the fire was ready for the fat" and that a host of writers then "fell to feeding the flames." Ida Tarbell's *History of the Standard Oil Company* was described at the time as "a fearless unmasking of moral criminality masquerading under the robes of respectability and Christianity." Upton Sinclair's novel, *The Jungle,* exposed the foul conditions in the meat-packing industry. Both produced violent public reactions. Such exposures gave Big Business a black eye, traces of which still linger. The public wave of protest and reform brought regulatory legislation and a wave of "trust-busting." Businessmen, long in the saddle, were forced to take the defensive. The corporations, the good ones along with the ruthless ones, had lost contact with their publics. For a while they sat helplessly by, inarticulate and frustrated, waiting apprehensively for the next issue of *McClure's Magazine.*

Business leaders, so long accustomed to a veil of secrecy, felt the urge

---

[1] For best account, see C. C. Regier, *The Era of the Muckrakers* (Chapel Hill: University of North Carolina Press, 1932). Regier neglects role of metropolitan newspapers in this muckraking. For generous sampling of articles, see Arthur and Lila Weinberg, eds., *The Muckrakers* (New York: Simon & Schuster, Inc., 1961).

[2] Vernon L. Parrington, *Main Currents in American Thought* (New York: Harcourt, Brace, and World, Inc., 1930), Vol. 3, pp. 404–405. For details on rise of mass media, see: Edwin Emery, *The Press and America;* Theodore Peterson, *Magazines in the Twentieth Century;* James Playsted Wood, *The Story of Advertising.*

[3] Richard Hofstadter, *The Age of Reform* (New York: Alfred A. Knopf, Inc., 1955), p. 185.

to speak out in self-defense but did not know how to reach the people. Their first instinct was to turn to their advertising men and lawyers. In the first stages of the Muckraking Era, many great corporations sought to silence the attacks on them from the press by the judicious and calculated placement and withdrawal of advertising. Thus, the newly established advertising agency was brought into public relations early.

The nation's first publicity firm, The Publicity Bureau, forerunner of today's public relations agency, was founded in Boston in mid-1900 by George V. S. Michaelis, Herbert Small, and Thomas O. Marvin "to do a general press agent business for as many clients as possible for as good pay as the traffic would bear." Michaelis, a Boston newspaperman once described by an associate as "a young man of many expedients," took the lead in organizing this new enterprise, and was with it until 1909 or thereabouts. The agency faded into oblivion sometime after 1911. One of the first persons hired was James Drummond Ellsworth, who would later collaborate with Theodore N. Vail in building the pioneering program of the American Telephone & Telegraph Co.

The agency's first client was Harvard University, which agreed in October, 1900, to pay "$200 a month for professional services." Harvard's President Charles W. Eliot knew the value of publicity and was a demanding person who insisted on accuracy in news releases. The Bureau's work for Harvard did not go smoothly and in 1902, or thereabouts, President Eliot quit paying the Bureau. However, it continued to provide service for the prestige of having Harvard as a client. Clients willing to pay for this new service included Harvard's rival, Massachusetts Institute of Technology, the Fore River Ship Yard, and the Boston Elevated Railway, the first American street railway company to establish its own publicity department.[4]

The Publicity Bureau came into national prominence in 1906, when it was employed by the nation's railroads to head off adverse regulatory legislation then being pushed in Congress by President Roosevelt. Ray Stannard Baker reported at the time: [5] "The fountainhead of public information is the newspaper. The first concern, then, of the railroad organization was to reach the newspapers. For this purpose a firm of publicity agents, with headquarters in Boston, was chosen. . . . Immediately the firm expanded. It increased its Boston staff; it opened offices in New York, Chicago, Washington, St. Louis, Topeka, Kansas . . . and it employed agents in South Dakota, California, and elsewhere. . . ." Baker records that The Publicity Bureau operated secretly, "careful not to advertise the

---

[4] For details and references to primary sources, see: Scott M. Cutlip, "The Nation's First Public Relations Firm," *Journalism Quarterly*, Vol. 43, Summer, 1966, pp. 269–280.

[5] Ray Stannard Baker, "Railroads on Trial," *McClure's Magazine*, Vol. 26, March, 1906, pp. 535–44. Also in Weinbergs' book.

fact that they are in any way connected with the railroads." This firm effectively used the tools of fact-finding, publicity, and personal contact to saturate the nation's press, particularly the weeklies, with the railroads' propaganda. The campaign was to little avail, however, because the Hepburn Act, a moderately tough regulatory measure, was passed in 1906. President Roosevelt used the nation's press and the platform to publicize a more persuasive case. Failure of this nationwide publicity effort caused railroad executives to reassess their public relations methods. This reappraisal led, within a few years, to establishment of their own public relations departments.

The loss of Harvard as a Publicity Bureau account in 1903 was offset when Frederick P. Fish, the new president of A. T. & T., retained the bureau. This move illustrates why there was a market for this new business. Fish earlier, in 1901, had succeeded the tactless John E. Hudson, who had brought A. T. & T. much ill-will by his public be damned attitudes. Fish's retention of the Publicity Bureau came some months after Theodore N. Vail had been brought back to the telephone company by the J. P. Morgan interests. Vail's views carried great weight with Fish, and Vail was keenly aware of the importance of good public relations to long-run business success. Ellsworth says: [6] "Thus a company that had previously been the most secretive, spent good money to have their affairs brought to the public's attention. This right-about change in policy was not without its underlying causes. . . . That people thought their [A. T. & T.'s] secrecy was to cover up discreditable conditions was the management's own fault. And when independent telephone promoters, capitalizing upon the Bell's unpopularity began to build competing and quite unnecessary systems, it was again the management's own fault, because in respect to public sentiment the management had had a blind eye."

Other industries took the cue and turned to the specialist who could tell business' story in the public forum: the newspaperman. It was a matter of fighting fire with fire. Thus began the large-scale recruitment of newspapermen to serve as interpreters for the corporations and other public institutions.[7] Some newspapermen took the Publicity Bureau's lead and organized similar firms. With waves of the popular revolt beating against Capitol Hill, the opportunity for such a firm in Washington became apparent. William Wolff Smith quit his jobs as correspondent for the New York *Sun* and Cincinnati *Enquirer* to open a "publicity business" in the capital in 1902. This agency, too, lasted little more than a decade. A New York *Times* reporter later recalled that the Smith firm solicited "press-

---

[6] "The Twisting Trail," unpublished mss. in Mass Communications History Center, State Historical Society of Wisconsin, Madison.

[7] "The 'Publicity Men' of the Corporations," *World's Work*, Vol. 12, June, 1906, p. 7703.

agent employment from anybody who had business before Congress." [8] The third agency set up in this Seedbed Era—Parker & Lee—had an even shorter life than the first two; it lasted less than four years, but the junior partner left a lasting mark on this emerging craft. Of him, more in a moment.

The Hamilton Wright Organization, Inc. dates from 1908 when Hamilton Mercer Wright, a free lance journalist and publicist, opened an office in San Francisco. He moved to New York City in 1917. His son and grandson, both carrying the same name, have followed in the founder's footsteps by specializing in promotion of foreign countries in the United States. The elder Wright's first publicity work was to publicize California for the California Promotion Committee. His agency's first account was the promotion of the Philippine Islands on behalf of U. S. business interests. The fifth agency started in this seedbed decade would, like Hamilton Wright's, endure; this was the one opened in 1909 by Pendleton Dudley, for half a century an influential figure in public relations. Dudley took his friend Ivy Lee's advice and opened a publicity office in New York's Wall Street district. Fifty-seven years later, Dudley was still the active head of his firm, Dudley-Anderson-Yutzy. He died December 10, 1966, at the age of 90. The second agency organized in Washington, D. C., was that set up by Thomas R. Shipp in 1914. Shipp, like William Wolff Smith and George R. Parker, was a native of Indiana and a former newspaperman. Shipp set out on his own after spending six years learning the arts of publicity and politics under two experts, Theodore Roosevelt and Gifford Pinchot. Shipp was opening his "publicity company" about the time Smith was closing his to return to law school.[9]

For the most part, these ex-newspapermen in the employ of business countered with whitewash and press-agentry. On the whole, they demonstrated little grasp of the fundamental problems in the conflict. There were some exceptions. One of these was Ivy Ledbetter Lee.

IVY LEE

The astute young Lee, son of a Georgia minister and a Princeton graduate, while a reporter covering the business world, shrewdly sized up the situation. He saw the possibilities of earning more money in the service of private organizations who were seeking a voice. After five years as a re-

[8] "Department Press Agents," Hearing Before the Committee on Rules, House of Representatives, May 21, 1912, 62nd Congress, 2nd Sess. (Washington, D.C.: Government Printing Office, 1912), p. 16. Also, see: William Kittle, "The Making of Public Opinion," *Arena*, Vol. 41 (1909), pp. 443–444.

[9] For details of Shipp's career, see obituary, *Washington Post*, Feb. 11, 1952, 2B.

porter, Lee quit his poorly paying job on *The World* in 1903 and went to work for the Citizen's Union, an organization supporting Seth Low's campaign for mayor of New York. Lee's work in this post led to a job in the press bureau of the Democratic National Committee during the 1904 campaign.

Ivy Lee had observed that the business policies of secrecy and silence were failing. He concluded that, in order to be understood, corporations must become articulate, open their books, and take their case directly to the people. *The New York Times,* years later, observed: "Lee brought something new to the business of publicity. When he was a young . . . newspaperman . . . there were numerous press agents in town who promoted the theaters and stage stars, but there was no specialist in publicity for corporations who conferred on terms of equality with the boards of directors of great corporations. His life spanned that change, and he had much to do with the change."

Ivy Lee teamed up with George F. Parker, former Buffalo newspaperman and veteran political publicist, some time after the 1904 Presidential election to organize a public relations firm in New York City. Parker directed the publicity for Grover Cleveland's three campaigns for the Presidency, but Cleveland was not wise enough to use him as a press secretary during his two terms as president.[10] In 1904 Parker was recalled to political battle to direct publicity for the Democratic National Committee in the futile campaign to unseat President Roosevelt. The young Lee was hired to assist Parker. Out of their association and conversations during the campaign came a decision to form a partnership. Pendleton Dudley recalled:[11] "Older than Lee and more widely experienced, Parker had quite definite ideas as to the practical functioning of an independent press agency and a sense of emergency about starting one. . . . Several clients were secured and the partnership prospered modestly for a year or more." However, the relationship of Lee and Parker was neither profitable nor happy, and the firm dissolved in 1908 when Ivy Lee became the Pennsylvania Railroad's first publicity agent. That year Parker set up another partnership with C. A. Bridge, then city editor of the New York *Herald.* Presumably the Parker-Bridge partnership folded in 1913 because that year Parker was appointed to handle publicity for the Protestant Episcopal Church, a position he held until 1919.

Editor & Publisher, which then took a dim view of space-stealing press agents, had high praise for Parker & Bridge:[12]

10 Gordon A. Moon II, "George F. Parker: A 'Near Miss' as First White House Press Chief," *Journalism Quarterly,* Vol. 41, Spring, 1964, pp. 183–190.

11 Pendleton Dudley, "Current Beginnings of PR," *Public Relations Journal,* Vol. 8, April, 1953, pp. 8–10.

12 *Editor & Publisher,* Vol. 7, January 18, 1908, p. 2.

. . . this publicity bureau has established itself firmly in the estimation of editors and publishers. . . . At its birth, this unique institution adopted the motto: 'Accuracy, Authenticity, and Interest.'

It has never made any attempt at deception; matter is sent to the press with the frank statement that it is in behalf of the client, and that no money will be paid for its insertion in the columns of any newspaper.

Ivy Lee, while working as a news reporter in Wall Street in the early years of muckraking, had sensed business' need for an articulate voice in the court of public opinion. Yet, in the early years of his publicity work, he found businessmen unreceptive to his ideas. The rising tide of protest against business gave force to his arguments. In 1906, a large industry—anthracite coal—sought Lee's help after taking a licking in public. He became spokesman for the corporations. This role was to make him rich and influential and to gain for him the dubious title of "father of public relations." Lee explained to all his prospective clients that secrecy was the cause of suspicion. He said he would not "press agent" them. Instead, he would attempt to advise them on how to correct their policies toward the public and to provide favorable notices in the newspapers. Ivy Lee wrote the platitudes while they were fresh.

Lee, using the occasion of his appointment to represent George F. Baer and his associates in the anthracite coal strike, issued a "Declaration of Principles" which was to have a profound influence on the evolution of press-agentry into publicity and of publicity into public relations. Eric Goldman observes that this declaration "marks the emergence of a second stage of public relations. The public was no longer to be ignored, in the traditional manner of business, nor fooled, in the continuing manner of the press agent." *It was to be informed.* Lee's declaration, mailed to all city editors, reads: [13]

> This is not a secret press bureau. All our work is done in the open. We aim to supply news. This is not an advertising agency; if you think any of our matter ought properly to go to your business office, do not use it. Our matter is accurate. Further details on any subject treated will be supplied promptly, and any editor will be assisted most cheerfully in verifying directly any statement of fact. . . . In brief, our plan is, frankly and openly, on behalf of business concerns and public institutions, to supply to the press and public of the United States prompt and accurate information concerning subjects which it is of value and interest to the public to know about.

[13] Quoted in Sherman Morse, "An Awakening in Wall Street," *American Magazine*, Vol. 62, September, 1906, p. 460.

This statement was revolutionary for its time. It offers a sound guide to effective press relations today.

Lee put this new approach to work in the anthracite coal strike. The work of reporters assigned to cover the strike was enormously simplified because all channels of communication were open. Although the press was not permitted to be present during the strike conferences, Lee did provide reports after each meeting. Lee was among the first to use the "handout" system on a large scale. Lee's success in getting a good press for the coal operators led to the retention of Parker and Lee by the Pennsylvania Railroad in the summer of 1906. Lee handled this account.

The railroad's reason for hiring the firm and its evaluation of Lee's services is indicated by a letter a Pennsylvania official wrote a colleague on the Southern Pacific: [14]

> We came to the conclusion, last June, that the time had come when we must take 'offensive' measures as it were, to place our 'case' before the public and we engaged a publicity firm . . . to perform the work for us under our supervision. The engagement was made, as an experiment for six months and we afterwards renewed it for an additional six months. Their work has been very satisfactory.

During this period Lee was using the term *publicity,* which, in his thinking, was public relations; his concept steadily grew, and his success grew with it. In December, 1914, at the suggestion of Arthur Brisbane, Lee was appointed as a personal adviser to John D. Rockefeller, Jr. At the time, the Rockefellers were being savagely attacked for the strike-breaking activities of their Colorado Fuel and Iron Company. Thus began a long career for him in the service of the Rockefellers. His starting salary was $1,000 a month. Contrary to popular belief, Ivy Lee was not hired by John D. Rockefeller. Nor did Lee originate the elder Rockefeller's practice of giving shiny dimes to children. In fact, Rockefeller, Sr., did not approve his son's hiring of Lee, but he adhered to his long-standing promise not to interfere with the son's decisions. In his long service to the son, Lee did, in fact, provide many services to the founder of Standard Oil. It was during the Colorado strike that Upton Sinclair dubbed Lee "Poison Ivy," a term that was to plague him all his life. That same year another pioneer, George Creel, then a crusading journalist, attacked Lee as a "Poisoner of Public Opinion." Although his work for the Rockefellers is the most publicized, Lee served a number of clients in the years from 1919 until his death in 1934. He was counselor to the Guggenheims and promoted their interests in the American Smelting and Refining Co., the Chilean Nitrate

---

[14] Ivy L. Lee Papers, Princeton University Library, Lee's Correspondence of 1907.

of Soda Educational Bureau, the John Simon Guggenheim Memorial Foundation, and the Daniel Guggenheim Fund for the Promotion of Aeronautics. He had other clients, but much of the work was handled by his staff.[15]

Ivy Lee did much to lay the groundwork for today's practice. Although he did not use the term public relations until at least 1919, Lee contributed many of the techniques and principles which practitioners follow today. He was among the first to realize the fallacy of publicity unsupported by good works and to reason that performance determines the kind of publicity a client gets. He saw the importance of humanizing business and continually stressed the human element. "I try to translate dollars and cents and stocks and dividends into terms of humanity." In his efforts to humanize wealthy businessmen and to put Big Business in the best possible light, Lee propelled the growth of publicity departments and trained publicity advisers in many institutions. And, in his 31 years as a public relations man, Lee changed the scope of what he did from "pure agency" to serving as "a brain trust for the businesses we work with." This work, he told his staff shortly before his death, amounted to "a new profession." Ivy Lee made a substantial contribution by establishing and publicizing the idea that there is a potential of service and money in public relations counseling.[16]

Lee, one of the craft's most forceful spokesmen, made an occupation of public relations by his practice and by his preachments. However, Raucher rightly warns: "Ivy Lee's reputation before World War I as the outstanding publicity specialist may easily obscure the general forces which created the new occupation. Lee built his career by exploiting problems of giant corporations in the early twentieth century."

Lee's record, although substantial, is not free from criticism. When he died, he was under public criticism for his representation of the German Dye Trust, controlled by I. G. Farben, after Hitler came to power in Germany and the Nazis had taken control of this cartel. Lee was paid an annual fee of $25,000 and expenses by the Farben firm from the time he was retained in 1933 until his firm resigned the account shortly after his death in 1934. The record does show that he never received pay directly from the Nazi government. Just before his death, Lee explained that his relationship with the German I. G. Farben came about as a broadening of his relationship with the American I. G. Farben, a subsidiary of the

---

[15] For definitive biography, see Ray Eldon Hiebert, *Courtier to the Crowd: The Story of Ivy L. Lee and the Development of Public Relations* (Ames: Iowa State University Press, 1966). Also helpful is Raucher's *Public Relations and Business*.

[16] For Lee's fumbling effort to define his work, see "The Duties of an 'Advisor' in Public Relations," *Printers' Ink*, Vol. 140, July 7, 1927, pp. 73–74.

German concern. Lee told a congressional committee: [17] "My relationship with them has been confined to advising the officers of the German Dye Trust as to what I considered to be American reactions to what had taken place in Germany and as to what, if anything, could be done about it." The record indicates that Farben hired Lee more in an effort to moderate the policies of the Nazi government than to function as a propaganda agent.[18] Lee's role in this case is still a matter of dispute. The propriety of American public relations firms' representing foreign nations in this country remains a troublesome issue to this day.[19]

The same year that flinty George Baer hired Ivy Lee to help him battle John Mitchell's United Mineworkers, John D. Rockefeller came to admit the need of a publicity man to defend him in the public prints. Businessman Rockefeller never appeared to mind criticism, but Philanthropist Rockefeller was cut to his Baptist quick by the accusation that his philanthropies were a means of buying public favor. When the "tainted money" issue flared anew in 1905, Rockefeller was hurt and angered. His philanthropic adviser, Rev. Frederick T. Gates, urged him to abandon his policies of secrecy. "While replying frigidly to Gates, Rockefeller gave way. He asked Gates to see (John D.) Archbold; and it turned out that he had sent Gates' letter to the head of Standard, and had frankly yielded the whole question." [20] This led to the employment of Joseph Ignatius Constantine Clarke, colorful Irish newsman, at a high salary of $5,000 a year. Clarke, attached to the legal department and given a staff of one stenographer, one office boy, and a man to paste clippings, worked hard to lift the veil of secrecy from Standard and its founder, and with some success. Rockefeller became more open and courteous with reporters and, starting in October, 1908, he published a series of autobiographical articles in *World's Work*. But as the legal and public attacks mounted in 1911, the company's executives quit giving Clarke information and he resigned in frustration in 1913.[21]

---

17 For testimony on this case, see *Investigation of Nazi and Other Propaganda: Public Hearings Before a Subcommittee of the Committee on Un-American Activities*, Hearings Numbers 73-NY-7 (Washington, D.C.: U.S. Government Printing Office, 1934).

18 *Trials of War Criminals Before the Nuremberg Military Tribunal*, Volumes VII and VIII, Case Six, *U. S. vs. Krauch, "The I.G. Farben Case"* (Washington, D.C.: U.S. Government Printing Office).

19 For contemporary closeup of this continuing problem, see *Activities of Nondiplomatic Representatives of Foreign Principals in the United States*, Hearings Before Committee on Foreign Relations, United States Senate, Parts 1–13, 1963 (Washington, D.C.: U. S. Government Printing Office, 1963).

20 Allan Nevins, *John D. Rockefeller* (New York: Charles Scribner's Sons, 1940), Vol. II, p. 547.

21 For full story, see Joseph I. C. Clarke, *My Life and Memories* (New York: Dodd, Mead and Co., 1955); "A New Press Agent," *Editor & Publisher*, Vol. 4, May 12, 1906.

INDUSTRY SEES PROFIT IN PUBLIC RELATIONS

Pendleton Dudley maintained, with considerable reason, that it was a gross oversimplification to explain the beginnings as a counterattack of Big Business against the muckrakers. He said that this conclusion was "hardly justified by the facts." Dudley admitted that such attacks did play their part, but he held that the dawning recognition of news and its force on public opinion was more basic. "On the side of business it was an awareness that news, in all its aspects, had become a fresh, strong determinant of public behavior" that induced the employment of publicity specialists.[22] Surely it is significant that virtually all the pioneers, from Amos Kendall on, had been recruited from the nation's newspapers. This substantiates the theory that the growth of the mass media was and is a basic factor in creating the need for the skilled communicator and intermediary with the press.

THEODORE ROOSEVELT

The part played by President Theodore Roosevelt in spurring the evolution has been too little noted. The colorful, swashbuckling President was a master in the art and power of publicity. He used that knowledge and skill to gain his political ends. Observers at the time claimed that Roosevelt ruled the country from the front pages of the newspapers. One of Roosevelt's first acts upon assuming the Presidency was to seek an understanding with the working press. One veteran newsman, David S. Barry, later observed: Roosevelt "knew the value and potent influence of a news paragraph written as he wanted it written and disseminated through the proper influential channels. . . ." A *Harper's Weekly* article of that time was titled "Theodore Roosevelt: Press Agent." Roosevelt's successful anti-trust suit against the Northern Securities Company turned the tide against the concentration of economic power. His conservation policies, effectively promoted by Gifford Pinchot in the government's first large-scale publicity program, saved much of America's resources from further exploitation.

With the growth of mass-circulation newspapers, Roosevelt's canny ability to dominate the front pages demonstrated a new-found power for those with causes to promote. He had a keen sense of news and knew how to stage a story so that it would get maximum attention. Not only did Theodore Roosevelt set patterns, but his skill forced those whom he fought

---

[22] Pendleton Dudley, "Current Beginnings." His retention by Trinity Episcopal Church, then caught in muckrakers' fire, tends to refute his generalization.

to develop similar means. Using these skills, Roosevelt advertised and dramatized to the country a point of view that was new and exciting. Frederick Lewis Allen said that this was Theodore Roosevelt's "most vital contribution to American history." Roosevelt fully exploited the news media as a new and powerful tool of presidential leadership, and he remade the laws and remade the Presidency in the process. His success begat many imitators.

This period, 1900–1917, saw an intensive development of public relations skills by the railroads and the public utilities. These businesses, particularly the local transit companies, were the first to feel the blistering heat of angered public opinion and to be brought under public regulation. The Interstate Commerce Act had set the pattern. In a five-year period, 1908–1913, more than 2,000 laws affecting railroads were enacted by state legislatures and by Congress. From 1897 on, the term *public relations* appeared with increasing frequency in railroad literature and in speeches of railroad men. In 1909, the *Railway Age Gazette* pleaded for "better public relations" in an editorial entitled, "Wanted: A Diplomatic Corps." On June 26, 1913, J. Hampton Baumgartner, another pioneer, gave a talk to the Virginia Press Association on "The Railroads and Public Relations." He was hired in 1910 to be "in charge of publicity and public relations of the Baltimore & Ohio Railroad." Baumgartner explained that railroads had, in response to the wave of agitation which had crystallized into antagonism, "endeavored to establish closer relations with the public, chiefly through the medium of the press and with its cooperation." As of 1909, the Illinois Central Railroad was employing an assistant manager who served in a two-way capacity to interpret the public to the company as well as to publicize the IC.[23] As early as 1905 Charles S. Mellen, president of the New Haven, had told fellow New England railroad executives: "Publicity, not secrecy, will win hereafter. Corporations must come out into the open and see and be seen. They must take the public into their confidence. . . ." The histories of the Pennsylvania and New Haven railroads make it plain that it takes more than preachments to build productive public relationships.

One of the first known efforts to define the practice was presented before the American Street and Interurban Railway Association in Atlantic City in 1907 by its "Committee on Public Relations." In 1912, James H. McGraw, writing in the *Electric Railway Journal,* advocated the open-door policy for utilities.[24]

[23] Ray Morris, "Wanted, a Diplomatic Corps," *Railroad Age Gazette,* Vol. 56, January 27, 1909, p. 196.

[24] See article, "Publicity," Vol. 39, July 1, 1912, p. 151.

In the most acute and difficult public relations in which railway managers find themselves there is, I believe, always the inner conviction that if the merits of the case could be conveyed to the public and its law makers, mercy at least, and possibly justice, could be obtained. The only medium of such communication is educational publicity.

Henry Ford pioneered in the positive use of public relations as well as in making and selling cars. He was quick to see the value of product publicity in selling mass consumer goods. His work dramatized the worth of publicity as a supplement to paid advertising. Professor David Lewis, who has chronicled Ford's public relations story, says: "The industrialist is revealed . . . as perhaps the most astute self-advertiser in the whole history of a land that has produced its full share of promoters and show-men." From 1908 on, Ford and his associates sought publicity, in sharp contrast to their publicity-shy business contemporaries of that era.

Ford sensed the value of racing events in publicizing performance of his new gas buggies. The house organ, *Ford Times,* was started in 1908 "to introduce hints among members of the Ford organization." Ford was among the first to use opinion surveys to give him guidance in marketing his cars. In 1912, he had 1,000 Model T owners queried as to why they had bought Fords. Interestingly enough, 842 of them reported that they had bought the car on the recommendation of a friend who had one. He organized Ford owners into clubs, as another promotional device. Ford pulled out all publicity stops in heralding announcement of his $5 a day for an eight-hour day in 1914, a story that was to shake the industrial community and make him a world figure.

Another businessman, Samuel Insull, was equally imaginative and innovative in the expanding utility field in these years. In the late 1890s his Chicago Edison Company relied on sales techniques, free wiring, and rate cuts to increase the use of electricity. In 1901 he created an advertising department to insure specialized treatment of his many messages to the public. The next year Insull built a demonstration Electric Cottage and in 1903 he started *Chicago, The Electric City,* an external house organ, "to gain understanding and good will" of the community. Insull began using films in 1909, perhaps the first to use movies for public relations purposes. He initiated "bill stuffers" in 1912, and in later years used these for political messages. He and his associates made countless public speeches, and many of these were reprinted for wider distribution. Insull knew well that those identified with an institution are the prime determinants of its public reputation. In 1912 Insull told the National Electric Light Association: [25]

----

[25] Reprinted in Insull's *Central Station Electric Service* (Chicago: Privately Printed, 1915), p. 356.

If our business is to be permanently successful; if we are to obtain and hold the good will of the communities in which we operate; if we are to be allowed by the governmental bodies . . . to extend our monopolies—we must defer to public opinion. I think that all our people should try to achieve the highest possible standing in the community in which they live. They should bear in mind that their personal conduct for good or ill is an addition or subtraction from the good will which the public bears towards the business on which we all are dependent. . . .

The pattern for the early development is illustrated in a study of the American Telephone and Telegraph Company, one of the first firms to develop a program. It organized its first press bureau in Boston, around 1890. It was officially termed a "literary bureau." After Theodore N. Vail returned as a director in 1902, the policies today identified with A. T. & T. began to take shape. These policies were brought to the fore when Vail became president in 1907. A program was undertaken to eliminate public criticism through efficient operation. Consideration for the needs of subscribers was directed. A systematic method of answering complaints was put into effect. Unlike other utilities, Bell did not fight public regulation; Bell accepted it as a necessary price for monopoly. Vail and Ellsworth, working in cooperation with the N. W. Ayer agency, pioneered in the extensive use of public relations advertising.

OTHER INSTITUTIONS SEE NEED

In this same period equally important public relations developments were taking place outside the business community. The Seedbed Years brought innovative publicity programs to colleges and universities. Yale and Harvard, among the nation's oldest, sensed the need for organized publicity programs, as the mass media made their power felt. At Yale, Anson Phelps Stokes in 1899 converted the office of secretary into an effective alumni and public relations office. At Harvard, Eliot, who in his inaugural address of 1869 voiced the necessity of influencing "opinion toward advancement of learning," retained the Publicity Bureau in 1900. Early that same year the University of Pennsylvania hired a Theodore Waters to "conduct the News Bureau of this University" but there is no evidence that the arrangement materialized. Pennsylvania's public relations program dates from 1904 when it set up the University Bureau of Publicity. That same year Willard G. Bleyer, pioneer journalism educator, organized a press bureau at the University of Wisconsin at the direction of public relations-minded President Charles R. Van Hise. But it was William Rainey Harper, dynamic builder of the University of Chicago, who did more than any other educator to harness the power of publicity to the cause of higher education. His methods and his resulting success were observed and copied by many other people.[26]

In this era of ferment and change, churches, too, began to perceive the need for a public voice. One cleric wrote:[27] ". . . we will find that if we believe in the fruits of publicity we must believe also in the potential power of human nature to achieve goodness." Nonetheless, as in the case of business, it was the sharp attacks of critics that brought about the first programs. The Seventh Day Adventist Church, responding to public attacks on its opposition to Sunday laws, in 1912 established a formal bureau, with a former newspaperman in charge, the first such bureau among religious organizations.[28] The Trinity Episcopal Church of New York City —under biting public attack since 1894 for its exploitation of renters in its church-owned tenements—in 1909 became one of the first clients of Pendleton Dudley, and thus the first church to employ an outside counselor.[29]

The whirlwind high-pressure campaign to raise money for charitable causes was first fabricated in 1905 in Washington, D. C., by Y.M.C.A. fund raisers Charles Sumner Ward and Lyman L. Pierce, in a drive to raise $350,000 for a Y.M.C.A. building. This initial whirlwind drive intensively demonstrated the power of publicity; for the first time, a full-time publicist was used in a fund drive. The Y's successful techniques were soon utilized in the annual appeals of churches, colleges, civic centers, and health and welfare agencies.[30]

In 1908, the first health association to appeal for public gifts, the National Tuberculosis Association, established a Publicity Program. That same year, the American Red Cross hired its first publicity man. The United States Marine Corps established a publicity bureau in Chicago in 1907 under Captain William C. Harllee, thus paving the way for today's large-scale public relations programs in our military services. There were undoubtedly others specializing in the field in these early years. Each ap-

---

[26] See: Richard J. Storr, *Harper's University* (Chicago: University of Chicago Press, 1966), and The President's Report for these years, in University of Chicago Achives.

[27] John J. Burke, "Publicity and Social Reform," *Catholic World*, Vol. 91, May, 1910, pp. 210–211.

[28] George W. Cornell, Associated Press column, "Religion Today," July 31, 1959. Also, Howard Weeks, "The Development of Public Relations As An Organized Activity in a Protestant Denomination," unpublished master's thesis, American University, 1963.

[29] Letter from Pendelton Dudley to Major Earl F. Stover, December 3, 1965.

[30] For full account of public relations' role in fund raising, see Scott M. Cutlip, *Fund Raising in the United States: Its Role in America's Philanthropy* (New Brunswick: Rutgers University Press, 1965).

pears to have broken his own ground. There was no sense or spirit of an organized calling in those days.

As this period neared its close, there was growing appreciation that high-pressure publicity was not the answer to good relationships with the public. In an effort to dispel public "ignorance," the American Red Cross in 1913 appointed a committee of three newspapermen to study the problem. The next year this committee recommended creation of an information division that would gather intelligence, disseminate information to the press, answer inquiries, and build public confidence through "proper and effective publicity."

Publicity had grown to considerable dimensions in these first few years of the new century, as reflected in the growing concern of newspapermen about the "perils of publicity." Don C. Seitz, business manager of *The New York World,* reported to the 1909 convention of the American Newspaper Publishers Association that the number of press agents was growing, that some were making $6,000 to $12,000 a year—high pay in those years. "Everybody was employing them; even the New York Orphan Asylum was paying a publicity man $75 a month. The advertising agencies —Albert Frank and Company, Lord & Thomas, N. W. Ayer & Son, J. Walter Thompson—had set up publicity departments which took fees for their services, fees diverted from the advertiser's newspaper advertising budget. Automobile manufacturers were sending a page of material each day to the *World,* and the cement, food, insurance, utilities, and other businesses were equally busy." [31]

WORLD WAR I AND GEORGE CREEL

Contemporary practice first emerged as a defensive measure. But World War I gave it great offensive impetus. George Creel and his effective Committee on Public Information demonstrated, as never before, the power of mass publicity and the techniques of mobilizing opinion. Creel emphasized the positive approach. The Liberty Loan drives, although based primarily on advertising techniques, taught businessmen and other executives how public relations practices could be used effectively. The Creel Committee trained a host of practitioners, who took their wartime experiences and fashioned them into a profitable calling. Among these were Carl Byoir and Edward L. Bernays. Byoir, who at 28 rose to the associate chairmanship of the CPI, after a decade's detour in other endeavors, founded

---

[31] Edwin Emery, *History of American Newspaper Publishers Association* (Minneapolis: University of Minnesota Press, 1950), pp. 125–30.

in 1930 what today is one of the nation's largest public relations firms. Bernays became the tireless advocate of public relations over the next half-century. Byoir played a much more influential role in the success of the Creel Committee than is generally recognized. A biographer of Byoir concluded that his skills and success in public relations stemmed in large degree from his experience and the lessons learned as a World War I progagandist.

The Committee on Public Information was set up by President Wilson in response to a suggestion from Creel, a journalist friend and supporter of Wilson. In this urging, Creel had the support of Secretary of Navy Josephus Daniels. President Wilson himself was aware of the importance of public opinion and knew the value of using the agencies of communication. Creel was chosen to direct this committee. The subsequent events are well described in Creel's book, *How We Advertised America,* and by Mock and Larson in *Words That Won the War.*[32]

> Mr. Creel assembled as brilliant and talented a group of journalists, scholars, press agents, editors, artists, and other manipulators of the symbols of public opinion as America had ever seen united for a single purpose. It was a gargantuan advertising agency, the like of which the country had never known, and the breath-taking scope of its activities was not to be equalled until the rise of the totalitarian dictatorships after the war. George Creel, Carl Byoir, Edgar Sisson, Harvey O'Higgins, Guy Stanton Ford, and their famous associates were literally public relations counselors to the United States Government, carrying first to the citizens of this country and then to those in distant lands, the ideas which gave motive power to the stupendous undertaking of 1917–1918.

Plowing new ground, Creel's successful demonstration was to have a profound impact on the American culture. As Bernays later commented, "It was the war which opened the eyes of the intelligent few in all departments of life to the possibilities of regimenting the public mind." Analyzing the influence of the Creel committee in spurring the growth of what it still termed "press agents," the *New York Times* commented in 1920: [33]

> Essentially the species, if not a war product, is one which the war has mightily increased. Liberty Loans had to be advertised throughout the country. Publicity did that. Five times, at short intervals, the newspapers of the nation stepped into line and "put across" to the man at the

---

[32] James O. Mock and Cedric Larson, *Words That Won the War* (Princeton: Princeton University Press, 1939), p. 4.

[33] February 1, 1920, p. 9, col. 1.

breakfast table, and in his office, in the factory, in the mine—in every phase of commerce and industry, in fact, the need of digging down deep into his pocket and "coming across." It worked. Beautifully and efficiently. Not only did he have a staff of press agents working immediately under him in a central office, but [Creel] decentralized the system so that every type of industry in the country had its special group of publicity workers. In this manner, more than in any other, were the heads and directors of movements of every type introduced to and made cognizant of the value of concentrating on publicity in so-called "drives."

It should be noted, however, that press agentry and publicity, as distinguished from public relations, grew even more rapidly after the war. This growth was mostly a corollary, although the line of demarcation may be a fuzzy one. In the immediate postwar years, men who had gained experience under Creel or had observed the efficacy of his techniques carried their knowledge back into civilian life. They began hammering out a new profession—even though it was still dimly seen.

BETWEEN TWO WORLD WARS

Vigorously generated by the wartime developments, this new public relations specialty quickly spread. It showed up in government, business, the churches, social work—now burgeoning in the war's aftermath—the labor movement, and social movements. The victory of the Anti-Saloon League in gaining national prohibition and the triumph of the woman's suffrage movement provided fresh evidence of the new-found power. The coercions compelling the development of this practice had also been enormously multiplied. The process of industrialization and urbanization had been pushed several notches further during the war. Things began moving at a faster clip.

With the war over and his duties with the American Red Cross ended, Ivy Lee resumed his practice in a newly organized counseling firm, Ivy Lee & Associates. Included was T. J. Ross, who joined the firm in 1919 and became an influential figure in his own right. In 1961, when Ivy's son, James, retired from his father's firm, this agency took the name of T. J. Ross and Associates.

Among those vying with Ivy Lee for prominence and for business in the 1920's was Bernays, long a central and controversial figure in this craft, who retired in 1962. Bernays was born in Vienna but was brought to New York City by his parents when he was still an infant. Bernays' mother was a sister of Sigmund Freud. Later Bernays also became a nephew-in-law of the famous psychologist when Freud married a sister of Bernays' father. His first effort at press-agentry, performed for Richard Bennett's sexy play *Damaged Goods,* opened young Bernays' eyes to the power of publicity. Prior to World War I, Bernays worked as a press agent, serving, among others, Enrico Caruso. He worked for the Creel committee during the war. There his ever busy mind was envisioning the possibilities of making a life's work of "engineering public consent," which is what he termed it.[34]

Bernays coined the term *public relations counsel* in his landmark book, *Crystallizing Public Opinion,* the first on public relations. Published in 1923, this book and others reflected the booming growth in this postwar period. Bernays broke more new ground the same year when he taught the first PR course at New York University. Bernays' book was preceded by one year by Walter Lippmann's classic *Public Opinion,* a book that has had a profound influence in this field. Lippmann reflected the awakening interest in the nature and power of opinion generated by the war. There were some eighteen books on public opinion, publicity, and public relations printed in all the years prior to 1917, but at least twenty-eight titles were published between 1917 and 1925. In 1921 the Library of Congress published a bibliography, the first one on the subject, *List of References on Publicity, with special reference to press agents.*

Equally influential has been the scholarly interest of social scientists, which dates from this period. [Here began the shift of interest from the power to the nature of public opinion and the role of communications in its formation] The work of social scientists in studying public opinion, analyzing propaganda, and observing the work of pressure groups in society has contributed much. Market research, social surveys, and public opinion polls gained headway during the postwar years. General Foods, a market research pioneer, set up a panel of homemakers in 1926 to test recipes for jams and jellies. The Lynds's historic social survey, *Middletown,* was made in 1925. The *Literary Digest* made its first presidential election poll in 1916. This poll had its heyday in the 1920s. Development of sound opinion-measurement methods was slow until the 1930s, but there were earlier beginnings.

Many other rapid-fire developments occurred in this postwar period. A number of new counseling firms were established alongside the existing ones of Wright, Dudley, Lee, and Bernays. In 1919 John Price Jones established his firm to direct fund-raising campaigns and to provide publicity service to corporations. Over the years, Jones made more money and gained more fame as a fund raiser than as a public relations counselor.

---

[34] For detailed chronicle of his career as he saw it, see: *Biography of an Idea: Memoirs of Public Relations Counsel Edward L. Bernays* (New York: Simon and Schuster, 1965).

When he started his firm, he billed it as "Organization and Publicity Counsel." He retired in 1956. In 1923, Harry A. Bruno, long-time aviation enthusiast and wartime flier, set up a firm in partnership with Richard Blythe, after the airline that Bruno was working for went broke. Most of Bruno's early clients were makers of airplane motors and instruments, and he aided them by promoting aviation. Bruno broke into national prominence when he and Blythe handled the press relations for young Charles A. Lindbergh's historic flight across the Atlantic in May, 1927. Bruno's publicity and public relations projects did much to speed America's acceptance of the air age. He also helped make motorboating a popular pastime.

In 1926, William Baldwin, after serving an apprenticeship in a shipbuilding firm and as a fund raiser, opened a public relations agency that was to serve corporate and civil clients—many of the latter gratis—over the next thirty-five years. Baldwin recalls that there were only six firms listed in the Manhattan telephone directory when he started. The next year, 1927, John W. Hill, Cleveland newsman, started a firm in that city. In 1933 he formed a partnership with Don Knowlton. A short time later Hill moved to New York to found Hill & Knowlton, Inc. Knowlton remained in Cleveland to run Hill and Knowlton of Cleveland. The two firms, connected only by overlapping ownership, operated independently until 1964. That year Knowlton retired and the Cleveland office was sold to a successor firm.

Similarly, advertising agencies started moving into the field, as product publicity became an important aspect of marketing. A few advertising agencies had set up publicity sections prior to the war. Now more were moving into this growing and lucrative field. The 1909 Seitz report noted that there were four agencies with publicity departments at that time. In the 1920's more developed this service for both advertiser clients and nonclients. Hower noted this in his history of the Ayer Agency, the pioneer in this development: [35]

> In some respects the Ayer agency entered the field of public relations about 1900 when it began to handle the advertising of such large concerns as the National Biscuit Company and the Standard Oil Company, for it soon had to take account of the attitude of the public toward these "big business" institutions. The agency strove to obtain goodwill principally by the use of advertising, but inevitably it was compelled to prepare publicity material as part of its regular work and also to prepare news releases. By 1920 the firm had a well-organized publicity bureau which became increasingly important during the next decade.

[35] Ralph M. Hower, *The History of an Advertising Agency* (Cambridge: Harvard University Press, 1939), pp. 297–298.

This period saw definite beginnings of institutional advertising as a tool. Probably the oldest continuous public relations advertising campaign is that of the Illinois Central Railroad which was started Sept. 1, 1920. These ads sought, in the words of IC's president, "promotion of a better understanding and closer relationship with the patrons of our lines." A latter-day successor, commenting in 1960 on the completion of 40 years' continuous advertising, said: "We believe this program, which we have often termed 'an investment in understanding,' has done much to take the mystery out of railroading. Taking the public into our confidence has earned many friends for the Illinois Central through Mid-America." In 1922, the Metropolitan Life Insurance Company started its good-health campaign, a series that also is still going. In 1923 General Motors began to use advertising to sell GM as an institution. GM did not set up a department until 1931, when it brought in Paul Garrett, another influential pioneer who retired January 1, 1957. In 1921 the American Association of Engineers held its first national conference on public information. Later it published the proceedings in a book entitled *Publicity Methods for Engineers*.

Another development of the early 1920's was the wholesale adoption of the Creel techniques by Samuel Insull and his cohorts in the utilities industry. Insull sparked a movement, beginning in 1919, to convince the American people of the blessings of his particular private ownerships.[36] Despite the cloud that later crossed this program, it embodied some forward-looking concepts. Insull's chief lieutenant, Bernard J. Mullaney, said in 1924: "Honest and intelligent publicity effort is a most important part of a public relations program . . . but not the whole program; and not even a part of it, as 'publicity' is commonly understood. . . . 'Publicity' that seeks to 'put over' something . . . is unsound; in the long run, it defeats itself." [37] Mullaney was more prophetic than he knew.

Among those pioneers shaping today's practice, Arthur W. Page stands at the summit. Page built three successful business careers, yet found time to contribute his talent to many public service endeavors. He was a writer and editor of *World's Work Magazine* and other periodicals of Doubleday, Page & Company from 1905 until 1927. That year, he ac-

[36] For this unsavory page in history, see *Utility Corporations: Efforts by Associations and Agencies of Electric and Gas Utilities to Influence Public Opinion*, A Summary Report Prepared by The Federal Trade Commission, 70th Congress, 1st Sess. (Senate Document 92, part 71-A) (Washington, D.C.: U. S. Government Printing Office). A popular summary of this probe is Ernest Gruening's *The Public Pays*. For kinder view, see Forrest McDonald's *Insull*, previously cited.

[37] Speech, "Public Relations in the Public Utility Industry," given at University of Illinois May 24, 1924. In files of Peoples Gas Co., Chicago.

cepted Walter Gifford's offer to become vice-president of American Telephone & Telegraph Co. to succeed James D. Ellsworth. He retired from A. T. & T. in 1947 after having integrated public relations concepts and practices into the Bell System. From 1947 until his death in September, 1960, he served as a consultant to many large corporations and gave much time to the service of his government, of higher education, and other causes. It was Page's work for A. T. & T. that left his lasting imprint on public relations.

At the outset, Page made it clear to Gifford that he would accept the vice-presidency only on condition that he was not coming as a publicity man, that he would have a voice in policy, and that the company's performance would be the determinant of its public reputation. The next year, Gifford spelled out this Bell System policy that "the service shall at all times be adequate, dependable and satisfactory to the user." Page's philosophy is summed up in this statement: "All business in a democratic country begins with public permission and exists by public approval. If that be true, it follows that business should be cheerfully willing to tell the public what its policies are, what it is doing, and what it hopes to do. This seems practically a duty." [38]

Late in the second decade a sense of identification and professionalism began to emerge in this new craft. The Bank Marketing Association, the first national public relations organization, was organized in Chicago on June 15, 1915, as a part of the Associated Advertising Clubs of the World. Seven bankers founded the new organization and called it the Financial Advertising Association. This reflects the fact that banking public relations in the era of World War I was seen as advertising and stiff, high-collar advertising at that. The organization changed its name in 1947 to the Financial Public Relations Association, again in 1966 to Bank Public Relations and Marketing Association and again in 1970 to Bank Marketing Association, to better reflect the work of the association. In its early years the association was mainly an "idea exchange" for its members.

The next group to organize is more reflective of the evolution of public relations. A handful of major universities and colleges had set up press bureaus prior to the war. More did so in the early 1920's, generally as an adjunct of a capital fund-raising drive. In March 1915, T. T. Frankenberg, then publicity director for the Western College for Women, Oxford, Ohio, planted the first seed for the American College Public Relations Association. Frankenberg's idea of a meeting for "an exchange of ideas that

[38] George Griswold, Jr., "How A. T. & T. public relations policies developed," *Public Relations Quarterly*, Vol 12, Fall, 1967, p. 13. Special issue devoted to A. T. & T. public relations policies and programs.

might be helpful" to those in college publicity did not take root until April 1917. In that same year he was able to stimulate sufficient interest to effect a new organization, the Association of American College News Bureaus.

It is indicative of this period that this name was selected only after vigorous debate. A strong minority wished to be known frankly as college publicity workers. The more conservative members prevailed. The "taint" of publicity in higher education was avoided! The outbreak of war soon vitiated this movement. It was not until the 1920s that it came alive again. At the 1925 convention, the organization took on vigor and strength, reflecting the growth of the practice in higher education. Symbolic of the growth in ensuing years, the organization's name in 1930 was changed to the American College Publicity Association and in May, 1946, to the American College Public Relations Association.

After World War I, the interest and utilization of publicity techniques spilled over into the new field of social work. This, likewise, had been given great impetus by the war and by the dislocations the war produced. As more and more money had to be raised to meet more and more needs of an urban society, there was a growing recognition of the importance of publicity and of the need for trained publicists. Advancement of social work publicity was spearheaded by Evart G. and Mary Swain Routzahn of the Russell Sage Foundation. The Routzahns played a key role in the birth of the National Publicity Council for welfare agencies and of a Health Education Section in the American Public Health Association in the early 1920s. What was first a committee on publicity methods in social work became, in 1922, the National Publicity Council for Welfare Services. From its inception in 1922 until 1940, the Council was the vehicle of the Routzahns and was used by them to transport new ideas, new techniques, and missionary zeal to the novices in health and welfare publicity work. The Community Chest movement which burgeoned after the war also provided employment for a growing number of publicists.

More religious leaders sensed the changing times. In 1918, the National Lutheran Council launched a strong national church publicity program. Later that same year a Catholic organization, the Knights of Columbus, organized a publicity bureau with John B. Kennedy as its director. *The New York Times* noted at the time, "They are quite frank in admitting that the 'biggest and most practical human lesson learned from the war is that nothing requiring organized effort can succeed without publicity and plenty of it.'" The quotes were attributed to Kennedy. The Y.M.C.A. and Y.W.C.A. had long had publicity staffs, and they formed something of a nucleus for the spread of organized church publicity. Astute leaders everywhere were observing this "most practical human lesson from the war."

Propelled by the wartime lessons and the changing nature of the American environment, the practice moved full speed ahead until the stockmarket crash in 1929. The ensuing Depression marks another milestone.

The economic catastrophe and Franklin D. Roosevelt's New Deal generated a fuller and broader development in many fields. Like his distant cousin before him, F.D.R. coupled strong leadership with consummate skill to harness the forces of protest into an effective political coalition. Roosevelt won his battles on the front pages and over the radio, a new medium which he used with matchless skill. Roosevelt's adroit moves in the public arena can be credited in large part to his unsung public relations mentor, Louis McHenry Howe. The astute, tough-minded Louis Howe served F.D.R. faithfully and effectively from 1912 until his death in 1936. He gave his life to being Roosevelt's right-hand man and did much to advance Roosevelt to the White House.[39] F.D.R.'s success in winning public support spurred the efforts of the conservative forces, particularly the business community, to counter his appeals. A new trend set in, marked by acceptance of an institution's or industry's social responsibility. It was increasingly realized that profitable public relationships could be built only by coupling responsible performance with persuasive publicity. Such a cataclysmic event as the Depression was bound to produce a sharp readjustment of values.

Events flowing from the Depression and the New Deal brought home to every group the need for building informed public support. The New Dealers soon found that this was essential to pave the way for their radical reforms. Government public relations had its greatest expansion under Franklin Roosevelt. School administrators were made to realize the dangers of an uninformed public as hard-pressed taxpayers chopped off "the frills" in education. The Depression brought a tremendous expansion in social welfare needs and agencies. These administrators, too, came to realize the need for better public understanding. Military leaders, looking apprehensively at the build-up of the Nazi and Fascist war machines, began to promote support for more adequate armed forces. Colleges and universities, caught in the web of financial woes, turned more and more to public relations to win contributions and to recruit students.

Business leaders turned increasingly to public relations men for help in fighting against Roosevelt's biting criticisms and his legislative reforms. There was a marked trend away from occasional and defensive efforts. There was a marked trend toward more positive and continuous programs, executed by newly established departments. A growing labor movement,

---

[39] For balanced view of Howe's contributions to F.D.R.'s career, see Alfred B. Rollins, Jr., *Roosevelt and Howe* (New York: Alfred A. Knopf, Inc., 1962).

too, soon found that it had problems and needed guidance. Growth was stimulated all along the line by the social and economic upheavals of the Depression.

WORLD WAR II

The onrush of World War II produced more violent changes in our environment. It accelerated this trend. Once more the government led the way with a breath-taking demonstration of the power of an organized informational campaign. This time it was called the Office of War Information. The capable Elmer Davis was its director. Davis and the OWI set the pace for extensive expansion of the practice in the armed forces, in industry, and in allied fields. More techniques were developed. Many more practitioners were trained in this gigantic program, which completely dwarfed the Creel committee. In the opinion of a public relations scholar, the "OWI's greatest significance lies in its work as the predecessor of the United States Information Agency. It was the OWI which pointed out the dangers in allowing distorted ideas of the United States to exist throughout the world." [40] This is a lesson other institutions learned in these tumultous years. Davis, veteran newsman and radio commentator, never effectively brought the warring forces in OWI under control, nor did he play the role Creel did in counseling the President.

In industry, emphasis was put on public relations to spur war production by promoting productivity and combating absenteeism. There were equally challenging tasks that could best be met by specialists. This, plus the excess profits tax then in effect, speeded organization of new departments in industry. War bonds had to be sold. Material and manpower had to be conserved. Rationing had to be imposed. Morale of those at the front and those at home had to be bolstered during the long, hard sacrifice of war. All these required intensive efforts. Lack of goods to sell and the need to keep the company name before the public spurred wider use of public-service advertising. Employee publications had their greatest growth during the war. In the expanded armed forces, thousands of men and women were recruited and trained in public relations. Everywhere more and more people discovered the value of the art. In World War II, practitioners were confronted with new challenges and new opportunities. That

---

[40] Robert Lee Bishop, "The Overseas Branch of the Office of War Information," unpublished Ph.D. thesis, University of Wisconsin, 1966.

they proved their worth is indicated by the booming growth of the practice which later ensued.

The accelerating developments from World War II on have been the most extensive yet recorded. Reasons for this growth will be underlined in the next chapter.

ADDITIONAL READING

ERIK BARNOUW, *A Tower in Babel—A History of Broadcasting in the United States,* Volume 1—to 1933. New York: Oxford University Press, 1966.

ROBERT J. BERENS, *The Image of Mercy.* New York: Vantage Press, 1967. History of public relations in American Red Cross.

ROGER BURLINGAME, *Don't Let Them Scare You—The Life and Times of Elmer Davis.* Philadelphia: J. B. Lippincott Company, 1961.

ELMER E. CORNWELL, JR., *Presidential Leadership of Public Opinion.* Bloomington: Indiana University Press, 1965. Traces presidential use of public relations to LBJ. Shows its impact on society.

ELMER DAVIS, "The Office of War Information 13 June 1942–13 September 1945, Report to the President," in *Journalism Monographs,* No. 7, August, 1968, published by Association for Education in Journalism. Edited by Ronald T. Farrar.

JOHN A. GARRATY, "The United States Steel Corporation Versus Labor: The Early Years," *Labor History,* Vol. 1, Winter 1960.

L. L. L. GOLDEN, *Only By Public Consent, American Corporations Search for Favorable Opinion.* (New York: Hawthorn Books, 1968.) Useful book gives history of A. T. & T., General Motors, Standard Oil of N. J., and DuPont programs.

ERIC GOLDMAN, *Public Relations and the Progressive Surge 1898–1917.* New York: Foundation for Public Relations Research and Education, 1965.

JOHN GUNTHER, *Taken at the Flood—The Story of Albert D. Lasker.* New York: Harper & Row, Publishers, 1960. Biography of America's pioneer advertising man who made many public relations innovations.

JOHN W. HILL, *The Making of a Public Relations Man.* New York: David McKay & Co., Inc., 1963. Part autobiography, part philosophy by one of PR's pioneers.

DAVID L. LEWIS, "Henry Ford, Publicity, and a $1 Million Libel," *Public Relations Journal,* Vol. 25, August, 1969.

PETER LYON, *Success Story: The Life and Times of S. S. McClure.* New York: Charles Scribner's Sons, 1963. Biography of the architect of the muckraking movement.

GEORGE K. TURNER, "Manufacturing Public Opinion," *McClure's,* Vol. 39, July, 1912. "Utilities Abandon Propaganda Work," *Editor & Publisher,* Vol. 65, February 18, 1933.

S. H. WALKER and PAUL SKLAR, *Business Finds Its Voice*. New York: Harper & Row, Publishers, 1938. (Reissue of articles in *Harper's Magazine* for issues of January, February, and March, 1938.)

CHAPTER 5

ECOLOGY— THE ENVIRONMENT

In its modern sense, public relations was brought into being by the
ever-increasing complexity of the economic, social and political problems
that have assailed the human race in the years since World War I.
Its roots are fixed in the basic fact that public opinion . . . is the
ultimate ruling force in the free world.

—JOHN W. HILL

The function of public relations continues to grow in scope and importance as the American environment accelerates in interdependence and complexity. And accelerate it will. Once society's needs are understood, the function's purpose and ability to help an entity adapt to a changing environment become clear. Moreover, as the nature of the function as a direct response to its environment unfolds, its essentiality can be plainly seen.

Webster's Dictionary defines ecology as "the mutual relations, collectively, between organisms and their environment." Ecology, which deals with the interrelationships of living organisms and their environment, once used mainly in the life sciences, is somewhat overworked. However, social scientists have found it an increasingly useful term to describe the interrelationships of environment and human institutions. We find it so in this effort to relate the practice to the environment which brought the developments summarized in Chapters 3 and 4.

Any public enterprise—profit or nonprofit—to prosper and endure, must (1) accept the obligations of public responsibiltiy imposed by an increasingly interdependent society; (2) find ways and means of communicating with unseen, remote publics over lines lengthened and distended by physical distance and psychological difference, and complicated by multiplying barriers to communication; (3) find ways of achieving integration into the total community that the organization was created to serve. In point (1) we find the source of *public relations thinking* in management enterprises. In point (2) we find the reason for the growth of public relations as a *specialized staff function*. In point (3) we find the *objective* of both the management philosophy and the specialized practice.

The twentieth century has brought an avalanche of change that has transformed the world beyond the wildest dreams of those who turned the calendar to this century—when the buggy was the means of local transportation and moon travel a Jules Verne fantasy. America has steadily and swiftly moved from an agrarian society of small towns, small organizations, and face-to-face relationships into an industrial society of big cities, big organizations, and impersonal relationships. For some 250 years (1620–1870), the United States was an agricultural society; over the next 90 (1870–1960) or so, it became the mightiest industrial society in the world. All this has been aptly described as "the Big Change" by Frederick Lewis

Allen.[1] *Fortune* termed it "The Permanent Revolution," in which a free people broke the power of capital as their master and put it to work as their servant.[2] Now America is moving into a post-industrial society, a term which little describes the vast changes at work. Daniel Bell defines this era "as one in which the economy has moved from being predominantly engaged in the production of goods to being preoccupied with services, research, education, and amenities."[3] In 1956, the United States reached a symbolic turning point—for the first time in any nation, the number of white collar workers outnumbered blue collar workers. The ratio has been steadily increasing since then. Industry is declining as the prime motive force in our society. A new social system is emerging. The net result of these complex forces has been: creation of an affluent society yet one wracked by 25-million persons living below the poverty line; a fluid, mobile society of overpowering size, impersonality, and interdependence; a society dominated by technology and troubled by conflict. Andrew Hacker, in his gloomy book, *The End of the America Era,* predicts: "The remainder of this century will witness a world in turmoil. Revolution and subversion, insurrection and instability, will continue to unsettle American sensibilities. . . . It will be difficult to be an American on such a planet."

Today's world is a world of complex organizations, big structures, and societies of scale. Increases in size change the very nature of organizations, give rise to multiple hierarchies, and introduce new problems of coordination and communication. Too often today's large-scale enterprise tends to resemble the Dinosaur—the body has become too large for its central nervous system. Compare, for example, the communications problems of a university of 3,000 students in 1910 with one of 30,000 students in 1971. It is a world of escalating changes which disturb and alarm large segments of society. We have shifted in this century from simple answers, Main Street, and colonial possessions to a complex world of international communications that has brought the world in instant reach of any listener or viewer, to a complex world of urban and suburban ghettos, to a complex world in revolution. Not all institutions have made the transition successfully. These rapid-fire changes encounter stout human resistance. Assisting institutions and individuals in coping with change is increasingly the task in public relations. *It is this environmental context that defines the problems and establishes the essentiality of this staff function in management.* Thus it becomes necessary to take a brief look at the relationship of the

---

[1] Frederick Lewis Allen, *The Big Change: America Transforms Itself, 1900–1950* (New York: Harper & Row, 1952). Readable, informative account of these changes.

[2] Editors of *Fortune, USA: The Permanent Revolution* (Englewood Cliffs, N.J.: Prentice-Hall, Inc., 1952).

[3] "Notes on the Post-Industrial Society (II)," *The Public Interest,* No. 7, Spring, 1967. See also his "Notes on the Post-Industrial Society I," *The Public Interest,* No. 6, Winter, 1967.

practice to its environment—its *ecology*. First we shall look at the *basic trends* in society producing change, next at those *consequences* of these trends that have importance for public relations, and, finally, how these consequences manifest themselves in the major sectors of our society.

THE BASIC TRENDS

Basic trends propelling a changing society toward the new century that have relevance for public relations are many.

WORLD POPULATION EXPLOSION

It took until 1830 to achieve a population of one-billion on Earth; by 1930, a century later, this had doubled to two-billion persons; and by 1960, thirty years later, the world's population totalled three-billion. If present birth rates are maintained, there will be four-billion persons by 1975, and nearly eight-billion persons by the end of this century. The United States population passed the 200-million mark in 1968 and is increasing by one person every 10.5 seconds. This may continue despite increased use of birth control measures because of increased numbers reaching marriage age in the 1970s. This population increase is occurring in a world that cannot provide adequate food and shelter for those already alive. In an era of rising expectations, current rates of population growth make lowered levels of living more likely.

URBANIZATION

The Industrial Revolution—the factory system, mechanization of farming, and speed up of transportation of goods—has produced the twentieth century phenomenon that crowds more and more persons into urban complexes, stretching down the East Coast, wrapping around the Great Lakes, and blanketing California. Today two-thirds of all Americans live in urban areas. Raymond Mack estimates that "if the present rate of urbanization continues until the year 2050, more than 90 percent of the world's people will live in cities of 20,000 or more." [4] This urbanization poses the nation's most troublesome problem. In the words of Eric Hoffer, longshoreman and philosopher: "If this nation decays and declines it will be not because we have raped and ravaged a continent, but because we do not know how to build and run viable cities. America's destiny will be de-

---

[4] In *Transforming America: Patterns of Social Change* (New York: Random House, 1967) p. 10. A readable, useful book.

cided in the cities." In 1970, according to U. S. Census estimates, the nation's suburbs became the largest sector of the population, their 71 million residents exceeding for the first time both central cities and the rest of the country.

SCIENTIFIC EXPLOSION

The greatly-increased manpower and money being devoted to research is producing changes in society at a far faster rate than man can accommodate. It is estimated that 90 percent of all scientists who ever lived are living today. U. S. government investment in research multiplied 200 times from 1940 to 1965. This scientific advance has brought space travel and cybernation. The latter results in a system of almost unlimited capacity. Its principles of organization are as different from those of the industrial era as those of that era were from the agricultural era. This scientific explosion has also brought a revolution in weaponry, the inhumanity of which precludes its use to win a war because it can obliterate civilization. Further, defense analyst Herman Kahn thinks military technology has supplanted the "mode of production" as a major determinant of social structure. Finally, Americans have learned that advances in science and technology alone are no guarantee of accompanying improvement in the human condition.

SEGREGATION AND AUTOMATION OF WORK

Unlike earlier times, today a person's work is remote and removed from his home and family life. Automation—machines running other machines—changes the nature of work and the requirements for the job; it basically alters the problems of investment capital and increases the need for steady, stable markets. Galbraith lists these imperatives of the new technology: [5]

a. An increasing span of time separating the beginning from the completion of any task.

b. Increase in capital that must be committed to production.

c. Growing in flexibility in commitment of time and money.

d. Requirement of specialized manpower.

e. Increased importance of organization to bring work of specialists to a coherent result.

f. Necessity for planning.

[5] John Kenneth Galbraith, *The New Industrial State* (Boston: Houghton Mifflin Co., 1967), chapter, "The Imperatives of Technology." This book offers a sweeping view of modern economic life.

SEPARATION OF OWNERSHIP AND CONTROL IN INDUSTRY

Ownership of industry is widely dispersed and the entrepreneur has been replaced by the professional, salaried manager who manages with precision and planning. In this he needs a corps of specialists. The corporation has become a dominant force in our society, one directed by a self-perpetuating oligarchy. "This New Industrial State," as Galbraith terms it, has required a "massive growth in the apparatus of persuasion and exhortation that is associated with the sale of goods."

EXPLOSION IN EDUCATION

At the turn of the century, most Americans left school at the age of twelve or thirteen. Today a college degree is a social expectation and a requirement for more and more jobs in this age of technology. In 1900, there were some 200,000 students enrolled in colleges and universities; in 1950 there were 2.2-million students; and the U. S. Census Bureau estimates that by 1985 there will be between 9.7-million and 11-million. That same study estimates that there will be 17.3-million pupils enrolled in high school. Within the next decade, fourteen years' free education will become the established norm in the United States, with expanded scholarship and loan funds to carry students beyond that to college. This explosion is "middle class-izing" our society, increasing the flow of new knowledge, and changing people's self-image. A group of opinion leaders queried on this point suggest: [6] "The better educated person will have more self-respect, will want to be treated more as an individual, will be far less tolerant of authoritarianism and organizational restraints, will have different and higher expectations of what he wants to put into a job and what he wants to get out of it." Hacker asserts education "undermines the preconditions for patriotism and piety."

SOCIAL REVOLUTION

The universal demand for full human rights is now clearly evident around the globe and particularly evident in the civil rights movement in the United States. The demand for equal rights and treatment for all, regardless of creed or race, cannot be fulfilled within the present context of society. Blacks and the cities have a complex of problems in common— poverty, unemployment, welfare, inadequate housing, schooling, and seg-

---

[6] General Electric Co., "Our Future Business Environment," April, 1968. A study of informed opinion outside the company on trends of the next decade—an example of public relations' interpreting the environment to management.

regation. A consensus of opinion leaders holds: [7] "There can be little doubt that this problem will be the dominant one . . . for the next ten years" . . . and "the threat of failure is a real one." The communications revolution has greatly accelerated the diffusion of these social demands. Modern mass communications often compels us to respond directly and immediately to social issues. Instances of police brutality, dramatized by scenes of snarling police dogs and cattle prods in Alabama, helped induce the Civil Rights Act of 1964.

These continuing trends are bringing changes great in number and magnitude. W. H. Ferry, long a practitioner, suggests there is "growing evidence that technology is subtracting as much or more from the sum of human welfare as it is adding." Yet progress can come only through change. Gaining acceptance of change is a difficult task. Tension inevitably accompanies change. Labor's opposition to elimination of jobs by automation, students' protests against outmoded university rules, and the debates on moral imperatives are examples. James E. Webb, former NASA administrator, has predicted: "The thrust into space will change the ideas and lives of people more drastically than the Industrial Revolution." Arthur Schlesinger, Jr. writes: "This constant acceleration in the velocity of history means that lives alter with startling and irresistible rapidity, that inherited ideas and institutions live in constant jeopardy." Kenneth Boulding put it succinctly: "If the human race is to survive, it will have to change its ways of thinking more in the next twenty-five years than it has done in the last 25,000."

CONSEQUENCES OF THE "BIG CHANGE"

Significant and far-reaching consequences were bound to flow from changes as profound as those just described. The fundamental consequences of this breath-taking and truly spectacular revolution have had great significance for public relations.

INCREASED INTERDEPENDENCE

Our industrialization has made us small cogs in one great industrial complex. Each segment is dependent upon countless others, unseen and remote. We all have a place on the American assembly line. A breakdown at any one point along this continent-wide assembly line quickly and directly affects all who man it. A steel strike in Pittsburgh quickly radiates its economic consequences to the automobile dealer in Phoenix.

---

[7] *Ibid.* This is a consensus of 60 influentials.

Little wonder that there has developed a strong public interest in labor peace or its unfortunate opposite, labor strife. Loss of income on the farm is quickly felt in the unemployment of the man who makes farm implements. A slump in the buying of refrigerators soon has its consequences for the men who make steel.

We have moved, in a half-century, from the general store to General Motors. Interdependence can be seen in the simple example of a neighbor's blaring radio or an industrial plant's smoke billowing across town. Its magnitude was dramatically demonstrated when the failure of one small component in an electric power system serving Ontario and Northeast United States blacked out 80,000 square miles and left 30-million persons in the dark. As *Newsweek* reported: "Elevators hung immobile in their shafts. Subways ground dead in their tunnels. Streetcars froze in their tracks. Street lights and traffic signals went out. . . . Airports shut down. Mail stacked up in blacked-out post offices. Computers lost their memories. TV pictures darkened and died. Business stopped. . . ." This interdependence is swiftly spreading around the world as the speed-up in communications and transportation hastens the day of Marshall McLuhan's "global village." Interdependence is blurring the lines of governmental boundaries and the divisions between the public and private sectors. Individually, we are no longer masters of our fate. Hence, there is a compelling need for each component to be responsible to all others. If this responsibility is shirked, society finds ways and means of enforcing it.

GROWTH IN THE POWER OF PUBLIC OPINION

Public opinion has long been an omnipotent force. Ortega y Gasset wisely wrote, "Never has anyone ruled on this earth by basing his rule on anything other than the rule of public opinion." It is this shadowy but nonetheless real force in society, *public opinion,* that is the source spring of public relations practice. Where public opinion counts for little, there is little concern for the state of one's public relationships. Any ex-GI or missionary who has served in New Guinea or Vietnam can confirm this.

That Americans are free to have opinions and to make them effective in shaping their destinies gives great force to public opinion. Using the techniques of organization and protest, small groups can catch the eye and ear of the nation with a Poor People's March, a sit-in, or a police confrontation. Persons in urban complexes are much more easily and quickly mobilized to vent their views than was possible in the days of agrarian protest. Because citizens have learned nearly everywhere how to dominate governments, or at least influence them, public opinion has become the dominant force in the late twentieth century. This power will grow, in the opinion of

Daniel Bell, for three fundamental reasons: [8] "We have become, for the first time, a national society . . . in which crucial decisions affecting all parts of the society simultaneously . . . are made by government, rather than through the market; in addition, we have become a *communal* society, in which many more groups now seek to establish their social rights— their claims on society—through the political order; and, third, with our increasing 'future orientation,' government will necessarily have to do more and more planning."

There is no more powerful office in the world than the Presidency of the United States. Yet President Harry Truman once observed, "You hear people talk about the powers of the President. In the long run, his powers depend a good deal on his success in public relations. . . . His powers are great, but he must know how to make people get along together." [9] President Dwight Eisenhower, said much the same thing, "We must mobilize public opinion to support and enforce highway safety. *Through such action, this problem, like all others to which free men fall heir, can be solved.*" President Lyndon Johnson recognized the same force when, as he left office, he lamented: "I know my biggest problem is communication. If I could just communicate with the people so they'd understand the problems we face. . . ."

ESCALATION IN COMPETITION FOR ATTENTION

As public opinion has grown in force and the ways of influence have multiplied, the competition for public favor has steadily escalated. The struggle to align people on the side of one's cause, client, or company has become increasingly competitive. When privately-owned utility companies launch a campaign to persuade the public to halt expansion of government power plants, the public power advocates counter with a like campaign. The high stakes in today's business and political competition intensify this competition. That people are governed and guided by public opinion in much that they do makes the practice of public relations mandatory. Once the power of public opinion as the supreme arbiter in public affairs is understood and the thesis that opinion is subject to change is accepted, public relations efforts of *communication, persuasion,* and *adjustment* inevitably follow.

Today's citizen, equipped with education, with access to information, and with organizations of strength, has considerable, if not full, power to enforce a public accounting on all institutions vested with a public in-

---

[8] In "Notes on the Post-Industrial Society (I)," *op. cit.*

[9] William Hillman, *Mr. President* (New York: Farrar Straus & Company, 1952), p. 11.

terest: not only business, but government, social welfare agencies, labor unions, schools, churches, and the like. The citizen exerts this power with his consumer dollars, his investment dollars, his philanthropic dollars, and his votes. Perhaps most important of all, today's citizen has the means to communicate his views to others with like interests and thus build organized support to enforce group opinions. This power reaches its zenith in what David Riesman has called our *"other-directed"* society.

Given the power, potential and demonstrated, of the mass media, access to their audiences has become a spirited struggle. In the view of one observer, "The battle now shaping up over the public's right of access to the mass media may well be the most important constitutional issue of this decade." She explains: [10]

> When a society is in ferment, as ours is today, pressure for equal access to public opinion through mass media increases as the old consensus splinters. New ideas and new minority opinion groups spring up everywhere. . . . The realization is now dawning on groups espousing these new ideas, that in a mass, technologically complex society, freedom of speech is only a technicality if it cannot be hooked up to an amplification system that only the mass media can provide. . . . A mimeograph machine can't get the message across anymore.

LOSS OF COMMUNITY

In Erich Fromm's opinion, man is suffering from his sense of alienation—"his feeling of being cut off, shut out, adrift, fragmentary." The secretary in New York City, the rubber worker in Akron, the salesgirl in Chicago, and the timber worker in the Pacific Northwest share a sense of helplessness. They seek the security of belonging, the respect of personal dignity. The rapidity of our urban growth has accentuated this problem. Not until 1920 did urban residents outnumber rural dwellers. Since then, virtually all our growth has been in the cities. Although we huddle together in cities or flee in droves to suburbia, we are more estranged from one another than ever before. A national longing for "togetherness" merely reflects this. The small town was also a neighborhood, but not today's large apartment building or urban housing project. Nor is neighborliness always found in suburbia, where today more than one-third of our people live. There, people do not, in the view of a thoughtful minister, meet heart to heart but meet at cocktail parties in a superficial way. The mechanization and automation of work have, likewise, depersonalized our society, leading to what writer Harvey Swados terms "the stultifying vegetativeness of the modern American work routine."

[10] Hazel Henderson, "Access to the Media: a Problem in Democracy," *Columbia Journalism Review*, Vol. 8, Spring, 1969, p. 6.

Today's citizen suffers a feeling of futility and frustration as he watches decisions being made for him by those beyond his reach. "There appears to be a tenuous line of communication between the governors of our society and the governed." Reflecting this, John Cogley asks this disturbing question: "Are our problems so vast, the technical aspects of modern life so tricky, access to the facts so slight, and the necessary knowledge so elusive that American democracy will become simply a matter of living one's private life and turning over the management of the public sector to professionals?" Much of public relations work involves efforts to supply this sense of "belonging" and a "line of communication between the leaders and the people."

A prime source of the bitter conflicts that beset our society are born in the lack of such lines of communication and in institutions that seem unresponsive. Onetime Kennedy aide, Richard Goodwin asserts: [11] "A people suffering from institutions that can't respond, problems that are virtually left untouched, and the myriad of uncertainties of their own private and public existence must inevitably rise in protest." Goodwin thinks it is "hard to overstate the extent to which the malaise of powerlessness has eaten its way into our society, evoking an aimless unease, frustration, and fury." Blocked lines of communication and rigidity of institutions bring ghetto riots, campus unrest, teacher strikes, labor strikes, and citizen protests. Individuals who feel they no longer control their own destinies are prone to dissent. James Reston thinks America's crisis is the feeling that the political system for dealing with our problems has broken down. Leo Rosten sums it up: "Each of us is a little lonely, deep inside, and cries to be understood. . . ."

We live in a world of fragments and factions, forever splitting off, one against another. Consequently, we retreat into the protective arms of groups where "we belong," where we can find a sense of worth, of dignity. The result of this often is not communications but groups rebounding from groups. Our relations with other human beings are conducted through organized groups, nation to nation, corporation to union, farm cooperative to the market. Fruitful public relations can serve society by helping to bring about a sense of communion in an integrated community.

MULTIPLYING MALADJUSTMENTS

The swiftly accelerating pace of technology and the consequences therefrom have enormously multiplied the number of adjustments required. These adjustments must be effected among widely separated people and organizations. A quick example would be the automobile and the chain

[11] Richard N. Goodwin, "Reflections, Sources of the Public Unhappiness," *The New Yorker*, Vol. XLIV, January 4, 1969. Provocative article.

of events that has brought us to critical urban problems of congestion, traffic control, safety, and air pollution. Once you get airborne, it is easier to fly across the country than to drive across town. The social and cultural lag caused by man's inability to adjust to the accelerating scientific and technological advances long has been a source of concern and comment. A tense world cowering in fear of atomic annihilation because scientists split the atom is a stark reminder of this inability. Today man is frantically trying to erect political institutions capable of controlling the scientific realities of atomic and hydrogen warheads coupled with satellite or submarine-launched missiles. The United Nations is such a vehicle. The "hot line" is another. On this race all else depends.

The maladjustments resulting from this social lag are to be seen in lesser but nonetheless critical ways. It can be seen in the continuing unemployment of unskilled labor, many of them young "school dropouts"; in the mounting populations in our mental and penal institutions; in the decaying blight of the central city ringed by new suburbs; in efforts to bring safety on the highways and in the airlanes; in the dislocations due to mechanization, automation, and changes in plant needs; and in countless other ways.

The swiftness of the changes has left a smaller and smaller span of time for adjustment. Our forbearers had a whole lifetime to adjust to the railroad and telegraph, then had a lifetime to adjust to the automobile. We whip across the ocean in a jet plane in about the time it took them to travel by car to the big city. In the span of a decade or more, America's space industry became bigger than the nation's seventy-year-old automotive industry. This generation has had to grapple with adjustments to mass communication, the automobile, the jet aircraft, data processing, automation, nuclear energy, earth satellites, and space travel, among others.

Lack of human ability to keep pace with this fast-flowing change has produced maladjustments aplenty. This harsh fact, too, has implications for the function of public relations. Introduction of change brings the need for winning acceptance of new ideas, new products, new ways of doing things.

SPECIALIZATION

To perform the myriad tasks required in today's highly scientific, computerized society, specialists are required. The knowledge used in managing today's large-scale enterprises is so vast, complicated, and abstract that few individuals have either the time or ability to master it. Instead each person tackles one small sector and masters that. Thus we have the specialist in data systems, personnel, planning, or fiscal management, the corporate lawyer, the nucleonic engineer, the high-energy physicist, and the astronaut. Each specialization has its own particular language, and this raises communication barriers. Specialists need translators of their jargon to communicate across their narrowing boundaries.

The specialty of public relations has attained its greatest impetus in periods of conflict, change, and major social progress. Discussing the increasing importance of the public relations specialist in American politics, Stanley Kelley wrote: "It is based on a solid demand. . . . More than anything else, public relations as an occupation owes its existence to the growth of the mass media of communication. Having committed themselves to the use of the mass media of communication for propaganda purposes, politicians and interest groups have found it an exceedingly complex problem to use them in such a way as to receive wide circulation for a point of view." [12]

COMMUNICATIONS FAIL TO KEEP PACE

We have moved in some seven decades to a society of separateness and abrasiveness. This has made the communications task increasingly difficult—from student to university administrator, from teacher to superintendent, from factory employee to company president, from citizen to government. A tremendous burden has been placed on the communication function. Today we are confronted by a paradox—unparalleled facilities but increasing difficulty and complexity in communication. Men can send televised pictures from the moon to the peoples of the earth but cannot communicate across neighborhood or national boundaries. Today's policeman is equipped with police radio and radar, but his squad car has cut him off from communication with the persons on his beat. One writer put it in the extreme when he wrote that we have reached the point where there is no communication between "the masses" and "the elite." A thoughtful publisher, Alfred A. Knopf, doubts that the activities of today's business corporation can be made meaningful to more than a handful of its shareholders, because the corporations "are all operating today in fields so highly technical that the average layman cannot understand what they are doing, much less its significance, no matter how simple the language." A philosopher, Charles Frankel, expresses a despairing sense "that events are outrunning the human capacity to understand them."

Thus the clear essentiality and urgent need for the communications specialist, capable of interpreting the publics to an institution's managers, and, in turn, interpreting the institution to its claimant publics. The pressure of events is demanding someone capable of bridging the chasms created in this twentieth century society. Your authors recognize the mag-

---

[12] Stanley Kelley, Jr., *Professional Public Relations and Political Power* (Baltimore, Md.: Johns Hopkins Press, 1956), p. 202. Now available in paperback. Also for discussion this development, see Leon D. Epstein, *Political Parties in Western Democracies* (New York: Praeger, 1968).

nitude of the problem. This is why we believe that the practitioner will come to be more and more the interpreter of the complexities of his organization and of the environment in which it will prosper or perish.

AREAS OF APPLICATION

The illustrations and implications of these basic trends and their consequences of relevance to public relations can be seen in several areas.

BIG BUSINESS

In early America, industry was a simple thing. The ironmaster of the Saugus Ironworks in Massachusetts in 1650 lived near the blast furnace, forge, and slitting mill. He attended to his own public relations with his few helpers. He did it on a personal, intimate basis, as part of his everyday contacts. He did it in his face-to-face dealing with his customers and in friendly chats with his neighbors going to and from work. He was his own director of public relations, just as he was his own production manager, sales manager, and controller. The New England cobbler who made shoes for people in his town and its environs dealt with his customers personally. They came to his shop to be fitted. They saw how their shoes were made. Any imperfections or any differences over price could be ironed out amicably across the counter. This cobbler employed one or two apprentices. He knew them and their families. Their respective "places" in the social scale were known and accepted. He knew their problems. In the daily side-by-side associations there was little chance for misunderstandings to grow roots. But as the cobbler's reputation for making good shoes grew, and as technology changed, his business grew.

The private-property system in production, which began with early America's farm and forge, has all but vanished in the vast area of our economy dominated by the industrial and financial giants of today. The rise of the large corporation began with the railroad systems, but it is almost wholly a twentieth-century development. As Adolf Berle notes: "Many of these corporations have budgets, and some of them have payrolls, which, with their customers, affect a greater number of people than most of the countries of the world." [13] These giants are managed by what he terms "an automatic self-perpetuating oligarchy."

What was once a small business with a few personal relationships has become a large corporation. The large corporation is divided into

---

[13] In "Economic Power and the Free Society," a pamphlet published by the Fund for the Republic, December, 1957. Also see: A. A. Berle, Jr., *The 20th Century Capitalist Revolution* (New York: Harcourt, Brace & World, Inc., 1954), and his *Power Without Property*, published in 1959 by the same publisher.

separate operating units. The units are often decentralized away from the main offices. The giant corporation has been chopped into precincts. Often some of the precincts are in foreign countries. Gone is the owner who lived in the community. In his stead are literally thousands of *shareholders* scattered across the nation.

The job of administering the business has been taken over by specialists called *management*. These professionals live in one part of town and move in one social orbit. Their *employees* live in another part of the city and move in an equally narrow orbit. Today's managers know few of the thousands of men and women whom it takes to make products and provide services for the mass market.

Today's *customers* are spread across the nation and around the world. They must be dealt with through a complex hierarchy of salesmen, distributors, and dealers. They must be persuaded to buy through mass-media advertising. We now have mass production, mass ownership, mass markets, and mass communication with a mass public.

General Motors, one of the world's largest enterprises, epitomizes what has happened. Organized in 1908, it produced its first 50-million cars in forty-six years but produced its second 50-million cars in twelve and one-half years. GM accounts for 1.3 percent of the nation's gross national product and makes almost half the automobiles sold in the United States each year. This industrial giant is owned by nearly 1.5-million shareholders. It provides jobs directly for more than 700,000 employees, who receive $5.5-billion a year in pay. It buys the goods and services of some 37,000 suppliers and thus partially provides jobs for many millions more.

The company measures its profits in billions. It holds the power of economic life or death over more than 15,000 franchised car and truck dealers. With all these and a host of others, including government, General Motors must do business. To do business, it must communicate. The communications between management, its employees, shareholders, suppliers, dealers, and customers must pass through a host of intermediaries and gatekeepers, up and down. For example, the lines of communication between the president and the car dealer in Seattle are long and complicated.

A business' publics have grown beyond the scope of personal communication. Today business firms are known to a mass public by the images they project through the news media and other means. These images are inevitably subject to distortion by intervening barriers and the news values and practices of the news media. An organization's image is not wholly of its own making.

BIG LABOR

Big Business has, in turn, produced Big Labor. To protect themselves against the growing economic power of today's employer, a large share of industry's workers have banded together in labor unions. After much travail, America's work force has forged a countervailing power to that of Big Business. In the labor union, the employee finds job security and, to some extent, a sense of belonging. Today nearly 19-million workers are joined together in organized labor unions, exerting a power far beyond their numbers. Organized labor is the articulate voice of the nation's wage earners. The rise of unions intensified the need for and the problems of industry's relationships with its armies of employees. Generally, industrial union membership has declined in recent years. The relationship of unions and industrial management have, to a great extent, stabilized over the past decade.[14] In the 1960s the unions had their greatest growth organizing public employees. Union membership in the private sector fell from 17,189,000 to 16,467,000 between 1956 and 1964, but union membership among government workers increased from 915,000 to 1,453,000 during the same period. In 1966, there were 17,409,000 members in the private sector, 1,717,000 in the public sector. By 1968, there were 2.2-million federal, state, and local government employees in unions. In 1968 there were 18.8-million union members, an increase of five percent over 1966. Strikes of public employees, once a rarity, are today common. Federal, state, and local governments are learning with difficulty the necessity and art of collective bargaining.[15] As was the case with industry years ago, unionization of public employees has compelled municipalities and school boards to develop more adequate internal and public information programs.

Effective internal communication between the AFL-CIO president and the union member in St. Louis is just as difficult as it is between General Motors' president and the car dealer in Seattle. The Rosens found in their study of one large union that "the failure of communications seems particularly acute in both directions with respect to what is actually being done in the union." [16] In those unions that are democratically run, member participation in union affairs is a difficult problem. Like industry, labor must demonstrate public responsibility and must communicate persuasively. Like industry, labor has felt that lash of angered opinion when it failed to measure up to its public responsibilities or abused its tremendous power.

Periodically labor unions stage strikes to gain their objectives in collective bargaining with employers. These strikes, however justified, often irritate if not injure the public and thus pose difficult public relations problems for the unions. Large strikes of long duration spread concern as to

[14] For elaboration, Jack Barbash, "American Unionism: From Protest to Going Concern," *Journal of Economic Issues*, Vol. 2, March, 1968.

[15] Everett M. Kassalow, "Trade Unionism Goes Public," *The Public Interest*, No. 14, Winter, 1969.

[16] Rosen and Rosen, *The Union Member Speaks* (Englewood Cliffs, N.J.: Prentice-Hall, Inc., 1955), p. 110. A study of one large union and the attitudes of its members. Still useful.

whether unions have grown too strong and whether their strength is applied without attention to the public welfare. It is harder for the public to see management's strikes against labor. Reflecting the integrated nature of our economy, a prolonged strike in a strategic sector can and often does create hardship for millions. For example, a walkout of 664 crewmen on railroad ferries and tugs in New York harbor stranded 100,000 commuters, forced an embargo on export freight, and stopped virtually all main-line service on the Penn Central and New Haven rail lines. To keep strikes in perspective, it should be recorded that only a tiny percentage of labor-management bargainings ever reach the strike stage.[17]

BIG AGRICULTURE

America was born on the farm, but it moved to the city. In the last century, more than half the people lived on farms, mostly small ones. Large families produced mainly for their own needs. Land was plentiful, labor was cheap, and little capital was needed. The farmer's interests did not extend much beyond the county seat, where he went Saturdays to buy a few necessities and to visit. All this has changed and is still changing. In 1870, 53 percent of our people were employed in agriculture. The 1900 census marked the first time that the industrial workers outnumbered those in agriculture. As late as 1933, when the New Deal came to power, 31 percent of our people lived on farms. By 1967, this had dropped to 4,903,-000, a bare 3 percent. It should be noted that, although the number of farm people is declining, the rural population is increasing owing to the increase of nonfarm residents. America's some four-million farms produce more than enough food and fiber for the other 95 percent of our people. In 1900, one farm worker produced food and fiber for himself and seven others. Now one farm worker supports himself and thirty other persons. Agriculture is no longer so much an individual's way of life. It is a heavily mechanized and capitalized business. The average farm in America in 1967 was worth $50,646, the average price per acre, $143.81.

These changes reach far beyond replacement of the old farm springhouse by a food freezer in the basement of the modern farm home. As an official of the United States Department of Agriculture points out: "The massive changes in farming are more than a shift from horse, mule, and human muscle to mechanical or electric power. They are a genetic revolution as well—witness the millions of acres of hybrid corn. They are also a managerial change of the first magnitude. Today's modern commercial farm is not just a face-lifted traditional farm. The skills required to manage

---

[17] For knowledgeable view of labor, see A. H. Raskin, "Labor's Welfare State," *Atlantic*, Vol. 211, April, 1963. For look at labor's PR, see Gerald Pomper, "The Public Relations of Organized Labor," *Public Opinion Quarterly*, Vol. 23, Winter, 1959–60.

its complex of technical, economic, and biological factors are of a high order." [18] The trend is clear. The independent farmer and his family are leaving the land. The homestead is vanishing. The business office is taking over. *Fortune* has said that agriculture today is comparable to "all industry, cartelized, subsidized, and rigidified," and "one of the most powerful blocs in American history."

These profound changes have brought a complex of interdependent relationships with people far removed from the American farmer. Today his economic livelihood depends on the needs and tastes of consumers in the election booth. Today's agriculture is a delicate mechanism. What the government does is soon felt in every township, although the impact varies from area to area. Changes in consumer tastes, such as the recurring reducing fads, quickly radiate their effects out to the farm. Consequently, we see America's dairy farmers uniting in the American Dairy Association to spend some $16-million annually on public relations. A far cry from 1900.

Today's farmer must communicate with consumers and voters far beyond the county seat. He must persuade the nation's voters to provide him with the subsidies, soil banks, and other help he insists that he needs. He must persuade the nation's consumers to buy his products. To meet these needs, the American farmer has need for—and through farm organizations employs—specialists.

BIG GOVERNMENT

Government in the last century was a narrow instrument. Governmental needs could be handled to a large extent in the town meeting and at the state capital. This, too, has changed markedly. Industrialization, accelerating technology, urbanization, and the concentrations of economic and political power combined to induce Big Government in our time.[19] This is particularly true of the federal government. Government—at the federal, state, and local levels—employs 12-million persons.[20] It spends billions to regulate and service more and more of our daily lives. Government has steadily grown in strength and shifted in locus. Public decision-making has ebbed from the town meeting, to the statehouse, to Washington. Likewise, because of the complexity of what government

---

[18] Philip F. Aylesworth, *Keeping Abreast of Change in the Rural Community* (Washington, D.C.: U. S. Department of Agriculture, October, 1959), p. 1.

[19] For a detailed picture of modern government, see James L. McCamy, *American Government* (New York: Harper & Row, 1957).

[20] See John M. Gaus, *Reflections on Public Administration* (University, Ala.: University of Alabama Press, 1947), a valuable series of lectures that offer clear insight into the changed nature of government. For scope of government employment, see "Federal Civilian Employment, Pay, and Benefits," published by Tax Foundation, Inc., 1969.

regulates and provides, decision-making has flowed from the legislative branch into the administrative arm of government.

The growth of positive, powerful government began in the last quarter of the nineteenth century. It started gathering real momentum with President Theodore Roosevelt. It has continued to grow in size and scope to this day, regardless of the party in power. This growth and its multiplying regulation of our lives are direct responses to our environment and the needs it brings. Man invents the automobile, and a whole host of government activities are the result. Man unlocks the atom, and a giant Atomic Energy Commission is inevitable. Space exploration brings a NASA. Daniel Bell sums it up: [21] "The major changes which have reshaped American society over the past 30 years—the creation of a managed economy, a welfare society, and a mobilized polity—grew out of political responses. . . . The result of all this is to enlarge the arena of power."

Because of the tremendous power gathered in government and thus into the hands of voters, public enterprises have had to conform more and more to standards of conduct imposed by voters. Its growth has meant more and more relationships with those who wield its regulatory powers and dispense its favors. Handling these relationships requires the talents of specialists in public opinion, as well as specialists in law.

The nature of government requires that those who make the rules and provide the services must communicate with those who are affected by the rules and those who should get the services. Enforcement of a public health law requires public understanding and support of its purpose. Promotion of soil conservation requires an understanding of its benefits and techniques by landowners if they are to cooperate. This takes skilled communication. The lines of communication between the citizen and the government official have been lengthened physically and psychologically. It is a long way from the Potomac to Puyallup, Washington. There is a big difference in the attitude toward apples of the bureaucrat in Washington, D. C. and the apple grower in Washington State.

This is illustrated, in the extreme, in the futile effort of an earnest citizen to communicate with his President in the White House. It is equally apparent in the effort of the President to escape the insulating barriers around him and to listen to the people. When President Woodrow Wilson started the White House press conference, March 15, 1913, he asked the reporters, "Please do not tell the country what Washington is thinking, for that does not make any difference. Tell Washington what the country is thinking." President John F. Kennedy, perhaps our most public relations-minded president, greatly extended the reach and impact of the Presidential news conference by putting it on television. He used this and other

---

21 "Notes on the Post-Industrial Society (I)," *op. cit.*

means to communicate his views and programs effectively to the voters. He also made a determined effort to keep in touch with the public through travel, wide-ranging contacts, public-opinion polling, and a sensitive reading of newspapers and magazines. President Richard Nixon employed the largest public relations staff in White House history. He executed a useful innovation by appointing Herbert G. Klein as Director of Executive Communications to coordinate the public information work of the executive branch of government. Previously, this had been an additional duty of the White House Press Secretary. Many on Nixon's staff had news media or advertising agency backgrounds.

In facilitating two-way communications with the voters and with other peoples, the United States president needs the help of this large staff of practitioners. Here again we see the environment compelling the development of special talents in opinion analysis and communication. There is a need to bridge the gulf from citizen or corporation to the government and back from bureaucrats to citizens or corporations distant from the scene of decision. Big Government has become the largest single employer of practitioners. Harold Brayman, veteran practitioner, asserts in his *Corporate Management in a World of Politics,* that government is the "most important maker of information for dissemination."

BIG PRESSURE GROUPS

Pioneer forefathers retreated into the stockade for protection against marauding Indians. Today's citizens have retreated into trade, interest, and professional groups to protect and promote self-interests and beliefs—in short, to win public opinion to a group point of view. Given the complexity and the competitive pressures of today's society, the trade association, professional association, cooperative, labor union, ethnic, racial, youth, and cause bloc—all pressure groups—are inevitable. There are more than 10,000 of these national, state, and local interest groups. They promote and protect every known interest and political view—through persuasion, pressure, protest, and politics.

Such groups are the political response to the need for individuals or institutions with common interests to match the power of opposing groups. These pressure groups are, in large measure, a response to the growing power of public opinion and to the growth of Big Government. If the natural gas producers combine to control production and fight federal regulation, it is inevitable that the gas consumers will combine to resist. The interest group or association has two functions. *One is to stabilize the relationships of its members through internal self-discipline. The other is to present the group's case effectively in public.*

The conventional view of the pressure group sees it as bringing pressure, direct or indirect, on the legislative or executive branches of government to get special-interest laws or regulations passed or to block adverse law or rule making. The conventional view is illustrated in the program of the National Rifle Association to prevent gun control legislation. This is a somewhat simplistic view in today's interdependent, complex society. A more realistic view is expressed by Joseph Kraft: [22]

> . . . there is a regular traffic back and forth between the lines, a ceaseless courting of allies and search for reinforcement in opposite camps, an unremitting effort to put together coalitions strong enough to tip balances. The lines of affinity that comprise this traffic are staggering in their diversity. Economic interest, of course, is a principal means of combination. . . . There really is a farm bloc, embracing lobbying organizations, Senators and Representatives, and most of the Department of Agriculture.

Thus, elements of Big Government, Big Business, Big Labor, Big Agriculture, Big Education and Big Pressure Groups interweave as well as interact, forming coalitions around issues of the moment. For example, forces in the Department of Agriculture join with Congressmen from tobacco-growing states to combat efforts by the U. S. surgeon general and the Federal Trade Commission to outlaw cigarette advertising. The sweep and power of such coalitions is seen in the Military-Industrial Complex. President Eisenhower warned against its power and dangers in his farewell address: "The total influence—economic—political, even spiritual—is felt in every city, every state house, every office of the federal government. . . . We must guard against the acquisition of unwarranted influence, whether sought or unsought, by the military industrial complex." At the center is the Department of Defense, which spends more than $80-billion a year—half the national budget—has some 2.5-million persons in uniform, and employs a million civilian workers. More than one hundred of the nation's industrial firms do more than $15-billion worth of annual business with the Defense Department, some of them wholly dependent upon the military business. Many communities depend on defense business or military installations for taxes, local commerce, and employment. In Los Angeles, for example, more than half the jobs come, directly or indirectly, from defense business. Reality suggests that the theory of interest groups as the balancing forces in society may be outdated.

Senator Eugene McCarthy broadened this complex, with some justification, to "the military-industrial-academic establishment" and called it "a kind of republic within the Republic." McCarthy held that since Eisenhower spoke "the situation has become more serious, more dangerous." [23]

---

[22] In *Profiles in Power* (New York: New American Library, 1966), xvi.
[23] In "The Power of the Pentagon," *Saturday Review*, Vol. LI, December 21, 1968.

Universities are tied into the complex through research and consulting contracts. The 100 largest prime contractors for the military in 1967 included Massachusetts Institute of Technology, in sixty-second place with $94.9-million in contracts, and Johns Hopkins University, in seventy-third place, with $71.1-million. Little wonder Eisenhower warned against the "prospect of domination of the nation's scholars by federal employment, project allocations, and the power of money."

The military-industrial complex also includes pressure groups, "led by men with strong emotional and careerist ties to the services and virtually financed by the defense contractors. The Association of the U. S. Army, the Air Force Association, and the Navy League—each with chapters throughout the country—are composed of active, reserve, and retired members of the Armed Forces, and of defense contractors, community leaders, and other supporters. These organizations are financed by membership fees, payments for contractors' exhibits at annual conventions, subscriptions to dinner meetings and rallies, and advertisements in official publications." [24] This is not a cohesive complex because often some elements will line up against other elements, for example the Department of Navy, the Navy League and Congressmen from districts with naval bases or shipyards will form a coalition against a like Air Force coalition in a battle for weapons money. Raymond rightly says, "The problem that confronts us is whether we can continue to depend on these countervailing pressures. . . ." These struggles within, for, and against the military-industrial-academic complex utilize talents of countless practitioners.

BIG EDUCATION

Education has become a major enterprise in the United States. Its influence radiates out to every cranny of American life and the pressures that pound schools and colleges reflect both the aspirations and discontents of Americans. Some 55.1-million persons five to thirty-four years old were enrolled in school or college in the United States in 1966. This represented 30 percent of the total population. U. S. Census Bureau estimates that there will be 47.7-million pupils in elementary and high schools and some 10-million students in colleges by 1985. This education establishment represents heavy public and private expenditures and is a prime influence on shaping our society. Its relationships are many, complicated, and full of conflict.

At the local level, parents are becoming increasingly critical about the content of curricula, and taxpayers are increasingly rebellious at the

---

[24] Jack Raymond, "Growing Threat of Our Military-Industrial Complex," *Harvard Business Review*, Vol. 46, May–June, 1968, p. 60. Raymond, former Pentagon reporter, is now head of a counseling firm.

ever-rising tax costs for education. Issues from segregation to sex education rile community after community. Introduction of an abstract concept, such as "flexible scheduling," can set parents, influenced by Puritan values, on their collective ear. Consequently, school boards have found it necessary to employ practitioners to educate the community about education.

As the university moved out of its medieval ivory tower into the mainstream of American life, it became caught up in the vortex of controversy. Gone is Woodrow Wilson's ideal university as a place where "calm science" sits "not knowing the world passes." Instead, in the words of President Charles J. Hitch of the University of California, "the modern university is both an extremely useful and a somewhat threatening instrument of society." This reflects the fact that the centrality of theoretical knowledge has become decisive in our swift technological age. The university's involvement in the military-industrial complex reflects this new fact of life. The university's relationships have greatly multiplied and have become greatly troubled in recent years. Yet, to be a free center of learning and research, the university must preserve its autonomy.

BIG MEDIA OF COMMUNICATION

Growth of mass media has come as a result of advancing technology, urbanization, and the rising level of education and income. Mass communication is another important element of massiveness contributing to the depersonalization of society. It is no coincidence that the extensive growth of public relations began with the emergence of large newspapers and magazines circulated on a national scale. In small-town, small-shop America, we could know people for their true worth. Today what we are and what we think are projected in the mass media in a matter of minutes to vast, unseen millions, by oversimplified images of us. A headline says, "Housewives in Arms Over Coffee Price Rise." The resulting image is, inescapably, compressed and thus bound to be distorted to a degree. Former Secretary of Labor Willard Wirtz spoke for most in public life when he complained that a considerable part of what the public sees, reads, and hears about the conduct of its public affairs is "a diluted and artificially colored version of fact and truth." Unless people know what truly motivates us and what values we hold, they cannot truly know us. And if they do not know us, they are apt to misunderstand us, and we, them. "They know not England who only England know." Yet we make many decisions each day on the basis of these second-hand images in the mass media. And therein lies their power.

Justice Learned Hand once observed, "The day has clearly gone forever of a society small enough for its members to have a personal acquaintance with one another and to find their station through the appraisal of those who have first-hand knowledge of them. Publicity is an evil substitute and the art of publicity a black art. But it has come to stay. Every year adds to the potency, to the finality of its judgments." Today the people are "incessantly peering at us through the magnified, but sometimes distorted, lenses of journalists, broadcasters, and motion picture procedures." [25] *The mass media of press, magazine, radio, television, and motion pictures have become the common carriers of decision-making information.*

The overpowering fact of our times is the thrust of television. It has become a dominant force in rearing of our young, the prime source of news and entertainment for most Americans, and a powerful soapbox from which citizens' protests can be communicated to the nation and the world. This medium has greatly altered presidential election campaigns and has diminished the role of the political parties. The national newswires and nationwide TV networks have created a truly national forum. Events made large by TV move and shape public opinion. Its power was demonstrated when it saved the political life of Richard Nixon,[26] was a crucial factor in President John F. Kennedy's election in 1960,[27] laid open the wounds of the Democratic Party in Chicago in 1968, and exposed police brutality to blacks in the South. Perhaps most illustrative of all was TV's role in making the Vietnamese War the nation's first televised war and its most unpopular one. This medium enables a nation to share its grief over a fallen president or its exaltation in landing men on the moon. The dimensions of its impact on society are yet to be fully documented, but their outline is clear.

Television greatly heightens citizen awareness of the conduct of public institutions and emphasizes the impersonal, interdependent nature of his environment. It also creates a sense of frustration for the citizen, who is witness to much that he cannot control—be it the Vietnamese War, a police-protestor battle in Chicago, the wretched life in ghettos, or developers' filling in San Francisco Bay. This frustration alternately leads to anger or apathy. TV is the most popular and credible source of news—a fact which many practitioners, most of whom once worked in print media, fail to reckon with. Television took the lead from newspapers as the source of most news in 1963. By 1968, based on a national poll, 29 percent of adults listed TV as the only source of news, while 19 percent said they

[25] Harwood L. Childs, *An Introduction to Public Opinion* (New York: John Wiley & Sons, Inc., 1940). His chapter, "What Are Public Relations?" remains a useful discussion of this field's ecology.

[26] For full account this historic political speech, see Garry Wills, "Nixon's Dog," *Esquire*, Vol. LXXII, August, 1969. For insider's account of Nixon's use of TV in 1968 campaign, see Joe McGinniss, *The Selling of the President 1968* (New York: Trident Press, 1969).

[27] Sidney Kraus, ed., *The Great Debates* (Bloomington: Indiana University Press, 1962). See Part II "Effects of the Debates."

relied on newspapers exclusively. Another 25 percent said they relied on both media.[28]

We have learned through research that the images and words these media carry determine, within the limitations posed by intervening factors, opinions of people and, thus, their actions. Woodrow Wilson saw this, too. He said, "Unless you get the right setting to affairs—disperse the right impression—things go wrong. . . ." It has become vital to all concerns subject to public opinion to project a favorable image through the mass media. And the media will not do this without assistance and guidance. Consequently, the effort to control and influence the content these media carry to the people has become an intense and spirited one. Growth of mass media, more than any other one factor, created the public relations occupation. It is *Fortune's* opinion, "When all is said and done, it is the public relations man's major job to help management deal with the various segments of that maddening and massive communication agency called the press."

Thus in this rapidly changing environment we see the forces at work which make necessary the role of the practitioner and the expanding dimensions of the challenge this role poses for those who undertake it. In this context—the age of specialization—public relations is no exception. Functioning across the broad spectrum of media, publics, and competing viewpoints, the intellectual, moral, and technical requirements for the practitioner are broad and severe.

ADDITIONAL READING

DANIEL BELL, *et al.,* "Toward the Year 2000: Work in Progress," *Daedalus,* special issue, Summer, 1967.

ADOLF A. BERLE, *The American Economic Republic.* New York: Harcourt, Brace & World, Inc., 1963. An analysis of the American economic system.

PAUL W. CHERINGTON and RALPH L. GILLEN, *The Business Representative in Washington.* Washington, D.C.: The Brookings Institution, 1962.

LEO CHERNE, "The Trillion Dollar Frustration," *Saturday Review,* Vol. LI, November 23, 1968.

MARQUIS W. CHILDS and DOUGLASS CATER, *Ethics in a Business Society.* New York: Harper & Row, Publishers, 1954. (Also available as a Mentor Book.)

CRAMPTON, JOHN A., *The National Farmers Union: Ideology of a Pressure Group.* Lincoln, Neb.: University of Nebraska Press, 1965.

[28] Roper Research Associates, "A Ten-Year View of Public Attitudes Toward Television and Other Mass Media, 1959–1968," Published by Television Information Office, New York City.

JAMES DEAKIN, *The Lobbyists*. Washington, D.C.: Public Affairs Press, 1966. Recent look at pressure groups in nation's capital.

WILLIAM H. FORM, "Organized Labor's Place in the Community Power Structure," *Industrial and Labor Relations Review*, Vol. 12, July, 1959.

JOHN K. GALBRAITH, *The Affluent Society*. Boston: Houghton Mifflin Company, 1958.

ANDREW HACKER, *The End of the American Era*. New York: Atheneum, 1970. Cornell political scientist sees U. S. as "embarked on its time of decline." Chapter on corporations illuminating.

FLOYD W. MATSON, *The Broken Image: Man, Science and Society*. Garden City, N.Y.: Doubleday & Company, 1966 (Anchor ed).

DAVID RIESMAN, *et al., The Lonely Crowd*. New York: Doubleday & Company, Inc., 1953. (Abridged from an earlier Yale University Press edition.)

MAURICE R. STEIN, *The Eclipse of Community*. Princeton, N.J.: Princeton University Press, 1960.

ARTHUR J. VIDICH and JOSEPH BENSMAN, *Small Town in Mass Society*. Princeton, N.J.: Princeton University Press, 1958.

CHAPTER
6

**PERSUASION
AND
PUBLIC
OPINION**

Public opinion, says Joseph Kraft, is "the unknown god to which moderns burn incense." Basically, there are three means of getting people to do what you want—*pressure, purchase,* or *persuasion.* The United States draft law got men into the armed forces by *pressure* or *force.* When a vice king bribes policemen to wink at law violations, he gets compliance by *purchase.* The campaign of the New York Stock Exchange which raised the number of common stock owners from six- to thirty-one million was one of *persuasion.* In public relations, persuasion is used. The basic objective of programs is either to *change* or to *neutralize* hostile opinions, to *crystallize* unformed or latent opinions in your favor, or to *conserve* favorable opinions.

Some years ago a number of harsh criticisms erupted in New York State against that state's welfare programs. To allay these criticisms, the State Communities Aid Association set out to bring the critics face to face with the grim problems of poverty, illegitimacy, illiteracy, and so forth. This is a modern version of citizen inspection of the poorhouses of yesteryear. The project's basic plan was simple: to let the community leaders see and talk to people living "on welfare," to watch caseworkers cope with the complex problems they face every day. The pilot project was sponsored in ten New York communities and financed by a grant from the Field Foundation. Other communities later adopted the plan.

In these communities on a given day community leaders—particularly those most vocal about loafers, chiselers, and loose-living women—are paired off with caseworkers. Critic and caseworker spend the afternoon visiting typical welfare recipients. These recipients are not tipped off in advance, but when asked if the observer may sit in, they readily grant permission. Typical, rather than "best" or "worst," households are visited. Then all visitors and welfare workers come together for a dinner and discussion of what has been seen during the day. This discussion often runs past midnight and the critics wind up with a different opinion about those living "on welfare." The State Communities Aid Association, after the pilot program, concluded: "This demonstration has proved its value in helping lift the fog of public suspicion about welfare." This is a *planned* effort to change what had been *hostile* opinion.

Public relations efforts to *create* attitudes where none exist was illustrated in the National Safety Council's campaign to get motorists to use seat belts. Basic research indicated that universal use of seat belts would save 8,000 to 10,000 lives each year and would reduce serious injuries by one third. Much of that educational effort met the ingrained resistance of human habit. The Joint Seat Belt Committee, consisting of the National Safety Council, the American Medical Association, and the United States Public Health Service, kept up a steady barrage of persuasive communication, using films, posters, public service advertising, news stories, TV documentaries, and spot radio announcement to get more motorists to use seat belts. Here the effort was to *crystallize* latent or unformed opinion. The presence of seat belts and their legal endorsement were not enough. Wisconsin was the first state to require seat belts in cars and supported the law with an intensive public relations effort from 1962 on, yet, a statewide survey in 1968 found that only 15 percent of adults reported using a safety belt every time they rode in a car. Changing fixed habits and attitudes is not the easy task that those who talk of "hidden persuaders" think it to be.

The diamond has long been a standard of ultimate value, fluctuating little more than money itself. When sales charts disclosed a trend away from the use of diamonds in engagement rings, the DeBeers Consolidated Mines Ltd. did something about it. To revive the concept of a diamond as a symbol of high fashion, publicity pointed readers and viewers toward the diamond that each TV, radio, and movie star received on becoming engaged. Fashion models were encouraged to wear diamonds with new gowns. Diamonds and St. Valentine's Day were linked in publicity. The jeweler was given special materials and booklets to use at service clubs and schools. All of these efforts had the object of *conserving* favorable opinion. Another example was the effort of IBM, long synonymous with computation, to *conserve* its favorable reputation when it was attacked by competitors and the U. S. Department of Justice for monopolistic practices. IBM took its case to the public through publicity and advertising.

The practitioner is striving constantly to start, lead, change, speed, or slow trends in public opinion. His problems are compounded of people's differences in outlook and opinion. The daily tasks of the staff are created by people who "don't understand us," who "won't cooperate," who "won't work as hard as they should," who "won't vote right," who "won't give as much as they should," and so on.

The term *public opinion* is a slippery one. Our ability to measure it is greater than our ability to define or manipulate it. Although the concept originated in the eighteenth century, it still has not been defined satisfactorily. *Public opinion* is difficult to describe, elusive to define, hard to measure, impossible to see. For this reason, the concept is utilized less and less in the growing precision of social psychology, sociology, and political science. Most writers agree that the force of public opinion is perceptible, though the concept is vague. Some scholars doubt that there is a field of public opinion separate from the psychology of attitude formation and change. Nonetheless, public opinion's pervasive power is easily felt. James Russell Lowell said, "The pressure of public opinion is like the atmosphere. You can't see it, but all the same it is sixteen pounds to the square inch." Another New Englander, Samuel Bowles II, added, "Public sentiment is a capricious, intangible thing, so hard to reach, so hard to manage when it is reached." The power must be faced, understood, and dealt with in a free country. *Public opinion provides the psychological environment in which organizations prosper or perish.* No one has better described it than did Lord Bryce: [1]

> [public opinion] . . . is a congeries of all sorts of discrepant notions, beliefs, fancies, prejudices, aspirations. It is confused, incoherent, amorphous, varying from day to day and week to week. But in the midst of this diversity and confusion every question as it rises into importance is subjected to a process of consolidation and clarification until there emerge and take shape certain views or sets of interconnected views, each held and advocated in common by bodies of citizens. It is to the power exerted by any such views, when held by an apparent majority of citizens, that we refer when we talk of Public Opinion. . . .

THE POWER STRUCTURE

This slippery abstraction, *public opinion,* finds its tangible expression in the decisions of a power structure concerned with a particular issue. Power, an ancient concept, is a relation among people. D'Antonio and Ehrlich offer this concept: [2] "Power in its most general sense refers to a capacity or ability to control others and, in this context, to control the decision-making process which implies the control of others." This relates *public opinion* to the *ecology* of public relations. The power structure, a comparatively new term, describes the network of influences existing among individuals and organizations involved in a given community's decision-making process. *The power structure, not some vague concept of "the public," must be the focus of the practitioner's work.*

There are many power structures, not just one elite group, and the power structure varies with the type of community. This concept was first

---

[1] James Bryce, *Modern Democracies* (New York: The Macmillan Company, 1921), pp. 153–154.
[2] William V. D'Antonio and Howard J. Ehrlich, eds., *Power and Democracy in America* (Notre Dame, Ind.: University of Notre Dame Press, 1961), pp. 132–134.

developed by sociologists C. Wright Mills and Floyd Hunter. Both developed the simplistic theory that each community is dominated by a single power group, the economic elite.[3] Another sociologist, Arnold M. Rose, took issue with Mills and Hunter by propounding a "multi-influence" hypothesis which is much more plausible. Rose wrote: [4] "The multi-influence hypothesis depicts social reality as a far more complex conflict than does the economic-elite dominance hypothesis." Rose saw the bulk of the population as consisting of integrated groups and publics, stratified with varying degrees of power, thus not subject to control by any so-called *elite*. Mills saw the public as an undifferentiated mass of inert individuals.

Political scientist Robert Dahl supports this pluralistic view in generalizations growing out of his study of the power structure of New Haven, Connecticut. He wrote: [5] ". . . Any investigation that does not take into account the possibility that different elite groups have different scopes is suspect . . . there is no doubt that small groups of people make key decisions. It appears to be the case, however, that the small group that runs urban redevelopment is not the same small group that runs public education, and neither is quite the same as the two groups that run the two political parties." Dahl sees this variation of influence in a community as a result of *dispersed inequalities*. Different citizens have different resources to influence public decisions; such resources are unequally distributed and usually no one influence resource dominates all the others. Nor is one influence source effective in all areas of decision-making.

Form and Miller list these independent components of community power: [6]

1. *The institutional power structure of the society*. This refers to the relative distribution of power among societal institutions.

2. *The institutionalized power structure of the community*. This is the distribution of power among local institutions.

3. *The community power complex*. This is a power arrangement among temporary or permanent organizations, special-interest associations, and informal groups emerging in specific issues and projects.

---

[3] The late C. Wright Mills' theory was expressed in *The Power Elite*, published by Oxford University in 1959, while Hunter's can be found in his study at Atlanta, Ga., *Community Power Structure*, published by the University of North Carolina Press, 1953. Also see Hunter's *Top Leadership U. S. A.*, published by same press in 1959.

[4] In *The Power Structure, Political Process in American Society* (New York: Oxford University Press, 1967), p. 3.

[5] Robert A. Dahl, "Critique of the Ruling Elite Model," *American Political Science Review*, Vol. 52, June, 1958, pp. 463–469.

[6] William H. Form and Delbert C. Miller, *Industry, Labor, and Community* (New York: Harper & Bros., 1960), pp. 437–438.

4. *The top influentials.* This refers to those persons who are reputed to be of most influence and power in community decision-making. In specific issues, particular decision-makers are drawn into various systems of power relations according to the community issues or projects that arise.

5. *The key influentials.* These are the acknowledged leaders among the top influentials.

Public opinion thus comes to be tangibly expressed in the decisions flowing from the interactions *within* and *among* integrated groups comprising the power structure that revolves about a particular issue.

A WORKING DEFINITION

There are countless definitions of public opinion. Most scholars in this field agree that public opinion represents a *consensus* among a varying number of persons and that this consensus exercises power. The consensus emerges, over time, from all the expressed views that cluster around an issue in debate. Hennessy holds: [7] *"for any given issue, public opinion is the collection of views, measurable or inferable, held by persons who have an interest in that issue."* Each of the two words that make up the term *public opinion* is significant. A *public* is simply a collective noun for a group—a group of individuals tied together by some common bond of interest—and sharing a *sense of togetherness.* It may be a small group or a large group; it may be a majority group. Ogle defines a *public* as "any group of two or more persons who demonstrate in any manner whatever that they are conscious of group solidarity." The term "public" is used frequently in public relations as a synonym for "a group." We talk about an "employee public," an "community public," an "alumni public," and so forth. There are literally an infinite number of smaller publics within the general public. The concept of a "public," was introduced by John Dewey in his *The Public and Its Problems.* He defined a public as a group of individuals who together are affected by a particular action or idea. Thus, each issue or problem creates its own public.

An *opinion* is simply the expression of an attitude on a controversial issue. Opinion implies controversy and dispute, whereas *fact* implies general acceptance. The law of gravity is a fact; the justice of a "right to work" law or a segregated schools policy are matters of opinion. One man's fact may be another's fiction. An *attitude* is simply a predisposition to respond in a given way to a given issue or situation. Rokeach, who defines attitude

[7] Bernard C. Hennessy, *Public Opinion* (Belmont, Cal.: Wadsworth Publishing Co., 1965), p. 20. (Second ed. 1970.)

attitude def.

as a relatively enduring organization of beliefs about an object or situation, suggests "that attitude change is a function not merely of attitude toward an object but also of attitude toward a situation." [8] The terms "attitude" and "opinion" often are used interchangeably. This leads to some confusion. They are distinctly separate concepts, although there is a continuing interaction between inwardly held attitudes and outwardly expressed opinions. Wiebe thinks, "Opinions adapt attitudes to the demands of social situations; but having adapted them, opinions appear to become ingredients in the constant, gradual reformulation of attitudes."

The attitudes of individual citizens provide the raw material out of which a consensus develops. Influencing an individual's attitudes is a prime task of the practitioner. Consequently, he must know the source of a person's attitudes, their organization as reflected in the person's value system and personality, and the processes which bring attitude change. All this is of basic importance in understanding the end product we glibly label "public opinion."

There are two main streams of thought with respect to the determination of man's attitudes: (1) one school assumes man to be an irrational being with limited powers of reason and thus susceptible to emotional appeals; (2) the second assumes man to be a rational being with strong powers of reason and discrimination. The early advertisers who relied heavily on the power of suggestion and exploited fear appeals reflected a belief in the irrational man. Those who believe that Americans are but puppets at the end of the "Hidden Persuaders'" string reflect this notion. Those who adhere to the rational model of man put their reliance on getting adequate information to people. Our educational system, for example, is based on the rational model of man. Practitioners who put their reliance on two-way communication of information demonstrate their belief in the importance of intelligence and comprehension in the formation of men's opinions.

In fact, most persons are influenced by both irrational and rational reasoning. A person who smokes may ignore overwhelming evidence linking cigarette smoking with lung cancer on one hand but go through a rational process in arriving at an opinion concerning a civic issue on the other. Either school of thought can point to evidence which supports its assumptions and undercuts the arguments of the other. There are elements of truth in both approaches in dealing with attitude formation and change.

On the psychological level, the reasons for holding or for altering attitudes are found in the essential functions they perform for the individual in enabling him to cope with his situation. These are the functions of ad-

---

[8] For elaboration, see Milton Rokeach, "Attitude Change and Behavioral Change," *Public Opinion Quarterly*, Vol. 30, Winter, 1966–67, pp. 529–550.

justment, ego defense, value expression, and knowledge. Daniel Katz, social psychologist, groups these according to their motivational basis: [9]

1. *The instrumental, adjustive, or utilitarian function.* . . . A modern expression of this approach can be found in behavioristic learning theory.
2. *The ego-defensive function,* in which the person protects himself from acknowledging the basic truths about himself or the harsh realities in his external world. . . .
3. *The value-expressive function,* in which the individual derives satisfactions from expressing attitudes appropriate to his personal values and to his concept of himself. . . .
4. *The knowledge function,* based upon the individual's need to give adequate structure to his universe. The search for meaning, the need to understand, the trend toward better organization of perceptions and beliefs to provide clarity and consistency for the individual. . . .

In sum, this functional approach is simply an effort to understand the reasons why persons hold the attitudes they do.

In dealing with the formation and change of attitudes, the practitioner will find Leon Festinger's theory of *cognitive dissonance* of value. This theory is based on the fact that human beings demonstrate a great desire for consistency and congruity in their attitudes and, conversely, they find inconsistency between what they know and what they have done disturbing and discomfiting. Festinger states his theory thus: [10]

Any time a person has information or an opinion which considered by itself would lead him not to engage in some action, then this information or opinion is dissonant with having engaged in the action. When such dissonance exists, the person will try to reduce it either by changing his actions or by changing his beliefs and opinions. If he cannot change the action, opinion change will ensue. This psychological process, which can be called dissonance reduction, does explain the frequently observed behavior of people justifying their actions. . . . When dissonance exists, dissonance-reduction attempts do occur.

Essentially the dissonance concept suggests that persons avoid information adverse to their views or situation and seek out information

---

[9] See Daniel Katz, "The Functional Approach to the Study of Attitudes," *Public Opinion Quarterly,* Vol. 24, Summer, 1960, p. 170.

[10] Leon Festinger, "The Theory of Cognitive Dissonance," in *The Science of Human Communication,* edited by Wilbur Schramm (New York: Basic Books, Inc., 1963), pp. 17–27. For a fuller discussion, see Festinger's *A Theory of Cognitive Dissonance,* published by Harper & Row in 1957.

consonant with their world. In recent years, Festinger and his associates have restricted the generality of the dissonance theory. They have postulated that the decision which produces the dissonance must have implications for subsequent behavior, that there would be little value in assuming value assertions favorable to action already foreclosed by commitment.[11] Much of the recent communications-opinion research suggests that persons seek out only that information which supports attitudes already held. The corollary of this is that any effect of the exposure is primarily in reinforcing values of the person, thus setting up a circular process, making it difficult to change attitudes.[12] Which indeed it is.

Others dissent from this closed circle notion. Sears and Freedman grant that "most audiences for mass communications apparently tend to over-represent persons already sympathetic to the views being propounded, and most persons seem to be exposed disproportionately to communications that support their opinions." But, they add, "a considerable amount of experimental research has uncovered no general psychological preference for supportive information."[13] Another theoretician, Richard Carter, suggests the answer when he holds that the supportive view focuses on the *expressive* function of the individual's communication behavior, but that in the second function, value *formulation,* one cannot readily accept that aversive information is avoided. Sears and Freedman conclude: "Perhaps resistance to influence is accomplished most often and most successfully at the level of information evaluation, rather than at the level of selective seeking and avoiding of information." This discussion makes clear that the opinion-formation-communications processes are inextricably linked. For clarity of discussion, they are separated in this book.

Each individual accumulates his predispositions to think or act in a certain way from many places, many sources. A person's attitudes remain latent until an issue arises for the group to which he belongs. An issue arises when there is conflict, frustration, or anxiety. Thus confronted, the individual takes his stand and voices his opinion. For example, university students have latent attitudes about what are proper regulations to govern visiting hours in dormitories housing the opposite sex. The dean of students sets rigid hours for such visiting privileges. A conflict develops. These attitudes crystallize into opinions pro and con. The opinion expressed represents the sum of a person's attitudes on a specific issue in debate tempered

[11] See Jack W. Brehm and Arthur R. Cohen, *Explorations in Cognitive Dissonance* (New York: Wiley, 1962) and Leon Festinger, et al, *Conflict, Decision and Dissonance* (Stanford, Cal.: Stanford University Press, 1964), for revisions.

[12] For this point of view, see Joseph T. Klapper, *The Effects of Mass Communication* (Glencoe, Ill.: The Free Press, 1960) and Bernard Berelson and Gary A. Steiner, *Human Behavior* (New York: Harcourt, Brace and World, 1964).

[13] David O. Sears and Jonathan L. Freedman, "Selective Exposure to Propaganda," *Public Opinion Quarterly,* Vol. 31, Summer, 1967, p. 212.

by that person's degree of concern for group approval of his *expressed* opinions.

Now that we have taken the term *public opinion* apart, let us try to put it together. The individual opinions expressed by members of a group with a common bond—be it a city council or voters of a commonwealth— are loosely bunched under the umbrella concept, public opinion. This is not the opposite of private opinions. Rather, *public opinion is the aggregate result of individual opinions on public matters.* Public matters are those which affect groups of people, not isolated individuals. A public is a group of people affected by the same affairs. Publics cannot have and do not have opinions, because a public is not an entity in itself. *Public opinion is the sum of accumulated individual opinions on an issue in public debate and affecting a group of people.*

The ultimate expression of public opinion, as indicated earlier, is not an arithmetical sum but rather the sum of active opinions working through power structures or social systems. For example, the opinions of the 15-million eligible voters who sat out the 1968 presidential election counted for little in the political decisions of that year. For the practitioner who must deal with this force on a daily basis, McCamy sets up three main categories: [14]

1. Public opinion in its broadest sense is the whole way of life in the nation, or what social scientists call the "culture" of a people.
2. Public opinion is the prevalent mood of a people, or at least a considerable portion of them.
3. Public opinion is the collection of individual opinions in a group of people whose attention is directed toward a common subject, purpose, like, or dislike.

The tides of public opinion are forever ebbing in and out, beating against the boulders of public issues as they ebb and flow. These tides move at slow, almost imperceptible speeds, for the most part. They are propelled more by events than by publicity. In Galbraith's phrase, "The enemy of conventional wisdom is not ideas but march of events." Events change values. Japanese bombs at Pearl Harbor destroyed not only our fleet but our isolationism. Thus, Americans support a United Nations when once they refused to join a League of Nations. Similarly, splitting the atom has weakened concepts of national sovereignty. Public opinion encompasses attitudes and supporting behavior that polarize around an issue in public debate. When goals are accomplished, the supporting opinions tend to disappear. Public opinion on one issue can be displaced by opinion on an-

[14] James L. McCamy, *American Government* (New York: Harper & Row, 1957), p. 462. These categories are expanded in his chapter on public opinion.

other. The episodic nature of our news coverage facilitates this. As issues change, so does public opinion. In this process, the practitioner plays an influential role.

The process of opinion formation goes something like this:

1. A number of people recognize a situation as being problematic and decide that something ought to be done about it. They explore possible solutions and do some fact-finding.
2. Alternative proposals for solving the problem emerge, and these are discussed back and forth.
3. A policy or a solution is agreed upon as best meeting the situation recognized as problematic. Agreement and a decision to promote its acceptance lead to group consciousness.
4. A program of action is undertaken, and this is pressed until the requisite action is obtained or the group becomes weary of the battle and its members turn to other projects and other groups.

ROOTS OF OUR ATTITUDES

Public opinion gets its power through individuals, who must be persuaded and organized. To deal effectively with this potent force, one must study it situation by situation and influence it individual by individual, group by group. This starts with the individual and the source of his opinions. It requires an almost endless exploration of heredity, environments, and the motivations of human behavior. People act on the basis of "the pictures in our heads" rather than in accordance with the reality of the world outside. What a person believes is *true,* moral or ethical *is true, moral or ethical for him.* To understand him, we start by digging out the roots of these "pictures in our heads." [15] What goes into the composition of these pictures of a world out of sight, out of reach?

PERSONAL FACTORS

We start with the fact that each person is an individual bundle of conscious ideals, life goals, fears, frustrations, hates, loves, habits, fixations, prides, and prejudices. Not all of these are visible or measurable—one of the factors making prediction or assessment of human behavior risky. The individual is primarily concerned with meeting the other's expectations of his performance, and he actually believes in the opinions and actions he

---

[15] The concept of the stereotype was introduced by Walter Lippmann in his now classic book, *Public Opinion* (New York Harcourt, Brace & World, 1922). This book has stood the test of time and offers lucid insight into the nature of public opinion.

adopts. Many psychologists believe that much human behavior can be explained by the numbers, intensities, and interactions of psychological and physiological needs. Just how these interact is difficult to ascertain because one cannot separate mind from body. This much seems agreed upon— the human personality has four primary determinants:

1. Biology or heredity.
2. Group membership, essentially one's environment.
3. Role, involving one's age, sex, social status, class, and color.
4. Situation, all the accidental things which affect people, which can make two brothers from the same environment quite different.

ENVIRONMENTAL FACTORS

Harwood Childs classifies the environmental factors that shape a person's attitudes into two categories—the *primary factors* of experience, the things we read, hear, or see ". . . the channels of communication and what comes through them—the ideas, reports, representations that constitute our world of verbal symbols." The *secondary factors* are those of culture, family, religion, race, school, class and status in the community. Our interpretation of issues is shaped by the glasses through which we view them. The lenses in the individual's glasses are ground by the secondary factors of environment—where we live, how old we are, how prosperous we are, and our biological, physical, social and psychological heritage. The primary factors are *active;* the secondary factors are *latent.*[16]

The roots of one's attitudes are many and extend in all directions and depths in the soil of our culture. Researchers can dig up and examine each of these roots. They still cannot, with any certainty, determine the amount of vitality or degree of variation that each root contributes to the living plant. Which has the greater force on what one thinks and says—his heredity? His environment? His family or peers? His church? His political party? The list of influencing factors is almost endless. The role each plays in relation to all the others is hard to calculate. It varies with each individual and each situation of conflict. The "pictures in our heads"—the symbols, codes, slogans, superstitions, and stereotypes that people live by —have their origins in many places.

In most attempts to enumerate and classify, the influence of heredity as against environment is a common starting point. From there such efforts take different pathways to answering the old question, "Why *do* we behave the way we do?" It is a question continually confronting the practitioner for a practical answer. Why do more people like coffee than tea?

[16] Harwood Childs, *An Introduction to Public Opinion* (New York: John Wiley & Sons, 1940). See chapter, "Formation of Opinion."

OUR CULTURE

No man lives unto himself alone. To demonstrate this to oneself, all a person needs to do is to be *absolutely* alone for 24 hours. From the crib to the casket, he is influenced by others. The newborn child finds an elaborate civilization awaiting him. He fits into historic institutions and is molded by them. The family, play group, school, church, city, state, and nation are organized ways in which the individual enters social relations. They make possible a richer life than could be attained if individuals lived in isolation. The necessities of civilized life, in turn, compel us to maintain cordial and cooperative relations with our fellows. We group ourselves together to work, to play, to worship. Without society, with its cultural heritage, man would be a beast.

These are the factors which determine a person's *mental set*—the screen upon which are cast the lights and shadows of what he reads, sees, or hears to form the pictures in his head. The basic institutions of family, church, school, and economic groupings are the portholes through which one views the world outside. They determine norms, standards, values. They transmit from one generation to another that which Bagehot named "the cake of custom." Man shapes these institutions and, in turn, is shaped by them. Public relations plays its role in this process.

There are two basic points to remember about the role of a nation's culture in shaping its opinions. As Cuber declares, the culture is "fundamental to the understanding of the human being and of groups. Most of the other social science ideas grow out of it or are dependent on it." The second is that culture is *learned* from time of birth onward to death. Illustrative of the cultural backdrop against which the drama of public debate takes place is what is generally accepted in the United States as the democratic creed. Two researchers found wide agreement on these propositions: "Democracy is the best form of government." "Public officials should be chosen by majority vote." "Every citizen should have an equal chance to influence government policy." "The minority should be free to criticize the majority decisions." "People in the minority should be free to try to win majority support for their opinions." [17]

The necessity of considering varying cultural patterns has been repeatedly demonstrated in the failures of well-intentioned outsiders to help the impoverished mountaineers in Appalachia. Many outside theorists have tried to bring change to these people without success. A minister who tried, later reflected about "the sullen and sometimes almost hostile

---

[17] Quoted from Prothro and Grigg's "Fundamental Principles of Democracy," pp. 282–284, by Robert A. Dahl in *Who Governs? Democracy and Power in an American City* (New Haven, Conn.: Yale University Press, 1961), p. 316.

way in which the people responded . . . when I tried to follow the procedures I had been taught . . . [and] . . . about the meagre results I
obtained from following the literature sent out by my church's central office. The people simply didn't see things—ordinary things—the way my
colleagues and I saw them. . . . They had good points and bad points,
but they were unmistakably different."

THE FAMILY

The family, the germ cell of society, is the first molder of opinions.
No person can escape the strong, formative influences of the family circle.
Certainly Henry Adams was not recording a unique experience when he
wrote that his father's character contributed more to his education than did
the influence of any other person. In many, many ways, some overt, some
subtle, the child acquires the parents' attitudes and outlook. A great many
people, for example, inherit their political affiliation.

"Within the family is to be found the germ of all those potentialities
which later ripen into love and hate, work and play, obedience and revolt,
reverence and agnosticism, patriotism and treason. It is the matrix which
molds the human personality and gives it the initial impetus and direction
determining its goal and means to its fulfillment." This influence is underscored by recent knowledge which indicates that many of our principal
characteristics are acquired before the age of five. It is the family that
bends the tender twig in the direction it is likely to grow. There are cautions to consider in assessing the role of the family in shaping attitudes.
One, members of a family are influenced by the same environments, the
same neighbors, and same neighborhoods so one can't be sure whether a
particular influence originates inside the family or outside in the neighborhood. Two, current social trends appear to diminish the influence of the
family. Childs writes: [18] ". . . many factors definitely lessen the influence
of parents: notably multiplication of outside diverting influences . . .
stronger emotional ties to peer groups, weakened parental authority, family
mobility, family instability, and the employment of women . . . outside
the home."

Many of our social institutions serve as reinforcing devices to re-
inculcate the lessons the child learned in the family circle. The neighborhood, mother's bridge-club companions, father's fellow workers, the evening
paper, network newscasts, the neighbors next door, and the breadwinner's
economic status—all shape adult attitudes. Similarly, the family shapes the
attitudes of the children.

---

[18] Harwood Childs, *Public Opinion, Nature, Formation, and Role* (Princeton, N. J.: D. Van
Nostrand Co., 1965), p. 141. This book has chapter on role of public relations and
advertising in molding public opinion.

RELIGION

One basic human trait binds nearly all people together. This is religion and the belief in a supernatural, universal power. Religion is a vital force. Both believers and nonbelievers are influenced by it. No effort to influence public opinion can omit or deny the strong influence of the church. The church is more influential in the formation of opinions than a mere survey of members might indicate. Religion is so important and pervasive that many Americans feel compelled to go through the forms though they may not subscribe to the substance. On the other hand, many religious persons have no formal church connection.

Religion has been a major influence in Western civilization. Who can doubt, for example, the Calvinist influence in shaping the ideals of industry, sobriety, frugality, and thrift which stem from America's frontier? R. H. Tawney held that the Protestant Revolution was one of the most decisive factors in the development of the capitalist ideology. He said, "Capitalism was a social counterpart of Calvinist theology." Who denies the indelible stamp placed upon American culture by Puritanism?

The influence of religion and dogma which permeates all strata of society is extended and underlined as the church increasingly turns to social issues in applied Christianity. Today clergymen—thought leaders—are active on many fronts in striving to generate and guide public opinion on social issues. The churches are concerned with teen-age gangs and with delinquent parents, with peace, slum clearance, civil rights, narcotic addiction, and racism. The important role which religion plays in shaping attitudes on public questions was clearly demonstrated in the 1960 Presidential election. Theodore White concluded: "There is no doubt that millions of Americans, Protestant and Catholic, voted in 1960 primordially out of instinct, kinship and past." [19] Religion's influence also was illustrated when the Rev. Martin Luther King took his into the streets. Its impact is seen in the debate swirling about programs of birth control as a means of slowing over-population of the world or in the periodic battles over fluoridation. Yet current social trends would suggest some slippage in the potency of religion, compared with past eras. A Gallup Poll in April, 1968 revealed that 67 percent of Americans think religion is losing its influence, a sharp shift in views expressed a decade earlier. America is increasingly a secular society. Yet who can doubt religion's influence when

[19] Theodore H. White, *The Making of a President 1960* (New York: Atheneum Press, 1961), p. 356. White's two subsequent accounts of the 1946 and 1968 presidential elections plus the one on the 1960 election give a readable, insightful picture of public opinion at work. All three were published by Atheneum.

one looks at the conflicts in Northern Ireland, the Middle East, or those involving India and Pakistan.

SCHOOLS

A teacher's influence stops only with eternity. The influence and importance of the school in the public-opinion process is underlined in a state which regards an educated, enlightened electorate indispensable to a free society. Whereas it seems that there has been some lessening of the influence of the family and church in recent decades, it appears that the schools have gained influence. More children than ever before are going to school. They are starting at an earlier age and attending for longer periods of time. Expanded and improved teaching methods, larger enrollment, and longer schooling account for the schools' increased influence.

Because of their key role in shaping tomorrow's citizens, the schools are getting increased attention from the practitioner. The philosophy or cause he represents strives for a greater share in the education of young people. This is reflected in diverse, greatly increased pressures on schools—with respect to what shall be taught, who shall teach, and what textbooks and films they shall use.

America deems it proper that the state shall have the right to take the child from the family and keep him in school until he reaches a certain age or a certain level of education. More and more parental responsibility is being shifted to the schools in the winter months and to the organized recreation programs in the summer months. In urban areas it is quite common for the child to leave the home for nursery school at the age of three, be enrolled in kindergarten at the age of four or five, and then be entered in the graded system at six. Any parent who has been bluntly told, "The teacher says you are all wrong, Dad. This is the way it is," does not need to be reminded of the impact of teachers and textbooks on a child's opinions.

Yet the schools do not exert an influence independent of home and family—a fact our nation has learned since the spotlight has been turned on the problem of providing adequate education for blacks. Sociologist William Sewell thinks: [20] "Schools bring little influence to bear on a child's achievement that is independent of his background and general social context; and that this very lack of an independent effect means that the inequalities imposed on children by their home, neighborhood, and peer environment are carried along to become the inequalities with which they confront adult life at the end of school. For equality of educational op-

---

[20] In his view of the report by James S. Coleman et al, *Equality of Opportunity* (Washington, D. C.: U. S. Government Printing Office, 1966) in *American Sociological Review*, Vol. 32, June, 1967.

portunity through the schools must imply a strong effect of schools that is independent of the child's immediate social environment, and that strong independent effect is not present in American schools." This illustrates the interaction of forces that shape attitudes.

ECONOMIC CLASS

Sometimes overlooked in exploring the roots of attitudes are *economic associations and status,* the individual's stake in the capitalistic economy. Although the "economic man" concept has been demolished, none would deny that economic motivation and influence are strong with most individuals. An individual's status as an unskilled laborer or as a management executive determines, in large measure, the way his attitudes are bent and shaped. Attitudes of the different income groups toward the role of government are proof of this.

The economic status determines, to a large degree, the particular social orbit in which people move. The pictures in a man's head will be shaped, too, by the nature of his affiliations. Is he a member of the National Association of Manufacturers, the AFL-CIO, or the unorganized "white collar" workers who now outnumber "blue collar" workers in America? One's place of work, pay, and security are vital factors in life. Their influence is strong.

Hennessy points out that, "Attempts to show the relationships between economic factors and patterns of opinion distribution often reveal the effects of differences in levels of knowledge. . . . Those of lower economic status usually have no knowledge or no opinion . . . and therefore fail to appreciate where their economic advantage lies." On the other hand, Alford found that the political importance of economic status is probably a function of how voters compare the personal consequences of social welfare measures with other influencing factors in their voting. He also found that war and personalities of candidates tend to soften strength of social welfare considerations by low income voters.[21] Here again we see environmental factors interweaving, overlapping in shaping attitudes.[22]

SOCIAL CLASS

Somewhat related, but not necessarily, is the influence of *social status.* Certainly one's position as a member of the yacht club set will determine

---

[21] Robert Alford, "The Role of Social Class in American Voting Behavior," *Western Political Quarterly,* Vol. 13, 1963, pp. 180–193.

[22] For candid close-up of America's lower middle class—some 23 million American families and their political values, see Peter Schrag, "The Forgotten American," *Harper's Magazine,* Vol. 239, August, 1969.

outlook, sources of information, and opinions. Those who belong to art circles, have big boats, and travel abroad see events differently from those without these or other status symbols that characterize each succeeding generation's "smart set." It is important not to confuse income with social status. High income does not necessarily mean high social status, although it often does. Determining factors are family background, education, occupation, home, and neighborhood. Status influences every phase of one's life.

David Riesman in *The Lonely Crowd* theorizes that there are three basic types in the American character structure, the "tradition-directed," the "inner-directed," and the "other-directed." The tradition-directed person is one whose conformity to the social order is assured by rigid adherence to the accustomed way of doing things. He "does what is proper." The inner-directed is one whose conformity is assured by early implantation—through parents, elders, and teachers—of goals and values which last throughout life. The other-directed person derives his character from the outside—from his contemporaries, peer groups, associates, friends, and the mass media. Riesman thinks that the "other-directed" character type is coming to the fore in America. This theory has important implications for those who would influence opinion. The inner-directed person has clearly formulated personal goals and relies relatively little on the approbation of others in reaching his decisions. The other-directed person who strives to "keep up with the Joneses" is more easily persuaded. Riesman's theory would appear to hold, despite the seeming contradiction posed by nonconformist rebels who, in turn, enforce a conformity of non-conformity in their membership, be it beards, beads, dress, or rhetoric. It remains important to know who the Joneses are. Every aspect of American thought and action is powerfully influenced by social class—be it the elite Domhoff described living in Scarsdale, Shaker Heights, or Winnetka, be it the new middle class or managers and technicians living in less affluent suburbs, be it the lower middle class living in the gray fringe areas of central city, or the poor living in the slums. To think realistically and act effectively, the practitioner must know the status system.

RACE

Another factor increasingly important in shaping our mental set in these days of schism and segregation, of black power and white backlash, is one's race. The growing gulf of misunderstandings and hatreds between the white and black communities of America bends and shapes opinions on most public issues. In the sober view of the Kerner Commission, "Discrimination and segregation have long permeated much of American life;

now they threaten the future of every American." [23] This issue will gnaw at the vitals of America until the some 22-million blacks get their share of the American good life: decent jobs, decent schools, decent homes, nothing less than integration across the board. As Brink and Harris predict: "With dark undercurrents of distrust and tragedy still running strong on both sides of the color line, the inescapable conclusion is that race will remain an overriding issue in America for decades to come." [24] The difficulty of white men and black men understanding each other is pointed up in this passage from *The Grand Parade* by black novelist Julian Mayfield:

> The wellspring of experience that drove one man was unknown to the other. Every second of every minute that had marched past since the black man was born in the slums of Gainesboro, every moment of self-hatred and frustration, of self-pity and pride and rejection, every night lain awake scheming and plotting after status and identity—all these had combined to make the black man a complete stranger to the white, and the total absence of this experience had made the white man a dangerous and unknown quantity to the black. . . . Thus each of the men had been chiseled by distinct realities, and they were conditioned to see different images when they looked at the same object.

American Indians, Puerto Ricans, and Chicanos have the same problems as the blacks and hold similar attitudes toward whites.

SOURCES OF MOTIVATION

Different people will respond differently to the same social pressures and persuasions. The appeals in incentives used will be effective to the degree that the individual has the necessary *motivational predispositions* to respond. These sources of motivation need to be taken into account.

The broad underlying social and cultural values developed in and expressed through the institutions of society serve to influence and determine needs of individuals. Robert K. Burns suggests that "These must be understood if we are to sense the essence of the motivation process. . . ." He states a few: [25]

---

[23] *Report of the National Advisory Commission on Civil Disorders,* with Foreward by Tom Wicker, published by Bantam Books, March, 1968. Essential reading for one who would understand today's public opinion environment.

[24] William Brink and Louis Harris, *Black and White* (New York: Simon and Schuster, 1967), p. 183.

[25] In "Management and Employee Motivation," *Public Personnel Review,* Vol. 20, April, 1959. For fuller discussion of our values, see Robin M. Williams, Jr., *American Society* (New York: Alfred A. Knopf, 1951).

1. An emphasis upon achievement and success, particularly occupational achievement. . . .
2. An orientation toward action, efficiency and the practical—with the tendency to view work as an end in itself.
3. A faith in change and progress with a tendency to identify change with progress.
4. An insistence upon equality of opportunity which decries extreme inequality.
5. A emphasis upon freedom as a basic value with an implicit suspicion of centralized authority. . . .
6. A tendency to judge conduct as right or wrong, ethical or unethical, stemming . . . from early American Puritanism. . . .
7. A somewhat materialistic measurement of happiness and progress.

A psychologist suggests that to motivate a person one must "emphasize the benefits and satisfaction he will gain, not the benefits to . . . your organization," and that "people behave to satisfy their real motives, not the motives they should have."

PERSONAL MOTIVATION

All the reactions of the members of a group, a public, occur within the individual. Le Bon's *crowd mind* theory has been discarded. To understand the opinion process, we must study, too, the individual's emotional and physiological drives. All people have these basic drives in common— among them *self-preservation, hunger, security,* and *sex.* Our basic emotional needs include the desire for *affection,* the desire for *emotional security* or *trust,* and the desire for *personal significance.*

The whole sum and substance of human motivation is not bound up in those three brief terms. But we can set them close to the center of a good working concept of human nature. Practitioners must and do devise ways of meeting these basic emotional needs in their day-to-day programs —employee communications, for example. Consider the emphasis on awards, promotions, and clubs. In these basic drives the individual seeks physical and social security, gratification of his human desires, and protection of his ego.

GROUP MOTIVATION

Communicators have found it increasingly necessary to take into account the group to which individuals belong. People, with rare exceptions, do not live in isolation but in constant association with others. There are essentially two kinds of groups, *statistical* and *functional.* It is helpful to enumerate the target audience both ways. An audience may be classified by age, sex, income level, educational level, occupation, and so forth. This is useful because members of the same statistical group *tend* to respond in the same general way to the same communications. Such classifications help to identify common bonds of interest which may be used in building a bridge between communicator and audience.

But the *functional* group plays the more vital role. Functional groups are composed of individuals who come together for some common purpose. It may be a construction crew, a political club, or the congregation at a church service. People desire to belong to groups and to find a sense of social security. In an "other-directed" society, we take our cues from our group associates. The group's influence appears to be on the rise; or else, through research, we are merely learning more about the group role in opinion formation. *To belong to a group, we pay a price. We conform to its standards, its consensus.* There is evidence accumulating in social science research of common attitudes among those who "belong together."

Our individual attitudes, and thus our opinions, are maintained in association with small numbers of others. We influence them, they influence us. An individual's relatedness-to-others has an important bearing on efforts to persuade him this way or that. For example, employers have found that workers will forego the increased pay possible under wage-incentive plans rather than be ostracized by their work groups as "rate busters." To "belong" can be as strong an incentive as money.[26] Thus, whether you change a person's opinions or not will depend to some degree on the resistance or support which the person encounters in his group. We are learning more and more that these interpersonal relationships intervene in the mass-communication process.[27]

A group develops standards for its members' behavior. These standards are shared. They represent the behavior and attitudes that members expect of one another. "There are some things you just don't do in *this* group." To the degree a person is dependent upon his group, he is *motivated* to conform. Also there will be found in groups "situational cues" which operate to arouse the motives related to conformity. Study of group dynamics and the group structure of our society is essential for the practitioner. The results of research can be summarized.[28]

[26] See William Foote Whyte, *Money and Motivation* (New York: Harper & Row, Publishers, 1955).

[27] See Elihu Katz and Paul F. Lazarsfeld, *Personal Influence: The Part Played by People in the Flow of Mass Communications*. This book introduced the two-step flow theory of mass communication and is essential reading for the public relations student. It will be referred to at several points in this book.

[28] Condensed by Herbert I. Abelson for Opinion Research Corp. in *Some Principles of Persuasion*, 1956, and based on research of Katz and Lazarsfeld, S. E. Asch, H. Guetzkow and Leon Festinger, *et al.*

1. A person's opinions and attitudes are strongly influenced by the groups to which he belongs and wants to belong.

2. The person is rewarded for conforming to the standards of the group and is punished for deviating from them.

3. People who are most attached to a group are probably the least influenced by communications which conflict with group norms.

It is important to note the distinction between the public-opinion process and the group-consensus process. Yet the distinction is not easily made. In the public arena, opinions form around a particular issue or a number of related issues, whereas the range of subjects on which the group demands conformity is broad indeed. A second difference is that the group interaction takes place among those who know each other well and are in frequent contact, whereas the public-opinion process involves those who may be in contact only one time on one campaign. Davison rightly concludes: [29] "The group opinion process is an extremely important component of the public opinion process but the distinction between the two must be maintained if public opinion phenomena are to be explained adequately."

A NATION OF MANY PUBLICS

It is a common mistake to think of The Public as one massive, monolithic assemblage. No money-spending, vote-casting, goods-buying unit of more than 200 million Americans waits as one vast audience to be molded into "public opinion." "We the People" consist of many publics, of many kindred interest groups, and of unorganized groups with like and unlike preferences in fashions, music, fiction, and so forth. Novelist Joyce Cary said the "mass mind concept" is our time's special bit of nonsense. Fortunately, this country is too large and too diverse for any single group, class, or ideological view to prevail.

A check of consumer purchases will quickly show the risk in fashioning national campaigns for national audiences. A product may have great appeal in New England and yet be ignored in California. Many public relations failures in the past resulted from the assumption that public opinion could be molded from New York City down. Millions of dollars have been wasted on this mistaken assumption. Our efforts to communicate persuasively with The General Public are, on the whole, inefficient and often ineffective. The total public is complex, heterogeneous. Within this

---

[29] W. Phillips Davison, "The Public Opinion Process," *Public Opinion Quarterly*, Vol. 22, Summer, 1958, pp. 91–106. Also reprinted in Christenson and McWilliams, *Voice of the People* (McGraw-Hill, Inc., 1962), pp. 6–20.

great mass, are smaller publics which can be defined and thus influenced.

The number of different publics is theoretically the number of distinct combinations of individuals within a given community. The number of key publics for any one organization is relatively small and manageable. For example, the university public relations director is primarily concerned with these publics: trustees, administrators, faculty, nonteaching staff, students, parents of students, prospective students, alumni, donors, community leaders, and legislators. On these groups he beams most of his communication. *The publics in public relations are those groups with common interests affected by the acts and policies of an institution or whose acts and opinions affect the institution.*

Individuals form themselves into publics in various ways—politically in parties, religiously in churches, socially in clubs and lodges, economically in trade associations, labor unions, or farm blocs. An individual can and does belong to a long list of publics simultaneously. It is dangerous to classify people rigidly as "employees" or "customers" when, in fact, these people play many roles. We are *whole* individuals. A person's overlapping memberships in many publics lend stability to this mercurial force, public opinion. Citizens are continually forming, disbanding, and re-forming into publics holding specific views toward specific issues.

Americans are great joiners and intensively organize themselves from Cub Scouts to Old Age Clubs. This makes it easier to focus on and communicate with individuals joined in groups. *To communicate with individuals in groups, appeals must be significant and relevant to a particular group interest in a particular situation.* Schramm says, "The kind of roles we play and the value and attitudes we build around them are largely determined by the groups we belong to." A person's group relationships provide the setting for most of the communication he receives and transmits.

Today's citizen has many interests. He can be a voter, a taxpayer, a Methodist, a Mason, a Republican, a Rotarian, a war veteran, a merchant, a member of the Chamber of Commerce, an employer, a parent, a fisherman, and a consumer all in the same day. Each of these "memberships" involves a special allegiance. The issue at stake determines which allegiance prevails in a given situation. All have their impact on a person's underlying attitudes. One minute a man may be a pedestrian crossing the street and mumbling about "those crazy drivers." A few moments later he may be driving home from work and angrily honking his horn at "fool pedestrians who never watch where they're going." Both roles will come to bear in shaping this man's opinions on a new traffic law. Quite often, too, a person's allegiances collide. When new taxes are proposed to build schools, will the individual respond as a taxpayer or as a teacher?

Individuals also react in unorganized groups. Some describe this as "crowds"; others refer to "the mass." Persons sharing an attentiveness to the same thing at the same time may be said to belong to an *unorganized public*. Certainly, under conditions of today's society, mass behavior has emerged in increasing magnitude and importance. The excited squeals of teen-agers excited about the latest recording idol are to be heard from Portland, Me., to Portland, Ore. There is mass advertising of mass-produced goods appealing to mass behavior. It makes people wear the same style clothes, drive the same kind of shiny, streamlined cars, and idolize the same TV stars. The strength of the "mass" influence is a matter of spirited debate in scholarly circles. Certainly it is an important influence on opinions, mores, and values.

GOVERNORS OF OPINION CHANGE

As pointed out earlier, the factors of *culture, family, religion, schools, social group, economic class* and *race* interact with the active, direct influences of what people *see, hear, or read—their experience*. The secondary environmental factors provide the glasses through which we see and interpret the public scene. Our environment and our experience fuse. These primary factors of opinion formation and change lead to the intense competition for public attention. The struggle for men's minds is waged with slogans, symbols, and stereotypes in all media of communication, in our schools, plants, stores, and offices. *Pragmatic agreement on the factors of what people see, hear, or read as the primary forces influencing opinions leads to the inevitable struggle as to what the public shall or shall not see, read, or hear.* This competition for men's minds becomes a battle of communication and censorship. Communication and censorship, or the lack of them, tend to regulate one's opinions and the rate of change.

COMMUNICATION

Social life is possible only through the ability to communicate, to transfer meaning between individuals. Group activity would be impossible without some means of sharing experiences and attitudes. Communication includes all the symbols of the mind, the means of conveying them, and the means of preserving them. To reach, to understand, and to influence another, a person must communicate. This is basic in the interacting process and is *the nub of public relations*.

Today's public-opinion market place is loud with the babble of men and issues clamoring for attention and consent. Every group faces strong, strident competition. Each person has less and less time, attention, and energy to give to more and more things thrust upon him. His time goes to those things that seize his attention and seem to merit his support.

The primary factors of what we see, hear, or read—the factors that *activate* our opinions—are selected out of a welter of things to see, read, or hear. Newspapers, books, and magazines are showered down upon us in an endless torrent. Radio programs fill our ears from sunrise to bedtime. Television, the movies, bowling, and baseball compete for what little leisure time is left after we've earned a living and given some time to our families.

The importance of communication is underscored by the fact that *each individual acts on the basis of that which he knows or thinks he knows*. The world is a big and casual place. To the individual, it frequently appears a confused and chaotic place. Each person can know with accurate, first-hand knowledge only a tiny fragment of the world's affairs. Yet he must have opinions and pass judgment. For this reason, one's judgments are rarely based on research and logical deduction. They are, for the most part, borrowed expressions accepted on the authority of others— a "talker" in the neighborhood, a union leader, the local paper, advertising, the boss, a TV commentator, a faraway "expert," or a favorite uncle.

CENSORSHIP

Censorship represents an effort to influence opinions by *suppression* of what persons might see, read, or hear. *Opinions can be affected by what one does not know as much as by what he does know*. Opinions based on no facts, part of the facts, or all of the facts are likely to be quite different. Thus, the tool of censorship is used to create or obliterate an individual's opinions. Dictators know this well. So do "managers of the news."

There are two kinds of censorship. *Artificial censorship* is deliberately invoked at the source or along the lines of communication. *Natural censorship* is effected by barriers of physical, psychological, and semantic distance and difference. The latter derive spontaneously from the environment of organized society. They intervene at many points in the communication process. Not the least of these is the individual's self-imposed *censorship of attention*.

People see what they wish to see, hear what they wish to hear, believe what they wish to believe. Research indicates that changes in opinion over short time spans are small in relation to overwhelming barrages of information. Opinions are highly influential in determining one's exposure to information. But, as indicated earlier, the research of Carter and his associates suggests that a person doesn't necessarily avoid adverse information when he is in the process of opinion *formulation*. Cantril holds: [30] ". . . the way we look at things and the attitudes and opinions we form are grounded on assumptions we have learned from our experience in life. . . . Once assumptions are formed and prove more or less effective,

---

[30] Hadley Cantril, *The Human Dimension, Experiences in Policy Research* (New Brunswick, N.J.: Rutgers University Press, 1967), pp. 16–17.

they serve both to focus attention and screen out what is apparently irrelevant and, as reinforcing agents, to intensify other aspects of the environment which seem to have a direct bearing on our purposes." Cantril usefully suggests that a person's "assumptive world" is the only world he knows. Research also indicates that persons easily and unconsciously remember those facts which enhance their views—thus *selective retention* of impressions and information follows the *selective exposure.*

It is easy—especially in the mass media—for people to avoid exposure to information. It takes only a flick of the dial or a flip of the page. Breaking through the individual's wall of isolation and insulation of fixed attitudes and limited scope of interest is not easy. Sales managers know this. Psychologists generally hold that emotional experiences far outweigh information in shaping opinions. If information is to have influence on attitudes and behavior, it must be related to one's values. Value judgments are essentially tied to the emotional processes.

The values each individual gives a situation determine what he perceives. This brings us to a key point. *Nearly every problem in public relations has its roots in the difference in perception—two or more people viewing the same situation in different ways.* Each person views the passing parade of public issues from a different place along the route. An individual's values stem from his heritage, his previous experiences, his sentiments, his likes and dislikes, his sense of obligation to others, his ideals, his goals, and his definition of self-interest. In short, his *mental set.* For each one of us, reality is whatever our values permit us to recognize as reality. We constantly seek to reinforce our beliefs and our values by selecting those facts from a situation which are consistent with what we believe. We ignore those facts which conflict with our beliefs. The business executive reads *Business Week;* the UAW member reads *Solidarity.* The factors of *awareness* and *evaluation* guide each person in what communications he accepts and in what he censors. This underscores a basic point for practitioners as enunciated by Gerhard Wiebe: "The persuasiveness of a public relations message is not inherent in the message, nor is it inherent in the rational quality of the organization's self-interest. The persuasiveness of a message is a function of compatibility of the message with the dynamic equilibria into which it is injected." Communication and censorship govern the flow of opinion change.

GENERATORS OF OPINION CHANGE

A host of forces and groups are constantly at work in promoting changes in old opinions and in creating new ones. These *generators* of opinion keep the opinion process in a state of ferment and flux:

a. Programs of industry, labor, agriculture, government, education, social welfare agencies, and so forth.

b. Political parties.

c. Pressure, professional, and interest groups.

d. Propagandists for partisan causes.

e. Press, including all mass media.

f. Churches.

It is necessary to keep in mind the continuing interaction of all the forces and factors. Man is a creature of culture, yet creates his culture. Attitudes shape opinions. Expressed opinions, in turn, reformulate attitudes. The family influences the child, who, in turn, influences the family. The group norms guide the behavior of the group's members, yet the members determine the norms. The press, through its content and emphasis, builds and changes opinions. Yet the content and emphasis in the mass media are selected in response to the opinions of the audience. Men create and direct organizations. Yet, as Chester I. Barnard once noted, when the efforts of five men become coordinated in an organization, there is created something new that is wholly apart and different from the sum of the five individuals. The "organization" shapes their opinions as they guide it. Political parties generate opinions, yet they spread and shape themselves to appeal to the most people. The way our two-party system aggregates opinions was seen by Key: [31]

> Each party leadership must maintain the loyalty of its own standpatters; it must also concern itself with the great blocks of voters uncommitted to either party as well as those who may be weaned away from the opposition. These influences tend to pull the party leaderships from their contrasting anchorages toward the center. In that process, perhaps most visible in presidential campaigns, the party appeals often sound much alike. . . .

It is this host of variables interacting upon one another with varying effects that makes this mercurial substance so difficult to grasp. "At all times it is difficult to determine whether public opinion is leading or being led, followed or manipulated." The answer is, both. *Public relations programs guide and are guided by public opinion.* The process will remain more of an art than a science until we build up what is now the imperfect knowledge and science of the mind.

[31] V. O. Key, *Politics, Parties and Pressure Groups* (New York: Thomas Y. Crowell Company, 1958), p. 241.

SOME "LAWS" OF PUBLIC OPINION

Hadley Cantril some years ago worked out "some laws of public opinion" on the basis of intensive study of the trends over a decade. Cantril holds that trends, as recorded by the polls, support these generalizations: [32]

1. Opinion is highly sensitive to important events.
2. Events of unusual magnitude are likely to swing public opinion temporarily from one extreme to another. Opinion does not become stabilized until the implications of events are seen with some perspective.
3. Opinion is generally determined more by events than by words—unless those words are themselves interpreted as "events."
4. Verbal statements and outlines of course of action have maximum importance when opinion is unstructured, when people are suggestible and seek some interpretation from a reliable source.
5. By and large, public opinion does not anticipate emergencies; it only reacts to them.
6. Psychologically, opinion is basically determined by self-interest. Events, words, or any other stimuli affect opinion only in so far as their relationship to self-interest is apparent.
7. Opinion does not remain aroused for any long period of time unless people feel their self-interest is acutely involved or unless opinion—aroused by words—is sustained by events.
8. Once self-interest is involved, opinions are not easily changed.
9. When self-interest is involved, public opinion in a democracy is likely to be ahead of official policy.
10. When an opinion is held by a slight majority or when opinion is not solidly structured, an accomplished fact tends to shift opinion in the direction of acceptance.
11. At critical times, people become more sensitive to the adequacy of their leadership—if they have confidence in it, they are willing to assign more than usual responsibility to it; if they lack confidence in it, they are less tolerant than usual.
12. People are less reluctant to have critical decisions made by their leaders if they feel that somehow they, the people, are taking some part in the decision.
13. People have more opinions and are able to form opinions more easily with respect to goals than with respect to methods necessary to reach those goals.

[32] Hadley Cantril, *Gauging Public Opinion* (Princeton, N.J.: Princeton University Press, 1947). See the chapter "The Use of Trends," pp. 220–30.

14. Public opinion, like individual opinion, is colored by desire. And when opinion is based chiefly on desire rather than on information, it is likely to show especially sharp shifts with events.

15. By and large, if people in a democracy are provided educational opportunities and ready access to information, public opinion reveals a hard-headed common sense. The more enlightened people are to the implications of events and proposals for their own self-interest, the more likely they are to agree with the more objective opinions of realistic experts.[33]

PRINCIPLES OF PERSUASION

Research in the social sciences has brought, in recent years, some tentative principles of persuasion based on experimental research.[34]

1. To accomplish attitude change, a suggestion for change must first be received and accepted. "Acceptance of the message" is a critical factor in persuasive communication.

2. The suggestion is more likely to be accepted if it meets existing personality needs and drives.

3. The suggestion is more likely to be accepted if it is in harmony with group norms and loyalties.

4. The suggestion is more likely to be accepted if the source is perceived as trustworthy or expert.

5. A suggestion in the mass media, coupled with face-to-face reinforcement, is more likely to be accepted than a suggestion carried by either alone, other things being equal.

6. Change in attitude is more likely to occur if the suggestion is accompanied by other factors underlying belief and attitude. This refers to a changed environment which makes acceptance easier.

7. There probably will be more opinion change in the desired direction if conclusions are explicitly stated than if the audience is left to draw its own conclusions.

---

[33] For sharp criticism of these "laws," see the chapter "The Behavior of Public Opinion," in Leonard Doob, *Public Opinion and Propaganda* (New York: Holt, Rinehart & Winston, Inc., 1948). Doob says it is premature to hazard a set of laws, and then proceeds to fashion some of his own.

[34] These are condensed from a number of sources, including: Herbert I. Abelson, *op. cit.*; Schramm's *Process and Effects of Mass Communications*, a reader; Katz and Lazarfeld's *Personal Influence, op. cit.*, and Carl I. Hovland, Irving L. Janis, and Harold M. Kelley, *Communication and Persuasion* (New Haven: Yale University Press, 1953). All of these sources are the research of many people in arriving at these "principles." These books cite, too, the original research upon which they are based.

8. When the audience is friendly, or when only one position will be presented, or when immediate but temporary opinion change is wanted, it is more effective to give only one side of the argument.

9. When the audience disagrees, or when it is probable that it will hear the other side from another source, it is more effective to present both sides of the argument.

10. When equally attractive opposing views are presented one after another, the one presented last will probably be more effective.

11. Sometimes emotional appeals are more influential; sometimes factual ones are. It depends on the kind of message and kind of audience.

12. A strong threat is generally less effective than a mild threat in inducing desired opinion change.

13. The desired opinion change may be more measurable some time after exposure to the communication than right after exposure.

14. The people you want most in your audience are least likely to be there. This goes back to the censorship of attention that the individual invokes.

15. There is a "sleeper effect" in communications received from sources which the listener regards as having low credibility. In some tests, time has tended to wash out the distrusted source and leave information behind.

Counselor Earl Newsom has compressed the relatively little known about public opinion into these principles: (*Interpolations are ours.*)

1. *Identification Principle.* People will ignore an idea, an opinion, a point of view unless they see clearly that it affects their personal fears or desires, hopes or aspirations.

Your message must be stated in terms of the interest of your audience.

2. *Action Principle.* People do not buy ideas separated from action—either action taken or about to be taken by the sponsor of the idea, or action which people themselves can conveniently take to prove the merit of the idea.

Unless a means of action is provided, people tend to shrug off appeals to do things.

3. *Principle of Familiarity and Trust.* We the people buy ideas only from those we trust; we are influenced by, or adopt, only those opinions or points of view put forward by individuals or corporations or institutions in whom we have confidence.

Unless the listener has confidence in the speaker, he is not likely to listen or to believe.

4. *Clarity Principle.* The situation must be clear to us, not confusing. The thing we observe, read, see, or hear, the thing which produces our impressions, must be *clear,* not subject to several interpretations.

To communicate, you must employ words, symbols, or stereotypes that the receiver understands and comprehends. This task will be discussed at length in Chapter Ten.

ADDITIONAL READING

BERNARD BERELSON and MORRIS JANOWITZ, *Reader in Public Opinion and Communication.* New York: The Free Press of Glencoe, Inc., 2nd ed., 1966.

REO M. CHRISTENSON and ROBERT O. McWILLIAMS, *Voice of the People. Readings in Public Opinion and Propaganda.* New York: McGraw-Hill Book Company, 2nd Ed. 1967.

G. WILLIAM DOMHOFF, *Who Rules America?* Englewood Cliffs, N.J.: Prentice-Hall, Inc., 1968.

LLOYD A. FREE and HADLEY CANTRIL, *The Political Beliefs of Americans: A Study of Public Opinion.* New Brunswick, N.J.: Rutgers University Press, 1967.

ROBERT T. GOLEMBIEWSKI, *The Small Group: An Analysis of Research Concepts and Operations.* Chicago: University of Chicago Press, 1962. Useful introduction to research centered on the group.

JOSEPH A. KAHL, *The American Class Structure.* New York: Holt, Rinehart & Winston, Inc., 1957.

DANIEL KATZ, ed., special issue, "Attitude Change," *Public Opinion Quarterly,* Vol. 24, Summer, 1960. (Also available in book form.)

ROBERT E. LANE and DAVID O. SEARS, *Public Opinion.* Englewood Cliffs, N.J.: Prentice-Hall, Inc., 1964.

CURTIS MacDOUGALL, *Understanding Public Opinion.* Dubuque, Ia.: Wm. C. Brown, 1966.

PIERRE MARTINEAU, *Motivation in Advertising: Motives That People Buy.* New York: McGraw-Hill, Inc., 1957.

JAMES N. ROSENAU, *National Leadership and Foreign Policy: A Case Study in the Mobilization of Public Support.* Princeton, N.J.: Princeton University Press, 1963.

HANS TOCH, *The Social Psychology of Social Movements.* Indianapolis, Ind.: Bobbs-Merrill Co., 1965.

JACK E. WELLER, *Yesterday's People, Life in Contemporary Appalachia.* Lexington, Ky.: University of Kentucky, 1966. A case study.

CHAPTER 7

THE FUNCTION'S PLACE AND PURPOSE

This chapter will discuss the place and purpose of public relations as these have evolved to meet organizational needs. The goals of the institution inexorably shape the function.

Essential to an effective public relations program are:

1. Commitment on the part of management.
2. Competence in the public relations staff.
3. Centralization of policy-making.
4. Communications from and to publics, up, down, across.
5. Coordination of all efforts toward defined goals.

The public relations function must be fully integrated into the organization. In the words of H. A. Batten: "Unless the business is so organized and administered that it can meet at every point the test of good citizenship and usefulness to the community, no amount of public relations will avail." Public relations cannot be compartmentalized; specialists cannot work in a vacuum. Their work and counsel is a support function which must be integrated into the operations of the organization.

The task of effectively integrating public relations in the daily work of an organization is a vital one. The *first task* of the practitioner is to earn and hold broad, enthusiastic support for the public relations concept *within* his organization. As one put it: "I find that I can afford to spend up to 75 percent of my time, if necessary, to persuade my associates as to what I do in the remaining 25 percent." Unless support is earned, there will be conflict, not coordination and cooperation. Conflict begets friction and frustration. Friction slows motion, frustration breeds ulcers.

Where the function is new, it is a matter of getting off on the right foot. Where the function is established, the need is for helpful collaboration with other departments. Integration applies whether the setup consists of outside counseling, an inside staff, or a combination. Successful integration depends far more on the personalities involved than on principles of administration.

Effective integration must be pursued through *patient persuasion and helpful service to all members of the team*. The function is still fuzzily

155

defined in many organizations. Its place and purpose in administration remain to be clarified through experience. Often there is a natural lack of understanding of how this new function meshes with older ones. The practitioner should strive to:

1. Assure public relations-mindedness of organization officials.
2. Obtain written definition of authority and responsibility.
3. Gain confidence and cooperation of associates.
4. Indoctrinate the entire organization in principles and programs.
5. Provide service to other departments, staff and line.
6. Develop a desire and opportunities for mutual participation in the program.
7. Promote a communication philosophy of candor.

A sound approach is offered in a paraphrasing of Ordway Tead's counsel. The job of the public relations executive in influencing and educating top managers is the most difficult of his tasks. To do it, he needs proper status, a personality which commands respect, easy access to top executives, and a sustained concern for all the educational influences he can bring to bear. These educational efforts should not be confined only to the top management; they should extend to middle-management and line people. First, however, there is need to have a realistic perspective of the practitioner's position in the organization.

EVERYTHING, NOTHING, OR SOMETHING

There is no unanimity, even among practitioners, on a single proper function common to all. The role performed and the stature enjoyed vary from client to client and from one institution to the next. Both are decided within each organization. The wide variety of assignments, ranks, and titles has given rise to confusion. And many efforts of public relations spokesmen intended to clarify have tended to confuse still more.

The occasional strident demand for a bigger or more universal voice in policy-making affairs has irritated some management people, misled some others, and made many shy away. Much of this confusion stems from the books administrators have studied in college and in short courses. Textbooks on management and personnel treat this new function superficially or ignore it altogether. For example, one widely used text, *The Social Psychology of Organizations,* makes only this reference to public relations: "The term *public relations* tends to be restricted to institutional advertising and is not an adequate concept to cover this important function of relating the organization to the total social system of which it is a part." [1]

At least two of the unfortunate results of the confusion merit consideration. *First,* the confusion of public relationships as an *end* result leads, inevitably, to the idea that public relations is everyone's job. This breeds the notion that no expertise is required, that everyone identified with an institution or group can and does handle public relations. *Everybody's job becomes nobody's job.*

Second, the lack of fixed boundaries for the working area leads to friction and conflict with the older, more solidly entrenched staff functions. This also is unfortunate. To be effective, the specialist, whether an advertising man, a psychiatrist, or a public relations man, needs cooperation.

Because of the failure of some managers to firmly fix the position and to delineate the scope of the function, some practitioners become embroiled in jurisdictional disputes. This is a failure of management to manage. All too often, a company "tries" public relations without knowing what to do with it, where to put it, or what to put into it. This is reflected when the president of a medium-sized company announces employment of a practitioner in a "position as yet unnamed and undescribed." Confusion about the function's place and purpose was compounded in the early 70s by a best-selling book by a one-time Avis executive who flippantly wrote that "the professional P.R. operation was as dead as the buttonhook industry." Yet all the while he was at Avis he was served by public relations professionals.[2]

Much of the difficulty stems from the lack of a universally accepted definition, reflected in this report of a panel discussion in *Editor & Publisher:* "They couldn't agree on a definition . . . but all agreed that public relations must occupy a top management position." This asks management to buy a pig in a poke. Lacking absolute boundaries, it can be said that the function of public relations is *not* to manage or to administer an institution. The practitioner is *not* in charge of all the institution's relationships. He is *not* qualified by training to be an expert in everything.

With reason a counselor warns: "The traditional organization and patterns of public relations behavior will just not be equal to the more extensive assignments expected in this period of change and growth. Professionals must consciously condition themselves to an attitude of 'enlightened dissatisfaction.' " [3]

Clarification of the position on the organization chart cannot be expected to emerge by virtue of statements supporting the importance of the

---

[1] By Daniel Katz and Robert Kahn, published by Wiley in 1966. Page 82.

[2] Robert Townsend, *Up the Organization.* New York: Knopf, 1970. He headed Avis Rent-a-Car for five years. His iconoclastic book had a saleable title.

[3] John F. Budd, Jr., "Public Relations' Mythology," *Public Relations Journal,* Vol. 24, March, 1968, p. 15.

function. If it is not clarified at the outset, it can be expected to emerge gradually, in direct proportion to its usefulness. Galbraith reminds us: "Group decision-making extends deeply into the business enterprise. Effective participation is not closely related to rank in the formal hierarchy of the organization." As the closed system of management in large enterprises gives way to the open system, the importance of formal internal organization will diminish.

Reflecting a basic insecurity, some practitioners spend much time fretting about the proper place of the function on the organization chart. Debunking the myth of the organization chart, Clarence B. Randall, late head of Inland Steel, had this to say: [4]

> . . . to know who is to do what and to establish authority and responsibility within an institution are the basic first principles of a good administration, but this is a far cry from handing down immutable tablets of stone from the mountaintop. . . . It is not the preparation of the organization chart that I condemn, but its abuse: this blowing up of its significance to a point where guidance ceases and inhibition sets in.

This perspective is important. *Managers determine basic policies.* Public relations executives work with them on matters having a strong impact on opinions of various publics, internal or external. They may be called on to counsel on other matters. Administrators make major decisions. When interpretation of the public opinion environment or communication are integral parts of the decision, the public relations specialist must participate if the organization is to be properly served. Authority should be delegated to him for implementation in those actions which depend on opinion analysis or communication for their effectiveness.

IT STARTS WITH MANAGEMENT

The management of an enterprise determines the scope, place, and, to a large degree, the effectiveness of all staff functions. A former president of New York Life Insurance Company said:

> When it is all said and done, a company's public relations office will only be as useful to management as management wants it to be. If management thinks of the public relations operation in a small way, then it will occupy a small place in the company's scheme of things, and its contribution will be small. If management thinks it is important, then it will occupy a prominent place and its contribution will be significant.

[4] In *The Folklore of Management* (Boston: Little, Brown & Co., 1959), p. 24.

Despite its evident essentiality, the function tends to go up and down like a yo-yo in some organizations. This reflects many factors—the differing values of succeeding executives, the intangible nature of public relations results, changing needs of the organization, and variations in competence of public relations specialists.

Inescapably, the function changes in scope and definition in response to changes in organizational needs. For example, in 1969, A. T. & T., a pioneer in corporate public relations, split its large department into a department of environmental affairs and a department of public information. The title "public relations" was dropped from the A. T. & T. organization charts a year earlier. The new environmental affairs unit's responsibilities include: relationship of advancing technology to the environment; aid to urban education; equal opportunity for employment and development; and special environmental factors affecting communications services in the cities. The information department has four divisions: advertising, news services and publications, Washington office, and information planning. This reorganization reflects the growing pressures of public opinion on all public institutions.

One who studied the ups and downs of one department in an internationally known company suggests these factors influence the *place* of the function: [5]

1. The attitudes of top management.
2. Capabilities and personalities of public relations staff.
3. General organizational structure and policy.
4. Organization's tradition, goals, objectives.
5. Company product and market areas (in case of businesses).
6. Company size and location.
7. Big Government.

Awareness of the importance of public opinion is characteristic of today's generation of organization executives. The importance of the function and its directing specialist have been recognized. Louis F. Hamele in an exhaustive study of public relations' place in corporate management found evidence to support this generalization. After a detailed study of a representative sample of American corporations, he concluded: [6] (a) Corporate management has recognized the essentiality of the public relations function and as a consequence has placed the function in the higher

[5] Robert Sullivan, "Evolution of a Corporate Public Relations Function" (Master's thesis, University of Wisconsin, 1967).

[6] In "Public Relations, Its Place in Corporate Management" (Master's thesis, University of Wisconsin, 1962).

levels of the organizational structure; (b) Corporate management has recognized the specialized nature of the function and as a consequence has practiced sound organizational principles by the establishment of separate public relations departments, headed by a specialist. Hamele's findings were substantiated in a similar study by Prof. Robert W. Miller of American University. In a nationwide survey of 182 corporations, 39 percent reported that the person in charge of public relations is a member of the policy-making group. More than one-third of these corporations reported that the person in charge was a vice-president.

Full-fledged acceptance also was underlined when President John F. Kennedy redefined the mission of the United States Information Agency. From its inception until 1963, the USIA was directed "to submit evidence to peoples of other nations by means of communication . . . that the objectives and policies of the United States are in harmony with . . . their legitimate aspirations." President Kennedy, advised by Edward R. Murrow, added to this directive the function of "*advising* the president, his representatives abroad, and the various departments on the implications of foreign opinion on present and contemplated policies of the United States." [7] His act in adopting the mature concept of public relations has been reaffirmed by succeeding presidents. This reflects the growing importance of the *intelligence* responsibility in public relations.

THE INTELLIGENCE TASK

Four basic problems confront the administrator of large scale organizations—determine the *goals,* develop a system of *controls,* encourage *innovation,* and collect and collate *intelligence.* The last is defined as "the problem of gathering, processing, interpreting, and communicating the technical and political information needed in the decision-making process." Wilensky elaborates: [8]

> The more an organization is in conflict with its social environment or depends on it for the achievement of central goals, the more resources it will allocate to the intelligence function and the more of those resources will be spent on experts whom we might call "contact men." The contact man supplies political and ideological intelligence the leader needs in order to find his way around modern society.

[7] The background of this shift in policy is discussed in Thomas C. Sorensen, *The Word War* (New York: Harper & Row, 1968).

[8] Harold L. Wilensky, *Organizational Intelligence* (New York: Basic Books, 1967), p. 10. Useful collateral reading.

This political intelligence function will grow in scope as crises, conflicts, and confrontations mount in our society. This suggests the need to shift from getting publicity to providing intelligence on the rapidly changing public opinion environment. Budd writes: [9] "The rapid pace of social change and the instability of values stemming from social mobility demand a new responsiveness and broader, more comprehensive service than can ever be rendered by the mimeograph machine alone."

Many practitioners are not equipped to meet increasing demands. A principal complaint voiced in Professor Robert Miller's 1968 survey of 180 corporations was that the practitioner's "background and training are not as broad as they should be . . . he lacks an understanding of the over-all economic picture and of the total corporate situation." [10] A veteran practitioner who rose to the chairmanship of the nation's largest financial institution, the Bank of America, has outlined the emerging role for tomorrow's practitioner: [11]

> . . . I think that there is a large and vitually important role that public relations can fill in our society, but it will require a broadening of vision and a willingness to shoulder a great deal more responsibility . . . in the future. . . . Nowhere in this society is there a profession that consciously attempts to look at the whole and relate all the seemingly unrelated bits of socio-economic-political minutiae . . . we need such a breed of men as never before. . . .
>
> In short, I believe that public relations can best serve by observing and studying the various trends in politics, economics, education, and social change, and by translating these trends to management. . . .

It is these same forces that are increasing management interest in the open system concept of management as contrasted with the traditional closed system. This trend, too, will have its effect in defining the place and purpose of public relations. One authority suggests that the closed system has "led to a disregard of differing organizational environments" and to "an overconcentration on principles of internal organizational functioning." The open system depends upon feedback of information from the environment which "enables the system to correct for its own malfunctioning or for changes in the environment" and thus to maintain a *dynamic* rather than static balance. In a society of change and conflict, of tension and turmoil the *intelligence* function will gain importance.[12]

[9] Budd, "Public Relations Mythology," op. cit.

[10] *Corporate Policies and Public Attitudes* (Washington, D. C.: American University, 1965).

[11] Louis B. Lundborg, "Management Looks at Public Relations," speech given at PRSA Conference, Denver, Colo., August 9, 1965.

[12] For explanation of these concepts, see: "Organization and the System Concept," chapter in Katz and Kahn, *The Social Psychology of Organizations, op. cit.* Also, James D. Thompson, *Organizations in Action* (New York: McGraw-Hill, 1967).

THE INFORMATION TASK

Only communication and actions that command a favorable response from the audience to the communicator can build a solid platform for congenial relationships. Today, the citizen is swamped and surfeited with causes and institutions. People are bombarded from all sides with pleas to listen, to buy, to give, to vote, to do this or not do that. Faster living permits less and less attention to these pleas. The day-to-day demands of making a living, taking care of family chores, engaging in multiplying recreational pursuits, and fulfilling growing civic obligations take most of the available time and energy. There is little time left to listen, less to read, and precious little to think.

The news media are pitched to these facts of life. These media, though vested with heavy public and social responsibilities, are primarily private businesses. In order to compete successfully, they find it necessary to emphasize that which excites and entertains. In determining content, they tend to headline the values of the sensational, the controversial, and the amusing. Factual, less interesting information tends to be subordinated. Values are hitched more to emotion than to reason. It is a sad but real fact that readers and listeners are much more interested in sin than in virtue. A felon is better copy than a professor of Greek.

The power of the news media has been greatly enlarged by television. This power is expressed in news values that emphasize the negative, in narrow confines that breed superficiality, and news judgments that are distorted by spirited competition. This powerful spotlight swings about somewhat capriciously and no institution or individual is long immune to its glare. This makes it necessary for all institutions invested with public interest to take the initiative in constructively telling their sides of the story to the public. The press will take the initiative to report strikes. Industry and labor must take the initiative in reporting peaceful, productive labor-management relationships. The press will take the initiative in reporting student protests. The universities must take the lead in reporting the substantial, though unspectacular, educational achievements. The press will quickly and fully report the conflicts of political personalities. Government must provide the less controversial story of its constructive achievements and of its services.

The various media do afford readily accessible channels for the institution that chooses to tell its story candidly and constructively. This is proof of an urge and an effort toward a more significant and balanced content. There is ample evidence that news values are undergoing steady re-examination and revision toward a more significant and more responsible definition of what interests people. The transition, however, is a long way from complete. The point is sharply illustrated by one capitol-city newspaper. It has four writers to cover spectator sports. It employs only one man to cover the state capitol with its more than eighty governmental agencies, whose functions and policies affect the lives of four-million citizens.

Hence, the need to tell the story of an industry or institution, is not so much born of the desire for "free publicity." It is the need to be accurately reported. Unless institutions make that effort, they run the risk of being misunderstood and misrepresented. Many misunderstandings can be traced not only to misinformation but also to the lack of information. This lack on the part of those with whom congenial relationships are sought can be the root of needless frictions and aggressions. *Informed support is strong, sure support.*

Thus, in the *intelligence* and *information-action* tasks, we see the all-embracing role of the practitioner.

THE PURPOSE

The purpose of this public relations function is to advance the objectives of the organization—be it a university in need of contributions, a government agency in need of political support, or a corporation in need of capital. The public relations program must be kept geared to organizational goals. The over-all program should be set down on paper in a form that is approved by the governors of the organization. *Effective programming requires an agreed-upon, clear-cut platform.*

Without a platform, public relations is, in one practitioner's view, "in danger of becoming tremendously expert in selling a grab-bag without having any clear idea of what our merchandise is." *Aimlessness is one of the main factors vitiating much of the effort and expenditure in this field.* Counselor Paul Garrett years ago said: "Set down on a sheet of paper the policies of your company you would like the public to know about. Then build supporting projects." The values of such a platform are listed by Oliver Gale: [13]

1. Opportunities are legion. If a company knows what it wants, it can do a more intelligent job.
2. The public relations department and . . . the whole organization can devote their efforts in the same directions.

[13] Quoted in Conger Reynolds' article, "And What Is Your Public Relations Platform?" *Public Relations Journal*, Vol. 11, October, 1955.

3. A written statement can be studied and accepted by top management and all departmental heads. There are also good reasons for having the basic policies of the enterprise known and understood internally. It invites support and collaboration from all hands.

In a study of twenty-four Chicago-area companies, A. Douglas Lyke found these the major objectives: [14]

1. To interpret the company, its goals, policies, practices, and types of business to the company's publics.
2. To interpret to management the attitudes and opinions of the public about the company.
3. To anticipate, ferret out, and prevent internal difficulties that might cause trouble for the company.
4. To obtain customer acceptance of company products, increase sales, and obtain franchises by winning customer friendship or improving service.
5. To take care of several miscellaneous company functions which don't belong in other departments.
6. To guide management in making the right moves for the company.

The framework for a highly successful public relations program is this statement of goals for the Caterpillar Tractor Co. (It uses the term *public affairs* to describe the function):

PUBLIC AFFAIRS OBJECTIVE

The objective of the public affairs activity is to help Caterpillar achieve the understanding and support it needs to operate a worldwide enterprise successfully. In pursuit of this objective, it is a public affairs responsibility at each operating unit to establish channels of communication with employees and other selected segments of the public, and to use those channels as effectively as possible to generate favorable attitudes toward Caterpillar's operations, goals, policies, and basic beliefs.

Seven Continuing Public Affairs Goals

I. Develop a better, truer public "impression" of Caterpillar . . . what we are, what we do, what we believe.
   1. A worldwide enterprise whose products are doing important, constructive work around the world.
   2. A strongly service-minded organization.
   3. A company placing heavy emphasis on research and engineering.

[14] *Public Relations as a Management Function in Chicago-Area Companies* (New York: Public Relations Society of America, 1954), p. 99.

4. A member of a highly competitive industry.
5. A believer in high levels of integrity, achievement, and quality.
6. A widely held company.
7. A well-managed enterprise.
8. A good company to work for.
9. A good company to do business with.
10. A believer in keeping the public informed.
11. A responsible corporate citizen.

II. Secure better understanding of the benefits of Caterpillar operations in localities in which facilities are located.

III. Establish better understanding of Caterpillar's viewpoint on important legislative and governmental matters.

IV. Promote better understanding of the creative role of profit in contributing to a better life for employees and the public.

V. Contribute to an improved climate for business operations . . . and an improved community attitude on factors that make settlement and growth in a given country, state or locale attractive to business.

VI. Build increased community confidence in and goodwill toward the Company, its operations and its people.

VII. Inspire greater individual participation in public affairs.

THE ROLE OF THE STAFF MAN

Public relations is a staff function. Thus, its practitioners need to understand the *staff role* in administration. The line-staff principle of management originated in the military but has been extended to most organizations of size. In industry, the product and profit producing functions—engineering, production, and sales—are the *line functions; staff functions* embrace finance, legal, personnel, planning, public relations, research, sales promotion, and advertising. The staff official to *assist* the chief officer became necessary as organizations increased in size and complexity, pushing the administrative burden beyond the time or capabilities of any one man.[15] Line executives have the authority and responsibility to see that the work gets done, but they need assistance in the form of plans, advice, and suggestions from staff executives. *The job of the staff officer is to support and assist the line officer.*

Staff work is the art of collaboration, and staff people justify their jobs by their total effectiveness. The burden is on the staff man to have the ability and willingness to assist line officers on *their* problems and to help *them* arrive at *their* solutions. Robert Sampson says staff people need "(1) a sense of business organization and operations; (2) an understand-

---

15 For elaboration see: *Management 2000* (New York: American Foundation for Management Research, 1968).

ing of people, their functions, their relationships; (3) an acceptance of managers as full-scale managers; (4) a humility about their contribution in their limited role; (5) a desire to relate themselves helpfully and dynamically to the ongoing management process." [16] The counselor must keep this basic objective constantly before him: *the continuity of the organization and its survival as a healthy entity.* All efforts must be bent in this direction.

The staff function embraces both *advisory* and *operational* tasks. In the advisory role, the practitioner *analyzes public opinion* and *counsels* line and other staff officers on the *public relations aspects* of organizational policies and problems. In the operational role, he handles the organization's communications *outside* the line function. In mature programs, the function embraces both. In too many cases, it is limited to communications.

Management and staff men have a right to expect certain things from each other. *Management should expect:*

1. Loyalty to the organization.
2. Help for management in exploring the public relations aspects of its decisions.
3. Skill in articulating principles, in interpreting, in explaining, and in enlarging understanding of the organization.
4. Inspiration for all members of the team to do their best and provide service cheerfully.
5. Influence to restrain line and staff people from saying or doing anything detrimental to the organization's welfare.

The staff man should expect:

1. Positive public relations leadership from management.
2. A definite policy supported by management.
3. A definite plan embracing all policies and programs.
4. A budget to do the job that needs to be done.
5. Funds for adequate public relations research.

The public relations aspect of each problem confronting an organization should be given due consideration—but no more than this—along with all other aspects of a particular problem or a proposed policy. The staff man can ask for no more. A standard operating procedure is the best way of insuring this. Here, for example, is the Summary Sheet which accom-

---

[16] Robert C. Sampson, *The Staff Role in Management* (New York: Harper & Row, 1955). A useful book on role, uses, and pitfalls in staff work.

panies all policy matters as these are routed for clearance in the Department of the Army:

| SUMMARY SHEET (DA Memo 340-15) | | | | | | | |

SUMMARY SHEET
(DA Memo 340-15)

TO			FOR	FROM	
DCSLOG	COA	CLL	APPROVAL	AGENCY	TELEPHONE
DCSOPS	ACSI	CHIEF OF STAFF	SIGNATURE		
DCSPER	ACSRC	___ S OF A ___	COORDINATION	GRADE & NAME OF CONTACT OFFICER	
CRD	TAG	SECRETARY OF THE ARMY			

FILE REFERENCE	SUBJECT	DATE

IMPLICATIONS (The implications checked below are involved in this action, are discussed below or in a seperate inclosure, and have been considered in the final recommendation.)

☐ CONTROL PROGRAM   ☐ MANPOWER   ☐ BUDGET   ☐ LEGAL
☐ CONGRESSIONAL   ☑ PUBLIC RELATIONS   ☐ MORALE   ☐ SECURITY   ☐ NONE

CLARIFY THE FUNCTION

Foremost of the measures to be taken is to clarify for the management group what the function is supposed to do, where it fits, and how it will go about its chores.

The following is a statement of responsibilities and functions sent around to the officials of a very large organization when a department of information was activated.

The responsibilities and functions shall be:

1. To serve as the central source of information about us and as the official channel of communication between us and the public.
2. To bring to public attention, through appropriate media, significant facts, opinions, and interpretations which will serve to keep the public aware of our policies and actions.
3. To coordinate company activities which affect our relations with the general public or with special public groups.
4. To collect and analyze information on the changing attitudes of key public groups toward us.
5. To plan and administer informational programs designed to fulfill most effectively the responsibilities outlined above.

In the same organization, the placement of the department of information under a director responsible to the president was announced. Outside counsel retained by the organization developed the statement and worked with the internal staff.

Here is a specific statement of responsibilities in Chrysler Corporation.

1. Assist corporate management in the development and maintenance of effective current and long-range policies, plans, and practices designed to project a favorable image of Chrysler activities to the public on a world-wide basis.

2. Provide top management with news and information of world-wide economic, political and social developments relating to and affecting Chrysler interests and operations.

3. Establish and maintain proper relations with the various mass communication media, gathering and releasing information to both general and special publics in furtherance of corporate acceptance.

4. Advise corporate management on the release and distribution of information to the public, including the review and assistance in the preparation of public addresses to provide appropriate quality and consistency with the Corporation's objectives and policies.

5. Develop and participate in press previews, special events, and other programs of public interest to further the Corporation's image to the public.

6. Provide information and liaison services between the Corporation and federal, state and local governmental activities, keeping management informed on government actions which affect the operations of the Corporation.

7. Maintain effective relationships with civic and educational organizations. Compile and distribute information to municipal and educational groups developing special programs and activities. Provide staff services in respect to contributions and Corporation memberships.

8. Develop, in conjunction with other functions in the Corporation, effective relations with the financial community, investors and shareholders; prepare shareholder reports and communications; advise management on activities affecting investors and shareholders' opinions.

9. Survey the Corporation's acceptance by various communities and publics; provide specific communities public relations services where appropriate.

10. Functionally supervise public relations activities in all Chrysler organizations; evaluate functional performance and recommend appropriate action.

The chart of a small business organization with a consumer product or service might look like the first diagram on the next page.[17] Variations are seen in the specific corporate charts.

---

[17] For examples of how the function is structured and its mission stated in 64 companies, see: National Industrial Conference Board, *Organizing the Public Relations Staff* (New York: NICB, June, 1961). (Now the Conference Board.)

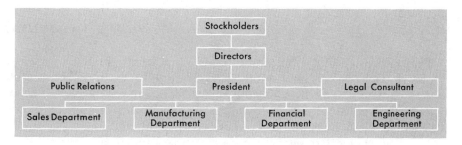

Motorola Inc. Public Relations

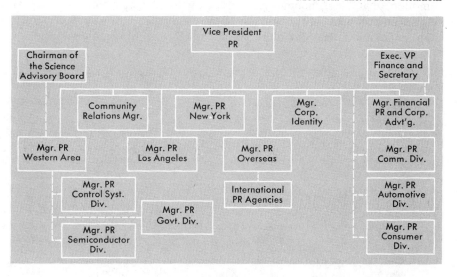

C.I.T. Financial Corporation Public Relations Department

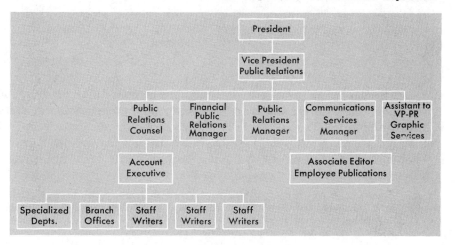

WHERE THE FUNCTION FITS IN

The relationship of the function to other departments is often a matter of history. One major firm has the staff reporting to the treasurer because the first man was hired to edit the annual report. In another, the function was an outgrowth of the employee publication. Often it is a matter of personalities. No flat rule can be set down.

The National Industrial Conference Board found, in a survey of the organizational relationship between the function, advertising and sales promotion, that "few managements treat lightly the problems of organizing their promotional and communication activities. . . . A number call for an open mind and flexibility in adapting . . . to changing needs and opportunities." [18]

Ford Motor Company Public Relations Structure

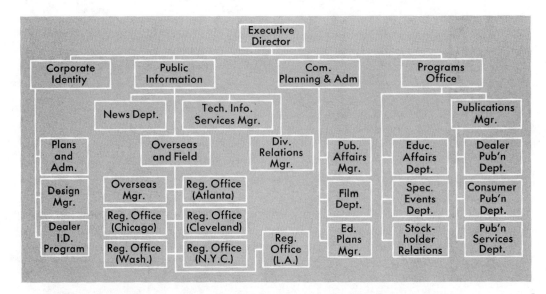

The important point is that for public relations to be regarded as rendering a mainstream service, it must feed into the mainstream in every sense of the word. This is as true of a small college or the American Civil Liberties Union as it is of the U.S. State Department or the General Motors Corporation. Wright and Evans maintain that "the line manager should regard public relations as a general rather than a special service.

---

[18] David L. Hurwood and Earl L. Bailey, *Advertising, Sales Promotion and Public Relations —Organizational Alternatives* (New York: National Industrial Conference Board, 1968), p. 14. Survey of 267 marketing executives.

The scope of public relations activities represents one of its chief assets." [19]

If the organization has a five-year plan on paper, public relations should have a five-year plan on paper. Its plans should be stated, at least briefly, in the master plan statement. If the organization has a formalized "goals and objectives" plan, public relations should be stated as one part of it. If the managers, or general officers, are periodically subject to performance review by a superior officer, the public relations manager should be reviewed equally or equivalently. If existing line departments or functions hold annual conferences to re-energize everyone, so should public relations. To attain organizational maturity, the function must be mainstream in every sense, not a side show.

Public relations staffers work most closely with the other staff functions of personnel, industrial or employee relations, legal, finance, and development. These functions intertwine and overlap in varying degrees. Sometimes the department finds itself in direct conflict with another.

Particular sources of internal friction are the departments of *legal counsel, personnel,* and *advertising.* Such disputes are costly to all concerned, especially to the employer. Each function needs the support and cooperation of the others if each is to discharge effectively its obligation to the team. Fortunately, such conflicts are not common—they are the exception. In most organizations, they have been resolved. But because the potential for conflict is inherent in the fluidity of the public relations function, practitioners should be aware of it and understand the reasons for it. The potential conflict of relationships between personnel, legal counsel, and public relations are found in most organizations. The advertising-public relations relationship is found mainly in business.

LEGAL COUNSEL

The conflict between public relations and legal counsel is an ancient one. In the days of the Muckrakers, corporate executives more often turned to their lawyers to "fix things" than to the emerging public relations specialist. Some still do. Ivy Lee felt strongly about this: [20] "I have seen more situations which the public ought to understand, and which the public would sympathize with, spoiled by the intervention of the lawyer than in any other way. Whenever a lawyer starts to talk to the public, he shuts out the light." Even in this day we can expect conflict when one corporation counsel asserts: "I am prepared to defend the position that the truly competent legal counsellor to the public relations division should be expected to express his opinion not only on matters of factuality which have potential legal impact, *but even on matters of good taste, logic, honesty,*

---

[19] Theon Wright and Henry S. Evans, *Public Relations and the Line Manager* (New York: The American Management Association, 1964), p. 174.

[20] In his *Publicity, Some of the Things It Is and Is Not* (New York: Industries Publishing Co., 1925), pp. 58 and 59.

yes even at times on the persuasiveness of your copy." [21] Usurpation of the public relations domain must be repelled.

On the other hand, there are many areas in which the close coordination of legal and public relations counsel are essential. Such cooperation is particularly urgent in the area of labor contract negotiations and other legally based or explosive situations—e.g., an antitrust suit, a campus riot, the threat of boycott, an accusation of discrimination, or a military court-martial. Additionally, there must be coordination and clearance on such matters as booklets explaining fringe benefits to employees, announcement of new facilities, legality of advertising or publicity claims, disclosure of financial information, and so forth. Public relations people find legal issues involved in their work almost all the time. As organizations—corporations in particular—deal with an ever more complex environment, the expanding scope of government, and urban problems, they need the combined talents of legal and public relations counsel. The Texas Gulf Sulphur's violation of Securities and Exchange Commission rules on disclosure of financial information; the unilateral action of General Motors' counsel in ordering a harassing investigation of critic Ralph Nader without knowledge of its public relations officer; and Consolidated Edison's problems with its proposed power project on the Hudson River are cases in point.[22]

Close cooperation of legal and public relations counsel, once mainly required in the business world, is now necessary in most organizations. For example, campus protestors frequently resort to the courts to achieve their demands or to escape punishment, posing a combined legal-public relations problem for the college. Parents often resort to the courts to protest grooming regulations or to block sex education in the schools, thus necessitating the school board's legal and public relations counsel to collaborate. Such collaboration has long been required in the military in publicized courts-martial or anti-war protests.

Given the cautious "admit nothing, deny everything" attitude of the lawyer and the policy of candor and openness advocated by the public relations man there is a built-in tendency to butt heads. This is costly to both and to the organization they serve. The foundation of effective cooperation must be mutual respect and understanding.[23]

---

[21] William Barron, counsel for General Electric, in speech given at PRSA Conference, Philadelphia, Pa., November 18, 1957.

[22] As of early 1967, Consolidated Edison had spent some $14 million dollars on legal counsel, studies, and public relations in an effort to gain public permission for the Storm King power project even though construction had not yet started. See: *New York Times*, December 13, 1966, p. 49. On August 19, 1970 the Federal Power Commission issued Con Edison a license to build the plant for the second time. For case history, see: Allan R. Talbot, *Power Along the Hudson* (New York: Dutton, 1972).

[23] For full discussion of relationships of public relations and the law, see: Morton J. Simon, *Public Relations Law* (New York: Appleton-Century-Crofts, 1969).

PERSONNEL

The relationships between public relations and personnel and/or industrial relations are many and the risk of friction is high. The fundamental problem concerns (a) whether communications in the community comprises an extension of the employee relationship, and (b) whether the employee is a "public" calling for public relations concepts of attitude measurement and communication. Compromise comes as practitioners and personnel specialists learn that the way an organization's personnel deal with their many publics shapes the external public's attitudes. The fears of personnel officials about invasion of their domain are understandable when they read in *Public Relations News:* [24] "Indoctrinating the worker and equipping him to assume and discharge his citizenship responsibility intelligently are most assuredly phases of employee relations, an established area of PR." Control of employee communication is the most frequent bone of contention between these two functions. Increasingly, this is being allocated to public relations which has the communications specialists on its staff. Such a transfer can breed resentment.

In a study directed by one of your authors, a survey of a representative sample of American corporations showed this breakdown of specific tasks which are often bounced from one function to the other: [25]

Public Relations Dominant
   Annual reports
   Open house, plant tours
   News releases on labor negotiations
   Maintenance of biographical data on key employees

Personnel Dominant, Public Relations Not Involved
   Suggestions systems
   Bulletin boards
   Reading racks
   New employee orientation
   Exit interviews
   Service awards
   Recruitment programs
   Pay inserts
   Christmas parties

[24] Issue, Vol. 21, March 29, 1965.

[25] A survey conducted by Scott M. Cutlip and Leroy Johnson to ascertain trends in the patterns of organizing the public relations, personnel, and advertising functions. Questionnaires were sent to public relations and personnel directors in seventy-three representative business firms, chosen on the basis of size, type of business, and geographic location. Seventy-four percent of the selected sample responded.

Personnel Dominant, Public Relations Advisory

    Employee attitude surveys

    Employee meetings

    Safety-promotion material

Responsibility Split

    Employee publications

    Employee newsletters

    Liaison with civic bodies

    Manpower for local fund drives, e.g., United Fund

    Conducting career days

The above distribution represents the dominant pattern found in this representative sample of thirty-five corporations and is based on questionnaires sent to and returned separately from personnel and public relations departments of these firms. The varying patterns of allocation of these tasks and the common interest of both personnel and public relations in them indicate the potential for conflict between these two staff functions unless clear, logical lines are drawn. When these specialists do collide, the top manager must thoughtfully ask: "Is it any wonder that management sometimes displays lack of understanding of human relations when the two departments of management that should be most concerned with this problem do not even understand each other?"

ADVERTISING

The need for these functions to be closely coordinated is readily apparent but there are many areas of potential conflict. This problem was discussed briefly in Chapter 2. Here the tussle is usually over control of public relations advertising and over product publicity in business firms. A company has three voices with which it formally communicates to the outside world—advertising, sales promotion, and public relations. The need for these voices to sing the same tune is plain. Effecting this harmony is not easy. Varied patterns of organization are to be found—public relations as a subfunction of advertising, advertising and sales promotion as subfunctions of marketing, combined public relations and advertising departments, and independent public relations, advertising, and marketing functions on a coordinate level. The NICB survey found:

"A majority of the companies . . . place advertising responsibility within the marketing (or sometimes the sales) department" with "the advertising head usually (reporting) to general management." The study also found of these 267 companies that "nine out of ten . . . report having a central public relations function, while only one in three maintains such a function within any of its divisions." [26] Such central control keeps public relations focused on all its responsibilities, of which supporting the sale of goods or services is but one.

Competition between these two functions is understandable. They compete for management recognition, for job advancement, and for bigger budgets. Often both seek to control the public relations (or institutional) advertising and often both seek to control product publicity. Public relations advertising to promote the general reputation of the company should be supervised by the public relations department but requires the expertise of the advertising department for its preparation and placement. Similarly, product advertising plans should be reviewed by the public relations department to insure that the proposed campaign will not offend the public or cause a consumer backlash as some ads have. The growth of articulate consumerism makes it important for companies to assess the public relations aspects of their marketing plans. The automobile industry's emphasis on speed to sell cars which backfired is a case in point. Cooperative planning and programming to advance corporate objectives is the sensible answer. Organization is secondary.

COMMITTEES HELPFUL

One quite useful means of controlling these conflicts is to form a public relations policy committee or consulting group which includes the opponents. The public relations counselor or staff director assumes the role of coordinator, executor of decisions, or secretary to the group. Others in the group tend by majority persuasion to overcome individual oppositions. The clash of personalities generally gets lost in the shuffle, for the moment. That is not to say that the formation of policy groups has no advantages to integration beyond removing conflicts. There is much to recommend such groups, on occasion, in bringing together the best minds available—all the specialists—to thrash out problems affecting the whole organization. They can swap ideas, and the best solution will emerge. More than that, when all is done, everyone is committed to the joint decision.

A main consideration in the formation of guiding groups is to keep them small enough so that they will not collapse of their own weight. Only those persons intimately concerned with communication should be brought in. And only matters that involve all participants in the group should be raised. For example, the treasurer of a university does not want to give an entire morning to discussion of how often the campus lawn should be

---

[26] *Advertising, Sales Promotion, and Public Relations—Organizational Alternatives, op. cit.*

mowed. Nor, for that matter, would the superintendent of grounds relish the idea of that particular subject, which he considers his exclusive domain, being tossed on the table for the opinions of uninvolved officials. Finally, in guiding group discussions toward a decision, a coordinator should lead off with the areas of common agreement, not the points of probable conflict.

A number of the nation's major corporations, in an effort to eliminate overlap and conflict, have tried combining public relations and personnel functions into one department under one director or vice-president. The General Electric Company led the way in 1956 when it merged public relations and employee relations under one vice-president. Two years later, this enlarged department was re-titled Staff Relations Services. The problem of organizing this function is illustrated by the fact that GE has put its relations services department through several subsequent organizations. Companies which combined these functions in the late 1950s and have since split them apart include General Foods, Quaker Oats, Eli Lilly, and Penn Central. At General Foods, the vice-president for public relations reports to the chief executive while the director of corporate personnel reports to the chief operating officer. As Robert Thurston of Quaker Oats suggests: Public relations covers so many different areas that "there is no logical reporting 'fit' other than at the top." Most of the people involved in this experiment agree that there is logic in combining these functions in small companies and in plant operations removed from corporate headquarters.

One large concern which has found one department for public and industrial relations most functional is Texaco. Its vice-president, Kerryn King, comments: "There are any number of arrangements that can work satisfactorily. . . . In a company that has strong centralized labor negotiations and a high concentration of its employees, I believe it is better to have a separation of the two functions. On the other hand, where the centralized department furnishes primarily functional guidance to the operating departments of the parent company and its affiliates, there are advantages to be derived from the combination setup." Other firms have combined public relations and advertising for the same reason. Penn Central is one example.

The Cutlip-Johnson study found a greater number of public relations departments merged with the advertising function than merged with personnel. One-fourth of the companies surveyed reported the latter organizational pattern. Some years ago Ford put advertising and public relations under one vice-president; a few years later it again split the functions. American Can and Borden's, both experienced users of these services, combine them under one executive. In fact, the majority of firms rely on informal exchange between these departments on a coordinate level. Close cooperation by specialists of competence and cordiality are by far the most effective solution to these jurisdictional disputes.

The internal relationships of the function are illustrated in this cataloguing by Boeing's director of public relations and advertising: [27]

BOEING AIRPLANE COMPANY

The director of public relations and advertising has the following relationships:

To: The President

He is accountable to the president for interpreting and carrying out his responsibilities and will fulfill any additional responsibilities assigned him by the president.

To: Public Relations Manager—Wichita Division

He will arrange for receiving reports and other coordinative information to assist him in carrying out his responsibilities for policy direction over the public relations manager—Wichita Division. He will develop with the public relations manager—Wichita Division—an understanding as to what material in the form of press releases, publications, or speeches should be cleared through his office prior to release.

To: Vice-president—Industrial Relations

On matters of industrial relations, particularly in connection with the publication of BOEING NEWS, he will coordinate general policy concerning employee relations with the vice-president—industrial relations.

To: Vice-president—Finance

He will coordinate reports to stockholders with the vice-president—finance—and the secretary.

To: Director of Sales

Coordination will be achieved with the director of sales on general policy of product promotion and customer relationships.

To: Assistant to the President

He will coordinate with the assistant to the president as to general policy on plant visits, use of the plant public address system, and management development activities.

To: Others

He will maintain liaison with the directorate of public information, United States Air Force; Aerospace Industries Association; Seattle Chamber of Commerce; and other civic organizations and committees.

---

[27] National Industrial Conference Board, *Public Relations in Industry* (New York: NICB, Studies in Business Policy No. 80, 1956). (Now the Conference Board.)

THE PRACTITIONER'S PERSONAL TASK

A public relations man can be prejudged harmfully if his personal, moral, and ethical standards are something lower than those he prescribes for others. A public relations man's personal principles and conduct loom large in the effective integration of his function. He and his staff must set the example.

He must gain the confidence of the thoughtful and influential people in the organization. He must learn their language, their problems, their thinking. He must enjoy at least the neutrality of all others. Respect for him and his judgment must reach from the top of the administrative down past the supervisory levels. The confidence of top management quite logically derives in part from the respect that people on down the line have for him.

To gain respect, *the effective public relations man or woman must operate through channels, keep promises, preserve matters given in confidence, and seek no partiality. He or she must lick his own wounds privately.*

The practitioner must have a bit of the crusader's fervor. The function is young. His or her own enthusiasm, coupled with results that support it, will go far toward instilling a public relations mindedness throughout the organization. Goodwill, prestige, and a good press can become everybody's desire. That has been achieved adroitly in many organizations. When the president or general officer makes a speech, everybody can prove that what he says is right. The spirit is such that ideas for programs are volunteered. Everybody wants to "get into the act." Personal popularity is much more difficult for the outside consultant to accomplish than for the staff man. The counselor is not on the premises daily to cultivate acquaintanceships. His visits are largely consumed by meetings with a relatively small number of people. He must make the most of his opportunities.

THE PRACTITIONER'S JOB

THE JOB STARTS WITH INFORMATION

Before an initial program is planned, the public relations man goes back to school, so to speak. He becomes a student of his environment. It may be that he has research performed by outside firms. But in his personal contacts, he is a researcher. He seeks out old-timers on the premises. He draws them out about their experiences. He listens to tales of changes in attitude and policy that have taken place through the years. He studies all the departments in the organization and their relationships to each other. In the process, he learns the motivations and the insecurities of the departments. Ideally he becomes the best informed person in the organization: *the answer man*.

The leg work is important in such personal research, but no less important is the desk work. The practitioner examines both complaint letters and testimonials from outsiders; reads the files on internal grievances, resignations, important meetings; goes through employee handbooks, statements of policy, typical letters going out, bulletin board notices, the organization's history, financial reports, and various brochures. He digs around in the file morgue and in the legends, the lore, and the keepsakes of the organization.

In the search the practitioner, of course, is looking for past or potential causes of breakdown in the communications of the organization with its publics. The search takes him walking . . . around the hometown, the post, or the campus. As he goes, he listens. He listens in the barber chair, at the corner grocery, in the bank, on the golf course, at the bus stop, and across the back fence.

THE INDOCTRINATION PROCESS

The public relations counsel is simultaneously a learner and a teacher. He is constantly striving to discern the public opinion climate and the winds blowing it one way or another. He or she is constantly striving to infuse colleagues with a public relations attitude. There are several ready-made vehicles.

1. Public opinion surveys—those commissioned by the organization, those published in newspapers or magazines, those published by other institutions—can be routed to executives.
2. Samplings of letters from critical parents or customers, from alumni or shareholders can be routed to all concerned.
3. Compilations of news media comment about the organization can be routed to executives.
4. Clippings of news about the organization and about its competitors can be routed among department heads.
5. News stories to be sent out should be cleared with the persons and departments involved. Copies of releases to executives not involved will prove to be a courtesy appreciated.
6. Professional publications can be routed with marginal notations for the attention of interested individuals.
7. Personal notes of congratulations and compliments can be sent concerning the civic activities of members in the organization. The same

for condolences. Not only are the notes indicative of thoughtfulness, but they also serve to remind others that it is effective to do likewise.

8. Participation in community welfare campaigns or civic enterprises can become the internal practitioner's hobby. Again, here is an example for others.

9. The house publication can emphasize, without heavyhanded promotional technique, that public relations is everybody's job. This is an old, well-worn theme. It has endured because its ultimate truth appeals to everyone's innate desire for participation. It can easily be demonstrated how the contacts of the purchasing agent, salesman, soldier on leave, or student do a public relations job for the organization he represents. The house publication can become an effective integrating force through constant and adroit development of the idea of mutual participation. In its own editorial staffing the house publication can include numerous reporters appointed through the organization, a voice-of-the-people column, a column of suggestions, by-lines for contributors, and the enclosure of questionnaires sincerely seeking guidance from readers.

10. Activities can be encouraged to bring together groups having objectives and functions in common. As prototypes, there could be a Better Letter Writing Clinic for business correspondents, a Leadership Forum for military noncoms, a Civic Council for Students, a Customers' Service Panel for utility office people, a Newcomers' Welcome Committee for the Chamber of Commerce, and Outing Clubs for members of a retail association.

RENDERING SERVICE

Within organizations there are many opportunities for personal service. Minor as they may seem, they are important to the recipients. They make the staff valuable to others, personally. This does not imply ingratiation, but rather attitude of service.

For instance, many a man is committed to give a speech who cannot put his thoughts well on paper. Consider the brilliant scientist who tries to put scientific terms into a vocabulary suitable for a group of small-town businessmen. That's where the public relations specialist comes in. He has a sufficient grasp of science and an acquaintance with the language of the layman. Speech-writing often provides needed access to top brass.

Another service is in liaison between departments and their publics, on occasion. Visualize the predicament of the people in a credit department confronted by irate customers who arrive on the premises with chips on both shoulders. The internal public relations staff can offer diplomatic service.

A third type of service is rendered in assisting reticent but capable people to participate in employee and community activities. A typical situation is that of the newcomer who wants to meet people of similar social interests and wants to be of service in community affairs. The public relations internal staff can handle introductions.

Then, there is the service of helping the introverts in the organization to have a share in some of those things that the extroverts take for granted. The public relations man exercises great influence on the content of the house publications, selection of the committees for employee events, handling visitor groups, and the staging of parties, conventions, and awards occasions. He can look out for the men and women who might otherwise get lost in the shuffle.

The "service" approach is effective, and limitless. For example, here are some ways public relations can assist, suggested long ago by a former public relations executive of Procter and Gamble.[28]

1. In a buying department, in the way it builds friends among suppliers even where it can't place orders.

2. In a sales department, whose management wants the customer to speak of the company as "fine people to do business with."

3. In a legal department, where, alongside sound law, the constant admonition of the head counsel concerns public opinion.

4. In an employment department, where unsuccessful applicants are not rejected like lightweight cattle at the stockyards.

5. In stockholder relations, where the shareholder is not by implication told to count her many blessings and be silent.

6. In a financial department, where a thoughtfully planned policy of contributions to health, education, and welfare causes is considered not an inescapable tax on the treasury but a means of building valuable goodwill.

7. In a traffic department, where people remember that the employees of the carriers can be customers and friends of the shipper.

8. In an adjustment department, where a patron helped is considered more important than an argument won.

9. In correspondence handling that signs letters—even form letters— that breathe warmth, friendliness, and understanding.

10. In a manufacturing department, where employees realize that sloppy shipments or disregard for plant-city neighbors have a direct bearing on a steady flow of orders.

11. In an advertising department, where, beyond the question, "Will it sell goods?" the question is asked "Will it make friends for the company?"

28 William G. Werner, "Can We Measure Up?" *Public Relations Journal*, Vol. 10, January, 1954.

12. In executive echelons, where a contribution of time and experience toward leadership in public-interest causes is considered not only a civic responsibility, but also a valuable public relations function.

THE LIMELIGHT

In the course of a year in most organizations, there is a variety of news of internal and external interest. In the ferreting out of such events, each facet of the enterprise, each department, should be explored. This is particularly important for the outside counselor. It helps him to be known favorably throughout the organization. The planned information program, using a wide variety of news outlets, can include releases about all phases of operations, all departments. On page 183 is a partial list of the news items released during the year by one business concern. Note the various departments within the company which shared the limelight.

COMPLETING THE INTEGRATION

A significant indication that public relations-mindedness is permeating the whole structure appears when people begin to say to each other that "candor" in communication is the best policy. "Those PR people know what they're doing," or "We've got to do more on the social problems" and so forth. This means that public relations consciousness is gaining ground. And, they have complete confidence in the staff to place the company in the right light, publicly.

With the appearance of this important symptom, the public relations group can actually apply complete candor in the communication structure, wherever it may have been lacking. The various groups sharing in the organization can be told anything they want to know. Outsiders can be helped to get any kind of look into the organization that they want.

The exposure to public gaze of a clean organization, operating in the mutual interests of itself and its publics, does not mean that all there is to say about the organization should be blurted out. In business, there are competitive considerations. In the military, there are security considerations. In institutions, there are rigid ethical considerations. Common sense is the yardstick.

CASE PROBLEM

You were employed six months ago to organize a department in the John O. Jones Co., a 50-year-old firm manufacturing heavy pipe, tanks, and

NEWS RELEASES	DEPARTMENTS MENTIONED
Announcement of spring advertising campaign	Sales, Advertising
Announcement of average wage in factory	All plant employees
Announcement of new technique in window trimming	Sales Promotion
Monthly meetings of supervisory people to hear outside speakers	Factory supervisors, union officials
Visit of foreign distributors to hometown plant	Export
Results of beauty contest among girls in office and plant	Factory, Office, Sales Promotion
Installation of plant safety devices	Factory Management, Personnel
Company participation in local industrial exhibit	Public Relations, Foremen, Beauty Contest Winners
Announcement of special promotion	Sales, Advertising
Announcement of company annual report	Production, Sales, Research, Finance
Attendance of engineers at industrial institute	Factory engineering
Award of product to high school valedictorian	Factory official
Bus-load of employees to neighboring festival	Factory assembly and others
Signing of a union contract	Factory management, union officials
Comparative figures on employment locally in plant	Factory employees
Visit of officials from foreign subsidiary	Management Export
Announcement of new product	Sales, Advertising, Promotion, Factory, Design group
Promotion of executive	Sales, Field force
Announcement of sales meetings	Field force, Divisional Sales Managers
Establishment of welfare fund	All employees
Human interest—employee father of three children born same day of different years	Factory employees
Article on proper care of product	Service
Policy statement allocating merchandise	Sales, Management
Plans for convention participation	Sales
Announcement of trend to higher-priced products	All employees
Disclosure of new material used in product	Research
Article on company aircraft	Administration
New display device	Sales Promotion
Factory methods	Factory management
Instructions on wrapping gift parcels for soldiers overseas	All employees, Office Management
Viewpoint of Latvian employee	All employees
Retention of prominent designer	Sales, Design group

other products made of steel. This firm set up a separate department when it entered the consumer goods field with a new product. Your staff consists of a press relations director and a secretary. Your function is new in this old, solid, and rather conservative firm. The firm has had excellent employee relations over the years, is known as a maker of quality products, and has always made a profit. In your initial fact-finding, you did find that it had the reputation in the community for being a dangerous place to work and a plant with a high accident rate. You learned that this is based more on hearsay than on fact.

You get a call at 9:30 a.m. from the local daily that an employee was killed in the plant an hour ago. The reporter says the ambulance crew told him that the man was crushed by a heavy pipe. He asks for the details. You ask time to check and promise to call back. You go to the safety supervisor. He blows up and insists that no details of the accident be given to the press. He insists on taking you to his boss, the personnel director. The personnel director— on the same level of authority with you—backs up his safety supervisor. What do you do now?

ADDITIONAL READING

AMERICAN FOUNDATION FOR MANAGEMENT RESEARCH, *Management 2000*. New York: The Foundation, 1968. Proceedings of a symposium.

ERNEST DALE and L. URWICK, *Staff in Organizations*. New York: McGraw Hill Book Co., 1960.

DAVID FINN, *Public Relations and Management*. New York: Reinhold Publishing Corp., 1960.

JOHN KENNETH GALBRAITH, *The New Industrial State*. Boston: Houghton Mifflin Co., 1967. Points up role of public relations in sale of goods in today's economy.

BERT C. GOSS, "Trial Outside the Courtroom." A talk given November 21, 1962, published by Hill & Knowlton, Inc. The antitrust suit as a public relations problem.

HOWARD F. HARRIS, "When Management Asks . . . ," *Public Relations Quarterly*, Vol. 8, July, 1963.

F. RHODES HENDERER, *A Comparative Study of the Public Relations Practices in Six Industrial Organizations*. Pittsburgh, Pa.: University of Pittsburgh Press, 1956.

JOHN W. HILL, "Corporation Lawyers and Public Relations Counsel," *The Business Lawyer, American Bar Association*, Vol. 14, April, 1959, 587–608.

EARL NEWSOM, "The Care and Feeding of Bosses," *Public Relations Journal*, Vol. 14, February, 1958.

CHARLES H. PROUT, "How to Organize and Run a Corporate Public Relations Department," *Public Relations Journal*, Vol. 19, February, 1962.

CHAPTER 8

THE PROCESS: FACT-FINDING AND FEEDBACK— THE FIRST STEP

THE PROCESS

Organized practice is the continuing effort to bring about a harmonious adjustment between an institution and its publics. This adjustment requires, among other things, exchange of opinions and information. This does not just happen in today's complex society. It must be *planned* and *provided for*. This is the practitioner's job. He serves, in turn, in the role of *listener, counselor, communicator,* and *evaluator* in this process. The process has four basic steps:

RESEARCH-LISTENING

This involves probing the opinions, attitudes, and reactions of persons concerned with the acts and policies of an organization, then evaluating the inflow. This task also requires determining facts regarding the organization. *"What's our problem?"*

PLANNING-DECISION MAKING

This involves bringing these attitudes, opinions, ideas, and reactions to bear on the policies and programs of an organization. It will enable the organization to chart a course in the interests of all concerned. *"Here's what we can do."*

COMMUNICATION-ACTION

This involves explaining and dramatizing the chosen course to all those who may be affected and whose support is essential. *"Here's what we did and why."*

EVALUATION

This involves evaluating the results of the program and the effectiveness of techniques used. *"How did we do?"*

Each one of these steps is as important as the others. Each one is vital to an effective program. Too often there is too little research, too little planning, and too much publicity. *Emphasis on fact-finding and planning largely distinguishes public relations from straight publicity.*

The program moves steadily forward in one *whole, continuing process.* The fluidity of the process does not permit a neat compartmentalization. As has been observed, the "public relations processes of analysis, synthesis, communication, and interpretation are continuous, spiraling, and overlapping processes."

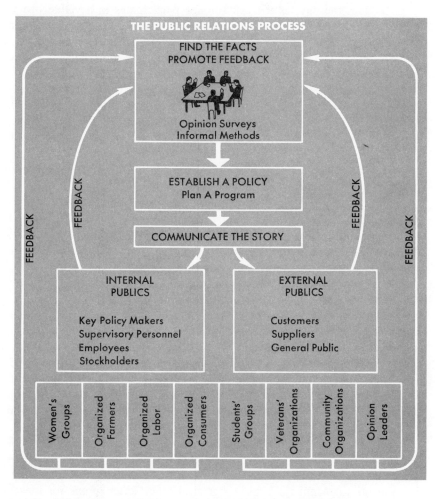

One minute the industrial practitioner will find himself called into the president's office and asked to ascertain, quickly, what the community's reaction will be if the company does not join the drive to eliminate discrimination in housing. This requires *fact-finding*. Next he may go into a conference with the sales and advertising executives to devise plans for introducing a new product. This requires *counseling* and *planning*. He may break away from this huddle to keep a luncheon date with a reporter from the local paper for an interview on the firm's new pension plan. Here he serves as *communicator* and *interpreter*. In mid-afternoon he may hold a meeting with his staff and representatives from Industrial Relations to reevaluate the purpose and content of the employee publication. This requires *evaluation*.

So goes the day, as the practitioner participates in a viable program. Between such tasks he may be answering a query from a financial magazine, arranging for a series of on-the-job safety pictures, cleaning up last minute details for a Boy Scout drive, digging out material for a speech, or checking proofs on the forthcoming annual report.

In order to understand the process, it is helpful to break it apart and examine each phase. That is the purpose of this chapter and the three that follow. The *unity, overlapping,* and *continuity* of the whole process should be kept in mind as the parts are taken out of the running machine for examination.

The four-step process is illustrated in this problem which confronted American Oil's public relations staff some years ago:

American Oil decided to close its Mankato, Minnesota, sales division as part of a company-wide reorganization to gain more efficiency. This meant that 600 *employees* would have to move or find new jobs. The Mankato *community* would suffer a loss in income. Minnesota *customers* would be concerned about getting equally good service under the new setup. The *public* would be curious about the meaning and implications of this move.

The first task was to marshal all the facts, through research, so the decision could be explained and justified to those concerned. The next step was to plan announcement of the decision. Timing was an important factor. The news had to be broken swiftly, before rumors started. Still, the news could not be released until plans were completed for its simultaneous release to all those affected. With plans completed, then came the task of communicating the decision in a manner calculated to gain understanding of the necessity and wisdom of the change.

Materials included: a procedure memorandum to guide its staff, a presentation script for meetings, letters to several different groups of employees, letters to all dealers, a news release, a statement on banking arrangements for Mankato banks, a general office letter, plans for meetings. The news was released through meetings, letters to all the different groups involved, and through the mass media. Finally, the department *evaluated* its handling of this problem with an eye to improving its procedures when the next move out of a community must be communicated.

FACT-FINDING AND FEEDBACK

There is an urgent need in today's practice to put more effort in the fact-finding and feedback step. As organizations grow in size, their executives become more insulated from the winds of the public climate. The busy executive has little time to read or meet persons outside his narrow circle. He is zealously guarded by protective assistants. Clarence Randall, longtime head of Inland Steel, saw the problem: [1]

"Responsibility breeds isolation. As a man's authority increases, so do the barriers that cut him off from direct contact with the world about him. . . . After he reaches the top, he is seldom seen in public and seldom heard. He becomes a myth. . . . The consequence is that when the great storm comes, as it does sooner or later to every large corporation, and he is driven out into the turbulence of public opinion, he may not be ready to go on deck."

The insulation of today's executive from public opinion is epitomized in the President of the United States. George Reedy, one-time press secretary to President Lyndon Johnson, has observed: "From the president's standpoint, the greatest staff problem is that of maintaining his contact with the world's reality that lies outside the White House. Very few have succeeded in doing so . . . it is only a matter of time until the White House assistants close in like a praetorian guard." [2]

Failure to monitor public opinion has resulted in many organizations being ambushed by crises. Several major public relations blunders of the 1960s make clear the cost when executives fail to sensitively interpret public opinion.[3]

The insulation of General Motors' management made that giant insensitive to the public's growing concern for death on the highway and, thus, unprepared for the predictable public anger at its efforts to harass its troublesome critic, Ralph Nader. In the view of one analyst, the corporation officers' expertise in business was "of little assistance when the company was confronted with a challenge whose nature was political and sociological rather than economic." He adds that as a consequence of management's reluctance to listen:

[1] In "Business, Too, Has Its Ivory Towers," *New York Times Magazine*, July 2, 1962.

[2] *The Twilight of the Presidency* (New York and Cleveland: World Publishing Co., 1970), p. 95. Reedy cuts away many of the myths surrounding the presidency.

[3] U. S. Steel's confrontation with President John F. Kennedy in 1962 was one. The details may be found in: Roy Hoopes, *The Steel Crisis* (New York: John Day, 1963); Richard Austin Smith, "Behind U. S. Steel's Blunder," *Fortune*, Vol. 66, August, 1962; "Big Steel's Blunder: How Big?" *Printer's Ink*, April 20, 1962; and Grant McConnell, *Steel and the Presidency — 1962* (New York: Norton, 1963).

The company's large, well-organized public relations staff has trouble performing one of its important functions: interpreting subtleties of the outside world to management. Instead, its considerable energies are employed to a disproportionate degree in interpreting management to the world.[4]

Insensitivity born of insularity is not confined to business. The campus revolt which has spread around the world had its beginning on the Berkeley campus of the University of California in 1964. Much, though by no means all, of the trouble at Berkeley was rooted in a president who had purposely insulated himself from the main campus so that he could view the large system as a whole, and was a result of a breakdown in communications. One observer wrote:

"As a result of size and circumstance, communication within the university has broken down—communication between student and teacher, between student and administrator, and even between faculty and administration. Students feel alienated from the university, mere numbers on an IBM card, figures in line at the library desk. . . ."[5]

In April, 1968, Columbia University was greatly damaged by student violence. Like most explosions, this one had roots extending into the past. Again, a breakdown of communications was central to the cause. A commission which probed the causes of the "Crisis at Columbia" makes observations such as these: [6]

"Columbia's organization and style of administration . . . created a wide unbridged gulf between the faculty and Administration. . . . Second, the faculty became more and more remote from the problems of student life and general university policy. . . . The authoritarian manner, on the one side, and aloofness, on the other, were mutually reinforcing. . . . Finally, . . . we are concerned by the lack of communication and understanding between faculty and trustees." The spark that ignited this explosive situation was the university's lack of concern and communication in dealing with its neighbors.

Nor are these communications breakdowns solely a matter of not encouraging or providing for feedback from the organization's intelligence machinery. Often the intelligence is collected but does not get to the decision makers. The U. S. Government had a public opinion poll taken early in 1960 in Cuba, showing that 86 percent of the Cubans supported Castro. Yet this information never reached those who made the Bay of Pigs de-

---

[4] Dan Cordtz, "The Face in the Mirror at General Motors," *Fortune*, Vol. 74, August, 1966.

[5] James Cass, "What Happened at Berkeley," *Saturday Review*, Vol. XLVIII, January 16, 1965, p. 67.

[6] The Cox Commission Report, *Crisis at Columbia* (New York: Vintage, 1968).

cision.[7] The U.S.I.A. had it but, not knowing of the invasion plan, did not send the study to President Kennedy.[8]

These are only a few available examples demonstrating the importance of fact-finding and feedback as the foundation for public relations planning and action. These examples show why executives, remote and removed from the public arena, need aides to supply political and ideological intelligence and to mediate organizational relationships with the outside world. Paul Lund of the Bell System says: "It is part of any PR man's charter to understand what's going on in society." President Duncan Wimpress of Trinity University expects his counselor "to supply current and condensed information on everything." Monitoring the public environment is the first step in public relations.

Public relations must bring more precision to its informational input, though the kit of tools for doing so may not be fully adequate. Walter Straley, vice president of A. T. & T. for environmental affairs, thinks "we're just on the threshold of understanding that the need exists for experimentation, research, evaluation, and intelligence mechanisms to bring environmental information into management." A study made in mid-1967 found that the behavioral sciences were not playing a dominant role, that use of pre-program research was limited, and very little post-program evaluation was being done.[9] Two practitioners maintain: "However lean the body of knowledge is in understanding people's reactions, attitudes and opinions, public relations has an obligation to use the best of it and to apply it." [10] Public relations will use with increasing frequency the knowledge of the behavioral sciences in much the same way the art of medicine uses knowledge of the life sciences.

RESEARCH ATTITUDE NEEDED

Public relations practice may be likened to an iceberg. Three fourths of it is unseen below the surface. The one fourth—publicity—that does show is too often taken for the whole iceberg. The unseen three fourths—research, planning, evaluating—are generally more important in the long run. Because of the high stakes, executives must increase the precision of their decisions. In business, for example, today's technology requires heavy in-

[7] Hadley Cantril, *The Human Dimension*, pp. 1–5.

[8] Thomas C. Sorensen, *The Word War*, pp. 140–141.

[9] Willard Bailey, "The Role of Behavioral Sciences in Public Relations Practice," unpublished master's thesis, Ohio State University, 1967. See his articles based on this study in *Public Relations Journal*, August and September, 1968.

[10] John F. Budd, Jr., and Robert G. Strayton, "Can Public Relations Be Measured?" *Public Relations Quarterly*, Vol. 13, Winter, 1969, p. 19.

vestment in machines and a lapse of time between a decision to produce and the emergence of the salable product. This makes it imperative that all steps be taken to foresee what will transpire. Institutions cannot afford to be taken by surprise and overwhelmed by the unforeseen. Staff officers are expected to provide facts upon which sound administrative decisions can be made. Executives are coming to realize that an organization's human relations problems are just as specific and researchable as other problems. Wilensky sees an increase in "information consciousness" among executives. David Ogilvy has observed "an increasing tendency on the part of clients to welcome candor, particularly when it is based on the results of consumer research." Counselor David Finn, in his book *The Corporate Oligarch,* takes a more pessimistic view. He says the business leader is deaf to constructive criticism. Nonetheless the demand for hard data is growing. This parallels the maturing fields of public opinion measurement, market research, and public relations. *Methodical, systematic research is the foundation of effective public relations.*

Counselor John F. Moynahan offers this example: [11] A New York department store's earnings were running above the level of previous years and an extra dividend was indicated. The store's employees belonged to a militant union, and the executives feared an extra dividend would create hostility among the employees. Accordingly, the advertising department prepared a brochure intended to gain the employees' "understanding" of management's view on profits. Just like that! Before the brochure was released, management wisely had an opinion survey made. The survey showed that most of the employees neither understood nor were impressed by the relationship of profits to gross sales, which was the main theme of the planned brochure. Depth interviews revealed that most of the store's employees thought of earnings in terms of the mark-up on the store's merchandise.

This opinion survey had three benefits: (1) It helped management plan a more effective brochure; (2) It provided a guide for a continuing information campaign to employees; (3) It provided a base against which changing employee attitudes could be remeasured in the future.

A great researcher who helped build the automotive industry, C. F. Kettering, once described this desired attitude in these words: [12]

Research is a high hat word that scares a lot of people. It needn't. It is rather simple. Essentially, it is nothing but a state of mind—a friendly, welcoming attitude toward change. Going out to look for change, instead of waiting for it to come. Research, for practical men, is an effort

[11] In "Opinion Research: To Solve a Problem, Grasp an Opportunity," *Public Relations Journal,* Vol. 19, June, 1963.

[12] "More Music Please, Composers," *Saturday Evening Post,* Vol. 211, No. 32, 1938.

to do things better and not be caught asleep at the switch. The research state of mind can apply to anything. Personal affairs or any kind of business, big or little. It is the problem solving mind as contrasted with the let well enough alone mind. It is the composer mind, instead of the fiddler mind; it is the "tomorrow" mind instead of the "yesterday" mind.

Much of President Franklin Roosevelt's success as a leader came from his "research attitude." He utilized analyses of the press, public opinion polls, and a field organization to provide an inflow of public opinion into the White House. Two political scientists who edited the proceedings of the National Emergency Council found that the leitmotif of these proceedings was "Roosevelt's overriding concern with his lines of communication with the public." They explain: [13]

"Under the National Emergency Council, a network of field organizations in all states and counties had been created. Roosevelt saw these not only as administrative instruments, but as a channel of regular reports on how things were going. He expected these reports to contain judgments as to whether the public was pleased, and secondly, whether the administration of the program was coherent."

According to Hadley Cantril who did much of his polling, FDR properly did not alter his goals to suit public opinion, but rather "utilized such information to try to bring the public around more quickly or more effectively to the course of action he felt best. . . ." [14] He also sampled White House mail and often had counts made on letters reflecting a response to a speech or incident.[15] FDR also relied heavily on his wife's reports on her frequent travels.

RESEARCH PROVIDES MUCH-NEEDED EMPHASIS ON THE
LISTENING PHASE OF PUBLIC RELATIONS AND GIVES SUBSTANCE
TO THE "TWO-WAY STREET" CONCEPT

One of the vitiating weaknesses in the past has been a misplaced emphasis on publicity. Communication starts with listening. This requires humility and systematic effort. Too often what purports to be communication is simply opposing ideas passing each other in psychological space— for example, in a management-versus-labor bargaining situation in which each side is merely waiting to score points, not listening to the other's views.

---

[13] Lester G. Seligman and Elmer E. Cornwell, Jr., *New Deal Mosaic* (Eugene, Ore.: University of Oregon Books, 1965). Proceedings of National Emergency Council, p. xxi. At first meeting FDR said the big problem was to get a reflection of nationwide opinion.

[14] Cantril, *The Human Dimension*, Chap. 6.

[15] Leila Sussmann, "Mass Political Letter Writing in America: The Growth of an Institution," *Public Opinion Quarterly*, Vol. 23, Summer, 1959.

Listening is not an easy task. Channels from the worker out in the plant or the car dealer in Seattle must be provided and kept open. Failure to listen leads to useless "communicating" on issues that do not exist to publics that are not there. Research can be used to find the bridge of interest capable of carrying a communications payload.

Before there can be rapport through communication, there must be empathy. Empathy is achieved by open-minded listening. As Thoreau put it: "It takes two to speak the truth; one to speak and another to hear." Public relations is a *two-way* street. Both lines of traffic must be given equal right-of-way. Unless you know the values, viewpoints, and language of your audience, you are not likely to get through. These values and viewpoints can be learned only through *systematic* and *sympathetic* listening.

RESEARCH PROVIDES THE OBJECTIVE LOOK
REQUIRED TO "KNOW THYSELF"

Public relations has been likened to a mirror, a mirror that reflects the public's image of the organization to its executives and reflects the image of the organization to the public. Today more wrong decisions are made on mistaken hunches of what the public thinks than on willful disregard of public opinion. Robert Burns said it so well:

Oh wad some power the giftie gie us
To see oursel's as ithers see us!
It wad frae monie a blunder free us, And foolish notion

The practitioner mirrors the publics of an organization by relaying the views and desires of those publics to its policy makers. To accurately interpret the publics of an institution to its policy makers, a practitioner must be able to look at problems from the *public viewpoint*. Objective research serves as a shoehorn in putting on the other fellow's shoes. It provides an effective stimulus to self-correction. Subjective assumptions of what "the public thinks" are risky.

RESEARCH EARNS SUPPORT FOR COUNSELING AND
PROGRAMMING AROUND THE POLICY-MAKING TABLE

The research-based approach is apt to be the most effective in gaining consideration for the public relations aspect of organizational problems. Executives are a fact-minded lot. The surest way to counter a controller's idea of "what the people want," when he is wrong, is with surveys and case studies of similar situations. Clarence J. Hicks, pioneer in industrial relations, once said: "It is characteristic of a profession that recommendations are of value in proportion as they are intelligently based upon a thorough diagnosis of the individual case or problem." Today's data-minded bosses want figures, not adjectives or hunches. *The need is for research-supported diagnoses, not new medicines.*

RESEARCH REVEALS FESTERING TROUBLE SPOTS
BEFORE THEY INFECT A LARGE BODY OF PUBLIC OPINION

Too often problems are allowed to define themselves in the form of a crisis. Too much effort goes into "fire-fighting" rather than "fire prevention." This is dramatized when deteriorating labor relations present the problem of a strike or a lockout or a student sit-in. Such situations usually have long histories. Sometimes neither party knows what caused the blow-up. Heading off "blow-ups" is part of the public relations task. The earlier a complaint is caught, the easier it is to handle. Continuous fact-finding will uncover many problems while they are still small enough to permit quiet handling without a critical public looking on. The same attentive listening will permit the catching of rumors before they become widespread.

RESEARCH INCREASES THE EFFECTIVENESS OF
OUTBOUND COMMUNICATION

Failure to provide feedback from various publics inevitably results in communications breakdowns and wasted public relations efforts. One of Britain's pioneer practitioners, Sir Stephen Tallents, saw the problem clearly: [16] "We must begin by studying the minds—the greatly differing minds—of those to whom our projection is addressed. . . . We must bring to our task a sensitive insight and a keen sympathy. And we must support them by the most carefully acquired knowledge of the different ways and tastes and needs of other peoples."

To obtain the maximum effect in communication and persuasion, each public must have special study and special treatment. Pimlott says: "This emphasis on the need to pinpoint the specific publics is one of the most useful contributions which public relations has received from the social scientists." Much of today's publicity effort is characterized by wasteful misses. Research enables the practitioner to pinpoint his publics, discover their leaders, learn their values, viewpoints, and language. These he must know if he is to beam his message in on its target. *A public relations effort increases in effectiveness in proportion to the specificity with which it is directed to a group.*

---

[16] In *The Projection of England* (London: The Olen Press for Film Centre, Ltd., 1955), p. 36.

RESEARCH PROVIDES USEFUL INTELLIGENCE—
AN IDEA SERVICE FOR EXECUTIVES

An intelligence service is an indispensable auxiliary to an information service. Increasingly administrators rely on the public relations department as a central source of information on the organization, the public's image of it, the industry or field, and the social, economic, and political trends. Such demands are to be encouraged. This service enhances the effectiveness of the total program. To provide this service requires fact-stockpiling and information analysis. One of the most useful services is to interpret the changing social-economic-political environment to executives. Research has two basic purposes: *First,* the collection and collation of facts used in planning a course of action and in determining channels and content of the informational program. *Second,* exploration of basic attitudes, opinions expressed, and information held by members of an organization's publics. Information gained in the latter type of research generally is used more for long-range planning.

Measurement and analysis of opinions range from the highly informal and impressionistic to the methodical and near-scientific. Progress in any specialized field is marked by its advance from impressionistic observation to objective testing, with accurate measurement techniques. Opinion research provides guidance at four stages of the process. Opinion Research Corporation lists these as:

1. *Current situation:* what people think today and why
2. *Basic principles:* how public opinion works
3. *Pretesting:* how people react to a given ad, article, argument, etc.
4. *Evaluation:* how people did respond and how attitudes changed, if they did.

WHAT ONE COMPANY DOES

In the Sun Oil Company, the public relations department has these responsibilities: (1) "to establish and maintain constant liaison with the managers of all departments of the company for the provision of counsel and assistance regarding their public relations activities and problems"; (2) "to conduct research in and prepare reports on social, economic, and political subjects and trends—which from a public relations viewpoint, may affect the activities or interest of the company, the petroleum industry, or business generally"; (3) "to keep company officials promptly informed of currently published or broadcast statements relating to the company, the oil industry, and business generally." To meet these assigned tasks and to carry out its specific programs to build goodwill, the Sun Oil public relations department established a research division—one of the first departments to do so. This research division performs various functions.

MAINTENANCE OF A LIBRARY

This library is directed by a trained librarian and houses standard reference books: general business and oil and chemical trade publications; works devoted to public relations practice and skills; reports on public relations programs; media analyses; public opinion and attitude surveys; definitive books on economic, financial, and other business subjects; a legislative reference section, including printed sets of congressional hearings on the oil industry, current volumes of the *Congressional Record, Federal Register,* and services listing legislation pending in Congress and in the states; more than 2,000 file folders containing accumulated reference material from newspapers, magazines, and such sources.

NEWS INTELLIGENCE

This section keeps track of what the daily and periodical press, radio, and TV are saying about the company, the industry, and business generally. News and editorial comment are abstracted from a representative list of daily papers in a *Daily News Digest* for top managers. Clippings and radio and TV reports are made widely available to public relations staff and management. Each week, the full staff reviews fifty weekly or monthly periodicals and abstracts items of interest. These are distributed in the company in a multilithed publication, *Periodical Highlights.* Annually the research section issues a *Company Encyclopedia,* a compendium of facts about company operations, history, etc. This is a desk bible for the several hundred managers who receive it. Another research division publication, *Petroleum Reference Sheet,* is a three-part document. It provides a weekly, monthly, and special case compilation of current statistics on oil industry operations.

SPECIAL REPORTS AND SURVEYS

The research division prepares reports on specific public relations problems, such as "Government Controls Over the Oil Industry." It also sponsors periodic surveys on attitudes toward the company and toward the oil industry. Surveys are being used increasingly to learn more about the impact and effectiveness of programs. For example, this division periodically sponsors readership surveys of company publications. Also, this staff is increasingly making pre-tests of communications materials before they are widely disseminated. The goal is to accomplish more at less cost per unit of results.

Obviously, only the large industrial and nonprofit organizations can afford to maintain research divisions of this scope. But every public relations job requires that these functions be cared for to some degree. Here's how.

FACT-FINDING

THE FIRST STEP: A FACT FILE

It has been said that all a man needs to become a counselor is a shiny office and a subscription to the *New York Times*. The grain of truth in this axiom emphasizes that it is important to collect, clip, and compile facts.

Locating, arranging, and analyzing information is important to a client or organization. Useful information is to be found in government publications, libraries, trade publications, newspapers, industry reports, and a multitude of sources. The painstaking fact finder will be greatly rewarded when confronted with an immediate need for information. Such demands are many and often unexpected. When the boss wants some information, he wants it now! Keeping a current organizational "World Almanac" is a useful idea. A common starting point in the organization of a public relations office is building of a fact file of resource materials. Daily requests will tell what is needed.

In practice, the department becomes the central information bureau in most organizations where there is no librarian or historian. Queries that cannot be answered by other departments wind up in this office. Newspaper, magazine, radio, and TV men have come to expect the office to provide quick answers. Such demands are met and encouraged. Media men should be encouraged to rely on the office for authentic information. Such practice has many valuable consequences. For instance, a reporter's query often gives a running start on a crisis in the making. Such demands should be anticipated.

From fact files come ideas and information for speeches, pamphlets, special reports, institutional advertising, exhibits, special events, and background information for special projects. The department is responsible for assembling the factual content of its communications program. Often these items have to be whipped up in a hurry. For example, a department of a bank had to get out in two weeks a brief history booklet to help mark the millionth depositor.

This department should have the over-all responsibility for developing accurate facts regarding company and industry policies, practices, and operations and for developing the dimensions of public relations problems on this basis. Increasingly, public relations departments are assigned the task of building and maintaining company or organizational libraries. Providing quick answers for tough questions can be a goodwill builder for the department, both inside and outside the organization.

DEFINING THE PROBLEM AND THE PUBLICS

The first requirement in research is to define the problem. Much waste in public relations practice is caused by attacking problems that don't exist and by aiming messages at audiences that don't exist. Joseph Kraft has observed, "Identifying difficulties is generally as important as solving them and usually much harder." Failure to accurately define the problem by ascertaining audience opinions and interests leads to what Dean Gerhard Wiebe calls "pillow punching"—cases where the PR program is devoting time, money, and creative energy in promoting a theme that simply is not perceived as important by the target audience."

Another essential part of research is in defining the publics. This involves, too, determining the effective channels of communication with each. Precise definition of a client's publics—their composition, and their prevailing attitudes—goes beyond simple classifications, such as trustees, faculty, students, alumni. Members of a given public are constantly shifting. *In public relations you must communicate with a passing parade not a standing army.* DeTocqueville observed: "Each generation in a democratic society is a new people."

Publics themselves change from time to time. There is a constant "toing" and "froing" in age groupings, economic interests, political interests, and geographic residence. The last is increasingly true in mobile America. New publics are always coming into being, old ones fading away. A discerning editor points out: [17]

> Basic changes have occurred in the past twenty years and have raised to power entirely new categories of Americans. The most significant new categories include: (1) college and university professors, (2) career government officials in all levels of government, (3) certain journalists . . . notably television commentators, TV producers, TV news editors, magazine editors, and newspaper columnists. These new influentials comprise a key public, described by Counselor Harold Bray-

[17] Peter B. Clark, "The Reporter and the Power Structure," *Nieman Reports*, Vol. 23, March, 1969.

man as "perhaps the most powerful and influential category in the nation."

Today's young people comprise another powerful bloc. In the 1970s half the eligible voters will be under thirty years old. The power of college students in the nation's political life was amply demonstrated in the political upheavals of 1968. Theodore White notes: [18] "By 1968 this campus proleteriat outnumbered farmers by almost three to one, coal-miners by fifty to one, railway workers by nine to one. Students were, in short, the largest working-class group with a single interest in the United States." The nation's more than seven-million college students exert themselves as a powerful force. Communicating with the young will be a prime task in the years ahead.

Typical of new publics coming into being is the new buying public with an interest in foreign-made cars. Introduction of a new product may, in the case of a manufacturer, create a new buying public. Establishment of a new branch plant brings a new community public to be studied and understood. No two are exactly alike. Normally, regroupings take place gradually, almost imperceptibly, such as the changes in family living brought on by television. Other times, the shift comes with lightning-like swiftness—when a whole nation is plunged into war or economic depression. Thus, it is imperative to keep current an accurate analysis of publics and their sentiments.[19]

Such analyses will reveal the group leaders or *influentials* in each of an organization's several publics. The importance of determining the real group leaders as against the presumed opinion leaders was underscored in Chapter 6. Too often in public relations there is a tendency to short-cut this task in an effort to "economize"—by tagging lawyers, doctors, clergymen, bankers, as the sum total of leadership or by assuming that a union leader is a leader in political or social affairs as well as in union matters. This short-cut is full of risks. For example, barbers talk to union members more often than their officers. So do bartenders. Persons may be influential in their groups and yet not prominent in the community. Each social stratum generates its own opinion leaders. Individuals look to different group leaders for guidance in different facets of their daily lives. Sighting respected group leaders requires laborious fact-finding. There is no short cut. The political graveyard is filled with aspirants for office who ignored, or sought to circumvent, opinion leaders.

In conducting this "publics" research, learn and recognize the interrelatedness of all these groups. The practitioner needs to know which of

---

[18] *The Making of the President—1968* (New York: Atheneum, 1969), pp. 68–69.

[19] For examples, see: Glen Perry, "Which Public Do You Mean?" *Public Relations Journal*, Vol. 12, March, 1956; Stuart Chase, "American Values: A Generation of Change," *Public Opinion Quarterly*, Vol. 29, Fall, 1965.

several appeals will be most effective with a specific public. He needs to gauge the reactions of this group and also of those that "listen in." What is said to one group may be heard by another. This presents a dilemma; the more practitioners appeal to different groups in terms of their self-interest, as they must, the greater is the danger of offending other groups. *Often organizations have to choose which groups they want on their side.*

Systematic definition of an organization's publics is needed, too, to determine order of priority. And priorities must be assigned to an institution's almost infinite number of publics. Rarely does a practitioner have the staff and money to do all the things he thinks need be done. This Nicholas Samstag terms "the perpetual priority problem."

PUBLIC RELATIONS WORKS FROM THE INSIDE OUT

The place to start in defining the publics is at the heart of an organization—in its power structure. It is there that the essential character of an organization's relationships is determined. The key policy makers must be the first concern. Working out from this inner circle, there are junior executives, supervisors, employees, home communities, consumers, investors, donors, and all others. From these immediate publics, attention moves along a broad front of special-interest publics within the general public. These include labor unions, industrial associations, farm groups, political groups, women's groups, professional groups, educators, veterans, youth and ethnic groups, and similar common-interest groupings. These special publics will be discussed in Chapter 15.

SELECTING THE AUDIENCE

Research is used also to determine the best ways of reaching publics, once they have been identified. This requires determination of channels of influence and communication. Pinpointing is essential if the message is to be designed in terms of what will gain the intended audience's attention. *It is not easy to attract the public's attention or to hold its interest.* Careless or casual determination of group and geographic boundaries is too common. *The more carefully one defines various publics, the more ways of reaching and influencing them one will discover. Research will best define the mutuality of interests that will serve as a bridge to carry an organization's persuasive communication.*

LISTENING IS AN INTEGRAL PART OF A SUSTAINED PROGRAM

An able practitioner of another generation, Abraham Lincoln, knew the importance of listening. Lincoln once advised a friend: "Keep close to the people—they are always right and will mislead no one." He followed his own advice. Lincoln, twice each week, set aside a period of his valuable time for conversations with ordinary folk—the housewives, farmers, merchants, and pension-seekers. Lincoln listened patiently to what they had to say, no matter how humble their circumstance or how trivial their business. An officer in the War Department once protested to the President that he was wasting valuable time on these unimportant people. Lincoln rebuked him, saying:

> . . . no hours of my day are better employed than those which bring me again within the direct contact and atmosphere of the average of our whole people. . . . all serve to renew in me a clearer and more vivid image of that great popular assemblage out of which I sprang and to which at the end of two years I must return.
>
> I tell you, Major . . . that I call these receptions my public opinion baths . . . the effect, as a whole, is renovating and invigorating.[20]

Prudence dictates the systematic listening to an organization's publics through scientific research. Yet many organizations still fail to utilize fully this tool. Why? Because:

1. Sound opinion research is expensive.
2. A time lag exists between the formulation of an opinion study and the time when the results are needed.
3. Management does not want to listen to the views of their publics.
4. There is a lack of knowledge about these research tools on the part of publicity-minded practitioners.
5. There is a lack of confidence in the precision of the research tools now available.

Typical is this comment found in *Trends in School Public Relations:* "Two-way communication is slim in some school systems because superintendents are afraid of it. They see it as organized back talk and a potential threat rather than an essential tool of modern management. But in most systems, the two-way flow is a trickle because it takes a lot of effort and skill to obtain reliable feedback."

INFORMAL METHODS

Pioneers in public relations lacked the precision tools that are available today to gauge opinion accurately. They were forced to fall back on what rough-and-ready means could be devised. Despite the development

[20] Carl Sandburg, *Abraham Lincoln: The War Years,* Vol. II (New York: Harcourt Brace Jovanovich, 1939).

of the more accurate measuring sticks, reliance on the informal methods still dominates many programs. It is not realistic to make formal research a part and parcel of the daily routine in a department or counseling firm.

This is due to lack of funds and to the necessity of making quick, on-the-spot evaluations. These informal methods include:

1. Personal contacts by telephone or mail or with persons you know.
2. Advisory committees or panels.
3. Analysis of an organization's incoming mail.
4. Evaluations by field agents or salesmen on opinions held about the organization.
5. Press clippings and radio and TV monitorings of what has been said on a particular subject.
6. Conferences of those involved in a particular problem or situation.
7. Study of national public opinion polls to gain a sense of opinion climate and trends.
8. Study of election and legislative voting which reflects public opinion on certain issues.
9. Speeches and writings of recognized opinion leaders.
10. Sales records.

These informal methods can be helpful. Recognize their weaknesses, however: Inherently they lack *representativeness* and *objectivity*—the keys to sound opinion research. Still, such methods can provide vital and significant clues to opinion trends and reveal sources of things people like and do not like.

PERSONAL CONTACTS

In 1893 Lord Bryce said, "The best way in which the tendencies at work in any community can be best discovered and estimated is by moving freely about among all sorts and conditions of men." Skill in sizing up the attitude of individuals has long been and always will be one of the prime qualifications of a counselor. There is great value in wide acquaintanceships with representative leaders from all walks of life.

It is a good practice to win friends in all publics. By probing, talking, listening, and analyzing as he moves freely about, the practitioner can learn a great deal. The politician has been doing this for a long time.

Many practitioners consult regularly with such influentials as editors, reporters, ministers, labor leaders, bartenders, civic leaders, bankers, and housewives.

IDEA JURIES, PANELS

It is only a short step from asking friends and associates for their reactions to organizing idea juries or opinion panels. These range from *ad hoc* to highly formal arrangements. The degree of formality and continuity in these sounding boards varies a great deal. The jury panel is one of the most economical "polls." Careful selection can provide a rough, working idea of opinion within these groups. Bringing such a group together for a lunch or dinner once a month can pay good dividends.

A Wisconsin dairy cooperative developed a fruitful variation of the opinion panel when it held a series of "Neighborhood Huddles" for its membership. An influential member was asked to invite the members in his neighborhood for a "Neighborhood Huddle." Current information on the dairy situation was presented and comments were invited. At the end, each member was asked to fill out a "feedback" form to evaluate the cooperative's program. Comments made during the meeting and these open-end evaluation forms were later collated and analyzed to draw a profile of member attitudes.

The panel technique can be used to establish communication with minority groups. The aspirations, needs, and demands of Chicago's black community were voiced when the Chicago Welfare Council staged a "listen-in" "to hear and understand from black leaders the needs and feelings of the black community." Another variation of this technique, used with increasing frequency, is to arrange for a panel of customers or clients to "tell it like it is" to an industry or profession at the annual meeting.

ADVISORY COMMITTEES

A variation of the idea jury device is the advisory committee. The honor of service on such a committee quite often will bring to an organization the services of an able group. An advisory committee can be helpful in preventing many a misstep. Advisory committees, representing public groups, also serve, on occasion, as heat shields to absorb public criticism. Nonprofit organizations can tap the aid of skilled public relations people in this way. Formation of such a group for a college or civil rights group can serve to win the interest and participation of influential persons in the community. Advisory committees create the opportunity for participation. Once interested and informed, members are likely to return to their own circle and carry the ball for the program. But there is a price to be paid in using such committees. Their advice must be given earnest consideration, or else the gesture will backfire. No one likes to serve as a show-window mannequin.

MAIL ANALYSIS

Another economical way of gauging opinions—one frequently over-looked—is a periodic analysis of an organization's incoming mail. The correspondence will reveal areas of favor, disfavor, and a lack of information. There is a tendency of letter writers to be critical rather than commendatory. This should be kept in mind in making such analyses. Letters often will hoist warning flags on sources of ill-will or service breakdown or detect the boomerang effects of a program. *Letters reveal indications of opinion, but they do not measure it.*

President John F. Kennedy borrowed a leaf from Franklin D. Roosevelt's book on keeping in touch with the public. Kennedy directed that every fiftieth letter coming to the White House be brought to him. Periodic mail samples helped both these leaders to bridge the moat surrounding the White House. Helpful studies have been made of mail coming to the U.S.I.A.'s Voice of America, studies that give indications of audience interest and belief in VOA's output.

Specific mail responses can be significant, too. A district manager of a large Western oil company became concerned about the large number of inactive accounts among credit-card holders. He sat down and wrote a personal, friendly letter to be sent to them. Thirty-four hundred letters were mailed and 1,100 responses came back, although no incentives or premiums were provided. An amazing response! Analysis of the letters revealed many implications for the program of that company.

FIELD REPORTS

Most concerns have salesmen, district representatives, or field agents who travel the organization's territory. These agents should be trained to listen. They should be provided an easy, regular means of reporting opinions encountered. In this way they can serve as the "eyes and ears" of an organization. Systematic reporting of opinions, complaints, and commendations should be part of their jobs. However, it should be noted that reports of such representatives tend to be optimistic.

For example, in an effort to measure the impact of a certain Progress Week, the industry's sales representatives in Bangor, Maine, were asked for an evaluation. Forty percent would venture no opinion. About half of those responding thought that the week's promotion had produced more favorable attitudes toward the industry. Actually, in a cross-section survey it was found that only eleven percent of the Bangor population were inclined to be more favorable toward this industry. In this case only twelve of the forty-two "grass-roots" observers were able to gauge opinions correctly. All impressionistic measurements must be studied with caution. Field reports can be helpful when the natural margin of inaccuracy is kept in mind.

MEDIA REPORTS

Press clippings and radio-TV monitor reports—all available from commercial services—have long been used as yardsticks. These devices will indicate what is printed or broadcast. They cannot report, however, whether the message was read or heard and, if so, whether it was believed and understood. Newspaper clippings are useful in measuring acceptability of releases sent to the press, but they cannot measure impact. These services can be used to detect what is being disseminated about your organization organization or about a competitor. One hundred percent coverage on newsclips is difficult to achieve, and returns from a particular service will vary.

The press, when used with extreme caution, can be a fairly reliable guide to current opinions, particularly those of protest and criticism. Still, the wide disparity between the voting opinions of the people and the editorial opinions of newspapers, as demonstrated in elections, should warn against uncritical acceptance of newspaper editorial opinion. The same is true of radio and TV news commentators. Caution should be used in accepting interpretive reporting as reflecting public opinion. Mass media can be used as indicators, not as yardsticks.

MORE RELIABLE METHODS

The surest way to learn opinion and underlying attitudes would be to sit down and talk things over face to face. This is not often possible. Instead, social scientists and market researchers have developed the technique of talking to a *small but representative* group in each public. *This is the sample survey*. Sampling is a great money saver and is accurate when the sample is *representative*. It is built on the laws of mathematical probability, which have equal validity in the social sciences.

By asking precise, understandable questions of a truly accurate miniature of a whole, public opinion can be measured with a high degree of accuracy. Just as the practitioner depends largely on the established channels to *talk* to the public, he surveys to *listen* to the public. Through such devices, representatives of the public are encouraged to tell their story to the institution. These survey tools offer an effective means of facilitating an inflow of information and opinion. Through these devices the practitioner interprets the public to the institution.[21]

CROSS-SECTION SURVEYS

A carefully prepared set of questions is asked of a cross-section sample of a given public. The questionnaire builds a bridge between an organization and members of the public. There are three ways to draw the sample to be interviewed: (1) *probability sample*—in which people to be interviewed are chosen at random by some mechanical formula, such as every *n*th name on the list; (2) *area sample*—a form of the probability sample in which geographical areas are listed, cities for example, then units to be surveyed are chosen at random; (3) *quota sample*—population in question is analyzed by known characteristics—sex, age, residence, occupation, income level—then interviews are assigned by quota in the same proportions as these characteristics exist in the whole population.

All these methods involve a degree of sampling error, which usually can be kept within tolerable limits. Such surveys are made by many commercial polling firms. They can be arranged through one of several universities. The results obtained through cross-section surveys are more quantitative than qualitative in nature; they often fail to reflect the depth and intensity of opinions expressed by respondents.

SURVEY PANELS

Under this method, a panel of people is selected and is interviewed several times over a period of time. The selection of participants is determined on a cross-section basis. Panels are used to learn what happens to people under varying conditions over a span of time. It is an effective device for controlled experiments. A panel could be used, for example, to measure the impact of a series of projects in community relations, or to follow people's buying habits in a grocery store. Panels are difficult to administer, and it is hard to keep all members interested over a long stretch. Panel members, in time, also tend to become atypical rather than typical.

DEPTH INTERVIEW

This is a qualitative instrument to probe the attitudes underlying expressed opinions. It is an informal kind of interview. The respondent is

[21] Discussion of the tools and techniques of surveys does not fall within the scope of this book. Suggested are such standard works as Mildred Parten's *Surveys, Polls, and Samples;* Hadley Cantril's *Gauging Public Opinion;* and A. B. Blankenship's *Consumer and Opinion Research.*

encouraged to talk fully and freely. This method takes highly trained interviewers and skilled analysts. Elmo Roper says: "Because of the informal nature of this technique and the fact that the most productive depth interviews are those which give respondents the widest range of latitude for responding, one major problem in its use is how to evaluate its meaning." He thinks the really qualified depth interviewer is rare. The depth interview is one of the techniques used in motivational research, one of the newer tools in the marketer's kit.

CONTENT ANALYSIS

This is a method of systematically coding and classifying the content of one or all of the mass media. This method can tell an organization what is being said and published about it and in what context it is talked about. Media content can be measured as to how much is descriptive, how much is favorable, how much is critical. Content analysis will show the pattern of mentions of an organization and can provide helpful clues to the kinds of information your publics are being exposed to, but not necessarily what they consume and believe. It is also possible to couple content analysis with a sampling procedure and obtain, from a sample of some 50 daily papers, an accurate picture of nationwide dissemination of a given subject. Content analysis also can be useful in periodically assessing content of informational output against stated objectives.[22]

MAIL QUESTIONNAIRES

Use of mail instead of face-to-face questionnaires is economical, and is thus tempting to the penny-pinched practitioner. The danger is that there is no assurance the respondents will be representative of the whole population. In putting questions by mail, you lose the flexibility and the interpretations possible in personal interviews. It is difficult to get an adequate response to many mail questionnaires. Many people have been polled in this fashion and there is some resentment. This economical device can be useful when used with due caution. It is most effective in soliciting opinions of homogeneous groups where the cleavage of opinion is decisive—such as of a group of employees on the question of overtime or night shift. This tool can be helpful in uncovering sources of criticism and praise. Space should be provided for additional comment at the end.

---

[22] For brief introduction to this research tool, see: Richard W. Budd and Robert K. Thorp, *An Introduction to Content Analysis* (Iowa City: University of Iowa School of Journalism, 1963).

SEMANTIC DIFFERENTIAL

This is a relatively new technique of measurement, one easy and economical to use—thus, one of great utility for the practitioner who invariably faces a "budget problem" on research. The semantic differential was developed by Professors Charles E. Osgood, George J. Suci, and Percy H. Tannenbaum and is presented in full in their book, *The Measurement of Meaning*. It is designed to assess variations in the connotative meanings of objects and words, and is based on the premise that such meaning constitutes one of the most significant variables mediating human behavior. The procedure consists of having the subject rate one or more objects of judgment (or concepts) against a set of scales defined by a pair of adjectival opposites, with seven steps between them. For example, one could obtain an index of an individual's opinion of Richard Nixon by having the individual allocate this concept on a set of bi-polar scales, such as *strong-weak, active-passive, valuable-worthless, heavy-light, pleasant-unpleasant,* and so forth.

The respondent rates the central concept in terms of what it means to him on each of a set of such scales, the particular selection and number of scales being unfixed. The seven steps between the pairs of opposites allow the subject to express both the direction of his association and its intensity, with a neutral point in the middle. Thus, confronted with a scale such as safe ____: ____: ____: ____: ____: ____: ____: dangerous, the subject can indicate whether he regards the particular concept to be *very* safe or dangerous, *quite* safe or dangerous, or *slightly* safe or dangerous, with the middle point reserved for the feeling of either equally or neither safe nor dangerous. With such sets of scales, measures of the connotations of various concepts can be obtained from specially selected individuals or groups, representative samples of the public. There is no basic restriction on the kinds of concepts that may be judged—individual personalities, corporation images, and so forth. The generality of the technique is attested to by the wide range of uses it has had in its relatively short existence— in attitude measurement, linguistics, psychotherapy, advertising, and image profiles in public relations.[23] Readers are cautioned that the semantic differential is a rough measuring instrument, not as reliable as a straight attitude measurement device.

---

[23] For elaboration, see Osgood, Suci, and Tannenbaum, *The Measurement of Meaning* (Urbana: University of Illinois Press, 1957); and Charles E. Osgood's essay, "An Exploration into Semantic Space" in Schramm's *The Science of Human Communication*.

OPINION RESEARCH IN PUBLIC RELATIONS

The oldest type of research of value is market research. Aimed at improving the distribution and marketing of consumer goods, it dates back more than sixty years. The pioneer N. W. Ayer Advertising Agency started to make market analyses for clients as part of its regular procedure around 1910. Opinion research which probes attitudes and the complexities of human motivation is considerably younger. It dates largely from the early 1930s. The emphasis is as much on the development of more reliable methods as on the findings themselves. Even though it is barely of age, opinion research offers vast potentialities.

It should be fully understood that opinion research is not a substitute for decision making. It is only a guide to it. The role of public opinion research is put in focus by Angus Campbell of the Michigan Survey Research Center: "Knowing your public is a difficult assignment. Leading your public is an even more exacting charge. Studies of public attitudes will give much more useful information to the administrator of public relations programs, but they will not relieve him of the responsibility of leadership. . . . The growth and development of all . . . institutions depends on the initiative of (those) . . . who are not content merely to keep the public satisfied with things as they are."

Opinion measurement has been used by a few pioneer practitioners for decades, but extensive utilization of this tool has been a fairly recent development in public relations. American Telephone & Telegraph, one of the longest and most imaginative users of opinion research, set up an opinion research unit of its own in 1929. Since that time, this organization has been developing improved survey methods and assisting Bell subsidiaries with their own studies. These Bell polls have varied widely in scope and purpose. All have been aimed at facts about customer opinions, employee opinions, and public opinions needed for current operations and policy decisions. Since 1946, Bell has conducted periodically a Customer Attitude Trend Study and since 1949, all the Associated Operating Companies have been conducting their own trend surveys. Early in its experience, Bell's opinion researchers learned:

1. That customers were willing to give their opinions when asked.
2. That the information the company got by going directly to the customers made sense.
3. That this information was useful to public relations and operating telephone people.

Generally, extensive use of opinion polls and attitude surveys in public relations has accelerated since World War II. The trend is growing. This is illustrated in the intensive use made of polling by political leaders—Richard Nixon, Lyndon B. Johnson, Hubert Humphrey and others. Too often, however, no one thinks of a poll until an emergency develops, such as an airline crash in the neighborhood of an airport. When such crises arise—and if there is still time—a poll can be used to define clearly the problem and to suggest its solution. A poll can reveal who is angry, who is not, who has the correct information, and who is off base. It can demonstrate the relationships of information, misinformation, and dominant attitudes. It will isolate urges and identify motives. It may indicate the positive and negative symbols to which people will react in a given situation. Usually time does not permit crisis polls. Opinion research is most productive when used as a guide to long-range plans and for improving communication techniques.

CASE PROBLEM

Let's assume that you are serving as director of public relations of your college or university. The president has accepted an invitation to give the main talk at the annual alumni banquet during commencement week. He asks you to prepare a 30-minute speech (approximately 10 typewritten pages) on "The Crisis Facing Higher Education Today." To carry out this assignment, you must:

1. Define your audience;
2. Determine themes to implement present and long-range objectives;
3. Assemble factual content through research;
4. Outline the suggested speech preparatory to a conference with the president on theme, tone, content, and so forth;
5. Write the speech.

ADDITIONAL READING

ROBERT O. CARLSON, "Public Relations Research—Problems and Prospects," *Public Relations Journal*, Vol. 26, May, 1970. A realistic view.

WILLIAM P. EHLING, "Public Relations Research: A Few Fundamentals," *College and University Journal*, Vol. 1, Fall, 1962.

CHARLES Y. GLOCK, ed., *Survey Research in the Social Sciences.* New York: The Russell Sage Foundation, 1967.

PIERRE MARTINEAU, "It's Time to Research the Consumer," *Harvard Business Review,* Vol. 33, July-August, 1955.

RALPH O. NAFZIGER and DAVID M. WHITE, eds., *Introduction to Mass Communications Research.* Baton Rouge: Louisiana State University Press, rev. ed., 1963. The chapter on "Field Methods in Communication Research" is especially helpful.

EARL NEWSOM, ROBERT O. CARLSON, and LEONARD KNOTT, "Feedback: Putting Public Relations in Reverse," in Dan J. Fenn, ed., *Management's Mission in a New Society.* New York: McGraw Hill, 1959.

EDWARD J. ROBINSON, *Public Relations and Survey Research.* New York: Appleton, 1969. Useful guide, with examples; subsidized by the Foundation for Public Relations Research and Education.

WILBUR SCHRAMM, ed., *The Science of Human Communication.* New York: Basic Books, Inc., 1963.

CLAIRE SELLTIZ, MARIE JAHODA, et al., *Research Methods in Social Relations.* New York: Holt, Rinehart & Winston, Inc., 1962.

CHAPTER 9

THE PROCESS: PLANNING AND PROGRAMMING— THE SECOND STEP

Planning requires a searching look backward, a deep look inside, a wide look around, and a long, long look ahead. Programming puts plans into a structure for action.

The second step in the process is laying plans. Once a particular problem is defined, then comes the decision of what to do about it. Effective plans, when they reach the action phase, become effective programming. As public relations matures, more emphasis is put on planning. Lack of thorough planning often leads into wheel-spinning busywork or into defensive spur-of-the-moment projects. Harried, hasty planning is makeshift at best. In times of crisis it tends to produce negative results. Prudent, long-range planning is more likely to result in:

1. An integrated program in which the total effort results in definite accomplishments toward specific goals.
2. Increased management participation and support.
3. A program emphasis that is positive rather than defensive.
4. Unhurried deliberation on choice of themes, timing, and tactics.

Planning is based on adequate fact-finding and the common-sense idea that people ought to know where they are going if they are trying to get somewhere. Even though the values of a planned program are clearly evident, there is still too little emphasis on this step. A survey made in Columbus, Ohio, found that only 53 percent of the practitioners were being guided by written objectives.[1] These appear to be the main obstacles to public relations planning:

1. Failure of management to include the practitioner in deliberations that lead to policies and programs.
2. Lack of clearly agreed upon objectives for implementing the public relations program.
3. Lack of time, which is stolen by the pressures of meeting daily problems.
4. The frustrations and delays which practitioners encounter in the endless task of internal clearance and coordination with other departments.

[1] William Carter Moore, "A Critical Analysis of Public Relations Practitioners in a Midwestern Metropolitan Area," unpublished master's thesis, Ohio State University, 1962. Brief summary of this study is found in "Testing a Test City for a Public Relations Profile," by Moore and Walter W. Seifert, *Public Relations Journal*, Vol. 18, September, 1962.

5. The practitioner's faith in the ultimate value of getting publicity as it develops in the organization day by day.

These obstacles block or distort planned programming in too many organizations despite the increased urgency in today's complex world to plan ahead. One of the nation's largest public relations programs underwent a public relations audit. Among the findings:

> Response and reaction are the key words in describing Blank's primary public information efforts. The news media, individuals, and organizations generate a steady demand for information—over 100 queries a day. Responsiveness is essential. . . . Emphasis on rapid response precludes an orderly, well-organized procedure to develop full story ideas or to plan comprehensive coverage. . . . What Blank does, where it centers its efforts and energies, is determined by activities and pressures external to it. . . . Coordinated planning to marshal total information resources of the public relations staff does not now occur within Blank's.

This situation in a large organization with a long-standing program is more typical than atypical.

In the business world, neglect of adequate public relations planning and programming reflects lack of full acceptance of corporate planning. A study of corporate planning in forty major corporations found: [2] "Organized corporate planning appears to be in its early stages of evolution, and it has not gained as high a stature or recognition in the organization as has been commonly assumed. Neither corporate nor operating managers have fully accepted formal planning as part of their job. . . . Corporate management is participating very little at the stage where plans are being prepared. . . . There has been some change in the direction of greater acceptance. . . ." The stakes riding on management decisions in today's volatile changing world will speed this trend. Yet this study found that only twenty-eight of the forty companies had formal planning documents. Planning will not eliminate risks, but it better insures an organization taking the right risks. The fact remains that planning—a formidable, amorphous, integral part of management—is hard to come to grips with. One practitioner observes: [3] "The biggest problem in planning a . . . program lies in the fact that public relations encompasses a whole universe of varied activities. . . . It is this nature of the beast—its unlimited possibilities—that sometimes causes its failure." Increased emphasis on "management-by-objective" puts like emphasis on public relations planning.

[2] Kjell-Arne Ringbakk, "Organized Corporate Planning Systems," unpublished Ph.D. thesis, University of Wisconsin, 1968, pp. 184–186.

[3] Richard R. Conarroe, "How to Plan and Organize a Public Relations Program," *Public Relations Quarterly,* Vol. 12, Summer, 1967. Helpful article.

The value of systematic planning was brilliantly demonstrated when the United States undertook to put men on the moon in less than a decade's time. This same comprehensive systems approach can be applied to the nation's social problems or to an organization's problems. George Hammond, a veteran counselor, isolated and identified the synergical elements of the space program which he thinks can be imaginatively applied to all planning:

1. Exhaustive study of every aspect of the problem in which all factors which led to situation under review are determined.
2. Determination of available resources to meet the need and of the source and amount of additional resources.
3. Acceptance of the magnitude of the task and commitment of the expense and time required for it.
4. An adequate organization fully staffed by specialists.
5. Determination to avoid short cuts or unrealistic schedules.
6. Passion for perfection by every participant.
7. Protection for human life at all costs.
8. Ability to learn from mistakes and rebound from failure.

Planning requires:

1. *A searching look backward*—to determine all the factors which led to the situation under study.
2. *A deep look inside*—in which the assembled facts and opinions are considered in the light of the institution's objectives and their validity weighed.
3. *A wide look around*—in which there is study of like situations in like organizations; political, social, and economic trends; and the mood of the times.
4. *A long, long look ahead*—in which goals for the organization and for implementing the program are set.

Where public relations is newly established, planning starts with the realistic aims of the organization. It encompasses a determination of goals, of strategy, of tactics. It sets up objectives, or targets, at close and long range. It decides between preventive and remedial activities in specific situations and works toward an atmosphere that is as nearly preventive all the way through as possible. Then there is the *staffing* and the *action* or follow-through to implement the plans.

A public relations firm that specializes in political campaigns once set down this outline:

While there is no master blueprint which can be followed in successive campaigns, there is a fairly definite table of contents. This applies to each plan of a campaign, and serves as a guide in drafting it. Here are some of the major requisites:

1. Careful delineation of the strategy which will be followed and of the steps which will be taken in the development of that strategy, so that the action moves with precision and reaches its peak of impact in the closing days before election.

2. Thorough appraisal and development of all the principal issues of the campaign and agreement on the relative importance to be given each issue. This keeps the focus of public interest on the objectives and issues which have the most widespread appeal.

3. A complete outline of all the organizational aspects of the campaign—the foundation and framework for the vast volunteer organization which will man the battle lines and carry the crusade personally to the voters.

4. Detailed plans for the use of all media—campaign pamphlets, newspaper and magazine advertising, direct mail, radio and television, billboards, moving pictures, newsreels, "literature" of all types.

Note the sequence of planning, programming, and action.[4]

A BACKDROP OF IDEALS AND AIMS

Without ideals to form standards of perfection, there would be no important incentive toward the things that make up what we call "progress." Without some definite, attainable goals, there obviously would be little advancement. People would concentrate on procuring the bare necessities. They would not seek to better their own lives or to help others. Thus, our constant process of linking ideals and goals gives promise of a better tomorrow. The process provides us both purpose and direction and imparts a certain drama to day-by-day living.

Organizations as well as individuals have ideals and goals. As a preface to the planning that goes into the organizational process, it is important to recognize these underlying motivations.

---

[4] For detailed examples of planning in political public relations, see: Harold Lavine, ed., *Smoke Filled Rooms, The Confidential Papers of Robert Humphreys* (Englewood Cliffs, N.J., Prentice-Hall, Inc., 1970). Contains the Republicans' 1952 campaign plan. Also, American Institute for Political Communication, *A Study of Political Strategy and Tactics* (Washington, D.C., the Institute, 1967). Discusses plans used in several campaigns.

To gain rewards.
To be meaningfully engaged and to help others.
To be supported within the organization.
To be respected within the community.
To deliver a necessary and a wanted product or service.
To be free from needless outside restraints.
To have an influence on public opinion.

Problems involving an organization's public relationships, including breakdowns in communication, relate readily to one or another of these basic aims. In a business, for example, a common problem is economic distress. Sales drop, or something else, causes earnings to slip. The business, in that case, is not *gaining rewards,* and its people are not *meaningfully engaged.*

In social welfare work, a problem arises if a charity cannot get volunteer workers to help solicit funds in the annual campaign. In that case, the undertaking is not *being supported within the organization.* For a military post, a problem exists if the residents in the neighborhood resent it as an intrusion. In such a situation, the military is not *respected within the community.* Or, if Congressional action were pending to ban women from military service, the organization would not be *free from needless outside restraints.*

In the perspective of an organization's basic aims, the specific problems threatening, or able to threaten, should be isolated for study. Three preliminary steps should be taken:

1. Determine by analysis the policy makers' attitudes toward publics with whom communication or understanding has broken down or failed to materialize.
2. Determine, with equal care, attitudes of the publics toward the organization.
3. Block out the areas of common agreement and common interest or of disagreement and strife. Work from these areas in devising a program to iron out differences and soothe hostilities.

The way in which planning and programming are integrated into an organization's work is illustrated in the program of the Skandia Group of insurance companies headquartered in Stockholm. A flow chart diagramming Skandia's public relations programming is on page 219. Rightly, all plans and implementing programs are geared to advancing the organization's purpose—sale of insurance through its forty-eight companies. A basic policy is stated to recapitulate the standards, to govern the decisions it makes, and to define the scope of the organization's actions. Within the broad organizational policy, a public relations policy must be agreed upon.

Skandia Public Relations Programming

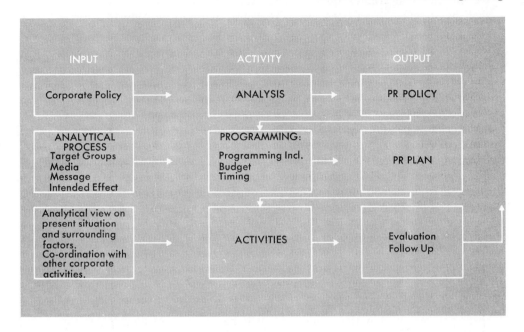

Analytical Matrix for Skandia Public Relations Programming

ANALYTICAL MATRIX FOR SKANDIA PUBLIC RELATIONS PROGRAMMING						
TARGET GROUP	INFORMATION INTEREST (most receptive to . . .)	INTENDED EFFECT (reaction or relation effect)	MESSAGE (policy and image values)	MEDIA (established and possible)	PRIORITY (long range or short term, permanent or temporary)	ACTIVITIES (rough outline)

Here is Skandia's: "The corporate image shall chiefly bear the impress of the Group's concern for quality, efficiency, and resources. Great weight shall be attached to an open and consistently pursued personnel-information program, and also to good and flexible channels of communication between the Group's different units." Within these policies Skandia is continuously engaged in planning and programming. This starts with the analysis, based on its fact-finding and feedback as indicated in the flow chart. Next comes determination of audience target groups, message to be conveyed, intended effect of message, media to be used, and budget necessary for implementing the plan with a program of action and communication. The matrix used in formulating plans and programs is shown on page 219. Timing is important in the program. Actions taken are then subjected to evaluation, and this leads to new analyses and new plans. The public relations wheel never stops turning. Through these systematic procedures, Skandia has developed an effective public relations program.

STRATEGY AND TACTICS

Planning takes two general directions. One is concerned with long-range programs to achieve the mission. These are defined by the institution's basic policies. Within this framework will be fitted short-term plans for specific projects. It is important to keep the short-range programming subordinate to the long-range plans.

The initial fact-finding and analysis compares with the "intelligence" function in the military. The planning compares with the strategy and tactics of a military campaign. Long-range planning relates to broad outlines of strategy, short-term projects to the tactics that make the strategy work. All are interrelated. Strategy is a master plan for winning a campaign. Tactics cover skillful use of tools and techniques in winning the several battles that make a campaign.

Long-term planning jells in decisions on ultimate aims. Although aims are usually couched in broad phrases, one must guard against the tendency to permit them to become vague, vaporous generalities. Sometimes these are formalized as a "Five Year Plan" or established as a basis for annual executive evaluation against specific goals or as qualification for income increase or promotion. John Budd maintains "Creative people, like public relations practitioners, need a solid, firmly oriented foundation for their planning. They look to management for this consistency of purpose. *Formulation of aims is the task of management with aid from its communications specialists.*"

Within the framework of organizational policies and long-range planning comes the implementation. For example, The Parker Pen Company, as one of its basic policies, supports the idea of free-flowing world trade. Long-range planning looks to the day when the markets of the world will be open equally to the pen makers of the world. Meantime, to dramatize the desirability of this ultimate aim, projects in the company's home community have included a "Peso Pay Day" for employees, a "Path of Nations" across the front of its plant, and a World Trade Fiesta in the community. This programming pursues the company's long-range goal by keeping attention focused on the basic policy.

Parker officials found in its free trade theme the guide to solving a difficult problem: How does a relatively small company compete with the giants of industry in an extravaganza like The New York World's Fair? After two years of planning talks, the firm set down these criteria which had to be met: tie-in with the fair theme, "Peace Through Understanding"; people-participation rather than just people-observation; involvement of non-fairgoers, too; an exhibit and pavilion that related to its primary business—selling pens. Parker's theme became "Peace Through Understanding . . . Through Writing," and it launched the biggest international letter-writing exchange ever attempted, using a computer to store and carefully match hundreds of thousands of names. Called the Parker Penfriend program, the company's dealers from all over the world helped collect names and thus won traffic to their stores by providing a welcome service. First, letters were written in Parker's pavilion at the Fair, which became a catalyst for Parker to gain attention and involvement, plus contributing in its modest way to world understanding.

The advantages of having definite public relations objectives and carefully planned projects to advance them is shown in the results Parker obtained. For less than one-million dollars—a fraction of what many competing exhibits cost—Parker lured more than three-million persons to its pavilion, got one and one-half-million persons to participate in the Penfriend program, and obtained world-wide publicity. The project won a PRSA Silver Anvil Award, and *Time* rated it as one of the thirteen best exhibits in the Fair.

TWO KINDS OF PLANNING

There are fundamentally two types of programs—preventive and remedial. In the past there has been too much remedial public relations—too much occasion for it—and too little preventive. Quite often, a matter calling for remedial action provides the spark that touches off preventive planning for the future. More than one public relations department has been born in a time of crisis.[5] Making good to consumers for a faulty lot of merchandise is a remedial action most manufacturers have experienced at one time or another. Usually that experience constitutes so much of a threat that plans are initiated for immediate corrective action. Controls—such as increased quality control checkpoints in the manufacturing process and periodic surveys that will provide early detection—are installed to minimize chances of a recurrence. The relationship of fact-finding and opinion surveys to planning can be seen in the following examples.

Some time ago the number of complaints about service began to increase in the Niagara Mohawk Power Corporation. On the recommendation of the public relations staff, an opinion and attitude study was conducted throughout the company's 24,000-square-mile territory. The study was divided into two parts: Part I was a "group dynamics" session of housewives and their husbands meeting in small groups in informal home settings to discuss the topic of service; Part II was a stratified random sample survey of all major markets served by the utility. These studies showed that many customers were not satisfied with the utility's office contact personnel, but that they had high opinions of its repairmen.

In response to the survey results, the company set up a committee composed of representatives of public relations, customer accounting, service, and office personnel to study customer service relations and to recommend changes needed. "This committee developed a three-point plan of action: (1) A training program for new contact representatives; (2) A follow-up training course for experienced representatives; (3) An observation center to maintain quality control in cooperation with the New York Telephone Company in Syracuse so that the quality of customer service could be observed and graded." [6] The program resulted in a decline in complaints and the grading of 90 percent of observed calls as "pleasant and helpful."

Counselor John Moynahan believes research is best utilized by public relations in planning, programming, mapping strategy, and validating audiences. Some years ago, his agency was counsel to a large bank with many branches. Signs appeared that the bank was encountering public relations problems with ethnic groups in its service area. One area, for example, had changed from predominantly white to predominantly black without the bank's taking cognizance of this shift. Moynahan persuaded the bank to retain a Columbia University sociologist to conduct field research to de-

[5] For examples of "crisis" public relations, see "Shock Treatment for Parke, Davis," *Fortune*, Vol. 48, September, 1953; "Ford's Fight for First," *Fortune*, Vol. 50, September, 1954; John Brooks, "The Edsel," *New Yorker*, Part I, November 26, 1960; Part II, December 3, 1960; Maj. Richard F. Abel, "Bad News—And How to Survive It," *Public Relations Journal*, Vol. 24, July, 1968.

[6] Robert H. Wells, "School for Courtesy," *Public Relations Journal*, Vol. 25, January, 1969.

termine various ethnic factors which were strongly influencing the bank's relations with the area it served. When Moynahan presented the findings, the bank officials were persuaded to make major changes in the personnel hiring policies of the bank.[7]

One city's United Givers-Red Feather organization failed to meet its fund-raising goal three years in a row. On advice of counsel, it sponsored an opinion survey. This poll revealed, among other things, that many persons thought that the agency's new headquarters were much too large and luxurious. Most of this criticism was based on the erroneous belief that only the United Givers staff occupied the building. A corrective campaign to publicize the fact that this building provided offices for many of the Red Feather agencies was planned and undertaken. This included placing on the front lawn a large sign listing all agencies headquartered in the building. As the result of this and other information projects planned on the basis of the survey, the organization's fund drive went over the top the next year.

CHECKLIST FOR PLANNING

Planning, its detail and procedures, too often appear an abstract, academic sort of business. It can be overorganized and thus become quite theoretical. It can also lead to rigidity. Informal planning is realistic but its danger lies in ignoring the necessity of planning altogether. There are a number of yardsticks that serve to measure programs or projects before they go into action. Well-planned programs should be:

1. *Sincere* in purpose and execution.
2. *Durable* and in keeping with organization's purpose and character.
3. *Firm* and positive in approach and appeals.
4. *Comprehensive* in scope and continuous in application.
5. *Clear and symbolic,* with simple messages.
6. *Beneficial* to both the sender and the receiver of the messages.

In planning a program to advance organizational goals, it is important that the content be devised so that it tells—over a period of time—the institution's history, ideals, and achievements; publicizes its people, its policies, and its products or services; and projects its plans for a better tomorrow. Unless such yardsticks are used periodically, emphasis is apt to

---

[7] Willard Bailey, "The Role of Behavioral Sciences in Public Relations Practice," unpublished master's thesis, Ohio State University, 1967.

become disjointed under exigencies of the moment. *To touch all bases, program content must be planned and devised.*

Computer technology can be utilized to keep information programs on the track. In the mid-60s, PR Data developed a system called Public Relations Electronic Planning and Review, or PREPAR for short. This was developed not as a measurement device, but as a means of controlling flow of specific messages to specific audiences. Mutual of New York, an insurance company, used PREPAR and later modified it to specifically relate output to input of clippings and to document the efficiency of the public relations staff. This output-input analysis enables the department to relate manpower investment to results. For example, one analysis showed that a week's work spent in sending stories on a manager's conference to 283 publications brought only 23 clips. This type story was abandoned. With computer data, MONY can determine the number of messages in each newsclip, the cost per thousand of stories printed, the program balance represented in publicity output and obtained, and the percentage of messages reaching targeted audiences.

PLANNING AND BUDGETING

Planning and budgeting for public relations go hand in hand. To prepare a budget for the next year, the department must plan ahead, and plans cannot be implemented without a supporting budget. Systematic budget-making requires planning in *advance* instead of on the spur of the moment. However, flexibility must be provided to enable a staff to capitalize on opportunities that cannot be foreseen. Budgets provide means of relating objectives with plans as these are shaped and limited by funds available. A sound budget includes all phases of management planning and results in a unified, agreed upon plan of action.[8]

Some organizations determine public relations budgets on a fixed formula, such as a percentage of sales. Others fix budgets on the basis of management objectives. The latter is preferable. The budgeting-planning process can best be illustrated in describing how the Caterpillar Tractor Co. plans and budgets to achieve the objectives stated in Chapter 7:

1. The process of management by objectives begins with an analysis of problems and needs by the leadership of the organization. In about August or September, Caterpillar's president defines *areas* for objective setting by management—in terms of over-all corporate

[8] For procedures, see: Robert H. Herrick, "Planning and Budgeting—Siamese Twins of Public Relations," *Public Relations Journal*, Vol. 17, January, 1961, pp. 14–15.

concerns such as: factory efficiency, sales, employment stabilization, return on investment, personnel development, safety, equal employment opportunity, scrap, etc.

2. Against this background, Caterpillar plants and departments around the world set objectives for the year ahead. These objectives are expected to meet the following criteria:

   (a) They should be profit or improvement-oriented.

   (b) They should be clearly defined and specific.

   (c) They should be practical and attainable.

   (d) They should be measurable.

3. The public relations function [which at Caterpillar is termed "public affairs"] is no exception to this process. Public affairs objectives are, therefore, expected to be *responsive* to the needs of the corporation . . . and *integrated* into its future plans.

4. When public affairs objectives have been completed and discussed with the appropriate corporate officers, a budget for the department is constructed.

5. The budget is then subjected to searching scrutiny by the president's office—which at Caterpillar includes the president and the two executive vice presidents. Out of this process, one or more of the following can result:

   (a) The objectives and accompanying budget may be accepted as is.

   (b) Flaws may be discovered in the objectives and/or in the projected costs of achieving these objectives.

   (c) Even if objectives and projected costs are not flawed, it could nevertheless be the case that the over-all program—though excellent—must be adjusted downward to suit business conditions and future prospects.

6. The budget is then adjusted as necessary. At Caterpillar, there is no attempt to build a continuing ratio or relationship between the public affairs budget and sales figures. If budget adjustments have been substantial, it is possible that some adjustment may also have to be made in objectives.

7. Out of the preceding, then, there evolves a set of objectives and projected costs for the year ahead that are responsive to corporate needs and appropriate to business conditions and prospects.

8. The technique of "flexible budgeting" is used . . . which is to say that, as time passes, the department head may seek a variance in the form of an increase or a decrease in order to do the best possible job of managing the public relations function in the light of current events.

9. The last step is that of follow up. In that connection, the Public Affairs Department is required to submit a brief monthly report commenting on the attainment or non-attainment of objectives, and the resultant effect on costs.

THE PRACTITIONER'S ROLE

The role of the counselor or staff director in executing programs is well established. His role at the earlier stages of fact-finding, analysis, and planning is not so clearly defined nor firmly founded. Ideally, he serves as *analyst* in the investigating phase and as *initiator and adviser* in the planning phase. Once the program and its projects move into action, he becomes *advocate.*

There are two reasons that stand out above all others why the practitioner should participate in the preliminary as well as the action stages. *First,* it is here that he brings the public's needs, desires, and opinions to bear on the policy-making process. He cannot later sell the organization to its publics if the organization's officials are deaf to what those publics think and feel. *Second,* only by participation in the planning can he fully understand and interpret fundamental policies. *No one can effectively explain or execute something that he himself does not understand;* it makes little difference how skillful or adroit he may be. Without such understanding, his efforts to translate are likely to be vague. Possibly they may not even relate to basic goals.

In actual practice, the practitioner is often confined to implementing plans with publicity. Often in the larger organizations, he cools his heels in the outer office while a major policy decision is formulated. He is called in and given a ten-minute briefing on the decision with a completely subjective analysis of why it was the "right" decision. Then he is told, in effect: "Now, you get your gang to explain to employees and the press why this decision was the right one, so that we'll get the credit we deserve." Obviously, in such cases the practitioner is, and is expected to be, simply a paid apologist.

Odom Fanning illustrates the consequences of this. A group of university experimenters were studying underwater explosions in a government-sponsored research project, but no plans had been made to explain to residents in the nearby-off-campus area that these would not be dangerous explosions. One night the scientists worked late. Their explosions shook the neighborhood, rattling windows and knocking pictures off walls. The alarmed neighbors called police. In due time the neighbors' fears were replaced by irritation at the university. For months the university's public relations director had urged the president to adopt an emergency plan in connection with this research project but to no avail. The president kept insisting, "We'll handle each emergency as it comes along." Fanning observes: [9]

[9] In "Planning and Candor—Key Words in an Emergency," *Public Relations Journal*, Vol. 17, March, 1961.

The president didn't realize that a lack of public relations planning on his part was accompanied by a widespread lack of public relations appreciation on the part of faculty and staff. So he discovered what many an executive in colleges, in industry, and in the government could have told him: Years of excellent public relations can be toppled in a moment under the stress of an emergency.

PROPER INDOCTRINATION

When a continuing program has been jelled at the policy level, it becomes necessary and desirable to indoctrinate the top echelons of executives in what is to follow. Otherwise, these important collaborators may wind up uninformed, like the counselor who is not allowed to participate in the planning. They would not be able to do their part nor would they be able to translate its importance into support from the people under their supervision.

The mechanical process of indoctrinating an organization is actually a test of personal skill in persuasion and coordinating. In this connection, some generally accepted tenets merit noting.

Starting with the top echelon of an organization, the basic problems should be explained in terms of the harm that can be done if they are left unattended. Then, the immediate remedial measures should be explained in relation to the long-term plans. The use of similar case examples is often very helpful. Surveys should be relied on to substantiate the plans. Personal opinion should be eliminated except as it applies to special knowledge already possessed. The program should be related to the climate in which the organization operates and hopes to enjoy in the future. It should be stressed that the activities to be undertaken will have a profound ultimate effect on public opinion. Explanations should be short and to the point. The practitioner should be *decisive,* a quality highly respected by managers and administrators.

Having gained the understanding and support of the top echelon, the next group to be tackled is that upper level of the organization in which executive collaboration for news preparation and the like is necessary. Such collaboration can best be acquired through informal sessions in which individuals can air their views and talk things out. Quite often meetings are arranged where the practitioner presents the programming then throws open the meeting to discussion. Where this is done, a summary should be supplied afterward to all participants in the discussion. This can take the form of meeting minutes, a program timetable, a roster of projects, or a brochure explaining the plans. It is important for the future relationship that the programming agreed upon be a matter of record. Getting it down on paper tends to put the details in the right places.

For an example of the whole process, assume that the A.B.C. Manufacturing Company, makers of parachutes, has decided to convert from the use of nylon to a new type of material called *Chemthin*. It is claimed to be better and is known to be lighter in weight and bulk. The raw materials for it are in free supply.

Assume, too, that the conversion idea originated years earlier. At that time the organization learned that the weight and bulk of standard parachutes was a source of concern to military officialdom and flight personnel alike. Consequently, a specific research program was activated. Chemthin was created and engineered by the A.B.C. Company as a private undertaking.

The prospect of introducing the new material posed problems involving relationships between the company and the military, the suppliers, the parents of flight personnel, and others. Long before the fabric was ready, the public relations man or woman presented a carefully planned program of information and events. These were devised to gain a sympathetic understanding from certain publics and the enthusiastic support of others. The program was approved.

Indoctrination of the organization followed. The plans were explained down the line from executives through supervisors to employees in the offices and shops. Auxiliary channels of information were used. A letter went from the president to each employee's home. Everybody in the organization, by being fully informed, became a front-line participant in the conversion.

Next, the practitioner opened the communication gate a bit wider. This might have been planned to happen in a rapid succession of events and news releases requiring no more than a working day or two for the full range. Or, it might have been planned to fan slowly out, first to the community, then to the national level.

In the dissemination of information externally, there were three basic components: (1) news, (2) media to carry the messages, (3) funds and staff adequate to get the job done.

Continuing the example, assume that it was agreed the informative phase should tell a story of research, product refinement, quality, durability, and safety. It was to emphasize that the company's action was in the public interest because it contributed to the national defense effort. The arrangements for external communication might have looked like this on paper.

Note that the specific target publics were those most keenly affected by what A.B.C. was doing: soldiers and parents concerned about safety, stockholders who bore the financial risk of the change, hometown residents whose livelihoods were linked with the ebb and flow of A.B.C.'s business, new suppliers whose materials would now be needed by A.B.C., and military officials and the general public shouldering the expense of the national defense effort.

TABLE 9-1

COMMUNICATION VEHICLE	IMMEDIATE PURPOSE
First, a statement to the home town press.	To relieve any anxiety about the community's economic security due to the changeover.
Second, a statement to the national press.	To confirm publicly that the move served the national interest as well as private interests.
Third, a special letter to the shareholders of A.B.C. Company.	To reaffirm the confidence of investors in the stability of the company.
Fourth, special magazine articles telling about the development of Chemthin.	To impress on segments of the general public the safety and quality features of the product; to establish leadership.
Fifth, an A.B.C. Hardship Committee.	To deal with employee hardship cases due to temporary layoffs during conversion.
Sixth, a plant visit by military officials.	To point up the progress of conversion and to identify activities with the defense effort.
Seventh, a booklet on Chemthin.	To reassure soldiers, parents of soldiers, educators, scientists, students, and others who might inquire.
Eighth, an open house on completion of conversion.	To demonstrate the benefits to the community and to reaffirm the interdependence of company and community.
Ninth, public demonstrations of the finished product.	To prove the safety, quality, and value aspects of Chemthin.

THE TIMETABLE CAN MAKE THE DIFFERENCE

It will be apparent from a re-examination of the program just outlined that the chronology was deliberate, not accidental. One reason is that people rebel against any sudden change of drastic proportion without some kind of reassurance that everything is going to be all right. Mental digestion leading to acceptance of change is normally a gradual process in human nature. A second reason is that communication, to obtain a desired reaction, should move out in waves from its original source. It should preserve, insofar as possible, its original form and integrity. It should be accurate. The normal path of information is from those most intimately involved to those who are only incidentally interested. A third reason is that news or advertising naturally follows the logical sequence of happenings.

TIMING IS A KEY ELEMENT

The several elements of a program, such as Chemthin's, must be spaced and timed to produce the desired effect at exactly the right time. In political campaigns the strategists and practitioners strive to bring enthusiasm and support for their candidates and their cause to a peak the weekend before Tuesday's voting. Like timing is sought in fund-raising campaigns. However, such plans cannot be made in a vacuum. They must be related to the total situation in which actions and communication will take place.

The calendar offers many opportunities for positive timing. For example, the public relations director of Atlanta's schools wanted to get the public's attention focused on the serious school-dropout problem. She prepared a documentary entitled, "The Ghost Story—School Dropouts," and it was broadcast on Halloween night. Shrewd timing is also used to smother a story rather than have it spotlighted, or to smother an opponent's story. Franklin D. Roosevelt, probably coached by Louis M. Howe, in 1932 held the hearings on the ouster of Mayor Jimmy Walker of New York the same day that Herbert Hoover was accepting the Republican nomination. The Walker hearings, highly sensational, overshadowed the Hoover story on the nation's front pages.

Here are some other examples: A leading manufacturer of home appliances took advantage of the news lull on Christmas Day to announce a sharp price cut effective January 1. Many a husband eyeing a shiny appliance by the Christmas tree and thinking of the higher price he had paid, was resentful. Many said so. A leading steel firm announced that it was boosting the price of steel $4.00 a ton because of increased labor costs. Forty-eight hours later, it released its annual report boasting of record profits. The coincidence of these two announcements brought public criticism that should have been expected. The time of the annual report was fixed. The price boost could have been delayed for a better psychological time. A few years ago the DuPont Company announced grants of nearly one million dollars to over 100 universities and colleges. This laudable act of corporate citizenship should have brought DuPont much favorable publicity. But the news was smothered. It was released the same day that the Ford Foundation announced a $500-million grant to educational institutions and hospitals. The public plaudits went to the Ford Foundation.

One of the many valuable guides that practitioners have learned from social science research is that *"Change in attitude is more likely to occur if the suggestion is accompanied by change in other factors underlying belief and attitude."* It is obvious that *the more we can make the environment give credence to our communication, the more likelihood there is of our message being accepted.* It is equally important to avoid, if we can, contradictions of our communication current in the environment in which they are received. Wilbur Schramm sums up implications of research on this factor in communications: [10]

---

[10] In *The Process and Effects of Mass Communication* (Urbana: University of Illinois Press, 1954) p. 214. A useful volume of readings edited by Schramm.

In general, (a) if we can make our messages appeal to individual
needs and wants, (b) if we can provide or point out social support for the
desired attitudes, (c) if we can *introduce our messages at such a time as
will let them be reinforced by related events,* (d) if we can point out or
provide a channel for action along the line of the desired attitude, and if
we can eliminate so far as possible or point out ways of surmounting the
barriers to such action—then we can be as confident as possible . . . of
accomplishing what we want to accomplish with our suggestion.

PLANNING FOR DISASTERS

It is usually possible to time an open house so that it will not conflict with
local events. It is usually possible to announce a decision of national significance at a time when it will not be crowded off the front pages and the
airways.

There is one type of event which cannot be forecast—a catastrophe.
But it can be planned for. Every institution and industry is subject to the
fate of a disaster and should plan accordingly. When it happens, time is
a key element in the handling of communication. There is no time to plan
cautiously and carefully a program of information. Plans made far in advance for calamity procedure must go into action. The on-the-spot planning, which would normally be given weeks, must be crammed into a few
minutes or a few hours at most.

Standard Oil Company of Indiana experienced disaster at its Whiting, Indiana, refinery years ago, when a hydroformer unit exploded.
Fragments of steel killed a boy, injured his brother, and smashed into
nearby houses. In the refinery, steel fragments tore into storage tanks.
Crude oil was soon ablaze in a 10-acre area. The fires lasted for eight days.
Smooth, skilled handling of the events which followed the explosion and
fires brought the company public understanding and its PR staff praise and
awards. The underlying policies called for *consideration* for those affected
and for complete *cooperation* with news media. The PR staff had *planned*
for just such an emergency and thus was prepared to act swiftly.[11]

Its first "Procedure for Reporting News of Serious Fires and Other
Unusual Emergencies" was drafted in 1947. It has been revised periodically since that time. After outlining the procedure for reporting such emergencies to management and to public relations officials—including names,
phone numbers, home addresses, and so forth, in sequence, the SO memo,
as last revised, carried this policy statement:

---

[11] John Canning, "The Whiting Fire, a Case History in Disaster PR," *Proceedings, Fourth
Annual Minnesota Public Relations Forum* (Minneapolis: Minnesota Chapter PRSA, 1955).
Also see John T. Hall, "A Fire Made Them Famous," *Public Relations Journal,* Vol 11,
July, 1955.

The general policy will be to receive all press and radio representatives courteously and to do everything possible to facilitate their getting the objective facts regarding the fire or accident.

Watchmen in particular should be courteous at such a time. They will generally be the first company representatives with whom reporters and photographers will have contact.

When press representatives ask watchmen at Refinery gates for permission to enter the Plant, as they always do at such a time, watchmen will tell them as politely as possible that watchmen do not have authority to grant such permission. They will suggest that for official information they go to the emergency press headquarters in the Personnel Office Section, Industrial Relations Div. Bldg., 1915 Front St., Whiting.

Reporters and photographers are not to be permitted inside the Refinery during emergencies.

There is to be no company interference with reporters and photographers at work outside Refinery fences. So far as our company is concerned, photographers have a right to take photographs from public highways, railroad property, and the like. Employees, particularly watchmen, are not to expose film or confiscate camera when photographers are working on property which does not belong to our company and is not inside Refinery fences.

Our representatives will not do any guessing or speculation. They will state only established facts.

In regard to monetary damages, they will make no statement until one has been authorized by the head of the Refinery or one of his superiors. . . . To inquiries regarding the cause they will reply with only such information as is clearly correct. Whenever the cause is in doubt, they will courteously request inquirers to defer their questions until there has been time to gather more information.

In proceeding cautiously in such matters, company representatives are to use their common sense and to be neither overly conservative nor too ready to jump to conclusions.

Whenever it is evident that the reporter is trying to make a sensation out of the incident, to represent danger or loss as being much greater than it is, our representatives are to endeavor tactfully to make him see the facts in their correct proportion. This is particularly necessary in case of oil fires, which are usually spectacular and look more dangerous than they usually turn out to be.

Despite the value of such plans, organizations continue to get caught flat-footed when disaster strikes. Such lack of foresight was demonstrated when three astronauts were burned to death while testing a space capsule in January, 1967. A critic of NASA's handling of this tragedy wrote: [12]

---

[12] James Skardon, "The Apollo Story: What the Watchdogs Missed," *Columbia Journalism Review*, Vol. 6, Fall, 1967, pp. 13–14. Also see his second article, "The Apollo Story: The Concealed Patterns," same publication, Vol. 6, Winter, 1967–68.

. . . there were no reporters or correspondents from any media on hand at Cape Kennedy when the fire broke out. . . . The question of informing the public . . . was thus left entirely to the institutional machinations of NASA. The agency reacted predictably. It not only shut down all lines of communication, but, either by accident or design, issued statements that proved to be erroneous.

Although NASA knew within five minutes after the accident that all three astronauts were dead, the information was not released until two hours later. It was nearly midnight before UPI and AP received a NASA picture of two of the astronauts entering the capsule for the last time. . . .

NASA claimed that the withholding of facts and its issuance of misleading and wrong statements resulted from the lack of a plan for handling information in emergencies. As hard to believe as this may be, coming as it does from an agency with a public information staff of 300, there is undoubtedly some validity to the claim.

NASA's information office has since maintained that an emergency plan was in effect and followed at the time of the Apollo 204 fire. NASA states that it has contingency plans for each mission. The agency refused to comment further on the above charges.

NEED FOR RUMOR CENTER

In recent years many institutions and industries, caught up in the crisis of conflict, have discovered belatedly the dangers of rumor and the need for a center to provide authentic information. When crisis comes, it is suddenly apparent that some seemingly unimportant facets of an institution's operation have been overlooked and must be given hurried attention. Inevitably, one such area of weakness is the availability of information for the general public. Spasm response usually results in a jerry-rigged rumor center which operates throughout the crisis period. Once the problems have faded, the rumor center goes the same route and is given no serious thought until the next crisis comes. This, in large part, explains why rumor centers, as they generally exist, are only partially effective.

There are three major points to remember in planning for a so-called rumor center. First, such a center must be recognized for what it is—a place where information moves from the institution to the general public. It is not a press operation. To saddle an organization's press office with an added responsibility to the general public reduces the effectiveness of both functions. Press and rumor centers must be closely coordinated, but they must be entities—each directed toward its own specific goal.

Second, the rumor center should be in two parts. Rumor centers are almost exclusively a telephone operation. To function most effectively, there must be an answering service, or information center. This group deals directly with the public, taking their questions and providing answers, or, in the absence of information, giving a promise to have it within a certain period of time. The second group is the coordinating agency. This is the point of contact between the information center and the institutional staff and agencies. The coordination agency goes into the institutional staff for information, checks material with the highest level of the administration for accuracy, coordinates it with the press office, and relays it to the information center for use. Hence all information—whether query or answer —flows through the coordinating agency, where it can be accounted for and logged. As the source, and the sole source, of material for the information center, it controls the information center and what is being said to the general public. Though not an official spokesman for the institution, in this way it does provide for "one voice" response to the institution's problems.

In addition to raw information—the factual material used to answer direct and simple questions—the coordinating agency should have qualified persons available to speak directly to callers who desire policy or philosophical discussions of current issues involving the institution.

Finally, and perhaps most important, any rumor center to be effective must establish credibility. It must be the accepted source of accurate information. This cannot be accomplished during the period of crisis alone. The flow of credible information must be established during routine times, and become an accepted part of the institution on a full time, continuing basis. Obviously, during troubled periods, the volume of queries will increase sharply, requiring an augmentation of the center staff. But the function should be identical in times of crisis to that during routine periods. It must, over an extended period, encourage both internal and external publics to use it with faith and confidence. This amounts to more than establishing a reputation for truth—it involves education. Externally, people with questions must come to recognize the center as a reliable source. Internally, all agencies of the institution must be made aware that such a system exists and encouraged to use it to make information available— information which they, due to their place in the organization, are aware of and for which they are responsible.

Such a program, operating normally over a long period of time, not only establishes credibility; it sets the pattern within an institution for quickly and efficiently moving information to a place where it becomes useful. If the institution is tuned to such an operation in routine times, the transition in troubled times is far less shattering.

You are an account executive in a local public relations counseling firm. You specialize in handling retail stores and in staging civic events. Your firm is retained on an annual basis by Duffy Enterprises, Inc., a realty and construction company. Your firm was hired because the Duffy firm is opening a new shopping center, The Eastgate, at the eastern edge of the city, in six weeks. You are assigned to the account. You don't have much time, but—

1. Study accounts of similar shopping center and like events in PR publications.
2. Assemble necessary "information" you need for planning.
3. Canvass and select, in cooperation with Duffy executives, an advertising agency to handle advertising for the opening.
4. Organize a Tenants' Committee to cooperate with you in planning and staging the opening celebration.
5. Draw rough plans for a gala opening of Eastgate to present to a conference of Duffy executives, other officers of your firm, representatives of the advertising agency, and the Tenants' Committee.

ADDITIONAL READING

LOUIS H. BELL, "Columbia's Magic Bicentennial Theme," *PR*, Vol. 1, October, 1955.

EDWARD L. BERNAYS, "What Every Executive Should Know About Public Relations," *Printers' Ink,* Vol. 240, September 12, 1952.

JOHN F. BUDD, JR., *An Executive's Primer on Public Relations,* Philadelphia: Chilton Book Company, 1969. Also: "Priority and Discipline, Keys to Programming," *Public Relations Journal,* Vol. 23, November, 1967.

GLEN PERRY, "Plugging Up the Holes," *Public Relations Journal,* Vol. 7, September, 1951.

PUBLIC RELATIONS SOCIETY OF AMERICA. "Budgeting the Public Relations Dollar." New York: The Society, 1960.

EDGAR STEPHENS (pseudonym), "Programming for Public Relations," *Public Relations Journal,* Vol. 13, May, 1957.

WILLIAM TAYLOR, "Long-Range Planning—Key to University's Celebration," *Public Relations Journal,* Vol. 18, July, 1961.

E. KIRBY WARREN, *Long Range Planning,* Englewood Cliffs, N.J.: Prentice-Hall, Inc., 1966.

BURT ZOLLO, "Setting Your Goals," *Public Relations Quarterly,* Vol. 7, Summer, 1962.

CHAPTER
10

THE
PROCESS:
ACTION
AND
COMMUNICATION—
THE
THIRD
STEP

*The fleeting attention today's citizen can offer is caught
by those in whom he believes and who talk to him in terms of
his self-interest in words that he can understand.*

In the third step of the going process, the public relations function moves on-stage from the wings of fact-finding and counseling. Once a problem has been defined and a program to solve it worked out, the next step is action. This action requires supportive communication to gain cooperation and to gain credit. This case study will illustrate.

A nationwide retailer began to get complaints on a baseboard heater it was selling. Research found a fault in the manufacture of these heaters that made them potentially dangerous. Action to recall these heaters from the stores and customers was decided upon. To effect this, a communications effort to reach all purchasers of this defective heater was required. The marketer bought advertising space in the nation's daily newspapers and saturated the news media with warnings to purchasers of this heating unit. Danger was averted and the giant retailer got credit for candor and prompt action. Communications and action comprise the main thrust in a public relations program. The other steps are designed to make this one effective.

THE NATURE OF COMMUNICATION

The dictionary describes communication as "intercourse by words, letters, or messages; interchange of thoughts or opinions." It would be difficult to think of anything that takes place, makes a sound or a gesture, that does not in some way communicate. Our social life abounds with communication, some of it overt, much of it unverbalized. The average American spends about 70 percent of his waking hours communicating verbally— listening, speaking, reading, and writing. Truly, Americans live under a waterfall of words. Inescapably, in our interdependent society, communications is the cement that holds society together.

The newborn infant's first cry communicates. It says, "I am alive." From then on through life a winked eye, raised eyebrow, smile, cupped ear, shaken finger communicate. Notice, however, that these simple human gestures are not in the form of actual words. Still, they inform eloquently. The same is true of sounds for which the audience forms words. There's no doubt what's going on when one hears a church bell, snap of a mouse-trap, or thunder.

Building from sights, sounds, and sensations, one finds the means to express himself, to be understood, and to understand. In the process, words and actions comprise the main carrier. Using words or taking meaningful action, whether the communicating takes the form of a news release or a protest march, constitutes the first common denominator.

Words are symbols. There are words which serve as symbols for real objects, *table, chair—thing words.* There are words which are symbols of abstract ideas, such as *freedom, love—nothing words.* Children are taught, for example, that a furry little animal with long ears and a short, fuzzy tail is a "rabbit." Once the word and the little animal are associated, the word will always evoke the image of that creature. Word symbols for real objects are readily understood with a high degree of agreement. Not so with symbols for abstractions. Abstractions, like "free enterprise" or "military morale," have no simple or universally agreed on referents in the real world of objects. It is difficult for people to agree on an image of free enterprise when they cannot see, touch, hear, taste, or smell it. This difficulty goes right to the heart of the communications problem. *To communicate effectively, the sender's words must mean the same thing to the receiver that they do to the sender.*

The word *communication* is derived from the Latin *communis,* meaning "common." *The purpose of communications is to establish a commonness.* There are three basic elements in communication: the source or *sender,* the *message* and the destination or *receiver.* A breakdown can involve one or more of these three elements. Effective communication requires efficiency on the part of all three. The communicator must have adequate information. He must be able to present it in forms the receiver will understand. He must use a channel that will carry the message to the receiver. The message must be within the receiver's capacity to comprehend. And it must motivate the receiver's self-interest.

When there has been no common experience on which to establish *commonness,* then communication becomes impossible. A sender can *encode* his message and a receiver *decode* it only in terms of his experience and knowledge. This explains a layman's inability to understand an Einstein and a non-baseball fan's bewilderment at the cry of "Bunt!" Common knowledge and experience provide the connecting links.[1] See next page.

Students should recognize that the illustration is a vast oversimplification of the communications process. Space does not permit the book-length treatment this process requires. A prime difficulty in understanding

---

[1] This process is elaborated in Wilbur Schramm's introductory essay, "How Communication Works," in *The Process and Effects of Mass Communications,* pp. 3–26.

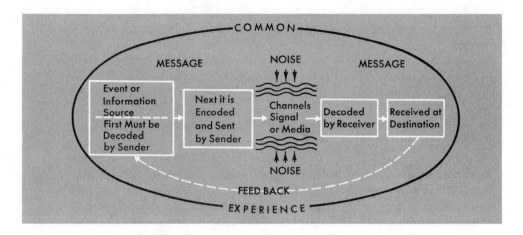

the complex communications process is its deceptive simplicity. Professor Edward J. Robinson suggests that we use the term "communications process" rather than "communications" to remind ourselves that communication is a complicated affair made up of many "parts" or "stages." The acts of *encoding, interpreting,* and *decoding* must be seen as one inseparable whole. Too many practitioners, by engaging in message sending only, put themselves in the position of a basketball player shooting at a hidden basket, unable to see the results of his shooting and, thus, unable to make necessary adjustments to insure accuracy.[2]

The greater the overlap in common interest and common experience, the easier it is to communicate. Where there is no commonness between sender and receiver, the message becomes virtually unintelligible. This explains why, despite the tremendous flow of words to and from Southeast Asia in the 1960s, Americans and Asians still little understand one another.[3] There are many barriers to achieving this overlap of commonness.

THE FUNDAMENTALS

Many fundamental factors in the communications process must be taken into full account by one who would effectively communicate. These will underline the complexity of this process.

---

[2] These concepts are introduced in his book, *Communication and Public Relations* (Columbus, O.: Charles E. Merrill, 1966). A useful book based on the assumption that "the public relations practitioner is an applied social and behavioral scientist."

[3] This is fully documented in John Hohenberg's *Between Two Worlds* (New York: Praeger, 1967). His comprehensive study showed that a heavy two-way newsflow doesn't necessarily effect communication.

Communicator. The credibility of the communicator is determined by his *expertness* and his *trustworthiness,* as these qualities are perceived by the intended audience. Research has shown that high credibility increases favorable attitude change and low credibility lessens the probability of favorable change. Many studies show that the audience's knowledge of the communicator's persuasive intent and bias do not necessarily impair his effectiveness. The more a communicator is known and liked by his audience, the more inclined the audience is to change its beliefs in the direction the communicator advocates. Personalized communications exert stronger influence than impersonal sources. Sargent found that communications identified by commentators' names are stronger than communications identified by name of newspaper, magazine, or network.[4]

Message. Persuasive communications must be supported by events. Facts alone do not persuade. Klapper concluded "facts may be successfully communicated without producing opinion changes that they are intended or expected to produce." [5] Nonetheless, facts and information may perform a significant role in eliciting, triggering, or rationalizing behavior. Davison thinks the communication of information, although limited in changing attitudes, has a great potential in promoting action and behavior.[6] Several studies have shown that more people are persuaded by an explicit statement of the communicator's position. Presentation of information after the need for it has been aroused is much more effective than the other way around. When both agreeable and disagreeable materials are to be presented, placing the desirable material first produces greater acceptance and better understanding of the total message. McGuire suggests that repetition of messages does increase acceptance of the theme, but only a small number of repetitions are necessary to produce maximum acceptance.[7]

Audience. The more interested people are in an issue, the more likely they are to hold consistent positions on that issue. The more a person is emotionally involved in his beliefs, the harder it is to change those cognitions by information or argument. Once a person commits himself to a position, the commitment becomes a barrier to change. People less interested in an issue hold weaker opinions and beliefs and thus are more likely to change their minds but the less interested take longer to make up their minds. A pressured person tends to change toward the prevailing attitude of his most favored group. The more pressured a person is, the less stable his opinions are during persuasion campaigns. An individual's behavior is

[4] Leslie W. Sargent, "Communicator Image and News Reception," *Journalism Quarterly,* Vol. 42, Winter, 1965, pp. 35–42.

[5] Joseph T. Klapper, *The Effects of Mass Communication* (Glencoe, Ill.: The Free Press, 1960), pp. 78–79.

[6] W. Phillips Davison, *International Political Communication* (New York: Praeger, 1965), p. 40ff.

[7] William J. McGuire, "Nature of Attitudes and Attitude Change," chapter in Lindzey and Aronson, eds., *Handbook of Social Psychology,* 2nd ed.

influenced by many different groups; at any given moment, the group with the strongest influence will be that group which is most salient. Persons tend to see and hear communications that are favorable or congenial to their predispositions. Berelson and Steiner asserted: ". . . the more interested they are in the subject, the more likely is such selective attention." The basic fact is that a message is perceived by the audience in accordance with its predispositions, desires, wishes, attitudes, needs, and expectations. DeFleur and Larsen suggest: "When contact is achieved and symbols are brought to the attention of a receiver, the content passes through a filter of selective perception by means of which ideas irrelevant or destructive to existing attitudes are suppressed or modified." [8] As noted in Chapter 6, Sears and Freedman question this selective exposure hypothesis. These processes are self-protective.

Chester I. Barnard long ago observed: [9] A person can and will accept a communication as authoritative only when four conditions simultaneously obtain: (a) he can and does understand the communication; (b) at the time of his decision he believes that it is not inconsistent with the purpose of the organization; (c) at the time of his decision, he believes it to be compatible with his personal interest as a whole; and (d) he is able mentally and physically to comply with it."

THE TWO-STEP FLOW THEORY

In this seemingly simple process, there are a number of intervening variables. Research, dating roughly from the 1920s, has successively isolated and identified them as: (1) exposure, access, attention given the communicator's message; (2) the differential character of the media of communication; (3) content of the message—its form, presentation, and appeals; (4) receiver's predispositions which cause acceptance, modification, or rejection of message; (5) interpersonal relationships of individuals as members of groups. Each one of these variables must be taken into account.

The most recent variable found to be influential is that of the receiver's interpersonal relationships. This has led to formulation of the *two-step flow of mass communication* theory.[10] Recognizing the spectacular

[8] Melvin L. De Fleur and Otto N. Larsen, *The Flow of Information* (New York: Harper & Bros., 1958), p. 27.

[9] *The Functions of the Executive* (Cambridge, Mass.: Harvard University Press, 1938), p. 165.

[10] For full discussion of this significant theory, see Elihu Katz and Paul Lazarsfeld, *Personal Influence: The Part Played by People in The Flow of Mass Communications* (New York: The Free Press of Glencoe, Inc., 1955), pp. 15–42. For later evaluation of this theory, see Elihu Katz, "The Two-Step Flow of Communication: An Up-to-Date Report on an Hypothesis," *Public Opinion Quarterly*, Vol. 21, Spring, 1957.

performances of the Creel Committee in World War I in mobilizing patriotism at home and support for war aims abroad, of the American Red Cross in raising unprecedented sums for welfare, and of the Liberty Bond drives in getting millions to buy bonds, communicators in the 1920s developed a mass communications model which is now outmoded. This Model T vehicle was built on assumptions that: (1) the people were an atomistic mass of millions of isolated readers, listeners, and viewers eager and ready to receive The Message; (2) every Message had a direct and powerful stimulus which would get an immediate response; (3) there was a direct relationship between information and attitudes.

In short, the growing mass media were looked upon as a new kind of unifying force. This force would reach out to every eye and ear in a society characterized by an amorphous social organization and a loss of interpersonal relationships. This vertical theory of communication presumed that the Message from the Mass Media beamed down in a direct line to the newly urbanized, isolated, and lost individuals—"the image of the audience as a mass of disconnected individuals hooked up to the media but not to each other." [11]

The naïve notion underlying the obsolete Model T theory is seen in this advice given to professional publicists after World War I: "Although clearness and logical arrangement toward a climax are necessary in presenting arguments, the chief thing is to emphasize a supreme point by which . . . a prospect is 'swept off his feet.' " [12] Research and pragmatic experience have shown this image of the direct effect of the mass media to be a great oversimplification. As Lazarsfeld says: "Paradoxical as it may seem, the closer one observes the workings of the mass media, the more it turns out that their effects depend on a complex network of specialized personal and social influences." [13]

Modern practice prefers a communications model that takes into account the *relay* and *reinforcement* roles played by individuals. This means less reliance on mass publicity and more on reaching thought leaders. Communications is both a *vertical* and a *horizontal* process. This was first noted in Lazarsfeld, Berelson, and Gaudet's study of the 1940 Presidential election when "it became clear that certain people in every stratum of a community serve relay roles in the mass communication of election information and influence." [14] To communicate effectively, more attention must

[11] See A. W. Van Den Ban, "A Revision of the Two-Step Flow of Communications Hypothesis," *The Gazette*, Vol. 10, 1964, pp. 237–249.

[12] Herbert F. deBower, *Advertising Principles* (New York: Alexander Hamilton Institute, 1919), p. 91.

[13] In the essay, "Mass Media and Personal Influence," by Lazarsfeld and Herbert Menzel, in *Science of Human Communication*, edited by Wilbur Schramm (New York: Basic Books, Inc., 1963), p. 95.

[14] *The People's Choice* (New York: Columbia University Press, 1948).

be paid to the group, its grapevine, and, particularly, its leaders. These leaders tend to specialize in issue areas.

A more recent testing of this two-step flow theory generally supported the hypothesis but suggests a re-interpretation of the group process as more opinion-sharing than opinion-giving by the leader. Arndt found: [15] "The two-step flow . . . hypothesis was tested in a field experiment involving diffusion of a new brand of a familiar food product. . . . The opinion leaders seemed to be more influenced by the impersonal source (the direct mail letter) than were the non-leaders . . . the data supported the notion of a first-step flow of influence. In regard to the second step, the leaders were found to be more active communicators, both as transmitters and receivers of word-of-mouth communicators. An unexpected finding was the relatively large amount of word-of-mouth flowing from nonleaders to leaders. This finding was explained in terms of the opinion-sharing nature of the communication situation. The word-of-mouth transmitters did not simply pass on the messages received from impersonal sources, but shaded the messages with their own evaluations."

These leaders, whether operating at local levels or national levels, serve as the key link between the official decision makers and the general citizenry. In the view of the late V. O. Key, political scientist, these leaders —"the talkers, the persuaders, the speculators, the philosophers, the advocates, the opponents—mediate between the world of remote and complex events and the mass of the public." He thinks, properly in our view, that the mass of citizens limit their participation in public affairs to supporting or vetoing the policy alternatives developed by the leaders. Practitioners must develop a more realistic model of the democratic decision-making process to guide their communications programs.

In relating recent research findings to America's communications efforts abroad, W. Phillips Davison lists these misconceptions that mislead communicators: [16]

1. That propaganda is an effective instrument for influencing opinion, because the media govern the sentiments of mankind.
2. That propaganda should be aimed at a mass audience with mass attitudes as the primary target.
3. That propaganda should be directed at those who hold opposing opinions in an effort to win them over when, in fact, this is most difficult, if not impossible to do.

---

[15] Johan Arndt, "A Test of the Two-Step Flow in Diffusion of a New Product," *Journalism Quarterly*, Vol. 45, Autumn, 1968, pp. 457–465.

[16] In "Political Communication As an Instrument of Foreign Policy," *Public Opinion Quarterly*, Vol. 27, Spring, 1963, pp. 28–36. For a full analysis of what has been learned about effectiveness and limitations of mass media in influencing opinions, see Klapper, *The Effects of Mass Communication*.

There are three fundamental facts the communicator must keep in mind: (1) That the audience for his communications consists of people. These people live, work, and play with one another in the framework of social institutions. Consequently, each person is subject to many influences of which the communicator's message is only one. (2) That people tend to read, watch, or listen to communication which presents points of view with which they are sympathetic or in which they have a deep personal stake. (3) That the response we want from our intended receiver must be *rewarding to him* or he is not likely to respond.

The Flow of Ideas

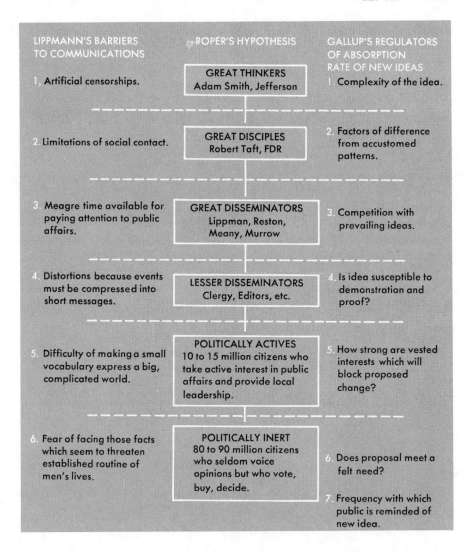

LIPPMANN'S BARRIERS TO COMMUNICATIONS	ROPER'S HYPOTHESIS	GALLUP'S REGULATORS OF ABSORPTION RATE OF NEW IDEAS
1. Artificial censorships.	**GREAT THINKERS** Adam Smith, Jefferson	1. Complexity of the idea.
2. Limitations of social contact.	**GREAT DISCIPLES** Robert Taft, FDR	2. Factors of difference from accustomed patterns.
3. Meagre time available for paying attention to public affairs.	**GREAT DISSEMINATORS** Lippman, Reston, Meany, Murrow	3. Competition with prevailing ideas.
4. Distortions because events must be compressed into short messages.	**LESSER DISSEMINATORS** Clergy, Editors, etc.	4. Is idea susceptible to demonstration and proof?
5. Difficulty of making a small vocabulary express a big, complicated world.	**POLITICALLY ACTIVES** 10 to 15 million citizens who take active interest in public affairs and provide local leadership.	5. How strong are vested interests which will block proposed change?
6. Fear of facing those facts which seem to threaten established routine of men's lives.	**POLITICALLY INERT** 80 to 90 million citizens who seldom voice opinions but who vote, buy, decide.	6. Does proposal meet a felt need?
		7. Frequency with which public is reminded of new idea.

ROPER'S CONCENTRIC CIRCLE THEORY

Gaining acceptance of an idea or point of view, then, is more than simply beaming it at an audience through a mass medium. There is still not sufficient evidence to be positive about how ideas are disseminated among Americans. Elmo Roper, after nearly 30 years of opinion research, formulated a hypothesis which he calls the "concentric circle theory." [17] Roper assumes that ideas penetrate the whole public very slowly. They do so by a process similar to osmosis. They move out in concentric circles from Great Thinkers to Great Disciples to Great Disseminators to Lesser Disseminators to the Politically Active to the Politically Inert. The flow of ideas as hypothesized by Roper is charted on page 244. This hypothesis assumes that American society can be stratified as indicated. It emphasizes the importance of using opinion leaders in the public relations process. His theory squares with the findings of Lazarsfeld, Katz, and others. It deserves further testing.

The *rate of flow* in the transmission and acceptance of ideas is governed by many factors. These include Lippmann's barriers to communication. They also include the "Regulators of Absorption Rate" named by George Gallup on the basis of three decades of opinion research, listed on the chart.

THE DIFFUSION PROCESS

The communications step in the public relations process requires influencing opinion among both sizable and distant groups. The United States Department of Agriculture has been working at this task longer than most. The USDA has learned that getting new ideas accepted involves more than simply discovering a new grain and publicizing it. It took 13 years to gain widespread adoption of hybrid seed corn on America's farms, for example. Out of their long experience and *evaluation*, agricultural sociologists have concluded that acceptance goes through five stages.[18]

---

[17] Outlined in "Who Tells the Storytellers?" *Saturday Review*, Vol. 37, July 31, 1954.

[18] This theory of the diffusion process has emerged as the result of research of many people over a number of years. It is summarized in Herbert F. Lionberger, *Adoption of New Ideas and Practices* (Ames, Ia.: Iowa State University Press, 1960); in E. A. Wilkening, "The Communication of Ideas on Innovation in Agriculture," in *Studies of Innovation and of Communication to the Public* (Stanford, Cal.: Institute for Communication Research, 1962).

1. *Awareness.* The individual learns of the existence of the idea or practice but has little knowledge of it.
2. *Interest.* The individual develops interest in the idea. He seeks more information and considers its general merits.
3. *Evaluation.* The individual makes mental application of the idea and weighs its merits for his own situation. He obtains more information and decides to try it.
4. *Trial.* Individual actually applies the idea or practice—usually on a small scale. He is interested in how to apply practice, techniques, conditions for application.
5. *Adoption.* If the idea proves acceptable, it is adopted.

STAGES IN THE ADOPTION PROCESS

AWARENESS	INTEREST	EVALUATION	TRIAL	ADOPTION
Learns about a new idea or practice	*Gets more information about it*	*Tries it out mentally*	*Uses or tries a little*	*Accepts it for full-scale and continued use*
1. Mass media radio, TV, newspapers, magazines	1. Mass media	1. Friends and neighbors	1. Friends and neighbors	Personal experience is the most important factor in continued use of an idea
2. Friends and neighbors mostly other farmers	2. Friends and neighbors	2. Agricultural agencies	2. Agricultural agencies	
3. Agricultural agencies, extension, vo-ag, etc.	3. Agricultural agencies	3. Dealers and salesmen	3. Dealers and salesmen	1. Friends and neighbors
4. Dealers and salesmen	4. Dealers and salesmen	4. Mass media	4. Mass media	2. Agricultural agencies
				3. Mass media
				4. Dealers and salesmen

Used by permission from Herbert F. Lionberger ADOPTION
OF NEW IDEAS AND PRACTICES, page 32.

They have concluded that information about new farm and home practices are communicated by these agencies in order of appearance: (1) mass media—radio, TV, newspapers, magazines; (2) friends and neighbors—mostly other farmers; (3) agricultural agencies—extension agents, vo-ag instructors, and so forth; (4) dealers and salesmen—purveyors of commercial products and equipment.

These media or agencies have a varying impact at each stage of the process. The mass media have their greatest impact and usefulness in creating *awareness*. For farmers and farm wives, at least, the mass media become less and less influential as the acceptance process advances toward adoption. In the *interest* stage, mass media still play an important part. But, to learn more, the farmer turns to agricultural agencies and friends.

In the *evaluation* stage, friends and neighbors play the dominant role. In the *trial* stage, agricultural agencies, friends, and neighbors are all important. Dealers and salesmen are influential in this stage when commercial products are involved. The time span in each stage varies.

This diffusion model, developed on the basis of extensive research among rural families, was confirmed in a comparable study of how doctors in four communities responded to the availability of a new "miracle drug." Despite the differences between a new seed and a new drug, and between farmers and doctors, the results are quite comparable. Comparing the study that traced the adoption of hybrid seed corn and that which traced the adoption of the new drug, Elihu Katz concludes that: [19]

> (1) Both studies plot curves of diffusion to map the spread of innovation, over time, within the social structure or various parts of it. The authors of the corn study inferred from the curve that interpersonal influence would appear to account for the observed pattern of spread. The drug study went one step further and, by comparing the curves for "integrated" and "isolated" doctors, could show that interpersonal influence was operative precisely where it would most likely be expected— among the "integrated" doctors.
>
> (2) Both studies find that "information is not enough"—neither farmers nor doctors accepted the innovation upon first hearing. It was shown that there are media which typically inform a potential adopter about an innovation, and that there are media which typically "activate" or "legitimate" the decision to adopt. The former tend to be more commercial and more formal; the latter more professional and more informal.

Professor Katz properly warns, "Whether these generalizations apply equally to the diffusion of other innovations remains to be seen."

The research conclusions demonstrate that communicating a new idea or practice is a long, tedious task. Different media are effective at different points and in different ways. The influence of the innovator or influential leader is great in every community. It is important for the communicator to know what media and techniques to use at different stages and how to mobilize these influences effectively. Taken together, these theories provide a much surer approach. *Effective communication is expensive in time, in understanding, and in emotional control. The cost is higher than is commonly supposed.*

---

[19] Elihu Katz' essay, "The Social Itinerary of Technical Change: Two Studies on the Diffusion of Information," in *Studies of Innovation and of Communication to the Public*, pp. 5–35. For details of drug study, see James S. Coleman, Elihu Katz, and Herbert Menzel, *Medical Innovation: A Diffusion Study* (Indianopolis: Bobbs Merrill, 1966).

THE BARRIERS AND DISTORTION

Barriers to understanding and to clarity of message exist in the communicator and the audience alike. *Each person lives in the protective shelter of a cocoon of his own spinning.* This cocoon insulates him from the communications babble that beats in upon him all day long, a babble steadily increasing in intensity. There are social barriers, age barriers, language or vocabulary barriers, political and economic barriers. There is the race barrier. The barriers and distortions that block communication are seen starkly in the gulf between American blacks and whites. There is peer pressure exerted within a person's groups, where "reality" is shared and interpreted —a factor discussed in Chapter 6. There is also the often overlooked barrier of the audience's capability to absorb the message. Discussing the widely prevalent notion that lack of information or ignorance can be remedied by more information, Gabriel A. Almond has observed that the problem runs much deeper: "A discriminating analysis of the evidence suggests that a large sector of the lower-income, poorly educated majority of the population is incapable of assimilating the materials of informational campaigns." Finally, there is the constant roar of competition for people's attention in the noisy public arena.

In a much-quoted article that has stood the test of time Hyman and Sheatsley codified the major reasons why many information campaigns fail. These are: [20]

1. Repeated social surveys have revealed a hard core of chronic know-nothings.
2. There are large groups in the population who admit that they have little or no interest in public issues.
3. People tend to expose themselves to material that is compatible with their prior attitudes and to avoid exposure to that which is not compatible.
4. Selective perception and interpretation of content follows exposure: persons perceive, absorb, and remember content differently.
5. Changes in views or behavior following exposure to a message may be differentially affected by the individual's initial predispositions and attitudes.

People have impressions about everything that touches the consciousness. Lippmann has bracketed these impressions into four groups. One is

[20] Herbert H. Hyman and Paul B. Sheatsley, "Some Reasons Why Information Campaigns Fail," *Public Opinion Quarterly*, Vol. 11, Fall, 1947. Also in Katz *et al*, *Public Opinion and Propaganda.*

the person's approach to the world, the second is his stereotypes, the third his personal interests, and the fourth his image of the world. Everyone lives in a world of his own symbols. Public figures, for example, during their lifetimes and afterward, are known partly through a personality created by images fixed in the public imagination. Astronauts and sports heroes are good examples. Their families and associates know them as people entirely different from their public personalities. People who live on one side of town tend to know people on the other side of town or in remote cities in a half-fictional, half-imagined way.

In communicating, nothing raises more problems than the fact that the audience has limited access to the real facts. Access, as Lippmann has made clear, is limited by the six main factors listed in the chart. With limited access, and with some information tending to confuse as much as it clarifies, people rely heavily on stereotypes. Specific and significant impressions become generalities.

From the cover of a magazine, for example, with a picture entitled "criminal," the person looking at it may pick out two or three sharply defined features. Perhaps he selects a low forehead, a squinting eye, a scarred face, or a mouth that curls at the corner. From then on, the impression may be so deeply rooted that he feels sure he knows the "criminal type" whenever he sees it. He can classify everyone, including his friends, as to whether or not they are criminal types. Indeed, he has classifications into which he can fit almost everyone he sees or hears about. Distorted stereotypes pose public relations problems. For example, the stereotype of the public school teacher as an old maid persists despite a recent survey showing that sixty-eight out of every one-hundred teachers are or have been married. The farmer in blue overalls with a straw hat little resembles today's farmer-businessman. The long-haired student and absent-minded professors are other stereotypes.

Lippmann emphasizes the sacrosanct regard that people have for stereotypes as "the core of our personal tradition, the defense of our position in society." Stereotypes tend, as a defense mechanism, to express the hopes of the audience. They form a moral code from which personal standards are derived. The specialist learns to recognize the influence and the presence of symbols and stereotypes in the seeming contradictions and contrariness of public opinion. *Stereotypes are used to counter stereotypes.*

Another system of barriers encompasses the superstitions, prejudices, and vanities to which we all cling. Considering superstitions alone, one man may laugh at another for his refusal to open an umbrella in the house. The same man who laughed at that superstition might well walk two blocks out of his way, however, to avoid letting a black cat cross his path. *We believe what we want to believe.* That is perhaps the best way to explain, in oversimplified terms, the grip that superstitions, prejudices, and vanities have on us.

THE ACT OF COMMUNICATING

It would be disappointing, if not futile, to establish any single set of sure-fire rules for swaying public opinion. Such a set could appear perfect in principle, yet be rendered ineffectual by an unseen characteristic of the audience. The timing could be bad. In the 1930s Chrysler introduced the streamlined automobile, a radical departure from the buggy-like cars of that day and the forerunner of today's styling. Ford emphasized auto safety in selling its 1956 cars. The public wasn't responsive, yet a decade later there was great public demand for safer cars. The audience could harbor an unspoken prejudice, such as confronts a Democrat campaigning in a Republican precinct. The wording of the messages could be such that it does not square with the images in the heads of the audience. Or perhaps the audience is not in a listening mood. Regardless of the specific barrier, results from standardization of programming are generally frustrating and futile.

Effective communication means tailor-made programming specially designed for the situation, time, place, and audience. It means careful selection of media and technique. No program, simply because it worked once before in a given situation, can be carted about like a trunk full of clothes and fitted to a new situation. With rare exception, the clothes will not fit the second wearer. If nothing else, they'll be out of style.

All public relations problems, however, do have people as a common denominator and require some communicating to bring the people and their viewpoints closer together. This applies whether the program calls for news releases, institutional advertising, meetings, or any other tool of contact.

Continuity is required in communicating. So are repetition of a consistent message in simple form, careful selection of time, place, and method, and a variety of media that converge on the audience from several avenues.

NEW PERSPECTIVES NEEDED

Emphasis should be centered on people's interests and mental capacities. The ideal is to keep publicity in perspective as a *part* of the whole process but to remain primarily concerned with the absorption of messages—the reaction. We must be more impressed by the *actions* that the audience takes than by the clippings and monitor reports. The pounds of clippings and the hours of air time mean very little if the organization is still misunderstood. Our focus must be on the audience.

Institutions are faced with the choice of doing their own telling or risking relationships that develop from gossip, rumor, and backfence and tavern conversation. In making that choice, the institution either succeeds or fails to invest itself with news interest. If the choice is in the affirmative, and a green light is given, it follows that, as a corollary, *everything newsworthy* about the institution becomes news. There is nothing but trouble and embarrassment ahead for the institution that tries to have the good things about itself invested with a headlining news value, and the bad things suppressed. The decision to undertake the communicating phase implies an all-the-way attitude. It represents acceptance of the need to put the public reporting of any institution into a more accurate perspective than is provided by the haphazard, superficial, sometimes sensational, and episodic reporting of the news media or by the careless and casual talk along the institution's grapevine. For example, a group of twenty-two young Republican congressmen who investigated causes of campus unrest on fifty campuses, found, among other things: [21]

> Most of the people we talked with stated the opinion that superficial mass media coverage was contributing to the widening disillusionment and misunderstanding between the public and the nation's campuses. The media, particularly those utilizing the visual impression, concentrate on the dramatic, the sensational, the vivid acts of violence or disorder. . . . Not only does this distorted coverage inflame the worst fears and stereotypes in the public mind, but it adds to the frustrations of those trying to work for progress and constructive change on campus.

Today's public relations, with its powerful and varied means of disseminating information, suffers from an overcapacity. Simon and Garfunkel sang to us in "The Sounds of Silence," that our problem is people talking without speaking, people hearing without listening. As repeatedly suggested in this book, there is an urgent need in this field to target *specific messages* to *specific audiences* to achieve *specific results*.

The practitioner must define his audiences with great precision, and he must use different strategies and techniques to accomplish different goals. Eugene F. Lane suggests "The communicator must vary his communications strategy in accordance with the intensity of concern with an issue felt by his audience." He suggests, for example, these techniques to reduce the discrepancy between the communicator's position and the audience's attitudes: [22]

[21] "GOP Congressmen on Campus," *College & University Journal*, Vol. 8, Summer, 1969, p. 4.
[22] *Public Relations Journal*, Vol. 23, July, 1967, p. 6.

1. Using media most closely identified with the audience's position.

2. Using a communications source that enjoys high credibility for the audience *on this issue.*

3. Playing down the differences between the communication and the audience's attitudes.

4. Seeking identification in vocabulary and anecdote with the audience in an area *removed from the issue.*

5. Establishing the communicator's position as being the majority opinion—defining the majority from the audience itself.

6. Bringing the audience's group identifications into play—when those identifications will help the development of a positive response. The converse is also true.

7. Modifying the message to fit the organization's needs—since you can't modify organizational objectives.

SEMANTICS

Semantics is the science of what words really mean. Word meanings change. Words are raised from the dictionary to popular usage. Other words wither away from neglect or are banished by abuse. In this text, this science of semantics can only be kissed lightly. Space denies a full courtship. Don't be misled, however; the subject really deserves and gets a great deal of attention from men and women in public relations. For, in communicating and interpreting, practitioners live by words. They make their living by them. Practitioners seek mastery of word meanings both as users and as understanders. For communicators, there is no escape from what T. S. Eliot described as "the intolerable wrestle with words and meanings."

The basic importance of semantics must never be lost. In communicating, a person is constantly making decisions on word meanings. Stephen Fitzgerald put it well: "When you decide whether the refusal of men to work should be called a strike, a work stoppage, or a damnable crime against the people, you are making a decision in semantics."

In selecting words to use as weapons, the practitioner must remember that the same signs and word symbols have different meanings for different persons. There is no one-to-one ratio between a word and its meaning; more likely, the ratio is one-to-fifty. Not only do signs and words have different meanings for different people; they have two different kinds of meaning—*denotative* and *connotative. Denotative* meaning is the common dictionary meaning generally accepted by most people with the same language and same culture. *Connotative* meaning is the emotional or evaluative meaning we read into words because of our experience and background. For example, all persons will agree that DOG *denotes* a four-legged, furry, canine animal. For most persons, the word DOG *connotes* a friendly, faithful pet and usually awakens nostalgic memories. To some people, however, the word DOG *connotes* a dangerous animal to be feared. Another example would be the term *bullfight*. North and South Americans fully agree on what the term denotes, but the connotative meaning of *bullfight* differs sharply in North and South America.

Words can be dynamite. There is evidence that a mistake in translating a message sent by the Japanese government near the end of World War II may have triggered Hiroshima and thus ushered in atomic warfare. The word *mokusatsu* used by Japan in response to the U. S. surrender ultimatum was translated by Domei as "ignore" instead of its correct meaning, "withholding comment until a decision has been made." A few years ago, a crisis between the United States and Panama was caused by semantic difficulties between the English verb negotiate and the Spanish verb "negociar." Panamanians interpreted negotiate as a commitment to negotiate a new treaty whereas our State Department intended it simply in its noncommittal sense of "to discuss." President Kennedy's 1961 conference with Premier Khrushchev at Vienna was abrasive, due in part to a wrong interpretation of "miscalculate." Repeatedly Kennedy warned the Russian leader not to miscalculate U. S. intentions. Literally translated, the word, which has no counterpart in Russian, implies the inability to calculate two and two and get four as an answer. Nor can the meaning of words commonplace in our language be taken for granted. David Ogilvy recalls using the word "obsolete" in an ad only to find that 43 percent of the women in the United States had no idea what it meant.

THE ROOTS OF MEANING

The source is the alphabet. It was man's greatest invention and has proved at times his most troublesome one. Though it repeatedly gets him into trouble with other people, the alphabet is potentially man's best means of getting along with other people.

As ideas and thoughts have become more and more complex, the language of words has broadened and grown more specialized. People have had to specialize language to talk about television, cybernetics, antibiotics, jets, automation, and atomic power. There will have to be more specialization in the years ahead to handle such things as earth satellites, microelectronics, facsimile, and computers. Meantime, there are already special language arrangements for scientists, immigrants, deaf and blind people, musicians, and even baseball fans.

THE PRACTITIONER IS EXPECTED
TO BE THE ANSWER MAN

In the midst of the struggle of words is the public relations man. Studying the words that leap out of people's mouths, stare up from newspapers, and smile out from a television tube, he's expected to react and then to be able to tell what those words mean . . . *not what they say, but what they really mean.* Then, he's expected to combine words and actions that will correct misunderstandings, educate where there is a lack of understanding, and, in general, clear up confusion.

A cardinal premise is that *you cannot tell anyone something he cannot understand. And you rarely can tell anyone something you cannot understand. You have to understand it first and then you have to make it understandable to the other person.* Whether you are dealing with one person or with a crowd, the same premises apply.

Public relations people must be tuned in to the various meanings of words used by all self-interested groups. The word *farmer* when used by a farmer is a compliment. It's not always a compliment when spoken by a city man. A "heel" is a different thing when tacked on a shoe or a man. There are several kinds of "Yankee"; ask a baseball fan, a Southerner, and a Connecticut farmer.[23]

Public relations people must be able to select and to transmit for various audiences words that will be received as kinfolk. Think of the harm that has been done, the confusion created, by legal language. A book could be written. Perhaps a single illustration will be enough.

Periodically, labor officials and management officials spend weeks talking out a new agreement on working conditions. Between them on the table at negotiation sessions is a contract. They're talking about the provisions in it. When it's all done, the union has a "new" contract, all properly drawn to stand up in court. *Not more than one of every hundred employees bound by that contract could understand all of it if they read it.* So, generally, they don't read it. They are told what it's all about in words they can understand. They're usually told in a manner that compliments the source, whether labor official or management spokesman. In one case, it's "Here's what we got for you." In the other, it's "Here's what we are giving you." The chances are that the employee is no nearer a real appreciation of the issues and solutions than he is when he gets through filling out an income tax form or reading an insurance policy, a financial statement, or instructions for claiming unemployment compensation.

---

[23] For a list of key positive and negative words used in our war of words with Russia, see Edward W. Barrett, *Truth Is Our Weapon,* Chap. 10, "The Problem of Words."

For example, here is an actual excerpt from the minutes of a labor-management bargaining committee meeting.

> It is agreed, in response to the request by the Bargaining Committee, to change past practice and policy so that in the future when an employee is absent from work on one paid holiday qualifying day on a leave of absence that includes that day, one of the excused absences as provided in the labor agreement may be used to cover such absence to qualify for pay for the holiday subject to the contractual paid holiday provisions, with the understanding that this agreement is in no way to be interpreted to mean that past practice and policy is changed to provide that an employee absent from work on a leave of absence on both qualifying days is to receive pay for the holiday regardless of remaining excused absence credit.

That may have made sense to the members of the bargaining group. They had been talking about it for several meetings. But it can't be transplanted, as is, for any other audience; to another audience it's just so much gobbledygook.

The same is true for the language of doctors, educators, the military, and government. Each has a special jargon not readily understandable to others—legalese, Pentagonese, educationese, and militarese. Then there are slangs, dialects, slogans, and exaggerations. The practitioner must work with his cousins in the press, radio, television, and on the platform to help straighten things out for the public.

HOW DO WE GO ABOUT IT?

There are, within every generation, wonderful examples of word mastery. There have been Franklin Roosevelt, Winston Churchill, and John F. Kennedy. In specialized fields of word usage, Stuart Chase has made sense of complex economic matters. Paul de Kruif did the same with medical science. Some popular magazines do a marvelous job with fiction and features.

Of the communicators mentioned, Franklin Roosevelt had no equal. He always found the right word in a tight situation. He was particularly skilled in his radio projection, but radio appeal was not all of it. He knew words. For example, the Social Security Act was first drafted as an "Economic Security" bill, but F.D.R. knew "social security" would be more acceptable. Another example of FDR's adroitness with words was shown when he termed the nation's military draft law of 1940 a "muster," thus evoking memories of the rugged farmers of Lexington and Concord, softening the introduction of conscription.

Winston Churchill had little resemblance to Franklin Roosevelt in choice of words for a mass audience. Churchill was dramatic in his "blood, sweat and tears," "the soft underbelly of Europe," and "the Iron Curtain," although he didn't originate them all. He, more than any other man, made "it's me" acceptable English. The fact that both Roosevelt and Churchill could draw an audience into a deep emotional kinship had to stem from something more than words or inflection. It did. Both men in their respective use of language represented the abstract symbols they embodied in the mass public conception. In their words and in their delivery, they lived up to their images.

In a later day President John F. Kennedy's polished prose aroused emotions around the world. His memorable inaugural address appeal, "And so, my fellow Americans, ask not what your country can do for you; ask what you can do for your country," will go ringing down the corridors of time. Kennedy's sensitive feel for the right word, the stirring phrase was reflected in the construction of that address. His collaborator, Theodore Sorensen, has recounted the way each paragraph was reworded, reworked, and reduced.[24]

The close attention paid to the semantics of his proposals by President Richard Nixon was illustrated when he changed the label of the much-criticized anti-ballistic missile system from Sentinel to Safeguard and when he introduced a controversial guaranteed annual income proposal smothered under the rhetoric of "work incentive plan" and the "New Federalism." One of Nixon's 1968 opponents learned this lesson the hard way: George Romney's candidacy collapsed after he admitted that he had been "brainwashed" by the military in Vietnam. Had he, instead, charged that he was "misled" by the military, his political fate might have been quite different.

Tagging your proposals with warm, favorable terms and the other fellow's with unfavorable ones is an important part of the communications contest. What one group calls a "program," an opposing group brands a "scheme." The proponent for paying farmers not to grow crops calls it a "soil bank." This couples two warm, respected words. Opponents call it a "subsidy." There's a difference in the impact of "sliding price supports" and "flexible price supports," yet both describe the same plan. Industries seeking tax postponements on new plants talk of "accelerated tax amortization." Critics of this law call it "fast tax write-off." Labor leaders plead the case for "union security" while industrialists plead for "the right to work."

The governor of New York pledges not to ask for higher taxes; he recommends an increase in "state fees" instead. The governor of Wisconsin

[24] In his *Kennedy* (New York: Harper & Row, 1965), pp. 241–242.

vows never to sign a sales tax bill; he signs an "excise tax" bill instead. Neither semantic trick fools voters. The campaign for national prohibition made "saloon" a dirty word, so today those who drink do so in taverns and cocktail lounges. Incidentally, the drys were too wise to campaign for *prohibition,* a harsh word; they advocated "temperance." A great coup in semantics was scored in coining the term "life insurance" to describe what could be called, just as properly, "death insurance." The latter would be harder to sell. Another ten-strike in semantics has been the successful effort of bowling promoters to change "bowling alleys" to "bowling lanes." Milwaukee's garbagemen got their title changed to "combustible truck loaders," a title with more dignity. Another successful semantic coup was changing "educational television" to "public television." The latter has a more popular ring to it. Semantic manipulation is an old art. In World War I Britain's propaganda boss, Lord Northcliffe, decreed that field hospitals be described as "evacuation stations," a less alarming term to kin of the injured.

Words change from one generation to another, from one context to another. In the Eighteenth Century, awful meant full of awe and officious meant graciously extending a person's offices. Today these words have quite different meanings. Once "bussing" was an affectionate pastime, now it is an angry word in racial conflicts. The way words are bent, like trees, by prevailing winds is illustrated in the word *dissent.* Long ago it meant speeches expressing unorthodox opinions or challenging ideas. In the 1970s it came to embrace a wide variety of physical acts, including violence. "Progressive" and "education" when used separately are warm, solid American words. Put them together and you get the sneer term, "progressive education." Inept choice of a word can have unhappy consequences. Some years ago, in a call-up of reserves, the Army referred to the casuals called to bring divisions to full strength as "fillers." This the troops resented. The railroads campaign against forced employment of more men than are needed calls it "featherbedding." The railroad unions counter with such terms as "dead man control" and a "full crew law." Today it is not good international public relations to describe any nation as "backward." Such nations are "emerging" or "underdeveloped."

A flair for the picturesque, memorable term and a feeling for words are important requisites for the practitioner.

SAY IT WITH SYMBOLS

Communication involves more than semantics; in large measure, it uses symbols and stereotypes. The symbol offers a dramatic and direct means of persuasive communication with large numbers of persons over long lines of communication. Symbols have been used since the dawn of history to compress and convey complex messages to the multitudes. The Star of David and the Cross of Christ remind us of this. Most persons need the shorthand of symbols to deal with that which is abstract, diffuse, or difficult. In David Berlo's view, this is the age of symbol manipulation. "In our grandfather's day, most people earned their living by manipulating *things,* not by manipulating *symbols.*" The need met by symbols was explained by Lippmann years ago: "This problem of the acquisition of meaning by things or of forming habits of simple apprehension is the problem of introducing (1) definiteness and distinction and (2) consistency or stability of meaning into what otherwise is vague and wavering. . . . We tend to perceive that which we have picked out in the form stereotyped for us by our culture. . . ." [25] A current example of Lippmann's point is given by Kenneth Boulding: "Black power is a powerful symbol because it condenses an enormous amount of information and experience into a little bit—there or not there, for me or against me, right or wrong."

The value and use of a venerated symbol is seen in the British monarchy. The British Commonwealth of Nations today is a free association of independent nations held together, not by legal ties, but by the symbol of the Queen of England. She symbolizes the traditional loyalties, the common interests, the traditional institutional forms held more or less in common, the family tie. The American flag, our cherished symbol, movingly and dramatically symbolizes all this nation stands for and means to us every time we see it. Think of the symbolic use we make of George Washington, Abraham Lincoln, of the Minutemen at Lexington and Concord, and of the Statue of Liberty in our patriotic and persuasive communications.

Symbols play an important role in the public relations and fundraising programs of health and welfare agencies. Probably the best-known symbol of its kind is the Red Cross, from which that agency takes its name. The Red Cross originated in Switzerland and created its symbol by reversing the white cross of the Swiss flag on a red background. The upright sword of the American Cancer Society, chosen in a nationwide poster contest, was created to portray its crusading spirit. Another crusade, that of the National Tuberculosis Association, is symbolized by the Cross of Lorraine that dates back to the Crusades. Another popular symbol is that of the Red Feather, used by our Community Chests and United Funds. Created by a local Community Chest in 1928, it was modified in 1955 to incorporate a large "U" to symbolize the merging of Community Chests with United Funds. A more recent example is the peace symbol of those protesting war, which quickly swept around the world—or its virtual opposite: the Green Beret of the U. S. special military forces.

[25] In *Public Opinion,* pp. 60–61, Pelican edition.

One of the most effective symbols ever created is that of Smokey Bear, used by the United States Forest Service to promote the preservation of our forests. The idea originated within a group of foresters and advertising people who were concerned about the need to protect our forests. After experimenting with drawings of deers, squirrels, and other small animals to carry fire-prevention messages, they hit on the idea of using a bear. A bear—with its human-like posture, its way of handling itself, its universal appeal to young and old—seemed ideal to build into a persuasive symbol. The Forest Service today has an artist who serves as "Smokey's caretaker" to make certain that drawings and pictures of him reflect the personality he is intended to convey. Smokey's personality, as determined by artists, has been changed over the years as various interpretations were fused into this one symbol. Although a created symbol, Smokey has had wide impact, especially among the young people of the nation. Smokey, shown below, keeps a half-dozen girls busy answering

his mail every day, taking care of his Junior Forest Ranger program, and sending out his fire-prevention campaign material—not only in the United States but all over the world. In a typical year, some 23-million printed items bearing his imprint are distributed by the Forest Service.

Increasingly business corporations are emphasizing their symbols in an effort to create a sharper, more favorable public image. Corporate identity is a phase of industrial public relations growth. Even so, many business firms are wasting millions in advertising and public relations dollars by using corporate marks that do not truly or effectively represent their companies. An industrial designer advises that a corporate symbol should be selected on the basis of (1) memorability, (2) recognition, (3) appropriateness, and (4) uniqueness. Surely the symbol should be distinct, different, and in character for the institution using it.[26]

THE 7 C'S OF COMMUNICATION

1. CREDIBILITY

Communication starts with a climate of belief. This climate is built by performance on the part of the practitioner. The performance reflects an earnest desire to serve the receiver. The receiver must have confidence in the sender. He must have a high regard for the source's competence on the subject.

2. CONTEXT

A communications program must square with the realities of its environment. Mechanical media are only supplementary to the word and deed that takes place in daily living. The context must provide for participation and playback. The context must confirm, not contradict, the message.

3. CONTENT

The message must have meaning for the receiver, and it must be compatible with his value system. It must have relevance for him. In general, people select those items of information which promise them greatest rewards. The content determines the audience.

4. CLARITY

The message must be put in simple terms. Words must mean the same thing to the receiver as they do to the sender. Complex issues must be compressed into themes, slogans, or stereotypes that have simplicity and clarity. The farther a message has to travel, the simpler it must be. An institution must speak with one voice, not many voices.

---

[26] Symbols, design, and printing all play a part in projecting an institution's image. For elaboration, see Dean R. McKay, "IBM Shows How to Create a Contemporary Corporate Design Theme," *Public Relations Journal*, Vol. 18, November, 1961; and Russell R. Jalbert, "How to Create a Graphic Identity—and Save Money," *ibid.*, Vol. 18, April, 1962.

5. CONTINUITY AND CONSISTENCY

Communication is an unending process. It requires repetition to achieve penetration. Repetition—with variation—contributes to both factual and attitude learning. The story must be consistent.

6. CHANNELS

Established channels of communication should be used—channels that the receiver uses and respects. Creating new ones is difficult. Different channels have different effects and serve effectively in different stages of the diffusion process.

7. CAPABILITY OF AUDIENCE

Communication must take into account the capability of the audience. Communications are most effective when they require the least effort on the part of the recipient. This includes factors of availability, habit, reading ability, and receiver's knowledge.

CASE PROBLEM

You are public relations director in an industrial firm which manufactures outboard and other small motors. Normally your firm employs 2,200 workers. Cancellation of a military order requires the firm to lay off 450 workers at the end of the month.

The personnel director works out plans for the layoff, which include a three-week notice to the men as a matter of fairness to them. Personnel also makes arrangements to try to find other jobs for them in the community and to provide the men laid off with a list of available jobs.

As public relations director, you are asked to work out a plan of communicating this information to company officials, foremen, union officials, the men, and the community. Your plan should include:

1. A timetable designed to squelch rumors and prevent confusion.
2. Themes and tone of announcement.
3. Wording of announcement to employees and to the local press.
4. Letter from the president to opinion leaders.

ADDITIONAL READING

RAYMOND A. BAUER, "The Obstinate Audience: The Influence Process from the Point of View of Social Communication," *American Psychologist,* Vol. 19, 1966, pp. 319–328.

BERNARD BERELSON and GARY STEINER, *Human Behavior: An Inventory of Scientific Findings.* New York: Harcourt, Brace & World, 1964.

DAVID K. BERLO, *The Process of Communication.* New York: Holt, Rinehart & Winston, Inc., 1960.

ERWIN P. BETTINGHAUS, *Persuasive Communication.* New York: Holt, Rinehart & Winston, 1968.

STUART CHASE, *Power of Words.* New York: Harcourt, Brace & World, Inc., 1954.

JOHN C. CONDON, JR., *Semantics and Communication.* London: Collier-Macmillan, 1966.

ERNST DICHTER, "How Word of Mouth Advertising Works," *Harvard Business Review,* Vol. 44, November-December, 1966.

MELVIN L. DE FLEUR, *Theories of Mass Communication.* New York: David McKay, 1966. Paperback. Second Edition, 1970.

EDWARD T. HALL, *The Silent Language.* Garden City, N. Y.: Doubleday, 1959.

S. I. HAYAKAWA, *Language in Thought and Action.* New York: Harcourt, Brace & World, Inc., 1949, rev. ed.

CARL HOVLAND, IRVING JANIS, and HAROLD H. KELLEY, *Communication and Persuasion.* New Haven: Yale University Press, 1957. Paperback.

MARSHALL McLUHAN, *Understanding Media: The Extensions of Man.* New York: McGraw Hill, 1964. Paperback.

CARL R. ROGERS and F. J. ROETHLISBERGER, "Barriers and Gateways to Communication," *Harvard Business Review,* Vol. 30, July-August, 1952.

EVERETT M. ROGERS, *Diffusion of Innovations.* New York: The Free Press of Glencoe, 1962.

WILLIAM H. WHYTE, *Is Anybody Listening?* New York: Simon & Schuster, 1952.

CHAPTER 11

THE PROCESS: EVALUATION— THE FOURTH STEP

The final step in the process is to seek, through research, answers to the questions: "How did we do? Would we have been better off if we had tried something else?" Evaluation leads logically back into the first step. The two aspects of fact-finding are separated here to emphasize the importance of evaluation. One of the weaknesses of contemporary practice has been the lack of yardsticks to measure results. As practitioners invest more time and money in evaluation, they will improve their precision. As they improve the precision of their efforts, they will enhance their professional status. *Extensive feedback is essential to an effective communications program.* The obstacles are, obviously, those of *time, money, tools,* and *knowledge.*

To keep costs down, managers must periodically reexamine the worth of each function. Administrators, particularly controllers, have a forceful way of asking: "What did we get for all the money your department spent?" Increasingly practitioners are being asked to *prove* that the effort has produced measurable and valuable results and that the cost is fair and reasonable. The late Stanley Baar listed four questions to answer in these periodic examinations: [1]

1. How much does this activity contribute specifically to the attainment of business goals? *What* specific goals?
2. Are we getting our full money's worth for each expenditure?
3. Is the over-all cost offset by its accomplishments? Specifically *what* accomplishments?
4. All of our public relations expenditures—how much do we really need them, *and why?*

As computer technology advances, management will become insistent upon getting definitive answers to these and similar questions. Lack of meaningful evaluation of programs causes executives to regard public relations with an unwarranted degree of suspicion and doubt. Study of the rise and fall of a program in one corporation found: "One major reason for the

[1] "Yardsticks for Public Relations," *Public Relations Journal,* Vol. 13, April, 1957, 20ff.

ambient attitude toward public relations by Blank's management is the absence of any yardstick for performance criteria." This finding echoed results of a Grey Public Relations' survey of the nation's top 500 corporations: "The need for better PR evaluation was voiced by nearly two-thirds of the respondents. First and foremost, the marketing executives surveyed said research was the key to improvement." Better evaluation tools are needed, but too few practitioners use the tools already at their disposal. In the view of Counselor John T. Cunningham, "Time and money spent in a ratio of 95 percent 'sending' to 5 percent 'evaluating' is probably par for most public relations departments." As Professor Otto Lerbinger suggests, "Evaluation of results is becoming more crucial because of development in the management field of the concept of management by objectives." The computer is being used by management to effect comparisons of results with objectives. Unless public relations can be subjected to this analysis, the function will suffer. Today's administrator is making increased use of such management tools as linear programming, PERT, critical path method, and simulation techniques. Two practitioners predict: [2] "As the communications function within an organization comes to be recognized as a principal top management function, we will see these tools . . . used in the communications area."

Counselor Cunningham suggests the following list of questions in evaluating the results of specific programs: [3]

1. Was the program adequately planned?
2. Did those concerned understand the job you wanted done?
3. Did all affected departments and executives cooperate?
4. How could you have made the results more effective?
5. Did you reach all pertinent audiences?
6. Did you receive desired publicity before, during, and after the completion of the program?
7. Could you have made better provisions for unforeseen circumstances?
8. Did the program stay within the budget? If not, why?
9. What provisions did you make in advance for measuring results? Were they adequate?
10. What steps were taken to improve future programs of the same type on the basis of this measurement?

---

[2] John F. Budd, Jr., and Robert G. Strayton, "Can Public Relations Be Measured?" *Public Relations Quarterly*, Vol. 13, Winter, 1969, p. 24.

[3] "Measuring Public Relations Results," in American Management Association Management Bulletin, *Measuring and Evaluating Public Relations Activities* (New York: 1968), pp. 4–5. Unfortunately, this helpful booklet is out of print.

Evaluation takes one of two forms—*pretesting* or *posttesting*. The devices used are still in the experimental stage. Even so, they can provide helpful guides in shaping appeals and selecting channels. Successful advertisers have long used these methods. Practitioners, limited by access, time, and budget, must make every item in the program count. Scientific checks, before and after, will serve this end.

Pretesting before launching an expensive, crucial informational campaign is likely to prove economical in the long run. Posttesting will uncover mistakes that need not be repeated and points the way to improved techniques. It is dangerous to rely on the number of clippings returned on a press release, the number of postcards received in response to a radio or TV program, and other equally rough indicators of impact.

Despite the broad developments in methods of evaluating program content and impact, professionals have been slow to adapt them to their needs. Westley Rowland reports: "A survey of 272 colleges and universities . . . revealed that few of them had developed any effective methods for evaluating their public relations programs." [4] A survey of large users of public relations advertising revealed that only a few sponsors had made a serious effort to gauge the impact of the expenditure of tens of thousands of dollars. Baar found a like result when he surveyed 150 practitioners to determine yardsticks they used to measure the value of printed publications in programs. He says, "it became painfully obvious that comparatively few had the vaguest notion of the impact or effectiveness of the words in question. Millions for printing, but not a penny for evaluation!" Moore's Columbus, Ohio, study revealed that only 42 percent of the practitioners studied made systematic efforts to determine the effectiveness of their work.[5] This weakness is world-wide. For example, the Swedish Government in 1966 distributed a brochure, "Your Right to Security," to all Swedish households to make its citizens aware of their social benefits. This program cost 1-million kroner but not one penny of this was spent on evaluating its effectiveness. Yet a similar booklet was prepared and distributed in 1969 at a cost of 1.4-million kroner without the guidance that could have been gained from evaluating the first one. All too typical is this "evaluation" found in the AHA *Public Relations Newsletter:* "Judging by the avalanche of material and clippings received at AHA headquarters, the 1966 National Hospital Week was one of the most successful in terms of increased recognition of the importance of the role of hospitals in our society."

[4] A. Westley Rowland, "Do We Know How Well We're Doing," *PR*, Vol. 1, April, 1956, pp. 24–28.
[5] William Carter Moore, "A Critical Analysis of Public Relations Practitioners in a Midwestern Metropolitan Area," unpublished master's thesis, Ohio State University, previously cited, p. 28.

Researcher Charles R. Wright pointedly reminds: "Unread leaflets, unheard broadcasts, unviewed films—however abundantly and skillfully produced—have no chance of influencing an audience that is not there. And volume of output does not guarantee that an audience is reached." [6] *Evaluation research will forcefully remind the communicator that dissemination does not equal communication.* Research may be conducted by practitioners themselves or obtained through commercial research services: Opinion Research Corporation, Roper Research Associates, Psychological Corporation, Alfred Politz, Crossley S-D Surveys, Daniel Starch and Staff, PR Data, Inc., Gallup's Public Relations Index, and many others. Outside counselors can be of help through critical public relations audits. These outside experts bring specialized knowledge, objectivity, experience in other organizations, and the prestige to gain management's attention. Many major universities and scholars also do such research. [7]

The need for "a merciless personal audit of the finished project" has long been recognized. Pioneer Evart G. Routzahn told the 1920 National Conference of Social Work: "After the returns are all in—when the last meeting has been held, the final distribution of printed matter made, and all activities of the immediate effort have been recorded as history—is the time to put yourself and your methods through the third degree . . . with prayerful solicitude that you will be able to untangle the lessons to be applied to the next project." His counsel has yet to be fully accepted, though its merit is obvious.

Many practitioners take refuge in the cliche that "public relations is an art, not a science" and in the fact that many results are intangible ones. As Edward R. Murrow once told a Congressional committee questioning U.S.I.A. expenditures: "It is very difficult to measure success in our business . . . no computer clicks, no cash register rings when a man changes his mind or opts for freedom. . . ." The variables involved also make measurement difficult; Kal Druck says: [8] "When you're talking about the broad marketing of a product, either consumer or industrial, you get involved in a number of factors which make it difficult to separate out the specific inputs and results of public relations activities, because you're involved in the whole pattern of marketing—the advertising, the salesmanship, the point-of-sale, the deals that are made, the pricing, the economics, the previous relationships of the company, and many other things." None-

---

[6] "Evaluation of Mass Media Effectiveness," UNESCO International Social Science Bulletin, Vol. VII, No. 3.

[7] For directory of commercial services available to practitioners, see Richard Weiner, *Professional's Guide to Public Relations Services* (Englewood Cliffs, N.J.: 1968). Unfortunately he does not list attitude and opinion research organizations, which may be reflective of the use made of research in public relations.

[8] Quoted in Willard Bailey's thesis, previously cited, p. 48.

theless, management's insistent demand for measurement and a growing kit of tools to provide it confront today's practitioner.

A careful precheck of material to be used in a project will pay off in detecting, beforehand, possible backlash effects. It will help in sharpening the understandability of the information for its intended audience. Sometimes an appeal or technique can boomerang with unanticipated, unfavorable results. David Ogilvy, a successful communicator, asserts: [9] "The most important word in the advertising vocabulary is TEST. If you pretest your product with consumers and pretest your advertising, you will do well in the marketplace. Twenty-four out of twenty-five new products never get out of test markets. Manufacturers who don't test-market their new products incur the colossal cost (and disgrace) of having their products fail on a national scale. . . . Test your promise. Test your media. Test your headlines and your illustrations. . . . Never stop testing, and your advertising will never stop improving." The same holds true for all communication efforts.

Backlash effects can be avoided by conducting a response analysis. This means using a sample audience to observe immediate reaction to specific communication content. As an example, an organization promoting tolerance prepared a series of anti-prejudice cartoons featuring an unsavory character, Mr. Biggott. These cartoons were pretested on 160 persons to determine their understanding and reaction. The response analysis showed that the cartoon message was misunderstood by nearly two-thirds of the audience and that the message boomeranged for 33 percent of the people.[10]

Catching potential boomerangs before they have a chance to do widespread harm is obvious common sense. A large insurance company published a series of articles in its employee publication on representative employees—a salesman, a stenographer, an accountant, and so forth. Its article on "The Management Man" boomeranged badly. The editors thought this was another routine article; how wrong they were! The article brought a heavy barrage of criticism, with these typical comments: "If this is the kind of a man——wants, I don't want——;" "I didn't know you had to be an egomaniac to be a manager;" "Mrs.——is a snob;" and so forth. A cautious try-out can head off such unhappy consequences.

---

[9] In *Confessions of an Advertising Man* (New York: Atheneum, 1964) p. 86.

[10] Cited in Patricia L. Kendall and Katherine M. Wolf, "The Analysis of Deviant Cases in Communications Research," *Communications Research, 1948–49*, edited by Paul Lazarsfeld and Frank N. Stanton (New York: Harper & Row, 1949), pp. 152–179.

Also, there is need to pretest the *understandability* of messages. What may appear to be a simplification of an instructor's manual may actually make it more complex in the eyes of the reader. The symbolism chosen for a public relations document may represent perfect clarity to its creator, but be both uninteresting and unintelligible to the reader. Or the symbol may be inappropriate. The latter proved to be the case when the United States Information Service put on an exhibit in India. The first panel featured a painting of Christ delivering the Sermon on the Mount, and the caption expressed the exhibit's theme, "Man Shall Not Live by Bread Alone." India's hungry Hindus and Muslims did not respond favorably.[11] A few years ago an experimental program of health education was undertaken in an isolated Peruvian community high in the Andes. As part of the program, a film on the transmission of typhus by lice, featuring graphic close-up shots, was prepared and shown to the villagers. It became apparent that the message wasn't getting through. A survey of the persons who had seen the film revealed that while they had many lice in their homes they had never been bothered by the giant kind shown on the screen.[12] To get results, appeals and symbols must be appropriate and understood.

The value of pretesting, which is relatively inexpensive, before making a heavy investment in a communications project is shown in this example.[13] The Equitable Life Assurance Society, like most life insurance companies, finds it profitable to promote health education. The company decided to issue a new booklet for national distribution on communicable diseases. The idea for such a pamphlet was stimulated by a U. S. Public Health Service report that more than 50 percent of preschool children were inadequately immunized against the common communicable diseases. Equitable probed more deeply. It found that the problem of inadequate protection against these diseases lay chiefly among the "lower socio-economic" groups in the population, groups difficult to communicate with. It needed a brief, lively illustrated booklet that would reach this audience.

All available data on these diseases were brought together. A professional free-lance writer was hired. The writer first submitted draft manuscripts to health authorities and to Equitable's medical department to insure technical accuracy. After these reviews, a pretest manuscript was prepared. The principal objective of the pretest was to determine whether the manuscript was "right" for its intended audience. One hundred and

---

[11] Arthur Goodfriend, *The Twisted Image* (New York: St. Martin's Press, 1963), p. 208.

[12] This and like examples are in Wilbur Schramm's *Mass Media and National Development,* published jointly by Stanford University Press and UNESCO, 1964.

[13] Based on Equitable Staff Paper, prepared by Caesar Branchini of Equitable's staff, 1965, provided by National Public Relations Council for Health and Welfare. For another example of the value of pretesting, see R. W. Coffman, "How's Your Impact?" in *Public Relations Journal,* Vol. 7, 1951.

forty-two typed manuscripts were distributed to a sample of the intended audience in a "geographic scatter"—Westchester County, New York; Stamford, Connecticut; Atlanta, Georgia; Seattle and Tacoma, Washington; and Los Angeles. These manuscripts carried no art work or sketches. This was done to save time and expense. The results of this pretest were used to shorten the manuscript from 5,000 to 3,000 words, to make it more readable and persuasive, and resulted in a highly successful pamphlet.

A cautionary note on the value of pretesting must be inserted here. The stream of public opinion rushes along swiftly. An idea that worked well on a pretest might possibly prove a fiasco upon widespread use because of the intervening time lag. Seasons change, and with them change people's buying patterns, recreational pursuits, interests, and so forth. The context of the public opinion market place can change markedly overnight with an unexpected news event. In using pretest results as a guide to a communications program, the practitioner ought to be as certain as possible that present conditions are akin to those which existed during the pretest.

POSTTESTING

Posttesting is valuable not only in determining after effects of a specific program but in advancing professional knowledge. Through such research the rough-hewn principles now relied upon can be proved true or false.

There are a number of maxims that are taken for granted in daily practice. But research tends to cast some doubt upon their validity. One is, "What people know about a subject depends roughly upon the amount said or published about it." An experiment designed primarily to find ways and means of extending support for the United Nations was carried out in Cincinnati, Ohio. A survey was taken to determine attitudes and level of information about the UN; then an all-out saturation information campaign was carried out over a six-month period. A postcampaign survey indicated no fundamental changes in the degree of support for the UN in Cincinnati, although the information level had been raised somewhat.[14] Such findings clearly indicate that increasing the flow of information does not necessarily spread information effectively.[15] Another maxim is, "If people know you better, they will like you more." Yet, studies of attitudes toward big business and of foreign attitudes toward the U. S. have indi-

[14] A summary of this landmark experiment can be found in: Shirley Star and Helen M. Hughes, "Report on an Educational Campaign," *American Journal of Sociology*, Vol. 55, 1950, pp. 389–400.

[15] Evidence of this generalization, as provided by Hyman and Sheatsley, was discussed on page 248.

cated the opposite.[16] Still another is, "The more employees know about their company, the better they will like it." Research has thrown doubt on this premise.[17] There hasn't been enough research to make flat generalizations about these maxims one way or the other. There is equal need to measure results of specific appeals, media, and methods.

Audience research can put you straight, however, if you are using words that don't communicate. Rensis Likert cites this example: [18]

> A particular company spent a substantial sum (I was told it was over a million dollars) advertising that its refrigerator was "dual automatic." But after a year's effort doing this, only 14 percent of the housewives could identify which refrigerator this was. "Dual automatic" is not a concept which is closely linked to the life sphere of most housewives. At the same time another company advertised that it guaranteed "Four years of trouble-free service" for its refrigerator. Trouble-free service entered the life spheres of housewives to such an extent that 60 percent of housewives interviewed could identify this refrigerator.

Another warning flag must be raised on the research mast. Research results must be used with discretion, tempered by value judgments. Discussing the value of readership research, Theodore Weber, Jr., vice president corporate communications for McGraw-Hill, Inc., cautions: [19] "While it can be interesting and useful to find out what employees want to see in a house organ and what pleases them most, the real job is not to give employees what they want always, but to get employees to like and read some of the useful and important information the company wants to communicate to them. The company paper cannot shape its sentiments to the pleasures of the public." Research must be *ruled*.

MEASURING IMPACT

A specific program's effectiveness can be evaluated by measuring in terms of four dimensions. They are *audience coverage, audience response, communications impact,* and *process of influence.* Wright points up the importance of each of these measurements this way: [20]

[16] For one bit of evidence, see Burton R. Fisher and Stephen B. Whithey, *Big Business As People See It* (Ann Arbor: The Survey Research Center, University of Michigan, 1951).

[17] Dallis Perry and Thomas A. Mahoney, "In-plant Communications and Employee Morale," *Personnel Psychology,* Vol. 8, Autumn, 1955, 339–46.

[18] In *Public Relations and the Social Sciences* (Ann Arbor: Institute for Social Research, University of Michigan, 1952), p. 13.

[19] In "Printed Material Readership Measurement," AMA Bulletin, *Measuring and Evaluating Public Relations Activities,* previously cited, p. 21.

[20] Wright, "Evaluation of Mass Media Effectiveness," previously cited.

1. *Audience Coverage:* To produce results you must first reach the audience. How large an audience is reached? What are they like? What proportion of the desired audience do they represent?

2. *Audience Response:* How do members of the audience respond? Does the content of the message strike them favorably or unfavorably? Does it arouse their interest? Does it bore them? Do they understand it?

3. *Communications Impact:* After an appraisal of these immediate reactions, you must consider the impact which a message has on its audience. What are the lasting, discernible effects upon people exposed to a message?

4. *Process of Influence:* What is the process by which a communication operates to influence its target audience? Through what channels of influence and mechanisms of persuasion does the message finally affect the individual? How effective is the program in setting into motion the social processes necessary to influence the opinions and behavior of its target audience?

EVALUATION TOOLS

For too long, measurement of impact of public relations' output has relied on a count of news clippings, broadened in recent years to include air mentions and film showings. Newsclips per se tell little beyond degree of media acceptance of publicity output. In recent years efforts to analyze publicity results have advanced beyond mere counting. A commercial firm, PR Data, Inc., took the first small step. An organization determines the objectives of its program and these are then fed into the computer to provide a yardstick against which results can be measured. This comparison serves to keep a program on the track. Then each release is coded for punched-card use, indicating the story number, the messages loaded in, the date, and the publication. The computer readout report, based on newsclips and monitor reports, covers several points: number of messages per story printed, total inches of newspace obtained, and the cumulative circulation. Management then gets a report such as this one: "During the past three months, we had exposure in 2,779 news stories carrying a total of 8,032 corporate messages—or an average of three each. Eighty-two percent of the circulation was in our primary market area. The return on our investment, expressed as cost per thousand readers, was 15.5 cents."

This small advance in using computers still does not measure the story's *impact* on the reader or viewer. Budd and Strayton put it in perspective: [21] "For all its space-age showmanship, the system at this juncture

---

[21] "Can Public Relations Be Measured?," previously cited, p. 20.

merely substitutes electronic muscle for human labor to analyze clippings, to add volume, tally circulation, 'readout' geographic coverage and aid in working out an array of percentages that gives an impression of scientific communications planning . . . (it) could not be regarded as a major step toward a definitive *measurement of results*."

In business the impact of product publicity can be gauged more accurately than it usually is. Carl Ruff, counselor for a furniture company, demonstrated this in analyzing inquiries about the firm's new office system, comparing those stimulated by advertising and those stimulated by publicity. He found that publicity outpulled advertising by a ratio of seven to one and that a qualitative analysis of public relations effectiveness by inquiry count, revealed that for a moderate fee the client had obtained $1.4-million worth of query-pulling, product-selling, and attitude-reinforcing exposure over a period of fifteen months. Ruff's effort to develop a method of analyzing results not only provided management with definitive data but further demonstrated the value of evaluation: [22] "The breakdown on inquiries by publications proved that some of these magazines which the client—and we—had considered to be prime targets were actually of little importance in producing queries. And magazines which one management group had not considered important turned out to be among those productive." All organizations can profit from such a systematic analysis.

In addition to these approaches and to the fact-finding, formal and informal, described in Chapter 8, the practitioner has several evaluation tools. Each one is based on the principle of making a survey of a *representative sample* of the target audience in a systematic way.

Reader-Interest Studies

What people read in newspapers, magazines, employee publications, and so forth, can be measured through reader-interest surveys. This technique was developed by the Advertising Research Foundation and a few journalism schools. The ARF, supported jointly by advertising agencies, advertisers, and newspapers, has made more than 150 such studies. These provide a wealth of data.[23] (The ARF's *Continuing Study of Newspaper Reading* did not include nonurban readers and readers under 18. The results should be viewed with these facts in mind.) This tool is more a quantitative than qualitative measuring device.

A reader-interest survey is made by taking fresh, unmarked copies

---

[22] Carl Ruff, "Measurement of Publicity Effectiveness by Inquiry Analysis," AMA Bulletin, *Measuring and Evaluating Public Relations Activities*, pp. 14–17.

[23] See, for example, Charles E. Swanson, "What They Read in 130 Daily Newspapers," *Journalism Quarterly*, Vol. 32, Fall, 1955. Many such studies are now being fed to computers and accumulated so the information becomes useful in showing trends.

of a publication to a representative sample of the total potential reading audience. After the interviewer makes the necessary introduction and qualifying statements, he goes through the publication with the respondent, page by page. The respondent shows the interviewer items he has seen or read. These are recorded on an interview form by code number. At no time does the interviewer point out items to the respondent. The key question is "Did you *happen* to see or read anything on this page?" Checks on this method have proved that readers are honest in saying what they have read.

Published reader-interest studies offer valuable insights into what potential readers actually consume. In using the results of such studies, it is well to keep in mind this advice of a veteran magazine editor, "A magazine cannot be edited by arithmetic alone." Reader-interest results are guides, not mandates, for the responsible communicator. This research ought to be followed up, after a given interval, to determine the comprehension and retention of the material read by readers. Both methods will provide healthy reminders that *readership doesn't equal circulation* and *readership doesn't equal comprehension and retention.*

Readability Tests

Yardsticks for the reading ease of printed materials have been developed. It is possible to grade a given message as easy to read at a given educational level, be it seventh grade or college senior. This yardstick enables the communicator to write his message for the reading ability of his intended audience. This should not be interpreted as "writing down" to people nor should a person's reading ability be equated with his intelligence. Making copy more readable definitely increases readership. This has been proved repeatedly. These yardsticks, too, should be used as guides rather than as commands to write inside a fixed formula.

It should be clearly understood that readability is only one aspect of getting readership. Equally important are *content, format, organization, and writing style.* These factors, coupled with the more fundamental understanding which the writer brings to his writing and the reader brings to his reading, all shape the reception and impact of the printed word. If used in this perspective, readability tests are helpful. There are four commonly used methods for measuring readability.

1. *The Flesch Formula.* Dr. Rudolf Flesch's method is divided into two parts; Reading Ease Score is determined by the difficulty of words used. This is measured by the number of syllables in words and by sentence length. Human Interest Score is measured by the number of personal words per 100 words and the number of personal sentences per 100 sentences.[24]

[24] Rudolf Flesch, *How to Test Readability* (New York: Harper & Row, Publishers, 1951).

2. *The Gunning Formula.* Robert Gunning's formula measures reading ease by the average sentence length, number of simple sentences used, verb force, portion of familiar words, portion of abstract words, percentage of personal references, and percentage of long words.[25]

3. *Dale-Chall Formula.* This one, developed at Ohio State, measures reading ease by analysis of average sentence length and the proportion of words outside the Dale List of 3,000 Words Most Commonly Used.[26]

4. *Cloze Procedure.* This test was developed by Prof. Wilson Taylor of the University of Illinois and is somewhat different from the first three. It measures help provided the reader by the context of the total message. It also can be applied to auditory as well as visual communication. This method tests readability by giving samples of the material to subjects with every *nth* word omitted. Success of subjects in filling in missing words on the basis of other parts of the message measures the item's readability. The "cloze procedure" is aimed at measuring reader's comprehension of material as well as its readability.[27]

In a review of the value of these formulas, Prof. Blaine McKee found that of those listed, Dale-Chall should be the most accurate but is the slowest of the three major ones and that the three major methods usually give results that are close. He thinks these formulas are particularly helpful for people who need to improve their writing but that practitioners should not continue to use them indefinitely.[28] Readability tests, when used in conjunction with reader-interest studies, will provide practitioners with useful guides for future projects.

Radio and TV Audience Research

There are seven basic methods for obtaining measurements of a program audience's size in the broadcast media.[29]

1. *The Diary.* This requires that some member (or members) of the household keep a written record or log of program exposure.

[25] Robert Gunning, *The Technique of Clear Writing* (New York: McGraw-Hill Book Company, Rev. Ed., 1968).

[26] Edgar Dale and Jeanne Chall, "A Formula for Predicting Readability," *Educational Research Bulletin*, Ohio State University, Vol. 27, January and February issues, 1948.

[27] Wilson L. Taylor, "Cloze Procedure: A New Tool for Measuring Readability," *Journalism Quarterly*, Vol. 30, Fall, 1953, 415–33, and "Recent Developments in the Use of 'Cloze Procedure,' " Vol. 33, Winter, 1956, 42–48 ff.

[28] In article, "Readability Formulas Can Aid Good Writing," *Public Relations Journal*, Vol. 23, July, 1967.

[29] *Recommended Standards for Radio and Television Program Audience Size Measurements*, p. 15. Copyright 1954 by the Advertising Research Foundation, Inc. Reprinted by special permission.

2. *The Recorder.* This method electronically or mechanically records automatically individual set tuning, including frequency or channel.

3. *The Personal Coincidental.* Personal interviews are made throughout the duration of a given program or time period. Respondents are queried regarding program exposure at moment of call.

4. *The Personal Roster Recall.* Respondents are shown a list of programs and stations. They are asked to indicate which they were exposed to during the measured time span.

5. *Personal Unaided Recall.* Personal interviews are made during which respondents are asked about program exposure for a preceding time span. Unlike the roster, the personal unaided recall uses no list of programs or stations. It depends entirely upon the respondent's unaided memory for exposure information.

6. *The Telephone Coincidental.* This method employs the same principles as the personal coincidental method except that interviews are made by telephone.

7. *The Telephone Recall.* This method employs the same principles as the personal unaided recall except that the interviews are made by telephone.

8. *Combination Telephone Coincidental and Diary.* This method combines broadcast exposure information obtained by the coincidental telephone method in one sample of homes with information obtained by the diary method in another sample of homes.

9. *The Combination Telephone Coincidental and Telephone Recall.*

10. *The Combination Telephone Coincidental and Personal Roster Recall.*

Among the leading commercial research organizations which use one or more of these methods in measuring audience size for clients are the A. C. Nielsen Company, American Research Bureau, Pulse, Inc., Trendex, Inc., and Sindlinger & Company.

Public confidence in the validity and honesty of audience research in radio and television got a series of jolts in 1963. Early that year the Federal Trade Commission obtained consent decrees from The Pulse, Inc., A. C. Nielsen Co., TvQ, Inc., and American Research Bureau that these firms would stop claiming that their findings are 100 percent accurate. In a series of public hearings weeks later, the House Commerce Committee presented evidence to show that radio and TV ratings were often based on faulty or dishonest research. Evidence presented indicated that the largest firm in this field was using a sample based largely on an outmoded 1940 United States Census. This use violated the basic premise that a sample must be truly representative if research results are to be valid. Another commercial firm could not present records to support rating surveys it had sold to clients as documented research. Still another admitted that it had fudged on the size of the sample needed for reliable results. One witness cynically remarked, "The industry doesn't want true figures, anyway." Chairman Oren Harris told one firm that its rating service "appears to me to be a con game." [30]

After these congressional hearings, both the Federal Trade Commission and the Federal Communications Commission expressed official interest and concern over the "ratings mess." These hearings made it clear that, in the heat of competition for the ratings business, many firms had cut the corners of research methods, with the result that their work was shoddy at best, dishonest at worst. This incident should warn practitioners that it is truly pound-foolish to expect a cheap buy in audience or opinion research.

Program Analyzer Tests

This is a mechanical device for recording an audience's reaction to a program while people are being exposed to it. Reactions are recorded in terms of Like, Dislike, or Indifference. The member of the audience indicates his preferences by pressing one of two buttons. These reactions are recorded on tape as the program progresses. Time lines on the tape serve to identify parts of the program to which the member is reacting. Through this device, audience response to specific items of program content can be determined.[31] This device can be used to pretest public relations presentations.

Measurement of Impact

The real test of a communications program is its results. Did it pay off at the box office? The sales counter? The voting booth? Did the program bring about the desired reaction and action? Did your message result in the desired modification of a group's attitudes? Actual results offer a sure test. They deserve to be studied and analyzed. In addition to observation of results *apparently* obtained, there are other ways of getting at the impact.

[30] "Is Pulse running a con game? Rep. Harris Asks That Question, Then Puts Nielsen on Hot Seat," *Broadcasting,* Vol. 64, March 25, 1963, 34–50. For details on hearing, see "Hearings, Subcommittee of the Committee on Interstate and Foreign Commerce, House of Representatives," *Broadcast Ratings,* Part I and Part II. (Washington, D. C.: The Committee, Government Printing Office, 1963.)

[31] See Tore Hollonquist and Edward A. Suchman, "Listening to the Listener," *Radio Research, 1942–1943,* edited by Paul F. Lazarsfeld and Frank N. Stanton (New York: Duell, Sloan, and Pearce, 1944).

1. *The Focused Interview.* This involves interviewing recipients of communication and getting them to relate their experiences to various parts of a program.

2. *Impact Analysis.* This involves studies to determine short-term and long-term effects of a given program. It includes determining the effects on individuals and on groups and subgroups. There are differences in impact to be studied in terms of time span and in terms of individual and group reactions.

3. *Experimental Studies.* The ideal way to measure the impact of a program is by comparing two groups which are exactly alike except for the fact that one group has been exposed to a program whereas the other has not. The critical feature is in matching two groups. In such experiments it is essential to control extraneous influences. Results are obtained by surveys and by panel studies.[32]

OVER-ALL REVIEW OF PROGRAM

The research tools described above are helpful, but they measure only the bits and pieces, not the over-all program. The total effort must be kept in view. An important step is to review, periodically, the total program and to measure its results against the assigned objectives. Several "report cards" have been designed for this purpose. One practitioner offers these check points as a guide in periodically evaluating a going public relations program:[33]

1. *Objectives*—Are they clearly stated and understood throughout company? Are there areas in which agreement on goals is needed?

2. *Organization*—Are related public relations functions organized as a single unit or scattered throughout various departments? Does the public relations director have adequate management backing to see that public relations responsibilities are considered throughout the company? . . . Is size and training of staff adequate to achieve desired public relations objectives?

3. *Content*—Do your programs and activities give adequate consideration to all segments of the public—customers, employees, stockholders, and the financial community, government groups, civic, educational, and community organizations, the press, and suppliers? . . .

4. *Measurement of Results*—Do you have adequate staff, budget and management backing to gauge results of your work? How do these activities compare with those of others in your industry and in other

---

[32] For illustrative study, see Hovland, Lumsdaine, and Sheffield, *Experiments on Mass Communication*, Vol. III (Princeton, N.J.: Princeton University Press, 1949).

[33] John T. Cunningham, "Evaluating Public Relations' Effectiveness," *Public Relations Journal,* Vol. 19, January, 1962, 21–23.

industries? Have you considered an outside specialist to review your public relations program?

5. *Control*—What steps have you taken to improve future public relations activities in the light of audit findings? What steps need to be taken during coming years?

CASE PROBLEM

1. Measure the readability of an employee magazine, handbook, annual report, or university brochure—by measuring samples of content, using:
   a. Flesch, Gunning, or Dale-Chall method.
   b. "The Cloze Procedure."
2. Compare results obtained by the respective methods used.
3. How does the reading level of the material square with the probable reading level of the intended audience?

ADDITIONAL READING

WILLARD BAILEY, "Program Evaluation," *Public Relations Journal*, Vol. 24, September, 1968.

RICHARD W. BUDD, ROBERT K. THORP, and LEWIS DONOHEW, *Content Analysis of Communications*. New York: Macmillan, 1967.

KEITH DAVIS, "A Method of Studying Communication Patterns in Organizations," *Personnel Psychology*, Vol. 6, Autumn, 1953.

WILLIAM M. DOMIN and JACK FREYMULLER, "Can Industrial Product Publicity Be Measured?", *Journal of Marketing*, Vol. 29, July, 1965.

FRANK E. HEWENS, "How to Audit Your Public Relations," *Public Relations Quarterly*, Vol. 8, Winter, 1964. Helpful guide.

JACK B. HASKINS, *How to Evaluate Mass Communication: The Controlled Experiment Field*. New York: Advertising Research Foundation, 1968. An ARF monograph.

HERBERT H. HYMAN, CHARLES R. WRIGHT, and TERENCE K. HOPKINS, *Applications of Methods of Evaluation*. Berkeley: University of California Press, 1962.

EUGENE F. LANE, "Social Science: Its Lack of Application Is Starving Public Relations," *Public Relations Journal*, Vol. 21, February, 1965.

ALVIN SCHWARTZ, *Evaluating Your Public Relations*. New York: National Public Relations Council for Health and Welfare, 1965.

CLAIRE SELLTIZ et al., *Research Methods in Social Relations*. New York: Holt, Rinehart & Winston, Inc., 1959.

DANIEL STARCH, *Measuring Advertising Readership and Results*. New York: McGraw Hill Book Co., 1966.

CHAPTER 12

THE
TOOLS
OF
COMMUNICATION

In his work the practitioner utilizes the printed word, the spoken word, and the image. He uses three avenues—~~personal contact, controlled media,~~ and ~~public media.~~

The importance of personal contacts and the part played by the people in communicating ideas already have been emphasized. The news media, through which the practitioner reaches the general public, are beyond the direct control of the practitioner. *For space and time in these media, he competes against all comers on terms set by the media.* The news media pose special problems which will be discussed in Chapter 17.

In this chapter we shall examine briefly the following 17 tools: Their content can be controlled by the communicator at the point of origin; their impact depends on the communicator's skill.

House Publications
Handbooks, Manuals, Books
Letters, Bulletins, Recordings
Bulletin Boards, Posters, Billboards
Information Racks
Inserts and Enclosures
Institutional Advertising, Identity Programs
Meetings and Conferences
Speakers' Bureaus
Public Address Systems, Telephone Newsline
The Grapevine
Motion Pictures, Slide Films, Tapes
Closed-Circuit Television
Displays and Exhibits
Open Houses and Plant Tours
Staged Events
Art Programs

These tools will be discussed in terms of *what they are*. Later on they will be discussed in terms of how and where they are used in specific situations.

THE PRINTED WORD

HOUSE PUBLICATIONS

Because of its versatility, the house publication has developed into a major medium. In the view of the *Wall Street Journal,* these publications have become "workhorses, instead of just management megaphones of intangible value." They meet the common need of all organizations to tell their stories through at least one medium, on paper, in their own words, in their own way, and without being interrupted. In each case, however, the sponsor must get the publication *read* and *believed.*

Exact figures on the number of company publications today are not available, but at least 11,000 can be definitely accounted for. It is the estimate of the International Council of Industrial Editors that publications sponsored by business reach a total circulation of more than 500,000 per issue. Industry is investing millions of dollars each year in this medium of communication to employees, customers, shareholders, dealers, thought leaders, and others. Of the some 11,000 company publications, the majority are published for employees, but many also are circulated to secondary audiences. The company publication is so common in business that there is a tendency to think and talk about its usage solely in terms of business. However, as organizations grow in size, the need for internal communication grows. There are thousands of publications put out by military units, governmental agencies, schools, colleges, welfare agencies, fraternal groups, and trade associations. Gebbie's 1968 *House Magazine Directory* estimates that there are some 50,000 house publications with the top 4,000 accounting for 16-million circulation, and the total of all exceeding 180-million.[1] These are estimates because, as *Fortune* says, "the house-organ publishing operation is so big and sprawling, no one has yet succeeded in measuring it."

There is increasing stability, sophistication, and specialization in this mushrooming segment of America's communications system. The *Wall Street Journal* has noted: "For years a hodgepodge of birth notices, bowling scores, and management messages, the house organ . . . today is improving in tone. At the same time, it is becoming more specialized with separate editions aimed at management, production employees, retirees, and other specific groups." For example, there is increased need for publications to disseminate technical information from one technical group to others in the same organization. The ICIE estimates that most of the 2,000

---

[1] Conley Gebbie, *Gebbie's House Magazine Directory,* 6th Ed. (Sioux City, Ia.: 1968). Particularly useful for those who can find publicity outlets in these publications.

new company publications which appeared in the late 1960s were specialized offshoots of existing house organs. Chrysler, in the mid-60s reorganized its internal communications and went from one to 38 employee publications in three years, adding, among others, Newsletter for Management.

Another reflection of specialization in the field is the prestige company quarterly designed for opinion leaders, such as IBM's *Think,* General Electric's *Forum,* and Standard Oil of New Jersey's *Lamp.* Some firms design their internal publications to serve both internal and external needs. For example, Price Waterhouse revamped its *Review* into an internal-external in 1962 adding 8,000 influentials to its mailing list. Of this list, some 1,000 are presidents and 3,000 vice-presidents; 2,000 copies go to libraries. These prestige quarterlies pay high fees to the nation's top writers for articles, and their unit cost ranges up to $1.75 per copy. IBM's *Think,* the pacesetter, has a carefully-screened circulation of 130,000.

Many of these corporate publications publish articles of general interest with no obvious tie to the company ledger. *The Grace Log,* published by W. R. Grace & Company, for example, includes articles on subjects ranging from Australian horse racing to the Peace Corps. Early in this decade the Kaiser Aluminum and Chemical Corporation re-styled its *Kaiser News* to deal with public interest subjects and to encourage creativity and innovation within the organization. The technique is to talk to "outsiders" and to rely on the staff catching the message. Others are breaking away from the old self-serving formulas; "The time is perhaps upon us when a corporate publication of genuine public interest, financed as only a great company can finance it, will do more for its sponsors, in a kind of inverse proportion of modesty, than the type of house publications that now prevail." [2] There is mounting evidence that company and organizational periodicals have become firmly established as integral parts of the public relations program.

The field's growth is reflected in a series of benchmark surveys made since 1948 by the International Council of Industrial Editors. The 1966 survey, Operation Tapemeasure No. 3, conducted by Dr. Albert Walker, showed that responsibility for these publications is steadily shifting to the public relations department, that increasingly the editor reports to a top official, and that editors' salaries have been sharply upgraded. The one negative finding in the 1966 survey was that there are few written policies governing corporate publications, a matter in which there was little change in a decade.[3] The 1966 survey showed increased emphasis on external

---

[2] Wilson Sullivan, "All in the Family," *Saturday Review,* Vol. 50, August 12, 1967.

[3] International Council of Industrial Editors, *Operation Tapemeasure No. 3* (ICIE: Akron, O., 1967).

audiences because the external editor tends to be a cut above his counter-part . . . external editors were more likely to be found in the public relations department, to have larger budgets, and to approach higher-ranking officers for policy clarification and story clearance. External editors also were better educated and drew larger salaries." [4]

As indicated, there are three types of publications: (1) *internal;* (2) *external;* (3) combination *internal-external.* Most are published for employees or members of organizations. Some are designed for general public consumption or for many specialized publics, such as alumni, dealers, contributors, reservists, or community leaders. Some serve *both* inside and outside publics. For example, Standard Oil's *Lamp* goes to some 125,000 opinion leaders as well as to its nearly one-million shareholders. *Gebbie's Directory* suggested that, in 1968, one half of organization publications were internal, one quarter external, and one quarter internal-external. The broader the audience sought, the more generalized the content must be. These publications are variously issued on a daily, weekly, bi-monthly or monthly basis.

ICIE's surveys show that there has been little shift in the type of publication over a decade, with most still primarily used for internal communications. *Operation Tapemeasure, 1956,* and *Operation Tapemeasure No. 3* show these comparisons:

PUBLICATION AUDIENCE

1956		1966
65%	Internal	65.89%
18%	External	17.39%
14%	Internal-External	10.59%
3%	Other	6.13%

The magazine remains the most popular format; of the 897 publications covered in the 1966 survey, nearly half used the magazine format; nearly 28 percent newspaper format; and nearly 15 percent the newsletter. The last figure is nearly double the 7 percent using the newsletter format in 1963, showing increased favor for this faster, more flexible means of internal communication. The majority of the publications are now printed by offset. Nearly 46 percent are issued monthly, 4 percent weekly, and nearly 17 percent bi-monthly. Nearly half use at least two colors in their publications.

Most publications are mailed to the homes of employees and to others

---

[4] Richard G. Charlton, "A Bigger Job for House Organs," *Public Relations Journal,* Vol. 25, June, 1969. Elaborates on *Operation Tapemeasure No. 3.*

on mailing lists. *Operation Tapemeasure No. 3* found that "nearly three out of five publications were mailed, while only 12 percent were distributed within the plant. Another 18 percent combined mail and within-plant distribution. Nearly 4 percent used first class mail."

In this staggering array of publications, there is little uniformity in format and approach. House publications take the format of daily newspapers, news magazines, and general slick magazines. Some are published as paid-for pages in local newspapers. There are slick-paper and newsprint publications; letterpress, offset, and multilith productions; special-cover, self-cover, and no-cover papers; four-syllable talk, picture talk, comics talk, cracker-barrel philosophy, preaching, personal items, gossip. Some publications stick to shop talk; some ignore it completely; some have a mixture. A few sell advertising space. A few, such as *Woman's Day* and *Arizona Highways,* have paid circulations. In Great Britain, some one-quarter of industrial firms publishing house magazines sell them rather than give them away. These firms range in size from the giants like Ford, Shell, and Guinness down to small companies. "The pro-sell group in Britain maintains that, psychologically, employees tend to place more value on a publication if it has a monetary worth. Even a nominal charge, they feel, establishes the publication as something too worthwhile to be given away." [5] The idea is worth consideration.

A recent innovation is the use of records to carry the sponsor's message into the employee's home, although the picture of weary employee at the end of the day taking trouble to put a record on his record-player to hear the company message is a bit hard to envision. These plastic records also are used by firms to send special holiday greetings to employees and customers. Still another variation of the employee-magazine format is Buick's *Factory Whistle,* an hour-long broadcast each workday morning of news and information for Buick's 18,000 employees over a local radio station. Buick pays for the radio time. *Factory Whistle* gives the time, weather, and traffic advice and transmits news of personnel appointments, promotions, retirements, employee awards, sales, and production successes. All this is packaged within the format of a radio show.

The content of house publications varies as much as the format. Two basic editorial schools of thought predominate. One is that content should be what readers will enjoy: news about themselves, for example. The other is that content should be what the publisher wants readers to know: for example, news about the organization and its objectives. Some industrial editors argue strongly for presentation of management's views on controversial political issues. Others argue as vehemently that company organs

---

[5] Jack J. Honomichl, "In Britain They Sell Their House Organs," *Public Relations Quarterly,* Vol. 10, Spring, 1965.

should avoid the controversial. Some company publications include union news; most do not.

As the ICIE surveys indicated, many of these publications lack the guidelines of definite policies and clearly-stated objectives. This leads, inescapably, to much waste of money and manpower. Counselor Fred Wittner has distilled these principles out of his quarter-century experience:

1. The publication should fill the needs of both the company and its employees.
2. It should provide useful, meaningful information, not small talk.
3. If distributed externally, it should go to the group leaders of the community, as well as to customers and prospects.
4. It requires the *joint* interest and effort of management and its appointed editor or counsel.

Professor J. W. Click studied the content of ten publications that won the Award of Excellence in ICIE's annual competition and found a wide variety of content being used. General company news and features accounted for nearly 44 percent of the space in these publications; general non-company features, the second largest category, accounted for nearly 15 percent of the space; recognition of employees got nearly 7 percent of the space, a distant third. Professor Click's analysis of content in these prize winners is shown on page 287.[6]

Most editors strive for a workable compromise between what the organization wants its publics to know and what they want to read. Properly viewed, the house publication is a direct channel to specific publics, not a vaguely conceived "morale booster." To justify the expense and effort required, a publication must accomplish something useful for the sponsor. There is growing realization that trivia accomplishes little for either reader or publisher. *A house paper has no intrinsic value.* Its only value is that put into it by the editor, guided by definite objectives. Intelligent editors do not confuse reader bait with the purpose and substance of the publication. *The content of a publication determines its character and impact.*

There is a trend toward making the publication two-way. This means inviting questions and making surveys of attitudes, then reporting them in print. It has been a tough job to sell management on the idea and an even tougher job to get readers to turn in questions.

In the average budget set-up, a most effective use of the house publication can be attained without straining for special effects. Four-color covers are not essential. The prime needs are for candor, intelligent selec-

[6] J. W. Click, "Employee Magazines in the Public Relations Program," *Public Relations Quarterly*, Vol. 12, Summer, 1967. Chart used with permission.

MAGAZINE:	ALCOA NEWS	SEARS EAST WIND	195 MAGAZINE	LONG LINES	B-A COM-MENTATOR	THE LINK	CAS-CADES	THE TRUNK-LINER	PER-SPECTIVE	FUSION	AVER.
A. EMPLOYEE CONTENT											
Wages, Hours, Benefits	.6	.5	.6	.7	2.2	3.2	...	3.2	...	...	1.10
Health, Safety, Finance	1.7	.7	1.7	.1	2.4	2.5	...	3.2	...	...	1.23
Employee Changes, Retirements, Promotions	1.1	...	7.7	5.8	25.3	4.1	...	...	1.1	3.3	4.84
Management Changes, Promotions, Transfers	.9	2.3	5.0	4.5	5.3	2.4	...	12.9	1.1	1.8	3.62
Recognition of Employees	16.3	6.0	8.3	1.8	5.6	11.4	...	6.4	8.3	4.2	6.83
Employee Recreation & Social Programs	2.4	...	1.4	1.9	6.8	...	...	...	2.2	2.4	1.71
Family Features	...	...	...	2.7	...	1.6	...	...	...	...	.43
B. COMPANY CONTENT											
Economic Issues	6.0	15.0	.8	.5	4.1	15.4	...	3.2	...	...	4.50
Elimination of Waste Time & Material	...	...	...	...	...	...	...	5.6	...	...	.56
Develop Pride in Job, Loyalty to Company	...	...	.6	...	...	...	2.2	4.0	...	...	.68
Company Policy News & Interpretation	.4	3.3	3.7	...	1.2	2.0	...	1.6	...	...	1.22
Labor Relations	2.2	...	...	...	1.4	...	...	...	...	...	.36
Letters to Editor, Employee Participation	...	1.0	...	...	.4	...	...	3.2	...	...	.46
General Company News and Features	46.8	53.4	50.8	60.6	27.5	44.7	19.6	21.8	45.0	64.5	43.47
Customer Relations	...	...	...	...	...	...	...	...	...	...	0.00
Political Issues	...	...	.8	...	...	...	...	...	...	...	.08
Editorial Comment	2.5	5.5	2.9	.9	.3	...	3.1	...	...	...	1.52
C. GENERAL AND MISCELLANEOUS CONTENT											
General Features (Not company-related)	9.4	...	8.1	10.6	9.3	1.6	63.5	11.3	23.5	9.1	14.64
Industry News (Not company-related)	...	...	...	1.1	.2	3.2	2.4	8.9	...	6.7	2.25
D. ADVERTISING											
Company Advertisements	.6	1.7	1.9	2.6	.7	.8	4.2	...	8.4	...	2.09
Public Service Adv.	3.1	.4	1.8	1.3	3.1	...	...	4.9	1.1	4.7	2.04
Employee Classified	...	...	...	...	...	...	...	...	...	...	0.00
E. COVER & MASTHEAD	6.0	10.2	3.9	4.9	4.2	7.1	5.0	9.8	9.3	3.3	6.37

tion of subject matter that combines the objectives of sponsor with interests of readers, simple format, and the constant purpose of helping readers learn as much about matters of mutual interest as they desire. Such a publication will almost assuredly break through barriers that isolate management from those who do want to think, to grow, and to share an understanding of the important things going on.

HANDBOOKS, MANUALS, BOOKS

There are three general types of booklets and pamphlets.

1. *Indoctrination booklets* welcome the new soldier, employee, society member, student, supplier, or visitor. Literature for the customer or product owner usually is served by the sales or advertising department. The beginner's booklet helps him to get off on the right foot. It tells him the rules of the game and the benefits of playing the game according to the rules. It seeks to instill a team spirit—the feeling that he has joined a winning combination.

2. *Reference guides* comprise a second type of handbook. These are useful to the seasoned member as well as to the neophyte. Reference handbooks concern themselves with details of a Group Insurance Plan, Pension Plan, Suggestion System, Hospitalization, Profit-Sharing, Housekeeping and Safety, Library Content, Recreation Program and Facilities, Contest Rules, Campus Geography, and the like. Handbooks enable members to look up specific information easily. In content, they tend to be definitive and instructive. They save time and encourage appreciation of the values of membership. They quickly provide information actually sought by the reader.

3. *Institutional booklets, books, and brochures* have subject matter devoted to the selling of an idea or a philosophy or to presenting the total entity rather than a product or service. Typical are messages related to the free-enterprise system, military recruiting, educational facilities, or charitable work. In another category are reports of dedications, celebrations, awards, history, success, expansion, and developments in science or the arts. Some contain statements of position on national issues. And there are the commemorative booklets and brochures on traditional anniversary occasions.

The format of booklets has the same wide variation as the house publication. The financial circumstances of the organization enter in, as do size of circulation, audience impression sought, and importance attached by officials to media and occasion. In most cases, the circumstances are such that an organization wants its literature to reflect both its success and its pride. They tend to be lavish. Budgets tend to be secondary. There are, of course, exceptions. University bulletins that reveal progress in a field of research, for example, are quite restrained in make-up and content. The information, rather than the appearance, is the thing. Similarly, there is a pattern of uniformity established for military manuals.

Prime among these publications is the presentation booklet which provides an over-all picture of the organization to visitors, prospective executives or students, prospective donors or customers, and other specialized audiences. Most institutions need a booklet which tells its story quickly and effectively to interested publics. One survey, in which 192 major U. S. corporations participated, found that 60 percent of them publish such booklets. Many non-users indicated they were considering doing so. Targeted audiences for these presentation booklets included: company visitors, prospective employees, community leaders, prospective customers, general public, stockholders, dealers, distributors, financial analysts, press, and educators.[7]

Another type booklet sometimes used is the comic book. It has readability, versatility, and economy to recommend it. Insurance companies use comics to provide insurance information, health information, and to teach safety. Utilities have used it with success to communicate safety information to non-English speaking customers. Comics, long a popular, effective means of communication, are the easiest of all printed forms to understand. The often-made criticisms made against this medium—poor writing, poor artwork, and bad grammar—are not inherent in the comic book.

There is no single method of distribution that has proved most effective for handbooks. Many organizations maintain libraries. Handbooks are seen in company cafeterias, reception lobbies, club rooms, and in wall racks. This distribution is secondary, copies having been mailed or handed to prime audiences. Employees get their handbooks variously at their place of work or in the mail at home. Dealers receive theirs by hand from salesmen or in the mail. The government catalogues literature and makes it available at nominal cost from the Superintendent of Documents. Large corporations mail literature to the homes of interested people in their plant cities. Trade associations issue literature at conventions and by mail to members and thought leaders.

The important thing to remember about these tools is that they are *supplementary, not primary.* A handbook for the new employee is no substitute for the personal handshake, a thorough orientation, and a personally conducted tour of introduction. Many organizations use the "buddy" system for newcomers.

A related medium being utilized more and more is the book or lengthy

---

[7] James K. Woodard, "Presentation Booklets: How They Are Used; What They Contain," *Public Relations Journal*, Vol. 24, May, 1968.

booklet tracing the history of an institution or industry or a biography of a founder. These books are written for business firms, universities, and trade associations. They are usually subsidized by the sponsor and published by a commercial publisher. The sponsor sees to it that copies are placed in libraries and freely distributed to influentials among his publics. These sponsored books are high in initial cost but pay a long-term dividend if they are accurate, well written, and widely distributed. Placed in libraries, such histories become source material for writers and historians. Examples include Procter & Gamble's story *It Floats;* Motorola's *The Founder's Touch,* life of Paul Galvin; Cybis Porcelain's *A History of American Art Porcelain;* Hallmark's *The Spirit of the Letter in Painting.* Effective examples of the use of reference books in public relations are Mobil's *Travel Guide* and Hertz' *Survival Manual for the Traveling Businessman.* Material for the latter guide was obtained from travel writers in each of Hertz' principal cities. Each of the twenty-eight chapters is offered as a free booklet in these cities. Another in this genre is First National City Bank of New York's *How to Survive in New York With Children.*

Basic questions must be considered: (1) Does the type of book under consideration fit the company's needs? (2) Will the nature and purpose of book attract a capable outside writer? (3) Is the book to be sold commercially or given away? (4) Should it have a prestige hard-cover or a paperback? (5) What are possible tie-ins to promote it? (6) Does it further organization's basic public relations objectives? [8]

LETTERS AND BULLETINS

Individually written, individually addressed letters have long constituted the backbone of interorganizational communication. Printed letters are being used in increasing volume to establish a direct, speedy line of communication with specific publics. Letters are used on a regular or spot-news basis to reach employees, dealers, alumni, or workers in a fund-raising or legislative campaign. As the *Wall Street Journal* observes: "An increasing number of corporations are finding the old-fashioned letter an answer to communications problems, a fact that may seem somewhat surprising in this era of electronics, high-powered press-agentry, and glossy company publications."

In industry the employee letter has been developed as a supplement to the slower, less frequently published house magazine. It offers an opportunity for the chief executive to talk to the employee and his family in a "you and I" conversational, newsy approach. James M. Black, writ-

---

[8] For more on this tool, see Richard Weiner, "Books Are Effective Public Relations Tools," *Public Relations Journal,* May, 1969.

ing in *Factory Management and Maintenance,* gives six advantages for use of the company letter: (1) *inexpensive,* (2) *direct,* (3) *important-looking,* (4) *intimate,* (5) *quick,* (6) *informal.*

A main type of letter used for public relations purposes is written by the chief official of an organization or the chief of a division for circulation among the members. The purpose is to establish a direct contact that spans the gap between the head man and all those who do not see as much of him as they would like to. Letters support line communication. They insure the accuracy of line transmission. Content points up what is important and newsworthy in the organization's affairs. Letters give added importance to line communication by proving that the line is well informed. This is increasingly important in international organizations.

Other letters go from organization officials to community opinion leaders, to members of selected professions such as medicine or education, to congressmen, suppliers, dealers, or newspaper editors. Common methods of reproducing letters include typewriter, multigraph, mimeograph, and printing.

More letters are mailed to the home than to business addresses. The home provides wider readership and a good climate for persuasion. There is a reluctance in some industrial quarters, however, to send letters into employees' homes. This exists mainly where there is a tense labor-management relationship. The reluctance is due in part to the possibility that union officials might seek to interpret the technique as a measure to weaken their organization.

Trade associations rely heavily on the circular letter to carry news to members. Charities take to the letter to solicit funds. Most educational institutions at the higher level have a periodic "president's letter" for alumni and one for parents of students. Crusaders for a particular idea or philosophy use letters in broad public mailings.

More important than these printed letters issued periodically are the larger number of letters that comprise an organization's daily correspondence. The endless flow of letters that goes out daily from today's organizations constitutes an important, influential, but too often neglected means of communication. The importance of effective letters that evoke a pleased reaction, not irritation or confusion, is obvious. Yet many organizations continue blindly in the rut of writing cold, stilted, hackneyed letters that do more to obfuscate than to clarify. Certainly one of the ways a person judges an organization is by the letters he receives in response to his requests for information or clarification or in response to a complaint. As American organizations get larger and automate more of their operations, the opportunities for personal contact grow fewer. The individually addressed letter, with a personal touch, is one of the few ways left. It should be more effectively utilized.

THE BULLETIN BOARD—POSTERS—BILLBOARDS

The use of bulletin boards is widespread: in college buildings, in every department of factories and offices, in military installations, in public buildings, and in the larger retail stores. The bulletin board is here to stay. If there were no other reason, laws requiring the posting of an ever-increasing number of notices would preserve it. Daily news bulletins posted on bulletin boards are one means of coping with the speed of the organizational grapevine.

The bulletin board offers a good place to corroborate information that circulates through interdepartmental channels. It provides quick access to the internal public, for spiking rumors and for making desirable information stick. The bulletin board gets regular attention if kept current and interesting. It needs to be serviced often so that the news on it does not get stale. There's a petty annoyance to a reader in seeing the same notice again and again after it has become history. Messages should be brief. Boards should be placed where traffic is heavy and the reading light is good. They should be at proper height for easy-eye-level reading.

In somewhat the same category as bulletin-board messages are the posters and placards placed on walls or columns of shops and offices. The theme of such posters is usually safety, housekeeping, economics, or security.

Assuming that the messages are personalized and appropriate to the audience, the poster can do a job. To do that job, it is important that these short messages be changed frequently and the phrasing be memorable. To keep posters from growing stale, one good system is to start with a series of them in various locations, rotating them regularly among the several stations.

INFORMATION RACKS

The information rack is used primarily for morale and employee education, with emphasis on economic education. It was started in 1948 by General Motors as "an idea cafeteria for offering mental and spiritual nourishment to employees." The idea caught on rapidly, and it was estimated twenty years later that at least 1,500 firms were using information-rack programs. Firms specializing in this service provide companies with booklets and reprints of magazine articles in wholesale lots which are distributed free to employees from these racks on a "take what you want" basis. The racks usually are placed in reception rooms and near plant and office exits so that employees may pick up a few on their way home. The usual procedure is to put out only enough booklets to cover 50 to 80 percent of the total number of employees.

One supplier for these information racks suggests these values for the reading rack: (1) The broad range of reading materials thus put in hands of employees tends to broaden the range of their reading and, consequently, their range of knowledge; (2) The voluntary pick-up has value for the employee, who has much communication forced upon him; (3) Home readership of these pamphlets and reprints gets the message to the wives and children of the employee; (4) It enables the firm to disseminate information on subjects the company would hesitate to take up in ordinary communication channels; (5) These booklets serve to reiterate and reinforce messages directed to employees through other channels; (6) It is a handy distribution medium that enables employers to get materials to employees quickly if need be. Granted these advantages, this supplier admits that most companies continue this reading-rack program pretty much on faith. The typical employer attitude is found in this quote: "If they are taking the material home and not leaving it around the plant, they must be reading it."

The booklets and reprints cover a wide range of subject matter—sports, hobbies, health, safety, how-to-do-it, economics, Americanism, and uplift material. Public relations and personnel practitioners hotly debate the worth of the considerable expenditure involved. In the words of one personnel director, "Reading racks are the ultimate in immeasurables." In a survey to determine extent and effectiveness of the reading rack, *Industrial Newsletter* found that, of 700 firms, responding to its questionnaire, 60 percent had made no evaluation of the rack's effectiveness. Another example of lack of evaluation!

INSTITUTIONAL ADVERTISING

The one certain way to get publicity printed or broadcast is to buy space or time—to use advertising. The $20-billion advertising business was developed initially to sell goods and services. Increasingly, paid advertising has proved useful as a public relations tool. Such advertising is variously termed "institutional advertising," "public service advertising," and "public relations advertising." Advertising to disseminate information or promote opinion change was first used in the early 1900s and on a small, spasmodic basis until World War II. Ivy Lee bought full-page ads in the Colorado newspapers in 1914 to tell the Rockefeller side of the story in the bitter Colorado Fuel and Iron strike. In World War II and in the decades since, advertising has been widely used on an increasing scale as a public relations tool.

The large plus of advertising is that it enables the sponsor to tell his story in his own words when he chooses and to the audience he selects. The headline and story are written exactly the way the advertiser wants them to appear, either in print or on the air. On the minus side, the citizen instantly recognizes this as paid pleading. Audience resistance thereby may be raised to some degree. News does not carry this handicap.

Advertising, first developed as a tool of public relations in business and industry, is still largely utilized by the corporate world rather than by other institutions, because of the expense entailed in buying media time and space. Yet, it is increasingly used in programs of public education by non-profit agencies. A dramatic demonstration of its effectiveness in recent years has been the anti-cigarette "commercials" of the American Cancer Society and American Heart Association on television. Television stations were required to show these by an FCC ruling, a ruling later upheld by the U. S. courts. Advertising by the U. S. Government is largely confined to the armed forces which spend several millions on recruiting advertising. The British Government utilizes advertising to a far greater extent. At the start of this decade the British Government was allocating nearly $15-million dollars to advertising in its public information campaigns, e.g. recruitment of policemen, highway safety, armed forces recruiting. Nonprofit public causes can, of course, hitch-hike by getting firms to finance advertising for a worthy cause. In such cases the advertisement does double duty. This kind of advertising has been found rewarding by many sponsors. The Sinclair Oil Company's advertising to promote and preserve the national parks and shrines brought that company much favorable public reaction and increased its business, too. The advertising industry's contribution to promotion of worthwhile causes through the Advertising Council has been especially noteworthy. Campaigns have promoted religion in American life; better schools; forest fire prevention, civil rights, anti-pollution, 1970 census. In twenty-eight years the nation's communications media have contributed more than $5 billion worth of services and facilities to such campaigns. Nonprofit agencies should utilize this agency when feasible.

Advertising is a versatile tool. Some uses have been catalogued by George Hammond, chairman of the Carl Byoir firm: (1) community relations—plant openings, plant expansions, plant open houses, company anniversaries, annual statements, promotion of community activities, such as clean-up weeks, safety, community chest campaigns, and so forth; (2) labor relations, including the company's side in labor disputes; (3) recruitment of employees; (4) promotion of art contests, essay contests, scholarship awards, and so forth; (5) statements of policy; (6) proxy fights for company control; (7) consolidation of competitive position; (8) records of accomplishment; (9) product difficulty or public misunderstanding which must be cleared up immediately; (10) promotion or opposition to pending legislation; (11) consolidation of editorial opinion; (12) supplier relations; (13) celebration of local institutions, such as the press during National Newspaper Week; (14) presentation of industry or professional activities and points of view. As Hammond says, "These 14 suggestions only scratch the surface of possible uses."

Is It Effective? This is a continuing question that defies generalization. Concrete examples of its power in specific situations are multiplying, but there are also examples of failures. There has been little research on its efficacy. Evidence to date indicates that *specific campaigns aimed at specific objectives by reputable sponsors are the most effective.* Ads with a "news" approach and using strong human interest pictures draw the biggest readership.

Many are using advertising to talk directly to the media gatekeepers by placing ads in the trade journals of press, magazine, and radio. Many have used this medium to place on record in convincing fashion their public relations policies for the benefit of the men and women in journalism.

Rules for Effective Public Relations Advertising. Hill & Knowlton has formulated these guides for preparing effective copy:

1. Be frank, fair, and honest.
2. Tell your story directly to an individual in his own language.
3. Don't talk up or down to anyone.
4. Use simple, unvarnished words and facts so that every housewife in the community will both understand and believe what you have to say.
5. Tell one story at a time—don't overload your copy.
6. Use figures sparingly—and only when illustrated by simple, everyday examples.

The use of paid advertising in public relations has been somewhat circumscribed by the regulation of the United States Internal Revenue Service providing that costs of advertising designed to promote or defeat legislation or to influence public opinion on pending legislation are not a tax-deductible business expense. This is true even though the proposed legislation may directly affect the advertiser's business, industry, or occupation. The I. R. S. regulation does not permit deduction from gross income for tax purposes of the cost of advertising designed to (1) influence members of a legislative body directly or indirectly, by urging or encouraging the public to contact such members for the purpose of proposing, supporting, or opposing legislation, or (2) influence the public to approve or reject a measure in a referendum, initiative, vote on a constitutional amendment, or similar procedure.

The I. R. S. regulation was upheld by the United States Supreme

Court. Advertising media, advertising associations, and the Public Relations Society of America strongly protested the regulation but to no avail.[9] In a ruling, the Federal Power Commission disallowed expenditures for institutional advertising by private utilities as a factor in fixing the rates of that company. Neither the I. R. S. regulation nor the Federal Power Commission ruling disallows deductions for goodwill advertising.

THE SPOKEN WORD

MEETINGS

Meetings bring people together, face to face. This not only provides an opportunity to communicate to a selected audience but also provides the opportunity to listen. The carefully staged meeting results in *two-way communication.* As more has been learned, this tool has come to the fore. Many organizations, for example, are shifting the emphasis in employee communication from the printed and visual media to work-group and study-group meetings. Industries have found, too, that the surest way to reach educators is to invite them in for conferences or fellowships. Such get-togethers are expensive, but if effective can prove economical in the long run. *Meetings, to be effective, require purpose, careful planning and staging, and skillful direction.*

The most impressive form of get-together is the mass meeting where corporate officials explain the annual report to employees, where the commanding officer explains to all troops why they are shipping out, where the college president tells the student body of the decision to drop football, where the office manager announces plans for the move to another city.

In these meetings, exchange of viewpoints is very carefully handled. The question-and-answer portion, if there is one, is controlled so that the meeting doesn't drag, and so that any discussion sticks to the important features. Otherwise, the discussion roams into other pastures or it explodes in personalities. The mass meeting has been most effectively used in middle-sized groups of employees or members and in cases where the one-big-boss really runs the organization. Effectiveness depends, too, on the top man's being a pretty good speaker.

Other meetings take the form of discussion groups, with a round table or panel of from ten to thirty-five persons. Among supervisory personnel, charity volunteers, and civic committees, these meetings are well attended even though held outside of normal working hours. For the hourly employee, the buck private, or the student—the man on the bottom rung of the ladder of success—such meetings are usually scheduled as a part of the work program. To avoid any inference of "captive audience," attendance should be voluntary.

Staging such meetings is often the task of the public relations staff. There are several check points:

1. Comfortable facilities
2. "Breaks" in the middle of long sessions
3. Exhibits, displays, charts, graphs, and films, or other playbacks wherever suitable to the subject-matter
4. Refreshments if participants give up their spare time
5. An opportunity for everyone to get into the act even if it's only through a note pad and a pen
6. Press notice of the occasion with credit to the departmental people who were responsible for it

There are many excellent case studies. The following are business examples, but the adaptation to other types of undertakings should be a simple one.

> Standard Oil Company (N.J.) for years assembled a Jersey Roundtable, a three-day conference of some twenty-five university teachers from all parts of the country and a like number of top-level Standard Oil officials on problems and philosophy of the industry.
>
> Motorola, Inc. has a fifteen-man Advisory Council of elected, middle-management people. They meet alternate Monday evenings, study corporate problems, and submit reports to the senior Board of Directors.
>
> Sergeant and Company stages group discussions to determine workers' attitudes toward the personnel program.
>
> Carrier Corporation, has an institute of business lecture series followed by small-group discussions.
>
> Pitney-Bowes holds job-holders' meetings for all its employees.

SPEAKERS' BUREAU

The speakers' bureau is a *planned* means for providing speakers for service club luncheons, evening cultural group meetings, schools, and special events—such as annual Chamber of Commerce meetings, graduation exercises, dedications, anniversaries, celebrations, and fetes for visiting celebrities. The requests for various areas of subject matter provide great latitude. The speakers' pool is also valuable in trade relations for the manufacturer, in civil relations for the military, and in general public relations for the government department, the educational institution, and the social agency.

There are few organizations of any size without some officials who can get on their feet and talk interestingly for a few minutes. There are, however, some commonly practiced alternatives. One is to engage outside public speaking specialists and pay their fees to fill engagements on the organization's behalf. Another alternative is for the organization to call on its friendly associates, such as public relations or public affairs counsel, management or legal counsel, or a nonresident director to fill engagements in its behalf. In all cases the kind of talent available determines its use. Practitioners are frequently called on to research speech material or to prepare an outline or a complete manuscript. In other cases, the public relations department collects appropriate material and functions as a speakers' library in the organization.

Here are four points worth remembering:

1. Select and coach the line-up of speakers with some care.
2. Select topics of broad interest which serve the needs of the potential audience and carry the organization's story.
3. Provide speakers with helpful visual aids—flip charts, flannel boards, slide films, etc.
4. Promote and publicize the availability of the speakers, to get maximum mileage.

Akin to a speakers' bureau is the increasing use of qualified employees as authors of magazine and newspaper articles. This is particularly apt for the scientist, scholar, or artist. The employee gets visibility, the employer gets credit for having such talent aboard, and for the breakthrough, program, or success described by the author. Many companies encourage this. For example, Convair established a Writing Award Fund, and within eighteen months the output of technical articles by its staff quadrupled. The Worthington Corporation has an Article Awards Plan.[10] Along this same line, qualified employees can tell the employer's story on radio and television programs by interview. This will increase as the use of video film and video playback tape become commonplace. The videotelephone, tied in with commercial television relay and display, will make this tool a handy one on the organization's premises. Employees are destined to become more and more personally involved in public relations programming.

[10] "When Employee Turns Author," *Management Record*, Vol. 20, February, 1958.

TELEPHONE NEWSLINES AND PUBLIC ADDRESS SYSTEMS

Telephone newslines and public address systems are utilized by many organizations to link the boss in the front office with employees in the office or shop or students on campus. Establishment of a telephone newsline from which persons can get late, authentic information simply by dialing has proved especially helpful in organizations caught up in conflict. For example, many universities have set up rumor centers where public and students alike can call to get accurate information from recordings in times of crisis. Illinois Bell Telephone has found that its management personnel make much greater use of its Telephone Communicator than do its non-management personnel. The recorded messages provided over telephone newslines, if kept fresh, can provide a fast, flexible means of communication to an organization of size scattered over a large geographical area.

The public address system, often used in conjunction with a recorded music service, deserves more experimentation in communication among working groups. Its effectiveness in promotional work and in stirring protests have caused practitioners to take a second look at this tool. There is a growing awareness of its advantages as well as its limitations. The PA system can be made mobile; the messages can be relayed. It can be tied in with closed circuit TV. But it requires a working knowledge of tape recorders, the turntable, and telephone relays.

THE GRAPEVINE

The grapevine is not a formal tool of communication. It is informal, but it really gets around. Keith Davis, Indiana University, reported in the *Harvard Business Review* the example of an official's wife who had a baby at 11 p.m. By 2 p.m. the next day, 46 percent of the management group knew it. It is a potent line of transmission. The grapevine is the channel that carries information much more exciting than the truth. Sometimes it is actually harmful or threatens to be. Rumors of lay-off, of friction among officials, of trouble, or of bad blood between factions can hurt. The word travels far beyond the local group; it becomes more and more distorted. The hints of trouble tend to breed trouble wherever there happens to be a chip on anybody's shoulder.

The public relations staff usually stays tuned in on the grapevine. When the gossiping and rumoring are harmless, nothing is done about them. When real trouble brews, the gossip is squelched by the release of full facts on the topic. Once in a while, a counterrumor or an exposé of the facts among the natural leaders of an organization is sponsored to offset a harmful rumor. A more positive use of the grapevine is that of the Indian Government in its difficult task of disseminating birth control information. The Indian Government first used the traditional channels—radio-movies, lecture—to educate Indian women. When these proved inadequate, India's Health Minister turned to introducing birth control devices to a few women in each village and then counting on them to spread the word along the grapevine. He terms this "indoctrination by gossip."

SIGHT AND SOUND

MOTION PICTURES AND SLIDE FILMS

Slides and movies grew out of the early nickelodeon and stereopticon, entertainment novelties of the late 19th century. So it followed logically that slide projection and the moving pictures were considered mainly as entertainment vehicles until the advent of sound movies in the late 20s. In the early stages of slides and movies, their education and information value was largely limited to travelogue lectures and newsreels, although some companies utilized their potential to inform and persuade as early as 1897, when Dewar's Whiskey and Columbia Bicycles showed films on outdoor screens in New York City. Early in this century, General Electric, Chicago Edison, U. S. Steel and Ford Motor Company began using films for public relations purposes. The Red Cross was a trail-blazer among nonprofit agencies. These were dubbed "non-theatrical" or "sponsored" films.

Sponsored films are those conceived within, and commissioned by, a business, government agency or a nonprofit organization as an investment in communication for a sales, training or public relations purpose. They are paid for by the sponsor not with the intent of reaping direct monetary return from the showings but in the hope of developing favorable ideas, motivations, attitudes, or reactions in the viewing audience.

Television provided the greatest impetus to the use of audio-visuals, particularly sponsored films and slide films, because it began to develop a generation of people more accustomed to receiving impressions and forming opinions from audio-visual media than the printed word. The Rev. John Culkin of Fordham University has estimated that by the time the average student graduates from high school today, he will have watched more than 15,000 hours of television and seen 500 movies, while spending a total of only 10,800 hours in school.

Television also pointed the way toward pictorial teaching and closed circuit TV classes. The basic factors that gave television its great potential are used in the motion picture to transmit ideas, stimulate imagination, and produce action. In the age of TV and pictorial journalism, a tremendous audience awaits the timely, skillful film presentation of a sponsor's story. It is an effective and economical means of reaching selected groups with real impact, and therefore has created an amazing growth in the use of films for public relations purposes.

The non-theatrical audio-visual business is more than a billion-dollar industry and grew more than 70 percent from 1965 to 1970. Eastman Kodak reported that 12,570 non-theatrical films were made in the U. S. in 1967 and the films produced by and for industrial firms accounted for 7,500 of the titles. Business-industry expenditures amounted to $241-million, followed by schools at $95-million, government at $72-million, community agencies at $23.1-million, religion in the amount of $10-million, and medical-health groups at $7-million.

Although the initial costs of production and distribution may appear high, the proper yardstick to use is the cost-per-viewer. Studies have shown this cost to be as low as 4.6 cents; when a sponsored film is also shown on TV, the cost per viewer drops to about 1.6 cents.

Not only has the use of sponsored films accelerated to an increased pace in the last decade but the acceleration has been matched by growth in audience potential. It is a rare club, business or educational group that doesn't use carousel or 16mm sound projectors frequently throughout its program season. Libraries, schools, resort hotels and motels, and even private offices and board rooms use audio-visual equipment with increasing regularity. All of which creates an ever-present need for new films, well-made films—films that not only educate and inform but at the same time entertain. United States Steel has estimated that, on the average, one of their films is shown every seven minutes of every working day to an audience of about sixty people.

The communications strengths of the motion picture are readily apparent. (1) It combines the impact of sight, sound, drama and movement, color and music with group enthusiasm. (2) It can present certain meanings involving motion which cannot effectively be described by print or audio means. (3) It attracts sustained, exclusive attention to a message for the length of the showing. (4) It clarifies the time factor in any operation or series of events. (5) It provides a reproduced record of events. (6) It presents processes that cannot ordinarily be seen by the human eye. (7) It can bring the past and the distant to the viewer. (8) It can enlarge or reduce objects and can use cartoons to dramatize abstractions. (9) Above all, it lets the viewer see with his own eyes and enforces the conviction that "seeing is believing."

It is estimated that there are more than one-million 16mm film projectors owned by organized groups meeting regularly—schools, colleges, churches, clubs, fraternal organizations, and labor, veteran, farm, and women's groups. Eighty-five per cent of all films shown in schools are sponsored. These outlets coupled with the possibility of sponsored films being used on TV stations, cable TV channels, in commercial theaters, in airport theaters, and in resort areas provides an almost unlimited potential. However, to be acceptable for all these uses, a film must be made with care and the commercialism handled with good taste. The quality of production and story line must be competitive with that of movies and taped programs for television.

There are many outstanding examples of sponsored films which meet and surpass this test. In 1969, Kaiser Corporation made a film, "Why Man Creates," based upon a series of printed essays in a company publication; in competition with other theatrical productions of comparable length, it won the coveted "Oscar" of the American Academy of Motion Picture Arts and Sciences. The film made did not refer to Kaiser products, and the only mention of the sponsor was in the credit lines at the end of the film. To encourage more world trade, Mobil Oil Corporation produced a film starring the famous pantominist, Marcel Marceau, with background music by the London Royal Orchestra. Without a single spoken word, the film tells its story gently and subtly and with no specific mention of the sponsor or its product except in credit lines. "The Challenge of Six Billion," by Allis-Chalmers, deals with the problems of providing enough power, water, food, transportation, and other necessities for the estimated six-billion people who will inhabit the earth by the year 2000.

To get the best public relations value from such a film, however, the film must get maximum exposure; therefore, the distribution of a film is extremely important. Films may be distributed through film producers that provide such a service, through educational film libraries, by the sponsor, or through firms specializing in this service. It is estimated that sponsored movies are shown to more than 200,000 different audiences, and there are many hundreds of titles available for immediate and free-loan showings.

Within the decade 1960–70, the number of sponsored films produced annually almost tripled. One reason for this growth is the willingness of TV stations to use commercially sponsored films at no cost. Films on drug addiction, ghetto and social problems, safety, pollution, health care, and hundreds of other subjects with mass appeal are particularly good for TV showing. One such film produced by the Walt Disney Studios for the sponsor, has been seen by nearly 170-million persons. Local TV stations, particularly, operate on limited budgets and cannot afford to produce documentary films. Consequently, TV program managers welcome films that are of the proper length—23 to 28 minutes or 14 minutes—to fit into program time slots and that do not contain blatant commercial plugs for the companies or organizations that produced them. The larger film distributing companies have divisions to provide TV program managers with films as a service to the station and at minimal cost to the film sponsors compared to the size of the viewing audience.

The growing use of public relations films in motion-picture theaters and drive-in movies parallels the drop in Hollywood's output of cartoons and short subjects. Hard pressed by TV competition, movie houses are much more receptive to free program material than they were as late as the early 50s. But theater managers insist that such films be entertaining. "Rhapsody in Steel," a powerful documentary tracing the development of steel, has been shown in most of the nation's movie houses. This 23-minute film was produced by United States Steel at substantial cost but the sponsor has been repaid by the vast audience exposure.

Sponsored films are also used for more specific public relations communication purposes. One company put its annual report on film for its shareholders. A newly merged company produced a film on all the operations of the combined entity for simultaneous showings to all its employees working in plants and installations throughout the world to let them see all the different activities in which their combined companies were involved. The community affairs function in public relations finds sponsored films to be a helpful ally, and in many cases, it is the one medium which reaches masses of underprivileged people in a way they understand, given their limited reading ability.

The number of firms producing non-theatrical films has mushroomed in the past several years and at rough estimate there are now at least several hundred. The breadth and quality of service that these firms offer vary greatly so sponsors should exercise selective care in choosing the right producers for their needs. Costs as well as expertise and an understanding of the public relations aspects of a film also vary widely.

Because of the expense and effort involved in a good film, the public relations department should weigh carefully the purpose of the film, channels of distribution available, and the potential audience. After it has been decided the film is worthwhile, and the target audience, method of reaching the audience, and general content has been determined, these questions should be considered:

1. Why is the film being made?
2. What special audiences do we want to reach with it?
3. How long should it be to stand best possible chance for exposure to our desired audiences?
4. What budget should we figure for production *and* effective distribution?
5. How much commercialism should the film include, if any?

6. Are we sure its excellence will be sufficient to successfully compete with TV shows and feature movies so as to gain exposure on these vitally important media?

While 16mm is still the most popular film for sponsored movies, and color is more acceptable than black and white, the use of 8mm and Super 8 film and projectors is skyrocketing. In 1967, investment in this new medium's projection equipment approximated $9-million, compared with $5.5-million in 1966. The number of 8mm projectors delivered in 1967 was more than 50,000, making a total of about 200,000 in use in the United States. About 80 percent are in schools. Eastman Kodak now produces a new Ektagraphic 120 Movie Projector that makes classroom movies as easy to use as a TV set, because there's no film to handle or thread and no reels. The teacher snaps a cartridge on the projector and presses a button. This makes movies as simple a teaching aid as textbooks, especially since the film is not only fully automatic but also controllable. The film may be stopped and reversed and may be held on a single frame for discussion and note taking.

The advent of relatively inexpensive video-tape produced by several manufacturers makes it possible to film speeches, interviews, panel discussions, instructional lecturers, or sales demonstrations in the offices of the company or a lecture hall and reuse these tapes hundreds of times to selected audiences.

The newest device in the audio-visual hardware field is CBS's Electronic Video Recording by which any motion picture, videotape or live television presentation can be recorded and stored in EVR cartridges for playback on an EVR player through a standard television set. The EVR cartridge is placed on the player, the television set tuned to a channel that is not broadcasting and the player button pushed. The film automatically threads itself past an electronic sensor which converts the film image to electrical impulses and transmits these impulses along with the sound into one or more TV receivers. RCA has a comparable machine, which it calls SelectaVision. The time is near when a person will be able to load the home TV set like a phonograph with modestly priced videotapes of his own choice. Experts predict that the 1980s will see a billion-dollar personalized communications industry. These economical reproduction methods also will bring complex problems in the protection of copyrights.

The rapid growth of film as a public relations tool plus the refinement in audiovisual hardware, makes it necessary for the large companies, and eventually the smaller ones, to use films as a part of the over-all communications program and to develop libraries of their own films as well as those produced by others. The outright sale and rental of prints of sponsored films to other film libraries in schools, hospitals and corporations is common and helps the sponsor recover a part of the cost of production and distribution to special audiences.

CLOSED-CIRCUIT AND CABLE TELEVISION

This tool, developed as a by-product of commercial TV, offers great potentialities. By means of a closed circuit, leased through A.T.&T., live pictures and sound can be piped from an originating point to one or more receiving locations across the country for viewing by selected audiences. This type of TV is not transmitted to stations for broadcasting to home viewers. It is simpler and less expensive than broadcast TV, yet it combines the power of TV with carefully designed programs for specific, invited audiences. It is as private as a telephone conversation. Tele-lectures are being used quite widely in education and in business.

The cost of staging a program or conference through closed-circuit TV is relatively high. It can, however, be more economical than staging a conference or convention in one city. This tool, too, can be a great time saver for busy executives. Robert G. Dunlop of the Sun Oil Company reported, "Our firm saved $125,000 by using closed-circuit TV to introduce a new gasoline to dealers, distributors, and employees in thirty cities throughout the country, as compared with separate dealer meetings before." By comparison, cost of eight meetings staged simultaneously for the same purpose by another oil company was $10,000. In the former case, use of this medium permitted "instantaneous break of a new product to all people in the field at the same time."

Dentistry and medicine are being taught through this medium. Firms use it to make annual reports to shareholders and staffs or to hold sales meetings. Political parties use it for nationwide and statewide fund-raising dinners and rallies. Educational institutions use it for teaching. More and more universities and colleges, pressed by mounting enrollments, are using closed-circuit large-screen TV to reach students across campus and across the state. The United Fund and Community Chest campaign has used this medium to kick off its annual fund drive by assembling the volunteers in groups across the nation. Where no TV outlets were available, kinescopes of the program were shown to the workers.

Canadian National Railways held a coast-to-coast press conference by closed-circuit TV to announce sweeping changes in its passenger-train services. Reporters were linked by two-way broadcast lines and TV monitors from Newfoundland to British Columbia.

Closed circuit television was first used on a world wide basis June 26, 1969, when more than 1,000 persons at functions in New York City, London, Tokyo, Perth, Sydney, and Melbourne "participated" in the official opening ceremonies of the Mt. Newman Iron Ore project in western

Australia. This world-wide circuit was made possible by the communications satellite system. Though expensive, it was cheaper than flying 300 key writers and officials to the mine site. Total cost of the event, including the satellite transmission, was under $200,000. The high costs and the difficulties caused by differences in time are the major obstacles to the use of this tool on a nationwide and frequent basis.

Cable TV showed remarkable growth in the 60s. A small-box cable converter, installed in the viewer's home at a cost of about $6.00 per month, not only improves TV reception in areas where interference is a problem but makes it possible for the set owner to view one or more channels that are closed-circuit cable only. Most metropolitan areas throughout the country are covered by cable TV and in some there are two channels, one programming weather, time and news reports, and another showing sports events, cultural programs like concerts and opera programmed live, and movies of the Hollywood spectacular variety. These cable stations also use sponsored films and are another prime and important outlet for public relations films well-conceived and well produced. While some consider cable television the forerunner of pay TV, a controversial development in the 60s, it provides still another method of communication as a vehicle for public relations messages.

For the future, even greater uses for audio-visuals are predicted, and more imaginative as well as more faithful documentary use may be a requisite of every public relations practitioner. The steady growth of the philosophy that every person should have more voice in how his government is to be operated, what his children shall be taught and who shall teach them, may demand a different sort of accelerated and almost instantaneous communication with the public. Politicians are fast feeling this need to appeal directly to the total public. During the 1968 elections, all candidates spent more than $16-million on television.

DISPLAYS AND EXHIBITS

In almost every factory, there is a reception room, a showroom, a museum, or an employees' lunch area. In every college, there is the equivalent of an "Old Main," a Students' Union, a museum, or a visitors' room. Every branch of military service has its sites to perpetuate its memories, receive its guests, and show its progress. These places are natural areas for displays and exhibits. For anyone who has ever taken a plant tour or visited a World's Fair, it is redundant to detail the content of such exhibits. The point to be made is that preparation and servicing of such displays usually fall in the province of the public relations staff.

In addition to the stationary or permanent displays, there are temporary exhibits in the community to mark a special event. There are national industrial shows, state and county fairs, and traveling displays. Some business houses have exhibits of materials, processes, or products that they lend their customers and their suppliers for use in special show-rooms of their own. The National Guard has equipment which it can put on display or wheel out for parades and local events. Occasionally a university takes a dramatic show to other cities. The welfare agencies usually are anxious to take part in exhibits where the nature of their work can be dramatized. A novel idea in exhibits is that developed by Public Service Electric and Gas Company. The New Jersey utility bought a Hudson River ferryboat, rechristened it "The Second Sun," and converted it into a Nuclear Information Center. The floating exhibit plies the Delaware River to promote a better understanding of nuclear energy and its peace-ful uses.

Exhibit users should remember that the objective is "to inveigle the footsore visitor (1) to stop in front of the display; (2) to remain long enough to look at the material; (3) to be stimulated to immediate or future action." Lynn Poole of Johns Hopkins University says that an exhibit to accomplish this must be something *different* that creates an *action* and promotes good *humor* while stimulating *participation*. The eye-getting, communicating exhibitor provides unusual, fresh ideas with a sense of showmanship.

EVENTS

Handling visitors is another direct-contact vehicle. Its most prevalent use is in open house events and in the day-by-day handling of plant tours. The idea behind the careful reception of visitors is to merchandise an organization's facilities and its practices. Open house events attract the community. Plant tours catch outside friends and relatives, vacationers, youngsters in school, foreigners here to absorb industrial know-how, finan-cial analysts, alumni, customers, and people who are just plain curious and haven't much else to do with their time. Plant tours have become interna-tional, too. To gain identity in the British farming community, Eli Lilly's British firm, Elanco Products, sponsored a fifteen-day, 2,000 mile tour of key U. S. agriculture research, production, and marketing facilities for twenty-five leading British and Irish agriculturists. This it dubbed the "Elanco Agritour." Planned tours for foreign visitors have become a main-stay of public relations for the U. S. Department of Commerce and the U. S. State Department.

Sponsors of these events have been quick to seize them as opportuni-ties to make friends at home. Most people are good hosts in their own houses because they work at it. The use of these tours is rapidly increasing, and there have been a growing number of circumstances urging their usage.

New plants and installations have opened. Old ones have been renovated. New products have been abundant. Organizations have reached important milestones. In short, there has been much to show off and much to talk about.

Techniques have become quite elaborate. Clever invitations, special transportation, celebrities, souvenirs, exhibits, motion pictures, and refreshments figure among the enticements. Then, too, the events regularly make news locally and nationally. In the community, an open house is a good story of civic spirit that the press welcomes. When visitors drop in from afar, their own hometown papers are glad to get word. If they are prominent citizens of some community, a photograph is in order.

STAGED EVENTS

Almost every city has some kind of annual occasion all its own, when everybody in town pitches in to make a staged event a whopping success. Perhaps it's Milkman's Day, Pickle Harvest Festival, Dollar Day, Fashion Parade, Founder's Day, Help Your Neighbor Day, Junior Government Day, Community Auction, or All-Sports Parade. Of all occasions, the most universally observed are anniversaries and milestone developments, such as inaugurations, dedications, and personal tributes.

These events are wonderful. They are crowd days. People shed their routines and some of their inhibitions to turn clown, auctioneer, beauty contest judge, auxiliary cop, hog caller, past champion pie eater, trombonist, or flag bearer for a few hours. On these occasions, the people in town who make most of the money the other 364 days of the year spend some of it freely.

These staged events can be international or national in scope as well as local. They serve to swing the public spotlight to an organization and its accomplishments. For example, KLM Royal Dutch Airlines observed its 50th anniversary by: staging a press conference at which its annual report and a press kit covering the past, present, and future of the airline were given out and discussed; sponsoring a jubilee exhibition at the Utrecht Fair which featured the winning entries in a school children's competition; printing 400,000 copies of a history of KLM; staging employees' parties in the Netherlands and abroad; striking a jubilee medallion; and getting the Dutch government to issue an anniversary stamp. The hundredth anniversary of a famed staged event—driving the Golden Spike in Utah May 10, 1869 to link the nation's first transcontinental rail line—was marked by an event staged by the Union Pacific and Southern Pacific railroads. The staffs of these companies spent three years planning a series of events under the aegis of the Golden Spike Centennial Celebration Commission. The staged event—criticized by Historian Daniel Boorstin for cluttering the channels of communication—must be newsworthy, in keeping with the character of the organization, and mutually rewarding to sponsor and public.

ART AS A PUBLIC RELATIONS TOOL

Although it does not neatly fit in this kit of communications tools, art is being used increasingly in public relations practice. Many institutions, mainly corporations, have found it advantageous to relate to the growing public interest in art, a part of the cultural explosion in the United States. Art can be used to gain public goodwill, to further the identity of an organization, and to make an employer's community more attractive. Richard Eells sees an "irreversible trend toward corporate involvement in the arts." Other institutions, likewise, find art helpful in advancing their objectives. Through painting collections, traveling collections, landscaping, sculpture, concerts, and lectures, organizations support the arts and link themselves in the public's mind with the finer things of life. Typical examples are: [11]

Twenty technological and industrial corporations in California joined with the Los Angeles County Museum to establish new art forms in new media. The companies provided $230,000 to place artists in residence in each corporation for three months to enable the artists to create new forms of art, using available materials and technologies.

Mead Packaging sponsors an Annual Painting of the Year Competition, open to all artists in southeastern states, from which it purchases paintings. Prints of the winning entries are mailed to customers and opinion leaders. Some 25,000 of these prints are given away annually.

Parker Pen Company, an international marketer, sponsored an art competition in Italy, selected sixty-four paintings, and brought these to the United States where they were shown in prestigious department stores with mutual benefit to artist, sponsor, and store.

S. C. Johnson & Sons, another international firm, put together a first-rate collection of contemporary American art, "Art: U.S.A.: Now," and sent the show abroad for five years in a cooperative effort with the United States Information Agency.

Illinois Bell Telephone, to attract public interest in its new Chicago headquarters, sponsored "The Art of the Poster" exhibit showing uses made of the poster from Cheret to the present day—political posters, travel posters, airline posters.

Container Corporation of America, the pioneer in this tie-in

---

[11] For recent examples, see "Esquire-BCA Fourth Annual 'Business in the Arts' Awards," *Esquire*, Vol. LXXIV, July, 1970, pp. 30–31.

with art, began its fine arts program in 1937 when it used a series of advertising designs by the French artist, A. M. Cassandre. Its more recent series of advertisements, "Great Ideas of Western Man" featuring original, commissioned paintings is widely and favorably known.

The United States Navy sponsored a combat art exhibit, called "Operation Pallette," containing 100 original paintings of battle scenes by professional artists. It put this exhibit on display in the nation's population centers.

Dayton's Department Store marked the opening of its St. Paul, Minnesota, store by dedicating a nine-foot-high bronze sculpture by Henry Moore.

New York University's College of Medicine created a medical art exhibit to help promote a $15-million medical center fundraising campaign. Its uniqueness intrigued the public.

Prentice-Hall, in its *Executive Report,* gives three reasons for using art in public relations programs: [12]

1. The material is highly mobile, can be directed at specific conventions, associations, meetings, and timed to dovetail with a particular promotion, introduction of new product, or plant opening.
2. Art has a general appeal to a wide range of individuals.
3. Art is relatively cheap. Most collections include new, unknown, and vital American designers and graphic artists. Their support contributes to a company's identity program, contributes to the community's well being, and brings public attention.

One executive observed: [13] "If business is to attract good people and keep them and to motivate them to do their best, the arts must become an important part of the business environment." This applies equally to nonprofit institutions.

CASE PROBLEM

You are in charge of written communications for the Apex Manufacturing Co. This firm employs 5,000 employees in a city of 35,000. It makes high-quality industrial pumps with a good reputation. Existing written communications consist of: (1) monthly two-color magazine of thirty-two pages, mailed to

[12] Prentice-Hall, Inc. *Executive Report,* "Business and Art," 1962, p. 4.

[13] George Weissman, "Good Art Is Good Business," *Public Relations Journal,* Vol. 25, June, 1969, p. 8.

employees' homes; (2) bulletin boards. You have an assistant, a photographer, and a secretary.

Six months ago, Apex experienced a drastic shake-up in management. The company has slipped and is losing its competitive position. Salesmen are finding it difficult to meet quotas. Wage negotiations will get under way in three months, and the union expects to ask for a 15 percent wage hike. Apex's wages are higher than those of competing firms, yet it has been the policy not to discuss these matters with employees. To cut production costs, Apex is installing new machinery which will cut down on manpower requirements. Rumors of layoffs are beginning. The accident rate has been climbing in the past year. There is unrest in the plant and in the community. Apex's situation is really not critical, but this is not generally known because the situation has not been explained to employees and the community.

The new president wants to change this. He wants to lay the company's cards on the table, but he cannot increase the communications budget at this time. He puts the problem to you and asks for a two-page memorandum on your recommendations. *Your recommendations must* (1) be within the present budget; (2) be effective within a six-month period; (3) be detailed sufficiently to give the president a clear idea of their objectives and your method of attack; (4) list the priority of actions. Your job with Apex may depend on the worth of the program you recommend.

ADDITIONAL READING

ASSOCIATION OF NATIONAL ADVERTISERS, *Advertiser Practices in the Production and Distribution of Business Films.* New York: The ANA, 1955 E. 44th St., Jan., 1965.

RUSSELL N. BAIRD and ARTHUR T. TURNBULL, *Industrial and Business Journalism,* Philadelphia, Pa.: Chilton, 1961. See the section on "Company Publications."

The Graphics of Communication. Typography, Layout, and Design. New York: Holt, Rinehart and Winston, Inc., 1964.

WALTER J. DeLONG, "Weyerhaeuser: A Nine-Year Record of Corporate Advertising that Pays Off," *Public Relations Journal,* Vol. 18, May, 1962.

RICHARD EELLS, *The Corporation and the Arts.* New York: Macmillan, 1967.

FRED W. FRIENDLY, "Asleep at the Switch of the Wired City," *Saturday Review,* Vol. LIII, October 10, 1970. Glimpse of coming changes in communication.

CHARLES F. HAMILTON, "Staging the Successful Community Anniversary," *Public Relations Journal,* Vol. 25, June, 1969.

GORDON L. HOUGH, "Handling the Delayed-Action Event," *Public Relations Journal,* Vol. 25, July, 1969.

ARNOLD GINGRICH, *Business and the Arts: An Answer to Tomorrow.* New York: Paul Erickson, 1969.

DOROTHY ROBERSON, "From Kitchen to Jet Set," *Public Relations Journal*, Vol. 25, May, 1969. Successful story of staged event, "Maid of Cotton."

JAMES J. WELSH, *The Speech Writing Guide*. New York: John Wiley and Sons, 1968.

Corporate Citizenship Expressed in Public Relations Advertising.

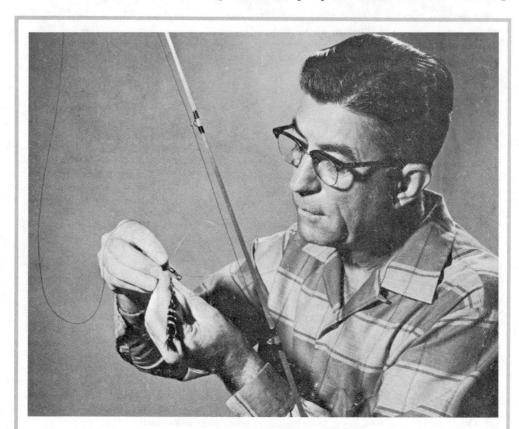

Sure he wants clean water.

And he's done something about *keeping* water clean.

Fisherman-citizen-employee Ray Bachman supervised the construction of the new water treatment plant at Caterpillar-Joliet.

This facility will make sure that Caterpillar doesn't release industrial wastes into the Des Plaines River. The treatment plant will remove impurities from water the Joliet Plant uses — and release it clean enough to meet or exceed all state water quality standards.

Clean water is what Joliet citizens want and need. Your neighbors at Caterpillar, like Ray Bachman, are committed to the goal of reducing water pollution.

Caterpillar, Cat and ▣ are Trademarks of Caterpillar Tractor Co.

CHAPTER 13

THE EMPLOYEE PUBLIC

The term *internal public* as used here means the people working in an organization—the governors and the governed. They are the managers, employees, members, teachers, and associates of organizations variously engaged in business, government, education, or social welfare. *Employee relations* is the short-cut term used to describe this internal relationship. Employee relations are a prime concern of management in every field.

THE BASIC RELATIONSHIP

Reaching the internal public is not difficult; the working relationship brings daily communication. In addition there is a wide variety of auxiliary tools. The effectiveness of the auxiliary communication depends to a greater extent than generally realized on whether or not the working relationship is a good one; that is, whether the audience is receptive and responsive. *Before there can be effective employee communication, there must be a climate of trust.* This is built or destroyed by day to day actions of those in authority.

Communications must be viewed as a tool of leadership. This starts with top management. Board Chairman Lynn A. Townsend of Chrysler says: "It is the chief executive who first must establish the right communications climate. It is he who should initiate and take an active part in the total communication program." This determination must be underwritten by formal statements of policy. For example, Westinghouse's corporate-policy manual includes this statement: "It is the direct responsibility of every member of management, at every level, to communicate effectively with employees under his supervision and to find out (their) thinking and reactions. . . . It is also his responsibility to maintain open communications with his line superior and his fellow supervisors." This need is as urgent in an organization of 300 persons as in one of 30,000. Yet, the barriers to free-flowing internal communication in organizations are many.

The most pressing need is for more adequate upward communications, a management that operates from the bottom up. Feedback channels must be provided. Such feedback invariably shows that members of an organization desire more information than they usually get. It also shows, repeatedly, a disparity in the views of management and staff. For example, one survey of supervisors and employees in twenty-four industrial plants revealed that supervisors thought good wages were what employees wanted most; the employees said full appreciation for work done was what they wanted most. Another survey, in which top executives rated themselves and their subordinate managers rated them, found that the executives saw themselves as better bosses than they were considered to be by their subordinates. For example, top management respondents were unanimous in stating that they encourage subordinates to suggest new ideas. Of 420 subordinate managers surveyed, only one in four said his superior encouraged suggestions. Management tends to seek self-assurance instead of communication.

Internal surveys of an organization's communications system will reveal its strengths and weaknesses. The Illinois Bell Telephone Company operates a comprehensive, intensive, internal communications program. This program includes an information bulletin, a newspaper, a monthly magazine, a telephone communicator and newsline, bulletin boards, company films and booklets. The program is directed by experienced communicators guided by systematic research. Yet with all these media and earnest effort, a 1968 IBT survey of employee attitudes toward company communication showed that only 49 percent of the management group got all the information they would like to have and that only 29 percent of the non-management employees got all the information they would like to have. This survey brought out that the supervisor is the most important source in an overall information program. Periodic surveys that enable employees to talk back will keep a communications program on the track. The 1968 IBT survey underscores the difficulty in effecting free-flowing communication up, down, and across today's organizations of size. This is management's central task.

Isidore Silver has written: ". . . one of the great problems of corporate life, and a cause for frequent grievance, is not the unfairness of management actions, but the inexplicability. It is ironic that in our over-communicative society, communications breakdowns frequently occur. Even in corporations—where internal communications networks are the lifeblood of their activity—decisions are sometimes made without adequate explanation. Often such decisions appear to be arbitrary when in fact they are not. Equally often, work discontent is caused by lack of understanding as to the reasons for such apparently unfavorable decisions. . . . The failure is by no means one-way." [1] What Silver says of the corporation applies with equal force to universities, governmental agencies, labor unions, and other entities. He advocates as a partial solution the establishment of an organizational ombudsman to hear grievances and to provide information. All

---

[1] "The Corporate Ombudsman," *Harvard Business Review*, Vol. 45, May–June, 1967, pp. 77–87.

managers must fully understand that an employee's ego is under assault from the time he enters the door until he leaves—the time clock, the badge or photographic I.D. card, and like instruments of regimentation bruise one's ego. Further, he or she comes to work freighted with the attitudes of associates and the community. Managers may choose to manage on the basis of the traditional closed system, but employees live much of their lives outside that system.

Common sense says, then, that practitioners need to know about the kind of working relationship that exists. Each organization is, within itself, a productive or service unit with production or service responsibilities. *It is also a social unit, with social responsibilities.*[2] Consequently, in any approach to the internal public, the social needs as well as the economic needs must be acknowledged and satisfied. A pay check falls far short of being the only thing an employee wants, although its importance should be recognized. Howard Wilson lists the social or psychological needs of man as: [3]

1. *Need to belong.* Man wants to identify himself with other people; he wants to be part of a group stronger than himself.

2. *Need for accomplishment.* Man wants to feel that he is making progress toward worthy goals, goals within his capabilities.

3. *Need for self-esteem.* Each man develops his own sense of worth, his own standard of pride and dignity.

4. *Need for acceptance.* Man must feel that he is accepted by the groups with which he identifies himself.

5. *Need for security.* The interdependence of modern life has sapped the once proud quality of self-reliance. Modern man is insecure and thus needs greater assurance of security.

6. *Need for creativity.* Too often in modern life the skill function has been taken from man and given to the machine. Without the chance to be creative, egos of men suffer.

Providing satisfying work is becoming an ever greater problem in our automated, productive society. There is no easy solution. Eric Fromm asks: [4] "Is man, during the next hundred years, to continue to spend most of his energy on meaningless work, waiting for the time when work will require no expenditure of energy? What will become of him in the meantime? . . . Is not work such a fundamental part of man's existence that it cannot and should never be reduced to almost complete insignificance?"

[2] For elaboration, see Burleigh Gardner and David Moore, *Human Relations in Industry* (Homewood, Ill.: Richard D. Irwin, Inc., 1955). A useful reference.

[3] "The Psychological Needs of Man," *PR*, Vol. 1, October, 1955.

[4] In *The Sane Society*, New York: Holt, Rinehart & Winston, Inc., 1955.

Those who would effectively communicate with employees must find ways of seeing work from their view. One who did this is Harvey Swados, writer and teacher, who went to work on an auto assembly line. He discovered how little we Americans really know of the texture of each other's working lives. He writes: [5]

> It came as something of a shock to discover that the one unifying force among all those men, so different from one another in ethnic background, educational attainment, and personal ambition, was hatred of their work. . . . I was doubly surprised that my middle-class friends found it difficult to accept this. . . . My friends of the middle class were frankly ignorant of the working lives of their fellow-Americans. . . . But when they heard what I had to say, they found it very difficult to accept it. . . ."

Another who did the same thing is Patricia Cayo Sexton, also a college teacher, who found that "the worker's world—as one lives in it—is very different." As a result of her three years in a Dodge plant, this sociologist concluded that "such phrases as 'powerful unions' and 'enlightened management' seem to me to convey very little of the essence of life on the assembly line." [6]

Equally tough problems must be faced in dealing with the expanding numbers of white-collar workers. Today nearly half of the employed civilian labor force are salaried personnel, yet these persons are too often overlooked in employee communications. Among the salaried people, the slow upward mobility of the college graduate has become a serious matter with which administrators are wrestling. The scramble for status has intensified. College-trained men between 25 and 34 now represent one-fourth of the total work force in that age group. The bright college graduate seeks meaningful work, early recognition, and advancement according to personal merit, not seniority.

Similar needs are felt by industrial and social service workers, soldiers and sailors, teachers and tellers, barbers and bartenders. Peter Drucker says that the corporation, as America's representative social institution, must satisfy two minimum requirements: "It must give status and function to the individual, and it must give him the justice of equal opportunities." One could have a college in mind and say the same thing.

Status and function require that each person have importance and dignity in his or her job despite the necessity for the jobs to be subordinated. This means that the floor sweeper in a dormitory realizes and feels sure that

[5] In "Work as a Public Issue," *Saturday Review*, Vol. 42, December 12, 1959, pp. 13–15 and 45.

[6] In "The Auto Assembly Line: An Inside View," *Harper's Magazine*, Vol. 224, June, 1962, pp. 52–57.

his job is worthwhile in the over-all scheme of things. The same is true for the filing clerk in the government printing office.

Parallel with this realization, there must be an understanding of the reasons why one job merits status different from another. A waitress may be required to wear a uniform. Another may be permitted to wear whatever she chooses. One executive may have a more sumptuous office than another. One secretary may work in a private office and another in a stenographic section. Understanding of the reasons for these symbols must replace envy of them. Along with this understanding there must be support of the promotion system, in which advancement from one job to another is possible and desirable.

Provision for the satisfaction of equal opportunity requires that each person's capabilities be known and measurable. It is not required, nor is it desirable, that all persons have equal opportunity for advancement regardless of their capabilities. It is not required or desirable that opportunities be opened in directions where people have unequal aptitude or training. An effort should be made to help the individual advance as far as possible in directions for which he is qualified. He cannot have a lasting working satisfaction if he is denied avenues of advancement or the hope of advancement, either socially or economically.

Giving the individual status, function, and opportunity establishes a wholesome working relationship. It satisfies the need of everyone for security, importance, individuality, and the friendship and esteem of others.

All this is good. But a practical approach must take into account that the supply of tangible forms of status, function, and opportunity is limited. The realistic approach must recognize that the United States socio-economic system is one of rewards in return for something—usually, time or effort in the form of productivity.

EFFECTIVE COMMUNICATION HAS A VITAL ROLE

Maladjustments and frustrations breed in large organizations. The lack of social integration leaves many workers asking: "Where do I fit?" "What does my boss think of me?" "How can I be a success?" *Communication which answers such questions helps reduce anxieties, create security, and bring job satisfaction.* But such meaningful, two-way communication becomes ever more difficult—from university president to student, from general to troops, from department head to field agent. Yet the glut and maze of communication grows. One large governmental agency estimates that it uses 12,000 sheets of interoffice stationery a day. As organizations escalate in size and complexity, internal communications efforts become ever more numerous and ever more difficult. A faculty committee pondering the question of enrollment ceilings in one major university said: "A special disadvantage associated with growth in numbers is the increased 'psychological distance' that threatens to isolate students, professors, and administrators from one another and from members of other groups. . . ." The problem is universal; the solution lies in a communications system tailored to the needs of a particular organization. Such a system ought to meet at least five basic needs:

1. To create among all hands an awareness of the organization's goals.
2. To keep all hands informed on significant developments that affect the organization and the employee.
3. To increase effectiveness of all hands as ambassadors on and off the job.
4. To encourage favorable attitudes in staff and to increase its productivity.
5. To satisfy desires of employees to be kept informed about what's going on in their organization.

Communications System

Typical of the internal communications systems required for effective operations in large organizations is that of the University of Michigan. It starts with listening. Utilizing the talent of its Survey Research Center, the university takes periodic opinion surveys to provide upward channels for the faculty, the non-academic staff, and the students. For example, a survey of student opinion in 1969 found, among other things: that nearly 67 percent of the students thought there was enough information provided by the administration to explain its actions, but nearly 28 percent thought not; that 90 percent thought students ought to be consulted on allocation of funds within the university; and that 40 percent regarded UM as "cool and/or impersonal." A faculty opinion survey found that, for this group, the greatest weakness in internal communication was lateral communication among departments, the most satisfactory communication was between professor and his department chairman. Similar surveys provide upward communication from the non-academic staff. Further, UM's administrators strive to meet faculty, staff, and students on an informal basis to facilitate a two-way dialogue. Michigan's downward communications program to keep its staff of more than 20,000, including 7,600 part time, ranging from physicists to plumbers—all part of an academic community with activists and an employer with unions—is described as follows by Vice-President Michael Radock, a veteran practitioner:

In the last year or so, U-M has initiated three regular publications: a weekly newsletter for faculty, professional staff and campus offices; a twice-a-month newspaper for non-academic staff that is mailed to homes; and a monthly *President's Letter,* sent to members of the faculty. The three publications are prepared by the university relations department and supplement three other established publications.

The newsletter, the *University Record,* evolved from a quarterly publication, which had been attempting to be all things to all staff. With a new format and a weekly schedule, the *Record* began in January, 1967, with a circulation of 5,000. As a result of requests, circulation increased by 50 percent in six months. At the end of a year, circulation was 7,900.

An apparent communication gap between the university as an employer and the non-academic staff—particularly the service and maintenance personnel—became even more apparent as public employee union activities intensified. A periodic newsletter, *Management Intercom,* was going to supervisory staff but no means existed for regular and frequent communication to employees generally.

The university's personnel office complained that the *University Record* was not doing the job for them. It wasn't, nor was it intended that the revised *Record* serve all staff.

To meet the needs of the personnel office, and to reach the non-academic staff primarily, a new publication was developed, the *U-M News.* The first issue came out in January, 1968, and was mailed to 9,800 employees' homes. Initially, the four-page tabloid-size newspaper will be published twice a month. It is generally in the style of a quality industrial plant newspaper, but it cannot be quite the same, because the academic community is different—even for the non-academics.

The third new periodical for internal communication is the *President's Letter,* a variation of a similar device that Michigan's president, Robben W. Fleming, used when he was chancellor of the University of Wisconsin's Madison campus. The *President's Letter* is normally four pages, 6¾ by 8½ inches, French fold, with a sketch of the president's house on the cover. The content is a personal message from the president on a subject of his choosing. The 2,400 persons on the U-M faculty senate mailing list receive copies.

Occasionally, a special edition of the *Record* has been published— for example, to provide information to the campus on the selection and background of a new university president. There is sometimes, however, the need to reach the staff more quickly. For "crisis communications," which can be typed, offset-printed, and circulated in a matter of hours, a "Report to the University Community" was developed. It has a standard heading, which may be attributed to the office of the president, or, when appropriate, to any of the university's vice presidential offices. Size is 8½ by 11 inches, one to four pages.

Supervisory personnel who interpret university policies and procedures to faculty and non-academic staff members need current and explicit information. A monthly *Management Intercom* was developed to meet this need. This 8½ by 11 inch, two-page newsletter goes to 1,400 managers and supervisors on the 10th of each month so that the information it contains can be relayed to all personnel before payday on the 15th.

Each week a "Weekly Calendar" listing all events scheduled on campus during the forthcoming week is mailed to deans, directors, and department heads. (Subscriptions are available to the public.) The calendar is 12 by 18 inches, and folds to 4 by 9 inches for mailing.

Another medium of general communication is the University's educational radio station, WUOM, also a division of university relations.

Still another medium are the university's three open phone lines. One line provides news briefs, another announcements of upcoming programs and events, and a third one specific information in response to queries. The first two provide recorded information. Stickers with phone numbers for this information are provided for each university telephone.

GAINING ACCEPTABILITY

Mutual confidence of employer and employee in each other is essential to the success of any enterprise. The main asset of any enterprise is the confidence of the men in their leaders, the confidence of the leaders in their organization, and the confidence of both in their product or service. Without such faith, there can be no permanent success.

In organizations with collective bargaining agreements, such confidence must embrace these fundamentals for industrial peace and productivity:

1. Full acceptance by management of collective bargaining.
2. Full acceptance by unions of private ownership and operation of industry for a profit, and nonprofit organizations for efficient productivity.
3. Strong unions that are democratically and responsibly run.
4. No management interference in union affairs.
5. Both parties demonstrate mutual trust in all dealings.
6. Neither party takes a legalistic approach in negotiations, which should be problem-centered, not issue-centered.
7. Full sharing of information and widespread consultation on matters of mutual interest.
8. Prompt settlement of grievances as these arise.

Many employers do not have to deal with unions. Nonetheless, they must gain acceptability by following the same basic approach of full sharing of information, consultation on matters of mutual interest, and prompt settlement of grievances. Enlightened management has taken most of the thrust out of organized labor's efforts to unionize all employees by providing voluntarily what the unions used to get through the power of collective bargaining. Union membership has been stabilized many years, although the nation's work force has been growing. *Fortune's* Daniel Bell ascribes this relative loss of strength by unions to "the increased sophistication of management, and because in this period of relatively full employment wages have been high in nonunion as well as unionized plants." Nonprofit agencies can write a comparable set of fundamentals and must, given the growth of unions in the public sector.

The process of earning acceptability for the manager or administrator is not complex. There are three components. One is an expressed interest in the employees' or members' affairs. The interest must be genuine, not simulated. It must be humane. It must be attentive to the employee's expressed desires and fears. It must be studious.

The second component is in the actions taken as a result of the problems of the employees. This implies no actions that are foolhardy or that consist of giving away something for nothing. It means, specifically, a regular review and appropriate overhaul of personnel policies. This gives positive action to the employer's genuine interest. Good intent is supported by deeds. An interest in employee health is backed up by actions providing for sanitation, safety, and medical services. An interest in his dignity means elimination of any thing he finds demeaning, whether that's the time clock, poor lighting, invasions of privacy, or racial discrimination.

The third component is a *free and candid flow of information between management and employee.* The flow uses the line organization and auxiliary tools. The purpose is to strengthen the wholesome working relationship. In practice, this requires an exchange of differing viewpoints. It requires efforts to reconcile the differences for the best interests of all. It requires a collaboration in realizing workaday satisfactions.

In analyzing the reasons for the long and harmonious relationships in the Marathon division of American Can Company, two specialists found this to be a key factor: "The company early established with its employees and with the unions when they arrived, a reputation for absolute integrity and a willingness to sit down and talk about any subject." [7]

An organization that takes these factors into account can get through even the most unpleasant situations. Take the way the George D. Roper Corp., Rockford, Illinois, handled a layoff of 450 workers. This firm had a military contract which was suddenly cut back. To gain time to ease the blow to the employees, the firm obtained a 30-day extension on the cutback. This enabled it to give the men three weeks' notice and thus time to look for other jobs. Personnel and employee communicators went to work to collaborate on *planning* the layoff and its announcement.

[7] Clinton S. Golden and Virginia Parker, eds., *Causes of Industrial Peace* (New York: Harper & Row, Publishers, 1955), p. 222. This is a valuable compilation of 13 case studies of good management-labor relationships.

A detailed plan of breaking the news was worked out. Efforts were made to line up other jobs for the men. Round-the-clock interviews were arranged for 900 other employees who had to be shifted to other jobs in the plant. Union officers were called in to help iron out complaints and to work out problems of seniority. When the layoff day came, the news was broken by this timetable: 8 a.m.—plant foremen; 9 a.m.—union representatives; 10 a.m.—office supervisors; 10:30 a.m.—notices went up on plant bulletin boards; 11 a.m.—news released to press, radio, and TV outlets in Rockford; 12—a letter from the Roper president was put in the mails, timed to explain the layoff to workers' families the following day.

By that date, the company's personnel people had completed 1,300 interviews. The 900 men to be kept were ready to step into their new jobs. Of the 450 let out, more than 200 had other jobs in Rockford within a week, owing largely to Roper's help. The final move was formation of the "Roper Veterans Club" for 21 employees who had passed or were near retirement. This club has been used to help retired employees find part-time jobs if they want them. It also has provided all retired employees an annual dinner. The reaction of employees—both those kept and those laid off—was most favorable.

Most organizations put their personnel policies down on paper. It is wise to do so. The forms vary, but the intent is uniform. Having the attitudes of management down on paper communicates a bid for acceptability. Administrators must remember that *these policies become a binding contract* in the employee's eyes. Such policies should be widely disseminated. There is a resultant awareness of management's attitudes on the part of employees or members.

Tone-of-voice in policy statements can be almost as important as what is said. The employee will interpret the attitude of the administration almost as much by the manner in which he is told as by what is provided in a policy. For example, the responses to granting a privilege can be considerably lessened if the announcement sounds like a threat against anyone who abuses it.

A QUESTION OF LAW

For employers of union workers, there is a troublesome legal question of how far management can go in its employee communications without violating the Taft-Hartley Act. This question, not fully resolved, was raised when the National Labor Relations Board found the General Electric Company guilty of unfair labor practices and cited its communications with employees during a bargaining period as evidence. The case has long been in litigation. This is the background.

Since 1947, General Electric has followed a firm policy *vis-a-vis* its unions, and it has backed this policy with an intensive program of employee communication. The program was formulated largely by L. R. Boulware after he took charge of GE's employee and community relations that year. He later brought public relations into his domain. Union critics labeled the program "Boulwarism." GE's stated purposes for this wide-ranging, hard-hitting program is: (1) Integrate and motivate the management team; (2) Develop supervisors as leaders of their people; (3) Build employee confidence in management. An industrial relations writer identifies "Boulwarism" by these characteristics: [8]

1. Management has a tendency to bypass the union and communicate directly with its employees on day-to-day problems.
2. Management attempts to win its employees' allegiance in competition with the union by convincing them that it is sincerly interested in their welfare and is doing its best to promote it.
3. Management follows a policy of firmness in negotiating with the union; for example, giving out a statement of its best and final offer with a deadline for acceptance and a warning that there will be no retroactivity for any later settlement.
4. Management communicates its offers directly to its workers and the public, independently of the union.

It was the latter that brought a citation for unfair labor practices from Trial Examiner Arthur Leff, who based his ruling on what lawyers call "the totality of conduct" doctrine. Leff found, in part: [9]

> Note has . . . been made of the great mass of employee communications to which GE employees were subjected during the period following the IUE convention, as well as of the apparent purpose of the communications to impair employee faith and confidence in the motives of the IUE top leadership, to induce a form of vote more to the Company's liking, and to impress upon employees the finality of the Company's position and the futility of strike action. . . .
>
> During the same period, the Company in its communications continued to plug hard on the merits of the company offer. The communications did not always confine themselves to arguments that had been

[8] Robert N. McMurry, "War and Peace in Labor Relations," *Harvard Business Review*, Vol. 33, November, 1955, p. 48. For full examination, con and pro, of this hotly-debated approach to employee relations, see: Herbert R. Northrup, *Boulwarism* (Ann Arbor, Mich.: Graduate School of Business, University of Michigan, 1964), and L. R. Boulware, *The Truth About Boulwarism* (Washington, D.C.: Bureau National Affairs, 1969).

[9] National Labor Relations Board, "General Electric Company and International Union of Electrical, Radio and Machine Workers, AFL-CIO, Case No. 2-CA-7851." Issued by NLRB, April 2, 1963, p. 47.

presented to union negotiators. In some instances the Company elaborated its arguments far more fully to employees than it had at the bargaining table. In some others, the Company presented arguments to employees that it had not presented at all to the union negotiators. . . .

The NLRB ruled December 16, 1964, that GE had "failed to bargain in good faith" with its union. The Board, in a four to one vote, "cited both major facets of the company's 1960 bargaining technique—an intensive communications campaign among the employees before and during negotiations to disparage and discredit the IUE as bargaining representative, and adamant insistence at the bargaining table on GE's 'fair and firm' contract proposal." [10] General Electric appealed the decision to the 2nd Circuit, U. S. Court of Appeals, where the case was heard June 3, 1969, and decided October 28, 1969. The court, in a two-to-one decision upheld the NLRB's findings.[11] The majority opinion stated: "We hold that an employer may not so combine 'take-it-or-leave-it,' bargaining methods with a widely publicized stance of unbending firmness that he is himself unable to alter a position once taken." The court further agreed with the NLRB examiner "that other aspects of the communications program also evidenced bad faith. . . ." In January, 1970, GE appealed the decision to the U. S. Supreme Court. Undeterred by the court decision, GE in 1970 launched an intensive communications program in its struggle with its striking employees in an effort to present its case to employees and public alike. The IUE responded with an advertising campaign urging boycott of GE products. The efficacy of "Boulwarism" continued in dispute.

This ruling raises the tough and vexing question, How far does the employer's right of free speech extend in competing with the union for the allegiance of his employees? Section 8(c) of the Taft-Hartley law reads: "The expressing of any view, argument, or opinion, or the dissemination thereof, whether in written, printed, graphic or visual form, shall not constitute or be evidence of an unfair labor practice under any of the provisions of this Act, if such expression contains no threat of reprisal or force or promise of benefit." What constitutes "threat of reprisal or force or promise of benefit" will never be an easy question to resolve. Professor Jack Barbash has wisely said, "It is the configuration of factors—the interweaving of the words themselves, the form in which communicated, the quality of the union-management relationship, the character of the community—which determines whether there is promise of reward and threat of reprisal or not." Barbash holds, rightly, that "the circumstances more

[10] News Release, NLRB, dated December 16, 1964, numbered R-992.

[11] USCA, 2nd Circuit, September Term, 1968, Docket Nos. 29502, 29576, NLRB vs. General Electric Co., respondent, and IUE, intervenor, October 28, 1969. G E lost appeal: Certiorari denied, 396 U. S. 1005 (1970).

than the words deserve the weight of consideration" in answering this thorny question.[12]

Resolution of this legal dispute will have an important impact on employee communication. The whole issue raises many questions. One commentator notes: [13] "One key issue is whether a company can take its case to its employees directly. If it cannot, then the whole structure of employee communication changes, for central to this problem is the question of a company's right to tell its workers where he stands on all issues affecting operations: working conditions, pay, profits, job security, management's position on a union's proposal."

Beyond the law, communicators must remember one basic fact: Neither administration nor unions can sell a bad case with good communication. General Electric is quite correct in asserting that "the public increasingly and properly expects more maturity and responsibility on the part of both management and union representatives in collective bargaining." [14]

COMMUNICATIONS IN PERSPECTIVE

Over the past twenty years, employers have steadily increased emphasis and expenditure on employee communications. The growth in number, size, and use of these tools is reflective. Too often "communications" are held out as the panacea to cure all the ills, frictions, and aggressions which breed conflict inside organizations. Management is quite concerned about its communications. Many employers have created special departments and have launched, periodically, intensive hurry-up campaigns. Most have active, large-scale programs. Communication specialists have multiplied. Nonprofit organizations have followed the lead of industry in headlong pursuit of this wonder drug. Millions of man-hours and of dollars are being spent. A lot of these are wasted.

This mounting barrage of employee communication in the case of industry is based on these premises: (1) that there is a need to "re-educate" employees in the values of America's competitive, capitalistic system, on the premise that they have become, somehow, ignorant of or hostile to the system; (2) that there is a correlation between the amount of information a worker has about the company and his attitude toward his company; (3) that there is a vital correlation between a worker's attitudes, or morale,

[12] In "Employer 'Free Speech' and Employee Rights," *Labor Law Journal*, April, 1963, pp. 317–18.

[13] L. L. L. Golden, "What Can You Tell Employees?" *Saturday Review*, Vol. 46, August 10, 1963, p. 50.

[14] General Electric's *Relations News Letter* for September 21, 1961.

and his productivity; (4) that employees who know the "facts" will be more reasonable at the bargaining table.

The validity of these premises is open to doubt and will remain so until there has been more *evaluation*. Much of the propagandistic political-social-economic education efforts of management have been shrugged off by workers as irrelevant and irritating propaganda. Industry's massive indoctrination campaign has had something of a benumbing effect on the intended audience. In Peter Drucker's opinion, most of these campaigns have failed because of these *mistaken* assumptions: (1) that employees consider the same things to be important and relevant that management considers relevant and important; (2) that employees are hostile to the free enterprise system.

Two researchers who tested the assumption that "good communications bring about high morale" concluded: "There is no significant relationship between employees' attitudes toward their company and their knowledge about the company." [15] Likewise, there is no firm proof that there is a relationship between worker morale and productivity. Two psychologists, after reviewing research testing this premise over a period of 20 years, concluded: "It is time to question the strategic and ethical merits of selling to industrial concerns an assumed relationship between employee attitudes and employee performance." [16] There is evidence to the contrary in both cases.

The reader should not leap to the conclusion that *all* employee communications programs are wasteful or ineffective. To the contrary, there is solid evidence of effective employee communications contributing to the successful operation of all kinds of enterprises. Shadows of doubt are cast here to bring the matter into reasonable perspectives. For the efforts that have failed, there are two questions: Did it fail in expecting too much of mechanical media? Did it fail in use of the media? The answer to both probably is: in varying degrees.

THE PRACTITIONER'S ROLE

Seldom does the public relations function embrace making and executing personnel policies, though exceptions exist. In most organizations, the staff is not *directly* involved in labor negotiations, employee recruitment, promotion, counseling, and training. However, the department has a large stake in productive, pleasant internal relationships. It can contribute much. The

---

[15] Dallis Perry and Thomas A. Mahoney, "In-plant Communications and Employee Morale," *Personnel Psychology*, Vol. 8, Autumn, 1955, p. 339.

[16] Arthur H. Brayfield and Walter H. Crockett, "Employee Attitudes and Employee Performance," *Psychological Bulletin*, Vol. 52, September, 1955, p. 421. Still worth reading.

role in employee relations includes: (1) an over-all concern for the success of the enterprise; (2) the attitudes employees reflect in their role as ambassadors of good or ill will for the organization in their relationships with outsiders; (3) responsibility for creating an environment favorable to the personnel, industrial relations function; (4) responsibility for encouraging and implementing two-way communication between managers and men.

Too often the emphasis in employee communications is on "selling" employees. Channels for an *upward flow* of employee opinion must be created and utilized. The employee must have adequate opportunity to tell: (1) what he would like to know about his job, his employer, and related matters; and (2) what he would like management to know about himself and the things that are bothering him. The public relations man should work to promote an understanding of the employee view inside management. Tactfully and without getting out of channels, he should encourage managers to *listen* to what employees have to say.

The staff can provide skilled assistance by sponsoring employee attitude surveys. S. C. Johnson & Son surveys employee attitudes each six years. The staff can promote use of the suggestion system, putting on "Why I Like My Job" essay contests, creating advisory groups, providing a Q.-and-A. box in the employee paper, and by other means.

Employee papers, letters, bulletin boards, and suggestion systems *supplement* but do not *supplant* the working communication system. Providing this system requires skill, tailored tools, and, above all, good ideas coupled with good timing. To do this job, the practitioner must work closely with the personnel department and must be informed on what is taking place on the line. He must know management's employee objectives if he is to promote them effectively.

One industrial relations writer, George S. Odiorne, sees these benefits in utilizing public relations skills in employee communications: [17] (1) Public relations people have a facility with verbalizing and writings; (2) They add color, vigor, style, and impact to their messages; (3) The department is staffed with people who have creativity and imagination, and these qualities show themselves in the ingenuity and *elan* which go into communicating information; (4) Many personnel people are not specialists in communications.

Odiorne also warns against these pitfalls which ensnare some practitioners when they move into employee relations: [18] (1) Failure to develop a clear image of who is "the employee"; (2) Undermining credibility by being too strongly antiunion; (3) Failure to know substance of employee

---

[17] In "Public Relations and Industrial Relations," *Personnel Journal*, Vol. 38, March, 1960, pp. 366–69. This relationship deserves more study than it gets.
[18] *Ibid.*

relations; (4) Tendency to indulge in "class" forms of communication and to see administration as a class of people rather than an activity which is necessary for the success of everyone in the organization. In short, the employee relations benefits are lost if the communications expertise is "rooted in inexperience and unrealism."

THE PERSONAL CONTACT IS SUPREME

Procter & Gamble, which has a long record of productive employee relations, holds that communications is a matter of having sound policies to pass on to employees and of receiving their reactions through man-to-man communication. At P. & G., employee communications is viewed as a personal function, not a mechanical one. It makes each member of supervision wholly responsible for communications in that portion of the operation assigned to him. To his people at P. & G., each supervisor *is* the company management.

THE SUPERVISOR

The supervisor, foreman or department manager has an increasingly important and difficult position in large organizations. He has counterparts in the top sergeant and the ward captain in a charity drive. He has an important role in internal communications, but he must be trained for it. The relationship is crucial, for it is here that management's objectives and employee attitudes interface. Auxiliary communications *must support, not undercut,* that relationship.

In sizable organizations, the people in the offices and shops seldom see the firm's administrative officials and only occasionally see the factory manager or office manager. The foreman and the supervisor have become the first link with management. These two key jobs constitute the counterpart of the factory boss in days when most shops were small and everybody saw the boss every day. Consequently, foremen and supervisors are objects of strong emotional attitudes.

The custom in modern management is to grant the foreman and supervisory people full membership in the factory managerial team. Common today are foremen-training programs in economics, labor law, and human relations. There has been a marked upward salary adjustment. There is participation in high-level consultation and action groups. Finally, there are social clubs and events bringing foremen into the executive circle. The National Management Association has done much to strengthen the foreman through the formation of Foremen's Clubs and through its public relations program.

THE EMPLOYEE COUNSELOR

Employee counseling is another vehicle for achieving face-to-face communication. Pioneer exploratory work in this field was done at the Hawthorne (Chicago) Western Electric plant. The employee counselor was an outgrowth of Elton Mayo's historic Hawthorne studies which had a profound effect on human relations. Many employers in and out of industry today have counselors who hear out employees, to let them get things off their chests privately. Many organizations without a full-scale employee counseling program retain the services of consultants in psychiatry or psychology. In the armed forces, the work performed by the classification sections, the Inspector General's office, and chaplains comprise a counterpart. In education, there are faculty advisers and student counselors. In social work, the caseworker counsels on a personal basis. Counseling provides an effective means of clearing away trouble.

PARTICIPATION IS THE KEY

An ounce of meaningful participation can be worth a ton of pamphlets. As organizations learn this, there is a consequent shift to group discussions. An affiliate company in the Bell System made a study of its presentation of a rate-increase request to its employees. This affiliate found that *participation-type* meetings were the most effective in getting this complex story to employees. The company's researchers found that "belief and knowledge were best in situations where employees said they had a 'whole lot' of discussion." Straight presentations with little or no discussion were much less effective.

This controlled study followed extensive research on employee attitudes in the parent Bell System by an outside research team. From this, American Telephone & Telegraph learned that: (1) When people get a lot of satisfaction out of their work, they reflect their feelings to outsiders, and they are more effective on the job; (2) Often important information fails to reach an employee because of employees' *lack of interest* or *lack of involvement;* (3) Employees want an opportunity to ask questions and express their ideas in small meetings. Out of this has come Bell's program of regular work-group meetings.

Situations in which employees can fully participate can: (1) provide means of two-way communication, including feedback of employee questions, mistaken notions, and so forth; (2) provide individuals with means of self-expression and tap the creative ideas latent in any group; (3) uncover opposition and obstacles to plans before they are effected; (4) encourage a sense of responsibility for the decisions made and thus pave the way for change. There is a price to be paid for these returns; the employees' views must be heard and given due weight. *Participation cannot be just a sounding-board operation.*

An aircraft manufacturer was losing large sums because 53 percent of his daily production of fins for jet motors was being rejected. In the motors then in production, there were 9,000 fins costing $50 each in each motor. A 53 percent rejection rate was appalling. The company put on a hurry-up campaign of communications and exhortations to cut this waste. Rejections declined slightly. Desperate, the firm brought supervisors and men together to decide how the problem could be licked. When solving the problem became a cooperative effort, the acceptance rate went up. Eventually it reached an acceptance of 89 percent. The savings added up to $300,000 in one year!

People's resistance to change poses tough problems. Textile firms have to make frequent changes in designs and products, and thus in jobs. The Harwood Manufacturing Company learned from its records that, after a change in operations, 38 percent of the operators recovered their standard rate of production. The other 62 percent became chronically substandard or quit. It made a controlled study using two groups. The group which was given *total participation* in planning and effecting the change was back to pre-change efficiency in fourteen days. Then it progressed to a production rate 14 percent above the former one. Members of the non-participating control group dropped off in production about 20 percent and improved little beyond their early efficiency ratings.

There are many ways of strengthening the line organization through group participation. This includes self-administered activities: music groups, parties, sports teams, outings, hobby clubs, credit unions, or contests. Selection of such activities, weighing one against the other, is of secondary importance.

Participation of internal groups by having a voice in the actual conduct of management-level affairs is another vehicle. This area, long considered sacrosanct, is being invaded more and more. College students are demanding a voice in making policies, in determining curriculum, and in selection of faculty. Public school teachers are demanding a voice in the selection of their principals. Union members are increasingly insistent upon a voice in management of their affairs. This self-assertion of the right to have a say in matters affecting one's livelihood or role will spread. Meaningful channels of consultation and communication must be the response. *Participation must be used with sincerity and not as a manipulative device.*

One internal communications task of increasing concern to management today is that of getting employees to appreciate and utilize employee benefits, more commonly termed "fringe benefits." The objective of these benefits is to get employees to stay with the organization and to motivate them to work with greater efficiency. Many employers complain that employees take the growing range of benefits for granted. The desire for communication on benefit programs is not one-sided. One survey, for example, showed that 85 percent of employees interviewed expressed a desire for more information about their benefits. Many of these employees were unaware that their employer matched their contributions to Social Security. Others were puzzled about provisions of the retirement plan. Explaining retirement plans is not an easy assignment, especially if the lawyers insist upon legal contract language. This task calls for imagination, ingenuity. For example the Minneapolis Civic Council issued a stock certificate with dividend coupons to its 4,842 "stockholders" one year—24 dividend coupons detailed its accomplishments for the year. Con Edison, the New York City utility, one year issued a four-color, spiral-bound calendar that used a few words of text and an appropriate cartoon to publicize a different benefit to employees for each month of the year. Several organizations have used the checkbook idea—to give employees a checkbook with each check showing the amount of money the organization had spent the previous year and the stub carries the explanation of the benefit. The check stubs show the payments accumulating from check to check.[19]

OTHER AUXILIARIES TO THE LINE COMMUNICATION

Employed with skill and in place, other *auxiliary* tools of employee communication contribute much. Use of the auxiliaries must be coordinated; one must reinforce the others. Their content must be beamed on specific objectives. For industry, Professor Wayne Hodges sets these over-all goals:

1. To promote unity, as defined by a sense of identity, of common purpose, of common loyalty, and of common benefit under the enterprise system.

2. To promote an understanding of management's problems, needs, duties, obligations, principles, and practices—and faith in the goodwill behind all these.

3. To maintain an atmosphere and a means conducive to genuine two-way communication.

4. To provide a permanent company record of actions and affairs not legally documented.

[19] For other ideas, see *National Industrial Conference Board Record*, "Employee Benefit Communications Get a New Look," December, 1965. For studies relating the world of work to behavioral sciences, see NICB's *Behavioral Science, Concepts and Management Application*, Personnel Policy Study No. 216, 1970. (Now the Conference Board.)

5. To inform employees concerning the role of their company and of themselves in community affairs.

Contrary to the opinions of some, *tangible* results can be and are accomplished with these tools. Take these examples:

> In a 1,300-man cellophane plant, a study indicated that power consumption could be substantially reduced. Management used the employee paper to spearhead a plant-wide power-savings program. Suggestions from employees were invited. The number of employee suggestions was double the number in the same quarter the year before. Management gave the paper most of the credit for resulting power savings, estimated at $100,000 a year.
>
> In a 3,000-man chemicals plant, when steps were taken to modernize a routine process, rumors began to fly to the effect that this conversion would result in wholesale layoffs. The full story was put before employees through the plant paper. Supervisors reported that rumors and speculation abated rapidly once the story was published.
>
> In another plant, supervisors reported to management a common problem, grumblings by employees that the cafeteria prices were too high, that the company was profiteering. An illustrated story gave a complete breakdown of cafeteria costs. It showed that the firm was paying out $1.02 for every $1 taken in. The complaints disappeared in short order, supervisors reported.
>
> Thomas J. Lipton, Inc. used its 3,500-circulation, semimonthly newspaper to improve the safety record of its car-fleet salesmen and other employees. The fleet accident rate went down, though the fleet grew 26 percent and mileage increased 52 percent. The insurance rates went down, too!

Examples could be multiplied many-fold. In using these tools, the practitioner should strive to keep the content *employee-centered*. It should be related to such specific goals as increased productivity, full use of fringe benefits, reduction of waste, reduction of accidents, reduction of absenteeism, elimination of misinformation and rumors, encouragement of employees to be *informed* ambassadors.

Above all else: *Employees should neither be overlooked in disseminating information nor should they be overloaded with information.*

CASE PROBLEM

You are public relations director for the U. S. Army's Strategic Communications Command (STRATCOM) in Washington, D.C. The unit employs 650 civilians. Many have owned their homes in the Washington area for years. Many have children in school and spouses who work outside the command. The Secretary of Defense decides to move STRATCOM to Ft. Huachuca (pronounced Wah-CHOO-kah), 75 miles south of Tuscon, Arizona, and only 20 miles from the Mexican border. Your commanding general informs you of the decision and makes it clear that it is his desire to retain as many of the civilians as can be persuaded to move. He sees this as internal communications task. You have six months to devise and implement a plan to persuade these 650 civilian employees to leave the exciting Washington area for a lonely outpost in Arizona. One of your first research steps is to examine the records of similar Army moves and you find that civilian participation had ranged from only 2 percent to a high of 19 percent. You resolve to do better by utilizing two-way communication between Army management and the civilian employees.

Draft a detailed plan, including themes, timetable, and so forth, for accomplishment of management's objective.

ADDITIONAL READING

BERNARD BASS, "Communications in Industrial Organizations," ch. 8 in *Organizational Psychology*. New York: Allyn and Bacon, 1965.

ROBERT BLAUNER, *Alienation and Freedom: The Factory Worker and His Industry*. Chicago: University of Chicago Press, 1964.

ERNEST G. BORMANN, WILLIAM S. HOWELL, et. al., *Interpersonal Communication in the Modern Organization*. Englewood Cliffs, N.J.: Prentice-Hall, Inc., 1969.

"Communications in Organizations," by Harold Guetzkow in *Handbook of Organizations*, (ed.) James G. March, Chicago: Rand McNally & Co., 1965.

VIRGIL B. DAY, "Communication in Labor Relations," *Public Relations Quarterly*, Vol. 11, Summer, 1966.

C. J. DOVER, "The Three Eras of Management Communication," *The Journal of Communication*, Vol. 9, December, 1959.

C. J. DOVER, *Management Communication on Controversial Issues*. Washington, D.C.: Bureau National Affairs, 1965.

ALAN C. FILLEY and ROBERT J. HOUSE, *Managerial Process and Organizational Behavior*, New York: Scott, Foresman Co., 1969.

EDWARD E. LAWLER, III and LYMAN W. PORTER, "The Effect of Performance on Job Satisfaction," *Industrial Relations, a Journal of Economy and Society*, Vol. 7, October, 1967.

DOUGLAS McGREGOR, *The Human Side of Enterprise*. New York: McGraw Hill Book Co., 1960. A landmark book.

CHARLES E. REDFIELD, *Communication in Management: The Theory and Practice of Administrative Communication*, rev. ed. Chicago: University of Chicago Press, 1958.

GEORGE T. VARDAMAN and CARROLL C. HALTERMAN, eds., *Managerial Control Through Communication*. New York: Wiley, 1968.

CHAPTER 14

THE COMMUNITY PUBLICS

Hometown relationships—inescapable
for industries or institutions—are a
something-for-something proposition.

Community relationships for all institutions—industries, utilities, governmental agencies, school systems, universities, welfare agencies—are increasing in importance and complexity as urbanization proceeds apace. Community relations work is distinguishable from public relations and public affairs work mainly in that it deals with a specific locality.

In an era when urban areas are threatened by the decay of the inner city, torn by discord between races, blighted by air and water pollution, strangled by traffic congestion and mass transit breakdowns, maintenance of productive community relationships is a most difficult task. Much of the community relations task for business falls under the title, Public Affairs; hence much of Chapter Nineteen is relevent here.

The community relations aspect of public relations confronts all practitioners. For example, consider the problems of universities forced to double in size over the past decade or so. This rapid growth causes dislocation in the neighborhood, increases the burden on city water and sewer systems, adds to traffic congestion, increases a city's costs and problems in police and fire protection, and at the same time takes more property off the tax rolls. These problems are exacerbated when student protests or hijinks spill over into the community. The *whole* process of public relations comes to a sharp focus in these first-hand community relationships. These are the tenets.

1. There is *increasing interdependency* of organizations upon the cooperation and esteem of many people, either in groups or as individuals. This works both ways. An industry, for example, cannot prosper without manpower, adequate municipal services, and freedom from strangling regulation. A community cannot live and grow without industries to provide expanding opportunities for its people.

2. The *continuous, interacting flow of the opinion process* starts at the top of an organization and flows downward through the ranks and then out into the community. An organization cannot have rewarding community relationships without healthy employee relations. Workers reflect community attitudes on the job and reflect job attitudes in the community where they live and play: one role reacts on the other.

For example, in the study of industrial peace between the Nashua Corporation, Nashua, New Hampshire and its workers, observers found a close correlation between community attitudes and attitudes of employees toward the firm. This company provided steady employment and high wages. Its workers were telling their friends: "They don't keep after you all of the time if you mind your own business." Or "They have a good union. The place is run by good management. My friends say if you stay there, there are chances to get ahead." This reputation gives "the Card Shop," as it is known locally, "the cream of the labor market" in the opinion of its employment manager.[1]

3. A positive effort to build favorable community relationships is not *do-goodism*. It is a profitable investment of the money and time it takes. Community relations is a *something-for-something* proposition, a calculated casting of bread upon the waters.

The community provides an institution with good employees, fair political weather, transportation facilities, housing for its employees, schools for their children, churches for their worship, health and hospital facilities, recreational and cultural facilities— a good community in which to work and live. In a tight manpower market, the community is often the decisive factor in job choice.

In turn, the community expects that the institution will provide people with good jobs at good wages, pay fair taxes, make local purchases, contribute to worthwhile causes, take leadership in community affairs, and behave as good neighbors.

Projects and programs to improve and strengthen institutional-community relationships must be mutually beneficial. One example is the Niagara Mohawk Power Company's promotion of urban redevelopment in upstate New York. Its community development and public relations staffs are cooperating in a program to promote better land planning and to arrest the decline of the larger cities in its territory. This utility has taken a major role in urban renewal in New York which, in the words of its manager of community development, "would not have been possible without an effective public relations program."[2]

Sometimes a clever community relations deed can appease the local citizenry. In the year 1956, the University of Wisconsin dedicated a $1.5-million sports building as a memorial to veterans of the Civil War! This was done to mute the aroused protests of the Sons of the G.A.R., a small organization, and a few Civil War buffs, who argued that erection of the building on a Civil War campsite was a desecration of hallowed ground.

---

[1] Golden and Parker, *Causes of Industrial Peace* (New York: Harper & Row, 1955), p. 190.

[2] J. Arthur Rath, "Speeding Up Urban Development," *Public Relations Journal*, Vol. 25, January, 1969, p. 29.

4. Sound relationships are not built upon gifts, gimmicks, or publicity alone. Good relationships are the product of *responsible community citizenship adequately publicized*. Elmo Roper found in a survey of community attitudes toward the "best" company in Terre Haute, Indiana, that: "The 'best' company in Terre Haute actually turned out not to pay the highest wages or to build the most playgrounds, but it did create the greatest number of opportunities and, therefore, 'did most for the town.' " This firm made its mark as a good employer "by paying good wages, by keeping management accessible to the workers so that grievances don't fester, and . . . by being an expanding, going concern that provides opportunities for jobs and advancement—and *letting everybody know it*."

As society's problems grow more intense, community leaders and active citizens look beyond financial contributions when rating organizations on whether they are doing their share in the community. One writer suggests: "Community relations today involve more than having the 'good will' of the community or traditional participation in civic organizations or large-scale contributions. . . ." Corroboration of this is found in an Opinion Research Corporation survey taken in an Eastern city and in a Southern city which found: [3]

MAIN REASONS FOR RATING A COMPANY "OUTSTANDING"—

	COMMUNITY LEADERS	GENERAL PUBLIC
Participation in local affairs	67%	48%
Financial contributions	41	23
Good employee relations	20	5

In what he admits is an oversimplification, Wayne Hodges say that there are two schools of industrial community relations: [4] (1) the "community-centered" or personal service school in which company presidents, and hence their administrative staffs, assume great responsibility for the development of the city and its institutions; (2) the "company-centered" school, concentrating exclusively on education of citizens in "basic economics" and on the use of public relations techniques to develop community attitudes favorable to the profitable operation of business and industry. As Hodges notes, "Each school holds vague reservations about the other." Few organizations today, profit or nonprofit, embrace the idea of isola-

---

[3] Al Vogel, "Urban Crisis: New Focus for Community Relations," *Public Relations Journal*, Vol. 23, September, 1967, p. 13.

[4] *Company and Community* (New York: Harper & Row, 1958), p. 42. This is a useful book with illuminating case studies in industry-city relationships in Syracuse, N.Y.

tion from the community in which they are taxed, legally controlled, and from which they recruit their manpower. The head of a trucking company put it in practical terms: "We need good relations or we find trouble with municipal legislation on ordinances for local delivery."

THE MAKE-UP OF COMMUNITY OPINION

The local community is a miniature of the entire public. An organization has, in its own hometown, a panel or jury whose judgments predict the opinions and interests of the national spectator. *This is where national opinions are born.* An apt definition of the community in terms of its motivation has been provided by Dwight Sanderson: "The community includes not only individual persons but the organizations and institutions in which they associate. The real community is the devotion to common interests and purposes, the ability to act together in the chief concerns of life."

Today community life is organized along the lines of interest groupings, whether the interest is in lower taxes, higher wages, a new civic auditorium, attraction of industry, cultural facilities, or whatever. These groupings come and go, shift and overlap. Each community is different and ever-changing. This calls for constant cataloging of the *influentials* in community affairs and requires programs tailored to fit the specific community—its people, history, and problems.

The first step in community relations is to tag the decision makers. Persuasion of these key individuals usually facilitates persuasion of their followers. *Each stratum in the community develops its own leaders.* The nominal leaders may not be the real leaders. In one town the mayor is a leader; in another, he is a puppet. Identification of opinion leaders requires probing.

In each city there are a series of influential power structures revolving about different issues—schools, urban redevelopment, cultural programs, etc. Each issue attracts different sets of leaders, pro and con. The influentials in the community—the active innovators—relatively few in number, deserve specialized attention. Floyd Hunter found this in his study of Atlanta, Georgia power structure, a study that Arnold Rose criticized as only "partial picture of the *image* of the power structure, as held mainly by the subordinates of the economic elite." [5] Nonetheless Hunter's listing of those influential in civic affairs is not without value: [6]

[5] *The Power Structure* (New York: Oxford Paperback, 1967), p. 9.

[6] Floyd Hunter, *Community Power Structure* (Chapel Hill: University of North Carolina Press, 1953), p. 109. For insight on power structure in a small town, see Vidich and Bensman, *Small Town in Mass Society* (Princeton, N.J.: Princeton University Press, 1958).

First Rate: Industrial, commercial, financial owners and top executives of large enterprises.

Second Rate: Operations officials, bank vice-presidents, public relations men, small businessmen, top-ranking public officials, corporation attorneys, contractors.

Third Rate: Civic organization personnel, civic agency board personnel, newspaper columnists, radio commentators, petty public officials, selected organization executives.

Fourth Rate: Professionals such as ministers, teachers, social workers, personnel directors, small business managers, higher-paid accountants, and the like.

Hunter was focusing on those who make community decisions. This is a concern of the practitioner. But of equal concern to him is the building of favorable attitudes in the city toward his enterprise. A favorable climate of opinion is compounded of many elements, many forces. A program is designed to win the favorable esteem of the *whole community,* esteem which holds an organization to be worthwhile, a good place to work, and a good neighbor. Millard Faught classified the "prime movers" in building such a climate:

1. Employee's or members' families.
2. The press, radio, and TV, their editors and reporters.
3. Thought leaders, including clergy, teachers, city officials, prominent retailers and professional men, union officials, bankers, civil workers, and industrialists.
4. Organizations, including city planning commission, welfare agencies, youth groups, veterans, fraternal, and service groups, cultural and political action bodies.
5. Crusaders, such as protest groups, petitioners, voice-of-the-people, special events, and the rumor factories.

THE BASIC APPROACH

Before thought leaders or the community at large can be persuaded in a specific direction or as a unified force, there has to be an understanding of the town's mutual interests. It is necessary to know what the community wants for its well-being, what part it expects each organization to contribute toward that, and how it measures those contributions. The interests of the community will all fit somewhere in these eleven elements:

1. Commercial prosperity
2. Support of religion

3. Work for everyone
4. Adequate educational facilities
5. Law, order, and safety
6. Population growth
7. Proper housing and utilities
8. Varied recreational and cultural pursuits
9. Attention to public welfare
10. Progressive measures for good health
11. Competent municipal government.

Accepting these elements as the scope of community interests, the communicating organization must somehow identify itself with them. It must show how it serves those interests. As a starting point, the underlying attitude of the organization must be one of a sincere interest in serving.

Organizational policies constitute a positive expression of attitude. They form the framework of a "personality" with which the organization is endowed in local opinion. The singular personality may be, in fact, composed of decisions rendered by a management policy committee. Most likely, the opinions will attach themselves to the personality of the head man. He becomes the symbol. People tend to identify actions and attitudes with people, not with buildings in which people live or work.

Beyond attitudes and personality, there is the factor of *participation*. The organization cannot stand aloof from the parade put on downtown by the local merchants or the town meeting discussing a new city auditorium. Nor can the officials of an organization neglect a responsibility to get into the blood stream of community life. *Community relations cannot be delegated* to one man or department. Participation requires a costly investment of executive time. In his study of community relations in Syracuse, New York, Hodges found that "ten to fourteen hours a week, more than half that spent at luncheons and evening sessions, was about par for the most active executives; and six to ten hours a week was fairly common in these managements." [7]

As pressures mount on organizational executives to give more time and energy to pressing community problems, the tendency to deputize subordinates—usually the public relations man—for these emotion-wearing chores increases. A public relations practitioner, James J. Bowe of Minneapolis, quit that city's Urban Coalition because the top businessman, active at the outset, withdrew and delegated the job to lower executives. Bowe said: [8] "The top executive himself must participate. He too often just

---

[7] In *Company and Community*, op. cit., p. 2.
[8] Quoted in *Jack O'Dwyer's Newsletter*, Vol. 2, Oct. 8, 1969.

sends a messenger. That's what we've done with all our middle-class social agencies for years. His opposite number across the tables knows damn well that this subordinate hasn't got the authority . . . and he's tired of fooling with these subordinates. Businessmen must change and that can come only through personal experience." This is equally applicable to the college president, the governmental bureaucrat, or superintendent of schools.

Executives have a choice of participating in *angelic* activities, such as heading the United Givers drive, the Red Cross chapter, or the Y.M.C.A., or of becoming involved in *controversial* projects, such as slum clearance, equal employment opportunity, survey of community health facilities, integration, and school bond referenda. Some leaders do both.

One businessman who enters the controversial arena is Daniel Parker, chairman, The Parker Pen Company, who said, "For years I have tried to work my way through to a personal understanding of the black dilemma. Scarcely a week goes by that I don't make my way into a ghetto to observe and listen and gain what I can."

Another businessman who accepts the new situation, Paul Lund of Illinois Bell Telephone, puts it this way: [9]

"To be sure, we still work actively with the Crusade of Mercy; we still support the Boy Scouts; and we provide advisers for Junior Achievement. These are traditional involvements. But to confine our commitments to movements such as these would be hopelessly anachronistic."

Community progress takes leadership and seldom comes without some controversy. The rebirth of Pittsburgh, Pennsylvania, is an example.[10]

Economic health is the first priority in the community, and the basic involvement of the institution must relate to the problems. Ford Motor Company set up employment offices in the heart of Detroit slums. AVCO, Control Data, IBM, Martin Marietta and Brown Shoe are among the companies deliberately locating plants in ghetto areas.

There have been unusual grants and uses of funds. Merck & Co., made a gift of $50,000 to the Inter-racial Council for Business Opportunities for a fund to guarantee bank loans to minority businessmen. Ford Foundation purchased $300,000 stock in an organization building black shopping plazas in twelve cities. In another action, $1-million in trust certificates were purchased from an organization that integrates housing remote from ghettos. Litton Industries Credit Corp. provided a $160,000 loan for black investors to open a cooperative supermarket in Harlem.

Every enterprise has a stake in the condition of the city's physical plant, the quality of service provided by government and social agencies,

---

[9] Speech at Mid-West Public Relations Conference, University of Wisconsin, October 20, 1967. (In proceedings published by Journalism Extension Division, Madison, Wis.)

[10] A. Steinberg, "New City Called Pittsburgh," *Reader's Digest*, Vol. 66, May, 1955, pp. 83–86.

the effectiveness of civic agencies, and the availability of community resources and facilities to improve the physical, mental, and moral health of the citizens. Most firms and institutions recognize this. Union Carbide is one. If it finds a lack of cultural activity in a community, its people will help organize a symphony orchestra or a small-theater group, or sponsor a lecture series. If it finds school facilities inadequate, it will lend its specialists as part-time teachers or provide classroom equipment.

Finally, there is the obligation of *continuous communication.* The affairs of an organization that mix with the affairs of a community are properly public domain. Silence on internal matters that affect the community is eyed by the hometown people with great suspicion. It is as if the person or organization had something to hide. Holding back bad news is self-defeating. One DuPont official has observed: "Bad news doesn't necessarily have a bad effect. You gain the sympathy and understanding of the community. And getting the facts out quickly avoids incorrect stories and damaging rumors." Officials of a chemical plant in Memphis, Tennessee, learned this the hard way. Many persons became ill when deadly chlorine gas escaped from a ruptured pipeline. The victims were hospitalized, but the company made no public explanation. The story became "news" when the State Board of Health closed the plant. A company official subsequently admitted to the community: "Chlorine brought the wrath of God down on our heads. Perhaps we were lax explaining what we were doing here, and we realize things that are unknown can create fear and suspicion about our activities." Enlightened management anticipates community questions with information.

A community looks around its own confines first for its news and opinions on grand-scale matters. Thoughtful analyses of national happenings come right into the home through the radio and television. Still, the hometown newspaper and local prominent spokesmen carry more day-by-day weight than the most highly paid outside sources.

This emphasizes the extreme importance of the hometown audience to business, government, and social welfare in their public affairs programs. Opinions formed at the community level are expressed up the line to the national level. The actual formation of opinions takes place in the local environment.

Businessmen, state officials, military leaders, and social agency heads have come around more and more to the idea of communication programs individually tailored within the community rather than modeled after a single pattern, cut in Washington or New York. There is much more work to the local tailoring, but there is a vastly more satisfactory result.

If each institution seeks and gains acceptability and popular support of its views locally, public opinion for that type of institution will follow suit on the national level. In almost every city in the United States, there is one or more industrial enterprise whose actions and attitudes locally determine pretty largely how the people in town feel toward the United States business system. Utilities nationally are judged by the behavior of the hometown power and light company. Manufacturers as a group are judged by what the local machine tool company does or fails to do. The Armed Forces are judged by observations of the nearest camp, base, or station. So it goes. *People judge the whole by the parts they know.*

In looking to a good reputation locally, the utility and the manufacturer are helping the national reputation of the business system. The local utility branch or manufacturer delivers a bloc of favorable opinions in much the same manner as the county political party chairman delivers a bloc of votes.

Let's look at how these fundamentals are translated into specifics by well-managed concerns. These elements are present in the "something for something" community relations program of the Ansul Chemical Company, a firm with 1,200 employees in Marinette, Wisconsin, a city of 16,500. Its dynamic president, Robert C. Hood, holds that a company must be a good industrial citizen "by determining its citizenship responsibilities and how to meet them." Here's a thumbnail sketch of Ansul's community relations program.[11]

1. COMMUNITY AT LARGE

An emergency rescue squad available 24 hours a day at no charge to anyone in the community; participation in activities of Marinette Chamber of Commerce; a daily radio program which carries free social and civic announcements for all local groups; large fire demonstration to highlight Fire Prevention Week each fall; plant tours and open houses; weekly advertising support of "Go to Church" campaigns; periodic community advertising.

2. COMMUNITY THOUGHT LEADERS

Regular mailing of company publication, special tours for specific influence groups; special mailings, such as company annual report or an outstanding national publicity "break."

3. LOCAL PRESS

Immediate dissemination of company news, both favorable and unfavorable; equitable, although modest, advertising support of all local communications media; impartial timing of news breaks, invitations to press

---

[11] Chamber of Commerce of the United States, *Effective Employee and Community Relations, A Report on Ansul Chemical Company* (Washington, D.C.: The Chamber, 1956). (Sketch condensed from pp. 22–23.) An instructive report on what a small firm can do.

to attend company functions; 24-hour-a-day availability to press; elimination of pressure to run company stories "as is."

4. CIVIC ORGANIZATIONS

Regular and proportionate donations to local charities; use of daily radio program; speaker's bureau, both for regular addresses and to fill emergency needs; free movies, projection equipment, and operator for use by nonprofit groups; plant tours and fire demonstrations for civic clubs.

5. STUDENTS, FACULTY, SCHOOL OFFICIALS

Plant tours by business, chemistry, and other school classes; regular advertisments in school yearbooks and newspapers; use of daily radio program by faculty; cooperation and leadership on Business-Education Day.

6. MUNICIPAL EMPLOYEES, OFFICIALS

Free fire equipment and recharging supplies to fire and police departments; use of fire test field for training and demonstrations; first aid training of firemen and policemen by Ansul Rescue Squad; availability of Ansul fire equipment for emergency use; personal leadership in city council, police and fire commission, civil defense, other municipal agencies; absence of pressure on tax assessments, zoning, special ordinances, and so forth.

7. LOCAL MERCHANTS, INDUSTRIALISTS

Mailing of *Ansul Fuse Plug;* avoidance of "pirating" employees from local business and industry; brief congratulatory letter when businessman is honored or promoted; welcoming visits to new merchants or industry officials; salutes to other industries in the company's employee publication.

8. NONEMPLOYEE LOCAL STOCKHOLDERS

Mailing of *Ansul Fuse Plug;* special mailing of periodic information about the company's progress; invitations to visit plant.

Ansul believes that building a reservoir of goodwill in its local community in these ways has helped to bring about dollars-and-cents returns:

1. Equitable tax rates, assessments, and other municipal actions which tend to regulate a company's operations.
2. Availability of labor, skilled and unskilled. People prefer to work for a company that's liked and respected.
3. Public support in case of trouble—labor difficulties, layoffs, accidents, plant disasters.

4. Increased employee productivity. Employees tend to reflect favorable community attitudes.

TRANSLATING ATTITUDES INTO ACTION

When all is said and done, an organization hopes to be known as a good outfit to be with—a successful operation in which citizenship and neighborliness are practiced. Getting that across is a big task in deeds and words.

The good outfit to be with is the one that knows how to make a *profit* while paying good wages. Nobody wants to work long for a company that doesn't know how to make a profit. In the case of a nonprofit organization, the "good outfit" would be one that has no serious trouble getting public funds and in paying its bills. There's no security in working for a business that cannot show a profit or get the funds it needs to grow.

Then, the good businessman is the one who hires his help locally, whether in U. S. or abroad, and doesn't import the kind of workers who turn out to be undesirable residents. Instead, he uses the local employment services to find people. He pays the going rates, but he doesn't pay so much that the retail merchants downtown can't afford to compete for help.

The good employer makes the work as steady as possible. If he finds himself shorthanded in rush seasons, he does not pirate workers from other establishments in town. He gets nonworking members of local families to fill in. He attracts desirable people from other towns.

When it comes to repairing the premises, remodeling, or buying replacement supplies, the good outfit gets as much of the work done by local people as possible. It buys as much of its supplies as can be purchased locally at fair prices. It calls on the local plumbers, electricians, office supply houses, hardware merchants, and automobile dealers. This is particularly important for military installations. Even so, it should be clearly understood that today community relations is more a frame of mind than a practice of buying goods from the local merchant, in this day of free-flowing world trade.

The good employer lives with his business. Absentee ownership in this period of decentralization is understandable. But the local managers should have the authority to make the same decisions as the owner would if he lived in town. There are still too many large organizations whose branch managers cannot approve a $50.00 contribution to the local Red Cross.

Contrary to the envious looks that local enterprises often cast at the large branch plants in town and their high-budget community relations programs, the hometown organization has many advantages. A good program doesn't necessarily cost a lot of money. Professor Wayne Hodges observes: "Because every city differs from all others in its pattern, structure, and needs, a CR-minded local management must become an integral part of its plant community in order to understand it and work with it intelligently. In this sense a locally owned company has an inherent advantage. But the outside company, if it puts emphasis on *community responsibility,* can do equally well." Hometowners are built into the community power structure. Outsiders have to work their way in.

Citizenship for the organization means that it does not try to dominate community decisions. Citizenship means observing the local laws without seeking special privilege. It means helping the town's elected officials. The community expects citizenship to be demonstrated through widespread participation in city planning programs, housing problems, land reclamation, and the like. The company offers support to charity fund drives and to the work carried on by local welfare agencies, school programs, and mercantile groups. Occasionally, the organization will be expected to offer some of its facilities for community undertakings such as conventions, evening meetings, and transportation. Cooperation is expected in matters of safety not only on the premises but nearby in reducing pedestrian hazards. And the good citizen is expected to cast his ballot.

The citizenship expected of the organization is particularly critical for the top people. When it comes to civic projects, they're expected to be aboard, again, without throwing their weight around. This is an area in which the official of an organization works alongside a wage earner from another organization. They have a common goal and a comparable status in civic work. They are joint participants in charity drives, the school board, the mayor's antipollution committee, or the tree-planting project for the parks.

Practicing good citizenship is not the simple matter it appears. Take the matter of contributions to the community's United Fund each year. This fund supports worthwhile agencies, its budget is determined by community leaders, and the contributor does not have to face the difficult task of deciding who's deserving and who's not. Then, say, for example, the American Cancer Society withdraws from the United Fund appeal. Now what do you do? Support the United Fund principle and antagonize the cancer society's membership? Or do you give to both and thus antagonize the United Fund believers? Such questions can lead to a reappraisal of a company's contributions program.

Financial contributions are but one way that a business expresses its interest in a community. Another is by taking, or not taking, stands on public issues. Here, too, the guidelines are fuzzy and the reactions some-times violent, as many business leaders who have taken the lead in bringing racial equality to their communities have learned. Even support of a useful, public-spirited organization can bring an unexpected public backlash. The Ford Motor Company and Sears & Roebuck discovered this a few years ago when the Committee on Economic Development, a forward-looking business group, issued a report suggesting that two-million farmers should quit farming and take jobs in industry. The National Farmers Organization picketed Ford dealers and Sears stores in many cities throughout the Midwest in protest of this CED report. Ford and Sears officials had served on the committee drafting the report.[12] Involvement in public affairs can also lead to the cynical charge that such involvement is only for public relations purposes. For example, Ralph Nader has said that Henry Ford is involved in urban affairs only because he recognizes this as "the new pr."[13] The role of the corporation and executive, seen in the framework of social responsibility concepts, is additionally examined in later chapters on Business and Corporate Public Affairs.

Neighborliness means more than the president of an organization's tipping his hat to the policeman when he runs through a red light. It means more than a speaker's bureau to accommodate the local service club meetings. There are expectations that the organization will make its plant, campus, or camp as attractive as practicable, that it will keep its trucks off people's lawns, that it will not smoke up, smell up, or dirty the neighborhood without first doing everything it can to avoid such nuisances. Those expectations include provision for parking facilities, waste disposal, smoke filters, noise controls, traffic planning, and safety devices.

Smoke and stream pollution are common causes of ill will among community neighbors. As the critical dimensions of pollution become clearer and more widely known, this irritation crystallizes into angry public action. And the fight against pollution enlists a broad cross section of the public. For example, Ashland, Wisconsin, businessmen joined ranks with Northland College students to march in protest against a DuPont plant's pollution in northern Wisconsin. The polluted creek was dubbed "Bloody Mary Creek." Even offensive odors bring protests, as the Mead Corporation learned when it decided to build a new plant in Escanaba, Michigan.[14]

These problems can be turned into public relations opportunities. After World War II, International Harvester built a new plant outside Memphis in open country. As inevitably happens to plants, air fields, and so forth, the surrounding fields were in time covered with homes and people living in them. IH recognized that its smoke and soot would soon become a problem and that it could not solve it by telling these people "We were here first, you had no business to move so close." The company took these steps.[15]

[12] For an example of what happened to one businessman who went into public service, see Hal Bruno, "Birth Control, Welfare Funds, and the Politics of Illinois," *The Reporter,* Vol. 23, June 20, 1963.

[13] William Serrin, "At Ford Everyone Knows Who Is the Boss," *New York Times Magazine,* October 19, 1969, p. 142.

[14] Barry Lando, "Save Our Air," *The New Republic,* October 11, 1969.

[15] James Robert Massey, "Smoke Can Lead to Understanding," *Public Relations Journal,* Vol. 10, September, 1954, pp. 13–14.

1. Company representatives rang all the doorbells in the affected neighborhood to talk over the problem with the housewives.

2. Samples of the offending dirt were taken from lawns and clotheslines. Then letters were written to the homeowners telling them that Harvester's powerhouse smoke was responsible.

3. The women were promised that Harvester would search for a solution. No promises of fast relief were given.

4. Harvester went to work on a solution and kept these women informed each step of the way. It put gas burners in the foundry cupolas, sprayed its coal with oil, put a warning bell in its smokestack, planted a park-like buffer zone of trees and grass. These items cost $70,000 and helped to alleviate the problem. Still, IH kept up its search for a solution and after three years found a type of air control equipment which would solve it. This was put in at a cost of $71,900.

5. When the solution had been found, the company called in its plant neighbors and community leaders. It explained the new equipment and thanked them for their patience and understanding.

In the end, Harvester came out a good neighbor. James Robert Massey concludes from this experience that: Industry can turn bad into good when smoke mars their community relations by (1) recognizing the serious public relations aspects of the situation; (2) being willing to spend the money necessary to provide relief, and (3) *maintaining frank, honest, and consistent communications with the community.*

Eastman Kodak has long acknowledged that its products pollute water, and its efforts to reduce pollution have been many. Opening a new treatment plant, a ground-breaking ceremony and the creation of a character "Terry the Trout" were undertaken partly to get credit for performance, partly to encourage others.

Industries and institutions face what a paper maker describes as "unremitting pressure from government for an ever higher degree of pollution abatement." The enlightened industry meets this need voluntarily. In the 70s, as pressure for clean air and clean water mounts, all institutions will be compelled to lessen or end pollution. Organizations will find it wiser not to wait for political solutions.

There are less costly ways of dramatizing a firm as a good neighbor. Allis-Chalmers for many years solved the problem of constructive post-prom activities for high schoolers by staging a post-prom party in its clubhouse. Employees of the Bekins Van and Storage Co., Pomona, California, on their time off removed more than 300 discarded refrigerators from the area. The company provided the trucks free.[16]

---

[16] Don O'Connor, *Community Opinion and the Trucking Industry,* A manual. Washington, D.C.: American Trucking Association, 1968.

Another facet of neighborliness lies in being host to the city's special visitors, holding open house on occasion, providing plant tours on request, and being available for visits from city officials. The good neighbor also takes part in exchange visits with merchants, educators, farmers, and other segments of the surrounding community. He attends other organizations' open house events, makes speeches in the city on invitation, and receives callers with courtesy on the telephone, at the front door, in the private office, and in the shop. If the official of an organization happens also to be a parent, he invites the children's teacher into his home. If he belongs to a cultural group, he gives it sincere attention, not merely dues.

Neighborliness means functioning as a partner in city recreational programs, milestone events, local holidays, and pet projects of civic groups. There is also the desirability of making awards recognizing the accomplishments of those whom the community wishes to honor.

No skeletons in the closet means having no secrets. The local press, radio, and TV should have access to all information that the townspeople want. Exceptions, of course, are pieces of information that could be damaging for competitive, legal, or security reasons. As a good reporter, the organization is expected to supply information to its own employees and principals, first, to its community, second, and to the outside public, third. The good reporter makes a point of knowing what the local press considers news. The main thing is to pursue a policy of candor and at the same time keep a check on the reactions to the news.

APPLYING THE AUXILIARY TOOLS

OPEN HOUSE AND TOURS OF FACILITIES

EXTENDED HOUSE-PUBLICATION CIRCULATION

DIRECT-MAIL LITERATURE

INSTITUTIONAL ADVERTISING

NEWS

CIVIC AND EDUCATIONAL PARTICIPATION

SPEAKER'S BUREAU

DISCUSSION GROUPS

There is an immense variety of ways in which the tools are used. Some firms, like Sears, Roebuck, award scholarships locally. Others train local youths for a career. The Bulova Watch Company has a school to train disabled veterans in watch repair. Many firms put on a Business-Education Day. General Motors brings noted speakers into a plant community on occasion for special events. Organizations foot the bills for local baseball leagues or new hospitals. National Cash Register donates space and supplies for local youngsters to have their own gardens.

The open house has the advantage of bringing large numbers onto the premises of the organization. Its weakness lies in that such large numbers do not have the opportunity for much personal discussion about interests they share.

The size of attendance suggests keeping arrangements for refreshments and personal services to a minimum. Hosts should go all out for devices that will facilitate pleasure and ease for the guests: exhibits that can be seen quickly, ample guides or signposts leading to appointed areas, seats for overflow crowd, and a carefully supervised method of regulating traffic. Of great advantage is the *participation* of employees. Many guests are relatives and friends of the rank and file. Participation as hosts gives employees a renewed pride in their working group.

The *tour* of facilities has as its most important feature the planning that precedes it. It is conducted as a special event, such as Business-Industry-Education Day, or as a routine system to handle daily visitors. *Planning* must include these factors:

1. An itinerary which is logical in telling the story.
2. A duration that accommodates the comfort of the tourist. Many tours are too long and arduous. If the tour requires great walking or undue exertion, there should be a break somewhere along the way with seating facilities.
3. Competent guides who not only understand the various phases of the operations *but can put them into words which laymen can understand.*
4. A running story which shows the interlocking of the organization's interests with those of the community.
5. Some sort of simple gesture at the end of the tour to make the occasion memorable. It can be a pause for refreshment, a handshake with the president, a product sample, an opportunity to operate a unique machine or device, or a pamphlet about the organization.
6. Above all, a visitor should be handled with enthusiasm.

Extended house-publication circulation is worthwhile. Little additional news matter is needed to make the employee publications of interest throughout the community. Among the readers close at hand are the people waiting a turn in the doctor's office, the barbershop, and the airport. Similarly, employees' activities are followed keenly by the clergy. Organizational activities are a matter of concern to merchants and to city officials.

Actually, there is no area of the community in which the house publication is not welcome. With the addition of such features as safe driving hints from the chief of police, comments on city-wide events, articles dealing with legend and lore, and perhaps a listing of future special events, a real service is performed without conflicting with the purpose of the daily or weekly newspapers. A few organizations have special publications. Motorola publishes a quarterly, *Volunteers in Civic Affairs,* recognizing employees who have made contributions in their community. The publication goes to all civic, education, and welfare officials in the community.

Thought leaders can also be reached by occasional *letters from officials* of an organization. These are quite helpful, especially in anticipating rumors and quieting harmful conversation. Topics in such letters are generally maintained at a high level of discussion. There should never be any intent to force thought leaders to serve the interests of the organization. Rather, the intent should be to place them in a better-informed position to serve the interests of their constituents.

A great deal of persuasion can be achieved through opinion leaders. Caterpillar Tractor's open house for barbers suggests that special audiences might have a good-sized hand in formulating community opinions. Barbers have the attention of all male residents for a half-hour, once every two weeks or so. Bartenders have a nightly audience. Then, there are the hairdressers, the local librarian, the auctioneers, the mailmen, the milkmen, and the hotel desk clerk. All of these people are in a position to influence others. All of them talk with the audience that organizations need to win.

Plant city advertising is becoming more popular. Plant city advertising is one answer to the problem of absentee ownership. It also serves a helpful purpose to the organization with employees who are swallowed after working hours by the remote sections of the city and have little contact with each other.

The stigma of impersonalization often attaches itself to paid advertising space. The reaction is that the organization did not have to air its views or fight its battles in that manner; it could have come closer to the people without resorting to advertising space. Organized labor is inclined to interpret such advertising, when subject matter touches industrial relations, as an act of bad faith—especially if it is used in time of crisis or strikes. Reactions depend on the use, not the medium.

To praise or discourage the use of the tool would be an unsafe generalization. There are many specific cases of success and failure. One success is a series by the Armco Steel Corporation, Middletown, Ohio, in a house publication with spill-over readership through the community. The headlines indicate the context (notes by the authors).

This Slot Machine Always Pays Off—in Cash (picture of time clock)

A Boy Who Needs $10,000 (amount invested in business per employee)

The Spade That Dug a Fortune (used to break ground for expansion)

Baby, You've Got a Future at Armco (planning for future)

Armco's $1,000,000-a-year Fishing License (retirement plan)

The Man Who Brings Us Paydays (plug for salesmen)

Henry, How is Armco Doing? (family's stake in company)

A Million Dollars from a Cornfield (monthly payroll at plant)

No Future in the Buggy Business (moving ahead for the future)

Bought Any Steel Mills Lately? (rising costs)

If Every Hen Laid Two Eggs a Day (plug for productivity)

A Sure Way to Get a New Pair (shoes pictured, plug for building surplus)

The *hometown news* is a large muscle in the local program. It cannot be said accurately that the public relations man exercises a control over this tool. He doesn't. But the local press, TV, and radio want news. They don't have to be sold on the idea. Local news builds circulation and listening audiences. The doings of any major organization is news. Organizational news comprises a service to the newspapers, radio, and TV.

Quite apart from the desire and need to cover the news, the local press takes pride in the community and is dedicated to the town's growth and prosperity. What helps the community helps the newspaper and the organization. What helps the newspaper and the organization helps the community. The interrelation is a close one. Recognition of that fact is a realistic one. It is well rooted.

CASE PROBLEM

Following severe floods in early summer last year, the Health Department of a medium sized city initiated a crash program to control mosquitoes. The program was the first really intensive control program in this particular community, which included both larviciding (spraying the surface of stagnant pools of water with insecticide) and fogging (spraying the air with a heavy mixture of insecticide which resembles a heavy fog).

The program aroused severe criticism from certain groups in the community, who claimed that the program had resulted in a great loss in the city's bird population. Most of the criticism was in letters to the local newspapers.

The city is the site of the state university, and the population is of above average education. In the past, letters to the papers have produced public concern and agitation and, due to the high number of citizens holding advanced college degrees, public issues have produced conflicting views argued at a high educational level.

You have been retained by the City Council to aid the Health Department in preparing a program to gain public acceptance of the pest control program for this year. You find that a neighboring city has been using the same type of program for several years with no adverse results. You also learn that the extension division of the state university has been conducting research into the development of an effective educational program concerning the use of agricultural chemicals.

What would you recommend to the City Council?

ADDITIONAL READING

TIMOTHY D. ARMBRUSTER, "Crisis in Cleveland: Rx: Instant Public Relations for an Ailing City," *Public Relations Journal,* Vol. 24, August, 1968.

SAMUEL W. BRYANT, "The Battle of the Jamestown Refinery," *Fortune,* Vol. 57, April, 1958.

"Closing Down the Plant: A Case History," *Public Relations Journal,* Vol. 13, February, 1957.

A. DICK DAY, "A New Plant Comes to Town," *Chemical Engineering Progress,* Vol. 56, November, 1960.

ALBERT S. FULLING, "Community Public Relations Defeats Proposed Jersey Jetport," *Public Relations Journal,* Vol. 18, March, 1962.

W. R. HILBRINK, "Sensitive Mission at Santa Monica Bay," *Public Relations Journal,* Vol. 25, September, 1969.

ESTHER C. LAWTON, "What Should Management's Policy Be Toward Participation of Employees In Community Affairs?" *Personnel Administration,* Vol. 20, November-December, 1957.

CARL LEVIN, "Give So That It Doesn't Hurt," *Public Relations Quarterly,* Vol. 11, Spring, 1966.

J. C. LONG, "Princeton University Programs Friendship," *Public Relations Journal,* Vol. 17, November, 1961.

JOHN T. McCARTY, "The Image in Your Community," in Lee H. Bristol, Jr., ed., *Developing the Corporate Image.* New York: Charles Scribner's Sons, 1960.

WILBUR J. PEAK, "Community Relations," chapter in Philip Lesly, ed., *Public Relations Handbook.* Englewood Cliffs, N. J.: Prentice-Hall, Inc., 1967.

JOHN CAMERON SIM, "Community Newspaper Leadership: More Real than Apparent?", *Journalism Quarterly,* Vol. 44, Summer, 1967.

JAMES TANNER, "One Company Town: Bartlesville Prospers Under Long Economic Domination by Phillips," *Wall Street Journal,* Vol. XLVI, August 4, 1966.

U. S. CIVIL SERVICE COMMISSION, *Community Relations: A Guide for Federal Agencies.* Washington, D. C.: The Commission, 1958. Management Series No. 12.

CHAPTER 15

SPECIAL PUBLICS

Any time more than two Americans meet on the street,
one of them is sure to begin looking around
for a gavel to call the meeting to order.
—WILL ROGERS

The American Public is ever growing, moving, changing. So is the American Mood. Every three seconds of the working day, a baby is born. Each day the equivalent of a town of 11,000 persons is added to America's population. This means more babies to be fed, clothed, and provided with toys; more children to educate; more young couples establishing homes that they must buy or rent and furnish; more people to buy cars and more highways for them to travel on; more people to open bank accounts, buy life insurance, take vacations, and use governmental services. And more targets for communications!

Based on the assumption that present fertility rates by age will continue to 1975, the Bureau of Census projects the population of the United States in one estimate as follows:

	(IN MILLIONS)
1975	221.5
1990	278
2000	300

Americans are the most restless people on the face of the earth. United States Census reports show that an average of 30-million Americans have moved each year since 1947. This movement means the shifting, far and near, of millions of families with everything they treasure—from pitchers to pianos. Car-equipped, mobile Americans are constantly on the go—for vacations in the South, in the North, in the East, in the West. And abroad, too.

Americans are moving from the cities to suburbs and exurbs. Some of them are moving back to the central city from suburbia. Others from farms to city. Social customs, hobbies, social groupings, and buying habits of our times are being radically changed by the most prosaic of men—the daily commuter. The spread to the suburbs and beyond is breaking up concentrations of population with common bonds of nationality, race, or custom. Increasingly, our people are rootless people. Also, people are living longer. This means more people to be guided in the difficult period of life—retire-

356

ment. More people will need to be provided for in the Golden Years. By 1975, it is estimated, there will be 20.5-million persons past 65 years of age.

These basic trends have profound significance. Communication with this massive, mobile Big Public would be nigh impossible—except for one thing. Americans have an unmatched penchant for organizing themselves into groups. Today's busy, busy citizen is organized and "committee-ed" almost to the point of frustration. Each organized activity represents a common bond of interest. *Practitioners use these common bonds as channels of communication and approaches of mutual interest.* In the craft, these groups are labeled "special publics."

One of the first chores is to identify and establish liaison with an organization's special publics. These may be many or few. Effective communication with the whole public is made economical and effective by this public-by-public approach. Americans are a many-sided people. They organize themselves into men's groups, women's groups, children's groups, parent's groups, racial and ethnic groups, labor unions, trade associations, professional groups, religious groups, service clubs, insurance groups, media groups, safety groups, transportation groups, ad infinitum. The membership and focus of these groups are constantly changing.

The American's urge to join and identify himself with the group is old and indestructible. De Tocqueville observed more than a century ago: "The Americans of all ages, all conditions, and all dispositions constantly form associations." Despite the impact of TV and other distractions of modern living on "lodge night," the number and membership of castles, camps, clans, circles, chapters, conclaves, groves, hives, aeries, and nests continue to grow.

More than 125-million Americans hold membership in nearly 300,000 different fraternal and social organizations. These orders range in size from the multi-million-member Masons down to a handful in the Liberty Boys of '76. Some are billion-dollar concerns, others have grocery-size budgets. Many employ public relations men. All are targets of programs. These groups have conventions, meetings, publications, and officers who provide channels of communication and influence with their members on matters of interest to them. Fraternal groups represent just one aspect of organized America.

Many persons are nonjoiners. Millions of Americans are not members of any voluntary association, civic or church group, union or veteran organization, according to one National Opinion Research Center survey. However, most *influentials* are joiners, and these are the persons whom the practitioner seeks to influence. Sociologists Charles R. Wright and Herbert H. Hyman report that "the persons most likely to join organizations are those who are married and have children, who are interested in public affairs such as public school or city planning problems, who have a high 'socioeconomic status' as measured by level of income, home ownership, and education."

Increasingly, practitioners target their messages to special publics through these organizational channels. This trend is being speeded by increased knowledge of the opinion-molding process and by the budget limitations confronting most practitioners. Typical is this delineation of special publics by the Sixth United States Army, headquartered in San Francisco: (1) civil organizations; (2) trade and industrial associations; (3) veterans organizations (Army alumni); (4) youth groups; (5) women's clubs; (6) clergy; (7) educators; (8) communities. Army commanders and information officers are advised: "The most efficient system by which the Army can retain and increase support of its publics is by working through the leaders of those publics."

SOME SPECIAL PUBLICS

TEACHERS, STUDENTS, ADMINISTRATORS

More than 52-million members of The Big Public are primarily concerned with going to school, teaching school, or administering schools. In 1970, education was a full-time occupation or a time consuming avocation for some 30 percent of the population.[1] Teachers and students, from the elementary grades to graduate schools, are the objects of an increasing amount of educational material, advertising, and public relations messages designed to shape the attitudes of tomorrow's citizens. Federal and state agencies seek to promote health, conservation, and racial tolerance through school programs. Insurance companies promote traffic safety and fire prevention. Manufacturers promote their industries and the capitalistic enterprise. Worthwhile causes find this important schoolroom audience increasingly receptive to *educational* aids and materials, increasingly critical of clumsy efforts to propagandize.

GOVERNMENT

The increasing size and scope of Big Government and its impact on the activities of every organization make it a key public for most concerns, especially business firms. From the president of the United States down to members of the county and town boards, elected and appointed government officials are the focus of much persuasion and pressure. What this powerful

---

[1] *The 1969 World Almanac and Book of Facts,* pp. 344, 345, 349. For overview, "The Magnitude of the American Educational Establishment," *Saturday Review,* Vol. LIII, September 19, 1970.

array of officials, elected and appointed, thinks and decides is often measured in dollars and cents. A government agency can grant or take away an airline route, a TV station license, or a tax rebate. It can build a power dam or let a privately owned utility build it. Government, with its billions to spend, is the nation's biggest customer.

In coping with the far-reaching power of government, organizations must deal with many officials, persuade many persons, and clear numerous hurdles. More than 100 agencies of the federal government alone regulate one or more aspects of business firms. Forty-three separate bureaus deal with business activities in foreign trade; 60, those in manufacturing; 41, those in labor relations; 62, those in transportation regulation. The same holds true for the legislative branch. In a typical session of Congress, there were 52 committees operating which filed 1,520 Senate Committee reports and 1,328 House Committee reports; the Congress enacted 45 internal revenue laws, 38 appropriations laws, and 191 laws affecting business; a total of 1,927 were enacted in all. The same extent and complexity of federal relationships confront other organizations. Today, for example, both private and state universities are getting a large share of federal support, and these grants and contracts involve countless relationships with many federal agencies. The same thing goes on at the state and local levels of government. Such figures underline the number and importance of relationships with the *government public*.

More and more, practitioners are involved in efforts to influence government bureaucrats and legislators. This is true of practitioners both inside and outside of government. Much of this comes under the emotion-charged word *lobbying*. Lobbying, as one writer notes, "is no matter of some florid operator buttonholing a Senator or Representative in the anteroom of the Capitol." Rather, as a lobbyist vouches: "The times are complicated. The problems are big. You've got to have more than an idea and a handshake. You've got to have a well-documented case. You're dealing with sophisticated men." The issues are complex—as complex as a trade expansion act, legislating sugar quotas, medical insurance for the aged, and farm support programs. Increasingly it is the practitioner's job to help counsel top management on long-run government economic, education, and research policies that might affect his organization.[2]

Congressional Quarterly asserts: [3] "By general acknowledgement, the influence of pressure groups and paid lobbyists on Congressional legislation

[2] For comprehensive look at lobbyists, see James Deakin, *The Lobbyists* (Washington, D.C.: Public Affairs Press, 1968; also see Paul W. Cherington and Ralph L. Gillen, *The Business Representative in Washington* (Washington, D.C.: The Brookings Institution, 1962).

[3] Congressional Quarterly, *Legislators and the Lobbyists* (Washington, D.C.: Congressional Quarterly Service, May, 1968), pp. 15–18. A valuable reference work.

in recent years has been great. Almost every bill considered by Congress has had its contingent of interested pressure groups which presented testimony, wired or met with Members of Congress, sent delegations or hired lobbyists to meet them, or carried on propaganda designed to sway public sympathy and thus eventually sway legislators." Behind the massive array of decision makers at all levels of government are some 15-million politically active persons in the two major parties. Government relations can be as direct as a lobbyist buttonholing a legislator or as broad as building nationwide support for reduction in the tariff. As government's rewards and regulations multiply, so will the relationships with its officialdom. The growth in number and importance of government relationships has given rise to the public affairs function discussed in Chapter 19. The stakes are high, the pressures intense, the relationships many.

WOMEN

The "hand that rocks the cradle" is increasingly clasped by those with goods to sell, stocks to promote, and votes to win. The 1967 census estimates recorded 101-million females, nearly 4-million more women than men. More of these women are working; more of them are taking part in public and civic affairs. Wise men never "underestimate the power of a woman."

It is often claimed, though not documented, that women do 85 percent of the nation's buying. The majority of corporate stockholders are women. Women make up one-third of the nation's work force. Employers know that the wife's attitude follows the husband to work. Political leaders have recognized the woman's role in winning elections. Approaches to this powerful bloc can be a feminine angle in a mass-media message, a feature in an employee magazine, or a plant tour for the wives. Or the approach can be through the scores of women's organizations.

Combined, United States women's clubs represent a membership of some 40-million—mostly middle- or upper-level women. Many of these are community, political, religious, and educational influentials. Women's organizations include Altrusa International, National Federation of Business and Professional Women, American Association of University Women, the League of Women Voters, D.A.R., N.O.W., Zonta International, and scores of others. The importance of this public is providing increasing opportunities for women in public relations work. The woman's counsel is imperative in an era of the Woman's Liberation Movement which is articulating the demands for more equal treatment in all walks of life. It takes a woman to know a woman!

VETERANS

The United States has more than 27-million veterans, who, on some issues, exert a pressure beyond their numbers. In 1969, there were some 6,000 Spanish-American War veterans still living. Nearly 15-million served in World War II, nearly 6-million in the Korean War, and more than 3-million in Vietnam. Another more than 3-million served in the armed forces between the Korean and Vietnam wars. Nearly half of the federal government's employees are veterans. With their families, veterans represent nearly half of the adult population.

The veteran's voice is heard through his organizations—the American Legion, Amvets, Disabled Veterans, Veterans of Foreign Wars, and smaller ones. These organized groups embrace a minority of those eligible for membership. They provide a direct channel to men with war service who are "veteran-minded." The veteran influence can be exaggerated. Military service is the common experience of a majority of adult males today, not the uncommon thing it was prior to World War II. Hence, there has been a diminution of men thinking as veterans.

These and other members of the public move in and out of these and a host of other specialized publics. Composition of The Big Public can be cataloged in many ways. It depends on the issue at stake. Predominant interests of people vary with sex, age, occupation, residence, marriage status, income bracket, church affiliation, and so forth. Beyond these general population groups, each industry or institution has its specialized publics within its Big Public. For a school system, these would include school board, superintendents, principals, teachers, pupils, parents, public officials, taxpayers, readers and listeners of local media, and so forth. Space does not permit detailing the ways and means of dealing with this almost inexhaustible list of special publics. Each organization's fact-finding process will identify its particular publics. We shall discuss two as being illustrative —Youth Relations and Black Relations.

THE YOUTH PUBLIC

Youth, defined statistically, encompasses at one end, young people of 15, who are in high school or starting to work steadily, seeking driver's licenses, making independent decisions, and in general pushing off from childhood toward adulthood. At the other end, it encompasses those of 25 who are, for the most part finished with educational and military commitments, settled into jobs, forming families and otherwise entering the mainstream of adult life.

This body of more than 41-million persons between 15 and 26 in the U. S., and equivalent percentages in every nation, represents various audience potentials to those who court it. Segments are variously perceived as "students," "draftees," "teenagers," "the affluent youth market," "legal minors," "new families," "recruits or trainees," and "juvenile delinquents."

To those responsible for public relations programs in the cosmetic industry, youth is a multi-billion dollar market. To those responsible for public education, youth represents a $21-billion investment annually in elementary and secondary education.

To the public relations wing of the President's Council on Youth Opportunity, in 1968, "youth" presented the practical problem of stimulating summer jobs for a great many of the 13.5 million students 16 to 21 who were seeking them.

For law enforcement and correction institution public relations practitioners, "youth" potentially involved nearly 30-million young people 10 to 17, and was actually concerned with, in 1968, the 1.2-million delinquency cases and more than 100,000 young people under 25 in correctional institutions. Public relations programs in social work had to deal with the presence of some 50,000 youths in training schools and in detention homes for rehabilitation.

Youth, for employers, comprises an audience of 14-million or more in the labor force of the U. S. For the federal government, there is the factor of $4-billion committed to higher education. For the Ford Foundation, there is $300-million annually allocated to education.

To the Ford Motor Company, however, youth represents a "first new car purchase." A soap manufacturer sees youth as an audience of 3.5-million new babies to be bathed daily. To a jeweler, youth represents a market for the 1,990,000 diamond rings and wedding bands sold annually. Banks see new accounts and mortgages on homes. In the investment community there are 1.5-million custodian accounts for minors. Politicians cater to youth. They style their hair, make speeches, and vote for legislation calculated to appeal to the youth vote.

And so it goes. Teenagers alone represent a $12-billion segment of U. S. purchasing power.

Studies are made regularly to analyze this audience and its complex reactions and responses. Common denominators are sought. Researchers say youth must be considered as "cool," "concerned," "action-oriented," "idealistic," "disenchanted with much in their parents' world."

At Seton Hall University, Senator Muskie said, "We cannot forget that there is much to dissent from in America, and that, when many of us were silent, the young spoke up." In contrast, Norman Cousins in the *Saturday Review* concluded that youth is "non-historical," lacking the discipline of history and a perception of the progress that has been made. Because of this, Senator Mark Hatfield expressed the concern that "more and more young people may come to view progress as the product of revolution."

The importance of this special public to the future of society—indeed it *is* the future—feeds the debate and the efforts to capture its attention and influence its views from White House to campus to counting house. The militant power of America's young people was dramatized anew in protests that followed in the wake of the decision to invade Cambodia and the tragedies of Kent State University and Jackson State College.

The point of view of many students was expressed thus by Jim Rittman, when editor of the student newspaper at the University of Alabama-Birmingham: [4]

> The youth of today are concerned—concerned about a society that seems to sicken daily. People seem to care less and less about their fellow man, almost as if non-involvement is to become an accepted standard of American life. As the generation that will be the backbone of the country in another ten years, we cannot accept the approaches of our elders toward solving society's ills; we have seen them in action and have seen them fail. We must try to utilize our own philosophies and methods to the best advantage. Of course, some of these fail, often miserably, but some failure is to be expected. However, a significant portion of these failures is not because the concepts are faulty, but are caused by rejection of these concepts because our elders are so stuck in ruts that they are afraid to try something new or different. This is what drives many alienated young people into the streets—if the channels of action and relevant communication are cut off, where else can someone who really cares go?

HISTORICAL PROGRAMS

Almost a permanent part of life in this country and in many others are such organized groups as the Boy Scouts, Girl Scouts, Sea Scouts, Camp Fire Girls, 4-H Clubs, Future Farmers of America, Boys Clubs of America, Y.M.C.A.'s, and Y.W.C.A.'s. The organized activities of such groups provide many public relations opportunities for sponsorship, contests, granting of awards, presentation of programs, tours, displays, and books. Support of these activities demonstrates social responsibility and bids for future customers or supporters.

The most direct example of this approach to youth by business is Junior Achievement. Founded decades ago by Horace A. Moses and Theodore N. Vail, it has been carried on by thousands of business leaders to show young men, by actual participation, just how the competitive enterprise system ticks. The Junior Achievement program calls for adult businessmen

---

[4] Reproduced in *Channels Forum* National Public Relations Council, April 1, 1970.

to function as advisers to companies formed by teen-agers. In these junior corporations, boys and girls 15 to 21 sign up for jobs, sell stock, and operate a corporate business. The jobs are rotated, and everybody gets paid if the enterprise clicks. There are directors' meetings, stockholder meetings, and all the problems and procedures of a corporate enterprise.

Classrooms from kindergarten to university provide access to the key public of teachers and students for nonprofit agencies promoting the causes of safety, health, conservation, wholesome recreation, and good citizenship. Business and the professions have developed large-scale *educational* programs to create understanding of the American business system, to promote consumer education, and to recruit talent.

One company that pays special attention to young people is Greyhound, because youth groups are a major source of chartered fares. Greyhound for many years has: distributed a cartoon booklet, "Driving Like a Pro," sent safe-driving posters to schools, and staged appearances of its "Lady Greyhound," a live dog which supposedly symbolizes the Bus Lines' "dependability and well-coordinated speed." One approach tried by Greyhound that did not work too well was a prose-poetry contest for school children. More recently, Greyhound has added booklets and speeches by its vice-president, Joe Black—first black pitcher to win a World Series game—to its youth program.

Typical college examples include the Ford College Roundtable in which up to 10 company executives meet with 100 representatives of faculty and students. A typical subject: "The Expectation and Realities of a Business Career." In a ten-year-period, there were seventy-seven round tables. TRW sponsored at forty colleges an English play, "By George," based on the life of George Bernard Shaw. Oneida Silversmith's presents "Community Service Awards" to co-ed organizations.

As indicated earlier, the some 7-million college and university students comprise a block of great potential, considerable power, and the source of professional manpower for society's needs. The activists among college students demonstrated their power in changing the course of the 1968 Presidential election and in turning public opinion against the war in Vietnam. The problems college students can pose for organizations is vividly seen in the series of protests against Dow Chemical Co. and military recruiters. More fundamental and widespread is the declining interest in business careers by college seniors. Headlines *The Milwaukee Journal:* "Selling Job Gets Tougher for Industry Talent Scouts." Campus recruitment needs the support of public relations as never before. Concerned about the reported decline of interest in business careers on the campus, Robert Galvin, chairman of Motorola, Inc., established a dialogue with representative students in a series of letters published as paid advertisements in the college press. This dialogue stimulated much interest and brought acclaim for its sponsor. It also elicited hundreds of letters from campuses, which Galvin answered personally. He visited scores of schools for face-to-face meetings. Subsequently, the heads of Goodyear Tire and Dow Chemical joined in sponsorship of the letters published in forty-eight university papers on alternate weeks throughout the school year. Radio dialogues aired over campus stations were also initiated by Mr. Galvin. The unique program examining business as a career and as a force for the progress of society echoed off campuses to parents, other businessmen, and the national press.

The once deep gulf between the worlds of education and business is steadily being bridged. Vehicles include corporate support of education, business-sponsored educator conferences, provision of specialists as part-time teachers, visits by teachers to industry, visits by businessmen to schools, and similar projects. Better rapport and closer collaboration on matters of *mutual interest* are the happy result.

Industry assistance to schools and colleges takes such varied forms as: [5]

INSTRUCTIONAL SERVICES

Student field trips to offices and plants; classroom and assembly speakers; student club programs; student work experience programs; vocational training and counseling; student award and recognition programs; facilities and equipment for meetings; curriculum advisors; teachers and professors on loan; substitute teachers and night teachers; student travel programs; seminars; research projects.

UPGRADING TEACHERS

Plant visits, workshops, conferences, research and work experience; special classes, travel programs, consultant service, summer employment, summer scholarships.

ADMINISTRATION AID

Membership on school and college boards, membership on advisory committees, aid in fund raising, aid in campaigns for bond issues, aid in planning buildings, cafeteria service, and transportation programs.

Other assistance to education by industry includes:

1. Grants and scholarships—often related to plant community relations, recruiting, or research.

[5] See survey, Albert L. Ayars, "How Business and Industry Are Helping the Schools," *Saturday Review*, October 17, 1964, pp. 57–58 ff. Also: Richard A. Stimson and C. Colburn Hardy, "How to Develop an Educated Approach to Business-Sponsored Materials," *Public Relations Journal*, Vol. 19, September, 1963, p. 20.

2. Personal participation—furnishing guest lecturers, encouraging company people to serve on school boards and advisory groups.
3. Plant tours, including annual business-education days.
4. Loaning or donating supplies and equipment.
5. Supplying information and photographs to textbook authors and publishers.
6. Instructional materials distributed free or at nominal cost.

Sponsored materials for schools—booklets, pamphlets, movies, and other teaching aids—have become big business. The volume is steadily mounting. Practitioners find teachers and professors receptive to *honest, useful* aids which are truly *educational* rather than propagandistic in nature. *Teachers welcome useful information; they rightfully resent indoctrination.*

Practitioners should approach collaboration with educators in a spirit of cooperation and helpful intent. Efforts to infiltrate the nation's schoolrooms with partisan pleading will backfire. Mary June Burton thinks: "Some of these 'aids' are clumsy and even dishonest, a nuisance to schools and largely a waste of money for the sponsors." She follows these "rules of the road" in preparing sponsored materials for school.[6]

1. Keep "advertising" to a minimum.
2. Avoid unfair slanting or bias.
3. Plan materials to fit the curriculum.
4. Keep materials easy to read.
5. Make them interesting.

Preparation of these materials is a task that the practitioner is seldom equipped to tackle unaided. He needs the help of teachers. Increasingly teachers are being employed on a part- or full-time basis to guide these programs. One educational program that attracted wide duplication was General Mills' health and nutrition project. This program can serve as a guide. From its inception, school administrators had an important role in this program. Directed by a former school superintendent, the project used the consulting service of the National Association of Secondary-School Principals. There was active participation by educators and nutrition specialists. The General Mills program was divided into four parts.

1. Testing

More than 100 test schools, from Minnesota to Georgia and ranging from rural one-room schools to city schools at all grade levels, were used

---

[6] In an article, "Sponsored School Materials Are 'Coming of Age,'" *Public Relations Journal*, Vol. 13, April, 1957, p. 9.

to experiment with techniques, to try out the program, and to *evaluate* its effectiveness.

2. Teacher Training

General Mills sought to show teachers how nutrition could be woven into regular classroom studies without disturbing the curriculum or the school organization. Demonstration programs for teachers were conducted at selected colleges and universities.

3. Teaching Aids

These were planned and developed by educators, nutrition and health specialists, and classroom teachers. They represented the framework for an inclusive nutrition and health program. These included a handbook, teacher's guidebook, wall posters, pupil leaflets, parents' leaflets, nutrition guide, the story of cereal grains, an outline of a suggested program, a film, and evaluation devices.

4. Promotion

The program was promoted by *advertising* in sixteen educational, agricultural, home economics, and health publications; by *direct mail* to key persons; by *personal contact* with key groups and individuals; by *presentations* to groups on city, county, state, and national levels; by *exhibits* at education and health conventions; and by a *publication* regularly circulated among some 28,000 educators.

There are other means of reaching this large, influential group of opinion makers and future citizens and customers.

BUSINESS-EDUCATION DAY

This is an educational relations tool of tremendous potential. B-E Days bring teachers and pupils to industrial plants and business firms for a close look and conferences. (The National Association of Manufacturers calls it Business-Industry-Education Day.) The idea started in 1946, when a Michigan State University professor took a group of school administrators on a flying tour of Michigan industries. The idea spread rapidly. The Chamber of Commerce of the United States, the N.A.M., and other trade groups have vigorously promoted it. Astute school administrators have turned the idea around to bring business leaders into the schools on Education-Business Days. It can work both ways.

Earl B. Steele counsels B-E Day sponsors: "Place the emphasis on those features which serve the real needs of the schools, teachers, and the students and those which develop a better understanding of our competitive system." [7] Such programs, like all others, must be *mutually rewarding.*

CAREER DAYS

This has become a standard spring event in many high schools. Such days offer another means of reaching tomorrow's citizens and employees. Community leaders are anxious to keep youthful talent in the community. Industrialists, editors, and engineers seek to attract young people into their callings. In these programs, businessmen, professionals, and scientists describe the many careers open to students. The Miami Beach Chamber of Commerce has added an extra twist to this idea. It sponsors a "Boss for a Day" program for high school seniors. This provides them with a close look at work in stores, professional offices, and business establishments.

The Evansville, Indiana, Manufacturers' and Employers' Association stresses career guidance in its educational relations program. In an effort to encourage young people to enter Evansville industry, this association published a 192-page book, *Your Career Opportunities in Evansville Industry.* This was a *collaborative effort* of a technical committee, representing industry, and an editorial board of five educators. Plenty of copies are made available through the high school libraries. The book includes a "Dictionary of Job Opportunities in Evansville Industry." The book is used as a text in a 10-week freshman course. This association also has sponsored a contest among high-schoolers for the best *career-planning notebooks.*

CONFERENCES

Industry-sponsored conferences which bring school teachers and university professors into the business for joint conferences, are growing in number. Standard Oil of New Jersey, DuPont, and International Harvester were among the pioneers. These conferences, conducted without strings, can be mutually rewarding.[8]

For example, the chemical industry of Delaware collaborated to get the opportunities in science known to high school students. These firms sponsored a "New Frontiers Day" at the University of Delaware. Every secondary school in the state, public and parochial, was represented by at least one teacher. Most sent two. Executives and scientists told of the opportunities and demands for young men and women in the chemical industry. To permit the teachers to attend, the companies provided chemists,

---

[7] Earl B. Steele, "PR Opportunities of B-E Day." *Public Relations Journal,* Vol. 11, May, 1955, pp. 12–13. Useful pointers.

[8] For an example of how high pressure tactics can backfire see Frederick S. Allis, Jr., "How Business Antagonized Some Teachers," *Fortune,* Vol. 50, September, 1954.

engineers, and physicists as substitute teachers for them. This provided a two-way impact.

One of the oldest and most successful of these industry-educator conferences is that started by DuPont in 1950 for university professors. The original guidelines are still followed. These include: No fewer than forty, no more than forty-four educators to be invited from institutions of various sizes and from all sections of nation; the letter of invitation goes to the president of the college or university, who selects those to attend; the groups are kept small enough for two-way discussion; top management of company participates, including nine members of DuPont executive committee; there is no ducking of the educators' probing questions. L. L. L. Golden thinks "the conferences have made management and the educators involved more understanding of each other's views."

SUMMER JOBS/INTERNSHIPS

An increasing number of industrial and professional organizations are providing summer employment for school teachers and university professors. This program has great potential for development of *rapport*. It provides the teacher with a realistic view to impart to his students. It provides those outside the academic world an opportunity to learn the educator viewpoint. Professions, newspapers, advertising agencies, and business firms are providing an increasing number of summer internships. Some firms lend executives to colleges as visiting professors.

The critical shortage of scientists and science teachers has been one spur for this increasing exchange. An executive of the National Science Teachers Association thinks: "When approached with no more caution than is required in any public relations activity, hiring teachers in science-related summer jobs promises rich rewards in increased understanding of the common problems of education, business, and industry." [9] Union Carbide has found that this program "achieves better community relations."

THE BLACK PUBLIC

As America's black population has developed pride and power through black nationalism, it has become a special public of great importance to the practitioner. It is a public that requires careful study, deep understanding, and great sensitivity. It is not easy to generalize about it, because it is not a monolithic public. Still, its members have in common growing pride

---

[9] John H. Woodburn, "Summer Jobs for Teachers Equals Public Relations Dividends," *Public Relations Journal*, Vol. 11, June, 1955, pp. 13–14.

in their race, mounting anger against the white man, and determination to attain equal citizenship. It is in pursuit of this goal that the splintering among blacks comes.

Effective communication with blacks is difficult for white practitioners and white institutions—which explains the rising employment of Negroes in public relations and emergence of black public relations agencies. The hard fact is that today white men find it difficult to talk to black men. One leader has defined "black nationalism" as the concept of "a nation within a nation." He adds: "This is neither a geographic area nor a political government. As black people, we are beginning to think of ourselves as sharing a common heritage and a common oppression." He explains: [10]

> We have rediscovered our African heritage, which is the only cultural stand that we can be proud of. It is important and we *choose* to make it our heritage. In what white people despise, we have found a basis for pride. . . . We can find a basis for pride in Africa, in the things that Africa stands for—in the culture, in the philosophy, in the religion, in the history, in the science of Africa. This is black consciousness in the sense of being a black people separate and apart from white people. . . .

Members of this "nation within a nation" comprise a public with steadily increasing political and purchasing power. It is a public of great potential—a public of some 22-million persons with a per capita income slightly more than the per capita income of western Europe, a public with 6-million families or households, of which more than half own automobiles. Forty percent of these families own their homes and some 75 percent have television sets. These families have more of their members studying in colleges than the total enrollment in Great Britain or Italy. Blacks constitute an important political bloc and a lucrative market. D. Parke Gibson gives four reasons why there is a "Negro market" in the United States: [11]

1. Forced identification of the people comprising this market.
2. Definable purchase patterns by this group of consumers.
3. The size of this market.
4. The location of this market within the United States.

American Negroes constitute more than 92 percent of the non-white population in the U. S. and 11 percent of the total population. The U. S.

---

[10] The Rev. Albert B. Cleage, "Black Power—an advocate defines it," *Public Relations Journal*, Vol. 24, July, 1968, p. 18.

[11] D. Parke Gibson, *The $30 Billion Negro* (New York: Macmillan Co., 1969), p. 9. A Negro public relations counselor provides a broad view of this key public with emphasis on its purchasing power.

Census estimates that by 1975 the non-white population will total 29,312,-000 persons, or approximately 12.2 percent of our population. Increasingly, Negroes are concentrating in northern cities. As of 1970, it was estimated that blacks constituted 40 percent or more of the population in fourteen of the nation's largest cities. Washington, D.C., and Gary, Indiana, had black majorities. Census projections indicate that New Orleans, Richmond, Virginia, would have black majorities by 1971; Baltimore and Jacksonville, Florida, by 1972; Cleveland, Ohio, by 1975; St. Louis, Missouri, by 1978; Detroit by 1979. In 1970 four northern cities had black mayors—Gary, Cleveland, Newark, New Jersey, and Washington, D.C. Blacks represent a market with $32-billion dollars spendable income. Black votes are often the decisive factor in elections. As they gain their rights, their purchasing and political power will increase correspondingly. To win market or political campaigns, requires effective communication with this bloc of citizens. As long as the dual society exists in America, it will be necessary for public relations programming to take this fact into account.

The most effective channels to the black are his political leaders, his religious leaders, his newspapers, his magazines, and his radio stations. Gibson advises: "Negro-oriented media offer communication with the Negro market, and their use gives messages conviction and believability that usually cannot be achieved in any other media. White-oriented media continue to ignore vital dimensions in the lives of non-white Americans, and almost without exception these media talk *about* Negroes and not *to* them." Blacks pay less than normal attention to print news media. One survey among Pittsburgh Negroes found that "the ghetto resident depended almost entirely on the television evening newscast for news outside his neighborhood." The Six-Day War in the Middle East broke out the day the survey started. Seventy percent of those interviewed first learned of this war on the 6 p.m. network newscast. Another fifth didn't learn of the war until late the next day—and by word-of-mouth. This researcher suggests: "The current channels for printed news-information are unused by the ghetto resident, but more communication might be established if newspapers increased material in regular news columns that might be of interest primarily to Negro readers." [12]

Although the practitioner must rely primarily on black channels of communication, there is much that he can do to interest and identify with blacks in the general news media. Advertisers have been doing this on an increasing scale since the early 1960s. This tack came in response to angry criticism of advertising by blacks. A 1963 survey found: "From the point of view of the Negro population there is virtually no general news-

[12] Thomas H. Allen, "Mass Media Use Patterns in a Negro Ghetto," *Journalism Quarterly,* Vol. 45, Autumn, 1968, p. 527.

paper, radio station, television station, or magazine which does not carry advertising that is discriminatory. . . . Strong negative attitudes toward advertising in general media, perceived by the Negro as being discriminatory, were expressed by 88 percent of the Negroes interviewed." [13] That same year, in the opinion of *Saturday Review,* the color line was irrevocably splintered in national advertising. Advertisers have been addressing messages to blacks and using black models with good results in more recent years. Such communication also has social value. The *New York Times,* commenting on the breaking of the color line in advertising, said: "The wider representation of Negroes in conventional middle-class settings will do much to erase the undesirable stereotypes of the Negro that exist in the white community." [14]

Since 1827 when the *Freedom Journal* was founded, the Negro newspaper has dominated black journalism, but with the growing power and affluence of the black his journalism now embraces several successful magazines and broadcast stations. *Ayer's 1969 Directory* of newspapers and periodicals lists 150 Negro publications, mostly weeklies. The more than 100 daily, weekly, or monthly Negro newspapers have a circulation of more than 1-million. An important addition to black news channels is *Tuesday,* a monthly magazine supplement for metropolitan dailies, which was started in 1965. This supplement is oriented to the black's interests and distributed in black neighborhoods by such large-city newspapers as the Cleveland *Plain Dealer,* Milwaukee *Journal,* and Chicago *Sun-Times. Tuesday* now has a circulation of more than 2-million. The leading black magazine is *Ebony,* with a circulation of more than 1.2-million published by the Johnson Publishing Co. of Chicago. Johnson also publishes *Jet,* a vest-pocket size weekly newsmagazine, *Tan* a women's and confession-type magazine, and *Negro-Digest,* a militant advocate of equality for blacks. The Good Publishing Co. of Ft. Worth, Texas, publishes *Sepia,* a monthly rival to *Ebony,* and *Jive, Hep,* and *Bronze Thrills,* all lively and physically smaller than *Sepia,* which like *Ebony* is *Life*-size.[15] A new magazine designed for black women, *Essence,* increased the opportunities for communication with this segment of the black population. There is an increasing number of black oriented radio stations in the cities with large Negro populations.[16]

[13] "Negroes Respond Negatively to Ads," *Editor & Publisher,* October 5, 1963, p. 22.

[14] *New York Times,* January 6, 1964, p. 88. Also see: William H. Boyenton, "The Negro Turns to Advertising," *Journalism Quarterly,* Vol. 42, Spring, 1965.

[15] Roland Wolseley, "The Black Magazines," *The Quill,* May, 1969. See: *The Black Press in America: A Guide* (Coralville, Ia.: Mercer House Press, 1972).

[16] For changes in black press, see: L. F. Palmer, Jr., "The Black Press in Transition," *Columbia Journalism Review,* Vol. 9, Spring, 1970.

The way these media can be used is illustrated in this case study recounted by D. Parke Gibson: [17]

B. F. Goodrich decided to introduce a new tire to the black markets of Pittsburgh and New Orleans in a pilot program to perfect its approach to these markets. In Pittsburgh, the advertising program was concentrated on a Negro station, WAMO, and in the Pittsburgh *Courier*. The *Courier* assisted in community relations promotion. A coffee hour was held, to which the newspaper, on behalf of Goodrich, invited some 150 black civic, social, and professional community leaders. The tire company's program was explained, a film shown, and door prizes awarded. A Goodrich Negro employee was presented a recognition award at this coffee hour. WAMO taped portions of it for a later broadcast. The *Courier* followed up with a mailing of a Goodrich advertisement along with a covering letter to its mailing list of three-thousand consumer families. A license-plate contest was also conducted over WAMO. Similarly in New Orleans, the black-oriented media were used to meet this marketing objective.

CASE PROBLEM

You are public relations director of the Dow Chemical Company and you find your company caught up in the protest against the war in Vietnam. Your company formerly supplied napalm to the U. S. Government for use in war for some years. Napalm represented less than 1 percent of Dow's sales volume and employed only ten persons in its farflung enterprise. In dollar volume, your company ranks 75th among Department of Defense suppliers, yet larger suppliers have not been similarly attacked. Last year, your campus recruiters were picketed, blockaded, or attacked on 55 campuses of the 330 visited. Because of its manufacture of napalm, Dow has become a hated symbol of those opposing the war. This has created a major public relations problem for your company.

It is June and time to sit down with your personnel officials to plan next year's campus recruiting campaign to get able college seniors to join Dow. It is your job to suggest themes to counter the Dow image, suggest ways of working with host colleges to handle these protests when they occur, and to persuade college seniors to consider a career with Dow. Prepare a memo for the Director of Personnel outlining the basic approach to next year's campus recruiting in light of these problems.

[17] Gibson, *The $30 Billion Negro*, pp. 155–156.

ADDITIONAL READING

JOHN W. ALDRIDGE, "In the Country of the Young," *Harper's Magazine*, Vol. 239, October, 1969.

JOSHUA D. BOWEN, *The Struggle Within Race Relations in the United States*. New York: Norton, 1965.

SALLY DICKSON and JOYCE CLARK, "The Image and Schools and Women's Clubs," in Lee H. Bristol, Jr., ed., *Developing the Corporate Image*. New York: Charles Scribner's Sons, 1960.

Encyclopedia of Associations, Vol. 1, National Organizations of the United States. Detroit: Gale Research Co., 1968.

JOHN J. GREEN, "Frank Seymour, a New and Necessary Kind of Businessman. . . ." *Detroit News Magazine*, Oct. 22, 1967. Profile of a leading Negro counselor whose background and success illuminate new requirements and opportunities in this field.

KENNETH KENISTON, "Youth, Change and Violence," *The American Scholar*, Vol. 37, Spring, 1968.

KATE MILLETT, *Sexual Politics*. New York: Doubleday, 1970. Gives clear insight to drives behind Women's Lib.

"The Negro Market: 23 Million Deep and $30 Billion Wide," *Marketing Insights*, January 29, 1968.

RICHARD M. SCAMMON and BEN J. WATTENBERG, *The Real Majority*. New York: Coward-McCann, Inc., 1970. A careful, revealing examination of the American electorate.

MUZAFER SHERIF, ed., *Problems of Youth*. Chicago: Aldine Publishing Co., 1965.

ROMNEY WHEELER, "The School Approach to Tomorrow's Customers," *Public Relations Journal*, Vol. 26, February, 1970.

RUDOLPH M. WITTENBERG, *The Troubled Generation*. New York: Association Press, 1967.

"The Woman in America," special issue of *Daedalus*, Vol. 93, Spring, 1964.

WHITNEY M. YOUNG, JR., *Beyond Racism*. New York: McGraw-Hill, 1969. A call to whites to respond to needs of blacks so that we may save an open society.

CHAPTER 16

THE MASS AUDIENCE

The economical, effective avenue of contact with the general public is through the mass media: newspapers, magazines, trade journals, radio, and television. To handle this part of his job, the practitioner must understand the role of publicity, these media, and those who control access to them. This chapter will be divided into two parts. The first will treat the role of publicity in public relations. The second will discuss the media. Chapter 17 will outline principles for successful relationships with the men and women who work in these media.

THE ROLE OF PUBLICITY

Publicity is an important—but not all-important—part of public relations. Successful publicity, over the long pull, must be grounded in works that the public defines as good, motives that the public accepts as honest, and presentation that the public recognizes as credible. As Cantril suggests, "opinion is generally determined more by events than by words. . . ." But there must be words and images, too—or else the good works are apt to be overlooked or misinterpreted by those with differing purposes or by those separated by distance. There can be quite a difference in impact between an act carefully explained and one that is not. A utility can simply go ahead and tear up a city's streets to put in larger gas mains. Or it can manifest concern and consideration for the inconvenience and noise and dramatize this work as proof of a desire to provide the community with better service. Publicity is not a cure-all, but effective communication can get results.

Publicity's role must be understood in the larger framework of the whole communications process. It cannot be used for any length of time as a substitute for good works or for desirable corrective action. It can only serve as a spotlight to focus attention on good works and to clothe institutions with personality. In publicity practice, the operator of the spotlight naturally tries to put highlights on the good and to soften the unfavorable with shadows. But the publicist must always remember that there are other operators with spotlights to cast a revealing glare in the dark corners of any institution or industry.

The objective of publicity is to make something or somebody known. The desire to be known stems from competition and from the mass media's partial failure, in terms of news coverage and values, to keep pace. The increased effort to make one's voice heard above those of others encourages an overemphasis on publicity. Publicity used as one means of attracting attention to one's wares and citizenship is a forceful tool.

Publicity is potent but not omnipotent. One says: "We live in an age of publicity. What we buy, what we do, what we think, and what others think about us are influenced by publicity. . . . Publicity makes you buy Fords or Plymouths, makes you buy tickets to a fight or a ball game, makes you vote the Democratic ticket, makes you want to take a train ride or spend your last dime, makes you feel patriotic." This is an oversimplification. Publicity will not, by itself, sell goods, raise funds for a charitable cause, or win elections. These things take a good product, a good cause, and a hard-working organization. But publicity can provide a voice to convey ideas to the people.

There are testimonials galore to the accomplishments of publicity. "Miss America" is one. The Rose Bowl Game is another. The "Blood Bank" is still another. When it was publicized that a United States president was eating beef bacon for breakfast, beef bacon sales skyrocketed and pork bacon sales slumped. One November, *The Reader's Digest* published an article about the Tracer Company of America, an organization which locates unclaimed bank accounts, legacies, and so forth. By the following May, this firm had received 438,000 letters as a result of this one article. A number of businesses trace their start to similar publicity breaks. These success stories can, of course, be matched by examples of efforts that misfired, or, worse, backfired.

Political and social history is replete with examples of the "big build-up." The techniques are many and varied, and most of them are easily mastered. This open sesame to "easy success" has led practitioners, on occasions, into an exaggerated idea of the power of being "known." Lyndon B. Johnson got to be pretty well known in his presidential years. But he didn't profit from exposure. Neither did Spiro Agnew. That's another side of the publicity rectangle. Getting an institution known by having it mentioned frequently in the press and on the air is a relatively simple and standardized procedure. "News" situations are fairly easy to contrive. Contrivance is a common practice.

Lavish testimonial to publicity breaks down, however, when one stops to consider that simple exposure of an institution to public gaze does not mean absorption of information, or support and understanding, by the public. There's a big gap between being heard and being appreciated. Contrast, for example, the public image of Romana A. Banuelos, whose name is publicized on every dollar bill, with that of Wilbur Mills, who is selective in the publicity he gets. The public image of Mills is proof of the power of good performance coupled with shrewd, dramatic reporting of that performance.

Excessive publicity can backfire by, *one,* irritating the media, and, *two,* creating false expectations in the public's mind. An example of this was the all-out publicity effort to herald the "War on Poverty." Two Washington newsmen sharply criticized the Office of Economic Opportunity's "merchandising" as outpacing the "agency's capacity to deliver the goods." O.E.O., at its peak, had a public relations staff of 46, "supported by a massive Xerox copying machine with a firepower of 2,400 handouts an hour," which "trumpets the smallest victory in the poverty trenches, conducts seminars for the press, and in general works hard." In these writers' view, the poverty program suffered "from too much and too effective salesmanship." [1]

In using and in evaluating the publicity tool, it is important to keep in mind the total *multi-step* mass communications process. Publicity items in these media soon become conversation pieces in offices, taverns, barber shops, and living rooms. Publicity provides a means of introducing your message into the word-of-mouth communications web. The publicity task should be approached with these thoughts in mind: (1) too much publicity can be, in fact, poor public relations; (2) it is the *content* and *absorption* of that content, not the amount of publicity, that eventually registers in public opinion; (3) publicity disseminated is not equivalent to information received; (4) publicity inevitably reflects the character of the institution it seeks to promote; (5) not all publicity that an institution receives originates within its control; (6) not all public relations activities result in publicity, nor should everything be so designed. In fact, there are times when avoidance of publicity is wisest. For example, when a large insurance company opened a 3,000-unit apartment project on a biracial basis in central Chicago, a highly volatile area, it chose not to use publicity. The decision proved wise, as the move came to be accepted without a single incident.

As emphasized in Chapter Nine, publicity to be productive must be planned to achieve predetermined goals. A guide to such planning is provided in Doyle's Communications Chart on page 379.

THE MASS MEDIA OF PUBLICITY

A READY-MADE AUDIENCE AWAITS

The mass media reach into every home in the land. They influence every literate person. The mass media appear to represent an easily used

[1] Erwin Knoll and Jules Witcover, "Maximum Feasible Publicity," *Columbia Journalism Review,* Vol. 5, Fall, 1966.

GROUP	OBJECTIVE	MANAGEMENT ACTION	PR ACTION	COMMUNICATION CHANNEL	TYPE OF MESSAGE
General Public	Good Will Respect Support	Conduct business in public interest. . . . Support community projects	Survey Plan Communicate Evaluate	Mass Media Mail replies Plant Tour folders	Institutional Ads News on basic information about company
Prospective Customers Clients	Sales	Produce Good Product or Service	" "	Mass Media Trade Journals Direct Mail Films	Sales Ads Product News Institutional Ads
Customers Employees Management Ranks	Loyalty Goodwill Efficient production Good morale	Help employees find work satisfaction, self respect, fun	" "	Company publications Bulletin Boards Mass Media Direct Mail Film	News and features about company and individual employees and employee groups Institutional Ads
Stockholders Bankers Investment counsellors	Operating capital Confidence Good Will	Good management	" "	Company publications Newsletter Mass Media	Progress reports Future plans Financial reports Institutional Ads
Government officials Civic Leaders	Good Will Support Favorable decisions	Conduct business in public interest Support community projects	" "	Personal contact Speeches Mass Media Films	News about company progress and plans Editorials Institutional Ads
Press Radio-TV	Respect Confidence in statements	"Open Door" policy Truth	" "	Personal meetings Memos Press tours General news tips *	Shop talk Background on company news
Educators	Respect Support Good Will	Host Plant Visits Serve on PTA Boards, etc.	" "	Personal contact Speeches Direct Mail	Offers to help educators

* The greatest favor you can do a reporter or editor is help him get a good story.

** Prepared by Robert J. Doyle, Wisconsin State Universities.

tool for bringing ideas and information to the public. This concept can be delusive. Just because the media exist and can convey your message does not necessarily mean acceptance or action upon it.

Sound practice requires extensive knowledge and full understanding of the mass media; it requires a first-hand acquaintance with the men and women who staff them; it requires a keen insight into the potentialities and limitations of each medium. The practitioner must know which specific medium or media to use. He must know, too, the rules of the game. He must have a *planned* program for use on a coordinated basis, using one to reinforce and supplement the others. Walt Disney's program is a good example. The Disney firm uses its TV programs to promote its motion pictures and uses both media to promote the sale of books, records, Disneyland, and other ventures.

NEWSPAPERS

When a person thinks of publicity, he almost instinctively thinks of the newspaper. The American press—daily and Sunday newspapers, weekly and semiweekly newspapers, black newspapers, labor newspapers, religious newspapers, collegiate newspapers, scholastic newspapers, and foreign-language newspapers—are read by virtually every literate person. Publicity in the press, day in and day out, 52 weeks a year, forms the strong backbone of any informational program. "Reading the newspaper" is as much a part of an American's daily habits as eating and sleeping. The influence of the press is incalculable. As an example, take this item from the wires of *United Press International.*

> BERKELEY, CALIF.—(UPI)—An elderly St. Paul (Minn.) man dying of cancer changed his will and left $21,000 to the University of California cancer research program *after reading newspaper articles about it,* the university disclosed Saturday. (The italics are ours.)

The newspaper is the moving force of current history. The late Justice Felix Frankfurter once said: "The unconscious, and therefore, uncritical absorption of print is much more powerful than any skeptical alertness which most readers bring to print. To an extent far beyond the public's own realization, public opinion is shaped by the kind, the volume, and the quality of the news columns." Edwin Emery gives the reason: "The power of the press is not in its persuasion by opinion, but in its dissemination of information and its arousal of interest in important issues hitherto submerged in public apathy."

The *strengths* of the newspaper are many. Newspapers are produced in local communities and are indigenous to those communities. They have a first-hand intimacy with their local publics. The local Y.M.C.A. can reach its community public through its local newspaper. The State Department of Health can reach its statewide publics through the daily and weekly newspapers of its state. A commercial concern with regional distribution can reach its regional publics by a regional selection of newspapers. Similarly, a national organization, such as the N.E.A., can reach that national audience through all newspapers. The number, locale, and variety of newspapers enable the publicist to pinpoint the geography of his publicity with precision.

There are other advantages. Newspapers reach more people more often than any other medium. A person buys his newspaper as something he wants, not as something thrust upon him. Newspapers constitute a medium of sustained interest and information. Readers are generally the interested, influential people. Because they reach their readers daily, newspapers are the most acceptable medium for a cumulative publicity build-up and thus are especially valuable in promotional campaigns. Newspapers are read at the reader's leisure and convenience. This is in sharp contrast with the broadcast media, where a program missed is gone forever.

The value of utilizing newspapers to build audiences for radio and TV shows can be seen in these facts. In a typical television season, some 400 companies will sponsor, with varying degrees of participation, several hundred network TV shows. These shows require multi-million-dollar investments. The network publicity staffs will provide routine promotion for these shows, but they cannot do an effective, intensive job for each and every sponsor. Counselor George Hammond observes: "To a corporation investing such sums in an entertainment medium, it is only sound business practice to spend the thousands additional that are needed to assure the maximum audience." [2] The smart sponsor will use newspaper publicity to push his message beyond the confines of the TV page and beyond the major marketing areas.

The newspaper also has its *limitations*. One important limitation is that the average reader reads only a portion of his daily newspaper; the typical reader spends 30 minutes reading one-fifth to one-fourth of the editorial content. Thus it is a mistake to assume that publicity in the press is publicity received by all. Basic though newspapers are, they cannot carry the information task alone. The press must be used in close coordination with other channels of communication. Another limitation is imposed by the press's fetish for speed and the resulting haste with which newspapers are put together. This pressure leads to many inaccuracies and fragmented, superficial coverage—a fact of life that the practitioner must cope with.

[2] In "How to Back Up the Television Advertiser," *Public Relations Journal*, Vol. 18, March, 1962.

As of 1970, there were 1,758 daily newspapers in the United States with circulations totaling more than 62-million copies, and 585 Sunday newspapers with a total circulation of nearly 50-million copies. Despite the highly-publicized deaths of a few metropolitan newspapers in recent times, the number of daily newspapers has been stabilized for a decade or more. There were seven more being published in 1970 than in 1969. Newspaper circulation has climbed slowly but steadily in recent years. Large city newspapers have lost some circulation as readers move to the suburbs. One study suggests that "daily circulation should increase more in the decade ahead than in any other decade in the history of the United States newspaper business.[3] Most dailies are monopoly newspapers. American newspapers—from the mass circulation giants down to the small dailies of 3,000 or so circulation—vary a great deal in content, character, and audience. Yet all have a fairly standardized concept of what makes news.

Knowledge of newspapermen, of newspaper practice, and of newspaper-reader interests and habits will enable the practitioner to use this medium effectively. The practitioner who works with the press needs a few indispensable tools. He ought to read regularly such professional publications as *Editor & Publisher, The Journalism Quarterly, Nieman Reports, The Columbia Journalism Review,* and *The Quill.* Among the essential reference books in every office must be the *Editor & Publisher Yearbook* and N. W. Ayer & Sons' *Directory of Newspapers and Periodicals.* These annual directories give detailed information on the names, locations, circulations, staffs, and so forth, of newspapers.[4] They should be used to *keep mailing lists up to date—a chore not to be neglected.* Outmoded and inaccurate mailing lists are a common source of complaint by newsmen.

In 1970, there were 7,612 weekly and semi-weekly community newspapers in the United States, with a total circulation of nearly 28-million copies (and an estimated readership of 111-million.) The average circulation of a community newspaper is 3,200. This segment of American journalism, like the daily field, is growing in readership. The death of weeklies in small villages of 1,000 or so population has been more than offset by circulation growth in the fast-growing suburbs. The weeklies claim a total readership of 75-million readers.[5] These newspapers offer an effec-

---

[3] Jon G. Udell, *The Growth of the American Daily Newspaper* (Madison, Wis.: Bureau of Business Research, University of Wisconsin School of Business, 1965).

[4] Also helpful: Specialized directories, such as Hudson's *Washington News Media Contacts Directory,* published annually; *Bacon's Publicity Checker,* 16th edition, 1968, includes 3800 magazine, 700 newspaper, and 40 syndicate listings; *The Working Press of the Nation,* National Research Bureau, Inc., Chicago.

[5] *1970 ANR National Directory of Weekly Newspapers,* published annually by American Newspaper Representatives, Inc., 404 Fifth Avenue, New York City, p. 11. Also see: Charles E. Hayes, "This Way to Suburbia," *Public Relations Journal,* Vol. 25, March, 1969. Discusses suburban press as a medium.

tive, direct, and intimate means of reaching the people of suburbs, small towns, and farms, who are often the source of grass-roots opinion. The weekly newspaper reader is a loyal reader who reads his paper through. Most experts agree that the weekly newspaper exerts a far greater impact on opinions in ratio to circulation than does the average daily newspaper. And these opinions count. This group exerts the dominant power in most state legislatures and has repeatedly demonstrated great power in Congress. Henry Beetle Hough, "Mr. Country Editor," counsels:

> It is well to abandon the fiction that ambition necessarily leads to the city, and the corollary that the people of the nation as a whole can be influenced by the old cliches and city symbols . . . as to the small town press, which is naturally important in any public relations thinking, it has a right to be judged functionally and not mechanistically or by fictitious or unrelated standards. Ordinary realism suggests the wisdom of relating it to its own purposes and environment, and not, by comparison, to magazines and city papers which rest upon different premises and different needs.

Most of these weeklies heavily emphasize news of local government, schools, public affairs, and personal news. A few militant ones have appeared in recent years.[6] The public relations practitioner, hedged in by the skyscrapers of the city, should not forget the people of small-town and suburban America or the weekly newspapers that help shape their opinions.

There are two standard directories that can be used as ready reference tools on names, locations, publishers, and so forth, of weekly newspapers: The Ayer's *Directory,* previously mentioned, and the *National Directory of Newspapers,* published annually by American Newspaper Representatives, Inc., the weekly papers' united advertising organization. Most state press associations also publish directories.

Labor journalism has developed extensively and matured considerably over the past 20 years. The exact number of labor newspapers is difficult to determine. Just about every union has its own magazine or paper. Recent estimates place the total at about 200 labor papers and magazines circulated on a national basis, in addition to hundreds of regional and local ones. Their total circulation is variously estimated from 16 to 20-million. It is safe to assume that every union member receives at least one labor newspaper. To get a story into a union member's newspaper increases its acceptability to him. Naturally, the information must be of special interest and must square with the policies of organized labor.

The following labor publications and press services offer important outlets for stories with a labor angle:

[6] "The Irrepressible Weeklies," *Columbia Journalism Review,* Vol. 7, Summer, 1968.

A.F.L.-C.I.O. News: A weekly paper published by the AFL-CIO, 815 16th Street, N.W., Washington 6, D.C.

A.F.L.-C.I.O. News and Mat Service: A mimeographed version of material prepared for the *AFL-CIO News*. It is sent to a list of official labor papers three times a week.

A.F.L.-C.I.O. American Federationist: A monthly magazine published by the AFL-CIO, 815 16th Street, N.W., Washington 6, D.C.

Labor: A bi-weekly labor paper published by the Railway Brotherhoods, 400 First St., N.W., Washington, D.C.

Press Associates, Inc. (PAI): A labor news and mat service, 312 Pennsylvania Avenue, S.E., Washington, D.C.

The vastly-increased importance of the Negro media in reaching this important segment of the public was discussed in Chapter Fifteen. Ayer's 1970 *Directory* listed some 150 black publications, mostly weeklies. More than 400 of the nation's 4,300 AM radio outlets devote at least part of their time to material directed toward Negroes. Most of these are white-owned. The first Negro-owned station, WCHD, went on the air in Detroit in 1957. *Broadcasting Yearbook* and Standard Rate and Data Service provide information on stations serving the black market.[7]

THE PRESS WANTS NEWS

This vast array of newspapers wants one thing from the publicist—*NEWS!* The press is not interested in providing people and programs with publicity. News and entertainment features are the life-blood of these publications. Although there is no precise definition, most journalists agree that news, essentially, is any material that an editor deems timely, of interest, or of consequence to his readers. The content of a newspaper provides the editor's definition of news.

The bulk of today's publicity output never appears in print. Large batches of publicity flood the newsrooms of our daily and weekly newspapers only to wind up in wastebaskets. To be specific, in studies made at the University of Wisconsin, it was found that: (1) out of approximately 300 releases received in a five-day period by a typical morning newspaper, 242 were rejected; (2) out of 339 publicity releases received in a five-day period by a typical evening newspaper, 218 were rejected outright, 32 were used as received, 42 were rewritten and used; (3) out of 113 publicity releases, totaling 363 pages, received in one week by a typical weekly newspaper, exactly *three* were used. A more comprehensive study of a repre-

---

[7] See Dave Berkman, "The Segregated Medium," *Columbia Journalism Review*, Vol. 5, Fall, 1966.

sentative sample of urban, suburban, and rural weekly newspapers in 1968 found that over 18.5 percent of the 1,072 releases received in twelve weekly offices in one week were used. The bulk of these releases came from educational institutions, the state and federal government, trade and professional associations, and business firms. Weekly editors interviewed said that two-thirds of public relations material is rejected because it lacks news value for their readers. Seventy-one percent of the releases were judged to have no local angle, an essential to get in the local-oriented weekly. Thirty-five percent of these editors found practitioners competent, another fifty percent thought them fairly competent. Of the total news content of these weeklies, measured by column inches, ten percent came from public relations sources, mostly non-profit institutions.[8]

Another researcher studying the input and use of publicity releases in five Milwaukee news media collected a total of 1,789 rejected releases in one full week. On the other hand, he found that, of the nonwire, nonsyndicated segment of the *Milwaukee Sentinel's* news content, some 30 percent came from publicity releases or phone calls. The *Milwaukee Journal* got 24 percent of its nonwire, nonsyndicated news content from public relations sources. The public relations content for WTMJ-TV was found to be 12 percent in terms of number of news items and 13 percent in terms of air time. For WTMJ radio, it was about 10 percent and 16 percent, respectively. Twelve percent of the items on the Wisconsin state AP wire came from publicists.[9]

The lesson of these studies is clear: If the editor thinks the story is newsworthy, he'll use it. The problem of releases flooding the nation's newsrooms has been accentuated since the prosecution of Texas Gulf Sulphur for violating the SEC rule on prompt disclosure. This rule has caused financial publicists to flood the media with releases. Thus, the problem gets tougher.

The reasons for these wholesale rejections are valid and well-known, yet the waste of effort and resulting irritation to editors continue. Professor James Julian surveyed 61 editors to determine the main reasons why more releases are dumped into wastebaskets than are used in print. He was given these reasons, in order of frequency:

Limited local interest
No reader interest at all
Story poorly written

[8] Stephen P. Zielke, "Public Relations and Wisconsin Weekly Newspapers," (Master's thesis, University of Wisconsin, 1969).

[9] Col. William Schabacker, "Public Relations and the News Media" (Master's thesis, University of Wisconsin, 1963). For brief account, see "P.R. News Content of Media Measured," *Editor & Publisher*, Vol. 96, June 8, 1963.

Reasons of policy
Disguised advertising
Material obviously faked
Apparent inaccuracy in story
Duplication of release
Material stretched too thin

Providing newspapers with news, pictures, and features of value and of timely interest to readers not only brings publicity but *builds good press relations as well.* James R. Sutphen, who served as city editor *of the Bergen, N.J. Record,* points the way to successful publicity practice with sound advice: "Daily newspapers labor continually under two serious shortages, lack of space and lack of time. There never is enough space to print all the news; there is never enough time to gather it, edit it, and publish it. So any aid they can obtain that will save space or time is welcome. . . . A responsible daily newspaper deals in only one commodity, news. Whatever agency helps editors and reporters obtain news accurately, completely, swiftly, they appreciate. Whatever agency blocks obtaining the news accurately, completely, and swiftly, they resent. Press relations is as simple as that."

Not to be minimized or overlooked in publicity is the photograph. This is an age of pictorial reporting. Reader-interest studies consistently show pictures at the top of the heap. The growth of TV as a competitive medium has forced newspapers to give increased emphasis to pictorial reporting. Greatly improved cameras have aided this development. Stories can be told dramatically and effectively in pictures. The power of a picture was amply demonstrated in the damage done Cornell University when a photograph of armed black students emerging from its student union was printed around the world. Cornell's president commented sadly: "We have learned that the news media exact a high price from those who neglect the tremendous impact of photographic shorthand." Good pictorial reporting will get a story in when a straight news story won't be accepted. Newspapers and magazines never have enough really good pictures.

AVENUES OF APPROACH

There are many different avenues for getting publicity into print. Each one has its special uses and its peculiar stop-and-go lights. Each one has a place in the going program. Knowledge of which avenue to use in a given instance and of the bumps and smooth places along each thoroughfare is a requisite.

The major press associations or wire services, *The Associated Press* and *United Press International* are the backbone of the nation's news system. AP and UPI provide daily newspapers, weekly newsmagazines, and the electronic media with the bulk of their news and feature content. Save for the network TV newscasts, most state, national, and international news read or heard by the citizen comes from these two wire services. The newspaper-radio AP and UPI wire services are the critical link between the public and the daily array of national and international public affairs.

For high reader-interest value, spot news of state, regional, or national significance, the wire service offers the most economical and effective outlet. Publicity with a "local angle" of local interest can be more properly directed to the individual newspaper where that interest exists. Getting a story on the wires assures immediate and widespread coverage. It also increases the acceptability of copy. Publicity that comes clacking in over the wire service printer or Teletypesetter tape is no longer "publicity." It is news! A well-written wire story can reach newspaper readers across the nation at little cost.

Feeding material to the press via the wire services generally means that it will be rewritten and compressed. Fat and puffery will be squeezed out. What starts out as an 850-word release in Washington, D.C., may wind up as a 50-word story in a Wisconsin newspaper. There is a steady compression and deletion of the tremendous bulk of material fed into the news wires as news progresses from Berlin, Germany, to Boise, Idaho. This is shown in the flow chart which was based on a five-day analysis of the content and flow of news in the Associated Press from trunk wire to state wire to daily newspaper.[10] The chart is on page 388.

Each of the two press services operates with national trunk wires, regional wires, and state wires in the United States. Each has its general headquarters in New York with bureaus and clients around the world. The best approach to the wire service is through the nearest bureau or "stringer" correspondent. With the spread of Teletypesetter wire circuits and the growth of wire transmission of photographs, the importance of using the wire services has greatly increased. The mailed release or mailed picture is, by the same fact, less and less effective. With the advent of T.T.S. the wireheads have become the key to effective newspaper publicity. Some agencies provide news releases on T.T.S. tape.

In the nation's major news centers, many practitioners use commercially operated publicity wires to speed their releases to the city's newsrooms. Today in the nation's principal newsrooms from Boston to Los Angeles, publicity wire teleprinters stand alongside the bank of clattering wire news machines. These teleprinters are bringing to the newsroom publicity releases fed into a teletype system from a central office. The first such

[10] For details of this study, see Scott M. Cutlip, "Content and Flow of AP News—From Trunk to TTS to Reader," *Journalism Quarterly*, Vol. 31, Fall, 1954.

An estimated 100,000 to 125,000 words of newscopy flows into the AP from staffers, stringers, member papers, publicists, etc. for each news cycle. The exact amount of copy processed is not known.

NEWS FLOWS INTO THE AP AND THEN GOES

Out of this glut of copy, the AP editors select and transmit an average (based on 5-day sample) of 283 items totaling nearly 57,000 words. This big volume of news rolls across the US on its A,B,D and Sports wires each news cycle.

FROM AP BUREAUS TO TRUNK WIRES

From the mass of AP trunk news, Wisconsin's AP bureau selects, as an average, some 77 items and 13,352 words for retransmission to Wisconsin's non-metropolitan AP dailies. This is a carryover of 27.2% items, 23.5% words from the trunks. To these, Wisconsin adds some 45 stories and 6,000 words of Wisconsin news so that Wisconsin's dailies receive 122 items totaling 19,423 words as an average.

FROM TRUNKS TO WISCONSIN TTS WIRE

From this reduced, revised news report, four typical Wisconsin dailies select and use as an average 74 items and 12,848 words of wire copy. The four papers studied used from 55% to 87% of the Wisconsin AP TTS wire.

FROM WISCONSIN TTS WIRE TO DAILY NEWSPAPERS

The Continuing Study of Newspaper Reading and other reader-interest studies show that the average reader reads a fourth to a fifth of the stories printed in his paper.

FROM NEWSPAPERS TO READERS (?)

publicity teletype service, started in New York City in March, 1954, has spread widely because it meets the common needs of the publicists and the press. These publicity wires, for a fee, provide the client with swift transmission of his news, simultaneous release to all media (which eliminates charge of favoritism), and lend a flavor of news to the release, at least as the newsman is accustomed to perceiving news.

At the start of the 70s, P.R. Newswire, the pioneer service, was serving 230 news media in 50 cities of the nation, linked in a 6,200-mile, 100-word-a-minute Teletype network. P.R. Newswire's success brought similar services in the United States and around the world. Canada is served by the Canada News-Wire headquartered in Montreal. The key Canadian circuit reaches 40 outlets, including 35 of the most important Canadian dailies. Canada News-Wire is partly owned by Universal News Service, started in London in 1959 by Alfred Geiringer, veteran Reuters' executive. UNS offers a world-wide business news service. Universal has offices in Bonn, Madrid, Paris, Los Angeles, Montreal, Vancouver, and Tokyo. In the United States, it operates through PR Newswire facilities. Unlike most of the other services, Universal reserves the right to "spike" a client's story if its editors do not deem it newsworthy. Given the swift growth of international business and the mounting requirements for prompt disclosure of business information, these services seem likely to develop into a world-wide supplemental business wire.[11] In the United States there are two nationally competitive companies—P.R. Newswire and P.R. Wire Service, Inc.—and five regional teletype distributing agencies in Chicago, Detroit, Washington, D.C., San Francisco-Los Angeles, and Dallas-Houston.

Use of this Teletype transmission of publicity releases has been hastened by the SEC requirements, discussed in Chapter Twenty and by traffic congestion in major cities. In 1966, PR Newswire started feeding its clients' releases directly into stockbrokers' offices on a separate broker line, thus giving the Dow Jones News Service its first competition in 80 years. PR Newswire states that its Prompt-Disclosure Broker Line "was expressly designed to aid publicly owned corporations in complying with stock exchange and Securities and Exchange Commission 'timely disclosure' requirements." Another way of disseminating such information as required by the SEC is that developed by the Financial Relations Board, a Chicago agency. After the business wires are given ample processing time, the Financial Relations Board transmits complete transcripts of press releases for publicly-owned companies to leading financial analysts over a "conference call" hook-up of A.T.&T.'s T.W.X.

Another large portion of newspaper content is supplied by the feature, photo, and specialized news syndicates. Here, as in the case of the wire service, placement of a picture or a feature with a syndicate assures wide, economical coverage and increases the acceptability of material. For example, the feature service, NEA—Newspaper Enterprise Association—serves some 800 daily newspapers in the United States and Canada and supplies colored comics to 386 Sunday and weekend papers. In addition, nearly 500 weekly papers use its features. A typical feature service, NEA provides pictures, comics, sports features, news features, woman's page features, columns, editorials—in fact, everything a newspaper needs, down to fillers. Material can be channeled to the press through such syn-

[11] For more on PR Wires: Victor J. Danilov, "The News Wire Story," *Public Relations Journal*, Vol. 16, December, 1960; Philip N. Schuyler, "Business Publicity Flows to Media via PR Circuits," *Editor & Publisher*, Vol. 93, July 30, 1960.

dicates as NEA, King's Feature Service, United Features, and many others. There are also feature syndicates which supply client-sponsored material to the press without charge to the newspaper. The client pays the bill. Typical of these is Derus, headquartered in Chicago.

A complete list of feature and specialized syndicate outlets for publicity is published annually in the *Editor & Publisher International Yearbook*. The 1970 edition, for example, listed 320 general feature services. Many of them deal in a specialized type of news, such as *Science Service, Religious News Service,* and *Fine Arts Features.* A story carefully targeted on the right syndicate will get a nationwide ride.

In dealing with the daily newspaper, the publicist quickly learns the importance of dealing with the specialist in the newspaper office. If it is a sports event that he seeks to promote, he works directly with the sports department. If it is a straight news story of local interest, he deals with either the city editor or the reporter on the specific assignment. If the publicity program is aimed at the feminine reader, then he channels material through the woman's editor or the society editor. It is helpful to remember that no two newspaper organizations are exactly alike. The same titles often mean different things on different newspapers.

The publicist should be especially alert to the publicity possibilities of the Sunday newspaper, which, in many ways, is much different. The Sunday newspaper generally gets a longer, more intensive reading on a full day of leisure. It tends to emphasize feature material—copy without a time element—more than the daily paper does. Special features and pictures without a time peg are supplied early in the week. Because of the now standard five-day work week, news is relatively scarce on Sundays and Mondays. Thus, newspapers are more receptive to material on these publication days. The publicist must also know and use the Sunday supplement magazines, such as *Parade* and *Family Weekly,* circulated nationally, and the local weekend magazine developed by large-city newspapers. In 1969, *Parade* had a circulation of 13,925,091, *Family Weekly* 5,860,714. The content of these two national supplements and the local "Sundays" —some are distributed on Saturdays—tends to be more magazine than newspaper. Most of them try to straddle the magazine and newspaper worlds. Some of their predecessors died from being too general, too bland.[12] Most of these supplements prefer to put their own writers on a story, rather than to take one from a publicist. They are eager for tips and story memos. Through them you can reach the major market centers of the nation.

[12] George P. Nicholas, "National Sunday Supplements: A Prime Publicity Target," *Public Relations Journal,* Vol. 24, December, 1968. Outdated by *This Week's* demise in late 1969.

THE MAGAZINE MARKET

The broad array of American magazines, from the giants such as *Reader's Digest, Life, Look,* and *McCall's* to the trade journals such as *Woman's Wear Daily* and *Furniture Digest* to the recreational magazines such as *Yachting,* provide another effective publicity medium. The number, variety, and circulations of magazines are almost limitless. There are more than 950 general consumer magazines in the United States. Of these, 40 percent are edited for general appeal; 10 percent provide news and commentary; 6 percent are aimed at the woman; 18 percent are for farmers and farm families; and 26 percent are comic magazines designed for children. Within each of these categories there is wide variation. In addition to these general magazines, there are thousands of trade and specialized publications.

There is a magazine or periodical catering to every known interest, vocation, and hobby of the American. For the promoter of pet foods, for example, there are these possible outlets: *All Pets Magazine, The Aquarium, Audubon Magazine, Cats Magazine, Our Dumb Animals, Popular Dogs,* and so forth. To reach the larger, more influential market of women —consumers, voters, and shareholders—there is a strong group of women's magazines. For the young girl there is *Seventeen, Co-Ed,* and others, reaching a group with much spending power; for the woman in her twenties, there is *Glamour;* for homemakers and career women the publicist can use the channels of *McCall's, Ladies Home Journal,* and *Good Housekeeping.*[13] The trend in magazines is from the general to the specialized publication. For example, *Homemaker's Digest* is aimed at women living in single dwellings with two or more children and living on incomes of $8,000 or more. For the youth market there is *Eye,* aimed at the 16 to 20-year-olds, *Careers Today,* for college seniors and graduate students, and *Outasite,* a pop music fan monthly. To reach today's college men, the publicist can aim his shots at *Esquire, Playboy,* and *Sports Illustrated.* The readers of each magazine have distinct, non-interchangeable characteristics. This is increasingly true as readers shift from the large general magazines of massive circulations to more specialized publications. This specialization of magazines enables the publicist to aim his message accurately at a specific group—a fundamental of effective communication,[14] particularly as the public becomes more segmented. Some see in this trend a decline

---

[13] See Robert E. Doherty, "Our Class-Conscious Women's Magazines," *Nieman Reports,* Vol. 17, September, 1963.

[14] For overview of magazines, see Theodore H. Peterson, *Magazines in the Twentieth Century,* Urbana: University of Illinois Press, Rev. 1964.

in the influence of the mass media and a corresponding rise in power of specialized media. However, it should not be overlooked that the mass media cater to various specialized segments of the total audience.

The publicist should not overlook the opportunities offered by a new breed of magazines—the slick city magazine, e.g. *Philadelphia, Atlanta, Los Angeles, New York*. Their approach to journalism has been described as a marriage between, say, *Harper's* and *Ramparts*. Many of course are inoffensive slicks that provide publicity outlets to reach the affluent in a city. The better ones, however, are providing a stimulating challenge to urban dailies and to national publications.[15]

Opinion leaders read many magazines. The survey, *Public Use of the Library and Other Sources of Information,* records that "seven out of ten adults report reading at least one magazine regularly." Lazarsfeld and Kendall reported in their book, *Radio Listening in America,* that 61 percent of persons interviewed read at least one magazine regularly. Magazines provide more durable information than newspapers. The magazine reader has the opportunity to read, reread, discuss, and debate the information gleaned from this source. There is a trend in general magazines away from fiction and entertainment features toward more investigative and interpretative reporting of current controversial issues. The vitality and force of magazines in shaping opinions, fashioning clothes, designing houses, setting standards for profession or business, and enlisting political support have been demonstrated since the first two American magazines were published in January, 1741.

Somewhat apart are the news magazines which want information of a spot-news nature and which emphasize the time element, except for special features in "the back of the book." From these, the practitioner builds a series of specialized mailing lists to reach his particular publics. Publicity placement should be preceded by a careful analysis of the publication's readers, its editorial formula, its advertising content, and the market it serves. As Clay Schoenfeld, both a magazine writer and practitioner, counsels: "The best hint on how to communicate with a particular magazine audience is the magazine itself. If the editor weren't communicating well, he wouldn't be in business." The smart publicist studies the magazine's topics, style, policies, trends, format, and so forth, and then translates this knowledge into slanting his pieces for a particular publication.

The practitioner can build a working list by using the resources of Ayer's *Directory, The Writer's Market* (published annually by *Writer's Digest,* a magazine for free-lancers), Bacon's *Publicity Checker,* also published annually, and the Standard Rate and Data Service directories.

Magazine publicity is supplementary to press publicity. In working

15 Bob Abel, "The City Slickers," *Columbia Journalism Review*, Vol. 7, Spring, 1968.

with mass-circulation magazines of general interest and those dealing with broad groups in our population—women's magazines, men's magazines, and so forth—the publicist generally does not submit prepared material. Rather he works on a tip or query basis when he has something which would have reader appeal for these broad audiences. He submits story outlines or feature suggestions. If one is accepted, he then works with the magazine's staff or free-lance writers in its development. The job here is one of selling an idea and then providing cooperation to writer and photographer, who build the idea into an article.

An avenue of approach often used, but sometimes overlooked, is that of dealing with a free-lancer. Free-lance writers who sell to the national magazines are interested in "a real *account* of an institution, a man, or an event which possesses at least one of these three qualities: (1) national importance or significance; (2) elements of struggle, conflict, contest, or drama; (3) anecdotal enrichment and entertainment value." It is common practice to give a free-lancer a good story to develop. The free-lancer gets a check; the publicist, a publicity break in a magazine. The Society of Magazine Writers, 520 Fifth Avenue, New York City, maintains a referral service through which public relations officials can tap a pool of professional writing skill for special projects.

BUSINESS AND PROFESSIONAL PUBLICATIONS

Several thousand publications serving the specialized needs of professional groups, trade associations, or business and industry offer countless opportunities to the alert practitioner. These publications generally will use prepared news releases, if the content serves their readers' economic or professional needs. The business press includes some 2,600 magazines, newspapers, and directories with a total circulation of more than 62-million. Each caters to a carefully-defined audience composed of highly motivated men and women.

Here, too, many publicists fail to do their homework and consequently miss their target. In a survey covering 348 editors of U. S. and Canadian business publications, Paul Wichterman found: [16]

> Fewer than 100 of those questioned received fewer than 100 news releases per month, while 19 publications get an average of more than 1,000 a month.
> Of the 346 editors, 99 said that 25 to 50 percent of the material they received was of at least some value.

[16] "A Quantitative/Qualitative Analysis of Industrial Publicity . . ." (Master's thesis, Ohio State University, 1964).

Many made the comment: "Too many public relations people use the 'shotgun' technique for sending out releases."

The great competition for editorial space is reflected in the fact that 161 editors use 25 percent or less of the relevant releases received.

The growth of business and technical publications to accommodate exploding knowledge in all fields poses productive possibilities for the publicist who has ideas and pinpoints his target. This requires a staff of writers who can make complex technology understandable and who provide accurate information. There is increasing demand from the public for scientific and technological information in easy-to-understand language. This publicity outlet will grow rapidly in the years ahead.

THE RADIO AUDIENCE

Radio broadcasts are a part of our daily life and exert strong influence. Radio broadcasting has adjusted itself to TV and reasserted its place in the mass-communications net. Radio offers a wide range of possibilities to the publicist. It reaches the breakfast table and living room, rides to and from work in the car, invades the bedroom, and goes along to the beach, to the woods, and even on fishing trips—a flexibility that TV finds hard to match. Its influence permeates every segment of society. Radio is a vital part of the American scene; it is a mobile medium in mobile America.

Radio's versatility is indicated by these examples. Texaco's long-term sponsorship of the Saturday afternoon Metropolitan Opera broadcasts has brought it the loyalty and patronage of opera fans—most of whom are affluent and influential in their communities. These broadcasts reach some two-million music lovers in the United States and Canada over a special network of 115 United States stations and 36 Canadian stations. Texaco's opera network includes both independent and network-affiliated stations— which illustrates how radio outlets can be tailored to a sponsor's market. Texaco views this program as a public relations vehicle and thus holds its commercials to the bare minimum. As one writer observes: "The commercials have a public relations impact that a hard pitch would destroy." [17]

Eastern Air Lines, like other carriers, was long plagued with the problem of its switchboards becoming jammed with calls from thousands of passengers and would-be passengers, all telephoning at the same time for information on departing and arriving flights. This communications jam resulted in irritations and lost customers. Eastern found its solution in

---

[17] L. L. L. Golden, "Ask the Man Who Listens," *Saturday Review*, Vol. 46, May 11, 1963.

radio. Eastern started *Flite-Facts*—announcements of approximately one minute each hour, seven days a week, from 6 A.M. and continuing 19 times through the day until midnight on one station in each of Eastern's ten key cities. To increase the reach of this program, Eastern made available, on loan, some 1,000 radios to the persons responsible for booking transportation in the large firms along its routes.[18]

Radio's vitality is reflected in the following figures. More than 98 percent of American homes, nearly 61-million in number, have radios. In 1970, there were nearly 200-million home radios in use, more than three per home. Another 75-million were in use in automobiles. These sets can receive programs up to 24 hours a day (a small number of stations operate around the clock) fed from more than 4,267 commercial AM stations, 2,070 commercial FM stations, and 391 noncommercial FM stations—a total of 7,599 radio stations. Radio stations blanket the nation, and today are almost as common in small towns as in larger cities. Radio is ubiquitous. Ninety-five percent of Americans over the age of 12 listen to radio and the average person spends 17 hours a week listening to radio. Though a mass medium, it possesses the qualities of a direct, personal touch, as it uses the spoken word, for the most part, to convey its message.

Arthur Godfrey, who has used radio effectively, put his finger on this *intimate* quality of radio in describing the turning point in his career. ". . . lying in that hospital listening to the radio, I realized for the first time how really intimate the medium is and how ridiculously ineffective most of the speakers were . . . they were not *talking,* they were *reading,* and therefore convincing no one. . . . I decided I'd do things differently. . . . When I face a mike I have a mental image of only one person listening to me and I talk to that one person."

Today's radio fare is largely built around music, weather, news, and sports, all heavily loaded with commercials. The disc jockey is a central figure in this program mix. Radio flourishes on conversation, debate, discussion, and talks. The increased emphasis on news and discussion-type programs—such as N.B.C.'s Weekend Monitor format—opens up many possibilities for the publicist. Talk shows and telephone interviews focusing on controversial issues have become increasingly popular in recent years, expanding opportunities for those with a message. Although radio offers a blanketing medium, it also can be used to select specific audiences— ranging from those who like classical music on FM stereo to those who listen to the rock stations.

One researcher has pointed out that ". . . although total program audience must always be of primary concern, a dissection of this audience

[18] Malcolm A. McIntyre, "How Eastern Keeps Its Seats Occupied and Its Phone Unoccupied," *Broadcasting*, May 14, 1962, p. 22.

is a tremendous value to many who would influence certain strata. Actually, the 'radio audience' is no more a homogeneous whole than is the population of the United States. It is composed of many 'cells' which can be stratified not only by economic group but also by geographic region, community size and character, family size and composition, etc." If you want to reach influentials, you sponsor classical music; if you want to reach a rural audience, you play folk music. If you want to reach today's lively, knowledgeable teen-agers, you do it through their favorite disc jockey. If you want to reach the broad span of the general public via radio, your best bet is the frequent newscast.

Radio is primarily a medium of news and of entertainment with commentaries, talk shows, and debate a growing factor. Its use as a public relations tool must be approached within this context. The ways to reach the radio audience are (1) through news and informational programs; (2) with programs of entertainment that will successfully compete with other program fare; and (3) through the feature programs, such as advice for the housewife. Methods of using radio include furnishing news, arranging for broadcast of special events, obtaining free "public service" time from the station for programs or from the sponsors of commercial programs, or by the purchase of paid time for a message.

Nonprofit organizations must depend primarily on public service programming. Public service time is seldom prime listening time, but it is not without value. In nonprime times, the competition with other stations is not so stiff, and one can still reach sizable audiences if the program fare attracts and holds listeners. In any event, radio requires a good bit of money in script and production costs as well as air time. These are the main possibilities in public service programming:

1. Special programs based on interviews, group discussions, demonstrations, and so forth, either in a series or in a one-time-only presentation.

2. Similar but shorter presentations inserted as "participating" features of other programs,

3. Brief spot announcements made at various times during a broadcast day. With radio's local format, the opportunities for free spots is much greater than it was formerly,

4. Personality spots made by on-the-air personalities, such as disc jockeys, farm directors, or directors of women's shows,

5. News items sent directly to the station or fed in by way of the station's news service,

6. Editorials prepared by the station endorsing your program or campaign.

Those who would use the broadcast channels to reach the public must bear in mind that stations are business enterprises operated to make a profit for their owners. Just as the newspaper has space to sell, the broadcaster has only one commodity, *time,* to sell. Except for bona fide public service announcements, the broadcaster ordinarily cannot afford to air free advertising. Thus, it is essential that the publicist seeking to use these outlets send genuinely *newsworthy* releases—written in the special style and format preferred for *on-the-air delivery*—to the news directors of stations or networks. United States broadcasters are complaining increasingly about the flood of so-called "news" releases and other efforts to get free air time. The publicist who gets his release back from a station or network along with an advertising rate card usually has no one but himself to blame.

Every listener survey shows newscasts at the top or near the top of the list of programs preferred by most listeners. By providing news for the radio newscast, the publicist can get a wide hearing for his story within the audience limits of a given station or set of stations. Radio newsrooms want news prepared for radio, not carbon copies or mimeographed copies of newspaper releases. They want news written for bulletin presentation. Radio news editors want all difficult names and words phoneticized for the announcer. A 100-word story is the headline story on the newscast. Radio must cover the world in 13.5 minutes; sometimes it does it in 4 minutes! Radio wants news written for the ear, not for the eye. Radio news must be informal, conversational, brief, to the point—and, above all, accurate! Once spoken, errors cannot be recalled and corrected. One never gets exactly the same audience twice in radio. Radio newsmen expect and deserve equal treatment with print journalists in the release of news and in the coverage of special events. Good results in radio news can be obtained by supplying tape-recorded interviews and news events.

Many institutions now provide stations a dial-access recorded newscast, which is kept updated as news develops. Stations serving the publicist's area are given an unlisted telephone number to receive these recorded newscasts. The playback system is automatic and does not require an attendant. Copy for the newscasts is prepared in the public relations office, then recorded on the tape. This then becomes available to the stations on a call-in basis. Many institutions have found it profitable to equip their publicists with cassette tape recorders so they can record interviews for this recorded newscast. This "hot-line" service is popular with radio stations in a day which emphasizes the "direct report."

Theodore Koop of CBS Radio counsels practitioners, ". . . for radio's sake, please call them news releases and not press releases. . . . The wordage of releases received in a single mail may equal those of a a novel. Yet CBS Radio News in Washington, for instance, broadcasts only about 8,500 words a day. . . . It is obvious that most releases are written by former newspapermen who think in newspaper terms. Many of them are only vaguely aware that radio and TV news have special requirements. . . . For radio and TV, the publicist must be content with hitting the high spots."

It is possible to get monitored transcripts on what radio and television are saying about one's clients. There are firms that provide "listening" service and will monitor specific stations or specific programs for a fee. The major one, Radio and TV Reports, operates in New York, Washington, Chicago, Los Angeles, Detroit, and San Francisco.

In working with the broadcast stations, the practitioner should know and observe the regulations imposed by federal law, particularly those 1960 amendments to the Federal Communications Act outlawing payola, plugola, and the rigging of question games. Also helpful to know are the FCC rules requiring equal time for "expression of the contrasting viewpoints," and the opportunity for an institution to reply to personal attacks and political editorials.

TELEVISION

The communication phenomenon of the century, television, has great force and scope as a publicity medium. Outstripping all other mass media, TV grew to full size in one decade—the 1950s. A medium which permits the use of the printed word, spoken word, pictures in motion, color, music, animation, and sound effects—all blended into one message—possesses unmeasured potency. It offers a vast range of possibilities for telling a story—from a terse, 60-second film clip on a TV newscast to a one-half-hour or one-hour documentary film. The powerful, pervasive impact of television was briefly discussed in Chapter Five. This impact is fast becoming world-wide with satellite transmission now commonplace.

Television has grown in scope and impact with incredible rapidity. It was developed on an experimental basis prior to World War II. The FCC authorized commercial TV to start July 1, 1941, but its full development was held back by the entry into World War II. Several stations went on the air soon after the war, but because of the problem of finding sufficient channels, the FCC froze all station applications from 1948 to 1952. From 1952 on, TV has grown rapidly in number of stations, size of audiences, and in perfection of its broadcast techniques, including color. In 1970, there were TV sets in 58,500,000 homes receiving programs broadcast from 877 TV stations—508 VHF and 187 UHF commercial stations, 182 non-commercial stations. There are nearly 100-million TV sets in operation in the United States, one-third of these color. No medium has ever developed so rapidly in size, scope, and strength. Yet many practitioners—most of whom formerly worked in the print media—do not fully comprehend and capitalize on TV's scope and strength. In one writer's opinion, "Of all the media presently at the disposal of the publicist, perhaps the least understood and most neglected are those of the electronic age—radio and television." [19]

TV's sharp impact on public opinion has been repeatedly and dramatically reflected in Presidential elections and in protests of the 1960s. The Presidential campaigns since 1956 have marked a definite break from the techniques that had been in vogue since late in the last century. The major candidates and parties today rely heavily on TV to get their message across. President Dwight D. Eisenhower helped shape the new campaign pattern with his reliance on television in 1956 in his campaign for re-election.

TV's power was clearly demonstrated in the 1960 election, when President John F. Kennedy turned the TV debates with his opponent, Richard M. Nixon, to his advantage. The "Great Debates" which brought the two contestants into direct confrontation in four nationally televised debates marked an important new development in American politics. If, as Theodore H. White suggests, "the TV debates did little to advance the reasonable discussion of the issues," they did give the voters a sense of participation in this contest. Dr. George Gallup estimates that a total of 35-million Americans watched one or more of the debates. Pollster Elmo Roper estimated that 57 percent of those who voted believed that the TV debates had influenced their decisions. President Kennedy himself testified following the election, "It was TV more than anything else that turned the tide." [20] His judgment is confirmed in research that found "the first debate appears to have set the pattern of change, with Kennedy's TV image becoming more favorable, while Nixon's becomes less favorable." [21]

Nixon, who had saved his political life with a dramatic TV appeal in the 1952 campaign, profited from his TV mistakes in 1960 to come back and win the Presidency in 1968. His skilled use of TV was a major factor in his narrow victory over Vice-President Hubert Humphrey. Guided by a large staff of TV experts, including Frank Shakespeare, now director of U.S.I.A., Nixon developed a warm, low-pressure, confident TV style. The main format chosen by his advisers was that of a controlled studio panel

[19] Jay Weitzner, "The Neglected Media," *Public Relations Journal,* Vol. 24, November, 1968. For glimpse of TV's power in selling goods see: Thomas Whiteside, "Annals of Television: Man From Iron City," *The New Yorker,* Vol. XLV, Sept. 27, 1969. Tells story of Rosser Reeves who developed hard-sell TV commercial.

[20] Quoted in Theodore H. White's, *The Making of a President, 1960* (New York: Atheneum Press, 1961), p. 294.

[21] "Candidate Images," a chapter by Percy H. Tannenbaum, Bradley S. Greenburg, and Fred R. Silverman in *The Great Debates,* edited by Sidney H. Kraus (Bloomington, Ind.: Indiana University Press, 1962), p. 281.

setting up questions for the candidate to answer. One who followed closely this TV work concluded: [22] "TV both reflected and contributed to his strength. Because he was winning he looked like a winner on the screen. Because he was suddenly projecting well on the medium he had feared, he went about his other tasks with assurance."

The powerful role of television in political campaigns suggests its power in any area of public discussion. This power also raises some basic questions for society. A total of $58.9-million dollars was spent for political broadcasting in the 1968 campaigns, 70 percent more than the $34.6-million reported spent in 1964. More than five-million political announcements were beamed over radio and television stations in 1968, according to the FCC. TV has skyrocketed campaign costs thus raising serious questions about the democratic process. TV's demand for colorful, photogenic personalities also raises serious implications for the nation's political process. There is growing indication that the mass media, particularly TV, have weakened the nation's political party system. Marshall McLuhan says, perhaps too sweepingly, "In all countries, the party system has folded like an organization chart. . . . The shaping of a candidate's integral image has taken the place of discussing conflicting points of view."

TV's power was noted in 1969 when the National Commission on the Causes and Prevention of Violence linked video violence to real violence, particularly in poorer families or in families that are disorganized or culturally deprived. In those cases, "in the absence of family, peer, and school relationships, television becomes the most compatible substitute for real life experiences," it noted. Much of this power flows from the fact that ninety-five percent of our homes have TV sets which are on forty hours a week. By the end of the 1960s, 59 percent of the persons in TV homes were getting most of their daily news from TV and 29 percent were getting their news only from TV. Further, 44 percent of the persons interviewed in a nationwide sample found TV the most believable source of news as against 21 percent who thought newspapers were the most believable medium.[23] Thus the publicist who gets his story told on TV news gets it told by a credible source.

A more comprehensive study concluded: "The average American viewer spends hours a day in front of his TV set and finds it a relaxing and pleasant—now an integral—part of his daily life: certainly not without important costs, but by and large, in his judgment, well worth them. . . .

---

[22] Joe McGinniss, *The Selling of the President 1968* (New York: Trident Press, 1969), pp. 39–40. Candid, unvarnished account of staff work behind Nixon's 1968 TV image. Provides many helpful hints.

[23] Roper Research Associates, "A Ten-Year View of Public Attitudes Toward Television and Other Mass Media 1959–1968," New York: Television Information Office, 745 Fifth Avenue, New York, N. Y.

The programs, on the whole, he considers good—somewhat better than satisfactory. . . . He would like TV to be more informative and educational but certainly not at the expense of entertainment. Aside from the day's news and weather—which he watches regularly—he rarely uses the set as a deliberate source of information." [24] Like radio, TV is primarily a news and entertainment medium and should be approached within this context.

Television has impact and realism, is welcomed into the home, and is readily available as a publicity medium for practitioners who will take the time and trouble to learn how to use it. An increasingly larger portion of TV time is being given to news broadcasts and to the news-documentary, social issues, and action coverage. These programs offer many opportunities to the alert publicist. Local stations find news coverage costly and welcome an assist from the source who can provide TV newsworthy film or relevant situations.

A United States Department of Commerce survey found that "All surveys indicate that television, in terms of (a) audience identification of the sponsor, (b) remembrance of, and understanding of, the sales point of the commercial, and (c) sales results produced, has greater sales producing impact per person reached than any other advertising medium." Other media dispute these conclusions.

On using TV as a public relations tool, Sydney H. Eiges offers this counsel.

> Networks have the glamour, the star appeal and the high-budget programs, but in public relations thinking, television should also be considered as a service provided in hundreds of communities by individual stations. Each of these stations is essentially concerned with its own community. . . . Identifying a story with that of the community at large arouses the interest of the local station and wins its cooperation. . . . Planning a campaign on a local basis can often be more productive than aiming only at networks which are of necessity more difficult to crack. Material and ideas should be aimed specifically at individual communities or regions. Stations should be approached individually and personally.

A local-station TV executive offers these tips to practitioners seeking time on local TV stations: (1) Approach the right person in the station. (2) Have a definite plan to discuss. (3) Have an idea with audience appeal, so that the station won't lose its viewers while your program is on the air. (4) Program idea must be within the station's capabilities. (5) Don't

---

[24] Gary A. Steiner, *The People Look at Television. A Study of Audience Attitudes.* (New York: Alfred A. Knopf, 1963), pp. 228–29. A voluminous report on a far-reaching study of attitudes toward this powerful new medium.

forget to say "Thanks." For the local nonprofit agencies without money and manpower, TV news and hitchhiking spot announcements offer the cheapest and easiest ways to reach the TV audience.

Thus far, TV has developed these formats for its programming: (1) Studio productions—musicals, comedy, drama, vaudeville, puppet shows, audience-participation shows, and so forth; (2) Remote broadcasts of sports events, public events, political conventions, congressional hearings, and so forth; (3) Films—old or reissued Hollywood movies, special documentaries, and films prepared for other audiences. As it has developed its own pattern of programming, TV has borrowed heavily from radio, journalism, Hollywood, and the stage. Selling story ideas to TV producers, getting personalities on the audience-participation shows, getting plugs on the conversation-type shows (for example NBC's *Today* and *Tonight* shows and the CBS and ABC nightly talk shows) and providing film for news and documentary programs are the most common methods the publicist uses to insert his message into this powerful medium. Most TV stations now broadcast in color, thus prefer color film and slides. Publicists must remember that the TV screen is a *horizontal,* not vertical medium; thus, the TV editor wants horizontal, not vertical pictures and slides. The TV newscaster also wants news prepared for TV, not lengthly newspaper handouts.

The expanded news-magazine type news program on TV, on both network and local stations, offers additional opportunities to organizations. On these 30-minute news-magazine programs there is need for short features as well as for spot-news film. The increased use of the documentary format enables organizations to "sell" program ideas to TV producers and sponsors that will carry their message to a large nationwide audience that believes what it sees on TV. One major obstacle to widespread use of TV as a publicity medium is the heavy cost of preparing and producing programs. Here, as in the case of films, the cost of per-person impact rather than initial outlay should be weighed.

Though it may be costly to sponsors and stations, TV programming is within the capability of nonprofit institutions if their counselors use initiative and imagination. The University of California, San Diego, has demonstrated this in recent years. A comparatively new institution, U.C.S.D. suffered initially from constant TV coverage of its protesting students who irritated the conservative San Diego community. U.C.S.D. hired a TV coordinator who showed that the University could make positive use of TV's power. She knew that TV needs and uses vast amounts of material; she saw that the problem was to make material available to the five local TV stations in such a way that it would be acceptable to both the program producers and the University community.

The TV Coordinator: Kept the stations informed on campus events;

provided background material; helped them locate principals involved in news stories; arranged news conferences before the TV film processing deadline; encouraged administrators to be available for short interviews; provided slides of newsmakers to be used with telephone statements; assisted assignment editors by finding professors who could be tied into national news breaks; looked for special stories with a high visual impact —e.g. the glass blower who makes special equipment for scientific experiments; studied local shows and looked for university persons who would fit into their pattern; and provided material and guests for the educational television station.

In one year, on a limited budget, U.C.S.D. provided over 300 segments of TV programming and balanced the news coverage of unfavorable news with news of positive accomplishments on the campus.[25]

The key to unlock the electronic media is knowledge of their news values, program needs, and changing technical requirements. For example, the Electronic Video Recorder (E.V.R.) discussed in Chapter 12, will greatly expand the opportunities to tell one's story on television. Here is a list of publications that will enable the practitioner to keep abreast of the electronic media so that he can tailor his publicity to their changing requirements:

> *AV Communication Review,* published quarterly by the Dept. of Audio-Visual Instruction, National Education Association.
> *Broadcasting,* weekly trade journal, and its annual *Broadcasting Yearbook,* which lists all stations, are essential tools in the practitioner's office.
> *Educational Broadcasting Review,* bi-monthly, National Association of Educational Broadcasters, Washington, D.C.
> *Journal of Broadcasting,* quarterly, Temple University, Philadelphia.
> *Television Age,* bi-weekly, Television Editorial Corp., New York City.
> *TV Guide,* weekly, designed for the listener.

CASE PROBLEM

Your university is sponsoring for the tenth summer a four weeks' course for utility-company middle-management executives. This is one of several such courses your school sponsors annually to provide the refresher training de-

---

[25] Mrs. Ardys Heise, "The New Look in Television Relations," speech in *Proceedings 1969 Mid-West Public Relations Conference* (Madison, Wis.: Journalism Extension Division, University of Wisconsin, 1970).

manded by businessmen. Enrollment is limited to thirty-five. Companies represented include telephone companies, Bell System affiliates and independents, gas, power, and light companies. Enrollees this year include accountants, engineers, sales managers, power superintendents, telephone district managers, and so forth. Those enrolled for this year's course come from Spokane, Seattle, and Bellingham, Washington; Boise, Idaho; Butte, Montana; San Diego, San Francisco, and Los Angeles, California; Denver, Colorado; Salt Lake City, Utah; St. Louis, Missouri; and Shreveport, Louisiana.

You have been asked by the Dean of the College of Business Administration to publicize this event in the daily and weekly press, trade journals, and house publications. Prepare a list of publicity outlets to cover your community, your university's region of influence, the enrollees' hometowns, and the trade journals in the fields represented. Use directories cited in this chapter as your sources.

ADDITIONAL READING

IRVING E. FANG, *Television News,* New York: Hastings House, Publishers, 1968.

ROBERT L. HILLIARD, *Writing for Television and Radio.* New York: Hastings House, 1967.

JOSEPH T. KLAPPER, *The Effects of Mass Communication.* New York: The Free Press of Glencoe, Inc., 1960.

Radio Television News Directors Association, *Television Newsfilm Standards Manual.* New York: Time, Inc., Joint product of RTNDA and Time-Life Broadcast, 1965.

Radio Television News Directors Association, *The Newsroom and the Newscast.* New York: Time, Inc., 1966.

CLARENCE SCHOENFELD, *Publicity Media and Methods.* New York: The Macmillan Company, 1963.

CLARENCE SCHOENFELD, *Effective Feature Writing.* New York: Harper, 1960.

JAMES W. SCHWARTZ, ed. *The Publicity Process.* Ames, Ia.: Iowa State University Press, 1966. One of the most recent and best books on "how to" aspects of publicity.

JOHN CAMERON SIM, *The Grass Roots Press: America's Community Newspapers.* Ames, Ia.: Iowa State University Press, 1969.

HARRY J. SKORNIA, *Television and the News. A Critical Appraisal.* Palo Alto, Calif.: Pacific Books, 1968. Strong criticism of present practices, past performance in TV news coverage.

CHARLES STEINBERG, ed. *Mass Media and Communication.* New York: Hastings House, 1965. Readings on how media function and how they serve society.

ROBERT E. SUMMERS and HARRISON B. SUMMERS, *Broadcasting and the Public.* Belmont, Calif.: Wadsworth, 1966. Complete description of our broadcast system.

ROBERT B. RHODE and FLOYD H. McCALL, *Introduction to Photography.* New York: Macmillan, 1965.

ROLAND E. WOLSELEY, *Understanding Magazines*. Ames, Iowa: Iowa State University, 2nd Ed., 1969.

HERBERT ZETTL, *Television Production Handbook*. Belmont, Calif.: Wadsworth Publishing Co., 2nd Ed., 1969.

CHAPTER 17

WORKING WITH THE MEDIA

Good media relationships are earned through honest, helpful news service provided in an atmosphere of mutual respect and candor.

News media relations represent an important part of the practitioner's daily work. The practitioner's standing with the media managers can shape and limit his accomplishments. Their confidence in him is one of his valuable assets, a fact too little appreciated. Though clients or employers come and go, the press and its gatekeepers are here forever. It is also important to understand the fundamentals. (In this discussion, the term *press* is used broadly to include all news media.)

THE MAN IN THE MIDDLE

To be effective in his role as go-between, the practitioner must have the full confidence of his organization and of the press. This is not easy. Their interests often conflict. Organizations want news reported in a manner that will promote their objectives and will not cause them trouble. The press wants news that will interest readers and viewers. Administrators complain: "Why does the press always sensationalize things?" "The papers never get things right." "They take things out of context." "You can't trust reporters." "I didn't say that at all." "Why do reporters enjoy stirring up trouble?" Newsmen counter-complain: "That organization will never come clean." "They won't give us the real news, only a lot of puffs." "They won't let you in to see the men with the news." "What are they trying to hide?" Both sides have a point. The man in the middle must *patiently* bring each side around to understand the problems and viewpoints of the other. This *is* public relations!

PRESS RELATIONS

It is important to keep in mind the underlying conflict of interest that always hovers in the background of this relationship. This basic difference between the publicist's advancing a particular cause and the newsman's representing the public point of view is a healthy thing. It should be so viewed by both parties. This clash of interest is often emotionalized beyond all proportion, but it does exist and is to be reckoned with. The irritation

407

of the press is understandable. It is all too often flooded with uninteresting, poorly written releases. Too often the publicist drowns a few facts in a sea of words in an effort to get more news space. Or a newspaperman may encounter a tightly drawn news-release curtain put up by an inept practitioner or by order of the boss. On the other hand, the media often fail to recognize the service provided in filling a void in comprehensive, constructive coverage. Practitioners comprise an influential and integral part of the nation's news system.

The basic conflict lies in the never-ending quest of the media for exciting news, in their efforts to keep the news stream uncontaminated, and the need for money coming into their cash registers. On the other side are individuals, institutions, and industries that find it imperative to have their stories told to the public with accuracy and fairness. For this task, the practitioner's expertise is essential. Much of the public relations effort goes into trying to put news about an institution into a total mosaic that lends perspective. Too often the news media are only interested in colorful fragments.

The media's definition of "news" is at the heart of this problem. Consider these examples: A Catholic archbishop criticizes, with reason, the two major wire services when they base their nationally-circulated story on seven lines of a twenty-page document issued after prolonged deliberation by America's Roman Catholic bishops. A Congressman who visited twenty-two of the nation's colleges, as part of a Congressional task force, later charged the media with having "dramatized, sensationalized, and vividly highlighted campus violence with the result that the public thinks violence is the only thing taking place on our campuses." Mayor Richard J. Daley of Chicago spoke for many administrators when he complained of the media's tendency to give page-one coverage to negative news of violence and conflict but, conversely, little attention to the constructive acts to ease tensions and to eliminate discrimination. An example of this kind of coverage was cited by Douglass Cater while serving in the Johnson Administration. Despite the dire predictions of congestion and chaos that Medicare would bring, its start was, on the whole, smooth and successful. Yet one TV network devoted five minutes of prime time to a twelve-bed hospital in Callaway, Nebraska, which had a grievance against Medicare— a newscast which left the viewer with an impression of nationwide bureaucratic blundering.[1] These examples could be multiplied many times.

Nonetheless, America's newsmen, generally speaking, are competent and fair-minded and do a good job reporting the day's news within the

---

[1] Douglass Cater, "For the Record," *The Reporter,* December 15, 1966, p. 26. Also: Lewis Donohew, "Newspaper Gatekeepers and Forces in the News Channel," *Public Opinion Quarterly,* Vol. 31, Spring, 1967. A case study in forces governing play of news. Max Ways, "What's Wrong With the News? It Isn't Enough," *Fortune,* October, 1969. Questions emphasis on outdated news practices.

limitations imposed by the nation's news system. Understandably, they are irked when criticized by those in high places who object to the ways of the news. For example, Secretary of State Dean Rusk, in a St. Valentine's Day interview in 1968, charged that newsmen seek only something to "bitch about" in hopes of winning a Pulitzer Prize. He taunted interviewers: "There gets to a point when the question is, 'Whose side are you on?' " [2] In November, 1969, Vice-President Agnew charged that "a narrow and distorted picture of America often emerges from the television news," prepared by "a little group of men . . . who admit their own biases."

But the media's news values are not the only source of conflict. The media's lack of manpower in numbers and in expertise to cover today's broad spectrum of complex news is part of the problem.[3] The limitations of time and news space, either print or electronic, also result in a condensation that often distorts a lengthy and complex story. Another important ingredient in this conflict is the frequent charge of denial of access to the news media altogether.

The wry view of the practitioner and his work held by at least some newsmen is reflected in the Associated Press Managing Editors' manual, *APME Guidelines:* [4]

> A flack is a person who makes all or part of his income by obtaining space in newspapers without cost to himself or his clients. Usually a professional . . . they are known formally as public relations men. The flack is the modern equivalent of the cavalier highwayman of old. . . . A flack is a flack. His job is to say kind things about his client. He will not lie very often, but much of the time he tells less than the whole story. You do not owe the P.R. man anything. The owner of the newspaper, not the flack, pays your salary. Your immediate job is to serve the readers, not the man who would raid your columns.

It might be helpful to list the grievances on both sides of the fence.[5] These are the complaints most often heard from the press:

---

[2] Quoted in DeWayne B. Johnson, "Vietnam: Report Card on the Press Corps at War," *Journalism Quarterly,* Vol. 46, Spring, 1969, p. 12.

[3] For example, the Associated Press has some 88 editorial workers in its Washington Bureau, the largest one in the capital, yet this staff can only "skim" the vast amount of complex news pouring out of the Federal government. For elaboration, see: Jules Witcover, "Washington: The Workhorse Wire Services," *Columbia Journalism Review,* Vol. 8, Summer, 1969.

[4] Loose-leafed manual prepared by APME for managing editors and their associates in 1969. Available from the Associated Press, New York City. Quote on page 44.

[5] See: Bernard E. Ury, "A Question for Editors: What are you doing to PR?" *Editor & Publisher,* February 1, 1969, pp. 18 and 22; Victor J. Danilov, "Business Editors List PR Likes and Dislikes," *Editor & Publisher,* September 14, 1957. For example of why editors continue to look with disdain on public relations counselors, see *Public Relations News,* Vol. 25, August 25, 1969.

1. Attempts by practitioners to color and check the free flow of legitimate news.

2. Space grabbing for "free advertising" with consequent loss of revenue to media.

3. Attempted "influence" and pressure methods of getting into news columns; indirect and sometimes direct bribery of reporters.

4. Gross ignorance of media's editorial requirements; no conception of what news is or how it should be written.

5. Raiding news staffs of experienced men with the lure of higher salaries.

Countercharges most frequently listed by the practitioner include:

1. Failure of the press to do its whole job; failure to increase its reportorial staff to keep pace with the expanding list of socially significant activities demanding news coverage (in the fields of industry, finance, education, medicine, and so forth).

2. The press's slowly changing definition of news which puts emphasis on conflict and minimizes the socially constructive events—the press's sensationalism.

3. Failure to treat news as news regardless of the source; that the attacks on publicity are only lip service to rationalize a basic money motive.

4. Failure to discriminate between the honest, helpful practitioner and the incompetent.

5. Increasing dependence of the press on the function it so frequently and lustily condemns.

PUBLICITY PRINCIPLES

Good relationships can best be achieved by the practice of a few basic principles: (1) *Shoot Squarely;* (2) *Give Service;* (3) *Don't Beg or Carp;* (4) *Don't Ask for Kills;* (5) *Don't Flood Media;* (6) *Keep Updated Lists.*

SHOOT SQUARELY

It is not just an academic nicety to counsel that "honesty is the best policy" in dealing with the press. It is plain common sense. The press men and women are alert, intelligent, critical, and, with very few exceptions, honest. They can spot a phony or shady practice a mile off. They see so many of both. It is their job to get the news and they generally get it, one way or another. Anyone who tries to thwart or block them through trickery, evasion, and censorship will encounter tough opposition. A publicist may win the battle in such instances, but he is likely to lose the war. The press fires the last shot. Unless a practitioner has the confidence and goodwill of the media gatekeepers, his value to an employer is minimal. This confidence is compounded of a record of *accuracy, integrity, and performance.*

Newspapermen are shrewd, understanding, and sophisticated people. They know the hokum of circus publicity but they play along with it, because they, like all Americans, love a circus. They recognize the inflated and artificial news pegs in the publicity output of a local charity or civic event, and they still use the stuff. They understand and appreciate the position of the man charged with making the most favorable presentation of his cause that the facts will allow. His stuff may be rewritten or tossed aside. If he is candid, he won't lose their confidence.

Out-and-out dishonesty is shortsighted and stupid. The first rule for sound publicity practice is to *be candid and cooperative.* The open-door policy is best. Holding that "the day-to-day stories about us in your local newspaper and on the air publicly measure Quaker's success at being a good business citizen," the Quaker Oats Company advises its staff: "The public, particularly in our plant communities, has a right to know anything about Quaker which is not confidential, as production figures are, for reasons of competition. And the press and radio wants to tell as much of Quaker's story as it considers newsworthy."

Here are some bad examples: (1) An Eastern plastics maker had a major explosion. Plant officials admitted newsmen to a plant meeting where they were allowed to wait but were told nothing. Reporters finally got the story from the hospitals, and, in many cases, they were the first to notify families of injured workmen. (2) A Midwest chemical plant call for fire protection while plant workers repaired a break in a chlorine gas line accidentally became exaggerated into a major poison-gas threat. School children were sent home as radio broadcasters flashed warnings. Plant officials, knowing the danger to be slight, could have eased this anxiety, but when the press called, they were not available!

The *Wall Street Journal* reports this example: A Cleveland company refused reporters' requests for a statement on how the company was doing during a period of slack demand. Shortly after, there was a rumor on Wall Street that the company was going in the red in the current quarter. It took a quick statement to the press pinpointing the less severe extent of the decline in earnings to halt an unjustified tumble in the price of the company's stock.

Another example: Ponder the consternation and ire of the British press when after months of advance publicity from both the Cunard Line and the Upper Clyde Shipbuilders about the Queen Elizabeth 2, newsmen were barred from the contract signing which turned the new luxury liner over to Cunard. This snub to newsmen apparently came in response to unfavorable publicity accorded the new ship in its shakedown period.

Despite the unhappy consequences which almost inevitably follow attempts to suppress bad news, executives—human as they are—persist. In a state hospital, a woman about to undergo surgery was killed when the anesthetic was exploded by a static spark. Hospital administrators persuaded the local press to suppress the story because of its possible effect on other surgery patients. Within 24 hours, the community was rife with gruesome rumors spread by the family, friends, nurses, and interns. The story, in three days, reached a metropolitan paper, which broke it on page one. The story rode high on the front pages of the state press for almost a week. The hospital was sharply criticized for its efforts to suppress a tragedy for which, in the beginning, it was blameless. And as is usually the case, _the rumors were worse than the published facts_.

In sharp contrast was the way a Milwaukee hospital handled a similar story a few years later. It quickly made available to the press an accurate and complete reporting of the death of a child in an anesthetic accident. The story was carried through two news cycles and then dropped. Public confidence in the hospital and respect for the medical profession were, if anything, enhanced. When a suppressed story is exposed, it is played far beyond its normal news value. And the suppressor is thought to be guilty of wrong because he tried to hide it. Executives must be counseled against efforts to suppress, to abuse the "off the record" tradition by using it as a gag, or to bottle up news to which the press has reasonable claim. Governmental agencies are being continually criticized on this score.

A perfect illustration of the folly of news suppression is seen in the celebrated case of Army Private William S. Girard, who killed a Japanese woman while she was picking up scrap metal on an Army range in Japan. Because an Army officer made the mistake of trying to suppress this unfortunate incident, the Girard Case became a serious political issue between the United States and Japan, brought our government great embarrassment, and brought the Army unfavorable publicity around the world. What would have been a small, routine one-day story was turned into an unfavorable banner-line story that lived for months.

Such efforts to balk newsmen breed attitudes reflected in this memo of a Detroit news bureau chief to his home office:

> The motto of the _____ corporation's press relations staff, according to one of them, is "We'll give you anything but information." He said it in jest, but the harsh fact is that too often this slogan is observed. _____ guys are, with few exceptions, personable, pleasant fellows. . . . But try for facts and you're up against a wall. Let it be quickly said that _____ is not alone in this regard. . . . The essence of each group's system is this: Avoid answering a question at all if pos-

sible. If not, give as vague and inconsequential an answer as possible. And always strive to keep the P.R. man in between the primary source and the newsman.

. . . This very quickly forces the conscientious and resourceful reporter into a couple of courses. He can battle the system frontally and spend all his time and energy fighting with public relations men in an effort to see the people he wants to see. This, in my opinion, is not the best course in Detroit. . . . The better method is to sneak around them. This system, however, has some real limitations.

Another fundamental principle is that *a publicist cannot favor one news outlet at the expense of others*. When he gets caught, he risks the confidence and good will of other news outlets. The publicity tune has to be played straight across the keyboard. This is not easy in a cacophony of stiff competition, wire service against wire service, newspapers against newspapers, or newspapers against radio and TV stations. The safest rule is that spot news should go out as fast as possible. Let the news determine the cycle in which it breaks. News and feature material for which the time peg can be fixed should be alternated evenly among the competitors. As a corollary of this, the publicist must protect a newsman's initiative in going after a story. If a reporter gets a tip on a story and asks for the information, it belongs to him. The same information should not be given to other outlets unless they come after it. This, too, will even out on the long pull. It is a policy with which no reporter can justly quarrel.

GIVE SERVICE

The quickest, surest way to gain the cooperation of media men and women is to provide them with *interesting, timely stories and pictures* that they want *when they want them* and in the *form in which they can readily use them.* Newsmen lean on and cooperate with the practitioner who willingly responds to a midnight call for a picture and biographical sketch of an executive who just died. News is a highly perishable commodity and occurs around the clock. Newspaper and newscast deadlines must be met around the clock. *The practitioner, likewise, must be on call around the clock.*

What does the press want? The *Syracuse Post-Standard* bluntly tells practitioners: "We don't want your publicity. We do welcome your *news*." William M. Hines, Jr., of the *Washington Star* explains: "We want ideas, truth and assistance." A *Newsweek* reporter advises: "We want reliable news and reliable background information. . . . We're interested in new developments, new products, new services, new enterprises, new methods of doing business." Another newsman counsels: "If you have a story a commentator likes, he'll take it. Have all the facts of the story ready when you suggest it. Know a man's deadlines."

DON'T BEG OR CARP

Nothing irritates media men and women more than a publicist who begs or carps. If the material is not sufficiently newsworthy to earn space in print or time on the air, it is not likely to attract interest in the audience. The editorial people get and hold their jobs by knowing what interests people. Don't beg to have stories used. Don't complain about the treatment of a story if it is used. Don't ask editors to serve as clipping bureaus by asking for tear sheets. One exasperated city editor expressed the irritation produced by these amateurish approaches when he wrote:

> Please, mister, if that's a handout in your hand, just give it to me. That's all there is to it. If we can use it, I'll ask a reporter to rewrite it. If we can't use it, I'll throw it away. Don't hold it under my nose and read it to me with your finger tracing every line. I can read. . . . And don't suggest that we have a little talk about it. I haven't got time for conferences. . . . No use standing there. There are sixteen more press agents waiting to see me.

Too many people who deal with the press try to be "editors" on the assumption that they know as much about defining or writing news as the editor or reporter. Too many executives insist on news releases as they would like to have them appear in print or on the air. They refuse to accept the fact that this is the newsman's job.[6]

The admonition, "Don't Beg," also covers a warning against trying to pressure publicity into news columns and newscasts by using advertising as a wedge or weapon. There is nothing an independent journalist resents more than to have the publicist work through the advertising department. In most cases, it won't work and will bring only resentment. Advertising belongs in the advertising department, and news—if it is news—will get in the news columns or newscasts. As Johns-Manville counsels in its press handbook: *"The press should not have to beg for news and Johns-Manville should never beg for free space."*

Despite the predictable backfire, some organizations try, from time to time, to use advertising as a club. Some business firms try to work out a publicity-for-advertising deal. On occasion they are successful. In most

---

[6] Robert B. McIntyre, "Good Press Relations Is Key to Good PR," *Editor & Publisher*, May 26, 1962.

cases the media willing to make such a deal are not effective vehicles for either publicity or advertising. A more common headache for the practitioner is in restraining executives who lose their tempers and withdraw advertising in retaliation for publication of unfavorable or undesirable news. Advertising stands alone. So does news.

Even the pros make this mistake once in a while. A few years ago the *Wall Street Journal* published six months in advance of the usual unveiling the details of the new car models of the Big Four car makers. The same day General Motors cancelled $11,000 worth of advertising scheduled for that paper. GM also took the *Journal* off its news-release list. This hasty action brought severe criticism. *Editor & Publisher,* voice of editors, said that General Motors's "sledgehammer retaliation through advertising dollars and control of news releases seems to us to be far below the dignity of such a mammoth corporation and more befitting the pique of a corner druggist." General Motors, in calmer wisdom, shortly restored its advertising in the *Journal* and called the matter closed. A Colorado brewery pulled its advertising from a newspaper which editorially criticized its labor policies and then put it back with due apology. A Portland, Oregon, department store did the same thing. Such instances underline the need for a "church-and-state" relationship between the public relations and advertising functions.

DON'T ASK FOR KILLS

A publicity man has no right to ask a newspaper, magazine, or radio station to suppress or kill a story. To any newsman this is a crude insult. It is asking media men and women to betray their trust. It seldom works and brings only ill will as a reward. *The way to keep unfavorable stories out of the press is to keep situations which produce such stories from taking place.* There are occasions when it is perfectly legitimate to request a delay in publication or to explain to the press any part of a story that might be damaging to the public interest. If there are valid reasons, cards should be laid on the table, face up. The newspapers will cooperate 99 times out of 100. If more than two people know a story, the chances of suppressing it are almost nil.

These principles or "rules of the game" can serve to establish profitable press relationships. One editor once told a group that the press wants *honesty, speed, brevity, confidence.* Another newspaperman advises: "Be frank, be as cooperative in giving bad news as the good, realize that what your organization does affects a good many people in the community and they have a right to honest reports about your activities." Good press relations flow from the unreserved acceptance that the public has a right to public information. *Good press relationships must be earned.*

DON'T FLOOD MEDIA

Study and experience teach the boundaries of news interest, and common sense dictates respect for them. If a financial editor repeatedly receives from the same source items appropriate for the fashion or sports editor, he loses respect for that source. A tendency of the inept and the opportunistic publicist is to flood all media with all releases and thus, theoretically, increase the potential circulation and exposure. This reasoning is fallacious. It identifies the publicist as being untrained or incompetent and his employer or client as being unreasonable, unknowledgeable, or unethical. As *Forbes'* editors complain: "We're constantly being plagued by PR men who come bounding into the office or who telephone bubbling over with 'a great story idea.' They're right; it's a great story idea—for them, but not for our readers who are busy men."

In the preparation of news material, the potentially interested audiences should be selected and catered to, and in the distribution those media which normally and naturally serve that audience should be thoroughly covered, with special consideration where a special "angle" is involved.

KEEP LISTS UP TO DATE

There is a transiency and mortality of press personnel and of media which require that distribution lists be dynamic. This means continuous updating. The purchase of annual media directories by departments and agencies represents a productive economy.

Few things could be more annoying to an editor than to receive news addressed to the person he or she had replaced in the job two or three years earlier. The same reaction occurs when a publication or station outlet receives news material forwarded from or misaddressed to a location it vacated years earlier.

The sophisticated practitioner will use modern data processing to keep his mailing lists up to date and to target his releases to specific audiences with interest in their content.

Perceptive practitioners have found it productive, also, to keep close track of key media and personal acquaintances in them. Not all do this. *Time Magazine,* in its 1967 "Essay on Public Relations," reported that "throughout the entire sixteen weeks that *The New York Herald Tribune* was struck in 1963, releases continued to pour into its offices—some of them by special messenger."

Student summer internships in public relations offices are often concerned with the updating and evaluating of mailing lists and the maintenance of an alert attitude toward special media relationships. It is an important experience, of value to the future practitioner.

THE NEWS CONFERENCE

Frequently used as the occasion for the release of news and as a vehicle to cultivate good media relations is the news conference. There is no better way to give out a story simultaneously to all media, provided the subject is newsworthy. When is a news conference justified? The best practical answer is, "Seldom!" Nothing could be more embarrassing to an educator, businessman, military or civil official than to find, on exposure to the press, that his viewpoint or his announcement contained scant news value. Both he and the press should be spared that. Generally, important controversial matters such as labor-management disputes, political pronouncements, and major industrial policy changes suggest a conference, because a discussion, rather than a one-sided statement, is in order. In this era of science, complex matters which require backgrounding, such as a technological breakthrough, often justify a conference. Simple matters which constitute no public issue or are not complex in nature usually can be handled without one. In this category could be such matters as a new consumer product or the results of a charity drive.

There are, of course, exceptions. A special event, like the annual introduction of new automobiles, lavish with showmanship or drama, may not contain a public issue or complexity. But the spectacle, the impact, broad public interest, and the opportunities for feature and photographic angles make it desirable that it be witnessed personally. The same applies for the exposure of celebrities on occasion.

Who should be invited to a news conference? As a rule of thumb: everyone representing news media who will not go away disappointed. If in doubt about a particular medium, it is well to make inquiry in advance. For local events having national significance, the local press should always be given the same welcome and courtesy extended those from out of town. In modern news networks, most local press is linked up with a national or international association.

With the high degree of mobility and instant-communications in society today, location of a press conference does not have the critical aspects of former times. Given a choice, a location handy for the newsmen involved should be a consideration. Their time is precious. Some firms have equipped trailers as press rooms, thus can take the press room to location of an event. This facility has proved popular with newsmen covering stories in remote locations.

As host for the conference, there should be an executive or official of the organization functioning as spokesman. On hand also should be experts and specialists capable of being interviewed in depth concerning the particular news matter at hand. All members of the organization participating in the conference should be briefed in advance on the most probable questions that will be put by press members. That will facilitate the answers, provide complete accuracy, place the organization in a favorable light, and put everyone at ease. If the conference takes place at a meal time, a meal should be served, and the conference should proceed during the meal. If refreshments are indicated, serve them. Neither should delay the news beyond the appointed time.

How should guests be invited? Invitations should be oral whenever possible. If written, they should be informal and friendly. A telegram, or follow-up telephone call sometimes lends a touch of urgency to an invitation.

What equipment should be on hand? For a spot-news break, telephones should be handy, and representatives of the wireless service should be standing by. Typewriters, paper, and working space will most likely be needed. For discussion groups, when the news does not have the same urgency, comfort is a prime consideration. For crowds over fifty people, public address equipment is indicated.

Kits containing information and photographs pertaining to the meeting should be passed out, preferably at the beginning, with time to examine them, so that reporters can know what questions they want answered. If the story is complex, exhibits or demonstrations are very much in order. They tend to lighten heavy news substance and enable reporters to interpret in language that readers can readily understand.

The conflicting requirements and spirited competition between reporters from radio and television as against those from the print media pose a difficult problem for the sponsor of a press conference. Space requirements and the distractions of TV cameras, lighting equipment, and so forth, make it difficult to accommodate both electronic and print media reporters in the same conference. Whirring TV cameras that muffle the interviewee's words and block reporters' views of the speaker and the eagerness of some reporters to be seen on TV are common causes of complaint by veteran news reporters. Some practitioners have developed the practice of having two conferences, one for the electronic media, one for the print media. Press invited but unable to attend should be sent the news material.

THE EXCLUSIVE INTERVIEW

There are many occasions in large entities, and in response to competition among media, which produce interviews between an official and a reporter. The principles cited earlier apply, with additional responsibilities on the part of whichever one solicited the interview.

When the newsman seeks the interview, the burden of guiding the discussion is on him. If requested he may submit an advance outline of the information he seeks, whether it be concerned with the university president's views on student alienation or the Army general's views of Vietnam.

When the newsmaker seeks the occasion, in hope that a profile of his organization or a white paper on his viewpoints, will result, he and his public relations advisor assume the burden. The proposal or suggestion to the reporter should state the general subject matter desired to be covered and render an opinion of its news validity. If it should be a union-management settlement, what is unusual or unique about it that recommends an interview? Areas considered secret or privileged should be mutually understood ahead of time. The union leader who seeks an interview to air a favorable settlement but does not wish to reveal the vote count of union members should preclude the question. The interview, itself, must be characterized by a maximum of candor on the part of the newsmaker. His ease and candor must indicate that he has done his homework. "Off the record," "I'd rather not comment on that" and disclaimers must be used sparingly. Otherwise, the newsman will use the option of seeking and quoting other sources for the information withheld.

When the interview and its subject matter lends itself to photography, this should be anticipated with whatever props or arrangements are relevant. Tape recording of interviews is desirable for both parties.

TWO FINAL NOTES

The *news conference* should not be confused or mixed with the *press party* or *junket*. Newsmen and women prefer not to mix their work and their fun. There is a time and a place for each.

Regarding souvenirs and gifts: To the extent that they are not expensive and are pertinent to the occasion, propriety and taste would approve. Items like imprinted plastic brief cases or note pads, key chains or holders with the organization's emblem, luggage tags or passport holders, food or confection samples, are safely free from criticism as being coercive. Extremely questionable, however, are irrelevant gifts such as boxes of candy on Valentine Day, cases of whiskey at Christmas, overpaid travel allowances when travel is in order, interest-free loans, costly product gifts, and ridiculous discounts.

PREPARATION OF NEWS

In preparing news for the press, radio, or television, the questions Who?, What?, Where?, When?, Why?, and How? should be answered. Preferably, they should be answered in the first sentence or the first paragraph with details following.

As an example, (who?) John Jones (what?) died (where?) in his home at 10 Main Street (when?) at six o'clock Wednesday evening (why?) of a heart attack brought on by overwork. (How?) He had returned home

Walter W. Seifert
School of Journalism
Ohio State University
242 West 18th Avenue
Columbus, Ohio 43210
  PHONE: 293-2683 (Area 614)

Immediate Release

Skip 2" for

headline

COLUMBUS, OHIO, OCT. 31---Basic rules for preparing
and placing effective news releases were suggested
here today by Walter W. Seifert, associate professor,
School of Journalism, Ohio State University.

Releases should be mimeographed cleanly on white
8 1/2" x 11" paper, Seifert said. They should be mailed
first class to all logical mass media, including radio
and television news directors, weekly papers and trade
magazines. Individually-typed copies should be
delivered personally to city editors of local dailies,
he suggested.

Other rules are:

IDENTIFICATION: The name, address and telephone
number of the author should appear at upper left.

RELEASE DATE: Most releases should be "immediate."
Only stipulate time when news obviously warrants holding
until a certain hour.

MARGINS: Use wide margins, so editors can edit.

HEADLINES: Do not indicate a headline. (That's
the editor's business.) Skip two inches between release line and body of copy so editor or rewrite
desk can insert desired headline.

---more---

$8\frac{1}{2}$" × 11"

Release Rules   2-2-2-2

    LENGTH: Never make a release two pages if one will
do. Edit your material tightly. Make sure it's accurate,
timely and not too pluggy. Don't split a paragraph from
first to second page. Put "more" at bottom of first
page.

    SLUGLINE: Put the traditional journalistic slugline
at upper left of second page. Indicate pages as shown
above.

    AVOID: Fancy tinted, printed news bureau stationery
is in poor taste. It looks commercial and doesn't fit
normal copy style. Don't shout NEWS. Editors decide that!

    STYLE: Use summary lead (Who, what, when, where, why)
most of the time. Doublespace. Prefer short, punchy
sentences with active verbs. Make sure spelling and grammar
are 100%.

    CHECK: Never trust your typist. Proofread every
stencil. Get client to initial a file copy of each release.
Don't hesitate to check your copy with your sources.

    PLACEMENT: Take general news to local city desks.
Don't arrive near deadline. (2 P.M. is good for most AM'S
and PM'S). Discuss special news with specialized writers.
Send comprehensive factsheets on major developments that
merit staff coverage. Query magazine editors on prospective articles to get their slant. Never place same story
twice with same publication!

    AT END: Put this
                    -30-

            Or this
                    ###

in midafternoon complaining of a difficulty in breathing and was dead when the doctor arrived.

To assure accuracy in transmission, news copy should be typewritten. Changes of text should be clearly indicated following the accepted rules of marking manuscript. Typewritten copy should be written on plain white paper of the standard 8½ by 11-inch size. Text should be double-spaced for print media, triple-spaced for electronic media. Paragraphs should be indented at least five typewriter spaces. Only one side of the paper should be used. If text runs more than one sheet, the word "more" should be placed at the bottom of each sheet except the last one, and page numbers should be used. The name, address, and telephone number of the person supplying the news should be written on the release so that it can be verified readily by the publication if desired. A sample release is shown on page 420.

The release must be tailored for its medium. Write news stories for newspapers; articles for trade and business publications; terse radio-style releases for radio; TV news scripts for TV. After many years of TV, practitioners continue to swamp that potent medium with newspaper releases, usually to no avail.

Practitioners should be alert to the practice of a few editors to serve notice to charge for printing releases. Jay Morton, a Florida weekly publisher, billed companies for printing publicity. When they refused to pay, he took them to court and won.

PHOTOGRAPHS

In an increasing variety of news, a photograph is invaluable. Quite often the photograph is, in itself, the news. If ever in doubt, a photograph should be included. The *matte-finish* still picture or one- to two-minute film clip is almost a must for television news. TV is primarily a visual medium. TV releases call for pictures, pictographs, screen slides, and film clips. The matte-finish photos for TV use should be horizontals in the ratio of 4 units of width to 3 units of height. This is the shape in which TV information is transmitted. This age of pictorial journalism has put a new premium on the good publicity picture. Ditto for the pictograph.

One successful practitioner counsels: "Good pictorial coverage is . . . the key. Photographers should never be assigned 'to get some pictures.' Pictures are an intrinsic part of any story, not a by-product. The two basic approaches in greatest demand by the print media are: the 35 mm human-interest approach that attempts to capture reality through the use of natural lighting and an unposed look at the subject matter; and the elaborately prepared, posed, and lighted 'setup' shot that depends for its impact on sharpness, clarity, and dramatic composition."

Photographs should be used by the publicist for what they are—*an economical, effective means of reporting a story*. Take, for example, the publicity photograph (shown on page 424) set up by a noted British firm to dramatize the strength of its renowned bone china. Wedgwood's public relations department arranged for this truck to be balanced on four china teacups to demonstrate their strength. The Tower Bridge of London added the authentic British background. Such a photo was bound to get wide coverage—as this one did. Another example of imaginative use of photos to get publicity was that of a transit company which took a night photograph of all its buses, lighted and arranged in the form of a Christmas tree, as a way of saying "Merry Christmas" to its patrons through the local newspaper. Photographs are especially effective in conveying the needs and values of welfare services. One such user is the Cincinnati Family Service Agency, whose photographer says: "Photographs 'spell out' a story more quickly, clearly, and powerfully than any other means of communication, perhaps because of their inherent capacity for conveying mood and evoking emotional response." [7]

Generally, the less descriptive matter needed to amplify or to explain the photograph, the better the acceptance. The best photographs of dramatic events are those that need no explanation beyond identification. An example would be a scene showing a wrecked car photographed from such an angle that the reader could see the street marker at the corner, the clock on a nearby store, a body in the street, and the upset bicycle nearby. That tells almost the entire story except for the name of the victim.

Photographs of groups of more than six or eight people discourage publication because of the space required for identification. Activity implied in a photograph will give it greater interest. This sometimes eliminates the need for identifying all persons.

People being photographed have great trouble with their hands and feet. If standing, they don't know what to do with their hands. If seated, their feet seem to get in the way. Objects held in the hand and objects placed in front of the feet tend to relieve the awkwardness.

Rarely will an experienced photographer provide for publication any type of reprints other than glossy ones. No other kind should be submitted for publication unless specifically requested. Many publicists use a standard-sized print, say 7 x 9 or 8 x 10, to effect savings.

A saying nearly as old as the press is that babies, animals, and pretty girls are sure-fire news pictures. A minority of projects are involved with the interests of these three subjects, but by clever arrangements it is quite often possible to tie in one of them with news subjects as seemingly remote

[7] Margaret R. Weiss, "Communicating a Community Service," *Saturday Review*, Vol. 46, September, 1963.

as a new wastebasket or an institution's participation in an anti-pollution campaign.[8]

ESSENTIALS OF GOOD COPY

Essentials of good publicity copy are essentials of good news writing. A few reminders can serve as a checklist.

CONTENT

Will the information or news really interest the intended audience?

Does the information answer every reasonable question that readers or listeners may ask?

Is the significance of the information explained in terms of audience?

Is the copy sufficiently newsworthy to survive stiff competition for public attention?

Will the information further the objectives of our institution? Is it useful?

[8] Mel Snyder, "How to Get the Best in Pictures," *Public Relations Journal*, Vol. 25, March, 1969.

Does the publicity accurately reflect the character and nature of the institution it represents?

Are the facts, names, and dates ACCURATE? Are technical terms explained?

STYLE AND STRUCTURE

Will the lead catch and hold the busy reader's attention? Will it produce a bright, eye-catching headline? Is the lead terse, to the point?

Do the facts of the story support the lead in fact and spirit?

Is it readable copy, stripped of superlatives? Good news copy must be CURT, CLEAR, CONCISE.

Has padding been stripped from the copy? (If you don't do this, the editor will!) Is the copy free of the charge that it is an effort to get "free advertising"?

Is the information presented as dramatically as possible with this set of facts? Squeeze all the news value you can into your story but don't exaggerate!

MECHANICS

Is copy legible, double-spaced, each page or ad correctly marked, end of story indicated?

Is source of release fully, correctly given? Easy for editor to check back with source if necessary?

If a fixed time is intended for release of story, is it plainly indicated on the outgoing release?

Is top third of first page blank, for editors who write heads directly on copy?

Is copy of genuine interest to readers of each publication slated to receive release? If not, don't send it.

Would the information be of genuine interest to an audience not provided for in present list? If so, what other outlets should receive copy?

Will the release reach intended outlets while information is still fresh, timely?

If you can answer these questions affirmatively, your copy should pass muster with the toughest-minded news editor. If you can't, you had better take another look at your story. *News is* anything *timely* that is *interesting* and *significant to readers* in respect to their personal affairs or their relation to society. The best news is that which possesses the greatest degree of this interest and significance for the greatest number.

AN EDITOR'S SCORECARD

On the basis of its *fact-finding* to determine editors' attitudes toward the press relations practices of business, Opinion Research Corporation has drawn up this score sheet by which an organization may measure its performance in the eyes of the press.

	(check one)	
	YES	NO
1. Does the company have a sense of what is newsworthy and what is not?	_____	_____
2. Is the company generally willing to give out information?	_____	_____
3. Can we rely on the company's word—are they honest in their dealings with us?	_____	_____
4. Is there someone in the company we can go to when we need information?	_____	_____
5. Is the company aware of *our* problems—deadlines, reader interest, how a release is written, etc.?	_____	_____
6. Are we well acquainted with the company—do we know their people and do they know us?	_____	_____
7. Does the company ever take the initiative—not always make us dig out the news ourselves?	_____	_____

Identical surveys conducted in 1962 and 1968 among the nation's leading business and financial writers by the Opinion Research Corporation made clear that for successful press relations "quality and selectivity must somehow replace quantity." These surveys showed a disturbing trend in corporate public relations: Editors thought there was less effort to provide a free flow of information in 1968 than in 1962. The results also showed that corporations do not make sufficient use of interviews with top officials. More editors would like features and would appreciate opportunities to visit the organization. Results of the 1962 and 1968 surveys are given below.*

MOST IMPORTANT FACTORS IN PRESS RELATIONS PROGRAMS

	TOTAL EDITORS	
	1968	1962
Provide free flow of honest information	39%	54%
Make top executives available to answer questions	30	27
Have competent public relations people	19	16
Acquire a better sense of what is news	15	17
Be prompt in dealing with the press	12	18
Send clear, concise copy	10	7
Don't withhold bad news	8	11
Have more personal contact	8	2

EDITORS' RATINGS OF INFORMATION SOURCES AND MATERIAL

	TOTAL EDITORS		
	Used too rarely	*About often enough*	*Used too often*
Interviews with top officers	63%	31	3
Features that are not necessarily "hard news"	50%	30	19
Visits to company installations	46%	41	9
Industrial photographs as "page brighteners"	34%	31	28
Biographical information on management	23%	52	23
Press conferences	19%	47	30
Photographs accompanying releases	14%	52	30
Mailed releases on financial results	7%	79	13
Mailed releases on general corporate news	4%	55	40
Mailed releases on product news	3%	50	45

LIKELIHOOD OF NEWS TOPICS BEING PUBLISHED

	TOTAL EDITORS		
	Very likely	*Somewhat likely*	*Not too likely*
Annual report of earnings	63%	20	15
R&D breakthrough	56%	36	6
Local plant or office construction	54%	16	29
Change in local executives	54%	7	38
Labor contract negotiations	54%	25	19
Wage hike or added benefits	50%	22	25
Quarterly report of earnings	49%	23	27
Financial outlook for the future	43%	46	10
Contract award, new business	42%	38	20
New product or service	36%	33	29
Litigation, patent suits	35%	38	25
Change in headquarters executives	32%	36	31
Scholarships, aid to education	22%	30	46
Participation in community affairs	19%	33	46
Government relations activity	13%	45	37
Contribution to charity	11%	26	61
Speech to other businessmen	9%	45	44
Construction, other than local	9%	39	51
New advertising campaign	5%	18	76
Company picnic or party	4%	9	83

* John S. Schafer, "What the Editor Thinks About Publicity,"
Public Relations Journal, Vol. 25, January, 1969.

A nationally known chemical manufacturer opened a plant in the hills of a southeastern state. The location was chosen on the basis of labor supply, raw materials, tax rates, and humidity conditions. Shortly thereafter, in an interview with local editors and wire service reporters, a top company executive said: "One of our major reasons for locating here—and thus one of our contributions to this community—was to help raise the standard of living of these hillbillies."

The story was widely reported. A storm broke. Nationally known natives of the state wrote burning letters to the newspapers. A syndicated columnist wrote a column, half in anger, half in fun. The governor, senators, and other politicians got into the act with duly indignant protests. People in the community expressed bitter resentment.

As public relations director, what do you recommend be done to remedy or repair this situation?

ADDITIONAL READING

JOHN BROOKS, "Business Parties . . . and the Free Loader," *Harper's Magazine,* Vol. 208, April, 1954.

MARION CRACRAFT, "If I Were a Public Relations Man Trying to Get Along with Newspapers," *Public Relations Journal,* Vol. 11, May, 1955.

DAVIS DOUTHIT, "Nationwide Insurance: Problem in Sponsoring a Television Program," *ibid.,* Vol. 19, August, 1963.

"How·to Prepare for a Press Interview," *Business Management,* April, 1964.

JACK B. KENNETT, "Pressroom on Wheels," *Public Relations Journal,* Vol. 25, February, 1969.

SONDRA K. GORNEY, "All-Out Service Provides for Large-scale Press Coverage," *Public Relations Journal,* Vol. 16, November, 1960.

"How to Handle Press Contacts During an Emergency," *ibid.,* Vol. 18, September, 1962.

CARROLL A. LAKE, "Planning Makes a Press Tour Click," *ibid.,* Vol. 14, January, 1958.

"School for Scribes," *Industrial Marketing,* March, 1967. Describes week-long course Hill & Knowlton conducts to provide writers with background knowledge of steel industry.

ARTHUR D. STAMLER, "Public Service Time—An Opportunity for PR," *Public Relations Journal,* Vol. 25, October, 1969. Suggests radio and TV welcome well-packaged, non-commercial material.

THOMAS WHITESIDE, "Corridor of Mirrors, The Television Editorial Process, Chicago," *Columbia Journalism Review,* Vol. 7, Winter, 1968/1969. TV's much debated coverage of the Democrats' 1968 Convention.

CHAPTER 18

THE PRACTICE: PUBLIC RELATIONS FOR BUSINESS

Public relations has had its most extensive development in business.[1] The
pervading concept has been that the immediate public interest and the
ultimate progress of all society is served in the successful and honorable
operation of business. The public relations efforts, therefore, have concentrated on interpreting the actions and policies of the corporation or industry
to the publics whose support is sought and on interpreting public reactions
and responses to corporate administration.

The efforts variously have included:

. . . identification with nonprofit sectors such as education, the arts,
health, and welfare.

. . . projects and publicity to reinforce marketing

. . . endorsement of, and nominal participation in, programs for
the resolution of social problems

. . . use of visual identification symbols to portray the unity,
modernity, or some other desirable characteristic of a conglomerate
or an entity undergoing renovation

. . . actions which portray personalized corporate statesmanship or
management or which popularize business views or personalities

. . . efforts to influence decisions on public issues or legislation

. . . staged events which commemorate or otherwise eulogize and
punctuate growth and progress

. . . the reporting of financial results

. . . participation in hometown improvements, celebrations, and
civic affairs

. . . programs concerned with international expansion

*Public relations mindedness, or its lack, has often been a crucial
factor in corporate success or failure.*

THE HISTORICAL BACKDROP

At the close of War II, the vast industrial machine reverted to peacetime pursuits. Big Business decided in 1946 that public good will had
diminished.

[1] For its beginnings in business in this century, see: Alan R. Raucher, *Public Relations and
Business, 1900–1929.*

To counter adverse views of the public, industry embarked on a grand scale economic education campaign to repopularize itself. The campaign, nationally advertised and publicized, explained the direct cause-and-effect relationship between the free enterprise system and the high standard of living in America, compared with the rest of the world.

The multi-million dollar effort was not effective in any significant way. It did convince many in industry that an abstract idea could not be sold in the same way as a new bar of soap. It raised a question among many professional communicators concerning the effectiveness of promoting high standards of living at a time when most people's stomachs were full.

In the latter part of the 1950s, industry tended to alter the theme of its postwar bid for popular approval from "how would you like to own this washing machine?" to "American ingenuity has taken the drudgery out of washday." The message became less concerned with whetting the appetite for material possessions in a nation of affluence and more concerned with the relationship between affluence and human "progress."

After analyzing some of the early efforts to resell "free enterprise," to reaffirm appreciation of the ultimate role of profits in our economic system, and to otherwise project a favorable image, *Fortune's* William Whyte concluded that better understanding hinged on closer cooperation between each corporation and its publics on matters of mutual concern. Whyte had seen part of the problem, but there was more to it.

INDUSTRY WAS INADEQUATELY INFORMED

Many industrialists, influenced by their practitioners, came to realize in the 1950s that they did not possess much useful and factual information about how their employees, hometowners, investors, or even their customers really felt about them: their bigness, their power, their integrity, the wisdom or objectivity of their views on public issues, or how well they were performing their role at any given moment, not in bygone decades or generations. *There was need for more sophisticated in-bound communication from industry's publics.*

Part of the void was occasioned by the traditional viewpoint that industry's destiny derived from keeping the consumer happy. This rationale held that, as long as business was good, the consumer was expressing his happiness.

A RETURN TO THE FUNDAMENTAL OF FACT-FINDING

On the positive side of the scales, research into public attitudes began to increase in the 1950s. Some depth studies showed interesting and promising results. A typical study was that by Social Research Inc., reported by Burleigh B. Gardner and Lee Rainwater.[2]

Gardner and Rainwater studied the "middle majority" or mass market, totaling 65 percent of the population, as distinguished from the factory wage earner. This middle majority was found to have five definite favorable attitudes toward big business.

1. Big Business is seen as the pace setter of the American economy.
2. Only Big Business can handle the job of production.
3. Big Business is good because the mass production techniques provide goods of uniform quality and at a low cost.
4. Big Business is good because it invests heavily in research and development.
5. Big Business provides many jobs and greater opportunity to work.

In another survey, Fisher and Withey found no clear-cut stereotypes, but a mixture of attitudes. They concluded that ". . . a large portion of those regarding the 'good' effects as more important lodge considerable criticism against Big Business activities, desire its power reduced and favor government control." The data clearly indicated also, that many good points in the functioning of business were seen by those who stressed the "bad" effects. The net sum found in this study was that "evaluation of Big Business arouses . . . a general tendency to stress good points."[3]

Other surveys through that period indicated that public opposition to government control of the economy had weakened and "because the inroads of government are a gradual process, people see no cause for alarm."

Businessmen were more concerned about government intervention in the economy than were the voters. Businessmen saw government as the umpire, who assures that rules of fair play are observed in the marketplace; the public showed itself receptive to having the federal government shoulder the burden, particularly on widely publicized needs. The public was pragmatic, not doctrinaire—rural citizens did not want "public ownership of utilities," they wanted electricity on the farms.

A VARIETY OF VIEWPOINTS

Granting business certain virtues, surveys in the 1950s and since have left little doubt that the individual retains anxieties of serious proportions about

[2] Burleigh B. Gardner and Lee Rainwater, "The Mass Image of Big Business," *Harvard Business Review*, Vol. 33, November–December, 1955.
[3] Burton Fisher and Stephen B. Withey, "Big Business as the People See It" (Ann Arbor: University of Michigan Survey Research Center, December, 1951).

bigness in almost any form that can be used against him, from whatever direction it comes.

For industry's part, there has been, and continues to be a reluctance to view its publics as comprised of many-sided individuals: *employee, voter, tenant, taxpayer, parent, soldier, borrower,* or *shopper,* as the case may be. With a multiplicity of roles, the individual has a variety of contrasting convictions and anxieties. He is an economic being, a social and political being. While shopping, he is the boss; while a tenant or an employee, he is dependent on others.

There is consequently the paradox of the same person in many roles, reacting differently in each one, changing views to fit a changing environment and life style.

Thus, in his job he may be uneasy about the power of the giant corporation over him; yet on payday, he may go to the grocery store and, freely choose the products made by giant corporations. He would like to feel that his free choices are not over-priced, misleadingly labelled or advertised. He expects them to be properly packaged and adequately warrantied. As a consumer the citizen has become increasingly articulate, and legislation has enabled him to act effectively.

The individual would like to believe that Big Businessmen share some of his anxieties and take their social and moral obligations as seriously as suggested in the words of one "Big Businessman," Lammont duPont Copeland.

> . . . business is a means to an end for society and not an end in itself, and therefore business must act in concert with a broad public interest and serve objectives of mankind and society or it will not survive.

EVIDENCE TO THE CONTRARY

Unfortunately, through the 1960s the performance of Big Business in the area of ethical conduct too frequently failed to reassure the publics of its good intent. Self-discipline was inadequate to preclude the threat and imposition of more and more legal restraints.

Critics and opponents have repeatedly been rearmed. One classic case occurred when some twenty-nine electrical companies admitted rigging their prices in a collusion which spanned *seven years.*[4] One writer said ". . . the electrical conspiracy is but one instance in a disheartening pattern of hundreds of similar antitrust violations in many industries."[5]

---

[4] The electrical price-fix story is recorded in two books as well as in the periodical press of that period. See John G. Fuller, *The Gentlemen Conspirators* (New York: Grove Press, 1962); John Herling, *The Great Conspiracy* (Washington, D.C., R. B. Luce, 1962).

[5] Harvey Bresler in a book review in *Saturday Review,* Vol. 45, March 10, 1962, p. 18.

Polls taken by Opinion Research Corporation in 1967, among 6,304 persons, showed "every indication of greater public receptivity for more government intervention, whether in the antitrust field or the consumer protection area." [6] Still, there is increasing need for freedom for business in its own eyes. J. K. Galbraith, in *The New Industrial State,* writes: [7] "The modern large corporation is adapted to the needs of advanced technology and the large amounts of capital and comprehensive planning which this requires. It reflects the need of its techno-structure for freedom from out-side interference." Preservation of this requisite freedom is the first task of today's businessman.

The flaunting of public interest persists. There have been nationally publicized cases of excessive profiteering on defense contracts, false and misleading advertising, inadequate and improper labeling, meaningless warranties, defective products, exorbitant service charges and poor service.

A piece of legislation, major in that it forecast the need for consumer protection by law, was the Kefauver-Harris Drug Amendments Act of 1962.

Several more laws followed. Among those enacted:

Fair Packaging & Labeling Act	1966
National Traffic and Motor Vehicle Safety Act	1966
Child Protection Act (toys)	1966
Drug Abuse Amendment	1966
Cigarette Labeling Act	1966
Wholesome Meat Act	1967
Flammable Fabrics Act	1967
Clinical Laboratories Act	1967
Fire Research & Safety Act	1968
Truth in Lending	1968
Natural Gas Pipeline Safety	1968
National Commission on Product Safety	1969
Public Health Smoking Act	1970

Consumer protection has been accelerating at the federal level. By 1967, more than 31,000 government employees were working on consumer oriented federal projects costing nearly $300-million. President Johnson added a Special Assistant for Consumer Affairs. President Nixon carried forward the effort. He sought legislation to establish the consumer office in the White House on a permanent basis, to enable consumers to band together to sue sellers for deceptive practices, and to establish a new division of consumer protection in the Department of Justice. Response to the growing demands of the consumer has been similarly reflected in state and local governments.

[6] *Public Opinion Index,* Vol. 25, November 15, 1967, O.R.C., Princeton, N.J.
[7] Published by Houghton Mifflin Co., Boston, in 1967. Fresh provocative look at the American business system.

The business response has been more defensive than corrective. For example, when an offshore oil operation polluted the waters along a stretch of California coast and killed thousands of birds, the ensuing public debate was more concerned with the misquoting of a Union Oil official about the value of bird life than with the question of pollution control or prevention by the oil industry. The threat of serious oil pollution from off-shore drilling and ever larger tankers—from the Atlantic to Alaska—has not been fully acknowledged by the industry.

In 1967, five leading drugmakers were convicted of fixing the price of a medicine so that for a long span of years it had sold at an exorbitant ratio to its cost. A capsule costing less than two cents sold for as much as fifty-one cents, according to Justice Department charges. In 1969, the companies, insisting that no antitrust law had been violated, nonetheless offered to settle treble damages claims amounting to $120-million.

From the actions of a few tend to come the labels put on all. When a nationally prominent businessman in the late 1960s was sentenced for conspiracy and perjury for falsifying financial reports, all those signing financial reports were suspect by those whose preconditioned attitude toward business was unfavorable.

One of the arguments advanced by business in its own defense has been that for every transgression of ethics or law by a company or individual there are hundreds of thousands of companies and individuals that very same day honorably and quietly pursue their calling. The point is well taken. However, bystanders paying higher and higher taxes, tenants paying rising rents, borrowers paying higher interest rates, and consumers experiencing increasing quality and service problems, find in the transgressions a corroboration of whatever unsatisfactory experiences they personally have suffered.

FACING THE FACTS

On the brighter side of the picture, a Harris Survey in 1966 revealed that 80 percent of the U. S. population expected business to provide leadership in resolving social problems. There is increasing evidence that, along a parallel path, business leaders are seeking to provide exemplary leadership in raising the moral tone of society.

There remains a long way to go and credibility has not been attained.

The refocusing of corporate effort toward social problems, with practical programs to combat them, is developing as a prime movement in the 1970s. Forecasts of the trend have been commonplace. As Sol Linowitz, Xerox chairman, put it in 1966, "to realize its full promise in the world of tomorrow, American business and industry . . . will have to make social goals as central to its decisions as economic goals; and leadership in our corporations will increasingly recognize this responsibility and accept it."

George Champion, chairman of Chase Manhattan Bank, said it simply, forcefully: [8] "Improving the quality of our society is simply another step in the process of taking a broader gauged view of return on investment . . . the distinction between capital investment and social investment is more a difference of degree than of kind."

G. William Miller, president of Textron, urged that action was vital to the survival of the system. "Management now is generally coming to understand that the forces of change will either destroy our system or that we shall shape these forces so that business can continue to be private and effective and productive."

Fundamental to the changing of attitudes have been several realizations:

1. Affluence has solved some kinds of problems and brought with it other kinds.
2. Beyond the attainment of material affluence is something more elusive, which looms as the next challenge.
3. Big Government, like Big Business, is a permanent factor to be accommodated. Both are growing. In 1967 there were 2,975 corporate mergers; in 1968, 4,462 and, in 1969, 5,400.
4. To be influential in the "new" areas of social needs, business must *earn* authority just as it earned preeminence in technology, finance, and production. Authority in dealing with human values can come only from the humans involved.
5. A "sense of social responsibility" is not enough. Managers must express their responsibility in programs of action and in their personal involvement. Managers must be trained in the humanities. Employees must be encouraged in pursuits of conscience. Concepts of recruiting, training, recognition, advancement, reward, and mobility all must be reevaluated.
6. The U. S. economy is shifting more to welfare and to services. Inherent in this is the need for a closer intermingling of business, government, and education functions.

THE CHANGING ENVIRONMENT

The overriding characteristic of the environment has been one of affluence without equivalent contentment. Advances spawned by science have come swiftly; adjustments to these have come slowly, with opposition.

[8] In "How Business Employs The Unemployables," *Nation's Business*, January, 1967, p. 78.

In the conduct of business, problems have included shortage of trained manpower, pockets of unemployment, mergers and acquisitions, movement away from central city areas, foreign competition, mechanization and automation, wage-price spiral, labor strife, and more. The internal problems have social implications and involvements.

In the external affairs of business, attention must be given to all major expressions of public sentiment, whether they concern equal job opportunities for blacks, the protests of college students against the military-industrial complex, the concentration of wealth in funds and trusts, the reduction of air and water pollution, financial support of higher education, the prospect of world starvation, the desegregation of public schools, or the gradual shift to a service-based economy.

The ability of business to have meaningful dialogue on these problems is complicated by the variety of approaches which the concerned publics bring to them. The range is from revolt, boycott, or protest march to editorials and intellectual questions about moral values and political systems.

THE CHANGING ROLE OF PUBLIC RELATIONS

In this dynamic environment, the role of the practitioner is vastly more complex and demanding than the issuance of information and the evaluation of response to it. Serious questions have been raised challenging the qualifications of public relations people to induce new or changed actions on the part of employers and clients.

Gibson McCabe, president of *Newsweek,* gave voice to the question before the Detroit Chapter of the Public Relations Society of America:

> "I think that business leaders—along with scholars, politicians and educators—are more and more coming to see the need for the private sector to move more actively toward getting at the roots of social discontent. And, as they do so, they should rightly be able to look to their public counselors for help in establishing goals and putting sound programs into action.
>
> "But, except in isolated instances, it seems to me that *this is precisely where public relations is at its weakest*—or, at least, has made its poorest showing to date . . . it is one thing to be able to report third quarter financial results, but quite another to inspire change on a social front."

There will be no lack of problems in which two-way communications is a factor: more than five-million U. S. families live in poverty: 45 percent of all children drop out before completion of high school: more than 700,000 arrests are made annually of young people under 17: one in ten persons encounters mental illness: nearly seven-million persons suffer from alcoholism: more than 50,000 auto deaths occur annually: millions are unemployed at any given moment: problems of racial strife, war, draft, a shift to a service-based economy, affluence, atmospheric pollution, and a myriad of fragmentations abound.

Broader intelligence will be required to understand the roots of social problems: merely knowing how to communicate publicly the details of social actions undertaken will not be enough. The function will require deep personal convictions and overt commitment as well as eloquence. There must be a questioning of old customs and ways however cherished. Personal integrity will be at stake when the economic or immediate interests of employers are at odds with public welfare. Practitioners will need higher than average moral and ethical standards of personal conduct. Finally, there must be extraordinary skill in the use of new communications technology.

A former public relations executive, James W. Cook, who became a senior official in the Bell System, said in 1968: [9]

"The **PR** man's job will grow even broader, even more complex, even more involved than it is now. He will need ever-increasing insight to recognize and understand what people are asking of our society . . . most visibly the minority groups and the younger generation. Above all, he will need the courage and flexibility to let go of the old when something new is the answer . . ."

Communications related to the social problem arena will increasingly challenge business practitioners. This aspect is discussed in detail in Chapter 19 "Corporate Public and Urban Affairs."

At the same time, an increasing emphasis in corporate practice will be concerned with the relationship between the corporation and investors. This is discussed in Chapter 20 "Corporate Financial Relations."

Meanwhile, corporate public relations also continues in its more traditional roles: reinforcing marketing, expressing the corporation's philanthropy, projecting the best possible image of the institution and its spokesmen, defending the values of the enterprise system, issuing news to all publics on which the corporation depends, and reflecting sensitivity to public opinion. Some examples follow.

PHILANTHROPY—AID TO EDUCATION, HEALTH, WELFARE AND THE ARTS

For those entities which depend on others for support, the corporation is the third largest source of funds, behind individuals and foundations. Cor-

[9] In "The New Public Relations," *Public Relations Journal*, Vol. 25, January, 1969, 6–9.

porate contributions to not-for-profit activities annually in 1969 were estimated at $900-million.

As enlightened corporate leaders know, the corporation is, in fact, a service organization. As one executive put it "The whole purpose of the corporation is to honorably serve social needs at a profit."

The greatest receiver of corporation benefits is higher education. Contributions for the improvement of education usually can be measured in dollar value, though they may assume a variety of forms other than cash. Among them: facilities and equipment, teaching aids, employee's time, scholarships, fellowships and internships, research grants, and matching the gifts of employees.

Recipients are variously selected, based on plant community relationships, the number of employees in each college or university city, the alma maters represented by employees or executives, judgment of excellence, the degree of alumni support mustered, or the simple whim of a top official.

An evaluation has taken place in recent years questioning whether the interests of the corporation are ultimately served best by the concentrated allocation of funds and effort in plant communities—on unrestricted terms where education, health and welfare are concerned—another view holds that the final gain would be greater if the funds were concentrated in areas of poverty and were clearly marked for education to improve the skills of the least qualified.

Public relations programming runs the kindergarten-to-adult education gamut and ranges from multimillion dollar projects to mailing folders.

There is "Reddy Reader," a preschool primer from Reddy Kilowatt, Inc., helping parents to teach reading. The New Detroit Committee gave $100,000 for sixth grade textbooks in poverty neighborhoods. Coca Cola prepared a slide film "Black Treasures" for distribution to schools, libraries, and youth organizations. Corn Products trained several hundred disadvantaged youths, and its educational subsidiary MIND upgraded reading and mathematics skills for thousands.

Scholarships lend themselves to communications programs. In 1969, General Motors granted nearly 300 scholarships, spread across 240 universities and colleges. Oscar Mayer provided a small number for the sons and daughters of employees. More than 175 companies have participated in a competitive National Merit Scholarship program.

Quite a record has been compiled by E. I. duPont de Nemours. Its aid to education program, in existence more than fifty years, made grants to 145 colleges totalling $2.1-million. A recent phase provided for postgraduate teaching assistant fellowships.

Corporate philanthropy directed to the privately supported health and welfare agencies and institutions is long established, and well known, as are the communications programs supporting fund campaigns and recognizing large contributions. Occasionally something exceptional pops up, such as the gift by Masonite Corporation of its $1.5-million Medical Center in Laurel, Mississippi to the people of the county.

Not so highly developed or known are the relationship between the corporation and the arts and imaginative communication vehicles for dramatizing and expressing the relationship.

The traditional pattern consists of regular monetary gifts for ongoing institutions such as opera companies and symphonies. It is reliably estimated that corporation gifts approached the $25-million mark in 1968. Support of the arts as a means of building good relationships is discussed in Chapter 12.

Occasionally grants are for specific projects. American Export Isbrandtsen Lines gave the New York Metropolitan Opera the cost of a new production of Aida. Eastern Airlines granted $500,000 for a new production of Wagner's Ring Cycle. Some corporations have pet projects. Johnson Wax and Container Corp. of America maintain traveling exhibits of contemporary art. Trane Company supports community theater in La Crosse, Wisconsin. Hallmark, the cardmaker, sponsors art competition and annually gives art awards to encourage promising artists.

Esso has had a major involvement when it presented a collection of Colombian art covering twenty-five centuries. Esso also has promoted a Peruvian tenor, produced eleven documentary cultural films on Peru's traditions and history, sponsored a literary contest in Colombia and supported an Inter-America Arts Festival.

T.R.W. sponsored performances of a live London-Broadway show "By George," based on the life of George Bernard Shaw, before some 50,000 students at forty colleges in a ten-week span. Its stated objectives were to extend the company's dialogue with students, broaden appreciation of the arts, and show that the modern corporation is interested in the cultural side of society.

Standard Oil Company of New Jersey won wide acclaim for its sponsorship on television of the "Play of the Week"—an eighteen-week series of serious two-hour dramas; its "Age of Kings," a fifteen-week series of Shakespearean dramas; and, more recently, its "Festival of Performing Arts."

Bamberger's Department Store in New Jersey initiated a program to bring the great artists appearing in nearby New York City to New Jersey audiences that won the respect and applause of audiences and performers alike. It first sponsored performances of the Ballet Russe in Newark, where the response was so enthusiastic that the department store kept the program going. Bamberger's pays all promotional expenses and prints most of the programs as its contribution to the community's cultural program.

Corporate support of the arts takes several other forms—providing exhibit space in lobbies or department store windows, purchasing art for corporate offices, the underwriting of costly TV programs furthering cultural interests, offering space and funds for community art shows.

REINFORCEMENT OF MARKETING

In the words of Steuart Henderson Britt at Northwestern University, "public relations is an essential part of the total marketing mix."

For some counselors retained by marketing officials, and for many departments reporting to marketing officials, reinforcement of marketing represents the bread-and-butter portion, if not the total, of their function.

The partnership of advertising, sales promotion and public relations efforts in marketing programs is well documented by success stories and well accepted by the partners. Divergence occurs over the question of whether public relations should be *part of,* rather than a partner in, marketing services when many of its other efforts relate to and are directed by non-marketing management. The resolution of this debate varies widely, from the consumer product company where marketing usually enjoys high rank, to the conglomerate or holding company where financial expertise ranks high, to the franchised utility or carriers where consideration of the community, public welfare and service, and government, are of top priority.

In many large corporations, separations within the public relations function have been accomplished, providing for a corporate staff and for separate marketing-oriented groups reporting within operating divisions. Middle-sized corporations frequently have a transitional setup, variously characterized by frictions and teamwork. Small corporations, for the most part unable to afford separation, assign the function to top management, or to marketing, dependent largely on the personal viewpoint and interest of the top official.

Regardless of structure, public relations has much to offer marketing in the process of creating, pre-conditioning, selling and serving a customer audience or area.

One Chicago counselor cites six supports of marketing: [10]

> . . . help a company and a product name become better known
> . . . help get new and/or improved products off to a good start
> . . . report those hard-core facts about a company that
>   bear on sales
> . . . help invest the product or service with benefits that
>   can help sales

[10] Ury, Bernard E. in an unpublished essay, "Strengthening A Marketing Program With Public Relations Techniques."

. . . seek out new markets and broaden existing ones
at relatively little cost

. . . create an over-all favorable image for the company

To this list could be added the values in third party endorsement or credibility gained by publicity in press, radio, or TV—bespeaking the organization behind the products, and linking the products and services to social progress.

The following examples illustrate the variety of projects.

Some efforts are directly related to a sales campaign such as publicity by Ford and General Motors in the introduction of the Mustang and the Toronado. American Express sought to boost sales with a "Fly Free For Life" contest, and United Airlines sought to increase sales by sending 2,500 executive secretaries a fresh rose "Roses to a First Lady" each Friday.

Alcoa had a newsworthy aircraft, a DC-7, outfitted as an exhibit of the company's products and capabilities.

The Men's Tie Foundation fought back competitively against turtlenecks with a campaign to identify ties with grooming and success. Among the vehicles were a $25,000 historical tie collection, a Presidential Tie Poll in 1968, a "Tie Tack" directory, and films, "Dressing Up" and "Good Grooming."

Many programs assist corporate marketing by indirection. Good examples include the U. S. Steel sponsorship of "Operation Snowflake" to help sell home appliances for Christmas, Goodyear's efforts to stimulate store traffic with a bargain album, "Great Songs of Christmas," and Oneida Silversmith's program to honor co-ed organizations for "significant service to the academic, civic or international communities."

To glamorize work clothes, Work Wear Corporation staged a fashion show tracing the history of work clothes, evolving to such modern interpretations as airline stewardess' costumes.

The Bicycle Institute of America has long conducted programs to popularize the use of bikes, by plumping for safety paths and by stressing the health and fun aspects of cycling. One stunt found the U. S. Secretary of the Interior leading a bike parade of congressmen on a ride to the Capitol.

CORPORATE STATESMANSHIP

Some programs are linked to marketing or products by the thinnest of threads but clearly bespeak the character of the corporation. On the retail scene, Neiman Marcus notified suppliers it preferred to deal with equal opportunity employers. Apollo Supermarkets in Colorado, adopted an eight-point policy of fairness, invited gripes on "Buyer Participation Day" each Friday, and answered them on the spot.

Safeway Stores went to the rescue of a co-op competitor in a black community in San Francisco. They lent a manager, gave training in recruiting, inventory and display practices, and became a management consultant indefinitely for $1.00.

Motorola, without seeking publicity, provided all the materials needed for hundreds of U. S. cities to activate a "community radio watch" program, in which vehicle drivers with two-way radios reported any potential crime situation so that police might head it off. Drivers were cited by the mayor, received awards, and were publicized by the press.

Chrysler contracted with the federal government to train blacks for dealership in fifty cities. General Motors bought several hundred thousand glove compartments from a predominantly black ghetto subsidiary of Aerojet General in Los Angeles.

INTERPRETING THE CORPORATION—
DEFENDING THE SYSTEM

This embraces those things said and done to project a favorable impression of the corporation's role in society and to negate the efforts of its critics.

Criticism of the corporation *per se* often centers on the dangers to the "little man" of wealth and power concentration. Critics do not lack for ammunition with: fewer than 500 corporations controlling two-thirds of the non-farm economy, gross sales of General Motors being larger than the gross national product of all but fifteen nations, IBM accounting for well over $2-billion of the $3-billion digital computer business while its nearest competitor has less than 5 percent, mutual funds with "faceless" managers having assets of $50 billion, and many Americans with incomes over $1-million paying no income tax.

Attacks on bigness and the abuses of power crystallize in legislation, regulation and threats of added controls.

Response has turned more and more to the entry of businessmen into public life—by executive appointment or by the election process—and to the use of the public forum, with businessmen speaking out on public issues, leading crusades, and identifying with the commonweal. Further discussion of this aspect is in the next chapter.

A vehicle coming frequently into the public relations realm is *Corporate Identity or Identification* embodying the use of slogan or graphic symbols to identify formally a conglomerate or changed corporation. Symbols have many practical benefits. They translate into other languages. They accommodate the computer.[11]

Thus, we see the Minuteman of an insurance company as a protective symbol, the distinction script-like style of the Coca Cola logotype, and easily remembered alphabetized names like IBM and RCA.

Corporate identification lends itself to modernization. Morton Salt has updated its girl with the umbrella, "When it Rains it Pours," five times in forty years. Each updating reaps publicity benefits.

Identity programs are frequently punctuated with symbolic events, souvenirs and exhibits. Campbell Soup on its 100th anniversary made extensive use of a collection of rare soup tureens requiring years to assemble world-wide. In moving painlessly from General Analine and Film Corporation to GAF, the company, among other things, sent novelty calendar paper weights to 10,000 key persons. But, as Howard Chase warns, "true corporate identity cannot be established or materially improved by drawing artistic lines around white space, designing new logotypes, etc."

Personalized spokesmanship, industrial statesmanship and crusades stem naturally from the need and desire to show that business is humanely oriented as well as efficiently managed. For example W. W. Keeler, president of Phillips Petroleum, for several years helped American Indians by urging his peers to put industrial projects on reservations. One tool was a booklet titled "Path of Many Ways."

William Miller, American Oil Co. official, sought to arouse his industry to clean up and beautify retail outlets and to eradicate abandoned ones.

Morris Milgrim, official of a real estate investment trust, pioneered a push for integrated housing.

David Rockefeller, Chase Manhattan Bank, plumped for the formation of a business committee that would lobby for social legislation.

A prevalent tool dealing with public issues has been the reprinting and wide distribution of testimony before government bodies, and speeches to campus, consumer, or trade audiences.

Efforts and media to show the position of business have been varied. Reliance Electric and Engineering sought to identify automation as a social "good" and to show itself as importantly involved. The program's theme was "Reliance Business in Automation." *Time Magazine* donated fifty-two pages of advertising space for agencies to use in expressing great social ideas. Equitable Life Insurance sponsored ads showing how social programs and business cohere.

There has been no abatement of business vigilance and communication

---

[11] See Joseph Selame, "The Corporate Symbol at Work," *Public Relations Journal*, Vol. 24, October, 1968.

on the matters of national interest, subversion, and patriotism. Many efforts have been directed in literary form to the elementary school child grade school age. Typical is a booklet "This Land of Ours," prepared by Greyhound Corporation.

Corporations and their members are increasingly committed in the political arenas. As Thomas Reid of Ford Motor Co. put it, "It is for them (the businessmen) to be active and articulate in working for the kind of government under which our free enterprise system can grow and prosper."

L. L. L. Golden, counselor and columnist, summed up the task in his *Only By Public Consent:* "To intelligent business leadership, good relations with the public involve continued concern by all who have an interest in the corporation's success. It is the road to public consent."

CASE PROBLEM

A main plant of a large food company with popular brand names has long been located in the central area of a major city. There are 5,000 employees, 20 percent black, reflecting the ratio between blacks and whites in the city. The company is an Equal Opportunity Employer.

Top management has decided to build a plant in a suburban village twenty-five miles away, where there are advantages in parking, taxation, and room for further expansion, and to vacate the central city plant.

The officials of the suburban village welcome industry but violently oppose open housing as deflating real estate values and otherwise downgrading the area.

The company has offered to give equivalent jobs to all employees at the central city location who wish to work at the new suburban location but has been unable to interest bus lines in running to and from the city to the selected village.

Within the central city plant, employee rumbles are beginning, ranging from sabotage of equipment to the organization of a product boycott. Minority group leaders and central city officials are showing interest and expressing sympathy for the employee's plight.

You are vice-president for public relations of the food company, located at headquarters in a city in another state. You've been asked to look into the situation, work out a plan with the personnel and marketing departments, and devise a communications program which will help make the move understood and acceptable to those involved.

What's the plan? The program?

ADDITIONAL READING

American Foundation for Management Research, *Management 2000.* New York: The Foudation, 1968. A collection of speeches.

RICHARD J. BARBER, *The American Corporation. Its Power, Its Money, Its Politics.* New York: Dutton, 1970.

HAROLD BRAYMAN, *Corporate Management in a World of Politics.* New York: McGraw-Hill Co., 1967. By veteran du Pont counselor.

JOHN BROOKS, "Annals of Business: The Edsel," *The New Yorker,* Vol. 36 issues of November 26 and December 3, 1960.

CHESTER BURGER, "Managing Public Relations in Diversified Companies," *Public Relations Journal,* Vol. 25, May, 1969.

"Business and the Arts," special issue *Public Relations Quarterly,* Vol. 15, 1970.

L. L. L. GOLDEN, *Only by Public Consent. American Corporations Search for Favorable Opinion.* New York: Hawthorn Books, 1968.

KENNETH G. PATRICK and RICHARD ELLIS. *Education and the Business Dollar.* New York: Macmillan, 1969.

HOLDEN, PEDERSON, GERMANE, *Top Management.* New York: McGraw-Hill, 1968. Based on interviews with top executives in 15 corporations.

ROBERT W. MILLER, ed., *The Creative Interface.* Washington, D.C.: The American University, 1968. Lectures on the new relationship between business and government.

BERNARD D. NOSSITER, *The Mythmakers: An Essay on Power and Wealth.* Boston: Houghton Mifflin Co., 1964.

JEFFREY O'CONNELL, "Lambs to Slaughter," *Columbia Journalism Review,* Vol. 6, Fall, 1967. How automobile industry misleads teenagers.

CHARLES A. REICH, "The Greening of America. 1. The Corporate State," *The New Yorker,* XLVI, September 26, 1970. Lengthy, caustic essay on corporation's domination of contemporary society.

PHILIP B. OSBORNE, *The War That Business Must Win.* New York: McGraw-Hill, 1970.

CHAPTER 19

THE PRACTICE: CORPORATE PUBLIC AND URBAN AFFAIRS— EMERGING FUNCTIONS

In a noteworthy public speech, Roger M. Blough, chairman of the U. S. Steel Corporation said, "Clearly we shall be in sorry shape if our nation is divided into two hostile camps with government and enterprise arraigned against each other. So, I should like to hope that we can create an additional group of revolutionaries—in both business and government—who can innovate ways of cooperation where only conflict grew before."

Coming from the man who had a celebrated confrontation with President Kennedy over the question of national interest in an increase of steel prices, Mr. Blough's after-the-fact statement represents a major shift by a senior official in the corporate approach to government relations and citizenship. Antagonism and belligerence are being replaced by attitudes of conciliation and partnership.

Mr. Blough's utterance expresses a synthesis of the philosophy being articulated in public affairs and urban crisis programs of industry: The rationale is that the enterprise system will be best served, as will all of society, by a spirit of collaboration rather than confrontation. Strengthening the business-government partnership is a big order.

As one expression of the changing relationships, the functions of public affairs and urban affairs have emerged in the past decade as increasingly important subsections in corporate public relations concepts. In many of the nation's largest corporations, they have been given separate departmental status. This development reflects reaction and response to the growing scope of government's role in business as a regulator and as a major customer, as well as the mounting demands for business's participation in the resolution of major social problems.

At the end of the 1960s more than a thousand companies told the National Conference Board that they had provisions in their management structures for public affairs. Hundreds had specialists working in urban affairs. In one notable situation, A.T.&T. set up a thirty-one person department of environmental affairs embracing minority, urban, and educational relations.

Demands for business's participation in government social programs, coupled with its continued concern about further government intervention and regulation of economic matters, will accelerate the public affairs trend in the 1970s.

William H. Eells, a regional manager of Ford's department of civic and governmental affairs, lists five reasons for the continued growth of public affairs: [1]

> First, the need for business to recognize its stake and its ability in helping to solve many of the socio-economic problems that are rapidly emerging.
>
> Second, the need for better business-government cooperation in setting up a practical, goal-oriented modus operandi.
>
> Third, the need for business to find ways and means of fully assimilating the hard-core poor into the mainstream of the economy.
>
> Fourth, the need to recognize and serve the growing sophistication and hardening demands of consumers.
>
> And fifth, the need to reconcile the role of business and industry with the ideals and high purposes of young people.

A BASIC CHANGE IN ATTITUDE

Traditionally a great many businessmen have resisted and resented the notion that their businesses should seek to fulfill social responsibilities not necessarily inherent in the products or services they purveyed.[2] Businessmen have variously labelled it as "phony," "lipservice," "outside our orbit."

Economist Milton Friedman at the University of Chicago has described the social responsibility notion as "a fundamentally subversive doctrine."

"If businessmen do have a social responsibility other than making maximum profit for stockholders," he said, "how do they know what it is?" [3] Friedman warned that if businessmen behaved like civil servants, they would eventually become nothing more than civil servants, elected or appointed like all others.

Nonetheless, the overlapping and interaction of business and government in almost all areas affecting the public interest has been increasing. Employment and unemployment are economic. They are also social, as are the psychological factors in automation. Exploitation of the consumer is a legal matter. It also gets into matters of moral and ethical responsibility. The over-riding problem business and government share is attaining pro-

---

[1] Speech given before Ohio Chamber of Commerce, March 8, 1969.

[2] See "The Corporation and Social Responsibility" a pamphlet summarizing a symposium at the University of Illinois, April, 1967, sponsored by the Illinois Bell Telephone Company.

[3] From "Business and Government: A New Balance of Power," *Business Week*, July 17, 1965, a special report.

ductive results while each preserves the independence in its own prerogatives, with neither taking on excessive power over the other, or over the public.

Carlton Spitzer, a counselor who has served both government and business, puts the value of collaboration this way: [4]

> It follows that each can serve best by serving together.
>
> Government can help business by reducing bureaucratic red tape, coordinating related and overlapping programs, and offering specific ideas. . . .
>
> Business can help the government by offering realistic plans and proposals that respond to general needs as well as to company goals.

Government has found increasingly that in responding to needs voiced by substantial segments of the whole nation, its role goes beyond that of a referee among the various self-interested entities. More and more, government finds itself, with assistance from the campus, defining social needs and problems, then turning to business, labor, and the professions for the solutions and the implementation of relevant programs.

Business, for its part, has been increasingly responsive, and for practical reasons. The relationship between social abuse and government regulations is a fact, not a theory. As for putting brakes on government's growth, George Champion, chairman of Chase Manhattan Bank put it bluntly. "I can think of nothing that would put the brakes on big government faster than for business to identify critical problems and take the initiative in dealing with them before Washington felt the need to act."

Automatic opposition to federal programs or regulations, labelling them as encroachment on the private sector, has proved a fruitless tactic at the worst, and a rearguard, delaying exercise at the best. Selective lobbying and dissent in the guise of a patriotic duty on the part of the "loyal minority" has too often faltered for lack of popular support which would stand up in elections.

The role of bystander for business was out of character. The enlightened view which has emerged is that for business to win support or sell its views, it must get deeply and personally involved in "social advance."

THE EMERGENCE OF PUBLIC AND URBAN AFFAIRS FUNCTIONS

The thrust for participation among some of the nation's 500 largest corporations, representing 70 percent of the total industrial profit and 60

---

[4] In "Wanted: A Business-Government Partnership," *Public Relations Journal*, Vol. 24, December, 1968.

percent of the sales, coupled with dread of increased federal intervention in the economic sector has sponsored the formal organization of the corporate public and urban affairs functions.

The roots of the function trace back in part to what a decade or two ago was often called "Economic Education." Home base was the "governmental affairs" department usually staffed with lawyers. Among the giants using this approach were General Electric, General Motors, U. S. Steel and duPont.

A significant formalization, or redefining, came in 1954 when a number of these companies gave birth to the Effective Citizens Organization (ECO).[5]

The ECO's stated purpose was to motivate businessmen to political participation. To this end, hundreds of workshops were conducted for thousands of businessmen. In 1966, ECO was renamed Public Affairs Council, attesting to the acceptance of the term "public affairs" as a fitting umbrella for the function. By 1967, the council could report that well over 500 companies had integrated public affairs into their operating budgets.

Workshop services and publications about public affairs have been sponsored by the U. S. Chamber of Commerce, and a Division of Public Affairs has been established in the National Industrial Conference Board. In Chicago, Public Affairs Service Associates provides a communications tie for those interested, with a monthly publication "Public Affairs Digest." A "Public Affairs Review" began publishing in 1967 to report on "public policy developments of today which have a bearing on national decisions of tomorrow." The semimonthly is edited by Charles B. Coates, a public relations consultant.

THE NATURE OF THE FUNCTION

The National Conference Board provides this all-encompassing definition of the public affairs function:

"A significant and substantial concern and involvement by individuals, business, labor, foundations, private institutions, and government with the social, economic and political forces that singly or through interaction shape the environment within which the free enterprise system exists."

Among some 1,033 companies surveyed by the NICB in 1968, 75 percent had identifiable public affairs functions.[6]

---

[5] "Public Affairs and Public Relations: Natural Allies." Richard A. Armstrong, *PR Quarterly*, Winter, 1963. See also "Public Affairs Council" a booklet. The Effective Citizens Organization Inc., 1601 18th St. N.W., Washington, D.C. 20009.

[6] "The Role of Business in Public Affairs" Study No. 2, National Industrial Conference Board, 845 Third Avenue, New York, 1968. (Now the Conference Board.)

Programs tend to fall in five areas: improving relations with government, encouraging employees in political activities, providing economic and political science education, rendering community services, and helping solve environmental problems.

The following objectives were stated by the National Association of Manufacturers for the guidance of members in formulating programs.[7]

1. Develop a more effective voice in community, state and national affairs.
2. Portray a positive business image dedicated to fostering the principles of the free enterprise system and Constitutional government.
3. Stimulate civic and political activity.
4. Inform employees, public and legislators, in human terms of the problems facing the company in its business development.
5. Foster a better understanding and appreciation of government.
6. Disseminate legislation information and maintain a practical legislation liaison.
7. Add an important and necessary dimension to the development of management personnel.

In a "white paper" on corporate public affairs, ten steps were cited as necessary for effective public affairs programming: [8]

First, public affairs must have the attention of top management.

Second, someone must be put in charge.

Third, a policy must be developed covering the full range of public affairs.

Fourth, the policy statement should be given broad circulation to employees and shareowners.

Fifth, the public affairs manager must set up information sources on legislation pertinent to the company.

Sixth, public affairs communications details should be determined.

Seventh, the employee training program in political economy should be planned.

Eighth, the public affairs manager should work out in-company procedures for political fund raising on a bipartisan basis.

---

[7] "Why Public Affairs?" a pamphlet, National Association of Manufacturers, 277 Park Avenue, New York, N.Y. 10017.

[8] "A White Paper on Corporate Affairs," Joseph J. Eley, president, Public Affairs Counselors, Inc., 350 Lexington Ave., New York 10016.

Ninth, cataloging of personnel trained and activities engaged in should be commenced.

Tenth, don't expect miracles of public affairs. On the other hand the company should expect performance in tangible terms.

In its survey, the N.I.C.B. identified three stages of development of public affairs programming.

First was the group of activities including review of legislation, presentation of views to government, political and economic education for employees, encouragement of voting and making political contributions.

Second was the encouragement of employee community service.

Third was corporate action to solve environmental problems.

In the first stage, NICB's survey showed that nearly all companies devote attention to pending federal legislation and shifts of attitudes in regulatory agencies. Continuous review is made by 43 percent of companies, frequently by 30 percent and occasionally by 25 percent.

There is little question in businessmen's minds that corporate views on legislation should be conveyed to legislators directly, or via trade associations and lobbyists.[9] A question does exist as to the propriety of conveying viewpoints to shareholders, employees other than executives, and the public at large. Also, the Internal Revenue Service questions closely expenditures for advertising designed to influence legislation.

On the matter of political activity, the corporation is prohibited by law from political actions. The question is how far to go in encouraging employee participation. Hughes Aircraft initiated an "Active Citizenship Campaign" with the stated purpose of making political participation more accessible to employees. A film "Who Cares" was produced to explain the campaign.

Experiences are not always beneficial to the individual and the corporation. New Jersey Bell Telephone reported in an annual report that among its ranks were 15 mayors, 58 councilmen, 68 school board members, 11 tax assessors and a state assemblyman. However one man, a Bell supervisor, as a school board member, urged publicly that residents vote against Jewish board candidates on the grounds "most Jewish people are liberals when it comes to spending for education." Other candidates accused the Bell man of being anti-Semitic, and the brief uproar made national news, causing harm to everyone involved.[10]

[9] "Effective Public Relations With Washington," Morris V. Rosenbloom. *The Public Relations Quarterly,* Vol. 12, Summer, 1967.

[10] "Company Politicans," a news roundup by *The Wall Street Journal,* March 21, 1967.

The NICB survey showed this degree of encouragement to employees:

Registering and voting	80%
Expressing political views	63%
Contributing to a political party	41%
Holding appointive public office	36%
Running for elective office	30%

Concerning political and economic education programs, the survey showed that 53 percent offer some form of political education on a non-partisan basis, and 46 percent offer economic education formally or informally, in-plant or outside.

Moving to the second stage, community service, this involves financial and other aids from the corporation, and the encouragement of employees to take part in local affairs. Nine out of ten companies made a financial contribution to community betterment. Eight of ten also contributed in kind, with donations of merchandise, use of office space and other facilities, and executive time and talent.

Some 87 percent urge employees to volunteer time and effort for social, civic and cultural pursuits. Forms of encouragement frequently include time off and recognition, usually in some form of publicity.

In the NICB survey, some fourteen areas of environmental or socio-economic problems were cited, together with percentages indicating corporate willingness to initiate action in each area:

Improvement and expansion of local school facilities	55.6%
Improvement of local school curricula	48.5
Problems associated with school drop-outs	53.9
Improvement of work/career opportunities for minority groups	69.2
Retraining of workers rendered unemployed by automation	72.6
Construction or improvement of medical facilities	62.1
Medical care for the aged	35.9
Provision for, or improvement of, low-income housing	31.3
More and better cultural facilities and activities	59.1
Purification and improvement of water supply	68.3
Reduction and control of air pollution	73.5
Improvement of urban and interurban transportation	60.4
Development of community recreational facilities	55.6
Improvement of law enforcement at local levels	61.4

It is stage three, solving environmental and urban problems, which will increasingly occupy the attention of corporate and urban public affairs programs in the decade of the 1970s.

THERE ARE NO EASY ANSWERS

As Herbert V. Prochnow, banker and writer put it: . . . "which things come first. . . . In what order do we place schools, defense, highways, housing, health, welfare, transportation, the conservation of water resources, agricultural subsidies and space programs? . . . with only 195-million people can we solve problems of poverty, illiteracy, disease, inadequate tax systems, inflation and land reform for almost one-and-one-half-billion people?" [11]

Businessmen are faced with puzzling philosophical and practical questions: What is the justification for using corporate funds in activities which do not directly benefit the stockholders? How can activities which do not fit into the ongoing business of the corporation be rationalized into the workday? What are the risks and the prospects for success in activities for which businessmen have no particular expertise? What are the consequences in raising public expectations and hopes beyond the ability of business to deliver?

One seasoned public relations practitioner puts his answer bluntly: "The business community may be painting itself into a corner . . . Corporations with all good intentions have taken on projects like job training for the unskilled and unmotivated. Each time a program is undertaken it cannot be given up without fearing accusation of abandoning the poor. Even if only partly successful or a failure, it tends to be replaced with another hopeful or wishful program . . . The core of the problem is that the expectations of all groups have been built up far beyond the reality of attainment."

High expectations have indeed been fostered by businessmen's professions of social conscience, by the publicity attending tentative and surface-scratching projects and programs, and by the assignment of increasing responsibility to business in areas of social need as deeply rooted as racial prejudice and as persistent as poverty.

The sharing of responsibility received emphasis in President Nixon's 1969 inaugural: "We are approaching the limits of what government alone can do. Our greatest need now is to reach beyond government to enlist the legions of the concerned and committed . . . not only in grand enterprises but more importantly in those small splendid efforts that make

[11] "Where We Stand," a speech at the Mayor's prayer breakfast, May 4, 1967, Chicago. Another thoughtful speech is "Business Involvement in Social Problems-Tokenism or Leadership," Wm. C. Stolk, chairman, Committee for Economic Development, before American Management Assn., March 5, 1969.

headlines in the neighborhood newspapers instead of the national journal."

Success and applause for efforts by the concerned corporation is by no means assured. Eastman Kodak has long been known for its generous paternalism in its employee relations and for its corporate citizenship in its Rochester, New York, homebase. Nonetheless, it was confronted in 1966 by a black organization FIGHT with a demand that the company hire and train 600 unskilled blacks selected by FIGHT. At the time of the demand the company had some 1,400 blacks on its payroll, or 3.4 of the total. In 1966, more than 11 percent of its new employees were blacks. Some 200 of the enrollees in its training programs were blacks. Obviously, Eastman had been moving up on the problem.

The demand touched off six months of confrontation, which generated national publicity, split the community, and, according to a report in *The Wall Street Journal,* "in the eyes of some people badly tarnished Kodak's reputation for concern for the commonweal." [12]

In retrospect, Thomas Robertson, the company's director of public relations, recorded several observations distilled from the experience:

> Top management's involvement, public involvement, demonstrates to everyone, inside and outside the company, that it is sincere and fully committed to facing the issues. . . . It must enlist the cooperation and support of all elements in the community which can make a contribution toward the environment. Most important, business should avoid going it alone. First of all, no company has the resources, economic or moral, to take on all the burden by itself. Secondly, community-wide problems call for broadly based efforts and solutions.
>
> Business, if it is involved with these inner city problems must brace itself for hard, frustrating, and often unsung efforts. There will be times when the full story behind an event cannot be told. As a result, the company may have to live with a temporary cloud of misunderstanding and unpopularity. Indeed, the efforts of management may not only be unappreciated, but even deliberately misrepresented or distorted by others.[13]

Direct, deep and continuing involvement, while recognizing the risk of controversy or failure, is the basic requirement. Businesses that have created formalized public affairs, urban affairs, and environmental affairs functions have had to restate corporate goals as applied to social problems. In some instances this is a general redefinition of corporate citizenship.

Illinois Bell Telephone early in the 60s set down on paper four guiding principles of management. One was:

---

[12] "Kodak's Ordeal," *Wall Street Journal,* Vol. 67, No. 181, June 30, 1967.

[13] From a speech by T. F. Robertson to Mid-West Public Relations Conference, University of Wisconsin, 1967.

"WE WILL ACTIVELY HELP THE COMMUNITIES WE SERVE."
This means that as a corporate citizen we are aware of our social responsibilities. We seek our full share of leadership and participation in
civic and public affairs—realizing that the good results of these activities
benefit the entire community, including our employees and our company.

It followed logically from this principle that in 1966 when Chicago
became the target for the open housing drive led by the late Reverend
Martin Luther King, Illinois Bell officials sensed the need for and spearheaded the creation of the Leadership Council for Metropolitan Open
Communities.[14]

This was but one aspect of a deepening involvement, with public-
urban affairs policy delineated and expressed in actions. Among others
were "I See Chicago" television documentaries, an advertising series "Take
Pride in the Promise of Illinois," fifty-two weeks of cultural programming
on Chicago educational TV channel, the Illinois Bell Volunteer Corps of
employees to help the aged, handicapped and disadvantaged, the Service
Activities of Volunteer Engineers to work on techniques and gadgets for
the physically handicapped, and a film "The Winners" to ease the drop-out
problem.[15]

To the credit of an increasing number of businesses and businessmen
it can be said that they are seeking ways to be effective in the "new" arena
where there is overlap and collaboration with government. Efforts are being
made to improve communications.

Indicative of the serious concern, after the riots of 1967 a group of
more than 1,000 leaders from the public and private sectors came together
to form the Urban Coalition. John W. Gardner, chairman, and formerly
U. S. Secretary of Health, Education and Welfare, said of it:

"Our distinction is that we bring together leadership elements that
do not normally collaborate in the solution of public problems; in fact we
bring together segments of American life that have been utterly out of touch
with one another—and in many cities, are still out of touch." [16]

Employment for the least qualified, in the heart of major cities, has
been a priority project of immense proportions. It has been the area in
which businessmen have found it easiest and most natural to scratch the
surface of social problems.

The National Alliance of Businessmen, later coalesced with Plans for
Progress, set out in 1968 to provide more than 600,000 jobs by mid-1971

14 For case study, see "Corporate Response to Urban Crisis," unpublished thesis by Linda
   Suzanne Brandt, University of Wisconsin, 1968.
15 See "Involvement in Community Problem's," Hale Nelson, The Public Relations Quarterly,
   Fall, 1967.
16 "Outlook," January, 1969. Vol. 4, New York State Department of Social Services.

in 125 cities for those who might otherwise be classified as unemployable.

Training for employment has been a major undertaking. Topping all others, General Motors, by 1969, had hired and trained 120,000 so-called unemployables, at its own expense. Small companies, often on contract with the Labor Department, have been particularly effective in the training and upgrading effort. The N.A.M. has had a training program for high school dropouts.

One particularly successful aspect of the GM effort was "Operation Opportunity," initiated after Detroit riots had resulted in 40 deaths. A "rule of reason," not educational background, was applied in cases of criminal record. Recruiting was in the ghetto. Wages were at union scale. A "Follow-up Committee" was formed. Sound trucks aided the recruitment.

THE EXAMPLES MULTIPLY

International Harvester provided several hundred blacks four weeks pre-employment and eight weeks on-the-job training. Procter and Gamble has openly sought to increase its Negro employment by providing training on and off the job.

Several companies have taken employment and training into the ghetto and areas known for segregation. Kimberly Clark put a $50-million consumer products plant in Beech Island, So. Carolina. Brown Shoe built a plant in the St. Louis ghetto and IBM in the unlikely Bedford-Stuyvesant area of Brooklyn. Notable efforts to upgrade the status of working minority groups include urging by Corn Products officials for the upgrading of salaries for employed Negros. A novel approach by Jewel Tea provided for employing college educated black management trainees with previous experience in teaching or social work. Their job was to counsel Jewel management and recruiters. The administrator of the program was a black.

Quaker Oats undertook a multi-faceted program in Chicago's ghetto to teach potential dropouts, combat malnutrition, encourage Black Capitalism, and meet in give-and-take sessions with leaders.

Businesses, with government and on its own, have also undertaken experiments in the renovation of slum areas on private capital, tackled problems of air and water pollution, converted undersea substances to edible food, produced pills to offset overpopulation and the world starvation it threatens, and sought to build an entire city from scratch.

In other actions, business handled the training of Job Corps recruits, administered part of the Medicare program, supported a ten-year study on the "Social Impact of Automation," and swapped jobs with Civil Service Commission and the Commerce Department.

The variety is large, but represents only a beginning.

Businessmen pledged $1-billion to improve slum housing. U. S. Gypsum on its own renovated an area of Harlem slums. Eastern Gas and Fuel Associates worked to rehabilitate 2,700 dwelling units. Boise Cascade, for $1 a year, acted as consultant to Boise's city redevelopment agency. Chicago businessmen mounted a Good Neighbor project to spur open housing. Eastman Kodak worked on a means of reducing water pollution at Rochester, New York. The Advertising Council undertook a campaign "Crisis in the Cities."

Among programs aimed at disadvantaged young people, New York City corporations funded a Playstreet program by the Police Athletic League. Aetna Life offered free driving lessons for minority youth. Ex-Lax launched a program to attract Negro high school girls into nursing.

Corporations are taking steps to communicate their concern for the human physical environment. Continental Can launched an anti-litter program with participants provided litter bags, stickers, speeches and press material. Cities Service made an eight-minute slide film on community beautification. The Central Ohio Coal Co. converted into lakes stocked with fish several areas which had been laid open by surface mining.

An original idea was expressed when the Bird's Eye division of General Foods helped 2,000 Arkansas farmers become okra growers by providing the seed at cost, giving planting and harvesting advice, and purchasing the product, thus adding $1-million to the farmers' income.

Programs concerned with social action have not been restricted to home communities. Massey-Ferguson and the Food and Agricultural Organization of the United Nations have trained personnel to help alleviate world hunger. Many companies through the International Executive Service Corps provide help to companies in trouble in the less developed nations.

Businessmen formed the International Executive Service Corps to send middle-management and retired managers to undeveloped nations to help their ailing corporations.

THE RELATIONSHIP OF PUBLIC AFFAIRS AND PUBLIC RELATIONS

The final relationship between the practice of public relations and public affairs is not yet clear.

Certain differences are obvious. The medium of public affairs has historically been through the political process. Practitioners have tended to be legally oriented. The medium of public relations is two-way communications. Practitioners tend to be journalistically oriented.

The crossover assumes significance considered in the light of facts revealed by an ECO survey of 110 companies. It showed that an average

21 percent of the public affairs man's time was devoted to communications. Equivalent information would probably document that a noteworthy portion of the public relations man's time is devoted to public affairs matters.[17]

The distinction grows fuzzier when it is considered that both functions, to be effective, must commit their efforts and their professional competence to problems of the social as well as the economic environment.

As one company president put it, "We feel that our company's responsibility extends beyond minding our own store. We want to improve the neighborhood in which we do business." The "neighborhood" obviously involves such problems as race relations, employment, tranquility, safety on the streets, housing, etc.

John W. Hill, who founded Hill and Knowlton, said in 1965, "The difference (between the two functions) is marked by an exceedingly fine line. Actually, the two activities are brothers under the skin."

Entering the 1970s, the question is which brother is slated to become head of the house. And what about community relations, which concerns itself with relationships in plant cities and homebases? A merging of interests, if not functions seems both natural and inevitable.

Avoidance of a three-way collision may rest on top management's appraisal of its own role in a changing social environment and where it wishes to place its emphasis. In companies where the head of a corporation is legally oriented and feels strongly about the dangers of further federal encroachment in the private sector, there is likely to be a public affairs man superior to the public relations man. Where the corporate head is oriented to marketing and to the persuasion process in general, most likely a public relations man would be placed superior to public affairs. In organizations where the philosophy generally is civic-minded and socially-responsible, the question of whether public relations or public affairs would be senior would tend to depend on which man or department held a perspective most closely attuned to the organizational philosophy.

In the very large organizations—whether business, labor or education—the team concept is both predictable and preferable. In smaller entities one executive, one department, can be expected to assume responsibility for both functions, drawing help from specialists in law, finance, personnel, and politics.

CASE PROBLEM

The Early American Oil Co., one of the nation's three largest producers and distributors, has long prided itself on its corporate statesmanship. A former

---

[17] This will be a worthwhile area to be investigated by graduate research.

president became an ambassador, and another ran successfully for mayor of a large city. The company's chairman has served on the National Committee for Parks and Conservation. The company loans executives to help troubled businesses in the less developed nations. It gives generously to welfare agencies, sponsors scholarships in geology and anthropology for needy students, has donated art treasures to national museums, has profit sharing for its employees, is civic-minded in its refinery communities, sponsors programs of tidiness for its retail outlets, once operated a Job Corps training center, and encourages employees to take part in the political process.

A federally appointed Safety Commission now reports publicly that the company's main oil refineries have been found to emit chemical vapors which pollute the environment to a degree hazardous to human health. The question of what constitutes a hazardous degree of air pollution is moot. However, the chairman, as spokesman, denies the allegation, and cites control measures voluntarily taken. The commission chairman responds that controls are inadequate. A congressman unfriendly to the oil industry calls for a congressional hearing.

Can the Early American Oil Co. make use of its long-standing, well-documented program of corporate statesmanship to offset or counteract the negative public relations ensuing from the action of the Safety Commission? If so, set forth the steps to be taken in appropriate sequence. If not, why not?

ADDITIONAL READING

ROGER M. BLOUGH, chairman, U. S. Steel, "The Public Life of Private Business," a speech. Available, PR Dept., 525 William Penn Place, Pittsburgh, Pa. 15230.

MARQUIS CHILDS and DOUGLASS CATER, *Ethics in a Business Society*, Mentor paperback. Harper and Brothers, 1954. Chapter VII, "Government and Business—The Uneasy Balance."

JAMES F. FOX, "Business in Public Affairs: What Dimensions?" *The Public Relations Quarterly*, Winter, 1966.

TOM M. HOPKINSON, "What is the Business of Business," *The Public Relations Quarterly*, Vol. 12, No. 4, Winter, 1968.

STANLEY KELLEY, *Professional Public Relations and Political Power*, a paperback. Johns Hopkins Press, Baltimore, 1966.

ROBERT W. MILLER, *Corporate Policies and Public Attitudes*, The American Univ., Washington, D.C., 20016, 1965.

———, "Public Affairs-Now" *Public Relations Journal*, Vol. 24, March, 1968.

"Prevent Political Drop-Outs," a kit. Public Affairs Department, National Association of Manufacturers, 918 16th Street, N.W. Washington, D.C. 20006.

THEODORE C. SORENSEN, "Corporate Leadership In The Public Arena," *Public Relations Journal*, January, 1968.

"The Role of Business in Public Affairs," a survey. Studies in Public Affairs, No. 2, National Industrial Conference Board, 845 Third Avenue, New York, New York 10022, 1968. (Now the Conference Board.)

U. S. CHAMBER OF COMMERCE, "Action Course in Practical Politics," 1615 H Street, N.W., Washington, D.C. 20006.

J. J. WUERTHENER, JR., *The Businessman's Guide to Practical Politics*, Henry Regery: Chicago, 1959.

CHAPTER
20

**THE
PRACTICE:
CORPORATE
FINANCIAL
RELATIONS**

A company's interests are ultimately best served by
supplying investors complete, current information,
whether good or bad, affecting their investment.

Investors, including individuals with small stockholdings, financial analysts advising others about their investments, and institutional investors holding large blocks of stocks, comprise a prime source of support or disapproval of corporate management.

The investing public provides capital and credit. These factors can become critical when a privately owned company goes to public ownership, when a corporation seeks to borrow money for its expansion, or on other occasions when major new funding is required.

Further, the investing public can use its proxies to endorse or discourage actions by corporate management requiring stockholders approval. Investors can voice views publicly and authoritatively on public issues affecting the enterprise system. Investors, sharing in the proprietorship of the corporation, potentially represent a pre-conditioned market for the products or services of the enterprise.

In the social ferment of this decade, the stockholders' meeting sometimes becomes the object of a noisy, staged protest. These protests require deft handling and, inevitably, put increased emphasis on investor relations.

On occasion, investors and the effectiveness of a public relations campaign hold the key to the survival of a corporate management. This was clearly illustrated in a classic battle for control of the New York Central in 1954. That struggle was characterized by opposing public relations efforts using news releases, paid ads, letters to stockholders, proxy solicitors, and more. There were many other contests for control in the 1950s, and, with the trend of the 1960's to industrial conglomeration by merger and acquisition, such battles have become commonplace. A take-over strategy which came into vogue during this trend was the generous tender offer for a controlling share of the outstanding stock.

The magnitude of the stakes involved in these situations is illustrated by the announced intentions of Gulf and Western Industries in 1968 of a tender offer for Sinclair Oil Corporation stock valued at more than $1.2 billion.

Public relations techniques and tactics have been used in these situations as well as in continuing communications and other contacts between corporate management and the investing public.

464

POWER OF STOCKHOLDER QUESTIONED

Corporate stockholders have not historically been organized into a mutual interest group with a collective voice, in the manner of employes in unions, or as financial analysts in a professional society.

There is basis to believe that the power and influence of the stockholders is overstated.

John Kenneth Galbraith debunks stockholder power as a myth. Writing in *The New Industrial State,* he asserted: "A small portion of the stock is represented at stockholders' meeting. . . . The rest is voted by proxy for the directors who have been selected by the management. The latter, though their ownership is normally negligible, are solidly in control of the enterprise." But this may change if the budding "ownerism" movement gains strength in the 1970s. Benjamin A. Javits, lawyer and economist, in a book entitled *Ownerism* advocates a "shareowners union" which would take over certain functions of government. Across the Atlantic, the British Labour Party in a policy document, *Agenda for a Generation,* argued that the shareholder should have a meaningful voice in the conduct of the firm in which he owns stock. There is increasing discussion of the fact that the public owns but does not control.[1]

Not all corporate managements feel equally obligated toward their stockholders, nor do all consider it vital to keep them informed about the company's doings. However, bitter proxy fights, dissident shareholders speaking up at annual meetings, successful tender offers, court actions by the SEC, and an expanded statement of disclosure policy by the New York Stock Exchange, have sharply reduced the number of managers who would in the 1970s say, "we make a profit, and pay our shareholders a good dividend. That's all they need to know."

As a manifestation of the changed attitude, the function of financial public relations has experienced major growth and increased responsibility. Entering the 1960s, there were a handful of counseling firms specializing in financial relations. The number was in hundreds entering the decade of the 70s. Practical reasons for this boom in financial public relations includes (1) a series of court decisions and government rulings requiring prompt disclosure of corporate information that might affect stock prices, (2) the wave of proxy fights in the trend to corporate conglomerates, and (3) steady increase in number of publicly owned companies. At the start of this decade there were more than 10,000 publicly owned U. S. corporations.

[1] A. A. Berle, *Power Without Property* (New York: Harcourt, Brace & World, Inc., 1959), p. 105. A realistic appraisal of the stockholder's role. Also Paul P. Harbrecht, S.J., *Toward a Paraproprietal Society* (New York: The Twentieth Century Fund, Inc., 1960).

THE COMPOSITION OF CORPORATE OWNERSHIP

The arena of competition for investors' support holds more than 30-million individual stockholders of U. S. corporations, an estimated 160,000 people in the securities industry, a few hundred funds, trusts, and institutions. The rate of growth is seen in comparative figures of 6,490,000 stockholders in 1952, 17,000,000 in 1962, 20,000,000 in 1965 and 30,850,000 in 1970. A.T.&T. has more than 3,100,000 stockholders, the largest number of any U. S. corporation.

Several factors stimulated the increase, all having public relations overtones. One was investment clubs. Another was inflation, which suggested common stock as an investment hedge against decreasing purchasing power of the dollar. Also the New York Stock Exchange spearheaded several efforts to expand public understanding of stock ownership. Major brokerage houses reinforced these efforts with advertising, mailing pieces. Brokers increased their personal contacts with corporate officers. This added to their effectiveness in dealing with potential investors.

OBJECTIVES IN PUBLIC RELATIONS PROGRAMMING

Considered on a grand scale, wide private ownership of corporate stock has political value for the capitalist system. "People's Capitalism" becomes a personal experience for millions of citizens, some unpropertied in any other way.

The fact that the numerical trend in shareowners continues up is both encouraging and significant. The significance is that this tends to counterbalance a trend in which an increasing proportion of industrial ownership has been concentrating in the hands of a few hundred giant institutional entities. Namely, mutual funds, pension funds, and other large institutionalized investors whose share of stock exchange total trading volume advanced from 33 percent in 1966 to 50 percent in 1969. The parallel uptrend in number of small shareowners would suggest that corporate managers in setting financial relations programs are seeking to counterbalance the weight of large investors, with programs designed to attract modest investors, who, on the average, will purchase no more than 100 shares in any company. Often corporate programs are aimed at employees.

The average stockholder, aware that an investment fund may own 150,000 shares of stock in the company when he holds 50, can be forgiven for a sense of helplessness and even apathy.

The minor stockholder, understandably, has welcomed the representation and the protection afforded him by individuals who have undertaken to champion his interest. Notable in this connection have been Lewis D. Gilbert and his brother who, since 1933, have been showing up at corporate annual meetings to pose perceptive questions for management. Questions have ranged from why a particular company did not number the pages in its annual report to why a management voted itself salary increases in a year when earnings decreased sharply.

Considered a nuisance at first by nearly all corporate officials, the Gilberts awakened them to the obligation of public disclosure as well as good performance. Their tactics aided managements in detecting blind spots and in anticipating areas of stockholder complaint. The tactics additionally provided an opportunity for management to capitalize on investors' desire to hear "the whole story" of a corporation's management.

The Gilbert crusade attracted others. Mrs. Wilma Soss, a public relations counsel, organized the Federation of Women Shareholders (more than 50 percent of stockholders are women). She once appeared at a U. S. Steel annual meeting dressed in a Gay Nineties costume satirizing the firm's antiquated custom of holding meetings in out-of-the-way Hoboken, N.J. The Gilberts issue an annual report of "Stockholder Activities at Corporation Meetings" which catalogs stockholders' complaints.[2]

Corporate response, at first bitter, was turned to constructive purposes through public relations planning and programming. Annual meetings were "readied" for the Gilberts, with charts and graphs, a line-up of articulate executives, comfortable seating in ample auditoriums, box lunches or light refreshments, invitations to the financial press. The annual meeting became a staged event projecting the kind of impression a company sought.

Attendance was spurred particularly among the over-65 investors not committed to an eight-hour working day. They welcomed an occasion which provided an importance to the individual, and often a pleasant social experience.

ADMINISTRATION OF FINANCIAL RELATIONS

Implicit in the trends and programming cited above is the significant role of public relations in attaining the rapport sought by top management.

Policies concerning what to reveal, under what circumstances, in what environment, by whom, are the province of management guided by law, by SEC regulation, and by attitude. Execution and implementation have

---

[2] Published annually by Lewis D. and John J. Gilbert, 1165 Park Avenue, New York 28, New York.

become increasingly the joint venture of financial officers and public relations staff or counsel.

In a survey of 196 companies, responsibility for Investors Relations was listed as follows: [3]

Financial Executive	77
Public Relations Executive	23
Secretary or Assistant	21
President	14
Secretary/Treasurer	9
Chairman of the Board	8
Assistant to the President	6
Executive Vice-President	5
Investor Relations Manager	4
Legal Executive	3
Vice Chairman of the Board	1
Outside Public Relations Firm	1
Shared by two or more Executives	24

The usual role for public relations in a shared responsibility embraces most or all of these functions:

1. Recommendations concerning communications strategy appropriate to management goals in investor relations.
2. Preparation in part or total of literature desired such as welcoming letter to new shareholders, interim and annual reports, dividend enclosures, financial news, and information for analyst's research reports. (The proxy statement, or a prospectus is normally prepared by financial or legal officials.)
3. Physical arrangements for analyst or stockholder tours of facilities and for the annual meeting.

EFFECTIVE PROGRAMMING

The first direct contact management can establish with a stockholder is at the time of the stock purchase. A *letter of welcome* can invite rapport. The letter can enclose the most recent financial report, or a booklet about the products and the history. The letter can offer to supply any information wanted personally, issue an invitation to visit the firm's offices or factories, pave the way for a sample product, submit a questionnaire, or merely reflect management's desire to justify the confidence expressed by the purchase.

[3] *Investor Relations,* A Research Report From the Conference Board. Studies in Business Policies No. 124. New York: The National Industrial Conference Board, 1967.

The keystone of any program is the annual report—this is the report card of business. This tool has been brought to a high degree of technical excellence. Much is due to the public relations emphasis in business. Some of the credit belongs to *Financial World,* which has stimulated improvement through its yearly survey and annual "Bronze Oscar of Industry" awards for the best reports. There remains room for imaginative improvement.

A comprehensive study some years ago by the then Controllers' Institute was discouraging. It found: ". . . when it comes to reading financial tables and forming his own conclusions about the soundness and prosperity of the company in which he owns stock, the typical stockholder loses interest—and his bearings!" The Institute report elaborated: "He (the stockholder) is oppressed by the complexity of financial data and frightened by what seems to him the incomprehensibility of accounting language." [4] The *Wall Street Journal* asserted a few years ago that stockholders find annual reports "a confusing jumble." One Opinion Research Corporation survey found that some 37 of every 100 stockholders do not even try to read them. There undoubtedly would be vehement stockholder protest if corporations did not issue annual reports that were accurate and attractive. The fact is that the diversity and technological complexity of today's corporation are difficult to explain in simple terms.

The trend is for reports to do more than reflect and compare the company's current financial results. Some reports show the company's international scope, or its impact on the economy of its plant cities. Some relate products and service to social problems such as air or water pollution, illiteracy, poverty or urban renewal. Some convey the position of management on public issues. The emphasis is on the role of the modern corporation in society beyond its own survival and growth.

Historically, the first annual report was published by the Borden Company in 1858 at the end of its first year of business. In 1903 U. S. Steel "rocked the caverns of corporate secrecy" when it published the first modern, informative annual report for its 1902 year. Judge Elbert Gary's trail-blazing was heatedly criticized by his fellow directors and by corporate officials who thought it was risky to take stockholders into management's confidence. All this is changed now. The annual report has become an important project for most firms over the past 20 years. It is required by law and by stockholder demand.[5]

---

[4] Reynolds Girdler, "18,000,000 Books Nobody Reads," *Saturday Review,* Vol. 46, April 13, 1963, p. 71. At the time, Girdler was vice president for public relations and advertising of Sinclair Oil Corp. For some useful hints on the annual report, see: Frank E. Hewens, "What's New in Annual Reports?" *Public Relations Journal,* Vol. 24, April, 1968.

[5] For interesting reading on annual reports, see John Brooks, "From Dance Cards to the Ivy League Look," *The New Yorker,* Vol. 33, May 18, 1957, 74ff.

An effective annual report ought to include most of these: a distinctive cover design to attract interest and reflect corporate character; a brief summary or table of highlights; a table of contents; identification of managers; an illustrated narrative review of the year; a breakdown of the sales dollar; comparative operating and financial statistics tabulated over a 10-year span; information on the nature and character of the company or expressed in employee policies; civic participation; posture on public issues; social responsibility; advertising and public service programs; aspirations and plans for growth and diversification; and an audited statement of income, financial condition, and number of stockholders.

PRACTICAL CONSIDERATIONS

1. *Readability*. This applies particularly to the corporation engaged in a complex technology, or structured financially in a complex manner. Technology (an integrated circuit) must be stated in terms of what it *does* (in a computer, or TV set) not what it *is* scientifically. The same for depreciation, amortization, the lower of cost or market, or sinking fund.

2. *Cost*. A small mailing list of 1,000 persons would make it uneconomical to put out a four-color, 32-page, slick paper booklet, particularly if the company's products were steamboat whistles. Conversely, a homespun, two-sheet multilith, one-color report to 50,000 stockholders of a firm making home appliances would be ill-advised. In the latter case, the 50,000 stockholders would be potential customers. The large majority of reports cost between 20 cents and $1.00 per copy.

It is common practice for companies to print substantially more copies than are needed for stockholders. The extra copies are for employee recruiting, financial press, analysts and funds customers, suppliers, libraries, trade associations, contract proposals to customers, students, and selected community and government officials.

There is correspondence with investors to be handled. Some submit thoughtful suggestions or inquiries about products, sales, processes, or research. Some others ask seemingly unnecessary questions about the current market price of the stock, the number of shares they own, the total number owned by people whose first name is John, or by people over fifty. Some are chronic gripers.

Among the specifics that stockholders are most likely to complain about, a National Industrial Conference Board study listed eight.

1. High executive salaries
2. Pension and option plans for executives
3. Ownership of stock by management, and possible conflicts of interest
4. Cumulative voting
5. Women directors
6. Selection of public accountants
7. Size of dividends
8. Discounts on products

Letter exchanges with stockholders can function as a splendid intimate communications tool. Perhaps it is this aspect that causes so many corporation presidents to handle responses personally.

Shareholder meetings constitute the means of contact enjoying the greatest amount of experimentation and refinement. Meetings have the undeniable value of face-to-face encounter in which personality, voice, kinship, and compromise all lend significance. Attendance is increasing. Stockholders, however, are scattered through the 50 states and beyond. The expense of attendance is often disproportionate to the stockholder's investment.

Some measure of the distance problem has been alleviated by issuing post-meeting reports. These take the form of meeting minutes, an informal letter from the president or board chairman, or a question-and-answer resume. General Mills, General Electric, Montgomery Ward, A.T.&T., Westinghouse, Gulf Oil, IBM, Woolworth, Xerox, U. S. Steel, and others have undertaken a solution of the distance problem with regional meetings. They have taken management to the population-hub areas where many can attend conveniently. Still other companies have sent representatives to call on selected stockholders, financial analysts, investment counselors, trust officers, and business-page editors. Western Union, with offices everywhere, has had an extensive program of personal calls on stockholders by local company representatives.

The *Wall Street Journal* has reported several complaints emanating from stockholder meetings. After some years, one firm cut out the custom of serving light lunches because stockholders complained loudly about the expense, yet other companies have been criticized because they did not serve lunches "like other companies." At one firm's meeting, stockholders complained about lack of samples and raided displays around the meeting room. Another firm's meeting overflowed the meeting room, and loudspeakers were provided to anterooms, but there were no microphones for these stockholders to use in asking questions. At an electric company's meeting, the film projector caused a short. The lights in the building went out—ironical in this context. Another firm planned to give plastic ice buckets to stockholders attending—but grossly underestimated the number and was painfully caught short. Stockholder meetings, like any other, must be carefully planned.

Some of the larger corporations have put out special publications. Extremely satisfactory results have been reported. Stockholder publications fall into three broad groupings. Some are issued regularly with somewhat the same continuity of format and content as employee house publications. Others are issued spasmodically, in booklet form, to point up some specific body of information such as a major program of capital investment bearing on the relationship between stockholder and the company. Then there are publications prepared for employees, dealers, or other groups, which are circulated among stockholders on the premise that they, too, would be interested.

The stockholder as a potential customer has been mentioned earlier. Among the specific tools harnessed to the task of persuading purchase of products are samples, discounts, sales-promotional literature, and special packages or services. The American Chicle Division of Warner-Lambert gives an assortment of its chewing gum to stockholders at Christmas. General Mills makes a special food assortment available at a special price.

Visits to the company are encouraged. Principal occasions are anniversaries and the opening of new or remodeled facilities. There need be no special occasion, however. Planning for such visitors should include a handshake with a top official, an opportunity to get thoughtful questions answered by qualified specialists, a tour, and a fitting souvenir. The open house is sometimes used.

Assuming that the receipt of a dividend is a happy contact with a stockholder, many companies use dividend enclosures for a sales presentation. Enclosures offer a suitable medium for a series of messages devoted to the inseparability of free enterprise and popular government, for a one-by-one exhibition of products, for photographic likenesses of management people, for branch plant or departmental operations, and a host of others.

ANALYSTS—THIRD PARTY SUPPORT

Financial analysts, bankers, fund managers and brokers in the professional financial community comprise a major third party support. Major investors represented by this fraternity account for more than 30 percent of the trading volume in the stock market.

Visits with individual analysts, presentations to groups, such as the Financial Analysts Society, and tours of facilities, are regular events for large corporations. A survey of 94 firms by the National Industrial Conference Board revealed that firms granted no less than 20, and as many as 100 personal interviews to analysts annually. Members of the financial community, and stockholders also, are frequently surveyed by corporations for their reactions to corporate decisions, actions, and communication with them.

William G. Maas, president, Investment Analysts Society of Chicago, in a talk before the Chicago Chapter PRSA, gave these do's and don'ts in presentations and other contacts.

Among the things to avoid were:

Long corporate history
Rehash of annual report
Enumeration of plants and properties
Industry statistics
Flag waving about free enterprise
Sales talks

Among the subjects that should be discussed:

Current sales
Interim statement
Sales breakdowns by divisions, types of operations, and customer classifications
New products and their potentialities
Plant expansion and modernization
Management
Existing problems
Forecasts

LEGAL AND ETHICAL CONSIDERATIONS

Public relations practice in the financial area is subject to legal considerations growing out of The Securities Act of 1933, Section 10 of The Securities Exchange Act of 1934, and Rule 10B-5 set down by the Securities and Exchange Commission.

The Securities Act of 1933 derived from the stock market crash in 1929. In essence, it required that a company publish a revealing prospectus about itself when it chose to sell securities to the public.

The Exchange Act of 1934 dealt with an aspect of the "conflict of interest" for a corporate official between his duty to fellow stockholders and his personal gain in benefitting through investment by personal posession of information not known to the public.

Rule 10B-5 set down in 1942 represented an effort to tighten up the Exchange Act specifically prohibiting fraudulent and deceptive practices in connection with the purchase or sale of securities.

Questions were raised concerning public relations practices under the provision of Rule 10B-5 when Texas Gulf Sulphur Co. *et al* were charged with violation by the SEC in April of 1965.[6] In this litigation the SEC charged that certain "insiders" traded on inside information concerning a promising ore discovery, and that persons privy to inside information passed on tips to their friends, allowing them to do the same. *At the same time, the company itself issued a false and misleading press release relative to the same information.*

A U. S. District Court ruled in the main favorably for the defendants in the Texas Gulf Sulphur Case. The SEC appealed. On August 13, 1968, a U. S. Court of Appeals found the defendants guilty of violating the disclosure laws. April 21, 1969, the U. S. Supreme Court let the ruling stand. Subsequently another Federal Court ordered Texas Gulf Sulphur to reimburse some stockholders who had sold out after the firm issued the press release minimizing the Canadian mineral find.[7] Again in May, 1969, the Supreme Court declined to rule on the legality of the SEC rule forbidding companies to issue misleading news releases that might affect the judgment of potential investors. This case involved Great American Industries which the SEC charged with creating exaggerated impressions about the company's program to acquire mining claims in Arizona, California, and Colorado. The Supreme Court, in effect, upheld a U. S. Court of Appeals ruling that the company's reports to the SEC said one thing, its news releases another.

There are two basic areas of uncertainty which confront practitioners on this matter of disclosure: 1. Definition of what is a material fact; 2. The timing of stock transactions by insiders. Critics of the SEC claim that it has been shifting its definition of the standards to be applied in both these areas. Spokesmen for the SEC assert that the lack of specificity in the rules should be of no concern to the ethical practitioner. In any event, the practitioner must be fully alert to the need for timely disclosure and the financial reporting requirements as these are set down by the SEC and the various stock exchanges. Robert W. Taft of Hill & Knowlton, Inc., and Craig S. Thompson have prepared the outline of reporting requirements which appears on pages 475–483.

[6] See complete text of the court's opinion in "U. S. Court of Appeals for the Second Circuit" No. 296, September Term, 1966. Published by LaSalle Street Press, 325 West Ohio Street, Chicago, Ill. 60610. See also "Annals of Finance," John Brooks, in the New Yorker magazine, Nov. 9, 1968. Complete day-by-day account of circumstances leading to and through T.G.S.—SEC litigation. Excellent case study.

[7] For further details on this landmark in financial public relations, see "A Press Release Goes to Court," *Public Relations Journal*, Vol. 24, October, 1968. Includes copy of disputed release.

Reporting required for:	Securities and Exchange Commission	New York Stock Exchange	American Stock Exchange	Midwest and Pacific Stock Exchange	—APRIL 1, 1973— Generally recommended publicity practice all companies
Accounting— Change in Method:	8-K * may be required if change in method results in or is related to a material reevaluation of assets or restatement of capital share account.	8-K if filed. Prompt notification to Exchange required.	Same as NYSE.	8-K if filed. Notice of any material change.	A.P.B. now requires statement of accounting policies in annual report. To anticipate new SEC requirements now proposed, give some publicity to accounting changes, be prepared to illustrate how alternative accounting methods would affect earnings. Also, effect of alternatives, where company's accounting method differs from that prevailing in its industry, and differences in tax and financial reporting.
Accounting— Change in Auditors:	8-K, reporting change in auditor and reason. Company must submit letter discussing any disagreements with former auditor on accounting practice, procedure or disclosure, and ask former auditor to submit letter stating whether or not he concurs with company version. Subsequent reporting of change in Forms 10-Q and 10-K.	Prompt notice to Exchange. 8-K when filed.	Same as NYSE.	8-K when filed.	Press release desirable at time of filing 8-K if differences are major. Consider discussion of change in annual or quarterly report to shareholders. Consider clear statement in annual report or elsewhere or when and how company rotates auditing firms.

* Generally speaking, Form 8-K must be filed within 10 days after the close of each month during which an event occurs which must be reported on this form. There are exceptions, which should be discussed with counsel.

Reporting required for:	Securities and Exchange Commission	New York Stock Exchange	American Stock Exchange	Midwest and Pacific Stock Exchange	—APRIL 1, 1973— Generally recommended publicity practice all companies
Acquisition or Merger:	8-K if company or majority-owned subsidiary acquires a significant (15 percent increase in total assets or revenues) amount of assets or business other than in course of business or if registrant issues more than 5 percent of additional securities. Proxy soliciting material or Registration Statement may also be required. Check application of Rule 145(b) to any such transaction involving exchange of stock.	8-K if filed. Immediate public disclosure. Notice to Exchange.	Same as NYSE.	8-K if filed. Timely disclosure provisions apply.	*Current NYSE policy requires immediate announcement as soon as confidential disclosures relating to such important matters are made to "outsiders" (i.e. other than "top management" and "their individual confidential advisors").
Amendment of Charter or Bylaws:	8-K if matter subject to stockholders' approval or if change materially modifies rights of holders of any class of registered securities.	Four copies of material sent to stockholders in respect to proposed changes. Appropriately certified copy of changes when effective. 8-K required for amendment to charter or bylaws.	8-K. Must file with Exchange when effective certified copy of a) charter amendment; b) directors' resolution as to charter or bylaws.	8-K. Certified copy and opinion of counsel, three copies of mailings to stockholders.	Recommend immediate publicity if change alters rights or interests of shareholders.
Annual Meeting (or Special) of Stockholders:	8-K when security holders' vote required except as to procedural matters, selection of auditors or uncontested election of management nominees as listed in proxy statement.	8-K if filed. Prompt notice of calling of meeting; publicity on material actions at meeting. Ten days advance notice of record date or closing transfer books to Exchange.	Same as NYSE.	MIDWEST: 8-K, if filed, three copies of proxy and notice to Exchange. PACIFIC: 8-K, if filed, four copies of proxy material to Exchange.	Press release at time of meeting. Competitive pressures minimize publicity opportunity except on actively contested issues; recommend wide distribution of special post-meeting report.

* Mechanics: On May 15, 1969 the NYSE modified its guidelines on distribution to the following: "To insure adequate coverage, releases requiring immediate publicity should be given to Dow Jones & Company, Inc., to Reuters Economic Services, and to Associated Press and United Press International. These releases should also be given to one or more of the newspapers of general circulation in New York City which regularly publish financial news."
The Exchange manual also states, "When the announcement of news of a material event or a statement dealing with a rumor which calls for IMMEDIATE RELEASE is made shortly before the opening or during market hours . . . it is recommended that the Department of Stock List of the Exchange be notified by telephone no later than simultaneously with the release of the announcement to the news media. If the Exchange receives such notification in time, it will be in a position to consider whether, in the opinion of the Exchange, trading in the security should be halted temporarily."

Reporting required for:	Securities and Exchange Commission	New York Stock Exchange	American Stock Exchange	Midwest and Pacific Stock Exchange	—APRIL 1, 1973— Generally recommended publicity practice all companies
Annual Report Form 10-K:	Required by Section 13 or 15(d) of Securities Exchange Act of 1934 on Form 10-K to be filed with SEC and exchanges where listed no later than 90 days after close of fiscal year. (Some schedules may be filed 120 days after.) Certain companies must submit four copies of printed annual report with 10-K.	No specific rules.	No specific rules.	No specific rules.	Form 10-K requires much new disclosure, and is available to the public through the SEC. Distribution of 10-K to stockholders or others is not presently required but may be desirable in some cases.
Annual Report to Shareholders:	Annual report to shareholders must precede or accompany delivery of proxy material. Seven copies to SEC with preliminary proxy material or when given holders, whichever is later.	Published and submitted to shareholders at least 15 days before annual meeting but no later than three months after close of fiscal year. PROMPTEST POSSIBLE ISSUANCE URGED. Three copies to Exchange. Recommend release of audited figures as soon as available.	Published and submitted to shareholders at least 10 days before meeting but no later than four months after close of fiscal year. PROMPTEST POSSIBLE ISSUANCE URGED. Ten copies to Exchange, Securities Division. Recommend release of audited figures as soon as available.	MIDWEST: Mail with or prior to notice of annual meeting a report containing balance sheet, income statement, analysis of surplus account covering period since last report. Consolidated, certified copy to Exchange. PACIFIC: Copies to Exchange and shareholders 15 days before meeting, not more than 120 days after close of year.	Recommend release of annual financial information as soon as available; second release at time printed report is issued. NYSE and Amex urge broad distribution of report to include statistical services so company information is available for "ready public reference." Check printed annual report and appropriate news releases to insure they conform to information reported on Form 10-K.
Business Purpose Changed:	8-K if registrant deems change of material importance to security holders (consult counsel).	Prompt notice of any material change in general character or nature of business. Public disclosure if securities values affected.	Same as NYSE.	8-K if filed. PROMPT notice of any change in general character or nature of business.	Timely disclosure required where change may affect market valuation of stock.
Capital Surplus: Charges Against—	See new detailed requirements of Form 8-K, item 10, revised 1/12/73. See "Extraordinary Charge."	Prior notice of any proposed substantial charge by company or by directly controlled subsidiary. Stockholder approval may be required.	Same as NYSE.	8-K if filed.	Prompt disclosure normally required if sufficiently material to warrant filing Form 8-K. See "Extraordinary Change or Credit."

REPORTING REQUIREMENTS (cont'd)

Reporting required for:	Securities and Exchange Commission	New York Stock Exchange	American Stock Exchange	Midwest and Pacific Stock Exchange	—APRIL 1, 1973— Generally recommended publicity practice all companies
Change in Directors or Officers; Change in Control:	8-K if change in control of corporation. New directors, officers or other insiders must personally file Form 3.	PROMPT written notice to Exchange of any change. 8-K if filed. Immediate release, if material.	Same as NYSE.	Same as NYSE.	Recommend immediate announcement of any change in directors, officers. However, no technical requirement for publicity except where control of company changes or key man is added or lost.
Collateral Removed or Changed:	8-K unless made pursuant to terms of an indenture qualified under Trust Indenture Act of 1939.	8-K Immediate notice to Exchange.	8-K Immediate notice to Exchange. Timely disclosure if materially significant for investors.	8-K.	Depends on terms of indenture.
Contracts: Defense and Major Long-term	Progress on contracts should be disclosed in such filings as 10-K, 10-Q, registrations. Should include earnings losses, anticipated losses and material cost overruns.	No specific rules	No specific rules	No specific rules	SEC urges that annual reports include disclosure on contract progress as complete as Commission filings. News release should be issued when any material developments affecting contracts become known. (See also "Extraordinary Charge or Credit.")
Conversion Rate— Changes in:	8-K if material change.	Prompt publicity on any change in convertible security, or termination of conversion privilege when conversions have been occurring or appear imminent. Notice by mail to holders of record. Immediate notice to Exchange.	Same as NYSE.	Same as NYSE.	Publicity should be timed to the event causing the change or termination of the conversion privilege. Immediate notice to statistical services.

Reporting required for:	Securities and Exchange Commission	New York Stock Exchange	American Stock Exchange	Midwest and Pacific Stock Exchange	—APRIL 1, 1973— Generally recommended publicity practice all companies
Default upon Senior Securities:	8-K if actual material default in principal, interest, sinking or purchase fund installment, arrearage in dividends for preferred, registered or ranking securities not cured within 30 days—and if indebtedness exceeds five percent of total consolidated assets. Note: SEC plans unilateral publicity for companies with qualified certifications or otherwise near bankruptcy.	8-K if filed. IMMEDIATE publicity and notice to the Exchange.	IMMEDIATE publicity and notice to the Exchange.	8-K if filed. Publish promptly to holders. Notice to Exchange a reasonable time in advance.	Immediate disclosure at time of Board action or when Board fails to act.
Disposition of Assets:	8-K if company or majority owned subsidiary disposes of a significant amount of assets or business other than in normal course of business.	8-K if filed. In addition, prompt notice if disposition materially affects financial position of company or extent of its operations.	Same as NYSE.	8-K if filed. Same as NYSE.	Immediate publicity, especially when assets consist of an entire product line, division, operating unit or a substantial part of the business.
Dividends:	Over-the-counter companies must provide advance notice of record date for subsequent dissemination to investors, extending comparable stock exchange requirements to OTC market. Failure to comply places issuer in violation of Section 10(b) of the Securities Exchange Act.	Prompt notice to Exchange and IMMEDIATE publicity. "Telephone Alert" to Exchange when the action is unusual and during market hours. "Immediate" means even while meeting is still in progress. Ten days advance notice of record date.	Same as NYSE. Notification to Exchange by telephone or telegram with confirmation by letter.	Publish promptly to shareholders any action. Notify Exchange.	Prepare publicity in advance and release immediately by a designated officer on word of declaration. Publicity especially important when dividend rate changes. NYSE manual implies announcement prior to formal board action may be required in case of a "leak" or rumor.
Earnings: Quarterly and Interim	Form 10-Q for each of first three fiscal quarters. Send to exchanges involved and to SEC within 45 days of close of period.	Quarterly. Publicity required. Shareholder mailing recommended but not required. No set time limit but four to five weeks after close of period considered usual. NYSE urges breakout of fourth quarter results for AP and UPI P/F ratio computation.	Quarterly. Should be published within 45 days after end of fiscal quarter. Quarterly breakout "urged" on 3/12/73.	MIDWEST: Three copies to Exchange. PACIFIC: Semiannual. Publish and submit four copies to Exchange.	Immediate publicity; do not hold data until printed quarterly report is published and mailed. Release no later than 10-Q filing. Information in news release must be consistent with 10-Q.

Reporting required for:	Securities and Exchange Commission	New York Stock Exchange	American Stock Exchange	Midwest and Pacific Stock Exchange	—APRIL 1, 1973— Generally recommended publicity practice all companies
Earnings: Forecast or Estimate	SEC presently forbids forecasts in filed documents; expects to develop forms for formalizing forecast procedure shortly.	No specific rules.	No specific rules.	No specific rules.	Forecasts should be either avoided altogether or widely circulated with all assumptions stated. Forecasts by others may require correction by company if wrong but widely believed.
Environment and Civil Rights Matters:	Where material, appropriate disclosure in Forms 10, 10-K, 10-Q and 8-K under sections pertaining to description of company's business and legal proceedings.	No specific provision.	No specific provision.	No specific provision.	Immediate public disclosure, where material. (See "Legal Proceedings.")
Exchange Offer or Tender Offer:	Conduct and published remarks of all parties governed by Section 13(d), 13(e) and 14(d) of the '34 Act and related forms.	Consult Exchange Stock List Department in advance. Immediate publicity and notice to Exchange.	Consult Exchange Securities Division in advance. Immediate publicity and notice to Exchange.	No rules codified.	Massive publicity effort required; should not be attempted without thorough familiarity with current rules and constant consultation with counsel.
Extraordinary Charge or Credit:	Detailed new rules on Form 8-K item 10 for more prompt and more complete disclosure of all material charges and credits to income of unusual nature, material provisions for loss and restatements of capital share accounts. Note special rules on handling disclosure of problems and losses on defense and other long-term contracts (6/22/72).	8-K.	8-K.	8-K.	Press release following information requirements of Form 8-K should precede filing of 8-K to avoid inadvertent partial publication of material information.

Reporting required for:	Securities and Exchange Commission	New York Stock Exchange	American Stock Exchange	Midwest and Pacific Stock Exchange	—APRIL 1, 1973— Generally recommended publicity practice all companies
Float: Increase or Decrease in	8-K if decreased more than 5 percent of previously outstanding amount by payment of indebtedness or decreased more than 1 percent by open market purchases. Over-the-counter companies carried on NASDAQ system must file Form 10-C with NASD and Commission if net change exceeds 5 percent. If company tenders for own shares, Form 13-D must be filed.	Prompt notice when occasioned by actual or proposed deposit under voting trust agreements, etc. and brought to "official attention" of officers or directors.	Prompt public disclosure if decrease is material. Copy of release to Exchange.	Same as NYSE.	Company statement on its intention to purchase stock in open market. Ads and releases where company tenders for own shares must conform with SEC filings. Publicity if change in control is involved or there is a sharp decrease in floating supply which could affect the market in the company's securities.
Form, Nature, Rights or Privileges of Listed Securities Changed:	8-K if constituent instruments defining rights have been materially modified or if rights are otherwise limited—including restrictions on working capital or dividend payments.	8-K if filed. At least 20 days prior notice of change in form, nature or right of securities or certificates.	Same as NYSE.	8-K if filed. 10-day prior notice. May require substitute listing application.	Timely disclosure of all relevant information as soon as "outsiders" are involved in planning discussions.
Legal Proceedings: (See also "Environment and Civil Rights Matters.")	8-K at start and termination of material proceedings (see exceptions in 8-K, item 3); also any bankruptcy, receiverships, reorganization or proceedings in which certain parties have interests adverse to company.	8-K sufficient unless proceeding bears on ownership, dividends, interest or principal of listed securities, or start of receivership, bankruptcy, reorganization proceedings.	8-K if filed. Public disclosure if material. Prompt notice to Exchange.	8-K if filed.	Public disclosure recommended if outcome of legal proceeding could have material effect on company, and news of proceeding has not already become public.
Listing: Initially or on Another Exchange	Involved and extensive legal work is required.	See listing requirements for each exchange involved.	See listing requirements for each exchange involved.	See listing requirements for each exchange involved.	Bulk of routine publicity handled by exchanges. Discuss other special opportunities with legal and public relations counsel.

Reporting required for:	Securities and Exchange Commission	New York Stock Exchange	American Stock Exchange	Midwest and Pacific Stock Exchange	—APRIL 1, 1973— Generally recommended publicity practice all companies
Prospectus:	Filed as part of registration statement. Copies distributed to underwriters and dealers in securities offering, and in turn to investors. (See Chapter 4, Public Offerings.) New rules adopted in 1971 expand presentation of data and specify rules in connection with photos of management, products, maps, other visuals.	Seven copies of final prospectus to Exchange. May be used as part of listing application if issued within past 30 days.	Copy of complete registration filing to Exchange. Recent prospectus may be used as part of listing application.	Prompt notification to Exchange of proposal to offer securities.	News release, if issued at time of registration, must state from whom prospectus may be obtained. It is not clear whether prospectus can accompany release at time of filing.
Proxy Material:	Five preliminary copies of proxy form and statement at least 10 days prior to shareholder mailing. Eight finals when sent to holders, plus three to each exchange where listed. Five preliminary copies of all soliciting material two days prior to mailing; eight finals, when mailed.	Immediate newspaper publicity on controversial issues, especially when there is a contest. Four copies of definitive proxy material to Exchange. Ask for advance review in major matters.	Same as NYSE. Ten copies of all material sent to shareholders to Exchange when change mailed.	MIDWEST: Three copies definitive proxy material. PACIFIC: Four copies definitive proxy material.	Normally publicity not needed on routine matters. Press release at time proxy is mailed becoming more common. Special rules apply in contests; use caution.
Public Offering:	Involved legal procedures and publicity practices. Decision to register may be announced prior to and at time of registration pursuant to Rules 135 and 134.	See Col. 1.	See Col. 1.	See Col. 1.	Publicity limited before, during and after registration; must not create illegal "selling climate" for issue. However, limitation does not exempt companies from disclosure obligations or bar "ordinary" publicity.
Redemption, Cancellation, Retirement of Listed Securities:	8-K. Over-the-counter companies carried on NASDAQ system must file Form 10-C with NASD and Commission if net change exceeds 5 percent.	8-K. Immediate press publicity. Prompt notice to Exchange of any corporate or other action affecting securities in whole or part.	8-K. Fifteen-day advance notice to Exchange. Prompt notice of corporate action that will result in any of these.	Prompt publicity to holders, and to Exchange a reasonable time in advance of redemption date.	Usually advertisement is required. Written notice to security holders.

Reporting required for:	Securities and Exchange Commission	New York Stock Exchange	American Stock Exchange	Midwest and Pacific Stock Exchange	—APRIL 1, 1973— Generally recommended publicity practice all companies
Rights to Subscribe:	Registration under the Securities Act of 1933. Prefiling notice covered by SEC Rule 135. Notice to NASD or exchanges 10 days before record date required under Securities Exchange Act anti-fraud provisions.	See regulations. Preliminary discussion necessary —immediate publicity. Important to work out time schedule with Exchange before any action taken. Notice to shareholders not less than 10 days in advance of the proposed record date.	Same as NYSE.	MIDWEST: Prompt notification to Exchange. Holders must be notified in time to exercise their rights, subject to Exchange satisfaction. PACIFIC: Immediate publicity. Ten days notice prior to record date.	Immediate publicity and mailing to stockholders to give all adequate time "to record their interest and to exercise their rights."
Stock Split, Stock Dividend or Other Change in Capitalization:	8-K required for increase or decrease if exceeds five percent of amount of securities of the class previously outstanding. IMPORTANT: Check with legal counsel. Notice to NASD or exchanges 10 days before record date under Securities Exchange Act anti-fraud provisions.	Immediate public disclosure and Exchange notification. Issuance of new shares requires prior listing approval. "Telephone Alert" procedure should be followed.	Same as NYSE.	MIDWEST: Notify of any proposed increase sufficiently prior to permit action on application for listing. Also if issuing securities on parity with or senior to listed securities. PACIFIC: Issuance of additional amount requires prior listing authorization.	Immediate publicity as soon as proposal becomes known to "outsiders" whether formally voted on or not.
Treasury Stock— Increase or Decrease:	Check Form 8-K, Items 7 and 8, for possible application. Note: special rules apply during tender battle.	8-K if filed. Notice within 10 days after close of fiscal quarter in which any transaction takes place. **Prompt** notice of any open market purchase above prevailing market price.	Same as NYSE. Recommend consulting Exchange on purchases above market price.	MIDWEST: 8-K if filed. Same as NYSE. PACIFIC: 8-K if filed. Notice within 15 days after close of fiscal quarter.	Normally no immediate publicity. Reason for action is normally given in annual or quarterly publications before or after event. However, see remarks under "Float," where applicable.

Concurrent with the final stages of the Texas Gulf Sulphur Case, The New York Stock Exchange expanded its policy concerning the adequate and timely disclosure of corporate information.[8]

This policy defines corporate information as "that which might reasonably be expected to materially affect the market for securities." It stipulates that a corporation should "act promptly to dispel unfounded rumors which result in unusual market activity or price variations." It states that a company "should not give information to one inquirer that it would not give to another or willingly give to the press for publication."

News on matters of corporate significance should be given national distribution by "one or more of the national news wire services." In case they do not carry the news, supplementary distribution is indicated.

These stipulations will continue for years to raise questions concerning relationships between public relations and press people. Interpretations range widely on what constitutes "material" information, and when it must be made public. Today no prudent executive would conduct an interview with an analyst or reporter concerning unreleased financial results unless both his lawyer and public relations representative were present.

Some practitioners have suggested that it no longer is proper to grant an exclusive interview to a trade or business magazine, if such matters as sales and earnings prospects, capital expenditures, or growth plans were to be discussed. The reaction and response of one large corporation is outlined in the Case Problem at the conclusion of this chapter. Some officials, both corporate and financial, including Philip A. Loomis, SEC General Counsel, felt there was "over-reaction" to the problem posed in the Texas Gulf Sulphur Case.[9]

Other cases, notably one involving executives of Merrill, Lynch, Pierce, Fenner & Smith Inc., have gone before the courts. Final conclusions will derive in the 1970s from court interpretation of the laws rendered in these and other situations.

CASE PROBLEM

The Widget Company has been a family enterprise for three generations. It now plans to offer stock in the public market.

---

[8] See New York Stock Exchange—Company Manual, July 16, 1968, Section A2, Part 1, "Timely Disclosure," and Part II, "Procedure for Public Release of Information."

[9] Philip A. Loomis, Jr., "Corporate Disclosure and Insider Information." A panel interview, October 7, 1968. The Financial Analysts Federation, 477 Madison Ave., New York 10002.

The chairman, George P. Widget has asked you, as public relations counsel, to draw up a years program which will help attract individual stockholders, and communicate properly with those attracted, interest and indoctrinate financial analysts, and guide all company executives in the legal aspects of financial reporting to the public.

What are the details of your program and the guidelines for executives?

ADDITIONAL READING

CORLISS D. ANDERSON, *Corporate Reporting for the Professional Investor*. Auburndale, Mass.: Financial Analysts Federation, 1962.

JAMES DERRIMAN, *Company-Investor Relations*. London: University of London Press, Ltd., 1969. A guide for British Companies.

C. JUDD HOLT, "How the Big Companies Stage Annual Stockholder Meetings," *Public Relations Journal*, Vol. 25, February, 1969.

SAMUEL A. KRASNEY, "Investment Clubs—A Growing Market Force," *Public Relations Journal*, Vol. 25, April, 1969.

GERALD M. LOEB, "Flaws in Financial Reporting," *Columbia Journalism Review*, Vol. 5, Spring, 1966.

BLAINE K. McKEE, "Reporters As Insiders: Financial News and Stock-Buying," *Columbia Journalism Review*, Vol. 7, Spring, 1968.

ELIZABETH MARTING, ed., *A Company Guide to Effective Stockholder Relations*, New York: American Management Association, 1953.

CLAYTON S. SCOTT, JR., and Frederick N. Robinson, "A Positive Approach to Annual Meetings," *Public Relations Journal*, Vol. 15, April, 1959.

"SEC Reports on Public Relations' Impact on Securities Markets and Public Investors," *Public Relations Journal*, Vol. 19, June, 1963.

T. C. THOMSEN, "The Care and Feeding of Financial Analysts by Public Relations People and Vice Versa," *Public Relations Journal*, Vol. 14, October, 1958.

MARTIN ZAUSNER, *Corporate Policy and the Investment Community*. New York: Ronald Press, 1968.

CHAPTER 21

THE PRACTICE: TRADE ASSOCIATIONS, PROFESSIONAL SOCIETIES AND LABOR UNIONS

> The concept of a business or professional association is a highly civilized one. It calls for what people do least well, subordinating their self interests to the betterment of all. And when members of the group are competitors, it seems an unnatural alliance that won't work. Yet it does, as the proliferation of associations has demonstrated.
> —HOWARD P. HUDSON

The fundamental purpose of the trade or professional association is to advance the interests of its members by providing information, promoting self-discipline in members' performance, and presenting the association's case to the public and to legislative bodies.

Modern trade associations, professional societies and labor unions employ public relations staff members and frequently retain outside counsel.

These associations and societies tend to have their national headquarters in such hubs of influence as Washington, New York, Chicago and Los Angeles. Regional and local units are most often found in state capitals and county seats.

Illustrative of this field of public relations practice is Manufacturing Chemists' Association, founded in 1872 to promote the "interests of the chemical manufacturing industry of the United States of America and Canada." The M.C.A. first employed a public relations official in 1953. By the 1960s its staff included a public relations director, a media relations director, and a woman's activities director. It issues news through both its New York and Washington offices. The public relations director works with a public relations committee of practitioners from the member firms. All M.C.A. public statements must be approved in advance by the government relations director, public relations director, and the technical director.

Typical activities for which the public relations staff are responsible: Issuance of a monthly newsletter; development of industry-wide public relations programs, such as those made necessary by a growing number of laws controlling use of pesticides and herbicides; preparation and distribution of instructional booklets and aids, such as a manual entitled *Keys to Local Publicity;* assistance to editors of employee publications; issuance of news releases; and preparations of presentations to be made to legislators or other specialized audiences.[1]

The magnitude of an association's efforts can be seen in the budget of the American Dairy Association, which spent $15-million to promote dairy products in 1970. Of this sum, $12-million was allocated for advertising and sales promotion; $265,000 for market research and economics;

[1] Digested from L. L. L. Golden column, *Saturday Review*, Vol. 48, June 13, 1964.

$620,000 for information and publicity; $775,000 for program support and field services; and $775,000 to collaborating trade associations.

Associations exist and thrive on the concept that there is inherent strength in numbers, and that public opinion can be swayed best by the unified voice of many. The validity of this theory can be seen in the growth of U. S. trade associations to 3,000 large national ones, and a total of some 40,000, counting local chapters and independent or local groups. There are more than 1,000 professional societies.[2]

The trade association is older than the nation itself. The first one, the New York Chamber of Commerce, was established by Royal Charter in 1768. But the idea didn't catch on right away. There were fewer than 100 trade associations in the United States at the turn of the century. The first major impetus came during World War I, when common purposes drew commercial groups together with common legislative goals. A second spurt came in the depression years of the 1930s. Some 874 codes dealing with such knotty questions as wages and prices were approved by the N.R.A. before The National Industrial Recovery Act was declared unconstitutional. Almost as an echo of the codes, 800 new associations came on the scene.

World War II had somewhat the same effect. Regulations, and the prospect of them, caused businessmen to seek mutual representation. By 1943, more than 1,900 trade associations were in existence. With some fluctuation, due to mergers, the pattern since then has been one of gradual growth.

Noteworthy early accomplishments of trade associations include the standardization of four time zones by the Association of American Railroads, and the cooperation of airlines in matters of reservations, ticketing, baggage, cargo, confirmations, standbys and alternate flights, arranged by the Air Transport Association of America.

By the time of the Civil War, national societies were flourishing for statistics, ethnology, homeopathy, engineering, medicine, architecture, education, and many more.

The increase of both societies and services in the late 19th century reflected the trend to job specialization and greater distribution of knowledge through periodicals and journals.

THE PROBLEM OF SERVING MANY MASTERS

In contrast with corporate internal allegiances—which serve a solidarity of interests, policies and problems peculiar to each corporation—the association or society, and to some extent unions, must serve memberships

[2] Craig Colgate, Jr., ed., *Directory of U.S. Trade and Professional Associations of the U. S.* Washington, D.C.: Columbia Books, 1969.

which may have widely differing views, shaped by a regional influence, a particular phase of a craft, or varying political, ethnic or proprietary predispositions.

The difficulties of a corporation in marshalling its employees or gaining the support of a few publics are multiplied in an association seeking to satisfy a diversity of members and public opinion groupings. The inability of the association to speak with authority is illustrated in an invitation of the attorney general of Iowa to the heads of GM, Ford and Chrysler to testify at a public hearing on auto safety. They declined. A representative of the Automobile Manufacturers Association declined to answer any questions dealing with the three companies because he was "not authorized to speak for any company's policy."

In the diversity of members lies the weakness of the association when it mounts programs on controversial issues. The managers of a corporation can decide with comparative ease whether—and the degree to which—the corporation's interests are affected by high or low tariffs, a drought in a southwestern state, a strike in the copper industry, or a change of administration in Washington. Such decisions are much more complex for an association executive and his staff, or for its presently elected officials. The views of all members, and perhaps an evaluation of which ones "count" most, must somehow be synthesized, represented, and weighted in the final decision. This is a lengthy process unless issues have been anticipated and viewpoints hammered out in the by-laws and policy structure of the organization.

This dilemma is reflected in this statement of policy of the National Council of Farmer Cooperatives:

> We recognize the wide divergence of political opinion among our employees, member cooperative personnel, and farmer-owners. It would be inappropriate for us to express a partisan viewpoint. Therefore, we will support non-partisan programs, as far as is practicable, and will encourage employee participation in partisan programs of their choosing.

Thus, the natural inclination of the association in its programming is to be limited to areas of action in which there is an obvious, predetermined unanimity, a substantial majority, or an effective militant minority. Consensus and compromise tend to be the order of the day.

DIFFERENTIATING TRADE ASSOCIATIONS AND PROFESSIONAL SOCIETIES

In serving the interests of its members, the trade association usually has a product such as tobacco, or a service such as rail transportation, as a common base of interest. The professional society is made up of individuals who share interest in a particular field of knowledge, such as physics or theology, or a skill like surgery or writing. Some professional societies are grouped into horizontal federations devoted to the same subject. The American Medical Association and the American Chemical Society are examples. Others are grouped vertically devoting their efforts to different subjects. For example, the National Research Council. Most learned societies are members of one or more national "councils" such as American Council on Education, and National Academy of Sciences.

Trade associations and professional societies tend to function together in the areas of public education, membership services, publicity programs, and public affairs.

In selecting and disciplining members, professional groups are more rigid. The aim is to gain professional stature and the rewards which flow from it. Levels of ethics for members in many professions preclude certain types of programming, for example advertising, available to trade associations. Some societies engage in group institutional advertising, though individual members may not do so.

In trade organizations, goals are more commercially oriented, with the admitted objective of increasing sales at the marketplace for the products or services of members.

THE OBJECTIVES

Within the framework of problems shared by members objectives fall in one of a definable set of categories.

1. To expand the association itself
2. To harmonize member viewpoints
3. To promote business
4. To influence government
5. To improve products and services
6. To gain popular support
7. To recruit young people
8. To train recruits and provide programs of continuing education for all members
9. To equate with social progress
10. To promote acceptable public behavior among members that will gain public credit and stave off government regulation.

ESTABLISHING A PROGRAM

The process of initiating a public relations oriented program is much the same as in a corporation, university, or government agency.

First, the situation is explored. What is the history in this field? What is the public reputation of the members and of the business or profession represented? Where are the problem areas? Are they critical, imminent, or slowly wending to trouble or catastrophe if not headed off? In short, what are the specific goals and immediate problems?

Second, a plan is needed. Media, tools, and a means of evaluation must be selected. The plan goes on paper. Members are persuaded to endorse it, to pay for it, to implement it as indicated.

Third, the plan should be tested if the stakes are high and time is available. Then it is implemented, with members kept informed of progress and of how they are to take part.

Fourth, results are evaluated and reported to the association management, as a basis for reporting to membership. Conclusions are in the report. The next steps to be taken are recommended. The next goal to be sought is outlined. The probabilities of success are delineated.[3]

FUNCTIONS IN THE PROGRAMMING

An objective analysis by the Public Relations Society of America lists twelve activities most frequently reported by associations. The analysis observes that the association provides "experience sharing" and "programs that in most instances could not be undertaken by individual companies or persons." [4]

". . . The preparation and dissemination of technical and educational publications, motion pictures and audio-visual materials.

". . . The sponsoring of conventions and meetings, instructional seminars and exhibitions.

[3] For a complete approach to a community relations program, see *Community Opinion and the Trucking Industry*, a 130-page booklet. American Trucking Association Inc., 1616 P Street, N.W., Washington, D.C. 20036.

[4] A booklet, "Association Public Relations," Business and Professional Assn. Section, PRSA, 845 Third Avenue, New York, N.Y. 10022, 1965.

". . . The handling of government relations, and the interpretation of the legislative and administrative actions of government agencies in terms of the members' interests.

". . . The compilation and publication of business and industry statistics.

". . . The preparation and distribution of a wide range of news and informational material to the press, radio and television.

". . . Public service activities of many kinds.

". . . The promulgation of codes and ethics.

". . . The dissemination of governmental and other standards to members.

". . . Cooperative research: scientific, social and economic.

". . . Institutional and/or product advertising on behalf of an industry and its products or on behalf of a field of professional or business endeavor, or in furtherance of such matters as public health, safety or welfare.

". . . The furtherance of good employer-employee relations.

". . . The promotion of accident prevention within the industry and among the public."

THE NATURE OF PROGRAMMING

Equivalently, as the emphasis has swung away from defensive postures and actions by corporations and professional men acting independently, the emphasis also has swung to aggressive and specific programs by associations.

Cigarette makers, a scant few years ago tended to deride efforts to determine whether there was a direct link between smoking and cancer. The industry's behind-the-scene efforts were ultra-sensitive to expressions of governmental interest in playing an investigative role. The Tobacco Institute, a public relations arm of the industry, appeared to bystanders to be a defense mechanism, not an instrument for positive public service. The Institute had no public relations office until 1968, and its outside counsel assisted solely in the area of smoking and health controversy.

In 1969, when the F.C.C. ruled that commercials must carry a warning message, the Kiplinger letter reported tobacco firms sought to have the ruling overturned on the grounds that *young people* were paying attention. Sales to young people were going down. The industry has, however, undertaken medically oriented tests and surveys at its own expense to discern whatever relationship may exist between the use of tobacco and disease. Although the timing is more than coincidental, the actions are nonetheless constructive.

Some strides have been made by trade and professional bodies in providing a base for credibility and a bid for support of their special interest programs. Examples follow.

The National Confectioners Association, with an assist from the American Dental Society, issued a booklet "How to Protect Dental Health While Enjoying Candy."

The National Institute of Dry Cleaning gave a "spirit of service" award to a Bay City, Michigan, cleaner. He had appealed on radio for the "shirt off your back" to make nurse gowns for Project Hope's Hospital Shop. He cleaned the shirts. The Bay City Junior Women's Club converted them to gowns.

The American Meat Institute took a position arguing for legislation concerning meat inspection that, in its view, would afford the public the best protection, not the least.[5]

The National Consumer Finance Association found that clergy were often sought by their parishioners for counsel on money matters, particularly matters involving debt responsibilities. Clergymen, however, were simply unequipped to counsel in this area. The Association helped establish "The Clergy Economic Education Foundation" offering a short course in money matters. An offshoot of this program was a counseling manual for the use of ministers, "Money and Your Marriage."

The Association of National Advertisers held for leading advertisers a day-long conference on "Changes and Inequalities in Our Affluent Society."

Less and less do associations mount automatic opposition to federal socially oriented schemes. More and more they seek to determine, and then to define for members, what particular part they might play in the total scheme.

The Electric Research Council and the National Coal Association have worked with the U. S. Public Health Service on the control of sulphur oxides in flue gases. Petroleum companies, through the American Petroleum Institute, have spent considerable time and money on pollution management and water conservation, in cooperation with government.

Public concern has been influential. Some auto association people have said that the investigation originally flamed by Ralph Nader was a blessing in disguise. It produced a public insistence on safety features, which the industry had been unable to add to vehicles because purchasers would not pay the cost. Nader, in 1969, was named by the U. S. Transportation Department to its National Motor Vehicle Advisory Council for a three-year term.

Enlightened industries, through their associations, are working hard

---

[5] Positions taken by associations in various industries on legislative matters is detailed by Henry Assael. "The Political Role of Trade Associations in Distributive Conflict Resolution," *Journal of Marketing*, Vol. 32, April, 1968.

on product quality, packaging, warranty and credible advertising—not on their congressmen—to preclude more consumerism in the form of legislated restrictions. Standards established by television manufacturers, via their association, to protect viewers from radiation are more stringent than those set down by the Federal Communications Commission.

Too often trade associations mistakenly presume an obvious public relations gesture will gloss over a fundamental problem. Typical is the custom of the American Mining Congress to present fifty Christmas trees, one for each state, for use in the annual Pageant of Peace in the nation's capital. The first gift commemorated the decision of over forty years ago to reclaim land devegetated by surface operations. Yet the scarring of the nation's land continues and mine disasters, often caused by lack of adequate safety measures, continue to take miners' lives.[6]

Wiser counsel is coming to prevail in many trade associations. Commenting on this shift, the late Philip Klarnet wrote: [7]

> "Many of the associations that most of us are concerned with undoubtedly did have their origins years ago in the need to establish a defensive posture for the business they represented. As time went on they found a thousand other functions they could perform. . . .
>
> "For associations in general, the issue is not always clear-cut. What *is* clear is that the nature of the new government-business interweave requires a new kind of thinking for both individual companies and associations of all kinds. Fire prevention is better than a bucket brigade. A foxhole is better than a tree stump. A useful public service is better than a good defense."

Professional associations are providing more educational services. In 1968, the Ohio State Bar Association published a 56-page booklet "The Law and You" and placed thousands in schools. Establishment of grievance committees by local medical societies and codes of cooperation between physicians and mass media are further examples of public service.

PROFESSIONALISM IN PUBLIC RELATIONS

Progress in the practice has been substantial. In soliciting fact-finding business from trade groups, Opinion Research Corp. was able to list a wide selection of survey types it has performed. Among them:

[6] For classic case of ineffective, negative public relations, see: Richard Harris, *The Sacred Trust*, New American Library, 1966, the story of the AMA's long-term campaign against government health insurance. Also see his *The Real Voice* (Macmillan, 1964) which details the public relations campaign of the Pharmaceutical Manufacturers Association against drug regulations.

[7] In "The Trade Association: Partner in Public Service," *Public Relations Quarterly*, Vol. 11, Winter, 1967.

 . . . a nationwide study of awareness and attitude toward major problems facing a manufacturing industry.

 . . . the value of present programs as seen by members in a financial association.

 . . . national marketing study on purchase and use of products for a consumer association.

 . . . analysis of a technical society's publications.

 . . . measuring impact of proposed campaign to gain support for a sales tax.

 . . . member evaluation of society's benefits, leadership, and communications.

 . . . survey of chief financial officers to study trend of financial communications.

Granting public relations maturity to many large associations, and progress to most, there remains a long way to go. Among the conclusions in a study by Katharine Abbott of programs in eighty-four professional associations representing 835,000 people, were these: [8]

> Activities promoting *professional ethics* ranked fourth among what members wanted done for them.
>
> Only half the organizations participating had bothered to spell out *long-range purposes* and methods for their public relations programs.
>
> *Members and legislators* were the prime audiences for most of the public relations efforts.
>
> Where programs were evaluated at all, it was usually done with *press clippings*.

On the positive side, in this study, respondents were quick to list public service projects—prepaid dental care, legal aid or lawyer referral, emergency doctor calls, poison prevention—ahead of publicity for effectiveness.

A public relations program, for long-term success, must be based on the association's accommodation of the public interest and a custom-tailored, two-way communications program. As the PRSA booklet, *Association Public Relations,* points out: "Considerably more is involved than the standardized programming and utilization of applicable communications tools. For example, careful consideration must be given to the legally permissible scope of an association's public relations activities. Federal income tax regulations often govern, and state laws vary. Continuing observation is necessary to insure compliance with all Federal and State regulations.[9]

[8] Paraphrased from "Professional Associations and PR," *American Management Magazine,* April, 1964. Based on an excellent thesis, "Public Relations Programs of Organizations in Eleven Professions." Katharine E. Abbott, Ohio State University, 1964.

[9] See Morton J. Simon, *Public Relations Law,* Chapter 23, "Lobbying."

J. Carroll Bateman, of the Insurance Information Institute, has put the status of the practitioner in perspective thoughtfully: [10]

"If anything has changed in association public relations in the intervening decade, it is that there has been general improvement in the status of the association public relations executive."

The improvement in status cited by Bateman is reflected in programs that are increasingly relevant to the environment in which corporations and professional men and women are functioning in the 1970s. The outlook for association practice is bright.

PUBLIC RELATIONS IN LABOR UNIONS

American labor is conscious of the importance of good public relations. This consciousness is manifested by a steadily growing expenditure of money and talent in public relations and public information programs. It parallels organized labor's growing role in civic and community affairs. In a real sense, public relations are the result of labor's awareness of a social responsibility transcending traditional labor-management relations.

Organized labor unions, with a membership of less than 20-million wage earners, represent less than a third of the nation's wage or salary workers. Yet organized labor speaks for and symbolizes the working men and women of America.

Labor's public relations apparatus includes radio "talk shows" sponsored by state and city central labor union councils. At the national level, the American Federation of Labor and Congress of Industrial Organizations (A.F.L.-C.I.O.) sponsors and produces a weekly network radio news conference on specific issues. Filmed documentaries and narratives of labor problems and programs are produced and distributed for public use and for educational and informational use by international and local unions throughout the nation. Filmed special programs also are produced for television.

Greater emphasis is placed on printed media. Production and distribution of brochures, bulletins, and pamphlets on specific labor-management relation subjects and social and political issues are an important part of labor's public relations program.

Nationally, the A.F.L.-C.I.O. publishes a monthly magazine (*The Federationist*) featuring in-depth commentary and analysis on current collective bargaining and social issues of the day. The articles it contains are written by professionals and experts outside the labor movement, as well as by labor's own specialists and officials. The national federation also

---

[10] *The Public Relations Quarterly*, Winter, 1966. "Association Public Relations Comes of Age."

publishes a weekly tabloid newspaper *The A.F.L.-C.I.O. News* and provides a national news service (a three-times-a-week mimeographed mailer) for its affiliates, practically all of whom publish their own monthly or weekly journals.

Labor unions also maintain personal contact with members of the working press and utilize press conferences and backgrounders with regularity.

Cooperative labor-management trade and industry shows have grown in popularity in the nation's larger cities during the past several years. One A.F.L.-C.I.O. constitutional department stages an annual Union Industries Show, involving participation of affiliated international unions representing virtually every segment of American industry. It is held in a different city each year, and its feature is product promotion and public relations, along with labor and management relations. Similar union industry shows are sponsored on a smaller scale by state and local union label councils. All stress harmonious labor-management relations and the fact that the union label (or shop card or button) is a hallmark of craftsmanship. Labor's public relations effort flows quite naturally from fundamental problems: getting and keeping working people organized into strong unions that can bargain effectively with management and promote employee participation in an industrial democracy. These problems continue to be given priority.

However, the role of unions and union members in community affairs, and the fact that union members represent a broad cross section of the community, increasingly require that organized labor's programs serve dual purposes. One is institutional and communicates directly with the membership in matters of collective bargaining and employment. The other is broad in scope and public affairs oriented. It relates the working man and woman to their community and nation, their governmental institutions and political processes and the social order in general.

This dual-natured function of labor public relations is not entirely different from the one labor faced in its early days as an underdog of power and influence, although arguments are mounted on both sides of the issue. Peter Drucker, a management consultant, has said, "Never before, it seems, has organized labor been as strong, as powerful, and as accepted in this country, as today. Yet the American labor movement faces its most serious crisis. It is a crisis of success, not of failure—but that may make it all the more severe. Our union leaders still live in the days when they had to fight for recognition if not for existence. But the problems they really face are those of labor's power and responsibility as a ruling group in industrial society." [11]

---

[11] Peter Drucker, "Labor in Industrial Society," The *Annals*. The American Academy of Political and Social Science, Vol. 274, March, 1951.

This viewpoint is counterbalanced by another: "There is equally impressive evidence that unions also recognize professionalization of the collective bargaining process. Each year, thousands of union leaders attend week-long training institutes so that they may be better informed of the requirements of their jobs. Union leaders of the last generation would indeed be surprised to see a group of union stewards being taught the intricacies of job evaluation on a college campus and by a regular university professor. Indeed, 'going to school' is now an accepted pattern in the life of the modern union leader." [12]

Indication that organized labor itself is adjusting to the changes of "The Era of Sophisticated Labor Relations" is perhaps best demonstrated by the A.F.L.-C.I.O.'s Labor Studies Center, opened in 1969 in Washington, D. C., to develop trade union leadership by education in a collective bargaining, labor law and history, grievance handling and economics.

With the right to organize and to bargain collectively generally assured in law and in public opinion, labor's familiar struggle with management over wages and working conditions has been expanded into such matters as: participation in the decision-making process to determine work rules and standards, safety and health in the job environment; severance pay; retraining programs and reduced work schedules to cushion the effects of automation. Ahead lie such questions as guaranteed annual wage, shorter work week, the effects of world competition in the labor market, and discrimination within unions.

New groups of employees—such as teachers, government employees, retail clerks, computer technicians, nurses and scientists—have broadened the base of organized labor in recent years.

The A.F.L.-C.I.O. has moved into this area by organizing specialized councils to serve the needs and functions unique to the new types of union members. One such council is the Government Employees Council—representing civil servants, letter carriers and postal clerks, and various skilled and semi-skilled employees of federal government departments, agencies, and the armed forces. Another is the Council of A.F.L.-C.I.O. Unions for Scientific, Professional and Cultural Employees—representing actors, dancers, musicians, writers, engineers and technicians. Each council determines its own internal and external public relations programs. Much of the success of allaying the traditional apprehension and hostility of unions held by middle and upper class Americans may be determined by the ability of these union members, themselves middle Americans, to participate effectively in various community endeavors and by attracting class and occupational peers into their organization.

---

[12] "The Era of Sophisticated Labor Relations," by Fred Witney, Professor of Economics, Indiana University, from *Critical Issues in Labor, Text and Readings,* Max S. Wortman, Jr., ed. (New York: The Macmillan Company, 1969), p. 445.

Labor's major difficulty in public opinion stems, of course, from the strike. Hardly anyone on the sidelines opposes the right to strike, in theory; but when the theory is put into practice, then the union's public relations problem grows.

While strikes can be precipitated by management's or labor's refusal to bargain, to yield, or to compromise on a bargaining issue, it is the union that appears publicly to have taken the first visible step. Its striking and picketing calls the public's attention to the worker's action rather than to management's action or inaction. In addition, labor's strength and the display of that strength as a pressure group and in political activity brought to bear in behalf of issues and candidates it favors quite naturally invokes opposition from those aligned against it.

It is apparent that organized labor's conflicting roles of representing employees on the job and of mobilizing these same employees as citizens involved in community, governmental and political affairs, makes its public relations problem a difficult and never ending one. Its barometer of public opinion support can be expected to go up and down over any given period of time, commensurate with events and issues, varying from locale to locale.

CASE PROBLEM

You are appointed public relations director of a state medical society, which has never had a professionally planned public relations program. Prepare a report to your directors (for oral delivery in class) that will detail your plans for research, action, communication, and evaluation during the next year. Be sure to include plans for actions intended to influence all publics involved and effective communications through all relevant media available.

ADDITIONAL READING

A Look at Association Committees, Chamber of Commerce of the United States, 1615 H St., N.W., Washington, D. C. 20006.

Association Operating Ratio Report 1967, compiled by Ernst & Ernst, The American Society of Association Executives, 2000 K St., N.W., Washington, D. C. 20003.

CLARK BELDEN, Public Relations and Association Executives, American Society of Association Executives, 1959.

PAUL W. CHERINGTON and RALPH L. GILLEN, *The Business Representative in Washington*. Washington, D. C., The Brookings Institution, 1962. Nineteen Washington representatives discuss their job as they see it.

JAMES DEAKIN, *The Lobbyists*, Washington, D. C. The Public Affairs Press, 1966.

LEWIS ANTHONY DEXTER, *How Organizations Are Represented in Washington*. New York: Bobbs-Merrill Co., 1969. Describes work of the Washington representative or lobbyist.

RICHARD HARRIS, "Annals of Legislation, If You Love Your Guns," *The New Yorker*, Vol. XLIV, April 20, 1968. Case study of National Rifle Association's campaign against gun control legislation.

JOHN M. HAVAS, "Counseling the Trade Association," *Public Relations Quarterly*, Vol. 14, 1969. This issue also has two other articles related to this chapter.

PHILIP LESLY, *Public Relations Handbook*, 3rd ed. Prentice-Hall, 1967. Chapter 17, "Public Relations for Trade Associations," by J. Carroll Bateman.

HUGH McCAHEY, *Association Public Relations Communications Guide*. Chamber of Commerce of the United States, Association Department, 1968.

BEN STERN, "Why There is No Travel Tax," *Public Relations Journal*, Vol. 25. March, 1969. Details successful campaign against proposed tax on overseas travel.

CHAPTER 22

THE PRACTICE: WELFARE AGENCIES, HOSPITALS, AND CHURCHES

Welfare workers can meet critics on at least equal
grounds if they do their jobs well and tell the
public about their work in everyday English.
—ARTHUR P. MILES

The fields of social welfare, public health, hospitals, and churches are expanding. The growing number of nonprofit agencies—either tax- or gift-supported, or both—is almost staggering. The practice of public relations runs the gamut from charitable organizations to social work agencies, health foundations, hospitals, libraries, religious bodies, and governmental agencies. These are served, in like range, with no formal programs at all, with simple promotional publicity, or with full-scale departments.

Generally, the concepts and practice in the nonprofit field are enlarging. These agencies and their activities are supported, to a large extent, by public gifts and by taxation. Most are staffed by a small corps of paid professionals directing large groups of volunteer workers. Some use lay citizens only as consultants and board members. Public welfare departments in government are an example of tax-supported organizations. The primary public relations objectives are:

1. To raise funds to keep going and growing as needs enlarge.
2. To broaden and maintain volunteer participation.
3. To win public acceptance of new ideas and new concepts, many of which are highly controversial.
4. To develop channels of communication with the disadvantaged cut off from society's mainstream.

In addition to churches, colleges, and hospitals, it is estimated that there are 500,000 gift-supported agencies. The United Way of America represents nearly 2,260 Chests and United Funds in the United States and Canada. In 1969, these community funds raised and spent more than $817-million dollars, about $707 million of it in the United States, to support more than 36,000 organizations for social welfare in 1970. About 84 percent was allocated to organizations with programs for family-children's services, general dependency services, recreation, informal education, and community planning. These figures represent an untold amount of promotion and participation in 2,270 campaigns. The United Way estimate that more than 4.1-million persons took part in the 1969 fund drives. More than 8-million persons serve as volunteers in Red Feather agencies year-around.

Philanthropic giving passed the $17-billion mark in 1969. That year American citizens, corporations, and foundations gave $17.6-billion to charitable causes, a substantial increase over the previous year. American giving passed the $10-billion mark in 1964. Contributions from the individual citizen represent three-fourths of the philanthropic dollars given by all sources, according to the American Association of Fund-Raising Counsel. Corporate contributions for philanthropy in 1969 were estimated at $900-million. In 1967 corporations deducted a total of $829.7-million for contributions, 1.03 percent of their total income. Corporations are permitted to deduct up to five percent of income for charitable gifts but such deductions have never exceeded 1.18 percent. More than one and one-half billion of the 1969 total came from the more than 6,800 tax-free foundations.[1] America's contributions to philanthropy have steadily increased in recent years. Total giving in the 1960s was estimated at $125.5-billion. One fund raiser observes, "We're nearer the floor of giving than we are to the ceiling." And there will have to be more such giving if the needs of nonprofit agencies are to be met. Much of this giving will come only in response to planned, effective public relations programs.

But these nonprofit agencies need more than funds. They need public understanding and citizen participation to attain objectives that are partly educational, partly remedial, and partly palliative. From the viewpoint of the practitioner, this vast range of social welfare activity has three important aspects.

First, there is the possibility of a career that offers deep satisfaction in the service of one's fellow man. It is one of broadening opportunities, especially for women. However, the financial rewards are comparatively smaller than in other fields. *Second,* as the social responsibility concept evolves for profit-making concerns, practitioners in industry give an increasing amount of time and talent to these public causes. *Third,* as the agencies multiply and competition for funds intensifies, the pressure on profit-making institutions likewise mounts. The decision as to which agencies to support and which requests to decline has become a tough problem for corporations, business firms, and labor unions.

The importance of expert public relations practice is slowly but surely being recognized. Progress has been a bit slower than in other fields, particularly at the state and community level. The emphasis has been on publicity and promotion rather than on education. The cramp of funds has been a large factor in slowing full-scale programs.

---

[1] American Association of Fund-Raising Counsel, Inc., *Giving USA, 1969* (New York: The Association, 500 Fifth Avenue, New York, N.Y.). A useful annual compilation of facts related to philanthropy.

WELFARE AND HEALTH AGENCIES

To see this field in its full dimension, there is need to understand that there were 10 million public dependents and $10-billion being spent on public welfare in 1970 through government agencies. These welfare recipients represented less than half of all Americans living in poverty. Further, there were approximately 22 million persons 17 years of age or older who were disabled to some extent by a chronic ailment at the start of this decade. Three million persons were totally unemployed. Public and private agencies represent a still imperfect response to society's needs and pose public relations problems of awesome complexity. A Pennsylvania official sees the lack of adequate collaboration of these agencies as a prime problem for the 70s. Norman V. Lourie, deputy secretary of the Pennsylvania Department of Public Welfare, asserted: "There is general consensus that, in relation to the complex and conflicting needs of our pluralistic society, the social services offered by the thousands of voluntary and governmental organizations . . . are not only inadequate in amount but also are generally poorly articulated and coordinated. . . . Over-simplistic, unplanned, uncoordinated solutions can lead to greater social fragmentation. . . . Responsible change is produced by cooperation of social forces."

The work of welfare, health, and religious agencies is society's response to the consequences of its social disorganization. Social welfare work is the affirmative answer to the question: "Am I my brother's keeper?" It is an outgrowth of the conflicts and maladjustments produced by America's high-speed urbanized living and a shedding of the notion of "survival of the fittest." The need to help those needing it dates from ancient civilizations. The humanitarian urge to give aid and comfort to those needing it is deep within us. Social work is maturing into a professional calling. Caught up in the turmoil and tension of today's divided world, it is in the midst of difficult problems and on the threshold of great opportunities.

Many older social welfare leaders still insist upon the cloak of confidentiality that shielded welfare recipients in years past. But the concept has undergone profound change with the new militancy of those on welfare rolls. The press has long insisted on access to welfare records as an essential safeguard against waste, inefficiency, or other misuse of relief funds. Today, welfare clients and others are eager to identify themselves and explain their problems. However, identifying them can also mean exposing them to the harassment of extremists and taxpayers' groups. Still, welfare workers' overlong insistence on confidentiality may account for the nation's slowness in recognizing and dealing with its acute social problems. Eve Edstrom, Washington *Post* reporter, told a National Conference on Social Welfare: "Social agencies used to shield and protect their clients from the press. . . . If you had told it 'as it was' in the past, things might be different today."

The barriers are coming down in many areas. Television and other forces have increased the frequency of public appearances by adoptive children, the handicapped, and even the mentally ill. For example, young patients at the Utah State Hospital for the mentally ill in Provo have taken the story of mental illness and the hospital's program to the community. These public appearances were found to be helpful therapy. In one year, adult patients provided guided tours through the hospital and participated in 126 panel presentations outside the hospital. Such novel ideas often meet resistance from the older generation of executives in health and welfare agencies.[2]

The development of public relations in this field has been spearheaded by the National Public Relations Council of Health and Welfare Services and the Department of Social Work Interpretation of the Russell Sage Foundation. Fund raising on a mass scale became big business after World War I. Writing persuasive messages and mapping of campaigns became, more and more, a highly specialized task, bringing the professional publicist to philanthropy. Evart Routzahn launched his drive for recognition of this function when he read a paper, "Elements of a Social Publicity Program," at the National Conference of Social Work in 1920.

Spontaneous response to his demand for "a new type worker in the social welfare field . . . trained in the technique of expressing social information in ways that will attract attention" led, ultimately, to formation of the National Publicity Council for Welfare Services in 1922; this title was changed in 1939 to Social Work Publicity Council, and then to National Publicity Council for Health and Welfare Services in 1943. In January, 1961, the title was changed again, this time to National Public Relations Council of Health and Welfare Services. These changes of title reflect the growth in this field. The Council, headquartered in New York City, publishes a twice-a-month newsletter *Channels,* sponsors conferences and workshops, and provides counsel to its member agencies. Its work speeds the advance being made in this field. By 1970, the Council had nearly 11,000 members.

Complete public understanding of social workers and their endeavors

---

[2] *Channels,* Vol. 20, June 15, 1968. For details of an information campaign to gain acceptance of Sheltered Workshops for the mentally retarded, see: Dorothy F. Douglas, et al, "An Information Campaign That Changed Community Attitudes," *Journalism Quarterly,* Vol. 47, Autumn, 1970.

is yet to be achieved. Much of the criticism of welfare agencies stems from general misunderstanding, but workers in the field have to accept a great deal of responsibility for creating these misunderstandings, in the opinion of Arthur P. Miles, professor in the University of Wisconsin School of Social Work. He lists these fountainheads of criticism: (1) intellectual confusion of the social sciences; (2) confusion over what should be held confidential in the public welfare field; (3) gobbledygook of social workers; (4) anti-intellectual trends in America.

Social agencies have yet to capitalize fully on thorough and frank accounting of their affairs to the public. Too many old-timers in this field demonstrate an attitude of "our noble motives and good works need no reporting to the donor citizen." There is need to distinguish between mass publicity-promotion campaigns once a year to raise funds and continuous and candid reporting week in, week out.

Agencies are constantly working against deep prejudices, deep fears, and ignorance, which characteristically breed rumors and gossip. The American Red Cross has repeatedly proved its dedication to humanity, yet it is frequently the victim of malicious rumors. Many of the charges lightly bandied about by Vietnam veterans are updated rumors common after the Spanish-American War. A child welfare agency must be steeled against the day when a newspaper will make a sensational crusade of the agency's withdrawal, before the end of the probationary period, of a child put out for adoption. The answer to such unfounded, emotional attacks is to establish credibility through performance and to build enduring support based on education rather than emotion.

Nonprofit agencies must have appreciation and tolerance for the plight of today's citizen, hounded by the multiplying demands of this cause and that agency for funds, while his tax bill to pay for like services continues to rise. They must realize that each person can give only so much time to the doorbell-ringing chores he is asked to perform by a multitude of agencies. *More effective two-way communication will bring the desired rapport between agency and citizen.*

A convincing demonstration of this principle was provided by the program of the State Charities Aid Association in New York to bring the critics of public welfare face to face with the grim problems of poverty, illegitimacy, and illiteracy, outlined in Chapter 6.[3]

THE PROGRAM

A welfare agency starts out in an enviable position. Its sole reason for existence is to help people. The agency can gain ready entry to mass

[3] *Is It Safe? Is It Wise?* Undated pamphlet, State Communities Aid Association, 105 East 22nd Street, New York City, circa 1963.

media and opinion leaders. It presumably has no selfish axe to grind. There are, however, organizations born to promote legal or social reform—Planned Parenthood, for example—which run head on into solid blocs of opposition. Those agencies and causes that are highly controversial have a more difficult path.

On the other hand, social agencies are "selling" intangibles. The Community Chest has widely proclaimed, "Everybody Benefits, Everybody Gives." Still, many people regard these agencies as existing for the "other fellow." Much of the service provided by social agencies is shunned because "it's charity." Many who could use the services of these agencies simply do not know of their availability. There is difficulty in making concrete presentations of the tangible benefits derived by the individual citizen. This difficulty is compounded for the charitable and family service agencies because of the confidential relationship that must exist unless voluntarily given up by the client. An increasing problem for the United Funds is mounting debate as to the relevancy of long-standing Red Feather programs. "Is too much being funneled into middle class institutions like the Boy Scouts rather than the ghetto?" "Must the organizations be dominated by the rich or wellborn or labor leaders, with minimum participation by the needy?" These are typical questions. There are questions from both blacks and whites about priorities and leadership.

Some social agencies have drifted into a heavy reliance on the "fear technique," exploiting the emotions in their fund drives. This approach may raise funds, but it doesn't serve well in the long run. The trend is in the direction of more positive appeals, but fear as a primary motive is being cast out too slowly by some agencies.[4] Use of emotional appeals has served to cloud the purpose of the agency in the public mind and to blunt its educational objectives. For example, people must be motivated to get periodic cancer check-ups, not frightened into an attitude of hopelessness. As *Channels* observed: "Pitying words used in fund-raising messages sometimes hurt the cause for which the funds are sought. Describing persons who have a particular deformity or disease, for example, as "helpless," or "hopeless" or "incurable" tends to dehumanize them, deters the rehabilitation process, and generally reinforces the harmful stigma that already exists."

More showmanship, less fear-mongering is emerging in social work. An example is offered in the showmanship of Detroit's Torch Drive. The Detroit community fund, on its annual lead-off, has staged a parade worth seeing, one that brings out millions of Detroiters.

Fear and showmanship sometimes can be successfully blended to produce an effective educational effort in these emotion-laden fields—to

---

[4] Helen R. Bitterman, "Slogans in Welfare," *Public Relations Journal*, Vol. 10, July, 1954.

wit: the campaign against cigarette smoking waged by the American Cancer Society and other health groups. The lead was taken by the American Cancer Society in the early 60s with production of TV spots warning against cigarette smoking because it causes lung cancer, emphysema, and heart disease. These spots got few showings until June, 1967, when the Federal Communications Commission ruled that radio and TV stations must give significant time to anti-cigarette messages, interpreted by the FCC counsel as one "anti-commercial" to every four paid cigarette ads. Actors and talented copywriters and publicists from advertising and public relations agencies volunteered their services. The Cancer Society spelled out the themes and provided the facts, and the volunteers wrote, acted, and produced the "anti-cigarette commercials."

One of the most compelling spots was made by actor William Talman, the district attorney of the TV Perry Mason show, who was dying of cancer when he recorded his warning to smokers. This spot, shown shortly after his death, hit the public like a bombshell. It has since been shown around the world. The influence of this anti-cigarette campaign on the social agency field has been marked. It produced results—the U. S. Health, Education and Welfare Department estimated that one million men and women quit smoking in the United States in 1968, basing its figures on a Census Bureau sample survey. These "commercials" appear on prime time and are widely discussed. Their professional quality and results have lifted the sights of publicists in the nonprofit field. Other agencies producing similar anti-cigarette commercials are the American Heart Association, the National Tuberculosis and Respiratory Disease Association, and the U. S. Public Health Service. The effectiveness of these campaigns was reflected in the drop in cigarette smoking in the United States in 1968, and again in 1969.

The Cancer Society has been innovative and imaginative in other ways. Conscious that it had to reach young people, it enlisted poster artist Peter Max, whose colorful anti-smoking poster quickly became a collector's item. Other agencies have enlisted young people in their campaigns. High school students in California, Minnesota, New York and other states have written and taped their own radio spots to fight smoking for the TB and Respiratory Disease Association. The Heart Association encouraged young people to create posters for the heart cause in Maryland. In its many faceted information campaign against drug abuse, the National Institute of Mental Health has recruited young talent from the ghetto to develop radio and poster messages for ghetto audiences. The Texas Health Careers program holds the attention of its high school assemblies with music and humorous audio-visual presentations.[5]

5 *Channels*, Vol. 22, October 1, 1969.

There are many other problems peculiar to this field. For one thing, there is the unflattering, untrue stereotype of the social worker. For another, there is social work jargon, full of clichés and meaningless abstractions. As one editor commented, "trying to catch such phrases as 'intergroup consciousness,' 'the weaving of the profession of social work into the community fabric,' ad infinitum, is like trying to catch a jellyfish in a net." More serious is the fuzzy notion in some quarters that these agencies are tax-supported. This is caused by the blurring lines between voluntary work and government programs.

Typical of the language problem is what to call the person the agency is trying to help—"client," "patient," "customer," what? The very term "client" or "patient" connotes a difference in hierarchy. One social worker who raised this question added: "People who are so categorized are placed in a seeking, supplicant role, which implies a superiority on our part and a more dependent role on theirs." She answers the question: [6] "Why don't we call them people?" "Perhaps this is one very important key to meaningful communication. People must be able to talk across the table in a free and sharing relationship, in which both participate with dignity and mutual respect. . . ."

Another problem is an overemphasis on publicity. This field pours out an endless flow of publicity. The national headquarters of such agencies as the United Way, Girl Scouts, Red Cross, Boy Scouts, Camp Fire Girls and the health foundations have strong, competent publicity staffs. These headquarters staffs promote national coverage in news media, both nationally and locally. At the local level, publicity is handled more often than not by volunteers with purely amateur standing. Many agencies could profit by putting more emphasis on the communication of ideas and less on getting publicity.[7]

The Camp Fire Girls, Inc. offer an example how the headquarters public relations staffs can assist local units. Each year the organization's small staff at New York City headquarters has developed a newsworthy theme for its annual birthday. One year it was "Make Mine Democracy," an economic education program. Another year it was "Discovery Unlimited—An Adventure in Creative Living," a program devoted mainly to better understanding of crafts and arts. For each birthday program, the headquarters group has provided guidance kits to all the local councils,

---

[6] Geraldine Gourley, "How Do We Communicate?", *Tennessee Public Welfare Record,* April, 1969.

[7] For a case study in national organizations, see Harold P. Levy, *Building a Popular Movement* (New York: Russell Sage Foundation, 1944). (The Boy Scouts.) For a glimpse of Girl Scout PR, see Natalie Flatow and Harriett Philmus Pitt, "World's Biggest Public Service Campaign: 50 Golden Girl Scouting Years." *Public Relations Journal,* Vol. 19, July, 1963.

promoted the theme in its magazine, *Camp Fire Girls,* and climaxed the event with a network radio broadcast on the birthday date. The press is fully briefed on the details. The Camp Fire Girls stepped up this program for their fiftieth birthday with a Golden Jubilee Celebration, which had four goals: (1) to increase public understanding of the organization; (2) to update and enrich the program; (3) to render an outstanding service to the nation; (4) to pay tribute to the vast body of dedicated volunteers across the nation. These goals were accomplished with a public relations staff of five professionals, two of them part-time, and four clerical assistants.[8]

Leadership from national and state headquarters, coupled with follow-through at the local level, makes an unbeatable combination. The California Division of the American Cancer Society brought out more than 186,000 California women to see showings of a film, "Breast Self-Examination," during a seven-week period. The success of this project was attributed to planning and local follow-through.

Although the problems may differ from the United Fund to Family Welfare Service to Red Cross to National Council on Crime and Delinquency to Girl Scouts, the principles of programming are the same.

THE YEARS AHEAD

Welfare agencies must tightly link their programs to educating the public to accept enlightened social concepts in fields such as poverty, mental health, crime and correction, child welfare, and the problems of aging. *Planned, consistent programs* are required to break the barriers of public apathy, superstition, and the deadweight of indifference on these fronts. For example, only enlightened opinion will bring acceptance of sound rehabilitation and parole procedures in the field of crime and corrections. To counter opinions blended of vengeance and sloppy sentimentality, corrections leaders must persuade the public of the values of modern prisons and the supervised return of prisoners to society.[9] What can be accomplished is dramatically illustrated in the progress made in mental health since World War II.

The expanded range of activity and the mounting public bill for philanthropy have been financed in an inflated war-and-defense economy. In an economic headwind, social agencies will be hard hit. The demand for their services multiply in time of financial depression, but sources of funds contract. Even with all the gains made, the pull on the citizen donor is

---

[8] Elizabeth M. McStea, "Camp Fire Girls Builds on 50-year Foundation," *Public Relations Journal,* Vol. 19, June, 1963. A case study.

[9] For illustration, see: James F. Donohue, "Social Action Makes a Prison Break," *Public Relations Journal,* Vol. 25, October, 1969.

still none too strong. Even in an economy loaded with cheap money, there is a strong tendency "to let George do it."

The tab for this vast range of social work no longer can be paid by the rich man or by the corporation. It is from the upper and middle income groups that donor-supported agencies must get the bulk of their budgets. It is in the middle income group that a strong sense of responsibility must be built. The alternative is to transfer the burden to government. Then all will pay through compulsory contributions in the form of taxes. The donor-supported, volunteer-manned agency has an important innovative function. It must be maintained in the years ahead. Leaders of these agencies must strive even harder to muster public support through public relations, support that will endure in good times or bad.

Foremost among the problems facing health and welfare agencies is that of building a communications bridge between the white and black communities, the inner-city and outer-city. The National Public Relations Council of Health and Welfare Services, under the leadership of Harold N. Weiner, has developed a plan to improve relationship and communications between social agencies and inner-city residents, which merits outlining here: [10]

I. *Why New Efforts Are Needed*

   A. "Come-and-get-it" services fail to reach inner-city adequately.
      1. Inner-city social disabilities and rates of mortality and morbidity from disease are far higher than in white urban and suburban communities.
      2. Most agencies lack service or information centers in inner-city.
      3. Services that exist there are frequently second class.
      4. Interests of inner-city residents are not directly represented on on boards of directors or staffs of most traditional agencies.
      5. Uncoordinated "marketing" of agency services compounds the difficulties of the poor in obtaining needed services.
   B. Traditional communication methods and messages rarely reach inner-city.
      1. "White" mass media are unreliable routes to inner-city.
      2. Pamphlets and other traditional materials are largely created by persons not in touch with inner-city needs, interests, language, etc.
      3. Distribution of materials frequently stops short of inner-city.
      4. Competition of messages from a host of agencies creates confusing static.

[10] Provided by National Public Relations Council, dated 1969.

5. Lack of involvement in inner-city problems has estranged many established agencies from that part of the community.

II. *What Kinds of Efforts Can Alter the Situation?*

A. Greater involvement of inner-city residents in affairs of social agencies.
   1. As aides, staff members, committee and board members.
   2. As advisors on agency communications and as communicators to and from the inner-city.
   3. As staff and volunteers in agency branch offices in inner-city neighborhoods.
   4. As partners in developing training programs in inner-city for civic leadership, for employment in social agencies.
B. Coordinated approaches by groups of agencies.
   1. Establishment of inner-city health and welfare councils, staffed by local residents.
   2. Creation of "Supermarkets" of services and information to make available one-stop centers in inner-city neighborhoods.
   3. Reallocation of agency services and budgets to make sufficient resources available to coordinated enterprises.
   4. Development of coordinated social action programs by groups of agencies to help fill expressed inner-city needs.
C. Use of varied communication methods.
   1. Work through inner-city organizations and institutions.
   2. Enlist paid and volunteer workers from the inner-city to help shape and deliver agency messages.
   3. Reallocate agency public relations budgets to defray costs of communication research in inner-city.
   4. Allocate public relations resources to joint communication action with other agencies to make services better known and used.
   5. Use black, Spanish-oriented media.

More effective communication with all sectors of society is an imperative for nonprofit agencies. There is growing public impatience with all inflexible, bureaucratic, and impersonal enterprises. There is increased demand for straight talk from those in social agencies.

PUBLIC RELATIONS FOR HOSPITALS

THE PERSPECTIVE

America's hospitals are thrust more and more into the public spotlight. They are gradually becoming sensitive to the importance of good public relationships. Medical men and hospital administrators, once coldly aloof and sternly professional, are developing a "public opinion consciousness" under pressure of mounting costs and criticism. Stung by such adjectives as "indifferent," "complacent," "smug," and even "arrogant," medical professionals, assisted by specialists, are coming to accept public relations as an essential part of medical practice. When charges against hospitals are catalogued in a widely-sold book *The Plot Against the Patient* [11] major newspapers editorialize on "The Crisis in Health Care," and patients protest skyrocketing costs, only the most blind would fail to see public relations' role in this vital field. There is, of course, a way to go, but progress in this field has been marked. Strong impetus was provided by the organization of the American Society for Hospital Public Relations Directors in 1965 under the auspices of the American Hospital Association. The A.H.A.'s *Public Relations Newsletter* stimulates many innovations.

Public relations for medicine is also spearheaded by the growing number of practitioners serving the American Medical Association, the American Hospital Association, the American Nursing Association, Blue Cross, and similar groups at the national, state, and local levels. There is still too much effort expended, however, in justifying rather than correcting the irritants. Medical public relations needs to be more concerned with the "diseases" which blight relationships than with their "symptoms." There is also need for closer coordination of the several active programs in the health field.

The advance made in hospital public relations is shown in a survey made at the University of Missouri in which twenty-four out of twenty-seven state university hospitals responding had public relations departments. Significantly, none of the programs was in existence twenty years prior to the date of the survey: eighteen of the departments had been organized within the previous decade. Twenty of the twenty-four directors were college graduates; eleven of these were journalism majors. Half of them had had prior newspaper experience. These twenty-four directors reported a wide variety of duties, but "two responsibilities seem to be basic. These include the release of information to the mass media and the preparation and supervision of production of publications. Other duties are as diverse as conducting tours for visitors and directing programs in postgraduate education." [12] On an average day, you can find more people than the combined populations of Boston and Cincinnati resting in United States hospital beds, plus some 45,000 newborn infants. The odds are that each of these infants will be confined in a hospital at least four times during

[11] By Fred Cook, published by Prentice-Hall, Inc., in 1967. Typical of several books in recent years which cite shortcomings in hospitals.

[12] Joye Patterson, "A Study of Communications Programs in State University Hospitals," Multilithed Report, 1962.

its lifetime. More and more people are requiring and getting hospital care. The public is "hospital conscious" as never before.

People do not have to be sold on the hospital; they want more hospital care. They do not have to be sold on doctors; they only want more of them and more opportunity to use them. What bothers people most is the problem of financing their health needs. Unless this problem is met, the rest will not matter very much. And this problem of costs is the central one facing hospitals, too. Hospital deficits are swelling as the average deficit per patient is multiplied by an ever-growing stream of sick folk entering hospitals. These deficits must be made up by either contributions or taxes. Despite shorter average patient stays in hospitals, bills are up. Hospitals receive much criticism from state insurance commissioners, labor unions, employers, legislators, and other public spokesmen. Most of this criticism is because of hospital charges, even though three-fourths of the population now has some kind of hospital insurance. Thirty million Americans do not. A few figures tell the story. Physicians' fees, rising about 3% a year until 1965, were increasing at twice that rate at the start of the 1970s. One day's stay in a hospital (not including physician's care) cost $44 in 1965, $70 in 1969, and was estimated to reach $100 a day by 1971. Senator Philip A. Hart of Michigan asserted that, from 1957 to 1970, prices for all consumer goods had increased 29.7 percent, doctors' fees had increased by nearly 60 percent, and the cost of daily hospital services had skyrocketed by more than 160 percent. At the start of this decade hospital care costs were climbing at the rate of 12 percent a year and nursing home care costs at the rate of 22 percent a year. The 1970 average cost of a hospital stay was quadruple that of the 1950s. The well-known financial writer, Sylvia Porter, has charged ". . . a majority of our hospitals still are guilty of gross misuse of available health care resources." These costs are compounded of advanced medical technology and of the cost of specialists to man it. In a sense, American health care is a victim of its own success. Medicaid, which serves 10 million persons, and Medicare, which serves an even larger number of the elderly who need more care, are illustrative. These costs must be justified to the public.

The Roger Williams General Hospital, Providence, Rhode Island, took its explanation to the citizens of Rhode Island in an eight-page supplement to the Providence *Sunday Journal*. In this annual report, which reached more than a half million readers, a four-page spread of pictures detailed the items in the hospital's then $45 a day charge. The back cover presented the annual financial statement. Some additional 10,000 reprints were distributed to influentials: legislators, staff, patients, and donors.[13]

---

[13] Raymond W. Caine, Jr., "The Why of Hospital Costs," *Public Relations Journal*, Vol. 24, October, 1968.

Demand for broader-based support comes in the face of the highest patient rates in history. Alden Mills wrote: [14]

> The voluntary hospitals have been expected to care for a larger number of free patients or patients who pay less than cost. . . . Increasing costs of operation have been particularly marked in the voluntary hospitals. These institutions have always been regarded as the pacemakers in hospital administration. . . . This country needs the leadership that they can provide. . . . To the voluntary hospital, adequate understanding, good will, and respect are today vital. . . . Lack of public support and generous respect may be fatal to voluntary institutions.

The tax-supported municipal and state hospitals, likewise, are confronted with multiplying demands for treatment and the provision of new and expensive facilities. In either type of hospital, public support determines the answer to these problems. There is increasing political activity to combat what the medical profession bitterly labels "socialized medicine" and there are the ever-persistent antivivisectionists. Adaptation of public relations practices to the needs of the medical profession results.

In presenting the views of John Q. Citizen toward hospitals, Frank Sinclair, former *Milwaukee Journal* writer, told a public relations conference of hospital administrators:

> Why is it necessary to awaken a patient a couple of hours before breakfast to wash his face? . . . He says that if it is a question of hospital routine or patient comfort, the hospital should make its routine fit the patient. . . . Why does it sometimes take many minutes for a nurse to answer the patient's light? . . . We've all seen nurses standing in the hallway talking and ignoring call lights. . . . Too many hospitals are drab.
>
> A more homey atmosphere is wanted. . . . Hospitals are too noisy. . . . Why can't more quiet be given the very ill? Hospitals that demand payment for care weekly or even at the end of the hospital stay, demonstrate a commercial quirk. . . . I know of one case where a husband was called upon to pay in advance before his wife was given a blood transfusion. . . .
>
> I've had people tell me that hospitals have become so professional that they are too impersonal, too cold and distant. . . . Some persons feel that hospitals overcharge on certain items. . . . The public can see no reason why any doctor who holds a license to practice medicine, and is capable, should not practice in every hospital. After all hospitals are tax-free because they support humanity.

[14] *Hospital Public Relations Today* (Berwyn, Ill.: Physicians Record Co., 1964). Pioneer book in this field. Mills died in 1969.

The sum of all this is that hospitals, from the smallest community to the largest, need continuing programs directed by trained practitioners. The medical profession needs the intermediary in dealing with the public more than most groups do. Mills argued, possibly with some exaggeration! "Without any attempt at melodrama, one can safely state that hospitals in the United States today face the most serious crisis in their history. The intelligent use of public relations programs may spell the difference between continued growth and stagnation."

THE PROGRAM

In no field is painstaking attention to detail and bird-dogging of loose ends more important. An individual's hospital experience is charged with emotion. The opportunities for irritations and ill will abound. On the other hand, the opportunity to gain everlasting devotion is unequaled. Every citizen is reached by the service of his community hospital at least once in every eight years. The basic requisite is considerate hospital service at reasonable rates. This means good medical care and efficient administration. In many hospitals, there is a broad gap between "public relations" and patient care. Hospitals, like others, must learn that good performance should precede the news of it.

Couple this principle to a planned program, and the hospitals have the means to meet their problems. Essentials of such a program are given in one planned for the Lancaster, Pennsylvania, General Hospital:

EMPLOYEE RELATIONSHIPS. Orienting an employee in the initial interview, providing a tour of the hospital, and giving him a personnel brochure. Informing employees through a weekly publication, movies, bulletin boards, panel discussions, and pep talks in pay envelopes. Providing employee incentives and understanding through a clearly established wage scale, a vacation policy, a security program, and an employee council as a channel of communication between management and staff, and plans for a termination interview. Using employees to tell the public the hospital story includes placing employee's family on mailing lists, hospital tours for families, and use of employees as speakers.

VOLUNTEER GROUPS. Informing members of the board of directors by providing full orientation, putting them on all mailing lists, and utilizing them as speakers and hospital representatives before public groups. Also providing appropriate recognition for their service. Keeping the volunteer auxiliaries thoroughly oriented, informed, and imbued with a sense of participation in hospital projects. Seeing that "Gray Ladies" are likewise given orientation, receive all hospital information, and are rewarded for their services.

MEDICAL STAFF. A contented staff essential to the best service and growth of the hospital. Definite and sound staff organization with working liaison between staff and hospital board. New staff men thoroughly oriented. Staff stimulated to help create means for the patient to better bear costs. Staff members continually made aware of variety of hospital problems. Staff, internes, and residents kept fully informed and educated as to importance of public relations consequences of their work.

PATIENTS. A voluntary hospital is a public utility. Patients are part of the society which owns and controls that utility. Demand the best of service. . . . Enter the hospital with a "combat mission" attitude. Their hospital experience a highly emotionalized one. Utilize this advantage. Admission interview to allay fears of hospitalization and financial worries. Understanding and appreciation of patient concept by all employees essential. The hospital interpreted to the patient, and convalescence is proper time to begin. Patient and visitors convinced that hospital is working in patient's interest. Services for visitors provided. Preadmission contacts also opportunity to win patient's understanding and goodwill.

In response to vociferous patient criticism, many hospitals are junking the custom of 5 A.M. reveille, speeding admission procedures, dropping requirement of payment in advance, providing tastier food, a choice of menus, and creating more pleasant surroundings. More medical people are coming to agree with Dr. Anthony J. J. Rourke, former president of the American Hospital Association, that "hospital rules must be set up for the benefit of the patient, not for the hospital or the doctor or the nurse." A writer found in a 100-hospital survey that those most affectionately regarded treated their customers as human beings, not as "symptoms with relatives attached." One of the urgent problems facing hospital practitioners is that of building two-way communication with the minority and poverty communities. This starts with listening to angry demands for equal care in equal surroundings for these disadvantaged citizens. Michela Robbins Reichman of San Francisco's Mount Zion Hospital and Medical Center urges fellow practitioners: "We must identify the real issues behind the rhetoric, instead of responding emotionally to the rhetoric."

Typical of the new approach in hospital public relations is the attention given expectant mothers by Chicago's Michael Reese Hospital. Two months prior to expected delivery, the hospital sends the expectant mother (1) a letter confirming her room reservation; (2) a pre-admission registration form, which keeps admission delays to a minimum; (3) information about a special birth announcement service sponsored by the hospital's Woman's Board; (4) general hospital instructions, policies, and services; (5) a folder about the availability of radio and TV sets with earphones. This is the positive approach.

To take the fright out of a child's first visit to the hospital, the St. Joseph Hospital, Albuquerque, New Mexico, organized pre-admission pediatric parties, scheduled on the second and fourth Saturdays every month. Parents accompany the future patients to the parties, and other children in the family are invited, if they have not recently been exposed to a communicable disease. The parties include introduction to personnel of the pediatrics unit, a tour, a visit to the playroom, and a slide show. Visiting regulations are explained to parents.

HOSPITALS AND THE PRESS

Doctors and hospitals, are a vital news source. Direct, daily relationship with news media holds great potential and poses equally difficult problems. Hospital administrators who maintain cordial cooperation with the press are virtually assured of access to the community through these media. A hostile newspaper or radio station can blast a hospital's reputation by the factual reporting of an unfortunate mistake which cost a life. Such things do happen. Take the case of a Woonsocket, R.I., hospital. The newspaper, using subtlety and restraint, told, with devastating effect, the story of how a missing oxygen-tank wrench cost the life of a prematurely born baby.

As acknowledged in one hospital-doctor-press code: [15]

> The community has a right to information about its hospital facilities and services. . . . It is the hospital's obligation to supply this information accurately, promptly, and willingly. . . . Each hospital should name authorized spokesmen to be available at all times (24-hours-per-day coverage) to answer inquiries from news media. News-media representatives should have the telephone numbers indicating where the appointed spokesmen will be available for information either day or night. After naming spokesmen, the hospital staff should be informed that the task of handling news has been assigned to specific persons. Others on the staff should not release information but should refer all inquiries to those named to perform the news function. Hospital telephone operators should be fully instructed to refer inquiries from news media to the authorized spokesmen—quickly, politely, and efficiently.

There is a gap between what the press wants for publication about personal injuries and illnesses and what the medical profession feels it can ethically reveal. The same is true in the matter of medical research and hospital innovations. The press demands for news run smack into the medi-

[15] State Medical Society of Wisconsin, *A Guide for Physicians, Hospitals and News Media* (Madison, Wis.: The Society, 1960), p. 3.

cal profession's code of ethics and the private relationship of doctor and patient. Hospitals, in turn, are circumscribed by doctors' attitudes and ethics. Leaders in both groups have been striving to gain agreement on mutually satisfactory procedures.

A number of codes have been worked out at state and local levels over the past few years. These codes are more guides than rigid rules. Such agreements recognize the press's obligation to report medical news adequately and accurately. Hospitals recognize the related obligation of serving as a cooperative news source. Both should be guided by three major considerations: [16]

1. To safeguard the private rights of the individual, so that no hospital patient will be caused unnecessary embarrassment or discomfort or be made the object of scorn or ridicule.
2. To report the news accurately, authoritatively, promptly.
3. To cooperate sincerely in all relationships.

PUBLIC RELATIONS FOR CHURCHES

REALLY NOT NEW

An increasing number of the some 238 church bodies in the United States are embracing the practice. In 1968, there were more than 126-million persons enrolled as church members, some 63 percent of the population. Communicating with this membership, with the public on social issues, and raising the funds to keep church work going requires the aid of specialists. Caught between inflation on the one hand and declining support from local churches on the other, many major Protestant denominations were forced to reduce size of staffs and missions in the early 1970s. The National Council of Churches trimmed its budget by $800,000 in 1970. This financial squeeze has underlined the importance of public relations. Nonetheless, there is still some tendency among the clergy and lay leaders to shy clear of anything as "modern" and "secular" as "public relations." Such churchmen ignore the past. From the earliest recorded history, religion has been spread by missionaries and travelers, hymns and sermons, parchment scrolls and books. The first book printed was Gutenberg's Holy Bible. The term *propaganda* originated in the Catholic Church in 1622 to describe the act of propagating the faith. Public relations, in reality, is but a new name for activities centuries-old in the churches. It was St. Matthew who long ago said: "Let your light so shine among men

---

[16] Chicago Hospital Council, *A Guide to Ethical Hospital Press-TV-Radio Relationships* (Chicago: The Council, 1956).

that they may see your good works and glorify your Father which is in Heaven." And it was St. Paul who wisely advised those who would communicate with their fellow man: "Except ye utter by the tongue words easy to be understood, how shall it be known what is spoken? For ye shall speak into the air."

The major religious bodies have large staffs in their national headquarters spending sizable sums on films and other media. The current emphasis is, in part, an effort to catch up with the refinements and the emphasis in industry, labor, government, and education. Donald C. Bolles observes: "The inventive genius that gave us newspapers, radio, television, films and magazines is being utilized by the churches to make its voice so powerful that it may rise above the din of daily life and point the way for all to a Christian sanctuary."

Adoption of public relations techniques to bring the church to the people and the people to the church is dramatized by Evangelist Billy Graham who gets a good press. The *Wall Street Journal* reports: "A Billy Graham crusade is based on public relations, meticulous attention to detail and almost down-to-the-minute advance planning." More and more churches and religious agencies are determined to regain communion with those who have strayed. This trend will broaden and deepen. Religion's problems are born of the sense of "lost community," the intense competition for acceptance of ideas, and competition for membership.

The church can make a choice in the matter of continuing publicity, but it has no choice in the matter of relationships with society. Everything about a church is open to public view—its attitudes, needs, purposes, deficiencies, mistakes, and achievements. Each contributes to collective opinion. Churches are not immune to the power of public opinion. They must participate in public debates on moral issues.

THE PROGRAM

So that "the whole Gospel might be brought to the whole world," churches are making increasing use of the mass media to express their spiritual message and views on social issues. In its public relations tasks, the church faces obstacles peculiar to it. These are the main ones: [17]

1. The intangible nature of many religious activities
2. The sacred nature of many activities, which demands a dignified approach
3. The problem of showing the practical worth of religious values

[17] Stewart Harral, "Public Relations for Religion and Religious Groups," in *Public Relations Handbook* (Englewood Cliffs, N.J.: Prentice-Hall, Inc., 1962), pp. 369–377.

4. The problem of interpreting a program that follows a more or less traditional pattern

5. The difficulty of knowing at which level to project ideas so that they will appeal to persons of all ages.

There has been a rather distant and sometimes strained relationship between pulpit and press. Much of the current stress centers on improving the relations by telling the story of religion within the framework of standard news values. In the nineteenth century, the church relied mainly on the religious press to carry its message to the public. It has been estimated that "in 1840 three-fourths of all the reading by the American people was religious." A century later, it was safe to say that the religious press's impact—in terms of copies published—was closer to one-tenth that of the secular press.[18] As the consequences of this shift in reading finally dawned on the clergy, they got busy. News media are responding to this effort.

The re-examination of news values, spearheaded by the Associated Press Managing Editors, is giving religion increased news value. The field of religious journalism is widening. As the mass media shed their traditional concept of religious news as church announcements, so must the clergy. As one newspaper editor once wrote: "Our newspaper, and I think it is generally true of others, is trying to improve its religious news. But, as in any venture, it is the old story of cooperation. The church news is measured in terms of cooperation between newspaper and clergymen." Religious news has moved from the obituary or church page to the front page. The church has not escaped the vortex of change, crisis, and confrontation, thus has become top news, often to a church's discomfiture.

This pressure for change and relevance in the church, and its present-day response, are vividly illustrated in William Jersey's exciting film, *A Time for Burning,* a film made for Lutheran Film Associates. This is a *verite* study of what happened to a Midwestern congregation when racial integration was introduced by its young minister. Many church bodies have modernized their communications programs by utilizing the power of film and TV to bring their message to media-oriented audiences. In 1969, for example, these bodies produced TV spot messages for national distribution: a group of Roman Catholic Franciscan religious communities, the Lutheran Church, the Southern Presbyterians, and the Mennonites. *Time* has observed: "It's a bit of a secret. Only those who on Sunday are not in church nor asleep nor buried in the papers know it: religious TV is more varied, skilled, sophisticated, and imaginative than ever before." [19]

---

[18] For a close look, see Lekachman, Marty, Deedy, and Silverman, *The Religious Press in America* (New York: Holt, Rinehart & Winston, Inc., 1963).

[19] "Excitement on the Tube," issue January 28, 1966, p. 70.

FUND RAISING

THE BIG EFFORT

There is a strong thread running through the warp and woof of these fields. It is the eternal problem of raising sufficient funds to enable the agency, church, or hospital to keep going, one year to the next. Fund raising dominates the practice in all these fields. Sometimes it dominates the agency itself. Much of the thinking, planning, and publicizing in social, health, and religious agencies is tied to the coin container and the collection box. There is fierce competition.

Philanthropy is "big business" in the United States, one of the biggest. To raise the money required takes a lot of publicity, promotion, organization, committee hours, and door-to-door canvassing. John Price Jones taught us: "Fund-raising is public relations, for without sound public relations no philanthropy can live for long. . . . It takes better public relations to get a man to give a dollar than it does to convince him to spend a dollar. Favorable public opinion is the basis upon which American philanthropy has been built. . . ." [20]

Some of this giving is spontaneous. By far, most of it is in response to carefully organized and promoted campaigns directed by professionals. Professional fund raising, a field closely allied with public relations, developed in the wake of World War I, when the potential of American philanthropy was realized for the first time. It has been estimated that, year in and year out, professional fund-raising agencies help raise twenty-five cents of every philanthropic dollar. These professional fund raisers may serve as counselors to an organization's staff or they may fully staff and direct the campaign. Ethical fund raisers work only on a fixed-fee basis, not on percentage of money raised. Generally, the professional fund raiser is brought in for one-time capital fund drives, although some agencies retain them on a continuing advisory basis. The professional brings with him the accumulated experience of many drives. The organized fund drive, born in the Y.M.C.A. movement, dates from the early 1900s.[21]

PROFESSIONAL OR AMATEUR?

There is no pat answer. There are advantages and disadvantages either way. The decision will depend on the organization and its environ-

---

[20] *The Engineering of Consent,* edited by Edward L. Bernays (Norman, Okla.: University of Oklahoma Press, 1955), p. 159.

[21] For full story, see Scott M. Cutlip, *Fund Raising in the United States: Its Role in America's Philanthropy* (New Brunswick: Rutgers University Press, 1965). This comprehensive history illustrates the impact of public relations on America's social institutions.

ment. The professional can furnish expert know-how, skilled personnel, carefully screened donor lists, large libraries, and proved procedures. On the other hand, the fact that an outside firm is sharing in the proceeds can hurt the cause among prospective donors. The local, indigenous staff, sparked by zeal and enthusiasm, if expertly counseled, often can do an equally good job.

The most generally used adjunct in either case is the volunteer solicitor.[22] Volunteer fund raising has the advantage of broadly extending individual participation and thus increasing the opportunities for goodwill. There is a simple formula for raising money. It is to "ask enough people to ask a lot of other people to ask for money." It is also difficult to make broad generalizations about the ratio of campaign costs to total funds raised. Two axioms of business apply in most cases: (1) The ratio of costs to receipts gets smaller as the campaign goal gets larger; (2) A noncontinuing operation costs more per dollar raised than a continuing one.

The professionals pretty well agree that it is impossible to run a campaign for funds at a cost of less than 5 percent of the total goal, and they regard 12 percent as a safe maximum. If costs appear to run over 15 percent, it is time to take another look. A recurrent source of criticism for some of the national health groups is that campaign costs eat up as much as one-fourth of the money contributed. Most experts agree that publicity and promotion should be allocated at least one-fourth of the total campaign budget.

PRINCIPLES ARE THE SAME

Whether the campaign is directed by a professional firm or the internal staff, the principles are the same. In most cases, however, it is unwise to leave the public relations planning and the publicity to amateurs, however zealous they may be. John Price Jones said: "Fully 50 percent of all the time and effort in the average fund-raising enterprise is in the field of public relations. Public relations in fund-raising demands a greater proportion of the entire effort than is required in industry." A successful campaign is compounded of a good cause, thorough fact-finding, careful planning, and skillful communication.

The American Association of Fund-Raising Counsel suggest that these steps must come before there can be a successful fund drive:

1. *The house should be put in order:* the service program tested for effectiveness and efficiency; business management checked; invest-

---

[22] For a scholarly study of the volunteer, his role and motivations in fund raising, see David L. Sills, *The Volunteers: Means and Ends in a National Organization* (New York: The Free Press of Glencoe, Inc., 1957).

ment policies scrutinized; governing boards and officers reviewed; the family assayed.

2. *The needs should be studied and documented:* what the institution proposes to "sell."

3. *The public relations should be "right":* a clear indication of favorable opinion is an essential prerequisite.

4. *The governing board should lead the way:* support given cause within the family.

5. *The area to be served should be defined.*

6. *Some estimate of total cost should be drafted.*

Common forms of fund-raising appeals include direct mail, sale of seals, benefits such as bazaars, balls, and dinners, radio and TV appeals and marathons, newspaper promotions, and direct door-to-door canvass.[23] An effective use of the door-to-door method has been the March of Dimes porchlight campaign. Another fund-raising device, employed by the Red Cross, Chambers of Commerce, and others is the membership campaign with various classes of membership. The annual membership drive is the backbone of several agency public relations fund-raising programs. It brings a sense of "belonging" and participation. This is why many organizations are reluctant to give up their separate drives and merge into united appeals.

The John Price Jones Company, one of the pioneer firms in the field, lists 25 principles of successful fund raising: [24]

Principles of Preparation

1. The five essentials of a successful campaign are a strong case, effective leadership, conscientious workers, prospects willing and able to give, and sufficient funds to finance the campaign during the preliminary period. These five essentials should be weighed with scrupulous care before outlining a plan of campaign.

2. Committee work and publicity work should be mapped out in advance. The correlation of these two lines of activity, all designed toward bringing a trained and enthusiastic worker face to face with a sympathetic and well-informed prospect, is fundamental to the success of any fund-raising effort.

3. The cost of a campaign, within reasonable limits, should be estimated in advance.

4. All campaign activities should be given a time limit. Dates provide the only insurance for a proper correlation of committee work, list work, publicity, and canvassing.

---

[23] For ways by which small groups raise money, see Helen K. Knowles, *How Groups Raise Funds* (Freeport, Me.: The Bond Wheelwright Co., 1961). For abuses in fund raising, see Ralph Lee Smith, *The Bargain Hucksters* (New York: Thomas Y. Crowell Company, 1962).

[24] In an undated pamphlet issued by John Price Jones Company.

Principles of Committee Work

1. The originating group, whether a committee or a board of trustees, should be a representative body.
2. The necessity for strong leadership is inversely proportional to the strength of the appeal.
3. The effectiveness of the group is conditioned by the degree to which individuals will accept personal responsibility.
4. The activity of the originating group determines the activity of all subordinate groups: the originating group is the inevitable yardstick both for giving and for working.
5. Committees are more responsive critically than creatively. In asking any group for ideas on a plan of action, for suggestions on a list of prospects . . . give each member of the group a copy of a plan.

Principles of Public Relations

1. The case must be bigger than the institution. The first object of publicity is to sell an idea; the second, to sell the means for its accomplishment.
2. Printed material should appeal both to the emotions and to the intellect.
3. Publicity must have continuity.
4. Publicity should proceed from the general to the specific. Interest in an idea proceeds from an appeal of general application.
5. Cheap publicity material is expensive. Quality in publicity pays dividends.
6. Publicity should be positive and not negative. Effective publicity always plays up elements of strength.

Principles of Operation

1. A campaign should not only solve immediate financial need, but should lay a firm foundation for the future.
2. Solicitation should proceed in six steps: listing, rating, assignments, cultivation, canvassing, and the follow-up.
3. Effective canvassing answers five questions—why, where, who, what, and how.
4. Campaigns should periodically reach a climax point. The climax is essential in arousing concentrated interest.
5. All canvassing, even for special gifts, should be conducted in an atmosphere of universality. "What are others doing?" is the common query of all prospects, large and small.
6. Campaigns should be conducted under a steady and constant pressure.
7. The time to be spent on a campaign varies directly with the size of the goal and inversely with the popularity of the appeal.

8. The direct appeal for help should be made when the interest is at its peak.

9. Ask for ideas, not for money. The canvasser should first interest his prospect in an idea.

10. There are four tests of the effective operation of a campaign: quality, quantity, cost, and time.

Even a cursory scanning of this blueprint will indicate the hours upon hours of planning and preparation and the amount of energy required. Such a well-organized campaign for a good cause will get members—and money. In planning the public relations part of the campaign, Jones counsels keeping these objectives in mind: (1) Appeal to the broad general public to create an atmosphere of universality, and (2) Endeavor to reach individuals for a direct response.

CASE PROBLEM

For many years now, University City's United Givers Fund has followed the conventional pattern of concentrating its publicity on the annual fund drive, which takes place the last two weeks of October. This fund embraces twenty-six nonprofit welfare agencies. Reliance for year-round educational efforts has been placed on the volunteer publicity chairmen in each of the twenty-six agencies. Because last year's fund appeal fell slightly short of the announced quota, fund officers have done considerable probing to determine the possible reasons. Among other things, they found a lack of public understanding of the needs of the individual agencies and of the relationship of the United Fund to such institutions as the local Y.M.C.A. The new chairman appointed a year-round public relations committee.

The purpose of the committee is "to evaluate public opinion and develop a program of activities which will create better understanding, goodwill, and acceptance by both the general public and special publics—agency boards, agency staffs, clergy, clients, givers, governmental leaders, labor leaders, business leaders, media personnel, etc." You have been called in as the public relations consultant to this committee of laymen. After the necessary fact-finding, including a study of the Community Chest, draft a year-round public relations program for the fund and its constituent agencies which will utilize available manpower and be most economical. The fund employs one woman to handle its publicity at present.

ADDITIONAL READING

WILLARD BAILEY, "Hospitals and Unions," *Public Relations Journal,* Vol. 25, February, 1969.

A. WILLIAM BLUEM, *Religious Television Programs.* New York: Hastings House, 1969. Survey of TV programming and guidelines for the program planner.

ROBERT H. BREMNER, *American Philanthropy.* Chicago: University of Chicago Press, 1960.

ABEL A. HANSON, *Guides to Successful Fund Raising.* New York: Columbia University Bureau of Publications.

B. F. JACKSON, ed. *Television-Radio-Film for Churchmen.* Nashville: Abingdon, 1969. How to use the electronic media effectively to further church work.

HAROLD P. KURTZ, *Public Relations for Hospitals.* Springfield, Ill.: Charles P. Thomas, 1969. A handbook for beginners.

National Recreation Association, *Communications and Public Relations.* New York: The Association, 1959.

National Public Relations Council, *Changing Society: Perspectives on Communication.* New York: The Council, 419 Park Avenue South, 1970.

WILLARD PLEUTHNER, *More Power for Your Church.* New York: Farrar, Straus & Company, 1952.

FRANCES SCHMIDT and HAROLD N. WEINER, eds., *Public Relations in Health and Welfare,* New York: Columbia University Press, 1966. An up-to-date treatment of this field.

HAROLD J. SEYMOUR, *Designs for Fund Raising.* New York: McGraw-Hill, 1966.

RALPH STOODY, *A Handbook of Church Public Relations.* Nashville: Abingdon Press, 1959.

WILLIAM F. ZORZI, "Why Nurse Bailey Came Home," *Public Relations Journal,* Vol. 24, November, 1968. Story of a recruiting campaign.

CHAPTER 23

THE PRACTICE: GOVERNMENTS AND CITIZENS

Public relations is one of the lubricants of democracy. Governmental and industrial processes are becoming increasingly complex. It is through public relations that these processes can be made intelligible to the people and enable them to leave their impress on the shaping of policies.

—MRS. INDIRA GHANDI

As the impact and extent of government increase, the need for adequate communication between public official and citizen becomes more urgent. Yet inescapable forces tend to drive them farther and farther apart. This problem is being met, to some degree, by public relations. Government has become increasingly a matter of administration. A vast machinery of commissions, boards, bureaus—*bureaucracy*—has grown up to meet our complex problems. There are some 86,000 separate units of government in America. The enlargement is quickened in a nation mobilized to discharge its leadership in a divided world and to deal with its mounting urban and racial problems at home. One of our crucial problems is to handle today's problems without destroying popular government. Central to this problem is communication from government to citizen, citizen to government. As William Rivers has noted, "information policy has been at the very center of governing the United States from the beginning."

Government today—federal, state, and local—is so complex and often so remote that citizens tend to become apathetic and bewildered. Who can determine the exact number of billions of dollars and kinds of weapons required to provide adequate military security? Who can assert, with confidence, the solution for difficult, delicate problems in foreign relations? It is hard for the busy, self-centered citizen to become interested in things he cannot easily understand.

The gulf between the citizen and his government tends to deepen as decision making moves away from him. Centralization and concentration of government produce a vitiating sense of remoteness. Government too often appears to the citizen as but a bundle of entanglements among special-interest groups. Urban renewal, for example, seems to be more a private fight between the real estate interests and the low-income groups than a significant public issue. Citizen apathy, well termed the "loss of citizenship," is sharply etched in each election by the millions of Americans who do not vote. For example, in the 1968 Presidential election 10-million eligibles were not registered to vote and 15-million others who were registered did not vote. In sum, only 60 percent of those eligible to vote did so. Sixty-five percent of American eligible voters don't vote regularly. There are other evidences of a default in citizenship and other reasons for it. Central to this problem is "the simple fact that the stuff of public life eludes the grasp of the ordinary man." [1]

The necessity and complexity of the government information task is clearly seen when a Secretary of Agriculture says that one reason people go hungry in America is their ignorance of food stamps. The difficulty of diffusing government information was underscored by a Health, Education and Welfare Department official who spent three days living in the poverty area of Baltimore: "Judging by observation and conversation with health and welfare clients—confirmed by workers—publications, newspapers, radio and TV do not reach the Baltimore poor. Word-of-mouth from a neighbor, minister, or block leader is the common channel." [2] Another aspect of the task's complexity is illuminated when Senator Mark Hatfield charges, with reason: "The confusion, alarm, and apprehensions over our involvement in Vietnam have not been relieved by the State Department briefings, the Pentagon 'handouts,' or the White House pronouncements about our commitments."

The breakdown of communication between citizens and their governments is reflected in the growing support for the *ombudsman* concept, developed in Norway and Sweden. In the view of the Thirty-Second American Assembly: [3]

> Millions of Americans view government as distant and unresponsive, if not hostile. Though often the targets of the resentment which ensues, government officials are usually not the cause of remoteness, but sometimes its victims. Dehumanized government derives from the impersonality of modern mass society. . . . there is a need in today's large and complex government for mechanisms devoted solely to receiving, examining, and channeling citizens' complaints, and securing expeditions and impartial redress.

The *ombudsman* was created as an independent, high-level officer who receives complaints, pursues inquiries without regard to channels, and recommends suitable action. Many countries abroad and a few local governments in the United States have adopted this means of facilitating two-way communication between government and citizen. [4]

---

[1] Joseph Kraft, *Profiles in Power* (New York: New American Library, 1966), p. 92.

[2] Wilbur J. Cohen, "Communication in a Democratic Society," in *Voice of Government* (New York: Wiley, 1968), p. 20. This book of essays on government practice, edited by Ray E. Hiebert and Carlton Spitzer, is useful.

[3] Final Report of the Thirty-Second Assembly, Columbia University, 1968, issued by the Assembly.

[4] For more on the *ombudsman* device see Walter Gellhorn's two books, *When Americans Complain* and *Ombudsman and Others*, both published by the Harvard University Press. Donald C. Rowat, ed., *The Ombudsman, Citizen's Defender* (London: George Allen & Unwin, 2nd. ed., 1968). The latter includes reports from thirteen countries.

The maze of government needs to be explained, interpreted, and clarified. Each person has only a small amount of time and attention to give to his government. Today's citizen needs a system of communications that will give him the same voice and understanding that his forefathers acquired in the town meeting. By the same token, today's administrator needs the face-to-face relationships that his predecessor of years ago had. He dare not lose the common touch. The bureaucrat must guard himself against isolation and insulation from the people of Punxsutawney and Prairie du Sac whose lives he so profoundly affects. This is an age-old problem, but one greatly magnified by the accelerating changes of today's Space Age.

Effective administration must grow out of the lives and problems of the people rather than be imposed from above. Skilled, conscientious practitioners can contribute much to solving these urgent problems. Zechariah Chafee, Jr. said: "Government information can play a vital part in the cause of good administration by exploring the impact of new social forces, discovering strains and tensions before they become acute, and encouraging a positive sense of unity and national direction." [5]

Reasonable people, in government and out, agree that there is real need and ample justification for a more effective transmission belt. In the words of one practitioner: *"Democracy will live where there is free communication of dependable information."* This problem raises anew a question posed by Aristotle centuries ago: "The environment is complex and man's political capacity is simple. Can a bridge be built between them?"

This old question today possesses a new urgency. In a real sense, as one observer points out, "while we Americans are many times as numerous as we once were and necessarily confront vastly more complex problems, our source of information and means for popular participation in the democratic dialogue are being ever more limited." This writer, John Cogley, of the Center for Study of Democratic Institutions, goes on to ask: "Do our growing bureaucracies, our galloping technology, our bigness, and the headlong advance of science make government of the people, by the people, and for the people irrelevant?"

The answer must be a resounding *No.* Much of the meaningful dialogue required to make democracy work today is shaped and phrased by the public relations practitioner. This imposes a civic obligation on him as he becomes, increasingly, the intermediary between the candidate or the public official and the citizens.

---

[5] In *Government and Mass Communications,* Vol. II (Chicago: University of Chicago Press, 1947), p. 736. These two volumes, by-products of the Commission on Freedom of the Press, provide helpful background reading. Often overlooked is that this commission recommended strongly that "the government, through the media of mass communication, inform the public of the facts with respect to its policies and of the purposes underlying those policies . . ."

As political campaign costs mount and the skills of persuasive communication become more specialized, the practitioner is playing an ever more important role in campaigns and in government. Political publicity is one of the oldest phases of the practice, but it never had the scope, shape, and reach that it has today. The public dialogue begins with the political campaign. Stanley Kelley observes: [6]

> Political campaigns are the principal institution in which this interaction between politician and electorate occurs, and the most striking role of the public relations man is that of a campaigner. The particular kind of campaign activity with which he is most often concerned has, in terms of the theory . . . of democratic government, an importance all its own. For the public relations man is occupied with directing the course of public discussion as it relates to the selection of government officials and the settlement of controversial issues of public policy.

The role of public relations in political campaigns and in government —the two are inextricably interrelated—is expanding, and public relations' impact on democracy is under scrutiny. Leon Epstein, a political scientist, thinks that the increased use of mass media publicity and of behavioral research permits a direct appeal to the voter that is making our political parties *"relatively* less important." He notes the increased criticism of public relations role: "Much of the criticism of the newer techniques is centered about the enterprise of public relations as such. The idea of selling candidates like soap is offensive to all those who . . . believe in the capacity of the voters to absorb information and make reasoned decisions. . . . Using the professional skills of public relations in political communication seems to involve an unusually frank rejection of rationalist assumptions about political behavior." [7] Epstein's assertion is amply reflected in Joe McGinniss' *The Selling of the President, 1968,* the inside story of Richard Nixon's use of radio and TV in 1968. Television has unbalanced the political system in favor of the men in office and the men of wealth. These matters merit discussion. The returns are not in yet.

PUBLIC RELATIONS' ROLE IN GOVERNMENT

Certainly, the foundation stones of Aristotle's bridge must be informative, candid, continuous reporting by government and more accessible channels

---

[6] Stanley Kelley, Jr., *Professional Public Relations and Political Power* (Baltimore, Md.: Johns Hopkins Press, 1956, paperback), p. 3. Recommended reading.

[7] Leon D. Epstein, *Political Parties in Western Democracies* (New York: Praeger, 1967), pp. 240–241.

to government for all citizens, not just those with an "in." The rise of the service state has had many profound implications. Some of these were sketched in Chapter 5. Two are of special concern here.

First, governmental power has steadily ebbed from the community to the statehouse to the federal government. Important decision making has likewise shifted from the more responsive legislative bodies to less accessible regulatory and administrative agencies. The result is to make government increasingly remote from the voter's reach. Trying to get a piece of information, to have a problem solved, or to make a need known, the frustrated citizen often gives up in despair. He fulminates against "red tape." Or else he turns to a lawyer, lobbyist, legislator, public relations man, or a political fixer. This new relationship is not satisfactory. This is demonstrated by widespread suspicion and distrust of government, attacks on bureaucrats (the word itself has a derogatory connotation), protests against the ever-mounting tax bill, and finally default of citizenship by millions. It also breeds, inevitably, influence peddlers who gnaw at the vitals of government.

Second, the mass media are grappling with the task of reporting under the heavy hand of news values fashioned in frontier days and with too few reporters. In days gone by, news of government was a relatively simple matter of personalities, oratorical political campaigns, trust-busting, and the like. It was entirely different from reporting world affairs, atomic energy, mental health, space travel, controversies over matters affecting equal opportunity, the environment, and other complex subject matter. Interpreting the complexities of government requires trained specialists and takes more time than deadlines often permit.

Much progress has been made by the media in government reporting over the past decade. But there is still need for government to strengthen and supplement today's reporting by the press. *Time* has observed: "The shortcomings in coverage (of Washington) are not always the fault of the reporters; they are due to the size of the job. In three decades the Federal Government has swollen like an explosion. And there just aren't enough reporters around to do a thorough job." Many editors dispute this.

Governmental activities embraced by the term "public relations" have developed naturally. They are part of the administrative system evolving to bridge the gap between popular and bureaucratic government. The objectives are *active cooperation in action programs* (for example, soil conservation); *compliance in regulatory programs* (for example, public health laws); and *voter support for the incumbent administration's policies* (for example, foreign aid). The justification for government public relations rests on two premises: (1) A democratic government is obliged to report to its citizens; (2) Effective administration requires citizen participation and voter support.

Utilization of public relations in government began with the presidency of Theodore Roosevelt, the first modern chief executive to see the power of the presidency and the necessity for mobilizing public opinion in order to use it. Roosevelt saw the White House as "a bully pulpit" and so used it. He created press offices in the White House, met regularly with reporters, and was the first to use the presidential junket as a calculated way of generating public support for his programs. He "saw the ebbing of the editorial and the growing importance of the cartoon and he tailored his actions accordingly." He initiated the Sunday release because he knew it would make the front page of Monday's otherwise drab issue. Cornwell concludes that "Roosevelt dramatized the potential of the office for affecting the course of public policy by means of a dynamic relationship with the electorate via the mass media." [8]

Typical was the campaign he and Gifford Pinchot, equally astute in the ways of public relations, organized to make conservation a popular cause and thus abate the looting of the nation's resources. Pinchot had launched an intensive publicity campaign in 1898 when he became head of the U. S. Department of Agriculture's Division of Forestry. When Roosevelt became president, this conservation campaign was stepped up. There was a continual outpouring of releases and editorials from the Forest Service; Pinchot and his associates spoke widely; the number of articles in periodicals multiplied; programs enlisted the cooperation of teachers; and outside groups to support the conservation movement were organized. The campaign culminated in the 1908 White House Governors' Conference, one of the nation's first public relations-staged events. This Conference: (1) Put the issue of conservation onto the front pages of the newspapers for the major part of a week; (2) Provided the major impetus for discussion of the issue in periodicals and the public forum for many years; (3) Firmly established the term "conservation of natural resources" in the public vocabulary.[9]

THE OBJECTIVES

These are the generally agreed upon objectives for a planned, continuing program in government.

1. To win consent for new laws and new reforms dictated by the needs of an everchanging, technological society. This involves a deep, fundamental shift in our theory of government and has dangerous implications.

[8] Elmer E. Cornwell, Jr., *Presidential Leadership of Public Opinion* (Bloomington, Ind., Indiana University Press, 1965), p. 14.

[9] Charlotte A. Wittwer, "The First White House Governors' Conference," *Public Relations Quarterly,* Vol. 14, 1970. Much of the above is based on the research of Felice G. Levin.

2. To overcome apathy and bewilderment toward new and complex functions of government; also, to provide reliable information for the voter seeking to make an intelligent decision at the polls.

3. To keep the citizen informed of the services and the functions provided so that he may participate and gain full benefit from them.

4. To provide the citizen usable devices for relaying his views and opinions to the administrator without employing intermediaries.

5. To interpret public opinion to the law enforcement agencies so that regulations will be realistic and acceptable.

6. To crystallize public sentiment and pave the way for noncoercive compliance. This requires convincing the citizen of the need for the administrative rules and assisting him in understanding them.

7. To build a reservoir of support for an agency which it may tap when the going gets rough; to have friends in time of need when a conflict develops with other agencies, with the legislature, or with the public.

These objectives involve debatable practices when viewed within the framework of a government of checks and balances. James L. McCamy points out: [10] "Administrative publicity in the past and now has been useful in the process of administrative leadership. Presidents and their assistants have gone to the public on many important issues, sometimes to enlist public pressure on Congress and sometimes to explain to the public the program advocated by Congress and the executive leaders." Actually, most of the impetus for public relations programs in governmental agencies comes from the need to marshal public support for the money and measures that must be voted in the legislative branch. Bureaucrats engage in lobbying just as surely as businessmen do, despite the myth that governmental bureaucracy is neutral. Peter Woll, who made a study of American bureaucracy, writes: [11]

> . . . through what might be called undercover devices, the bureaucracy engages in extensive lobbying and propaganda activities. . . . Administrative agencies function to a considerable extent as freewheeling interest groups, and in their use of propaganda activities they are no exception. They not only seek to apply pressure at critical points in the political process, but also strive to maintain a favorable image of themselves before the public generally and before specific groups which they consider important in the battle for political survival.

---

[10] In *Government Publicity* (Chicago: University of Chicago Press, 1939). A landmark book, now out of print.

[11] In *American Bureaucracy* (New York: W. W. Norton & Company, 1963), pp. 134–135.

HOSTILITY TO THE FUNCTION

The public relations function has been established longer in government than in any other field of practice. Yet it has not been as effectively used as it might be. Government practitioners face more hostility and suspicion than do practitioners in most fields. This hostility stems from four fundamental conflicts of interest embedded in our democratic government. These have a long history.

1. The continuing struggle between the press fighting for "the people's right to know" and the officials of government, who insist upon discretion in deciding what public business should be exposed to public scrutiny.

2. The unrelenting struggle for balance of power between the legislative and executive branches of government. This contest is present whether it is between mayor and council, governor and legislature, or the President and Congress.

3. The continuing struggle for power between the major political parties. The "out" party fears the power of an army of "propagandists" in keeping the "ins" in and the "outs" out. As Oscar Ewing, then National Democratic Chairman, wrote President Franklin Roosevelt in March, 1943, the party in power gets the benefit from a "good job of selling and pays for the consequence of a bad one."

4. Industries, institutions, and other vested interests when threatened by proposed legislation or government regulation will often decry the use of public funds and government machinery to carry the day against them.

Beyond these conflicts there is the inevitable association of government information programs with that dirty word *propaganda*. Americans have long been deeply suspicious of anything labeled "propaganda." Suspicion and distrust have been intensified as this power device has been used in other countries to gain and hold despotic control. Thus, public suspicion of information as "nothing but propaganda" is especially strong when the information comes from government. After a thorough study of this field, Professor Donald Krimel drew these conclusions.[12]

The idea that governmental propaganda can be and should be eliminated stands in the way of open, careful, and efficient use of this

[12] From his Ph.D. thesis, "The Public Communication Function of the Federal Government," Madison: University of Wisconsin, 1955.

administrative tool. In addition, negative stereotypes attached to governmental propaganda also are attached to governmental information services by persons who understand no distinction between the two kinds of activity. These negative stereotypes are a major deterrent to more effective use of the whole of governmental public relations.

Also involved in this opposition is the double standard that many citizens have for government and for private enterprise. The public generally accepts the right and propriety of business to publicize and advertise even though the customer pays for it. On the other hand, many people regard government information work as a waste of tax dollars. Citizens generally see no need for government to hawk its wares. There is no way of telling just how deep-seated and widespread this citizen attitude is. The average person is probably unaware of the problem at all. However, some politicians think that they get votes when they flay "government propaganda."

FROM THE PRESS

It is the continuing task of the press to ferret out and publicize the actions of public officials. Officials, in turn, insist that not all acts should be open to public view. One day a metropolitan newspaper will assert that "the amount of federal money and manpower devoted to publicizing government . . . has reached staggering proportions." Another day New York State newspapermen will join in a "move to tear apart the paper curtain which shields government officials at Albany from inquiring reporters." And on still another day a Florida weekly editor will announce "a boycott of all state agency handouts." Periodically there are magazine articles about "How Government Pressure Boys Squander Your Money" and blasts from TV commentators. This historic conflict runs from the village school board to the statehouse to the federal government. It reached a new level of intensity in the past two decades.

The conflict stems from the growth of government at all levels and from the uneasy tensions and recurring crises of the world conflict. Decreasing access to news of government is thought by many newsmen to be the major threat to freedom of the press today. This alarm is frequently and stridently sounded by newsmen in their meetings and in their journals. Three professional groups—American Society of Newspaper Editors, Sigma Delta Chi, and Associated Press Managing Editors—have given much attention to reporting of government by making studies and issuing reports. At the federal level, the attack has been on the abuse of security classification to hold back news which the press insists the public is entitled to know. At the state and local level, the campaign has been to get laws requiring all agencies to hold open meetings and to maintain open records. The complexity of this problem and its meaning for freedom of the press have been well defined.[13]

The conflict between press and government gained new intensity in September, 1951, when President Truman issued an Executive Order 10290 giving all civilian agencies of the Federal government authority to classify information, thus empowering each agency to act as its own censor. The press vehemently denounced the order. President Eisenhower, in Executive Order 10501 on November 5, 1953, reduced the number of agencies empowered to use this classification authority. President Kennedy, in Executive Order 10964, September 20, 1961, further modified the basic directive by setting up an automatic declassification and downgrading system. The twice-modified version of Truman's original directive was continued in force by Presidents Johnson and Nixon.[14]

The continuing campaign against secrecy in government has been led by Congressman John Moss of California and his House Subcommittee on Government Information since the mid-1950s. Moss thinks that the "major cause of the restrictive situation is a 'papa knows best' in federal agencies." More realistic are the reasons inherent in human nature and in the realities of politics. Executives find it more comfortable to do their jobs without the public looking over their shoulders. Subordinates find it safer to suppress information than incur the boss's wrath for releasing it.

When the Moss Committee started its campaign against secrecy, it found executive agencies using three legal justifications for not releasing all information sought by the news media: (1) The President's executive order giving authority to many department heads to classify information on the grounds of national security; (2) President Eisenhower's letter of May 17, 1954, to Secretary of Defense Wilson (written in connection with the famed Army-versus-Senator McCarthy hearings) holding conversations and documents involving strictly the executive branch to be confidential; (3) The public records law (5 U.S.C.A. 1001-1011) dating from 1872, which provides, among other things, "matters of official record shall be made available (to the public) . . . *except* when required to be held confidential."

In the mid-1950s the press's "freedom of information" groups, the

---

[13] For helpful background reading, see: Harold L. Nelson and Dwight L. Teeter, *Law of Mass Communications*; Harold L. Cross, *The People's Right to Know*; James Russell Wiggins, *Freedom or Secrecy*, 2nd ed.; Douglass Cater, *The Fourth Branch of Government*; Francis E. Rourke, *Secrecy and Publicity*; Herbert Brucker, *Freedom of Information*; and William L. Rivers, *The Opinion Makers*. It was Brucker who introduced the concept "managed news" in this context.

[14] President Nixon issued a modifying order March 8, 1972, effective June 1, 1972. The new order limits power to classify material "top secret" to 12 agencies, the power to classify material as "secret" to another 13. It also cuts number of officials empowered to classify documents.

American Bar Association, and the Moss Committee joined forces to get
the long-standing barrier to government information removed by effecting
a "true public records law—a law which not only spells out the right of
the public, press and congressional access but also has enforcement provisions." [15] Mentor for the campaign, the late Harold Cross, believed:
"Citizens of a self-governing society must have the legal right to examine
and investigate the conduct of its affairs, subject only to those limitations
imposed by the most urgent public necessity." The uphill campaign culminated in the passage of the so-called Freedom of Information Act, which
President Johnson signed into law July 4, 1966, and which became effective
one year later. Technically this law was an amendment to Section 3 of the
Administrative Procedure Act of 1946. The new law was hailed as being
an "about face" both in theory and substance, as changing a "withholding"
statute to a "disclosure" statute.

Ramsey Clark, then Attorney General, saw these as the chief benefits
of the new act: (1) that disclosure be the general rule, not the exception;
(2) that all individuals have equal rights of access; (3) that the burden
be on the government to justify withholding information; (4) that individuals denied access to information have the rights to seek relief in the
courts; (5) that there is reflected a change in government policy and
attitude.[16] The law's meaning was somewhat clouded by a series of changes
quietly passed by Congress in June, 1967.

The long-term effect of this law remains to be seen. In the first year,
thirty-one court cases were filed against the government for alleged withholding in violation of the Act. Of the eleven closed cases, six upheld the
government, two plaintiffs withdrew charges, one plaintiff got the information he was after as a result of his suit, and two decisions ordered disclosure. Congressman Moss reported that "journalists . . . report bureaucratic barriers are noticeably being lifted." Yet a scholar who has closely
followed this Freedom of Information struggle is much more pessimistic.
Professor Robert O. Blanchard observes: [17]

> As FOI (Freedom of Information) advocates have studied the provisions
> of the law more closely, they have found it ambiguous at best. One of
> the chief problems is the indeterminate character of the law's nine phrases
> describing exempt categories of information. Several of the phrases seem

[15] Freedom of Information Center Report No. 189, *A History of the Federal Records Law*
(University of Missouri School of Journalism, 1967), p. 7.

[16] Sigma Delta Chi, "Report of the 1967 Sigma Delta Chi Advancement of Freedom of
Information Committee" (The Society, Chicago, Ill.), p. 5.

[17] In "Freedom of Information Act—Disappointment and Hope," *Columbia Journalism
Review*, Vol. 6, Fall, 1967. Professor Blanchard elaborated on this in a paper given
before the Association for Education in Journalism convention, Lawrence, Kansas, August,
1968.

bound to encourage continued, perhaps more sophisticated federal agency discretion in release of information. Ironically, the court-enforcement provision of the law adds to the possibilities of blockage. In fact, eight of the exemptions violate the blueprint for a public records law laid down by such originators as Harold L. Cross.

V. M. Newton, Jr., a founder of the FOI movement, lambasted the Act's exemptions as "nothing more than an open invitation to the federal bureaucrat to withhold legitimate information from the American people." In another assessment, Professor Blanchard concluded: "The FOI Act, in reality, is of little relevance to the interests of the press in effectively checking executive withholding of information relevant to vital public issues." He also sees the Moss Committee as a "watchdog in decline." [18] In the late 60s, Congressman Moss narrowly averted an effort by the chairman of the House Government Operations Committee to abolish the Subcommittee on Government Information.

In these clashes between newsmen and governmental agencies the public relations man, inevitably, is caught in the crossfire. Typical of this conflict is the battle over "management of the news" that boiled up in the wake of the Cuban Crisis of October, 1962, and in the reporting of the Vietnam conflict from the White House and the Defense establishment. In such crises there are no clear, meaningful precedents.[19] Still debated is then Assistant Secretary of Defense Arthur Sylvester's assertion that, "in the kind of world we live in, the generation of news by the government becomes one weapon in a strained situation." This statement fueled the "news management" controversy for the duration of the Kennedy-Johnson administrations. The "news as a weapon" debate, in Pierre Salinger's view: "illustrated once again the fundamental chasm that exists between the interests of the press and the government in a crisis situation." The debate flamed anew when Vice President Spiro Agnew repeatedly attacked the news media, particularly the TV networks, and asserted that the president had a right to communicate directly with the people "without having the president's words and thoughts characterized through the prejudices of hostile critics before they can even be digested." Countless charges and countercharges flew back and forth as the "news management" debate continued into the 1970s. Many newsmen concur with Britain's Lord Shawcross that "The tendency of governments is to shield themselves behind a curtain of secrecy

---

[18] "A Watchdog in Decline," *Columbia Journalism Review,* Vol. 5, Summer, 1966.

[19] These articles are typical: Arthur Krock, "Mr. Kennedy's Management of the News," *Fortune,* Vol. 67, March, 1963; Hanson W. Baldwin, "Managed News, Our Peacetime Censorship," *Atlantic Monthly,* Vol. 211, April, 1963; "The News Management Issue," special issue of *Nieman Reports,* Vol. 16, March, 1963. For two harshly critical books, see: Bruce Ladd, *Crisis in Credibility* (New York: New American Library, 1968) and William McGaffin and Erwin Knoll, *Anything But the Truth* (New York: Putnam, 1968).

in which the only window is controlled by a public relations official trained in the art of conveying a minimum of information with a maximum of selfrighteousness."

Hovering across press and public relationships with government has been the "crises in credibility," which began in the Eisenhower Administration with the U-2 incident, gained intensity in the Kennedy Administration's "Bay of Pigs" fiasco, and reached a crescendo of charges and countercharges in the Johnson administration. It recurred in the Nixon Administration with the President's decision to invade Cambodia. The common thread here is the United States' role in the world power struggle. William McGaffin and Erwin Knoll, writing in *Anything But the Truth,* hold: "The garrison state attitude that has tainted public policy since the cold war has also done much to undermine the traditional concept of the open society." Fortunately, as Bruce Ladd notes in his *Crisis in Credibility,* "public opinion in a free society has a way of developing an instinct for the truth." Study of the "credibility gap" will demonstrate that candor remains sound public relations policy.

Nonetheless, the press puts great reliance on government information for its coverage of public affairs. An analysis of twenty-two major newspapers, published in eleven metropolitan centers and representing every sector of the nation, showed that one-fifth of the stories published in both the foreign affairs and health-education-welfare fields were traceable in whole or in part to formal releases or statements issued by the State Department and HEW. The over-all averages were 21.2 percent for foreign affairs, 21.3 percent for HEW releases. If White House statements and press conferences are also considered, the figure jumps to 38.6 percent for foreign affairs articles. The authors of the study conclude: [20] "The daily press is heavily dependent upon the federal bureaucracy's generative or creative capacities for the news it carries, and this dependence is more the product of broad evolutionary forces operating on the American society than of reportorial habits, editorial biases or the nature of the press itself." [21]

Newsmen hold that there is an equally strong trend toward increased suppression of government information at the state and local levels. Closed meetings of state and local boards are a frequent item of editorial protest. Efforts to break down the news barriers by the news media have been more successful at these levels, where no national security matters are involved. Sigma Delta Chi's Freedom of Information Committee has spearheaded a campaign to get open meetings and open records laws passed in the states.

---

[20] American Institute for Political Communication, *The Federal Government-Daily Press Relationship* (Washington, D.C., The Institute, 1967), p. 108. Another study showing that public relations is an integral part of the nation's public information system.

[21] Robert U. Brown, "ASNE Spells Out Broad Scope of the People's Right to Know," *Editor & Publisher,* Vol. 90, July 20, 1957, 9.

As of 1969, 32 states had adopted both open records and open meeting laws. Eight states had enacted only open meeting laws; six states, only open records laws. The laws are far from uniform. In no state are all public records and meetings open at all times. Those states still without adequate protection for public access, in the committee's view, give "ample proof that American politicians across the country still have an abiding love of secrecy."

The press lacks the resources to report comprehensively and constructively all the affairs of government. First, there is lack of manpower to cover the multiplying agencies and activities in government at all levels. A press service attempts to cover a state government of more than sixty separate agencies with a two- or three-man staff on a forty-hour week. Obviously this is an impossible task if the reporters are to dig below the surface and get the real news. Second, there is the outmoded set of news values which puts the spotlight on the negative, controversial, and wrongful aspects of government. For example, the press will quickly mobilize to report in detail a state prison riot. The lack of an effective parole program, lack of adequate penal facilities, and the mismanagement which led to the riot are not reported prior to the outbreak. Joseph Kraft thinks the improvement in public affairs reporting must come from the media. "The central requirement is that the press and TV find and promote more intelligent and better trained people . . . the chief danger of a kept press lies in the intellectual poverty of the press itself."

A veteran Washington reporter once said, "By and large government information agencies have been invaluable to the Washington newsgatherers and therefore to the public. Without them, the comprehensive coverage of government affairs would be impossible." The working press in city hall, state capital, and Washington know that government information men are essential, and they seldom share the bombastic views of the editor. As one veteran public relations man in Washington put it: "I have never found the working press to be hostile. The publishers and editors sometimes talk hostile, but the reporters, correspondents, and commentators want and ask for and use the public information services of the agencies."

The skilled, specialized reporter qualified to interpret the scientific and technical aspects of government today is rare and expensive. A sufficient number is beyond the payroll of most news agencies.

FROM LEGISLATORS

Almost from the beginning, the public relations function in government has been handicapped by the opposition of legislators. Their continuing opposition prevents maximum effectiveness in government practice and prevents an accurate accounting of the function's cost. Attacks on public relations by legislators are less frequent but perhaps more damaging than those of the press.

Legislative opposition often is stimulated by other sources of hostility. The Roosevelt-Pinchot campaign for conservation of the nation's lands soon brought Congressional reaction from the spokesmen of lumbermen, mine operators, and cattle grazers who had been exploiting the nation's public lands. Congressman Franklin Mondell of Wyoming, a spokesman for sheepmen and stockmen, in 1908 won adoption of an amendment to the Agricultural Appropriation Bill dealing with the Forest Service which read: [22]

> That no part of this appropriation shall be paid or used for the purpose of paying for in whole or in part the preparation of any newspaper or magazine articles.

Thus the first systematic use of public relations to promote acceptance of an Administration's policies brought Congressional hostility to the function in the executive branch.

Congressional ire next erupted in 1910 when Rep. Joseph T. Robinson, Arkansas, demanded an investigation of the Census Bureau for its employment of Whitman Osgood in 1909 as a special agent at $8.00 per day to explain to the public the purpose of the 1910 census. The director of the Census Bureau, E. Dana Durand, rightly insisted that it was essential, if the census was to be complete, that all citizens and aliens be reached —through newspapers, the foreign language press, and agricultural weeklies—and be assured that their replies would not be used for taxation purposes.[23] The Committee, after hearing from the Census Bureau, tacitly approved the employment of a publicity agent.

By 1912, the number of publicity agents employed by executive departments was clearly growing, and some campaigns were not beyond reproach. In May of 1912, Congressman John Nelson of Wisconsin gained passage of a House resolution to investigate meat inspection in the Bureau of Animal Industry in the Department of Agriculture. In the early part of the hearings, Nelson was angered by a circular criticizing the resolution and defending the department; the pamphlet had been published before the hearings opened. He charged the department was using publicity to discredit one of its accusers. He then introduced a House resolution to investigate "the expenditure of public moneys for press bureaus, postage, stationery, and employees by the Department of Agriculture and by other departments; and that said committee be directed to make recommendation

---

[22] *U. S. Congressional Record,* 60th Cong., 1st Sess., 1908, Vol. 42, 4137.

[23] U. S. Congress, House, Committee on the Census, *Adverse Report to Accompany H. Res. No. 236,* House Report No. 296, 61st Cong., 2d Sess., 1910, 2.

to the House as to what steps are necessary to protect public funds from newspaper exploitations." [24] The resolution did not pass.

At the hearings on his resolution, Congressman Nelson declared "If there is any warrant of law for the maintenance of these press bureaus, which I very much question, this provision ought to be speedily repealed by Congress." [25] Three Washington reporters testified in support of Nelson's charges. Congress was awakened to the growth of public relations in the executive branch, but wasn't ready to act.

A year later, the Civil Service Commission advertised for what *Editor & Publisher* described as "a press agent to help boom the good roads movement" in the Office of Public Roads. The Civil Service Commission circular called for a "publicity expert" whose ". . . affiliations with newspaper publishers and writers is extensive enough to secure publication of items prepared by him." This triggered the amendment to an appropriations bill by Rep. Frederick H. Gillett, which provided that no money could be spent for publicity unless specifically authorized by Congress. The 1913 Gillett amendment became embedded in law to hamper and cloud the function from that day to this. This opposition comes from both the legislator engaged in a struggle for power with the executive branch and from the legislator of the minority political power seeking majority control. Legislative investigations are not frequent, but they are effective in intimidating or driving government information men underground.

This conflict is born in our government of checks and balances. The legislative body cannot view calmly the skillful use of public relations by the executive to achieve his legislative goals. On the other hand, the executive cannot dispense with them and do his job. Congress would do far better to recognize honestly the facts and to make intelligent and integrated provision for the proper function of publicizing government activity than to be incessantly trying to bottle up administrative publicists. Pimlott writes of this conflict: [26]

> The controversy over the limitations which should be set upon federal government public relations springs from the fear lest programs undertaken in the name of administrative efficiency should result in an excessive concentration of power in the Executive. This fear is shared by Congress, the states, and pressure and other groups which, though unrecognized by the Constitution, compete with the constitutional organs in

---

[24] U. S. Congress, House, Rules Committee, *Hearing on H. Res. 545, Department Press Agents,* 62nd Cong., 2d Sess., 1912, 3–4.

[25] *Hearing on H. Res. 545,* p. 6.

[26] J. A. R. Pimlott, *Public Relations and American Democracy* (Princeton, N.J.: Princeton University Press, 1951), p. 72. Part II has thoughtful discussion of government public relations by a longtime British civil servant.

the de facto exercise of power. What is more, government public relations threatens the member of Congress not only in Washington but in his constituency, where he has traditionally been the chief medium of communication with the capital. The controversy over government public relations is one facet of the perennial controversy over a strong central Executive.

Illustrative is the sustained attack Senator J. William Fulbright launched against the Department of Defense's "vast apparatus" for public relations. Fulbright said: [27] "It is one thing for the Defense Department to have employees available to provide—quickly and responsively—factual information both to the public and the press—upon request. It is quite another when that Department and the individual military services use taxpayers' money to generate and promote public support for military weapons and military programs."

On the state level, a senator will slap an expensive booklet on the desk of a department head and ask, "What right do you have to spend the taxpayer's money to pressure us into spending more of his money for you?" In Michigan several years ago, the governor was called "in and down" by a legislative committee because he was "sending political propaganda to local newspapers in order to put the legislators on the spot." As a result, "the Michigan civil service put some sugar coating on this pill by making 'publicists' into 'public information specialists'. . . . Hiding these publicists has been facilitated by a regulation which allows each state agency two unclassified positions." [28] The effect of this legislative opposition is seen in this reply from a Michigan department in response to a query: "We do not have any PR unit or budget. Public relations is a dirty term in state government—we avoid it entirely. . . . We are not really in the image-making business." Not only does this title-dodge blur the function's purpose, it hurts the morale of the practitioner. One in the federal government writes: "We have brought this confusion about our job on ourselves through use of ambiguous terminology. It is a waste of effort and manpower; even worse it confuses the public."

Yet legislators utilize public relations to advance their own political careers. Virtually every member of Congress has at least one public

---

[27] "Public Relations in the Department of Defense," *Congressional Record*, December 1, 1969, S15144-15157. See also his detailed examination of the services' public relations programs: "Pentagon Propaganda," *Congressional Record*, December 2, 1969, S15306-15333; "The Public Affairs Program of the Air Force," *Congressional Record-Senate*, S5649-S15674; "S.3217—A Bill Requiring Secretary of Defense to Submit Regular Reports . . . ," *Congressional Record*, December 5, 1969, S15804-S15845. These statements give a full account of Pentagon public relations' expenditures.

[28] Gerald J. Keir, "Government Public Relations and the Press in Michigan," *Journalism Quarterly*, Vol. 43, Autumn, 1966.

relations aide on his staff, and state legislative leaders are coming to recognize the value of such aides. Less often do legislators see the need for a systematic public relations program for the legislative body, but this, too, is changing. For example, a 1966 Utah Legislative Study Committee concluded "A legitimate expenditure of modest public funds for a report to the people is in order. . . . Total inaction . . . carries with it . . . penalty—a continuation of the decline of the Legislature as a branch of government." The Wisconsin Legislature in 1969 adopted the suggestion of a study made by the Eagleton Institute of Politics to provide information aides for party leaders in both houses. This legislative opposition has led to legal restriction, circumvention, and under-the-table practices which are wrong and wasteful. Much of the waste and ineffectiveness which can be justly ascribed to government public relations is directly attributable to legislative restriction. This hostility also causes many competent men to shy away from government practice. *Public relations should be a legitimate, aboveboard function of government.*

Four specific legal restrictions tend to confuse and cloud the practice in the federal government:

1. An act of Congress, passed in 1913, forbids spending money for "publicity experts" of any part of an appropriation unless specifically appropriated by the Congress. (*See* 38, U. S. C. 3107.)

2. The "gag law" of July 11, 1919 prohibits using any part of an appropriation for services, messages, or publications designed to influence any member of Congress in his attitude toward legislation or appropriations. (*See* 18 U. S. C. 1913.)

3. The law, also passed in 1919, but not strictly enforced until 1936, requires that all duplicating of material, including multilith and multigraph, must be done by the Government Printing Office or at least farmed back to the department for reproduction by the G.P.O. (*See* 44 U. S. C. 501.)

4. Restrictions on the privilege of executive departments and independent establishments in use of the free mail frankly prohibit any executive department mailing material without a request. (*See* Title 39, U.S.C.A. Sec. 321n.)

Any one of these measures, strictly enforced, could virtually paralyze an information program. It would not be hard to interpret, for example, a quite legitimate informational release as "designed to influence" a member of Congress. The barest of facts can influence a person's opinion. Although the legislative rule on printing has much merit, it causes lost time and waste motion. The 1913 law has led to the parade of titles which cloak and camouflage the practitioner in the federal government. "Public Relations" as a job title is avoided. One who made a study of the Congressional attitude toward the public relations function in the federal government concluded: [29] "The attitude of Congress toward government publicity was a negative, restrictive one, even though it prodded the executive branch to make information available. . . . Congress's failure to recognize and endorse the positive values of government publicity resulted in the executive branch's continuing the subterfuge of obscuring public relations under 'information' titles. . . . Congress continued to consider information problems on a piecemeal basis."

The same situation exists to a lesser degree at the state level. A number of states have had or do have legislative restrictions. Legislative opposition—often coupled with executive disapproval—leads to the same cloaking under innocuous titles in state government. One survey found that in at least four states the information function was completely covered. In six other states with public relations personnel, there were no public relations titles or civil service classifications for such positions. In 18 states reporting public relations as a staff function, there was some degree of conformity in title and function. Although the function is not extensively utilized in municipal government, it is usually accurately titled.

Underneath the editorial bombasts and legislative scrutiny are solid questions of public policy that must be kept in mind. Public relations, as a staff function, must be justified on the grounds that it will not give undue power to the executive branch of government and that it will provide the public with useful information. Most vital of all is it that the programs do not interefere in the slightest degree with freedom of speech and freedom of information. The opposition must have full opportunity to oppose, counter, and criticize. So long as all sides have equal access to the citizen, there can be no real danger to freedom from the "government propagandist." [30]

FROM VESTED INTERESTS

It is natural that those interests who are the object of government regulation or legislation which they deem hurtful would protest the use of the government's public relations machinery to promote such legislation. This was

[29] Walter N. Moore, Jr., "Congressional Attitudes Toward Government Information Policies in the Eisenhower and Kennedy Administrations," master's thesis, University of Wisconsin, 1968, p. 212. There have been no prosecutions under provisions of the gag law.

[30] For differing views on this fundamental point, see Chapter IX in McCamy's *Government Publicity, op. cit.,* E. Pendleton Herring, *Public Administration in the Public Interest,* and an article, Harold W. Stoke, "Executive Leadership and the Growth of Propaganda," *American Political Science Review,* Vol. 35, June, 1941.

first illustrated by the efforts of the lumbermen and cattlemen to deprive Gifford Pinchot of funds for public information in 1908. This source of opposition is most dramatically illustrated in the long fight of the American Medical Association against what it termed "socialized medicine." This struggle, lasting two decades, cost the A.M.A. and its affiliates some $50-million and a somewhat tarnished public reputation. Repeatedly in this long fight, the A.M.A. decried the expenditure of public funds for "government propaganda." [31] The A.M.A. was influential in initiating the Harness Committee investigation of government public relations in the 80th Congress. Given the A.M.A. ammunition, it is not surprising that the Harness Committee found: [32] "At least six agencies in the executive branch are using Government funds in an improper manner for propaganda activities supporting compulsory national health insurance, or what certain witnesses and authors of propaganda refer to as socialized medicine in the United States."

THE FUNCTION MATURES

This necessary emphasis on the hostility and restrictions surrounding government public relations may have produced a distorted picture. Despite this opposition, the practice has steadily grown in concept, in ethics, and in practices. The press continues to use the information and services provided. Public relations in government has grown apace with the practice in other fields. Its necessity and usefulness in government make this inevitable.

Congress, state legislatures, and city councils recognize and accept the function by their annual appropriation of large sums for public relations. For example, when Congress passed the National Aeronautics and Space Act, it provided that NASA make all information available to the public except that limited by national security. In fiscal year 1969, NASA employed sixty-four full-time information officers and had a budget of $2.2-million for public relations. In 1966, a Senate Appropriations Committee commanded the National Institutes of Health "to undertake a more vigorous and imaginative public information program dedicated to the public understanding of their activities." A student studying recent press attitudes toward the function in government concluded: [33] "The government information

---

[31] This epic pressure group-government struggle was fully chronicled by Richard Harris in *A Sacred Trust* (New York: The New American Library, 1966).

[32] U. S. House, 80th Congress, 1st Sess., Committee on Expenditures in the Executive Departments, *Investigation of the Participation of Federal Officials in the Formation and Operation of Health Workshops* (1947), p. 1.

[33] Francis R. Cipolla, "Press Attitudes Toward the Public Information Function in the Federal Government, 1953–1963," master's thesis, University of Wisconsin, 1968, p. 173.

function was increasingly accepted by the press. Reporters, being concerned with facts, needed dependable sources and accurate reference material. Government information organizations willingly provided these services, within limitations placed upon them by policy-making officials and by Congressional appropriations, and therefore, were accepted as necessary expediters."

NUMBERS EMPLOYED

No accurate figures are available on the number of practitioners employed in government. The camouflaging of titles and budgets—born of legislative and press hostility—make it impossible to get accurate data in the federal government and in many state governments. In 1967, the Associated Press asserted that there were 6,868 federal employees working full or part time in public information. The same expose claimed that the government was spending $425-million a year on public information. The accuracy of these figures was hotly disputed by government officials. One agency that made no secret of its public relations budget was the Department of Health, Education and Welfare, which reported that year that it had 892 employees in public information and was spending nearly $8-million a year for this purpose. Approximately 3,000 of these information officers were employed in the Department of Defense and the armed forces.[34] The Associated Press figures presumably did not include those employed in United States Information Agency (USIA)—the nation's public relations agency—which has more than 10,000 employees, most of whom are nationals employed in posts abroad. The USIA budget for 1969 was approximately $178-million. No accurate count has yet been made of the number of federal employees performing this function. A like difficulty exists in trying to collect and collate a full picture of the practice in state and local governments. There are few reliable data in this area, suggesting (1) caution in accepting such figures, and (2) research opportunities for the scholar.

GOVERNMENT PRACTICE

The practice varies widely from local to state to the federal level and from department to department. It is a long way from a city's explaining to voters where its tax dollar comes from and where it goes to the United States Department of Agriculture's informational system radiating from

---

[34] Unsigned AP dispatch, "Tax Bill for U. S. Publicity: 425 Million a Year," *Chicago Tribune*, March 19, 1967, Sec. 1a.

Washington to 3,000 county agents. In government there is the one-man-plus-secretary operating on a simple publicity basis to the complex, far-flung mission of the United States Information Agency, which serves as America's public relations arm around the world. The necessity, potential, and difficulties inherent in government practice are sharply illustrated in the USIA's stormy history.

From World War II on, the United States as leader of the free world has been concerned with the problems of international communication, particularly with getting the people of other nations to understand our way of life and our fervent desire for peace. America's overseas public relations program has two main objectives: (1) countering Soviet propaganda and bringing other countries to a fuller and more friendly understanding of American policies; (2) making technical knowledge available to assist underdeveloped countries. In the words of the Smith-Mundt Act of 1948, this agency has the responsibility of presenting to the world "a full and fair picture" of the United States. While trying to accomplish this, the agency has been subjected to several reorganizations, repeated budget cuts, sharp congressional attacks, and undercutting from inside and outside government. It has had several different directors since World War II. The USIA has no lobby to defend it from its critics.

Under the late Edward R. Murrow and Carl Rowan in the early 1960s, the USIA achieved a stature and stability more commensurate with its mission. In the view of an aide, Thomas Sorensen, the USIA under Murrow's leadership: ". . . put confidence, excitement, and new hope into America's message to the world; built up its operations in Latin America and Africa, two areas previously neglected; ended diffusion of effort and output that had previously characterized USIA; and began to participate significantly in the formulation and execution of foreign policy." [35] It was at Murrow's urging that President Kennedy broadened the mission of USIA to embrace "advising the President, his representatives abroad, and the various departments and agencies on the implications of foreign opinion . . . ," thus bringing to USIA the mature concept of public relations. There is evidence to suggest that the advisory role lessened under Presidents Johnson and Nixon, though the 1963 mission statement was in effect in 1970. Even in the Murrow years, USIA had its critics. One was John Kenneth Galbraith, U. S. Ambassador to India in those years, "USIS [overseas it is known as the U. S. Information Service] in all its aspects [is] deadly dull. Magazines, books, film subjects . . . are totally pedestrian." The chorus of criticism has grown louder in recent years. At the end of the decade, Nixon-appointed Director Frank Shakespeare was

[35] In *The Word War* (New York: Harper & Row, 1968), p. 219. Sorensen, formerly in USIA, gives illuminating account of agency's policies and the internal differences over them.

under fire for banning several controversial books in libraries abroad. This agency suffers from a "split personality" because it is continually caught between demands for credibility abroad and domestic political demands that it soften America's ugly blemishes in foreign countries.

Accept the premise that peace begins in the minds of men and you accept the need for a stronger, more adequately supported agency to tell America's story and to interpret other peoples to Americans, particularly to our top policy makers. To achieve its purposes, the USIA employs all the aboveboard techniques of modern mass communications: press, radio, film, television, libraries, books, the arts, exhibits, and, most important, personal contact by its officers overseas. At 239 posts in 106 countries throughout the world, some 1,300 Agency officers are hard at work as spokesmen for America.

USIA operates an international wireless file, which radios some 10,000 words daily in several languages to these overseas posts, where they are adapted for local use. This wire news is used to supplement and balance that transmitted around the world by AP and UPI. Similarly, a constant flow of photos—some 750,000 prints and 160,000 copy negatives a year—is kept moving to the field for use in local publications. The agency produces four major magazines in Washington, and USIA posts overseas produce sixty-two other magazines in twenty-five languages, as well as twenty newspapers, wall posters, and other periodicals. USIA operates libraries and distributes American books by the millions of copies. Best known of USIA programs is the Voice of America, the radio broadcasts carrying the U. S. A.'s message to the world in thirty-six languages 761 hours weekly to an overseas audience numbered in the millions. It also makes and widely distributes films and exhibits to tell our story. Professional practitioners have assisted USIA through participation in its "People to People" program.

On the domestic front, the United States Department of Agriculture is one of the government's oldest and most intensive users of public relations. The department's director of information told a Senate committee in 1960 that his staff of 232 practitioners produced 3,600 news releases in one twelve-month period. This figures out to more than ten a day, not counting Sundays and holidays. The U.S.D.A. staff also produced 600 different printed publications, distributing more than 34-million copies. The agency supplied radio and TV stations with material every week and sent out 6,000 photographs to news media. Other Agriculture Department divisions also have information staffs. In all, the U.S.D.A. employs some 300 practitioners in Washington plus many more in field offices across the country. An increasing part of the U.S.D.A.'s assignment is to win public understanding of agriculture among the fast-growing urban population.

In most government programs, the emphasis is on disseminating information. Less attention is given to opinion analysis and policy making. Krimel gained the impression in his study that "the agencies of the Federal Government which carry on broad programs are almost entirely lacking in systematic, modern means for opinion measurement." Yet the Bureau of the Census and the Division of Special Surveys in the Department of Agriculture pioneered in opinion sampling. One of the pioneers was Dr. Rensis Likert who reminds administrators "The acceptance and support that a program receives depend not only upon its soundness and how well it meets the needs of the public but also on the understanding that the public has of the program. Fundamentally sound programs have failed because of misinformation and ignorance on the part of the public."

The same forces—press and legislative critics—that compel government agencies to camouflage their work as to cost and numbers employed also hinder full utilization of the research tools. Several agencies, including the armed services, do use surveys despite criticisms. Not enough do. Information sections in many agencies regularly provide their colleagues with editorial opinion digests, with the result that many officials tend to think that press opinion *is* public opinion. By and large, however, government agencies rely on political channels to bring in the people's views. This is unwise.

The value of public opinion surveys as a means of making government responsive to the views of its citizens was recognized by Canada when Prime Minister Trudeau reorganized that government's public relations machinery in 1970. He established a central public relations agency, Information Canada, with four branches: planning and research, information dissemination, public opinion surveys, and an administrative branch. The prime minister based his action on recommendations of a report of a Task Force on Information, significantly titled, *To Know and Be Known*.[36] Similarly, the British Government has long utilized public opinion research to guide its public relations programs. Its surveys unit was born May, 1941, as part of Home Intelligence in the wartime Ministry of Information. After the war it became the Department of Social Surveys in the Central Office of Information. It was made an independent agency in 1967. Its longtime director, Louis Moss, states: "The basic techniques of survey research are democratic in every sense of the word. They are rooted in representativeness, personal involvement, and consultation."

There are wide disparities in planning. In many agencies the information official is a strong and able personality. He will earn an influential voice in the agency's policy making. More frequently, the information man will

---

[36] *To Know and Be Known*, The Report of the Task Force on Government Information. Vol. I, Panorama, Vol. II, Research Papers. Ottawa: The Queen's Printer, 1969.

be relatively remote from the policy level. He is thus hampered in effectively interpreting the public to the agency and vice versa.

Informational programs in government generally take the form of (1) a campaign on particular topics—for example, revision of the state's deer-season law; (2) a steady play on a central theme for a long period of time—for example, conservation of the natural resources; (3) issuing news without any specific objectives—for example, a personnel change. There is a tendency to place too much stress on formalized communications and not enough on actual face-to-face communications. One state highway commission takes great effort to prepare an attractive, readable annual report. The same commission ignores a red-tape licensing procedure that irritates large numbers of citizens in the annual license "rush."

All communications must be understandable. A major weakness in government informational programs, generally, is continued use of gobbledegook, still the trademark of the bureaucrat despite all the fun that has been poked at it. There is urgent need for plain English and conversational writing in government correspondence and communications. Government jargon is a real obstacle to meaningful communication. Stripping it away involves more than clarity of writing: it is equally a matter of attitude. Agencies tackle the problem periodically. Several years ago the Internal Revenue Service brought in Dr. Rudolf Flesch. More recently the General Services Administration hired a former college English teacher to show the government's 750,000 letter writers how to write less like government letter writers.

Little wonder that newsmen and citizens become impatient with government language when the Pentagon describes the bombing of Hanoi and Haiphong in Vietnam as "merely an incremental adjustment to meet a new stimulus level." On the other hand, publications can be too readable—at least in the eyes of Congress and bureaucrats. In the Johnson Administration, HEW put out a 54-page pamphlet that was catchy, colorful, and crammed full of Presidential photographs and Johnsonian wisdom. One hundred thousand copies were sent to places like government clinics, doctors' waiting rooms, and Social Security offices. The *Wall Street Journal* reported that old-line bureaucrats feared that the "Madison Avenue methods" would destroy public confidence in HEW.

What can be correctly termed "Madison Avenue methods" are sometimes used. For example, the alcohol and tobacco tax division of Internal Revenue Service prepared an intensive publicity campaign to support an effort to crack down on moonshining, dubbed "Operation Dry-Up." As part of the promotional effort, The ATT division of IRS prepared thirty 30-minute radio programs designed not only to entertain but "to brainwash the citizenry and escalate the image of the ATT special investigator."

The division's information officer admitted the programs might be "corny and over-dramatic." Understandably, this campaign brought Congressional ire.[37]

The government practitioner uses the conventional tools of personal contact, annual reports, bulletins, films, publicity, education, consultation, and demonstrations. Many would do well to emphasize personal contacts, consultation, and educational programs. Not to be overlooked in the dissemination of government information is the practice of "leaking" information to get into public debate without revealing its source. "Leaks" through press officers and "plants" at informal dinners with a few chosen Washington correspondents are being used increasingly in the capital. Legislators as well as administrators use this technique. It can backfire badly, and frequently does.

Because of the increasing complexity of public affairs, public officials, usually at the urging of their advisers, use the background conference with increasing frequency. The "backgrounder" is fraught with peril—for the practitioner and for the public. One who is protected by anonymity can, if the press cooperates, grind an axe, float a balloon, or denigrate another department and still protect himself by fuzzing the source. Another danger is public confusion—how can the public judge the validity of information which comes from "a reliable source," or a "high government official." Yet the backgrounder is useful and necessary. Bill D. Moyers, who served as President Johnson's press secretary and counselor, lays down these guidelines for the backgrounder: [38]

> ONE: "Backgrounders" should be designed to *explain* policy rather than *announce* policy. This rule would discourage the use of unattributed quotations.

> TWO: "Backgrounders" in subjects other than national security and foreign affairs should be the exception rather than the rule.

> THREE: The contents of a group "backgrounder" should not be disclosed for at least one hour after the conclusion of the session. This would permit time for cross-checking.

> FOUR: The rules should be clearly stated before the "backgrounder" begins by the principal or by his press spokesman.

> FIVE: There should be only two levels of concealment. Either the reporter uses the information on his own—a practice that should be

---

37 From Memorandum prepared in the Information Office, ATT Division, IRS, and reprinted in *Congressional Record*, U. S. Senate, June 7, 1966.

38 In "Press or Government: Who's Telling the Truth," *Television Quarterly*, Vol. 7, Summer, 1968, pp. 24–25.

reserved for the most sensitive issues of national security—or it should be attributed as stated in the following principle.

SIX: The source should be identified by his specific agency. The loose anonymity of "high U. S. official," "top government officials," "friends of the President," or "visitors who've talked to the President" would be replaced by "A Defense Department spokesman," or "A U. S. Army official," or "White House sources."

SEVEN: The reporters should refuse to deliberately increase the obfuscation through such tactics as withholding the information until the source has left town, or by attributing the information to plural sources when it comes in fact from one source.

EIGHT: When a public official in a "backgrounder" refuses to permit attribution of material that is patently self-serving but reporters nonetheless feel obliged to carry the story, they should carry a sentence attributing the information to a Pentagon (or State or White House) official "whose name is withheld at his insistence."

There are many examples of skilled programs and useful techniques to be found in government, some borrowed, some homegrown. The public relations-minded John F. Kennedy made many innovations to promote his political fortunes. One was the introduction of the Regional White House Conference, which took federal officials to key cities of the nation for public conferences on current government problems. These conferences served the double purpose of publicizing the Kennedy Administration's view and of subjecting top officials to public opinion as reflected in these rather lively conferences. Secretary of HEW Wilbur Cohen adapted this idea by taking several key HEW executives to live in the inner city of Baltimore for three days. Many governments are acting to make information more accessible by opening "storefront" information centers in cities.

President Nixon brought an important innovation to the Federal government when he split the functions of White House Press Secretary, a position created by Herbert Hoover in 1929, and created a Director of Executive Communications. First holder of the latter position, Herbert G. Klein, former newspaperman, served as public relations adviser to the President, endeavored to coordinate release of information among the several departments, not always successfully, and fielded reporter's complaints. Klein saw his job thus: "My main responsibility is coordinating the flow of information from various departments of executive branch, as well as maintaining a liaison role with the Republican National Committee, maintaining contacts with the Republican side of Congress, and serving as a member of various policy committees in the White House." The Press Secretary, Ron Ziegler, serves as a spokesman for the President and tends to the needs of the White House press corps.

The State of New York has borrowed industry's open house. One year, the state held Open House Week, putting out the welcome mat for its 17-million residents to visit some 500 state offices and institutions. Employees provided guided tours, showed films, gave talks, and provided literature on their work. Some years ago the Kentucky Department of Revenue used an information program to pave the way for a needed overhaul of its 55-year-old tax laws. Another good example is the story of Ralph Gates, who, as governor of Indiana, took "the state capitol to the people" in the manner of a corporation taking its annual meeting to the stockholders. John Reynolds, when governor of Wisconsin, borrowed and modified this idea by holding his budget hearings in the various state institutions as a way of dramatizing the needs of Wisconsin's colleges, mental hospitals, and penal institutions. Governor Nelson Rockefeller developed the practice of holding "Town Meetings" in various parts of New York. In one such meeting, the governor, according to the New York *Times,* "parried the complaints of New Yorkers disturbed about crime, narcotics, pornography, insurance rates, airplane noise, and migrant workers."

Typical of the way in which the function is maturing in state government is the program of the Oklahoma State Department of Health. Its public relations program, directed by a coordinator of public affairs, has these objectives:

A. To establish a system whereby newsworthy information on public health may be disseminated through all appropriate channels of communication.

B. To develop a capability for technical assistance, advice and consultation to line programs within the State Department of Health, and to local health units on informational materials, public relations and other appropriate aspects of informational activities.

C. To provide a focal point, or clearinghouse, for both the mass media and departmental staff on consistency of information to be released and policy statements representing the department's over-all posture and attitude.

D. To effectively measure trends, attitudes, needs and reactions of the general and specialized public on their acceptance of departmental programs and objectives in order to meet these changes.

Governors have long accepted the need for a press secretary, most of whom function in the full public relations sense. A 1966 survey found that only five states—New Hampshire, Florida, Virginia, North Dakota, and Nevada—did not have such a position in the executive office. The Florida governor maintained he could handle his own public relations; the Nevada governor reported that the legislature had refused to approve such a post. The survey found: "Specific titles and duties appear to support the fact that there is still confusion about what constitutes press relations, public relations, promotion and other work areas." [39] A later study found that forty-three of forty-seven reporting governors have a staff to maintain liaison with newsmen. This study found: In twenty-four states one person works in the press section; in twelve states two persons are employed; and in three states the governor employs more than four persons in public relations. Nearly half of the state executives employ personnel with a background in radio and television news.[40]

At no level of government is citizen understanding and cooperation more essential than at the local level, where government provides schools, fire and police protection, safe streets and expressways, recreation facilities, urban renewal to combat inner-city decay, low-rent housing, and a host of other services. Today our cities are caught in crisis and their administrators in the vortex of conflict: taxpayers demanding a halt in rising property taxes one moment, demanding more services the next; municipal employees, now organized into unions, demanding higher wages and more fringe benefits; the needy demanding more adequate welfare payments; policemen frustrated by their inability to cope with the new tactics of confrontation and protest. Yet it is at the local governmental level that public relations has developed most slowly. A 170-city national survey conducted by the American Municipal Association found little agreement on the role of public relations. This survey found that in four out of every ten cities over 50,000 in population, no one had been assigned to public relations on a full-time basis. The survey also found excessive reliance on such time-worn gimmicks as presenting a key to the city and student government days. Regardless of city size, the AMA survey showed that the four most needed improvements are: (1) employee training in public relations techniques; (2) more effective communication of the municipal story; (3) a trained staff; and (4) better press relations.[41]

In the view of one practitioner: "The news media is local government's first and most effective line of communication with the taxpayers . . . and the news media can provide local governments with information on the effects of its policies so that mistakes can be corrected and needed city government improvements supported." This Lincoln, Nebr., official observes: "The simple fact is that much of the misunderstanding arises because many city officials, mayors to meter readers, don't know how

---

[39] John Behrens, "Governors Prefer Trained Newsmen," *Editor & Publisher*, May 14, 1966, pp. 28–30.

[40] Thomas F. Baldwin and Lowell Newton, *State Governors and Broadcast News* (East Lansing, Mich.: Michigan State University, January, 1968).

[41] Richard Oakland, "Public Relations: a 170-City Survey," *Nation's Cities*, March, 1966.

news media representatives operate, how to work with them, or the importance of good press-government relations." [42] How public relations can be utilized to assist local government was shown by the city of Birmingham, Alabama and a construction company, who put on a public relations campaign to get motorists' cooperation in closing a busy intersection for nine days, thus lopping off a full year's time on a major expressway. Employment of practitioners to smooth the stormy relationships between police and civilians has brought calm to many cities. Yet many chiefs resist this development, insisting rather naïvely that "community relations is a task for the whole department."

CASE PROBLEM

You are public relations director for the State Department of Public Welfare. Its division of corrections long ago decided that the state boys' school was grossly inadequate and a dangerous firetrap. The State Board of Public Welfare launched a public relations campaign three years ago to win legislative support for a new facility in a better location. After three years of effort, the State Legislature appropriated six-million dollars for a new reformatory. The Board of Public Welfare, in collaboration with the governor, decided to locate it in a state forest. This would provide attractive surroundings, isolation from cities, and constructive work for the boys. When this decision is announced, conservation groups, headed by the Izaak Walton League, issue vehement protests and threaten court action to block the move. The community in which the present reformatory is located organizes a committee to keep it there. Conservation groups start a public campaign to force the governor and welfare board to reverse the decision. The much-needed new reformatory appears to be in jeopardy. The director of public welfare and the head of the corrections division turn to you to ask: "How do we head this thing off?"

What are your recommendations?

ADDITIONAL READING

LOUIS ALEXANDER, "Space Flight News: NASA's Press Relations and Media Reaction," *Journalism Quarterly*, Vol. 43, Winter, 1966.

SAMUEL J. ARCHIBALD, "Rules for the Game of Ghost," *Columbia Journalism Review*, Vol. 6, Winter, 1967–1968. Critique of the "backgrounder" which shields Washington sources.

[42] Leo Scherer, "Better Press-Government Relations," *Wisconsin Counties*, September, 1969.

HERBERT M. BAUS and WILLIAM B. ROSS, *Politics Battle Plan*. New York: Macmillan, 1968. Manual for political publicist.

WILLIAM O. CHITTICK, *State Department, Press, and Pressure Groups*. New York: John Wiley & Sons, 1970. Examination of information officer's relationship with press and with fellow bureaucrats quite illuminating.

DELMAR D. DUNN, *Public Officials and the Press*. Reading, Mass.: Addison-Wesley Publishing Co., 1969. Examines relationships of Wisconsin government officials and press.

ROBERT E. ELDER, *The Information Machine. The United States Information Agency and American Foreign Policy*. Syracuse, N. Y.: Syracuse University Press, 1968.

RONALD T. FARRAR, *Reluctant Servant. The Story of Charles G. Ross*. Columbia, Mo.: University of Missouri Press, 1969. Includes Ross' years as Press Secretary to President Truman.

JOHN W. HENDERSON, *The United States Information Agency*. New York: Praeger, 1969.

LAWRENCE S. HOBART, *Governor's Press Secretary: A Profile of Paul Weber*. Ann Arbor, Mich.: University of Michigan Bureau of Government, 1958. Papers in Public Administration No. 25.

PAUL HOFFMAN, "The Neglected Statehouse," *Columbia Journalism Review*, Vol. 6, Summer, 1967.

DAN D. NIMMO, *Newsgathering in Washington*. New York: Atherton Press, 1964. Chapter II especially pertinent.

JACK REDDING, *Inside the Democratic Party*. New York: Bobbs-Merrill Company, Inc., 1958. Story of the 1948 Presidential campaign as seen by Democrats' public relations man.

HARRY W. REYNOLDS, JR., "Some Neglected Aspects of Public Relations in Local Government," *Public Relations Quarterly*, Vol 12, Summer, 1967. Shows importance of power structure in municipal public relations.

WILLIAM RIVERS, *The Adversaries: Politics and the Press*. Boston: Beacon Press, 1970. Conflict between press and government examined in several readable essays.

JOSEPH ROSAPEPE, "How to Collect $155 Billion Dollars," *Public Relations Journal*, Vol. 24, April, 1968.

IRWIN ROSS, *The Loneliest Campaign. The Truman Victory of 1948*. New York: New American Library, 1968. Good account of this upset election.

RONALD RUBIN, *The Objectives of the United States Information Agency*. London: Pall Mall Press, 1968.

PAN DODD WHEELER and CLIFF P. GREENWOOD, *A Municipal Public Relations Program That Works*. Knoxville: University of Tennessee, 1954.

CHAPTER 24

THE PRACTICE: PUBLIC SCHOOLS

The nation's public schools are caught in a web of difficult relationships in this era of rapid change and shifting social patterns. News of public education has moved from the inside pages to the front page. Headlines tell the story: "Desegregate Schools at Once, Court Rules," "In Ten Years, Americans Double School Spending," "Sex Education Banned," "Taxpayer Revolt Closing Schools," "Teacher Strikes on Mass Upswing," "School Bond Issue Defeated," "Rulings on Student Dress Anger School Officials," "Parents Oppose School Shifts," "Teachers Strike in Florida," "Jersey Reverses Sideburns Ruling," "National PTA Shaken by Loss of Members," "Parents Protest Bussing Decision."

The growth in news coverage of education in part reflects the public's increased awareness of schools and their impact on society. With the rapid evolution of the civil rights movement and protests in the streets, the discovery of the poor, the rise in industrial technology, and swiftly changing social patterns, the social urgency of public education has been firmly established in the public mind. These developments have brought a broadly-supported revolution in education, which has increased its costs, broadened its role, and made it the object of much criticism.

Education is a major enterprise. Enrollment in public and private schools and colleges of the United States in 1970 exceeded 58-million students, more than one-fourth of the population. Increased enrollments at the high school and college levels are expected to boost this total to 63-million students, kindergarten through college, by 1977.[1] Nearly three-million teachers and administrators serve in our elementary schools. Roughly 50 percent of the nation's families have children in some kind of school. For the nation as a whole, 41 percent of local taxes are used for schools.[2] An increasing percentage of state-collected taxes are, likewise, spent for education. Also, an increasing amount of federal tax money is being channeled to the education enterprise. In higher education there are almost 2,500 colleges and universities with some 524,000 faculty mem-

[1] *Projections of Educational Statistics to 1977–78* (Washington, D.C.: U. S. Government Printing Office, 1969).

[2] Juan de Torres, *Financial Local Government* (New York: National Industrial Conference Board, 1967). (Now the Conference Board.)

bers and more than 7.5-million students.[3] The net result is that virtually every citizen is touched directly by the schools in one way or another. The relationships of education with the people are many, direct, and diverse. The opportunities for frictions, misunderstandings, and communication breakdowns abound.

The need for understanding and support of education is urgent in a time when demands for freedom and equal rights have penetrated the schools, when a generation gap has developed, and when school dollars have been sapped by inflation. Consequently, education public relations is expanding in scope and concept. The problems in the 1970s loom large.

The National School Public Relations Association in 1970 polled state school administrators and state school board associations to determine the most difficult communication problems facing school districts. Here are the top-ranked communication problems in the combined opinion of these two groups:

1. Communication with teachers and other employees.
2. Getting voter support of local finance issues.
3. State legislative relations.
4. Lack of a year-round, planned public relations program.
5. The communication of negotiations.
6. Public "image" of the school board.
7. Student communications (tie).
7. Adult pressure groups (tie).
8. Federal legislative relations.
9. School integration.

EDUCATION—A JOB FOR ALL

The key to sound relationships is development of the idea that education is the job of all citizens. In achieving this, *educators must take the public into partnership,* using wisely the tools of persuasion, information, and cooperation. Responsibility rests primarily with the educator. He is increasingly aware of this.

Surveys repeatedly show that education ranks among the most valued symbols in American life. In fact, there have been disturbing signs that Americans expect too much from education. Many presume education to be the panacea for all the ills that beset the nation.

---

[3] *Digest of Educational Statistics, 1969* (Washington, D.C.: U. S. Government Printing Office, 1969).

One tends, too easily, to turn to schools for relief from weaknesses, for protection against feared enemies. If the accident rate zooms up, people demand safe driving courses. If juvenile delinquency breaks out in a community, people insist that the schools do something about it. Threatened from without and within by Communism, people turn, frightened, to the schools for courses in "Americanism." They join forces with extremists to advocate loyalty oaths for teachers and probe feverishly into the content of textbooks. Those concerned with the rising rate of illegitimate births press for sex education in the classroom, a movement spearheaded by the Sex Information and Educational Council of the United States (SIECUS). Those who fear such instruction coalesce in protest groups, Concerned Parents Committee, Movement to Restore Decency, etc.

In the face of these attitudes, serious shortcomings in the schools have fostered the growth of a vast educational gap. Edward J. Steimel, executive director of the Public Affairs Research Council of Louisiana, Inc., attributed this gap to questions such as curriculum relevance to the students, quality of education available to whites and nonwhites, achievement opportunities for the affluent and the poor, and availability of special education for the handicapped.

Years ago Walter Lippmann predicted the magnitude of the responsibility which the schools would be called on to assume: [4]

> It (education) promises to solve the problem which is otherwise so nearly insoluble—how to educate rapidly and sufficiently the ever-expanding masses who are losing contact with the traditions of Western society. The explosive increase of the population in the past hundred and fifty years, its recent enfranchisement during the past fifty years, the dissolution, or at least the radical weakening, of the bonds of the family, the churches, and of the local community have combined to make the demand upon the schools almost impossibly big.

Never was the need for strengthening the schools greater, a need underscored by at least three factors. *First,* in the battle for freedom and peace, United States citizens face problems of unequaled perplexity and difficulty. The need for educated, informed citizens capable of charting a safe course for the nation was never greater. One of the prime functions of education is to develop informed citizens equal to their responsibilities. Schools should offer every child an education up to his capacity.

Second, because our system is grounded in free education, schools represent the first point of attack. This requires vigilance and common

[4] In *The Public Philosophy* (Boston: Little, Brown & Co., 1955), p. 73.

sense to safeguard against subversion and against injury from well-intentioned but ignorant zealots.[5]

Third, the educational system, from kindergarten to university, is confronted with lack of adequate facilities and *qualified* teachers. The accelerated birth rate, from World War II on, has swamped present facilities and staffs. There are more young people, more of them going to school and more going longer. In 1967, there were nearly 44-million pupils in public schools. In 1977, there will be 48-million children enrolled.[6] For a typical city of 100,000 population, this means one new school building every few years. For example, in Huntsville, Alabama, school enrollment increased rapidly enough to require one additional teacher and one additional classroom a week for five years out of ten. Urban mobility also complicates the building problems for school boards.

These problems are critical in large cities. Robert Bendiner, in his book, *The Politics of Schools,* wrote: "It is the paradox of education in metropolitan America that where the needs are the greatest, the resources are scarcest; the children needing education the most are receiving the least!" The problem is complicated further by the expectation that the coming enrollment increases will be at the most expensive levels—high school, technical college, and college. These requirements impose a heavy burden on the taxpayer—and on public relations. To persuade taxpayers to vote the money required for new buildings and to pay salaries to attract well-qualified teachers is a task of the first order.

"The Youngstown syndrome" describes the taxpayers' revolt in large city schools such as Chicago, Los Angeles, Philadelphia, and others threatened with closing because of lack of funds.[7] In Youngstown, the schools were closed for five weeks. Finally on the seventh try, the voters passed a 12-mill operating levy—but not before the citizenry had been humiliated by national attention focused on their plight. Similar taxpayer resistance forced Fremont, Ohio, to close its ten public schools for the last two months of 1969. From May to November, 1969, only eight of nineteen bond issues voted on in Iowa passed; from July to November, 1969, only twelve of twenty-five school bond campaigns in Ohio were successful. Columbus, Ohio, voters rejected a bond issue for the first time in thirty years.

Evidence of the need for and value of effective two-way communica-

---

[5] For examples of misguided efforts to censor what is taught and read in our schools, see: Jack Nelson and Gene Roberts, Jr., *The Censors and the Schools* (Boston: Little, Brown & Co., 1963); "Facing the 'Facts of Life,'" *Life,* September 19, 1969; Thomas J. Cottle, "The Wellesley Incident, A Case of Obscenity," *Saturday Review,* Vol. 52, March 15, 1969; "Hell Breaks Loose in Paradise," *Life,* April 26, 1963; Joseph A. King, "Books and Banners: Case History," *Saturday Review,* November 9, 1963.

[6] *Projections of Educational Statistics, op. cit.,* p. 1.

[7] For a brief account of this campaign, see: "The Youngstown Story," *Trends in School Public Relations,* June, 1969.

tion between schools and the taxpayers supporting them abounds, as shown in several exhaustive studies carried out by Stanford University under the sponsorship of the United States Office of Education. Two of these studies, directed by Richard F. Carter, were based on interviews with community leaders in eighty-two school districts in the nation and interviews with a representative sample of voters in four widely spread cities. These studies found, among other things: [8]

1. The voter thinks schools are good in general, but he criticizes them in particular areas: frills, too much play, curriculum, and discipline.
2. The voter thinks the most important task of schools are to teach the fundamentals—reading, writing, spelling, arithmetic, and speaking— and to instill loyalty to the United States. He also thinks that these are the jobs done best.
3. The voter thinks the least important tasks of the schools are to teach about the local region, to afford enjoyment of cultural activities— art and music—and to provide industrial arts education.
4. The voter's evaluation of the local schools, his evaluation of school costs, and his pride in the schools are most closely associated with likelihood of voting and of voting favorably.
5. About half the voters show no evidence of any participation in school affairs and no interest in such participation. About a third of the voters participate actively. The more the voter participates, the more knowledge he has of school performance.

Summarizing many studies, dated over a half-century, of what the public thinks about its schools, Steven Chaffee and Scott Ward make these points: [9]

> It is difficult to assess the over-all adequacy of public knowledge about schools, since no "baseline" of comparison is available. Parents seem to feel generally well-informed but show some desire for more information. In a study of seven communities in Washington . . . one elementary school parent in four could not name his child's teacher. Over-all, parents tend to be more informed than others.

[8] Richard F. Carter, *Voters and Their Schools* (Stanford, Calif.: Stanford University Institute for Communication Research, 1960). Findings summarized on pp. 4–16. Other studies in this long-term, fruitful research project include: Carter and William G. Savard, *Influence of Voter Turnout on School Bond and Tax Elections* (Washington, D.C.: U. S. Government Printing Office, 1961); Carter, Bradley S. Greenberg and Alvin Haimson, *Informal Communication About Schools* (1966), Carter and Steven H. Chaffee, *Between Citizens and Schools* (1966). The studies are summarized in Carter and William R. Odell, *The Structure and Process of School-Community Relations: A Summary* (1966). The latter three were published by the Stanford Institute for Communication Research.

[9] "Channels of Communication in School-Community Relations," *Journalism Monographs*, No. 8, September, 1968. A review of the research literature and bibliography.

Knowledge is greater on "external" and formal aspects of the school's operation, than "internal" and subtle aspects. For example, in one study more people knew more about fire drill and the age for entering kindergarten than about teacher tenure and school board business; the PTA was better understood than the citizen advisory committee; and there was more knowledge of driver training than of courses for the handicapped. Opinions about schools are not limited to areas in which the citizen is informed. In one nationwide survey, half the sample knew nothing about the membership of the school board, yet . . . expressed opinions about the representativeness of the board.

Accurate knowledge of school operations may lead to less favorable opinions. In one predominantly black community, the parents were poorly informed about schools but generally favorable; their children, presumably well informed, were considerably less favorable.

Public opinion supporting schools is most likely to come from citizens who are close to schools in some way or have benefited from education.

There is abundant evidence that the average citizen has only the vaguest notions of what constitutes "good education" and that half of the population takes scant interest. Fact-finding provides provocative insights for the school practitioner and should be studied with care. For example, a national survey made in 1969 indicated: 30 percent of those interviewed did not know how many students dropped out of their high schools; a third did not know the percentage of high school graduates going on to college; 57 percent did not know how much it costs to educate a child each year. The survey showed the public about evenly divided in willingness to pay more for schools, and that citizens are so uninformed about educational innovation and "so lacking in objective ways of judging school achievement that little, if any, pressure is exerted by them to make improvement."

The poll, conducted by Gallup International, was sponsored by CFK, Ltd., a Denver-based foundation devoted to education and headed by Charles F. Kettering 2d. This was the first in a series of annual surveys which will provide, in the years ahead, a national profile of school opinion against which local districts may design their programs and measure their results.

Developing adequate support for more funds and needed changes requires public persuasion. One problem is the need to demonstrate that the modern, consolidated school with a modern curriculum is essential. Then, there is the problem of safeguarding the integrity and freedom of those who teach and those who learn. Those who confuse sex education with birth control and eroticism demand removal of sex education courses from the curriculum. Attitudes on racial integration of the schools makes cooperative effort difficult. Student activism is confused with student disorder.

THE PURPOSE

The Depression of the 1930s provided rough jolts for educators. It was a period of cutbacks in school budgets. When taxpayers in revolt made cutbacks in schools, they attacked not the least useful activities but generally those they understood the least. As the taxpayer association steamroller passed over them, schoolmen began to realize their failures in public relations. They ruefully admitted that if the required economies were made on the basis of emotion and misunderstanding, they, not the taxpayers, were primarily at fault.

A new generation of administrators has learned much the same lesson the hard way: communities refusing to vote the tax monies required for sufficient classrooms and trained teachers; teachers going out on strike; a number of communities refusing to consolidate small, uneconomical districts into larger, more feasible school districts; protests against educational innovations, such as modular scheduling; parental protests against dress codes; and a number of misguided but successful attempts to throttle the freedom of teachers.[10]

Yet, even now, there is disturbing evidence that many school boards and administrators still do not recognize the need for a *planned program* to build public support. This starts with the state departments of education. In 1967, Project Public Information—a U. S. financed three-year program to improve school public relations—surveyed the states to ascertain the state of educational public relations at that level. Forty-three states responded to the questionnaire. Of these, ten states did not have a full-time public relations official, and in four other states the information officer handled the task as a part-time duty. Highlights of this survey included: [11]

> Most state school chiefs emphasized publicity and media relations in their concept of public relations. Few of them embraced the mature concept of public relations. Few had provisions for feedback from the public.
>
> These state school heads, when asked to indicate the immediacy of their public information needs, placed an effective external communications program first, an internal communications program second.
>
> Ten state departments of education said they could not provide public

---

[10] For a case study showing the cost of a failure in public relations, see: David Hulburd, *This Happened in Pasadena* (New York: The Macmillan Company, 1951).

[11] *The State of the Art. A Survey Report on Public Information Programs in the State Departments of Education* (Madison, Wis. Project Public Information, 1968). Includes evaluative comments by Scott M. Cutlip and H. Thomas James, formerly of Stanford University.

relations assistance to local districts, despite the growing demand for such counsel.

In seventeen states, the superintendent said the public relations officer was included in the administrative council of the department; in fifteen states he was not.

Of the thirty-three information officers covered in the survey, only two had over ten years' experience in their present jobs. The median level of experience was less than one year.

In an analysis of this forty-four-state survey, one of your authors noted: [12]

> The data clearly show an urgent need to expand the public relations horizons of the state departments of education by demonstrating to them the value of public relations in achieving their objectives and in recruiting and upgrading the public relations personnel in education to implement the mature concept of public relations. The pool of mature, experienced education-oriented personnel is shallow indeed. The newness of the function in many states is apparent.

The same thing can be found at the local level. For example, a study made in Wisconsin in 1963 showed that few Wisconsin school districts follow a planned policy for disseminating information. This study, based on a questionnaire sent to a representative sample of Wisconsin's 395 districts containing both secondary and elementary schools, found: [13]

1. Few Wisconsin public school districts follow a pre-determined information policy. Concern for such a policy may be increasing; but, as yet, most school districts handle communications problems as they arise.

2. Most school districts have some method of allocating informational duties, but in many cases communicating is considered as just another duty to be performed.

3. The attitudes of school district administrators are not always on the side of the people's right to know.

4. The most frequently used channel of communication of the school districts is written press releases, whether or not an information specialist is employed.

5. Only three school districts in Wisconsin employed full-time practitioners. Many schools use teachers on a part-time basis to handle publicity. Most specialists replying in the study said that they needed

---

[12] *Ibid.*, p. 20.

[13] Digested from a master's thesis, "Public Information Policies and Practices of Wisconsin High School Districts," by Timothy J. Burke (Madison: University of Wisconsin, 1963).

more time to do their public relations tasks, particularly for external communications.

A somewhat comparable study of public relations attitudes and practices in ten school systems around Boston led Professor Albert J. Sullivan to a comparable conclusion. The sound view that "the prime objective of public relations for schools is mutual cooperation of all segments of the community" was neither widely held nor practiced in the Boston area, he found. He writes: [14] "Educational public relations in its best sense envisions inter-communication and mutual cooperation. Too often this view, in practice, becomes diluted: one segment does all the 'communicating,' the other segments are conceived as receivers or listeners, or at most, as groups to be persuaded to some action."

In an earlier survey of 200 school systems, John Moran found that most of them had no organized program.[15] On the other hand, Roy Carter's survey of California found that half the superintendents in the state's daily-newspaper towns had a person on their staff to prepare publicity releases. Full-fledged departments were less common.[16] An increasing pattern, especially in large high school districts, is employing a journalism-trained teacher to teach journalism, supervise the student newspaper, and "handle school publicity." In a 1965 survey, Mrs. Mary Ericsson of the Pittsburg, California schools, found programs in districts as small as 1,000 pupils. In her random sample, she found that school public relations was "increasingly becoming a specific assignment for a trained person" and school public relations budgets range up to $300,000 a year. Forty-six of the 69 school districts she queried had one or more persons working full time; the others had part-time employees.[17] Over-all, there is marked progress in developing full-time programs; the question is whether the progress is fast enough.

The magnitude of the problem is becoming clearer as educators step up their efforts. Nationally, advances are being spearheaded by the nation's political and educational leaders, the National Education Association and its affiliate, the National School Public Relations Association. Founded in 1935 to further public understanding of the public schools, NSPRA has grown rapidly and has done much to clarify and elevate the status of

---

14 In an article, "What's Wrong With School Public Relations," *Quarterly Review of Public Relations*, Vol. 7, Fall, 1962, pp. 21–29.

15 A survey of 200 school systems indicated that "90 per cent viewed public relations as just another term for publicity." See *Public Relations Journal*, Vol. 9, December, 1953, p. 12.

16 Roy E. Carter, Jr., "The Press and Public School Superintendents in California," *Journalism Quarterly*, Vol. 31, Spring, 1954.

17 "The Changing Face of School P. R.," April, 1965, mimeographed.

the practitioner. Even with the tremendous gains of recent years, this progress is neither broad enough nor fast enough to meet the critical challenge.

Many schoolmen, to their sorrow, have too often taken public support for granted. They have assumed that the public would foot a bigger and bigger bill for an ever-expanding program and plant. They have assumed that the public comprehends objectives and methods—despite ample evidence to the contrary. Or worse, they often have assumed that courses and teaching methods were none of the public's business. And worse yet, many school boards have refused to allow teachers and students a voice in curriculum or teaching methods. Schools are social, public institutions with broad impact. Consequently, they cannot escape conflicting pulls and tugs.

These are the common problems of American educators. Schools in the South and in the border states face even tougher problems born of geography and history.

Educator's influence in improving education rests upon their ability to guide public opinion and to be guided by it in meeting society's needs. Failure to establish this cooperative partnership frequently results in defeats of bond issues needed to provide more classrooms and more teachers. Terry Ferrer, an education writer, put it succinctly: "Much of the school financing opposition, much of the recurring criticism about education stems wholly or in part from an uninformed public." Miss Ferrer recognizes the fact that the mass media cannot provide information on education unaided, and she urges a year-round school public relations program.

Lack of this cooperative partnership is also the source of much of the unbridled criticism of teaching methods and curricula content. Over the years public forums have resounded with stinging criticisms. A book attacking the teaching of reading, *Why Johnny Can't Read,* was a national best seller in the 1950s. In the 1960s, Vice-Admiral Hyman G. Rickover's book, *American Education—a National Failure,* was widely sold and discussed. He aimed his shots at course content, curricula, and teaching methods. In the words of one educator: "Critics have loudly denounced the schools as godless, Communistic, unamerican, unenlightened, and subversive." [18]

Robert M. Hutchins has said: "One reason why educational institutions are vulnerable to economy drives and Red scares is that the purpose

---

[18] For a sampling of these critical books, see Rudolf Flesch, *Why Johnny Can't Read;* Hyman G. Rickover, *American Education—A National Failure;* Arthur E. Bestor, *Educational Wastelands* and *The Restoration of Learning;* Arthur Lynd, *Quackery in the Public Schools.* For a more recent and telling indictment, see: Charles E. Silberman's *Crisis in the Classroom.* (New York: Random House, 1970.) For one rebuttal, see Paul Woodring, *Let's Talk Sense About Our Schools.*

of education is not generally understood." Yet Hutchins frequently criticizes the practitioner whose skill is needed in building such understanding.
Public disputes repeatedly demonstrate that the public does not fully understand modern educational methods and objectives. Too much attention
has been focused on the sideshows—athletics, baton-twirling, extracurricular activities, social events—and too little attention on the show in the
main tent.

The board of education members occupy a strategic position in the
public relations program. They determine the educational policies upon
which the program must be based. The board, comprised of lay citizens,
who have accepted responsibility for public education in their communities,
is the intermediary between the public and the professional administrators.
It is essential that a board agree on an adequate statement of public relations policy. The board must serve its function of interpreting the community to the school staff and, in turn, interpreting staff ideas and policies
to the community. Influential, articulate board members can be a valuable
asset to a school system. Self-seeking, opinionated members can be harmful.[19]

Many school boards bring suspicion, criticism, and ill will by insisting on a "closed door" at board meetings. Conversely, they fail to utilize
this newsworthy means of focusing public attention on school policies and
problems. Basil Walters, veteran news editor, once advised schoolmen:
"Maybe if you really had debate on some of these problems . . . if you
would invite in citizens to debate out the issues, it might be beneficial. It
would be painful . . . but it is the only way in which to educate the
American people in such a way that they can form an enlightened and
intelligent public opinion." Newspapers are increasingly insistent on this
point. The New Bedford, Massachusetts *Standard-Times,* for example,
hammered away publicly at its board for eighteen months before the board
opened its doors. The Florida Supreme Court in 1969 ruled unanimously
that boards of education cannot hold secret meetings, executive sessions,
or even informal gatherings where public business is discussed. The case
arose and received support from the Florida Education Association when
a reporter was arrested for refusing to leave a "closed" meeting of the
Broward County Board of Education.

The able school executive must recognize that if he must go against
popular opinion to serve the best interest of the pupils, and if the decision
is for the welfare of the children, it will be the right decision over the long
pull. But the public must be persuaded that it is the right decision. The
able executive recognizes that performance is basic and does not confuse

---

[19] For details of a long-range, well organized program for school innovation in Fullerton,
Calif., see "No Surprises Wanted," *Trends in School Public Relations,* Jan. 15, 1969.

publicity with the whole of public relations. There are also practitioners in education who tend to mix cart and horse.

A comprehensive set of objectives for a school public relations program set down by experienced school administrators some years ago is still valid: [20]

1. To inform the public about the work of the schools
2. To establish confidence in the schools
3. To rally support for proper maintenance of the educational program
4. To develop awareness of the importance of education in a democracy
5. To improve the partnership concept by uniting parents and teachers in meeting the educational problems of children
6. To integrate the home, the school, and the community in meeting the needs of the children
7. To correct misunderstandings as to the aims and objectives of the schools.

Inside these continuing, long-range objectives fall more specific, short-range objectives determined by current needs. For example, in the years just ahead, these would be specific, short-term objectives: (1) greater financial support to meet the increased pupil load; (2) higher teachers' salaries and teacher tenure to attract more qualified people to public school teaching; (3) equal pay for elementary and high school teachers; (4) improved teacher education; (5) improved facilities; (6) broadened, more realistic courses of study; and (7) needed expansion of school plants.

PUBLICS AND PROGRAMS

The chief executive of a school system needs skilled assistance in planning and directing the program. In too many systems public relations is left to individual schools with no central direction and coordination. *A public relations program requires direction,* and the superintendent must provide it.[21] He must:

a. Accept personal responsibility for planning and coordinating the public relations program

[20] American Association of School Administrators, *Public Relations for America's Schools,* 28th Yearbook (Washington, D.C.: The Association, 1950), p. 254. Though old, still a useful reference.
[21] *Ibid.,* p. 17.

b. Adapt leadership activities to his ability and personality and to community expectations

c. Merit community recognition and acceptance by performance and competence

d. Delegate the proper public relations functions and commensurate authority to staff assistants without relinquishing his own responsibility

e. Make effective use of available technical assistance from staff members and laymen in the community and assign specific responsibility to specific persons

f. Encourage and expect the staff of each school in his system to maintain good public relations in its own service area.

A school program, like any other, starts with the system's policies and performance.

The public relations responsibility of boards and superintendents is taken for granted. However, a powerful new leadership force has emerged in the form of teacher and student activism. More and more, when school boards and administrators fail, the teachers are stepping in—using their own resources—to "tell it like it is" to the community. Increasingly, teachers seek a voice in selecting their administrators. Similarly, high school students are vigorously demanding more say in shaping their school programs. The Research Council of the Great Cities—a body representing twenty urban school districts—has recommended active student participation in public school operations. Some boards of education have seated high school students as *ex-officio* members to establish better rapport with students.

The professional association is the spokesman for teachers. They have mustered the courage and strength to stand united for quality education—"fighting city hall" if necessary to accomplish needed reforms, working tirelessly on school bond campaigns, becoming politically active on issues concerning the schools, and seeking a voice in the development of policies affecting the students they teach and their profession. Teacher militancy has been a prime force in bringing new emphasis to the public relations function. The ideal climate exists when the board, superintendent, teachers, and students work together as a team.

Basic to sound programs are fact-finding and opinion research. As educators have repeatedly said: "The community should be so organized that citizen control of its public school policies is respected in principle and facilitated in practice." One of the surest ways to facilitate citizen control is through periodic surveys of community opinion. The Denver public schools, since 1951, have made such surveys at three-year intervals with profitable results. Through these polls, in the words of the Denver superintendent, Denver's administrators and teachers "obtain a sort of group concept of what parents want and what citizens of this community want—their concept of what good schools are." The results of these surveys, fully reported to staff and the community, serve as guides for Denver schools in their program and public relations planning.

Ned Hubbell, a consultant from Port Huron, Mich., stresses that it is necessary to get information before one can give information. This doesn't have to be a formal opinion poll, he says, but even an inventory of information obtained by teachers in conferences with parents or other groups.

The starting point of any program is the careful determination of the publics involved, channels of two-way communication with them, and agreement on objectives. There are various publics in school relations that must be reached.

INTERNAL	*EXTERNAL*	
School board	Parents	Churches
Teachers	Taxpayer groups	Alumni
Children	Service clubs	Athletic boosters
Staff employees	Patriotic groups	Labor unions
	Civic groups	Legislators
	Industry	Government administrators
	School neighbors	

First, there should be rapport between the school hierarchy and the teachers. That such a relationship often is lacking is evident, however, by the introduction of federal legislation to make it mandatory for school boards to negotiate with teachers. The necessity for enacting laws to accomplish this communication is indicative of administrative and communications breakdown. A sound program cannot be built if the teacher is excluded.

Many teachers spend vacations and holidays in workshops and university courses to enhance their skills. If allowed a voice, this training often can be shared for the benefit of the entire system. But most important, the teacher in his day-to-day activities is in a position to relate effectively to students, parents, and others—and, in turn, to provide valuable feedback to those responsible for the program.

One useful approach in bridging the gulf between administrators and teachers, which grows as districts increase in size, is a requirement that superintendents and principals take frequent turns as substitute teachers. This enables them to see the teacher's problems in a fresh way.

Children are perhaps the most influential of a school's publics. Much of the information and the attitudes held by the general public are transmitted from pupil to parent to public on the community grapevine. There is no surer route to a person's heart—or resentment—than through his child. When the program of a school system rests on a foundation of classroom accomplishment, it is like a house built upon a rock. Ill-founded criticism will not overwhelm it. The pupil's role as an intermediary is a strategic one. Public relations, *truly,* starts in the classroom.

The school executive should determine whether students are enthusiastic boosters. He should see that pupils are well informed about policies, that courses satisfy their needs and challenge their abilities, that individual attention is provided for those who need it, and that the overall atmosphere engenders pupil and parent pride in the school. Proud, satisfied parents will ring doorbells to win a school bond vote.[22]

It is important that pupil and parent get off on the right foot. This starts with kindergarten. Many schools have effective programs for introducing parent and child to the school. A typical one starts with preregistration in the spring before the child starts school. This includes enrollment by the principal so that he can get acquainted, a visit by the mother and her child to the room the child will enter in September, and a leisurely cup of coffee with the principal and other teachers who may be free that hour. This is followed in August by mailing the parents a Kindergarten Handbook which tells them what is expected of the budding pupil. *Informality, information,* and *consideration* are the keys to a pleasant introduction.

Schools dare not rely upon the child's often twisted reports to keep parents fully, accurately informed. Good parent relationships are built by frequent, frank communication between teacher and parent. Although teachers and parents share the same goals, there are many blocks to communication. Care must be used in report cards and in parent conferences. In a study of parent-teacher conferences, it was found that standard practices "boomeranged" unless the teachers were well prepared in interpreting data about the child.[23] Communication means include report cards which report, not merely score; conferences; encouragement of parent observation of normal classroom situations; special programs for parents; and home visits by the teachers to handle ticklish problems. P.T.A. meetings with a purpose—not just excuses for a social hour—are a tool of proved worth in school-parent communication. Too many P.T.A.s fail to serve this need.

Constructive relationships with parents are best built on annual parent-teacher conferences. In this connection, a ticklish problem has developed concurrently with our schools' extensive testing programs—"To

---

[22] For an excellent "how to" booklet on school bond campaigns, see *School Finance Campaign Handbook* (Washington, D.C.: National Education Association, 1969).

[23] Claud E. Kitchens, "The Parent-Teacher Conferences as an Instrument for Changing Perceptions of and Attitudes Toward Schools and Teachers," Ph.D. thesis, University of South Carolina, 1961.

what information are parents entitled?" As Paul Woodring comments: [24] "Parents in several American communities have charged that the schools are withholding important information about their children. Some have taken legal action to require that the full record on each child be made available to his parents. Teachers and administrators are troubled and frightened by these demands because they have compiled a great deal of . . . information about each student and many school systems have no clear policy regarding what may be released to parents." The only prudent course is to develop carefully thought-out, clearly stated policies in this matter and then enforce them.

Another effective way to build school-parent understanding is to hold special night courses for parents. In recent years many high schools have instituted such courses to introduce parents to new concepts and new teaching methods. Such courses have met with an enthusiastic response in most cities. Parents are anxious to know the content of their sons' and daughters' courses and thus to be able to assist the students with their homework. Smart schoolmen capitalize on this parental interest.

Each member of the school staff, from principal and teachers to bus driver to custodian to school nurse, must be brought into the program. This can best be accomplished through a continuing in-service training program. Also, the qualities and attitudes of a person should be given due weight in staff recruitment. Finally, it should be remembered that the happy, satisfied teacher or employee is the one who generally makes the best representative.

A given school district's residents, who foot the bill, provide the children, and shape the school's environment must be the ultimate targets. This public is composed of many groups: parents, taxpayers, and citizens with positive ideas about "what our schools ought to be teaching." The public can be reached through the pupil, P.T.A., press, service clubs, church groups, and in countless other ways. Community influentials can be involved most effectively through consultation on school matters.

Changes in school policy, organization, and curricula and plans for new schools should be cleared with key public groups. The counsel of lay leaders should be sought as often as possible and practicable. Location of new schools directly involves city government, real estate developers, businessmen, bankers, and others. Cooperative planning can be coordinated through councils, committees, and commissions. It should be based on a continuous process of self-analysis. Broadly based planning makes available a wealth of good ideas. It also serves to clear the path for important changes. Public hearings on major issues can be a profitable, if at times uncomfortable, procedure.

[24] In Editorial, "The Parent's Right to Know," *Saturday Review*, Vol. 44, November 18, 1961.

For example, the Pasadena, California, school system set up a number of citizen-staff advisory committees to deal with particular problems or issues. One was created to deal with the system's multi-million-dollar building program. Another was organized to advise on how best to develop a vocational education program. These citizen-staff committees also have been used on the problems of equitable districting, released time for religious education, and programs for the retarded. In this way, many fresh ideas are obtained, possible criticism are eliminated beforehand, and two-way communication is firmly established with the community's influentials.[25]

The Columbus, Ohio, school district took another approach to this objective of closer citizen-school ties when it instituted a series of successful neighborhood seminars. These seminars were an outgrowth of a series of Saturday morning conferences held the year before by the school board president and carefully chosen Columbus civic leaders. The neighborhood seminars, sponsored by a City-Wide Seminar Committee, were devoted to discussions of the Columbus schools' program and financial needs. Study guides were prepared and distributed ahead of time. These served as the basis of the discussions. When the series was announced the first time, some 4,000 Columbus citizens signed up; when the seminars were held, another 3,000 turned out. Columbus officials have found these neighborhood ideas highly productive.

Another example of cooperative planning—one of many—is found in the constructive contributions of Detroit's Better Schools Association. Committees of this association delved deeply into Detroit's school problems. One committee found ways of cutting costs of building construction. Another found a better site than the board had chosen for a new school, and the board made the shift. Ways were found to cut some red tape and waste in school operation. The association put great stress on getting the facts about the public schools and publicizing those facts. Constructive groups are to be encouraged. Those with an axe to grind must be either converted or repelled.

National awards for outstanding projects developed by local education associations are made each year by the Association of Classroom Teachers (ACT) during the annual convention of the National Education Association.

In 1969, twenty-one awards were made. For instance, the Pryor, Oklahoma, teachers developed a program using modern media to familiarize the community with the school program; the Ashland (Ohio) City Teachers Association promoted public support of increased funding for

[25] For ways of developing and using citizen advisory committees, see Herbert M. Hamlin, *Citizen Participation in Local Policy Making for Education* (Urbana, Ill.: University of Illinois College of Education, rev. 1960).

better schools; the Klamath Falls, Oregon, ACT conducted a project to increase public knowledge and appreciation of its schools.[26]

It is imperative that local businessmen be included in programs. To help overcome the Youngstown crisis, one industrial firm provided the services of its advertising department to assist with the school bond campaign.

John Riefler, vice-president of the Thom McAn Shoe Co., says, "Businessmen and educators both have to get involved in the problems that are real and are of high priority. Thom McAn annually finances the national School Board Awards program, coordinated by the Association of Classroom Teachers of the National Education Association, in which local education associations may nominate their school boards for recognition. There is a high incidence of teacher and community involvement in the projects cited.

A milestone occurred in 1969 with the development and adoption by the National School Public Relations Association of a set of "Educational Public Relations Standards for Programs and Professionals." [27] This provides an authoritative guide for school programs and personnel. Organizations covered by these standards include school districts; community colleges; and national, regional, state, and local educational associations and agencies. The professional personnel standards have been developed:

> To elevate the profession of education public relations
> To provide professional development and guidance to the educational public relations professional
> To provide assistance to administrators of educational organizations seeking to recruit competent public relations professionals
> To provide assistance to institutions of higher learning in establishing and improving curricula for the training of educational public relations professionals.

COMMUNICATIONS

The objectives of educational publicity have been listed by Benjamin Fine as follows: [28] (1) to build good will for the schools; (2) to gain public support for sufficient funds; (3) to acquaint the public with new educational trends; (4) to add to the reputation of the schools through

---

[26] For a description of the projects, see: *Local Color, 1969* (Washington, D.C.: Association of Classroom Teachers, NEA).

[27] This helpful handbook is available from the National School Public Relations Association, 1201 16th Street, N.W., Washington, D.C. 20036.

[28] In his book, *Educational Publicity* (New York: Harper & Row, Publishers, rev. ed., 1951). Book deals only with publicity aspects of education public relations.

full reporting of accomplishments; and (5) to build sound working relationships with the press.

Yet press coverage of schools still emphasizes athletics and student activities—by a wide margin. Several years ago the school news content of a representative sample of Michigan newspapers (daily and weekly) was measured and analyzed for one year. Authors of the study concluded that school news is one of the least well-written portions of the newspaper and that the absence of "significant news" is a more acute problem. In the opinion of the director of the study, these figures "speak eloquently on the failure of some vital school problems to receive sufficient treatment in the Michigan press." [29]

In another study, two researchers studied nineteen well-known newspapers for one month and clipped all education news except sports. Each of these newspapers had a full-time education writer and the researchers concluded that the quality of stories was good but, by and large, the news was not substantive. They found that these newspapers concentrated on "student extra-curricular activities, teacher appointments and activities, school finance and buildings, scholarships and honors, awards, the school bus, P.T.A. notes, and a variety of news about colleges." [30] They noted that little was said about educational speeches, what teachers think, their preparation for teaching, and their stands an educational issues. In these authors' view, only about five percent of the clippings exhibited imaginative, informed reporting. A journalism educator, commenting on the Dapper-Carter study, asserts: [31] "If you depend on your local newspaper for information on education, chances are that you have virtually no information or perspective on the major national issues in education and only the most fragmentary view of the local school picture."

"It is appalling that the story of education is being told so poorly, when it is told at all," says G. K. Hodenfield, former Associated Press education editor, now at Indiana University and executive director of the 500-plus member Education Writers Association. He feels that the schools and the press may both be to blame. "Too many superintendents believe their job is to cover up news, not disclose it. They would rather be misunderstood than to create any waves," he said. On the other hand, he observes that "for every *New York Times* with four top-notch education reporters there is an entire state with only one or two." [32]

[29] See William H. Roe, ed., *Schools Are News*, Michigan Communications Study (East Lansing: Michigan State University, 1957).

[30] Gloria Dapper and Barbara Carter, "Is Education News?", *Saturday Review*, Vol. 45, March 17, 1962, pp. 103–106.

[31] George Gerbner, "Teachers and Schools in the Mass Media," *Phi Delta Kappan*, Vol. 44, February, 1963.

[32] G. K. Hodenfield, "The Superintendent and the Press," *The School Administrator*, October, 1968.

George Gerbner made a study of education news for the U. S. Office of Education and concluded: [33] "The celebrated 'Boom on the School Beat' appears to have been limited to metropolitan dailies and to have been more a sign of recognition than a rise in the proportion of all special editorial employees holding school news assignments on American daily papers. . . . Mobility on the job is still generally high. The 'hard news, local angle' policy sets the style of reporting on most papers. The local orientation of the American daily paper assures a fair amount of community school news. . . ."

Another researcher, Steven H. Chaffee, found that the newspaper is providing the public with more school information than any other source but suggests it could do more. He also suggests that the news media provide an impersonal mode of contact with schools that may help transcend social barriers. He adds that the news media fail most in providing a feedback from the public to the schools, suggesting: "the press might well consider giving more attention to this feedback function." [34]

The press is slowly revising its news values to include more news of positive educational developments. The trend was started some years ago by the news magazines. It needs to be speeded. The local newspaper is the primary means of informing the public what the schools are trying to do and what they contend with in doing it. This requires continuous reporting. If this job is to be done, the schools must take the initiative. This requires a planned informational program directed by a trained practitioner.

Martin Buskin, a New York education editor and a president of the Education Writers Association, compares education writing to science writing. He says, "the press cannot just react; they have to get behind events and find out why these things are happening. . . . The education writer has to know what is really new and significant." [35] The public relations officer can be of great service to this end.

Increased coverage of the hard news of education is being encouraged by reader demand and by the National School Bell Awards program, which provides recognition for distinguished service in the interpretating of education to the public. The program is coordinated by the National Education Association with other educational and media bodies and provides for awards at the national, state, and local levels. Many state education associations are establishing state School Bell Awards programs.

33 George Gerbner, "Newsmen and Schoolmen: the State and Problems of Education Reporting," *Journalism Quarterly*, Vol. 44, Summer, 1967.

34 "The Public View of the Media as Carriers of Information Between School and Community," *Journalism Quarterly*, Vol. 44, Winter, 1967.

35 In interview, *CBE Bulletin*, Vol. 13, April, 1969, Council for Basic Education, Washington, D.C.

News—disseminated through the school paper, community papers, over radio and TV, through personal contact, and in public meetings— forms the hard core of the informational program. In Bedford, Michigan, the teachers bridged a credibility gap between the school system and the community by converting their own association membership newsletter into an open letter to the township citizens. The media coverage of education must be strengthened and supplemented. One method is to get a readable annual report into the hands of parents and community leaders. The Kalamazoo, Michigan, schools have found it effective to publish an annual report as a supplement to the local daily paper. Reasons given were (1) reasonable cost; (2) broad distribution; (3) low cost of extra copies; (4) newspaper personnel assistance in preparation, layout, and so forth; (5) ease of publication during American Education Week increases focus on this annual event. Other cities have copied this plan with good results.

Many schools use American Education Week to stage open houses and to gain the community's attention. Education-Business Days represent another effective adaptation of a tool by educators. Filmstrips and motion pictures, which need not be expensive, are another effective tool. One administrator, an amateur photographer, took a series of pictures of the school day, starting with the bus pickup and showing every school activity. The slides were grouped according to grade levels and extracurricular activities. No planned script was used for narration, and this informality and lack of education jargon strengthened the presentation. Such slides can be used at P.T.A. meetings.

Motion pictures on a variety of subjects of interest to parents—or, for that matter, any citizen concerned about his schools—are readily available. State education associations, state departments of education, and many colleges and universities maintain film libraries, well-stocked with reels on all aspects of education. Many of these come from the National Education Association, which produces films specifically for the general public, to help citizens understand the goals and problems of education.

An imaginative way of reaching the public by using its channels of communication was a daily radio program initiated by Lindley J. Stiles, when he was dean of the University of Wisconsin School of Education. For several years Professor Stiles had a daily fifteen-minute program in which he mixed relaxed comments about education with music. The program was first carried on a radio station appealing primarily to devotees of rock 'n roll, jazz, and folk music. Asked about this program, subsequently carried on a large number of stations, Stiles said: "Being identified with rock doesn't bother me. We're trying to entice people to think about educational problems, and I think it is important to reach high school and college-age people." His fan mail told him he was on the right track. For nearly a decade the National Education Association, in cooperation with the state associations, has produced a series of weekly, three-minute radio tapes highlighting current education topics through recorded comments of persons making or interpreting news of education. More than 700 stations carry these highlights. The Fairfax County, Virginia, public schools has for several years produced a Radio Report Card, cooperatively financed by the system's public relations department and the cooperating radio stations.

The informational task cannot be assigned to any specific medium. The prime importance of personal contact between school personnel and public must be kept foremost. A survey of California educators showed that they regard personal contact as "the most important channel in keeping the general public informed about the schools." Those interviewed rated the daily newspaper and reports carried home by children next in importance.[36] Further, it is essential that the relationship between the publicity objective and the base objective of wholesome two-way relationships of school and community be kept clearly in mind. The program should be developed so that there is direct contact with every home in the community.

The two-way communications task between school and patron is sufficiently important and demanding to deserve the full-time efforts of a trained practitioner. But many school districts insist they cannot afford this. Effective programs can be developed by part-time specialists if they get the cooperation of administrators and teachers. One such program is that directed by Mrs. Mary Ericsson of Pittsburg, California. An able teacher, she was given two days a week. "How could she, in two days a week, handle all the public relations and publicity requirements of nine schools?" she asked herself. Her imaginative solution was to make her fellow teachers partners in her project. With only one group meeting of a ten-member faculty public relations committee, this is what Mrs. Ericsson and her co-workers accomplished in one school year:

1. Radio series of six weekly broadcasts with teachers as speakers.
2. Teachers appeared before local civic and service organizations to tell the school's story under the auspices of a Teachers Speakers Bureau.
3. Development of a visual school story, using teacher-taken slides and motion pictures.
4. Arranging classroom work in a traveling display case for exhibition in downtown banks and department store windows.
5. A series of articles written for local newspapers by teachers under their own by-lines.
6. A teachers' talent show to raise funds for a music camp.

[36] Roy E. Carter, Jr., op. cit.

The informational task must be indigenous to and modified by each school's environment needs, problems, and personnel available to do the job. *It takes public relations-mindedness and planning more than it takes money.*

EVALUATION

Jerome C. Kovalcik, New York City assistant superintendent and former NSPRA president, gives the following checkpoints for evaluating a school public relations program:

> Is the program child-focused? Is the child the primary client?
> Is reporting accurate and truthful?
> Is the program based upon what goes on in the schools—and not on window dressing?
> Are weaknesses as well as strengths reported?
> Is it a multi-media program?
> Is it sensitive to various publics?
> Is there in-service public relations training for *all* staff members?

CASE PROBLEM

You are director of public relations for University City's school system. You have a secretary and a small budget.

The city's voters will be asked to approve a bond issue of $4,420,000 at a city election two months hence. This will provide two additional grade schools and an addition to one junior high school. It is estimated that University City will have to provide for an *additional* 1,000 pupils each year for the next five years. The city has doubled in population and tripled in area since 1950. This bond issue will cost the taxpayer eighty-nine cents per $1,000 assessed valuation. The alternatives to providing additional schools are half-day sessions or oversized classes and more bus transportation. University City voters approved a similar bond issue four years ago by a vote of three to one.

Plan an informational campaign to win voters' interest and support for this bond issue. The P.T.A. Council has promised to provide needed manpower. The superintendent and principals will provide organizational leadership.

ADDITIONAL READING

ROBERT BENDINER, *The Politics of Schools: A Crisis in Self-Government.* New York: Harper & Row, 1970.

GEORGE GERBNER, "The Press and the Dialogue in Education," *Journalism Monographs,* No. 5 (1967). Austin, Tex.: Association for Education in Journalism.

GRACE GRAHAM, *The Public School in the American Community.* New York: Harper & Row, Publishers, 1963. The school in its societal setting.

JAMES HYMES, *Effective Home-School Relations.* Englewood Cliffs, N.J.: Prentice-Hall, Inc., 1958.

M. KENT JENNINGS, "Parental Grievances and School Politics," *Public Opinion Quarterly,* Vol. 32, Fall, 1968.

JAMES R. JONES, *School Public Relations,* New York: Center for Applied Research in Education, Inc., 1966.

JAMES J. JONES and IRVING W. STOUT, *School Public Relations: Issues and Cases.* New York: G. P. Putnam's Sons, 1960.

LESLIE W. KINDRED, *How to Tell the School Story.* Englewood Cliffs, N.J.: Prentice-Hall, Inc., 1960.

CARROLL G. LANCE, *Educators Meet the Press: A Communication Gap at the State Capital.* (Madison, Wis.: U. S. Office of Education, Project Public Information, 1968.) A survey of capitol newsmen in 35 states.

MARC LIBARLE and TOM SELIGSON, eds., *The High School Revolutionaries.* New York: Random House, 1970.

GORDON McCLOSKEY, *Education and Public Understanding.* New York: Harper & Row, Publishers, 2nd ed., 1967.

MERLE R. SUMPTION and YVONNE ENGSTROM, *School-Community Relations: A New Approach.* New York: McGraw-Hill, 1966.

CHAPTER 25

THE PRACTICE: HIGHER EDUCATION

> The need for public understanding of the colleges has never been more urgent than it is today. For as the nation grasps the complex problems of colleges, so will the legislators who vote funds and the private donors react.
>
> —L. L. L. GOLDEN

The nation's colleges, caught in recurring crises of confrontation, protest, distorted electronic images, and swift change, face public relations tasks unparalleled in the history of higher education. The student revolt, which began at the University of California in mid-1960, has swept around the world, bringing profound changes as well as painful crises to universities in all lands. Essentiality of the function in higher education is no longer debated.

Institutions of higher learning were among the first to set about winning public favor on a systematic basis. The emergence of the strong public university, dependent upon taxpayer support, in the latter part of the Nineteenth Century brought with it increased concern for popular support. The University of Michigan led the way when it established a publicity office in 1897. Increased competition for funds and students forced the private institutions to counter with like programs.

Public relations's Seedbed Years brought innovative publicity programs to many colleges and universities, among them Harvard, Yale, Columbia and Pennsylvania in the Ivy League; Chicago, Michigan, and Wisconsin in the Big Ten. As classical education gave way to curricula responsive to the needs of the Twentieth Century, as the demand for extension grew, and as the need for money increased sharply, the college administrator turned, sooner or later, to the use of publicity, and, ultimately, to public relations.[1] Today's millions of college students—armed with more knowledge and more power than their predecessors—along with the research explosion are markedly changing the course of higher education.

Colleges often become the target of youthful discontent, sometimes in terms of legitimate complaints about the deficiencies of the institution, sometimes as a convenient tactic for assault upon the general society. Dealing with these interlocking crises has become a major public issue and the cause of angry and bewildering debate. The undergraduate, for his part, increasingly demands that education meet his personal requirements

---

[1] See chapter, "The 1920's . . . Cash for Colleges and Cathedrals," in Cutlip's *Fund Raising in the United States* (New Brunswick, N.J., 1965).

and society's. He cares little for long-established curricular rigidity. Much of the student revolt also is born of a deep-felt desire to have a greater part in decisions affecting their own lives.

The patriarchial college president is gone. Today's president must lead not direct, faculties, students, and governing boards. Today's president or chancellor is caught in the crunch of conflicting values and demands from his constituent-claimant publics. To thread his way through these conflicts, he must be an effective communicator and mediator. The role is a difficult one. Former California President Clark Kerr has ruefully observed: "This mediator is always subject to some abuse. He wins few clear-cut victories; he must aim at avoiding the worst rather than seizing the best. He must find satisfaction in being equally distasteful to each of his constituencies; he must reconcile himself to the harsh reality that successes are shrouded in silence while failures are spotlighted in notoriety." College presidencies are not the nation's most desirable jobs.

The two-way communications task confronting colleges and universities is difficult and demanding, one that does not permit glibness. A sociologist suggests the complexity of the task: [2]

> With (its) sizes, (its) purposes, and (its) duties, the university campus becomes an extremely complicated social arrangement of the relations of men at work. The formal structure is bound to be full of overlap, gap, and contradiction. It becomes somewhat like a confederation of tribes that have wandered into the same campgrounds. Bureaucracy enforced from the center is, at the level of the professoriate, not fully in control, since the centrifugal forces of profession and discipline are strong. . . . The campus is a setting for a hundred, several hundred, distinctive clusters of experts. With this as its primary nature, it is fractured rather than integrated. . . .

The colleges face communication breakdowns with external publics of equal magnitude—with communities crowded by campus growth and traffic congested by student cars, with legislators angered by student protest and student mores, with alumni whose sons and daughters cannot be admitted, with taxpayers growing weary of the mounting bill for higher education. This breakdown in communications has had and will continue to have serious consequences. Allen H. Barton asserts: [3] "The effect of alienating a generation of students and a large section of intellectuals from normal political channels can be very serious, both for universities and for nations,

---

[2] Burton R. Clark, "The New University," *American Behavioral Scientist*, Vol. 11, May–June, 1968, p. 2.

[3] "The Columbia Crisis: Campus, Vietnam, and the Ghetto," *Public Opinion Quarterly*, Vol. 32, Fall, 1968.

as demonstrated in other countries as well as in the United States." These problems, on the positive side, have done much to reinvigorate and freshen educational thinking, to bring education to the disadvantaged, and to make colleges and universities more relevant to society's needs.

New, more effective channels are needed to provide an inflow of information from students, faculty, townspeople, taxpayers, and other constituent-claimant publics. A trustee, John C. Corson, suggests "What an institution needs to cope with this new condition is an organizational capacity to listen." Also new and more imaginative ways of facilitating communication between community and college must be found. One example is the Dialogue Center set up at San Fernando Valley State College to provide a place where students, faculty, and residents of Northridge can get together for informal and frank discussion. Formal programs also are held in this center.

Morris B. Abram, formerly president of Brandeis University, observed that university administrators have been compelled to move from talking about the need for communications to actually communicating with their publics. He said: [4] "Communication alone will not provide the solution to our problems. . . . I think that on our campuses today there is so much distrust and suspicion that most (communication) is rendered sterile." Speaking from a campus wracked by conflict, Steven Muller, vice-president of Cornell University, observes that one effect of the recurring crises on campuses has been to place "universities and colleges under the lens of public scrutiny with an intensity that is relatively rare in their long history." The new problems impose a heavy burden on the function.

The development of the professional association in this field is significant. Organized in 1917 as the American Association of College News Bureaus, in 1930 it became the American College Publicity Association. In May, 1946, it evolved into the American College Public Relations Association. It is on public relations and fund raising, rather than on publicity, that its emphasis is placed today. At the end of the 1960s, this association had a membership of 1,244 institutions and some 3,650 men and women, professionals responsible for their institutions' public relations, financial support, and development programs. The institutional membership was nearly three times the 451 in 1939–40. These figures graphically reflect the growth in this field. The association is a strong force in the development of public relations for higher education. Its central office provides many services: *College & University Journal,* a quarterly with in-depth articles; *Techniques,* a bi-monthly, how-to magazine; a *Newsletter;* a wide variety of workshops, institutes, and conferences; sponsorship of research; maintenance of a lending library of case studies; and a placement service for its

---

[4] In address, "The Restless Campus," *College & University Journal,* Vol. 8, Fall, 1969.

members. An increasing percentage of its members are college fund raisers or development officers. There is a resultant shift in emphasis.[5]

More and more, the selection of college presidents is taking into account the candidates' abilities in public relations. More institutions are moving the function to the policy-making level. More institutions are converting old-line publicity bureaus into effective public relations agencies. More college presidents are thinking and talking public relations with their trustees, with their faculties, with their alumni, and with their students. These are fairly widespread trends. This definition of campus governance emerged from the American Association of State Colleges and Universities Summer Council of Presidents in 1969: "Governance involves communication among the various groups on the campus concerned with the over-all education process. . . . Those institutions that seem to have had more success in dealing with the problems of institutional governance were able to maintain open lines of communication."

The dimensions of the task in higher education have been outlined this way by one of its veteran practitioners, Michael Radock of the University of Michigan: [6]

> Today's educational administrator must deal with all echelons of government, with trade unions and professional associations, with virtually every kind of staff member, with a conglomerate of autonomous units, with private donors, with alumni, with parents, with vendors, with a governing board which may be publicly elected or politically appointed, with recruiters of the students and competitors for his staff. *And* he's working with society's most highly volatile and precious resource—talented youth.

There is still too much emphasis on publicity in college practice. And much of the publicity smacks of press-agentry. Higher education still has a few press agents who put the spotlight on the college sideshows of beauty queens, athletics, and contrived gags. A picture of a pretty coed throwing books and legs in the air to celebrate the end of exams does little to tell what higher education is all about. Many institutions still have their "public relations offices" in some remote temporary set-up instead of in the administrative suite.

Many collegiate practitioners, prodded by books, professional journals, and their association discussions, are spending themselves on the barricades of faculty and administrative resistance. Scope and skill of performance, not the place on the organization chart, will decide the ultimate role.

---

[5] The story of the Association's first thirty-five years is told in M. Charles Seller's *The American College Public Relations Association: A Study of Its Development from 1915 to 1950.* A master's thesis written at Pennsylvania State and distributed by Marts & Lundy.

[6] "Behind the Ivy Curtain," *Public Relations Journal,* Vol. 24, October, 1968.

The professors' cooperation is essential. Yet, many faculty members remain aloof, others merely indifferent, and a few plainly hostile. For many younger faculty members, public relations is a weapon of "The Establishment." To some faculty members, the function smacks of *propaganda* or *press-agentry*. The coldness of a few stems from their distaste or hostility for the news media, not an uncommon attitude among intellectuals. Sometimes it is the result of overzealousness on the part of the practitioner. As one university director admits: "Publicity people occasionally overextend themselves, even against the conservative background of a university. Inadvertently, a few unsteady practitioners assault the basic rights of the professor without the professor's knowing it." An example of such an assault is the occasional misguided effort to "centralize" or "coordinate" all faculty expressions through the central information office. This is especially irritating in a day of vocal faculty dissent.

The best way to win the faculty's cooperation is through patient internal education and through the provision of help when the professor needs it.

Emanuel Goldberg suggests ways in which the public relations department can serve the professor: [7] "It can serve as a buffer between a potentially articulate and socially useful scholar and the raw press; that is, it can at least prepare a release in a manner satisfactory to the professor's wishes, even though there is never a guarantee that newspapers or broadcasting media will cast it in the same form, or even use it. Whenever a faculty member takes the trouble to document and deliver a speech . . . the news bureau can reach a larger and more general public. Books, articles, travel, papers, institutes, research, pet projects, civic and governmental service—all these are grist. They can be turned nicely to the professor's, the University's, and the community's advantage." The practitioner must strive, ceaselessly, to clear away faculty and administrator misconceptions.

One of the strongest misconceptions is the idea that to have a strong program is to pander to public opinion and thus undercut a university's true purpose. Robert Hutchins reflected on this:

> The most dangerous aspect of public relations work is its reflex action: we find that the public does not like something about the University; our temptation is to change this so that the public will like us. Our duty is to change public opinion so that the public will like what the University does, and, if this cannot be immediately accomplished, to hold out against the public until it can be. Public relations work in a university is a phase of its efforts in adult education.

[7] "The Professor and the Press," *College & University Journal*, Vol. 2, Summer, 1963, pp. 57 and 59.

Over-all, the public relations function is widely accepted on the college campus and is daily demonstrating its worth. President David D. Henry of the University of Illinois correctly observes: [8] "The importance of an informed public opinion about the individual institution and higher education in general is now quite widely accepted among educators. The hostility toward the lay adviser has disappeared; the resentment of the journalistic interpretation of science is nearly gone; the isolation of the academic community is no longer celebrated as a major virtue."

FREEDOM, FUNDS, AND FRESHMEN

Higher education faces three continuing problems. Its academic freedom is frequently in question, if not in danger, from within and from without. Its financial support is precarious and insufficient. The competition for qualified students is spirited; their selection difficult.

Clark Kerr, one of the early victims of the student revolt, has listed ten problems facing higher education, which illustrate: [9]

1. The problem of public control and influence over public institutions which are threatened by a loss of autonomy to legislators, governors, and federal agencies
2. The problem resulting from neglect of undergraduates the past two decades
3. The problem resulting from excessive pressure now put upon students
4. Excessive specialization in curriculum and in research
5. The geographic imbalance in higher education
6. Financing higher education in a time of high taxes, competing social needs
7. Adjusting to and accommodating the New Left
8. The increasing gulf between the intellectual and society
9. Equal access to education throughout the United States
10. The problems posed by the new technology which can bring changes as far-reaching as those brought by the printed book.

The need is clear. The task is formidable; the progress, slow. In an exhaustive survey of attitudes, the *Fortune Survey* found unbounded faith

---

[8] In *What Priority for Education?* (Champaign-Urbana, Ill.: University of Illinois Press, 1961), pp. 76–77.

[9] In address at meeting of Educational Writers Association, February 9, 1967. Reprinted in *Swarthmore Alumni Magazine*, March, 1967. Also see: *Daedalus*, Winter, 1970, special 200-page issue with articles by Kerr, Morris Abram, Edgar Friedenberg, and others.

in collegiate institutions but little real understanding of their function. *Fortune's* pollsters found great interest in, but little information on, education. They found great faith in education's ability to enable a person to earn more money but little concern for its objective of enabling a person to live a fruitful, enjoyable life. The *Fortune Survey* concluded that "the subject of higher education is very little understood by the American people generally." More recent public opinion polls only serve to emphasize the same lack of an adequate understanding of education.

NEED FOR FREEDOM

Free inquiry as the fundamental of scholarship has long been recognized, generally observed. The teacher must have freedom to teach, not merely for his own sake or for the sake of his students, but for the future of America and what America can mean to mankind. Yet, the freedom of the student to learn and of the teacher to teach comes under frequent attack. It is sometimes abridged, frontally or indirectly. Protecting and defending intellectual freedom is a continuing task.

The defense becomes doubly difficult in periods of internal tensions fed by threats of external aggressions, when fear and hysteria break loose. In an emotionally tense social climate, all ideas that diverge from the *status quo* become "dangerous" and open to suspicion—and pressure. In the years following World War II, there were numerous legislative committee investigations, requirements of loyalty oaths for teachers, and similar incursions on academic freedom. Periodically the political extremes, the Far Right and the Far Left, assault academic freedom.

These limitations on free inquiry take a variety of forms. "Their net effect," as the *New York Times* points out, "is a widening tendency toward passive acceptance of the status quo, conformity, and a narrowing area of tolerance in which students, faculty, and administrators feel free to speak, act, and think independently." The consequences pose a grave threat to education. Such attacks must be repulsed. A former president of the University of Kentucky once said that the most important activity a president has to perform is to keep the university free.

This has become increasingly difficult with the eruption of conflict on campuses across the land and the resulting backlash of legislators, trustees, and the public. Maintenance of a rule of law on the campus is essential not only to preserve the rights of all but to fend off external threats. President Robben Fleming of the University of Michigan put it plainly: "If the university community, including both faculty and students, is unwilling to face the responsibility which internal discipline requires, it is clear that the public will insist that order be imposed from the outside." Angry public demand resulted in much restrictive legislation enacted in the late 1960s and early 1970s, stiffened Federal requirements on loans and grants, and in Congressional tax restrictions on philanthropic foundations. One practitioner has observed that "Threats by alumni and donors are rampant."

The college or university that is fearlessly seeking the truth out of the conflict of ideas cannot escape pressure. It must have the backing of an informed public that cherishes free inquiry to reckon with such pressures. Education cannot, like the ostrich, safely hide its head in the sands of the past. Such a position is both undignified and vulnerable. It is the public relations function to persuade the people that, as Bernard de Voto said, "On this campus all books, all expressions, all opinions are free." An institution of learning cannot dispense with controversial ideas and live. Research and teaching cannot be totally bland.

The task is to demonstrate the vital necessity of freedom for the student to learn and for the scholar to search for the truth without restriction. Too often, college men tend to make academic freedom appear as a special license for the professor. The emphasis needs to be placed more on the by-products of the denial of academic freedom. Citizens need to be reminded forcefully that, as academic freedom has disappeared in other countries, so also has the freedom of all citizens. Freedom is indivisible.

College practitioners man the front lines in the defense of academic freedom. Defending a loyal American professor's refusal to sign a non-Communist oath or staging a "teach-in" as a matter of principle is no easy task. The state can abolish the freedom of learning only if the people are uninformed and inert. Loyalty oath controversies and protest backlash, painful though they are, do provide an opportunity to dramatize these fundamentals.

For many institutions, political pressures beat most violently around the problem of providing education for the disadvantaged. One practitioner, John A. Griffin of the Southern Education Foundation, points out: [10]

> Whether or not we have so far admitted it, colleges and universities have responsibilities in race relations, both on the campus and in the communities. . . . Thus for urban institutions and for many nonurban colleges and universities, North and South, race relations is increasingly a fact of life. This means that the colleges and universities, like the armed services, need staff persons who are specialists in race relations. . . . The problems that need attention range all the way from accreditation to football. . . . Public relations and development people need to give thoughtful attention to their responsibilities of sensitizing their institutions in regard to their responsibilities and their opportunities in race relations.

[10] In speech, "Higher Education and Race Relations," American College Public Relations Association convention, June 25, 1963.

NEED FOR FUNDS

It is almost trite to talk about "the financial crisis" facing collegiate institutions. This has been a pat phrase since Harvard held its first fund-raising lottery in the 1700s. Yet the years ahead pose problems of truly critical proportions. The facts are simple; their impact staggering. Today's full-time college enrollment of some seven-million students is expected to reach some eleven or twelve-million by 1980 and then to stabilize near that figure. John Leslie summarizes the problem for the 1970s: [11]

> A dollar pinch is developing for higher education. The 1970s will bring larger student bodies . . . , greater demand for services and research, and continued rapidly rising costs. Competition for the education dollar will become acute. Budgets will be squeezed and all aspects of higher education will have to become more effective and efficient. The challenge to programs and personnel devoted to the furtherance of understanding and financial support will be equally as great. Interpretation of the educational program will be increasingly difficult as institutions grow more complex and the public more sophisticated. Added demands are being placed on the tax dollar, and education will find other agencies competing strongly for funds in the state house and on Capitol Hill. . . . Just to stay even, the management of educational fund raising and public relations programs will have to be improved greatly.

This new crisis is compounded of three trends converging on the campus: (1) the exploding increase in enrollments and in scientific research; (2) the mounting burden of educational costs; (3) the drying up of traditional sources of support. The United States Office of Education estimates that colleges and universities will have to spend close to one-billion dollars per year in *new money* over the next decade. Where will this money come from? There are only three major sources: (1) tuition fees, (2) the federal government, and (3) gifts and bequests.

Privately endowed and sectarian colleges are especially hard hit. Gifts and incomes from endowments fail to keep pace with the inflationary costs of frogs, footballs, and faculty members. America needs the strong, independent college, free of political control and influence. These colleges have already raised their tuitions to the limit—if not beyond. Some have been forced to shift investments from securities to common stocks. Others have dipped into reserves to keep going. The Carnegie Commission on Higher

---

[11] In *Focus on Understanding and Support* (Washington, D.C.: ACPRA, 1969), p. 2. A survey of the status of advancement programs in higher education. Leslie is executive vice president of ACPRA.

Education found, at the end of the last decade, that costs were rising faster than income for the private universities. The cost per student was then rising at a rate of about seven and one half percent each year. Private institutions are leaning more and more on gifts from corporations and annual alumni fund drives.

A new development in the fund raising of private colleges is the united college fund. The idea, first tried out in the 1920s, emerged anew in 1944 as the United Negro College Fund. The idea was given new dimension in the 1950s by Frank H. Sparks, then president of Wabash College. With some difficulty, he persuaded other private colleges in Indiana and a few corporations of the worth of the idea of a united fund for private colleges. The idea caught on. Nearby Ohio was quick to follow suit. Although Indiana gets credit for the idea, Ohio was the first state to start a united fund appeal on an incorporated, organized basis. The Ohio Foundation, started in 1951, had, by 1961, twenty-nine colleges participating. Cooperation through consortiums is another approach to this financial problem. Corporations giving to colleges promote the idea because it eliminates the sticky problem of deciding which colleges to support and which ones to turn down in a particular region. Within a decade, Spark's idea had grown to multi-million-dollar dimensions. In 1970 there were forty such funds operating on a regional or state basis. The dimensions of philanthropy in financing higher education is seen in the report of the *Chronicle of Higher Education,* January 13, 1969, that at least 114 colleges and universities were conducting or had recently completed fund-raising programs which raised more than $2.3-billion. The John Price Jones annual report, *American Philanthropy in Higher Education,* for fiscal 1968–69 showed only a 7.7 percent increase in giving over the previous year. Private giving may be slowed by the provisions of the 1969 Tax Reform Act which took away some tax incentives for charitable giving.

State-supporting colleges are finding the going tougher all the time as their costs go up. They are faced with strong competition for the taxpayers' dollars. More and more state tax monies are going into pensions and benefits for the aged and handicapped, for improving institutional care and mental health programs, to public schools, highways, and hard-pressed cities and counties. Consequently, state universities are putting more emphasis on voluntary support and are intensively promoting alumni giving. Private support is increasing markedly for all state universities.

In a time of increased demands on governmental resources, private support is seen as more critical than ever by leaders of public institutions. Howard R. Bowen, former Iowa University president, observed: "Legislators do not look with favor on the extras that will make the difference between adequacy and excellence. The public institutions, which wish to strive for exceptional performances are therefore forced to look to private

sources for the funds needed to lift them above the commonplace . . . ."
Similarly, private institutions campaign hard for increased help from public
funds. In fact, the line between private and public colleges and universities
has become quite blurred. Both rely, increasingly, on the federal government. In 1966–67, for example, the federal government provided $3.3-
billion in support of higher education. Public and private institutions divided this sum nearly equally: public universities got $1.7-billion, or 52.2
percent, of distributed public monies; private institutions got $1.6-billion,
or 47.8 percent. Federal funds have become the second most important
source of private university revenue. Thus, the competition for the donor's
dollar and for the tax dollar has intensified in both sectors of the higher
education establishment. The following table reflects this changed situation: [12]

WHERE THE HIGHER EDUCATION DOLLAR COMES FROM

PUBLIC INSTITUTIONS		PRIVATE INSTITUTIONS	
State and Local Government		Tuition and Student Fees	44.1%
(Taxes)	43.3%	Federal Government (Taxes)	25.9
Tuition, Student Fees	20.1	Private Gifts	14.1
Federal Government (Taxes)	19.7	Other Sources (Auxiliary	
Other Sources (Auxiliary		enterprises)	13.9
enterprises)	15.2	State and Local Government	
Private Gifts	1.7	(Taxes)	2.0

The solution cannot be found in higher tuition fees. These fees nearly
tripled in the 1960s. In 1970, for example, Yale University's undergraduate
tuition and fees totaled $3,900. A study made by the National Association
of Land Grant Colleges and Universities showed that the average tuition
in these colleges for resident students increased about 39 percent from
1963–64 to 1969–70, and for non-residents tuition went up about 38 percent in the same period. Fred H. Harrington, former president of the
University of Wisconsin, thinks public education is "threatened by national
and state proposals that the student be required to pay the full costs of
instruction." This proposal, he adds "would mark the end of public higher
education as we have known it." Despite the increase in scholarships and
loan funds, today's high tuition charges are pricing many qualified young
persons out of a college education. A survey by the U. S. Office of Education a few years ago confirmed that "the nation's loss of talented, potential
college students is due primarily to lack of money."

[12] . . . *for your information,* Circular Number 42, September 8, 1969, issued by Office of
Institutional Research, National Association of State Universities and Land Grant Colleges.

Dr. Alvin C. Eurich, of the Fund for the Advancement of Education, warns that the competition for the federal and local tax dollar is such that we cannot expect anything like a sufficient flow of tax money to diminish the pressure on institutions to build more financial support. Developing mass public support for mass giving on a regular basis seems to be one of the hopeful trends in this situation. It certainly spells more emphasis on public relations.

WHAT FRESHMEN?

In years past, much of the college effort was on recruiting students. Often these campaigns to get students used the techniques of advertising more than those of information and interpretation. The emphasis in the past has been too much on getting students and too little on the social responsibility involved. The intense promotional publicity to get new students is responsible, in part at least, for the questionable notion that to "get ahead in the world" one must go to college.

In student recruitment we have a paradox. On one hand, colleges are worried about their overcrowded classrooms. On the other, they are trying to persuade still more students to enter. But there is an explanation. College officials know that something like 250,000 gifted high school graduates do not go on to college each year. Half are prevented from doing so by lack of money. Educators want to encourage and finance the brilliant and talented students because they know that this nation requires more *educated manpower* than is available to meet America's post-industrial-society needs.

In the decade ahead, the student problem will not be one of recruiting numbers but in the far more thorny task of deciding who should go to college and of financing the talented poor. The recruitment problem is complicated by vocal demands that admission to a college or university is a right, not a privilege. Increasing demands for waiver of requirements for the disadvantaged pose another problem. Solution of today's "freshmen" problem will take statesmanship, not salesmanship.

THE PUBLICS

The pitch and emphasis to the different publics of a collegiate institution will vary according to the size, base of support, and philosophy of the institution.

STUDENTS

Foremost of the public relations agents are the students, first as students, later as alumni. Student attitudes and conduct are powerful factors in determining public attitudes. Students come from the farms and the mining camps, from the metropolitan city and the village, from all parts of the nation. These students become "authoritative" interpreters of their college in their hometowns. If they have pride in them and enthusiasm, it will be mirrored. If they have an unhappy educational experience, that, too, will be reflected—and for years to come.

The student's role in shaping public attitudes was amply demonstrated in the late 1960s and early 1970s when student protests brought public anger and legislative retribution. For example the slaying of four students at Kent State University and two at Jackson State College in the wake of this nation's invasion of Cambodia caused strikes and protests to erupt on some 760 campuses—about 30 percent of all colleges and universities. The anger such protests bring is plainly shown by the fact that 32 of the 50 states had enacted laws by mid-1970 to prevent campus disorders. In the course of these protests, students brought down college presidents, erased outmoded student regulations, gained effective voices on faculty committees and, on the governing board. The confrontation politics of this era emphasized dress, language, and mannerisms designed to offend and antagonize. As one veteran practitioner observes: "Bizarre tactics, dress and language employed skillfully by a few naturally get the publicity, especially through television—the perfect device for confrontation politics." Unfortunately for institutions of higher education—and for society—too many citizens accept this bizarre behavior as typical. Students who go about their business of learning, working part-time, and having fun are not as newsworthy as pot parties, "arrangements," and firebombings.

The public is heavily influenced by the news media, which spotlight the protest and neglect the quiet academic achievement. A task force of twenty-two young Republican congressmen who visited fifty campuses to probe causes of student unrest found: [13]

> Most of the people we talked with stated the opinion that superficial mass media coverage was contributing to the widening disillusionment and misunderstanding between the public and the nation's campuses. The media, particularly that utilizing the visual impression, concentrate on the dramatic, the vivid acts of violence or disorder. There is altogether too little effort made to thoughtfully explore the underlying issues and problems that concern the vast majority of students and educators. . . .

[13] "GOP Congressmen on Campus," *College & University Journal*, Vol. 8, Summer, 1969.

The public record must be balanced by examples of students' public service, and by representation of the college in a constructive way winning goodwill and gifts are many.[14]

A university must develop an enthusiastic, responsible body of students as good will ambassadors. With the fast turnover of the student body, this is a difficult task. The surest way to develop the student's appreciation of his responsibility is to bring him into active participation in the program. Personable college students are the most effective public symbol a college can have. Students can be involved in the program through organizing of campus host and guide groups. High School Day, Legislator Day, or Parents' Week-end; through touring college choirs, glee clubs, or drama groups; and in many other ways. College administrators, faculty members, and student leaders must guide the student in this responsibility.

There is another important aspect. A student may be in school from one to four years, but he is an alumnus for his life. Too many institutions wait until a student is an alumnus before they start to woo him. The student who has good teachers, who is given wise counsel and helpful individual attention, generally becomes a loyal alumnus. An educational program revealing the sources of educational support could do much in developing a sense of responsibility in future alumni.

Fundamental to effective student relationships is to maintain, despite an institution's size, free-flowing channels between the administrator and the student. Too often, with bigness, these break down. A study of the National Association of State Universities and Land Grant Colleges, released in 1970, suggests greater student involvement in university policy and curriculum decisions as an effective way of dampening student protest and alienation. It listed these reforms of recent years: student committee membership, including those to select new presidents or chancellors; more effective communication with students; appointment of university ombudsman,[15] and enactment of student suggestions.

Among public universities, Kentucky led the way in giving students a vote on the governing board. Then, in 1969, the University of Connecticut and the University of Maine followed suit. The University of Washington and the University of Wyoming have added students as non-voting members. A survey of American Association of State Colleges and Universities members in 1969–70 found that "On at least half of the 120 campuses included in the survey, students will take their places without question in faculty and administrative councils which were unquestioningly closed to

[14] Janet Rich and D. C. Tork, *Student Power and How to Use It.* Notre Dame College of Staten Island, New York, 1969. Survey of student involvement in development and public relations in a cross section of colleges.

[15] For one example, Paul L. Montgomery, "Cornell's New Faces Turn to Student Unrest," *New York Times*, October 13, 1969, p. M 41.

them previously." In the words of one: "Now, from Harvard to Salem State, from Stanford to Azuza Pacific, the role of the student both as a participant in the process of education and as the object of its intent is receiving widespread attention." [16]

For the large university, a President's Council of student leaders, meeting informally in the president's home, has worked well on many campuses where presidents have been willing to listen. There is a danger in selecting such students and in their being labeled as "Uncle Toms." In many instances, a minority group gets control of the campus newspaper and shuts out other points of view, particularly the administration's. Many universities have started official newspapers aimed at getting administration views across to the student body. Columbia, for example, has a university newsletter that is available wherever the daily *Spectator* is distributed. Effectiveness of these internal communications channels depends on existence of a climate of credibility.[17]

FACULTY AND STAFF

The college or university president and the custodian—each plays an important role. People think in terms of people, the personal symbol, the concrete. The personalities of people identified in the public mind with an institution will largely determine the kind of confidence and support the institution has. The personal symbol is particularly important for a college, whose leaders and teachers are constantly in the public spotlight, free to speak out as they see fit.

College presidents and professors are a prolific source of news. Developing the staff of an institution into an effective team is the starting point for the program. The college or university president, by reason of his position and prestige, must be the leader. The president personifies the institution. A strong personality can bring prestige, stature, and public confidence. A president whose mental radar is sensitive to public relations can contribute much to developing this awareness.

The faculty member can contribute most by inspired teaching, by counseling his students, by research accomplishments, and by lending his talents to public service. Faculty members, especially those of the younger generation, are increasingly aware of their responsibilities. Members of the university's housekeeping staff, the secretaries, the telephone operators, the policemen, must be imbued with the spirit of friendly service. The important thing is that these staff members be kept adequately informed of the uni-

[16] Wallace Roberts, "Patterns of Reform" in symposium on the Academic Revolt, *Saturday Review*, October 18, 1969.

[17] "Campus Administrations Develop Their Own Newspapers to Communicate With Faculty, Students and Staff," *Chronicle of Higher Education*, February 2, 1970.

versity's policies, programs, and problems. This requires a continuing internal information program. The college staff must be gently, but *persistently,* reminded of its public relations responsibilities.

Today faculty members insist upon a voice in college policy-making. If this participation is to be meaningful, they must be kept informed by the administration so that the faculty can, in turn, take informed positions. Without a steady flow of information from those who have it to those who need it, cooperative decision making can never amount to much.

Members of the governing board constitute an important internal public that functions as the official intermediary between key publics and the college. A good board serves as a heat shield. A strategic group, generally recruited from opinion leadership, they must be convinced of the need for giving consideration to public relations aspects of policy making. Consistent but subtle pressure is required to prompt the board to give full and sympathetic consideration to public opinion. This key group must be kept adequately informed of the university's aims and problems so that they may interpret these aims correctly. Informing the board is primarily a task of the president.

COMMUNITY

Next, in planning a program, come the important external publics to be reached and influenced. "Town-grown" relationships provide the environment. These relationships have been made difficult and sometimes abrasive in recent years by institutions' needs to expand and by the police problems posed by student protest and campus drug traffic. Colleges and universities are lagging well behind industry in recognizing the importance of good community relations. There is a real need to do more to win and keep the support of local citizens. Support can be won by giving the citizens a voice and a sympathetic hearing, through consultation, on college matters directly affecting the community. There are a number of natural irritations that may develop if town-grown relations are neglected: for example, the tax-exempt status of educational institutions may appear as a sign of partiality. Municipalities are increasingly hard pressed to find adequate revenues to pay for their expanding services. Many institutions have wisely taken steps to dramatize their recognition of this problem. One state university, for example, arranged to buy a new fire truck for its community and to employ a third of the firemen.

Another problem is faced by metropolitan institutions that must expand in already built-up areas. This growth means just one thing to the taxpayer: removal of property from the tax rolls and, hence, more taxes. It means dislocation to the residents. Such moves should not be suddenly thrust upon a surprised community. The moves, of course, are ultimately of great benefit to the community. The college must properly explain them to its neighbors. Traffic congestion created by university facilities or activities has caused harsh irritations in some college towns. There are many other examples.

On the other hand, there are many positive advantages which the college can and does offer the community. Townspeople need to be reminded of these, lest they take them for granted.

Robert G. Miller, vice mayor of San Jose, California, expressed the relationship between the university and community this way:

> A broad and comprehensive goal should be to integrate the campus both physically and socially with the surrounding area and the downtown, rather than to isolate itself from the city it serves. The campus should make efforts to relate itself to the large community in terms of the special skills available from the sub-community of the scholar. In the broadest sense, this means assisting the city in its search for a better and more meaningful life.
>
> In return, the city can offer support to its college or university in a myriad of ways, and a new spurt of growth is started as industry and capital, attracted to the university centers of the nation, locate and make available their resources for further support of the university.

PARENTS

Parents of students are a ready-made nucleus of support. They have a vital stake in the institution. They can be welded into an effective group of allies. Providing a good home away from home and giving sons and daughters kindly, personalized attention win parental support. But this potential good will needs to be activated and reinforced. Parents' Week-end, frequent letters from president to parent, and Parents' clubs bring parents closer to the school. Spot newsletters are in order when trouble breaks out on campus.

ALUMNI

Maintaining the interest of the alumni has long been given emphasis —with varying degrees of success. Too often the alumni interest centers almost exclusively on the fortunes of the football team. The problem seems to be to get the alumnus as interested in education as he is in football. Practically every college has a going alumni association. Often its sole concern is keeping alive the flames of loyalty. Sometimes the alumni influence can be—and is—mobilized to override sound educational policy. Sometimes alumni associations tend to become vested interests and ends in themselves. The alumni association must be kept harnessed to its basic objective—support of Alma Mater through organized effort. Emerson Reck has pointed this out: [18]

> The alumni form the most important off-campus public of most colleges and universities, and there is no limit to the good they can do for their institutions provided (1) the experiences of their undergraduate years can be recalled with appreciation and pleasure; (2) they are kept fully informed regarding the objectives, policies, progress and problems of their Alma Maters; (3) they are given an opportunity to perform challenging tasks for their institutions.

The critical problems faced by higher education make it essential that alumni groups and universities forge a stronger bond. Informed alumni can be a strong base of support. Uninformed alumni can represent a disturbing interference in the conduct of the college. Those irresistible drives to fire the coach have led many faculties and administrators to fear alumni influence. There is a real need to do a better job of keeping alumni informed of more than merely his classmates' doings and the football statistics. Alumni magazines reach millions of persons annually. Many of these contain little intellectual meat with the traditional chroniclings.

The objective, vis-a-vis alumni, should be one of getting more than dollars. Colleges should strive to gain loyalty, interest, and counsel from their alumni. Win those, and the dollars will follow. Charles P. McCurdy, a former president of the American Alumni Council, has said: "I do not believe that we can continue to beseech our alumni or anybody else to contribute for *things*. We will have to begin asking them to contribute for *principles.*"

When a college is caught up in the vortex of a crisis or controversy, it is imperative that it get the full story to its alumni and other publics as quickly as possible. For example, when Cornell University had a crisis in 1969, it arranged to reprint the news stories in *The Ithaca Journal* and quickly mail 115,000 copies of these stories to alumni and other key publics. In this era, the alumni magazine can and must become a channel of candid communication between an institution and its alumni. The day of the bland, rah-rah magazine, carrying college puffs, sports, and class notes, is dying. Typical of the new day was Editor George Keller's account of Columbia's 1968 crisis in *Columbia College Today*. The Ohio State alumni magazine campaigned vigorously against the trustees' outside speakers rule until it was rescinded. This represents, says Charles Helmken of the American Alumni Council, "a revolution that has not been easy." Emory's Virgil Hartley says "many alumni don't welcome candor."

---

[18] In one of early books in this field, *Public Relations: A Program for Colleges and Universities.*

OTHER PUBLICS

Other publics include prospective students, parents of prospective students, present and prospective donors, opinion leaders, the various philanthropic foundations, sister educational institutions, legislators and state officials for the state-supported school, the armed forces, and various agencies of the federal government—particularly those with research programs.

Institutions of higher learning face many difficult but not insoluble problems in the foreseeable future. These problems can be fundamental, such as definite decisions concerning the true function and purpose of the college and university. They can be specific, such as developing a sound relationship between the main function of education and the extracurricular activity, athletics. The evils of proselyting, commercialism, gambling, and over-emphasis, which cloud intercollegiate athletics from time to time, represent a tough but typical problem for the practitioner.

For years ahead, institutions of higher learning must grapple with other problems. Funds must be raised to pay professors, to build buildings, and to buy expensive research equipment. Emotional attacks on teachers and doctrines by the Far Right and New Left must be beaten back. The right of faculty and student dissent must be preserved however angry elements of the public become. There will be the squeeze of doing more and more research and public service—particularly continuing education to enable society to cope with the escalating technological and social changes in America. An increasing number of applicants will be denied admission to colleges, especially private ones. The demand that colleges do more for disadvantaged young people will grow. The fierce competition for public and philanthropic funds will increase, not lessen. This adds up to a need for all the confidence and support that can be mustered through effective public relations. Never has the task confronting the college practitioner been as difficult as it is today; never has his opportunity to serve and advance society been greater.[19]

CASE PROBLEM

Monday seven black students, representing the Afro-American Action Committee, demanded an appointment with the president of the college. He

---

[19] The task is well stated in "Communication Challenge: A Survey," *College & University Journal*, Vol. 7, Summer, 1968.

was out of town, but the vice president for student affairs met with them and heard these demands: (1) that a Department of Afro-American Studies be established with black students to be given control of its program; (2) that the college provide support for a black students conference to be held next month; (3) that black athletes be assured of financial support for their college careers whether they continue to play or not; (4) that at least 500 black students be admitted next September whether they meet admission requirements or not. The students set a deadline of 1 p.m. Tuesday to have answers to these demands, described by a spokesman as "non negotiable."

The president met with the group at 1 p.m. Tuesday. He made clear that actions were under way in the college to meet demands 1 and 2 but that demands 3 and 4 were unreasonable and could not be met. The students left peaceably though protesting that their demands were not being met. Then they entered the Bursar's Office and Office of Records on the first floor of Administration and established a blockade. Occupation continued all night. During the night the occupiers caused $11,000 damage to building and equipment.

University administrators sought to seek settlement by negotiation Wednesday and Thursday but without avail. College trustees, when interviewed by newsmen, criticized the administration for being "soft and too permissive." A state senator lambasted the president, saying the college suffers from "a limp hand on the tiller."

Campus militants take up the cause of the black students. A campus strike is proposed. Sporadic fights occur among students and campus police. Four are arrested. Tension mounts. Parents of students begin phoning the college to ascertain whether their sons and daughters are safe.

Prepare a communications plan to get the college's position and policies in this crisis to key publics as promptly as possible and to maintain open channels of communication.

ADDITIONAL READING

AMERICAN COLLEGE PUBLIC RELATIONS ASSOCIATION. *Case Studies.* Beginning with 1964, ACPRA's award winning case studies of public relations and development programs have been abstracted and published annually in paperback. The Association, One Dupont Circle, Washington, D. C. Particularly helpful for beginner.

JACQUES BARZUN, *The American University. How It Runs, Where It Is Going.* New York: Harper & Row, 1968.

COX COMMISSION REPORT, *Crisis at Columbia.* New York: Vintage, 1968. Report of the Fact-Finding Commission Appointed to Investigate Disturbances at Columbia University in April and May, 1968.

JOHN EGERTON, *State Universities and Black Americans*. Southern Education Foundation, 811 Cypress St., N.E., Atlanta, Ga. 1969. An Inquiry by Southern Education Reporting Service Into Desegregation and Equity for Negroes in 100 Public Universities.

LEWIS S. FEUER. *The Conflict of Generations: the Character and Significance of Student Movements*. London: Heinemann Educational Books, 1969.

SIDNEY HOOK, *Academic Freedom and Academic Anarchy*. New York: Cowles, 1970.

GEORGE KELLER, "Six Weeks That Shook Morningside," *Columbia College Today*, Spring, 1968. A definitive, candid account of the crisis at Columbia.

KENNETH KENISTON and MICHAEL LERNER, "The Unholy Alliance Against the Campus," *New York Times Magazine*, November 8, 1970.

DOUGLAS M. KNIGHT, ed., *The Federal Government and Higher Education*. Englewood Cliffs, N.J.: Prentice-Hall, Inc., 1960.

JAMES SIMON KUNEN, *The Strawberry Statement: Notes of a College Revolutionary*. New York: Random House, 1969. A student view of the showdown at Columbia.

SEYMOUR MARTIN LIPSET, *The Berkeley Student Revolt*, Garden City, Doubleday, 1965.

MICHAEL V. MILLER et al. *A Campus Divided: Revolution at Berkeley*. New York: Dial Press, 1965.

DELBERT C. MILLER, "Town and Gown: The Power Structure of a University Town," *College and University Journal*, Vol. 2, Summer, 1963.

ROBERT E. NELSON, "Aumni?", *College and University Journal*, Vol. 1, Fall, 1962.

MICHAEL RADOCK, "University of Michigan's 150th Birthday Observance," *College & University Journal*, Vol. 7, Winter, 1968.

RICHARD W. SMITH, "Campus Leadership 1968: A Critique," *College & University Journal*, Vol. 7, Fall, 1968.

FRANKLIN H. WILLIAMS, "The University's Black Crisis," *College & University Journal*, Vol. 8, Spring, 1969.

CHAPTER 26

THE PRACTICE: THE ARMED FORCES

> No organization so directly concerned with the public interest can hope
> to escape the effects of popular opinion, nor can personnel . . . do
> their best work without adequate knowledge of where they fit in.
> —GENERAL OMAR BRADLEY

For their common defense, the people of the United States support a large and costly military establishment. The armed forces drain heavily upon the nation's wealth, manpower, and natural resources. Since 1946, taxpayers have paid out more than one-trillion dollars for national security. Each year, the Federal Government spends more than seventy cents of every budget dollar on the Defense Department. This drain of funds will require sacrifice on the part of the American people for the foreseeable future.[1] People must be convinced of the need for paying taxes and having sons drafted. They must have confidence in the spenders and the commanders. *It is mandatory, therefore, that the armed forces gain public understanding of their mission.*

No organization faces a stiffer, continuing public relations assignment. In gaining support, the armed forces must fight uphill against the intense dislike for military force inherent in American culture. The enormity of this task was clearly seen by the first Secretary of Defense, James Forrestal, who said: "I know of no task that is more complex, except possibly the task of government itself, than that of engendering in a democracy an appreciation of the role of the armed forces."

To cope with this problem, the military has developed a large public relations organization. Its scope is reflected in these figures: in the fiscal year of 1969 the Department of Defense and the military services spent at least $27,953,000 on public relations—a ten-fold increase in a decade. In the same period some 2,800 persons were in public relations assignments in the defense establishment. The latter figures does not include the time and expense that other officers, especially commanders, put into public relations.[2] Senator J. William Fulbright, who spread the detailed account of military public relations upon the public record, said he thought these figures "conservative" because ". . . they often leave out the cost of using military aircraft and many overhead costs." Likewise, there are many

---

[1] For critical view of much of this expenditure, see: William Proxmire, *Report from Wasteland: America's Military-Industrial Complex.* New York: Praeger, 1970.

[2] In 1969 Senator Fulbright got from the Department of Defense and the military services a detailed accounting of their expenditures and personnel assignments for public relations. He put these in the *Congressional Record.* See issues December 1, 1969 (S15144-S15157), December 2, 1969 (S15306-S15333), December 4, 1969 (S15649-S15674), December 5, 1969 (S15804-S15845).

shifting and "additional duty" assignments, which make a head count difficult; additional clerical personnel are not usually included. The pressure to camouflage government practice operates here, too, to prevent accurate accounting.

The nation's military history is replete with illustrations of public opinion prevailing over what is deemed sound military strategy. In the Civil War, for example, widespread fear among the Eastern seaboard compelled the fragmentation of Union Naval forces and abandonment of what Naval leaders deemed sound strategy. Military leaders were taught anew in the Vietnam War that public opinion shapes and limits battle plans.

Today's top military men provide a leadership responsive to public opinion. Consequently, they are keenly aware of the place and purpose of public relations. This trend represents a sharp break from the insulation which largely prevailed until War War II. The attitude at the top is gradually permeating the whole establishment.

The unpopularity of the Vietnam conflict intensified the need for a sensitive understanding of public opinion. The military's public relations task has been made difficult in a day when the U. S. military budget totals more than $80-billion and pressing social and educational needs go unmet. Dissents and dissatisfactions born of the Vietnam War have compounded the problem, both inside and outside the armed forces. The bitter fight against the Safeguard Anti-Ballistic Missile System, faulty weapons, charges against "cost overruns," and the threat of "the military-industrial complex," are examples of the serious problems facing military public relations officers.

It should also be apparent that the military has a unique problem in the area of disasters or accidents. For no matter how severe or routine a mishap may be, it always involves taxpayers' investment and often the lives of citizens serving in the armed forces. Either of these factors increase public attention when circumstance, mismanagement or misunderstanding create crisis: a number of Marines drown in a routine training exercise; a Congressional committee claims that a new Army tank costing millions to develop catches fire too easily; an American destroyer collides with an Australian aircraft carrier, costing nearly 100 lives; an Air Force bomber carrying nuclear weapons crashes on foreign soil. These and countless other incidents create instant requirements to lay the record bare—to provide reams of factual information to the Congress, the press, and the people. Such sensitivity of all segments of American society to problems of the military compel a recognition of the role and responsibility of those personnel who are directly responsible for moving information from the military establishment into the public domain.

In the military the term IO, Information Officer, is widely used; the military also uses PIO, Public Information Officer, to indicate those officers specifically dealing with the news media. IO, is in general use inside the services because the word *information* is used in the official titles of the public relations chiefs of the Army, Navy, and Air Force. This neutral title "Information Officer" appears to attract less flack from Congress and the press—the basic reason for its use. Public Affairs Officer (PAO) is used to designate public relations officers in the Unified and Specified Commands. These officers take their titles from Defense, where public relations is directed by an Assistant Secretary of Defense for Public Affairs. Command Information Officer is used to indicate those charged with communicating to the internal audiences of the services—officers, troops, and civilian employees. In large commands, the IO is likely to have both a PIO and a CIO serving under him. The terms *internal* (command) and *external* (public) information are common informal usage inside the Army and are well understood in other services. The purpose and programs vary slightly among the services.[3]

In response to congressional criticism, the term *public relations* was abandoned—in formal documents, if not in informal talk, almost two decades ago. In recent years the term *public affairs* has been used with increasing frequency. The military concept has progressed beyond publicity to include internal, community, and public relations in the full sense of those terms. In 1964, the Army changed the term for troop information to *command information* to emphasize the commander's responsibility in the area of internal information. The Air Force uses the term "internal information."

FROM THREE PIO's TO NEARLY THREE THOUSAND

Growth of the function has a long, up-and-down history. In the Revolutionary War, little was done, once the war started, to mobilize public support for the fighting forces. Revolutionary political leaders put great stress on gaining support for independence but made no efforts on behalf of the Continental Army. The military was slow to recognize the importance of molding a favorable public opinion. In the Civil War, for example, reporters continually complained of their lack of standing and mistreatment

---

[3] Troop information and education were split by the Army in 1956. Education was assigned to the personnel function (G-1). Congressional relations and public relations were separated—organizationally—earlier in all the services. The Marine Corps public information organization does not include the internal relations function, which is viewed as a command function. The entire Navy Department thus conducts internal information partly in the Office of Information and partly in the Bureau of Naval Personnel. Additionally, all services use materials prepared by the Director of Information for the Armed Forces (IAF) of the Department of Defense. After Secretary McNamara assumed office, the Department of Defense exercised more control and coordination over service public relations programs.

by the military. " 'West Pointers' were especially unfriendly to the press." One reporter wrote his editor: "Until it is clearly settled that an accredited journalist, in the legitimate exercise of his calling, has just as much right in the Army as the Commander himself, he will be considered by a large majority of Regular Army officers as an unauthorized hanger-on and treated accordingly." [4] Today's newsman is accepted.

The United States Marine Corps led the way in the early years. The initial impetus was to outbid other services for recruits. This branch is justly famed, both for its heroic exploits and for its skilled practice of public relations. The Corps established the first military public relations office when it set up the Chicago Publicity Bureau in 1907. This office provided releases, pictorial material, and other publicity matter to newspapers throughout the Midwest. Today such practice is commonplace; then it was unusual.

The Corps pioneered in building today's concept. In 1920, a Marine Corps sergeant, Percy A. Webb, a pioneer, said: "We must not forget that it is the cumulative effect of what the Marines do in the battle zones coupled with what is said or printed about them, radio programs, motion pictures . . . and every report about them, good or bad, which help to formulate public opinion." In 1925, Major General Lejeune phrased today's concept when he said: "The future success of the Marine Corps depends on two factors: First, an efficient performance of all the duties to which its officers and men may be assigned; second, promptly bringing this efficiency to the attention of the proper officials of the government and the American people."

A Marine Corps officer was among the first to recognize the distinction between publicity and public relations. In 1927, Capt. Jonas H. Platt wrote: "At its worst, publicity is the cunning art of putting one's best foot forward—and lying about the foot. At its best, publicity is the science of so governing one's public relations that the average citizen will have no reason to think of one with anything but the deepest respect. Why not jettison the word publicity once and for all? Public relations is a better term. . . ." [5]

Historically, the Army initiated reports to Congress as early as 1777. It did not formally report directly to the people until the outbreak of the Spanish-American War. Then, an unnamed correspondent persuaded the War Department to publish information for the press daily by posting it on a bulletin board outside the office of the Secretary of War. This was the casual beginning of today's extensive information program.

[4] Louis M. Starr, *Bohemian Brigade* (New York: Alfred A. Knopf, Inc., 1954), p. 119.

[5] The foregoing information on the Marine Corps is taken from Robert Lindsay's, *This High Name: Public Relations and U. S. Marine Corps* (Madison: University of Wisconsin Press). Recommended reading.

In 1904, the Adjutant General of the Army made the first formal press release to newspaper correspondents. The press release constituted the Army's "public relations" program until the eve of World War I. In June, 1916, Secretary of War Newton D. Baker was busy getting ready for what looked like war. News interest in the War Department had perked up. To get inquiring reporters off his neck, Baker called in a promising young major, Douglas MacArthur, and appointed him Press Release Officer of the War Department. MacArthur had an instinctive feel for news.

The demands of the press led to the creation of a press section in the A.E.F. Headquarters in France in 1917. Near the end of the war, in October, 1918, public relations was formally recognized as an Army staff function. It was given definite status on the General Staff level with the creation of the Public Relations Branch in G-2, Military Intelligence. With the peace of the 1920s, the Army's interest withered. The military crawled back into its shell.

Public interest and support of the armed forces languished. The armed forces' interest in public support was rather indifferent until the mid-1930s. Then the gathering Nazi war clouds in Europe brought the nation's military weakness into public focus. In 1935, General MacArthur, then Army Chief of Staff, brought in Major Alexander Surles, on duty at the War College, as head of the Public Relations Branch. Surles' staff totaled three: another major, a captain, and himself. Major Surles and his two aides took on, with skill and enthusiasm, the "dual job of getting before the public the War Department's anxiety over the shape of things to come in Europe and of helping newspapermen to pry stories out of the War Department."

In January, 1941, General Surles was asked by the War Department to draft a plan for setting up a "man-size bureau of public relations." A month later, Major General Robert C. Richardson III, one of the Army's top commanders and organizers, was ordered to Washington to organize the War Department Bureau of Public Relations. Richardson served in this post until August, 1941, when he took command of an Army Corps. Surles replaced him and was Director of the War Department Bureau of Public Relations through World War II. In the words of one Washington editor, Surles "came through with laurels and the affectionate respect of the newspapermen with whom he had to deal." The WDBPR directed the Army's far-flung public relations operations during the war.[6]

The Navy's first formal step toward a public affairs program was taken during the U-boat raids prior to World War I when the Secretary of the Navy, Josephus Daniels, began holding two press conferences a day in his office. Soon after America's entry into the war, Secretary Daniels

---

[6] Information based on Colonel Sidney A. Knutson's thesis, "History of Public Relations Program of the U. S. Army," University of Wisconsin, 1953.

established the Navy News Bureau, staffed by civilian newsmen and directed by the Secretary.

After World War I, the Assistant Secretary of the Navy, Colonel Theodore Roosevelt, Jr., created an Information Section within the Office of Naval Intelligence. In 1939, this section was renamed the Public Relations Branch, Office of Naval Intelligence (ONI), and subsidiary branches were established in all Naval districts.

In 1941, Secretary of the Navy Frank Knox transferred the responsibility for public information from ONI to a new Office of Public Relations, directly responsible to the Secretary of the Navy. In the same year, the Chief of Naval Operations declared public relations to be a function of command.

During World War II, Navy public information activities were expanded, but there was little long-range planning. As a consequence, many public information aspects were overlooked. In 1944, the Navy public affairs structure was reorganized, and the following year the first signs of a carefully thought-out national program, emphasizing both long-range and immediate objectives, appeared. Many of the Navy's most experienced public affairs personnel left the service at the end of World War II.

The Army Air Corps, headed by General H. H. Arnold and less bound by tradition, moved rapidly to capitalize on the glamor and color of this new weapon of war. General Arnold had started blazing the trail for air force public relations as far back as 1925, when he was chief of the information division, office of the Chief of Air Service, in the War Department. His successful career reflected a shrewd grasp of public relations. The Army Air Corps, as war broke, quickly recruited a large number of skilled public relations and advertising men. The Army Air Corps' public information shop was consolidated with the War Department Bureau of Public Relations in September, 1942. The Air Force did not operate independently until it became a separate force in 1947.

Even though the armed services went into World War II ill equipped for public relations, they acquitted themselves well. The work was largely a matter of publicity, censorship, and assistance to war correspondents. Naturally, mistakes were made. Senior commanders, with brilliant exceptions at the top, were not public relations-minded. They had matured in an era when the services were relatively unconcerned about public opinion. The result was that many commanders gave little support or personal attention to the efforts of their PIO staffs. In a few cases, they opposed such efforts.

Initially, public information staffs were recruited overnight, many were experienced newsmen or practitioners in civilian life. Others had had little training and held the fuzziest of concepts. Some of the amateur PIO's brought about bruised public relationships. Given the size of the task and the rapidity of recruitment, it was amazing, actually, that there were not more square pegs put into round PIO holes.

Additionally, the PIO staffs were put under the secrecy-minded G-2 and A-2 intelligence staffs who often sought to suppress too much on the grounds of military security. Intelligence officers had a broad, rubbery definition of military security. Some PIO's confused information endangering military security with that endangering the reputation of fellow officers who made mistakes. Despite mistakes and handicaps, public relations personnel made significant contributions to soldier morale, home-front morale, and war production.

The incompatibility of the public information and intelligence functions was ultimately recognized. Consequently, the functions were separated and public relations was recognized as a staff function in its own right.

Military public relations has experienced a sounder, more orderly development since World War II. In response to public opinion, the armed forces were quickly stripped down after the war's end. The public, understandably, assumed victory in war meant peace. Those charged with providing national security saw the necessity for rebuilding the machine.

Arthur W. Page, veteran corporate counselor, was influential in effecting a more professional approach to public relations in the military. Early in the spring of 1945, he was asked by Secretary of War Henry L. Stimson, a long-time neighbor and friend, to study the Army's public relations set-up. In a memorandum dated May 30, 1945—still referred to in the Army as "The Page Report"— the vice president of A.T.&T. told the Secretary: "It is vital that if we are to have any effective national defense that the Army be reasonable, articulate, and public minded, for the public is quite capable and quite likely to risk its existence from an enemy rather than accept defense on a basis it neither likes nor understands." [7] Page recommended a reorganization and improved staffing of the function. He wrote Secretary Stimson: ". . . a fundamental change can be effected if the Army (1) puts a fair sample of its best regular officers in public relations jobs, (2) recognizes them for effective service in that capacity, (3) makes a good public relations background part of the basis of every officer's continuous training, and (4) carries out the positive duty of explaining itself to the public all the time, which will naturally flow from the new attitude." The Army adopted his recommendations, created the position Director of Information and put the Bureau of Public Relations, the Legislative and Liaison Division, and the Army's Information and Education Division under him for policy purposes.[8] The other services were in-

---

[7] Memorandum dated 30 May 1945 to Secretary of War Henry L. Stimson, in Army files, Washington, D.C.

[8] Memorandum dated 8 September 1945 to Deputy Chief of Staff, from Maj. Gen. A. D. Surles, in Army files, Washington, D.C.

fluenced by this Army reorganization and reorientation and, to some degree, followed suit.

The Navy, for example, established the Fleet Home Town News Center, an innovation the other services copied in due time. In 1947, the Navy created a Public Information Officer specialist category. A year later, in 1948, the enlisted Journalist (JO) rating was established as an outgrowth of the Specialist (X) (Journalist) or (Naval Correspondent) and Specialist (X) (Public Information) ratings which had been in effect during World War II.

Early in 1949, following the establishment of the Department of Defense, many of the functions of the Navy's Washington Office of Public Relations were consolidated into the Defense Department. In 1950, the name was changed to the Navy Office of Information.

Interservice rivalry for talented recruits and Congressional support has been one of the sharpest spurs in advancing public relations in the armed forces. It is also the source of some glaring public relations mistakes and bitter public fights. The Air Force, once it gained independent status, took the lead in publicizing and proselytizing, but all services vie spiritedly for the public's support. The Secretary of Defense, operating through the assistant secretary for public affairs, tries to mute service disputes in the public arena, but is not always successful. The organization extends from this assistant secretary to junior officers at Army posts, Air Force and Marine bases, aboard Navy ships, and in unified commands.

IT STARTS AT THE TOP

Direction and impetus for the military's large staff and extensive program is centered in the Department of Defense. The President, as Commander-in-Chief, inevitably plays an important role in setting the tone and themes of defense information. The Secretary of Defense "regards public information as a *prime responsibility* of the Office of the Secretary of Defense and of each of the military departments." From 1949 until 1954, the program was directed from the Office of Public Information in the Defense Department. The O.P.I. was abolished July 30, 1954.

James Forrestal, first Secretary of Defense, set up the O.P.I. in March, 1949, to unify and coordinate the programs of all services. One of his aims was to eliminate the feuding which had been rampant in the scramble for funds and manpower. His successor, Louis A. Johnson, moved to implement the Forrestal order. Through his Assistant to the Secretary, he set up eight divisions in O.P.I. and stripped the service staffs in the Pentagon. The Army was left with about sixteen PIO officers and civilians, and the other two services retained about thirty officials in the top echelon. It was a sharp cut for each service. Johnson envisioned O.P.I. as the public relations office for the whole military establishment in Washington. He ruled O.P.I. would be "the sole agency of the Establishment at the seat of government for dissemination of public information."

However logical centralized control of military information may appear to the President and his Secretary of Defense, the service secretaries will insist, properly, on their need for a staff. Likewise, military reporters will always insist, properly, on dealing with the service experts, not with spokesmen one or two steps removed. Nor is it wholly against the public interest to have service differences aired in public. Taking these factors into consideration, Department of Defense (DOD) has since returned some of the public information capabilities to the services.

With the expansion of the armed forces for the Korean War, the setup in each service was steadily built up again. The O.P.I.—with all its elaborate organization—operated mainly as a referral agency for persons seeking information. Its primary tasks were to communicate top defense policies, to counsel the Secretary and his staff, and to mediate conflicts with the press over security regulations—a recurring headache. As of September, 1969, there were several hundred persons assigned to public relations duty in the Pentagon. These included 206 in the office of the Secretary of Defense, excluding those assigned to the Office of Information for the Armed Forces.

Secretary of Defense Robert McNamara, operating through the Assistant Secretary for Public Affairs, was more effective than his predecessors in tightening his control over the service public relations staffs. In 1964, after a public airing of the rivalries of the Army and Air Force over military air support control, the Secretary cut the number of civilian and military personnel assigned to public relations duties, moved the service book-magazine and organization liaison sections to DOD, and eliminated the separate military service desks in DOD.

The conduct of military public relations in the Kennedy and Johnson administrations shared most of the same criticisms applied to governmental public relations in other years.[9] The furor over Arthur Sylvester's use of "news management" as a weapon in the Cold War has been discussed. The Berlin call-up of 1961 and the Cuba Crisis of 1962 created opportunities for a test of public relations finesse in the military establishment. This was increased many-fold by the war in Vietnam.

This period of revamping of military strategy to meet changing de-

---

[9] For first-hand account of military public relations in these years, see informative book by Phil Goulding who served Secretaries McNamara and Clark Clifford as assistant secretary of defense for public affairs: *Confirm or Deny, Informing the People on National Security.* New York: Harper & Row, 1970. Goulding now heads the Earl Newsom firm.

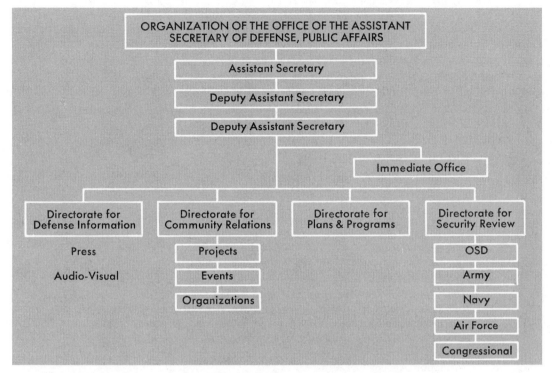

ORGANIZATION OF THE OFFICE OF THE ASSISTANT
SECRETARY OF DEFENSE, PUBLIC AFFAIRS

Assistant Secretary

Deputy Assistant Secretary

Deputy Assistant Secretary

Immediate Office

Directorate for Defense Information	Directorate for Community Relations	Directorate for Plans & Programs	Directorate for Security Review
Press	Projects		OSD
Audio-Visual	Events		Army
	Organizations		Navy
			Air Force
			Congressional

fense needs, especially for the Air Force and Navy, brought a return to
fierce budget battles for new weapons and men, which had been so much
a part of the Eisenhower administration. In their battles for what they
consider their rightful share of the multi-billion-dollar defense budget, all
four services utilize the help of military manufacturers and their "alumni
associations." Woll notes: [10] "For example, Lockheed Aircraft, prime con-
tractor for the Polaris submarine missile, has used its public relations and
advertising departments to help publicize the importance of the Navy,
while Douglas Aircraft has boosted the Army or the Air Force, for which
it is building missiles. Defense contractors are often willing to boost any
service that uses their products. . . ." In such a situation, the service
public relations organizations get close scrutiny. This was shown again in
the fierce ABM debates of 1969 and 1970.

Melvin R. Laird, Secretary of Defense under Nixon, proved an astute
politician, keenly conscious of the value and problems of public affairs.
Among the innovations begun by him was the practice of holding daily
press briefings for the Pentagon news corps. While these have been con-

[10] In his *American Bureaucracy* (New York: W. W. Norton & Company, 1963), pp. 134–35.
Also see: Joseph Kraft, *Profiles in Power*, "The Change at the Pentagon."

ducted by the Assistant Secretary of Defense (Public Affairs), Secretary Laird frequently dropped in at these sessions for an informal discussion with newsmen. In October, 1969, Secretary Laird announced he was abandoning the "backgrounder press conference," a long established device, which permits officials to float trial balloons without having them directly attributed to the source. Laird preferred to talk on the record. Laird also recognized the importance and complexity of the function when he made Daniel Z. Henkin, a holdover from the Johnson Administration, Assistant Secretary of Defense for Public Affairs, thus encouraging men to make government public relations a career.

The functions of the Assistant Secretary of Defense (Public Affairs) are stated in the July 10, 1961, directive enumerating his responsibilities: [11]

> The Assistant Secretary of Defense (Public Affairs) is the principal staff assistant to the Secretary of Defense for public information and community relations. He is responsible within the Department of Defense for an integrated DOD public affairs program which will:
> 1. Provide the American people with maximum information about the Department of Defense consistent with national security.
> 2. Initiate and support activities contributing to good relations between the Department of Defense and all segments of the public at home and abroad. These activities will be carried out in overseas areas in collaboration with the Department of State and the United States Information Agency.
> 3. Plan for Department of Defense national public media censorship activities during a declared National Emergency.

THE SERVICE SETUPS

Experience gained in World War II, the Korean War, and in Vietnam, unification of the services, and creation of a centralized coordinating agency in the Department of Defense have served to modify the organization of the function in the services. These organizations remain rather fluid and are periodically revamped. Even so, it might be helpful to outline briefly the pattern of the service programs.

AIR FORCE

The United States Air Force program originates in the Office of Information in the Office of the Secretary of the Air Force. This is abbrevi-

---

[11] Department of Defense Directive 5122.5, Assistant Secretary of Defense (Public Affairs), dated July 10, 1961. Since then this basic directive has had only two minor modifications.

ated: SAFOI. A major general is director. Three primary divisions handle most of the work. These are entitled "Public Information," "Internal Information," and "Community Relations." Also reporting to the director are the offices of Reserve Forces Liaison, and Security Review; special assistants for information who are assigned directly to most offices of the Air Staff; and field extension offices in New York, Chicago, and Los Angeles. SAFOI plans, policies, and programs are implemented in the field by information staffs at major commands, numbered air forces, and bases.

The division organization of the top echelon is generally duplicated at all command levels down to air bases. History on an Air Force-wide basis is handled by a separate organization. The Air Force keeps the information function at a special staff level and avoids having it regarded as an "additional duty," except in small, detached units. Air Force commanders use the information program to keep their personnel informed and motivated for maximum production and service, and to fulfill the obligation to keep the public informed of Air Force activities. Strong emphasis is placed upon the internal information program as a management tool. This is done to instill in each member the sense of personal dedication to country and duty necessary for him to be efficient in his job at all times.

ARMY

The Army centers its program of public and command information in the Office of the Chief of Information. The mission of this office is to discharge "Army staff responsibility for all matters pertaining to public and command information, and for Department of the Army Information plans and programs in support of Army basic plans and programs." In plain language, the Chief of Information advises the entire Army leadership in the Pentagon, military and civilian, on the conduct of public and command information activities. In this role, the Army operates under policy guidance from the Secretary of Defense.

The over-all objective of Army information is "to insure understanding of the importance of the Army's role in a sound national military program, and to win support for the Army as part of the Armed Forces of the United States." The Army office includes division of public information, command information, community relations, and policy, plans, and programs.

The Army organization is similar in its principal field commands— the Continental Army, Army Materiel, and Army Combat Developments Commands, and other Army Field Commands. Under the Information Officer at CONARC are branches for plans and programs, public affairs, and internal information. The public affairs branch breaks down into sections for community relations, special projects, press, and audio-visual. Smaller offices organized along the same lines are located in the headquarters of the five continental armies. Much smaller information staffs are used at posts, camps, and stations, with divisions in the field.

Army regulations provide that information officers will be appointed to the staff of each battalion and of all commanders down to and including the battalion or unit of an equivalent size. A full-time information officer is authorized at division level or higher. Below this level, it is an additional duty assignment. Those specifically provided for in tables of organization have the status of special staff officers when information is their primary duty. The Army states that "*direct access* to the commander at all times is essential to the information officer for him to perform properly his duties." Within the military organization, this rapid entry matches problems with decision authority but unfortunately the exception is as true as the rule.

NAVY

At the apex of the Navy organization is the Office of Information in the Department of the Navy. The Navy Chief of Information reports directly to the Secretary of the Navy and has additional duty as Chief Public Relations Advisor to the Chief of Naval Operations. The public affairs mission of the Navy is to inform the public and members of the naval service as to the Navy's role as an instrument of national policy and security; the operations of the Navy, as much as is compatible with military security; and the responsibilities and activities of naval personnel as United States citizens. The objectives are to promote: public support and understanding of the importance of seapower, particularly in the nuclear age; the Navy's role in preserving U. S. security and in fulfilling U. S. national objectives; an efficient and effective modern Navy; the high caliber of personnel needed in today's technologically complex Navy; career advantages of Naval service; the many contributions of the Navy to scientific research, particularly its leading role in oceanography and nuclear propulsion.

In Washington, each Navy bureau, office, or command (the Bureau of Naval Weapons, for example) has a PI officer or a civilian information specialist. The size of the staff varies according to need and includes civilians, naval officers, and enlisted men. Ashore, the Commandant of each naval district or river command has a public information office, and the Commandant has coordinating authority for all Navy public information within his area of responsibility.

All commanders and commanding officers are encouraged to designate an officer to handle public information as a collateral assignment if the command does not have a full-time public information officer. Afloat, fleet commanders have public information officers assigned to their staffs, while aboard ship a qualified officer handles information either full time or as a collateral duty.

All services operate centralized news centers. The Navy's Fleet Home Town News Center was opened in 1945 at Great Lakes, Ill., which serves the Marine Corps and Coast Guard as well as the Navy. The Army set up a similar center at Kansas City in 1951, and the Air Force established one at Oklahoma City in 1961. These centers take the news in the rough from ships at sea and units. They edit or rewrite news releases, prepare pictures and mats, duplicate recorded radio and TV tapes, and distribute these to the hometown media of soldiers, airmen, sailors, and Marines. One writer in a critical essay estimated the output of two of the news centers at 15,000 releases a day.[12]

In 1946, the Army set up an information school at Carlisle Barracks, Pennsylvania, with courses for officers and enlisted personnel. With unification, it became the Armed Forces Information School. It was moved to Fort Slocum, New York, in 1951 and until 1954 served all the Armed Forces. In 1954, it became the Army Information School again and subsequently trained few men of the other services. The Navy had a separate school at Great Lakes, but both the Navy and the Air Force sent some students to the Army school. In 1964, the Secretary of Defense directed that all service training in public affairs again be conducted within a single military school but excepted graduate-level schooling for the requirement. Accordingly, the Army was designated the executive agent for the Defense Information School, which is located at Fort Benjamin Harrison, Indiana. The school is staffed by members from all the services.

All services have sent officers to universities for graduate education in journalism and public relations to prepare these men for military public relations assignments.

PUBLICS OF THE ARMED FORCES

The services divide their several publics into "Internal" and "External." For example, the Army considers its internal publics to be: Active Army, Reserve Components (U. S. Army Reserve and National Guard), USMA Cadets, ROTC Cadets, civilian employees, retired personnel, and families of all these. External Army publics are Congress, the news media, community organizations, business, industry, labor, education, and the general public. Military public relations officers formally recognize the overlap between and within the two but sometimes forget this in practice.

[12] William Stucky, "How to Collect Military Information," *Harper's Magazine*, Vol. 210, February, 1955, pp. 55–61. Critical of PI output.

INTERNAL

The armed forces fully realize that the officers and enlisted men and women are their most important goodwill ambassadors. The best—or worst—representative of the Army, Air Force, Navy, or Marines is the soldier, airman, or sailor. This is reflected in assignment of command information to the information staffs. Secretary of War Patterson once said: "What he knows, what he thinks and what he feels about the Army will be reflected in the attitude of the public. The soldier comes from the people and he goes back to the people, not only by his eventual return to civilian life but by his visits, his letters, his very presence on the street. You cannot have an informed public until you have an informed Army."

Military leaders recognize that it takes more than information programs to make a good soldier. It takes *action*. It takes good leadership and good treatment. American soldiers and sailors are the best fed, best clothed, and best cared-for military men in the world. The Army has made great strides since World War II to improve the status of the soldier and to clothe him with dignity. As Omar Bradley once said: "We cannot induce men to become soldiers if in the process they are divested of their dignity and human rights."

Military leaders recognize, further, that the soldier is the most important link between the public and the military. Crude, carousing soldiers, sailors, airmen, and Marines playing tough in nightclubs at home or abroad can do much to offset the leadership of a commanding general. At the end of the 1960s, American troops were in effect "on trial" around the globe. In 1970, more than a million U. S. airmen, soldiers, and sailors were stationed abroad at 2,270 air, naval, and army bases, major and minor, scattered in 33 nations. Commanders are bearing down hard to make their men behave while off duty and to deal in a friendly, respectful way with host country populations. Drunken servicemen, so prevalent in World War II, have all but disappeared. Before troops leave the United States, they are briefed on their new stations, customs of the country, and reminders of their role as representatives of America. Training in how to get along with the local citizenry continues overseas. Operations labeled "Friendship" have been launched in many foreign countries.

Such constructive efforts are more than wiped out by such disgraceful episodes as the My Lai Massacre perpetrated by U. S. soldiers in Vietnam in 1968, but not exposed until late in 1969. This and similar incidents of barbaric behavior in that war brought discredit to the Army in the United States and to the nation in the world. The Army's efforts to suppress details of the senseless killing of Vietnam civilians was ultimately of no avail. The suppression served only to magnify the crime in the eyes of the public.[13] Similarly, front-page scandals of widespread looting of NCO clubs by officers and enlisted men brought public distrust.

A problem much more difficult than that of troop behavior off post or ship is the relatively new problem of officer and soldier-sailor dissent to national or military policies. Amidst the tension and turmoil of the 1970s, the military, once rigidly authoritarian, found itself engulfed in the spillover of dissent from the civilian community. The new tendency of officers and enlisted personnel to question orders and the sympathetic treatment given to such dissent by civilian courts has, on occasion, disrupted discipline, created doubt as to available courses of action on the part of commanders at all echelons, and, in the opinion of some military leaders, lessened morale at all levels. Typical examples include: The court suit of two staff members of the Fort Dix Coffee House and two members of the armed forces against the Army to stop "harassment" of coffee house employees and of person involved in distribution of an underground newspaper, *Shakedown;* a court suit by the North Carolina Civil Liberties Union contesting the right of military officials to prohibit civilians from passing out leaflets on Army bases. This dissent is also reflected in many publicized defections.

In September, 1969, the military took cognizance of the increasing expression of dissent on and off post. The Secretary of Defense, in a directive dated 12 September, 1969, laid down these guidelines to all commanders: [14]

A commander is not authorized to prevent distribution of a publication unless "there is a clear danger to the loyalty, discipline, or morale of military personnel." The fact that a publication is critical of Government policies is not grounds for banning a publication. Commanders may not prohibit the possession of "an unauthorized publication." Commanders have the authority to place establishments "off limits" when, for example, activities taking place there include counseling members to refuse to perform their duties or to desert.

Commanders may not discipline members of the armed forces who work off post on their own time and with their own money on "underground" newspapers.

Members of the armed forces are prohibited from participating in off-post demonstrations when they are on duty, or in a foreign country, or when violence is likely to result.

[13] This grim episode was first and fully told by Seymour M. Hersh, then a correspondent for the Dispatch News Service, for which he received a Pulitzer Prize. The full story is in his book, *My Lai 4: A Report on the Massacre and Its Aftermath*, published by Random House in 1970. A shorter account may be found in *Harper's*, May, 1970.

[14] DOD Directive 325/6, 12 September 1969. Also see Department Army publication, TAG Letter, "Guidance on Dissent," 28 May 1969.

Commanders must recognize that membership in a "serviceman's union" is not against current regulations, although commanders "are not authorized to recognize or to bargain with a so-called 'servicemen's union.'"

Typical of the channels of internal communication used in the services are those of the Navy. The Navy Office of Information puts out a "news service" for ship and station newspapers; *Direction* magazine, a monthly containing public affairs guidance, timely articles, and features for commanding officers and public affairs staffs; and NAVANEWS, a twice-a-month service of news, features, and editorials on Navy-related material. The latter also includes a Family Editor section for dependents.

Although heavy-handed attempts to control and censor internal channels of communications, including Armed Forces radio, occur from time to time, the Department of Defense has repeatedly affirmed the right of military personnel to have access to all news not jeopardizing national security. In February, 1967, a general of the "public be damned" school relieved an able public relations officer because he refused to kill a story in the European edition of *Stars and Stripes*. The story involved the son of a U. S. Ambassador. On May 1, 1967, Secretary of Defense McNamara issued a directive which in effect over-ruled the general.

RESERVISTS

Reserve personnel and the National Guard units offer an excellent bridge between the armed forces and the public. Reserves are primarily civilians but still possess a strong, continuing interest in the armed forces. This reserve membership reaches down into every city and hamlet of the nation, from Maine to McAllen, Texas. These reservists offer a ready-made transmission belt to carry information to the public and back again. In the immediate postwar years of 1945–1950, the armed forces failed to use this public relations opportunity. During this period, reservists were ill-informed, confused, and largely ignored in the post war military establishment. For example, the 1961 call-up in the Berlin Crisis also produced some confusion, irritation, and controversy.

Increased use of National Guard units to quell protests, particularly in cities and on campuses, has brought grave problems. These militia units, under state control unless federalized, sometimes are unable to cope with these situations because of inadequate training. And on occasion guardsmen prove trigger-happy. The needless slaying of four students at Kent State University in May, 1970, brought the Guard vehement criticism across the nation.

All the military departments direct special attention to reserve personnel. The Army has made a special effort to recognize the importance of the reservists, both Army Reserve and Army National Guard, to the effectiveness of its forces. The contribution of all components of the Army family, part-time, full-time, military, and civilian, has been highlighted as essential. The Army has placed this "One Army" concept as one of its major annual information themes since 1959. It has yet to put the idea across effectively. The Berlin call-up re-emphasized the need for such special information effort for reserve personnel, and the Army recognized it with an expanded program designed for this audience alone.[15]

"Naval reservists in civilian professions related to public affairs work maintain mobilization readiness and training while contributing to the Navy's public affairs program through the performance of various projects and local public affairs tasks. Naval Reserve public affairs personnel frequently perform specific public affairs assignments while serving on temporary active duty or on active duty for training."

Important sources of information for those with special interest in the military are the military service associations and other organizations with close military ties. Among the largest of these are: the Navy League, Air Force Association, Association of the United States Army, Marine Corps Reserve Officers Association, American Legion, Veterans of Foreign Wars, and Military Orders of World Wars. Their annual conventions become top news stories and are often the forum from which important defense stories emanate. Each of these groups maintains local chapters and conducts public relations activities of varied sorts. These groups are often called upon by the military when support in Congress is needed.[16]

EXTERNAL PUBLICS

CONGRESS

Congress, which grants funds for the armed forces and determines their respective roles, is the smallest but most vital public of all. Public support, or its lack, eventually comes to focus in Congress. Actual relationships with the Congress are the responsibility of small, compact legislative liaison units in the top echelons. Their pitch and their problems are ultimately reflected in the information units. Every PIO must keep this

[15] For a case study, see Col. Joseph F. H. Cutrona, "Information Program for Released Reservists Produces Good Will," *Public Relations Journal*, Vol. 19, July, 1963.

[16] For an account of one civilian supporting arm, see Armin Rappaport, *The Navy League of the U. S.* (Detroit: Wayne State University Press, 1962). Also see: Jack Raymond, "Growing Threat of Our Military-Industrial Complex," *Harvard Business Review*, Vol. 46, May–June, 1968.

key group constantly in mind. Public relations and legislative liaison are parts of the same whole. The effort to win congressional support is intense and unremitting. *Each public relations program and each policy guiding that program must be weighed in terms of the ultimate reaction in Congress and in the Executive Branch of government, the seats of civilian control.*

EMPLOYEES

From World War II on, the armed forces have employed thousands of civilians, from topflight specialists to maintenance workers. In the process, the military has learned the problems and procedures that go with good employee relations. Military leaders have learned the difference in dealing with a civilian free to choose his employment and with a soldier drafted to serve wherever he is assigned. Civilian employees form another important link with the general public, particularly at the post and base level. They must be included in the program's publics.

INDUSTRY

America's industrial machine provides the sinews for the national security. The relations of the armed forces and American industry are close and complex. As the military machine becomes increasingly a mechanized machine, these relations grow in importance. The armed forces recognize this and have special industrial relations sections in all top headquarters. The officials of the military and of industry have many problems and projects in common. They find themselves, with increasing frequency, working together. Just as the armed forces form an important public for industry, so does industry constitute an important public of the armed forces.

To bridge the gap between defense policy makers and industrial leaders the Defense Department initiated some years ago the Joint Civilian Orientation Conference. The JCOC plan originated with Secretary Forrestal and has been followed through by his successors. Once a year some seventy to eighty civilian leaders are invited to participate in an orientation program as guests of the secretary. The purpose of the week-long program has been to acquaint opinion leaders with the activities, programs and problems of the department and the place of national defense in world affairs. The exchange of information and ideas is encouraged all the way through. The JCOC program has been broadened to include leaders from all walks of life.

COMMUNITY RELATIONS

This phase of military public relations is getting increased emphasis. There has been a complete about-face from the days when the Army post was an isolated island in an unconcerned community. The key to this policy of being *a part of* instead of *apart from* the community was laid down by the Doolittle Board shortly after World War II. It recommended: "Close contact and association with civilians should be encouraged and maintained, since a citizens' army is a result of combined interest, effort, and contribution of both military and public. A mutual exchange of information will enhance the military organization. . . . A maximum of military personnel living in civilian communities rather than on Army posts will accomplish this." Military forces, more and more, are "living off the post."

All information offices now include a community relations section. Service directives on such programs are based on Department of Defense directive 5410–18, "Community Relations," dated February 9, 1968, and DOD Instruction 5410–19, "Armed Forces Participation in Public Events Supporting Community Relations Programs," dated November 26, 1968. The services are required to submit their implementing directives to the DOD Public Affairs for approval. The Army program is typical. It was outlined in Army Regulation 360–55, issued on January 23, 1957, the first such regulation. In advising top Army leaders in 1963, the then Army Chief of Staff, Gen. Earle G. Wheeler, said:

> The community relations program is intended to promote abiding cordial relationships between the Army and the citizens of cities, towns, and villages adjacent to military installations. Army men and women in uniform and our Army civilian employees who take an enthusiastic and active part in community affairs enhance the prestige, influence, and public understanding of the Army as a whole. Command interest, attention, and supervision are essential to a successful community relations program.

The Air Force and Navy put similar stress on community relations. Navy shore-based commands conduct intensive community relations programs, and many of the Navy's ship visits to domestic and foreign ports are used to generate public understanding of the mission of the Navy. Military bands and exhibits are a familiar sight, and the Army's "Golden Knights" parachute team, the Navy's "Blue Angels," and the Air Force's "Thunderbirds" flying teams have thrilled spectators throughout the country.

But military community relations problems involve far more than being a good citizen in local communities. There are some real sticklers. Some were posed by the difficult problem of maintaining adequate worldwide facilities for all military forces. When, early in the Johnson Administration, Secretary McNamara announced a list of installations to be closed within the states, the announcement generated mixed comment. The move was praised as a long needed economy in all places unaffected by the closures. Congressmen want economy in someone else's district.

Although some of the large military reservations are on lands of small commercial value, the large number of small installations that all military services have maintained near or in major metropolitan areas have been the focus of criticism.

The Presidio of San Francisco would make a fine residential project adjacent to Golden Gate Bridge; Fort Sam Houston is now surrounded by the burgeoning suburbs of San Antonio. Some industrial-type facilities remain that might be needed for future emergencies—yet they represent sites for industrial complexes that are unavailable elsewhere. Within the national capital alone, the Washington Navy Yard, Bolling Air Force Base, and the Anacostia Naval Station remain as monuments to the history of the earlier military era—at greater cost than some think is warranted. The real estate holdings of the American military forces—valued at $35.4-billion, located at 7,000 installations on 30.6-million acres—make DOD a landlord having all the difficulties attached to that role.

With the Kennedy administration's instructions to the Secretary of Defense to take actions to secure equal opportunity for all their personnel, the military services moved into an area of special sensitivity. This action, directed at the Negro segregation problem, caused political controversy when the President's committee, headed by Gerhard A. Gesell, in the summer of 1963 pointed the finger at off-post discrimination against military personnel as a major inequity. Discrimination within the services had been largely eliminated shortly after World War II. The national conscience was impaled on the twin prongs of desire to insure fair treatment for all service personnel and the traditional fear of any incursion of military authority into the civil domain.

The services faced the quandary of "damned if they do and damned if they don't." They did—and continue to—receive embittered salvos with each step taken, both from segregationists and from those concerned about a possible loss of military subordination to civil authority. Secretary McNamara bore the brunt of the attack but he struck a promising theme when he commented that there was no intent to reform society, that what he was trying to do was to look after military morale and efficiency.

PRESS

Relationships with the mass media constitute an important and sometimes difficult phase of military public relations. Clashes occur between the press's insistence on the public's right to know and the military's obligation to prevent release of security information which would be of value to the nation's enemies. Much improvement has been made, but this basic conflict is not likely ever to be fully resolved.

The Office of the Assistant Secretary of Defense (Public Affairs) maintains a Directorate for Security Review to review material prior to public release for security and policy. There is frequently room for argument as to whether material is classified to avoid release rather than for security reasons. Also the review for policy is always controversial.

That this is not new can be seen from the following quotation:

> I write to suggest that you request and advise all officers of the service, whether active or retired, to refrain from public comment of any kind upon the military or political situation on the other side of the water. I would be obliged if you would let them know that the request and advice comes from me. It seems to me highly unwise and improper that officers of the Army and Navy of the United States should make any public utterances to which any color of political or military criticism can be given where other nations are involved.

While these words could be written today, they are in fact from a letter written by President Woodrow Wilson to the Secretary of War on August 6, 1914.[17]

In 1962, Senator John Stennis' Preparedness Subcommittee conducted a thorough investigation of this problem. The Subcommittee report on policy review of military information prior to release, stated: "If we fragment and undermine our national policy by allowing thousands of military officers publicly to express views not in consonance with established policy, our enemies will be comforted and aided and our friends confused and bewildered."

An example of an outdated military gag attitude was offered in the case of then Major General Samuel Anderson's actions while in command of the Carswell Air Force Base, home of the Eighth Air Force. Because General Anderson objected to the *Fort Worth Press's* treatment of a B-36 crash near Albuquerque, New Mexico, he ordered the *Press* reporters barred from the base and issued orders that the *Press* was to get no information from the base. No question of military security nor the publication of classified news was involved. The General's anger and action were based on what he termed "sensationalism." It took a flying trip from Washington by the Air Force public relations director to straighten out the General and to get the ban lifted. General Anderson had given the military another black eye with press and public alike.[18]

Here are some other examples. A few years ago an Assistant Secretary of Defense for Public Relations refused to release to the W.C.T.U. a list of military bases at which liquor was sold to servicemen. The Eleventh

---

[17] War Department General Orders No. 60, August 8, 1914.

[18] For this story see Delbert Willis, "The Press vs. The General," *Nieman Reports*, Vol. 5, July, 1951.

Naval District headquartered in San Diego once invoked, without warning or explanation, wartime censorship on news of Navy plane crashes and issued a "gag" to the Coast Guard in that district. This reversal of the Coast Guard's peacetime practice of promptly making public the nature of its search and rescue missions was cancelled by the Naval District commandant after strong protest from the press. In Oakland, California, an Army officer ordered M.P.'s to keep reporters and photographers away from the wedding of an Army captain and a Japanese girl. Reporters were threatened with guns, and one photographer was thrown into the guard house for an hour for trying to take a picture at the church.

Clashes between news photographers and military authorities at scenes of disaster on and off military reservations are all too frequent. Sometimes this represents an effort by military police and air police to prevent the photographing of secret equipment or to avoid identifying military victims through the press rather than through appropriate notification of next of kin by the service; sometimes the abrasive actions are less justified. In October, 1963, the Department of Defense, prodded by Congressman Moss' committee, made a new effort to modify military policies on this score. The new directive bars military and air police from using force against reporters or photographers at the scene of a plane crash or other accidents. The rule enforces a principle basic to a democratic society— that the military has no right to exercise authority over civilians in civilian areas. All services were advised to call on civilian law enforcement officers if and when necessary.[19]

Considerable progress has been made in recent years as the number of trained information officers increases. The military information programs are infinitely better than several decades ago. Graduate schooling for key officers and the Defense Information School (DINFOS) have been a major influence. Also contributing to the communications improvement is modern management of the armed forces, cognizant of the necessity for good public relations. Yet in the military, as in other institutions, not all top officers fully accept the management concept and its implementing staff. The crunch comes for some public relations officers in the unfavorable attitude of senior commanders and in the denial of promotion to those officers who make a career of public relations. Arthur Page's advice to "put a fair sample of its (the military) best regular officers in public relations jobs" and "recognize them for effective service in the capacity" is still not fully heeded.

If sympathetically administered, there can be no quarrel with the military policy that *"a minimum of information will be withheld from the*

[19] Department of Defense Directive No. 5410.14, October, 1963.

public consistent with security." But relations with the press often involve more subtle problems than direct clashes of opposing interests. A military officer making a scholarly study of the Pentagon press corps' performance found that the accuracy and completeness of reporting on defense matters are a function of the reporter's energy and trustworthiness, news deadlines, and the accessibility and responsiveness of official sources. If primary official sources are uncommunicative, the reporter relies on lesser sources, usually at a loss to the public, the Defense Department, and the press.[20]

Responding to sharp press criticism for the over-classification of a public relations plan to promote the military's anti-ballistic missile system, Secretary of Defense Laird, March 4, 1969, reaffirmed the "public's right to know" about all military matters consistent with maintenance of national security. Rightly so, because censorship is abhorrent to the American press and public alike. But both the press and the public recognize its necessity in time of war. No American ever wants, knowingly, to be the cause of death and destruction among his defenders. Even so, wartime censorship is a difficult task at best. Press censorship preserves the security of American and allied combat forces by *temporarily* delaying or withholding from public dissemination any information that might aid or comfort the enemy until such time as this information will be of no value to any enemy.

Military men need to accept fully the democratic principle of the public's right to know compatible with genuine security requirements. One editor, J. Russell Wiggins, says: "Wise censorship, by democratic definition, ought to be a censorship that yields the most security with the least interference with the news. The military cannot have all the security it wishes without denying to the people the information they must have to maintain their understanding of and support for an effective defense. The people cannot have all the information they would like to have without endangering security." [21] This adversary relationship is part of a larger conflict, "The Information War," used to describe "a much broader and more profound conflict, that between the democratic imperative of full public disclosure and those forces and tendencies which act to constrict, control, and manipulate the information the public gets." Dale Minor puts the major burden on the press, suggesting doubt as to the press' ability to meet the demands made upon it by contemporary society.[22] William Rivers agrees that the major burden rests with the press: "Without a challenging

---

20 Information based on then Colonel, now Lieut. Gen. George V. Underwood's thesis, "The Washington Military Correspondents," University of Wisconsin, 1960.

21 See "Wise Censorship Must Be a Compromise," *Quill*, Vol. 38, October, 1950.

22 Dale Minor, *The Information War* (New York: Hawthorn Books, 1970), p. vii. He terms military public relations apparatus "The Snow Machine."

journalism, officialdom is quite likely to win public sentiment for its own goals." [23] Nonetheless, the public official has the obligation to provide quickly, fully public information about public business.

Although the basic conflict between the interests of the press and what the military considers to be their own best interests can likely never be fully resolved, the military, like other organizations, have long recognized that to best serve the press, there must be a foundation of mutual understanding and trust. This comes about only when military commanders and information officers are aware of the place and purpose of the media in the American society; when information officers deal with the press on a friendly and candid basis; and when information forthcoming·from military sources establishes itself in the long run as reliable and factual.

CASE PROBLEM

You are the public information officer at Fort Jackson, South Carolina. On Sunday afternoon you are called by the bureau chief of the Augusta, Ga., *Chronicle-Herald* requesting information about a leaflet being distributed in downtown Columbia, S. C. You are told the leaflet invites persons who have doubts about the U. S. participation in the Vietnam War to attend a meditation and discussion of the war at Fort Jackson's chapel Number One at 7:30 p.m. Tuesday night. You have no information but promise to call back first thing Monday morning.

You check the next morning with your chaplain and find that the chapel has been reserved for an interfaith prayer meeting. You learn that the chaplain had no knowledge that this was to be a Vietnam "pray-in." Your investigation indicates that this request for the chapel had been part of a planned move to make the U. S. Army a part of the proposed discussion on the war. It indicates to you an attempt to embarrass the Army through the implication of official sanction. You and your commander see this as a "loaded gun" situation: If the Army allows the anti-war demonstrators use of the chapel, it will lend credence to their cause; if the Army denies the right of these individuals to worship and peacefully meditate, the public will criticize the Army and the Fort Jackson commander for having denied a basic freedom to a group of young people, some of them wearing the uniform of their country. In the meantime you stall the press with the statement "the matter is under consideration."

The Commanding General has called a staff conference Tuesday morning to hear your recommendation. What is it?

[23] In *The Adversaries*, previously cited, p. vii.

ADDITIONAL READING

MAJ. RICHARD F. ABEL, "Bad News—And How to Survive It," *Public Relations Journal*, Vol. 24, July, 1968. Two cribbing scandals at the Air Force Academy—one handled the wrong way, one the right way.

JEFFREY D. ALDERMAN, "The Army Way: News Management at Fort Hood," *Columbia Journalism Review*, Vol. 7, Winter, 1968/1969. An example of heavy-handed efforts to manage the news.

RICHARD J. BARNET, *The Economy of Death.* New York: Atheneum, 1969.

MALCOLM W. BROWNE, "Vietnam Reporting: Three Years of Crisis," *Columbia Journalism Review*, Vol. 3, Fall, 1964.

MARTHA DERTHICK, *The National Guard in Politics.* Cambridge, Mass.: Harvard University Press, 1965.

FREEDOM OF INFORMATION CENTER, "Freedom and the Military News Media, Report No. 222," Columbia, Mo.: University of Missouri School of Journalism, 1969. Detailed discussion of problems of insuring free flow of news to troops.

WILLIAM J. FULBRIGHT, *The Pentagon Propaganda Machine.* New York: Liveright, 1970. This book includes speeches from *The Congressional Record* cited in footnotes in this chapter.

WARD JUST, "Soldiers," *The Atlantic*, Vol. 226, Oct.–Nov., 1970. A critical look at the Army system.

DAVID R. INGLIS, "H-Bombs in the Back Yard," *Saturday Review*, Vol. 51, December 21, 1968. Tells angry reaction to efforts to locate ABM sites near large cities, illustrating delicacy and difficulty of military-community relations.

ROBERT LINDSAY, "Perspectives on Public Relations," *Marine Corps Gazette*, Vol. 40, January, 1956.

CLARK R. MOLLENHOFF, *The Pentagon: Politics, Profits, and Plunder.* New York: G. P. Putnam Sons, 1967.

CAPT. R. B. MORRISEY, "Pub Info—A Command Function," *Marine Corps Gazette*, Vol. 41, February, 1957.

BARNEY OLDFIELD, *Never a Shot in Anger.* New York: Duell, Sloan, and Pearce, 1956. (Reminiscences of an Air Force PIO who retired in 1963.)

U. S. House of Representatives, Subcommittee on Government Operations, Eighty-Eighth Congress, *Government Information Plans and Policies.* Part I—*News Media Panel Discussion;* Part II—*Office of Emergency Planning;* Part III—*Information Procedures in the Department of Defense;* Part IV—*Vietnam News Coverage* (Washington, D.C.: The Committee, U. S. Government Printing Office, 1963).

JULES WITCOVER, "Surliest Crew in Washington," *Columbia Journalisim Review*, Vol. 4, Spring, 1965. Study of Pentagon correspondents.

CHAPTER 27

THE PRACTICE: PUBLIC RELATIONS AROUND THE WORLD

A NEW FRONTIER BECKONS

Public relations around a fast-shrinking world is the bright new frontier
beckoning young people with ability and a sense of adventure. International
practice will accelerate to meet the needs born of a hotly competitive
world market and of a spirited economic and political struggle in a world
linked by rapid international telecommunication and transportation. In a
day of satellite-relayed worldwide radio and television, supersonic jet-
liners that make intercontinental trips a matter of a few hours and world
travel commonplace, international public relations is bound to grow at a
fast pace.

Advances in telecommunications and transportation have brought
people into the closest contact in the history of civilization. Never before
have ideas and information had such rapid and far-reaching impact. The
same ecological factors that compelled the development of public relations
in the United States are operating to bring it about on a global scale—
only more quickly. Public relations is being adapted to the needs of
business firms, nonprofit institutions, and nations of the world at a breath-
taking rate. Our business firms and the U.S.I.A. are leading the way in
spreading the practice to what once were far corners of the world.

In ever-growing numbers, U. S. companies are operating abroad
through subsidiaries, branches, distributors, and in partnership with local
and multi-national corporations. Business firms doing business across national boundaries and in different cultures find public relations more imperative abroad than at home. Corporations abroad have to buck the onus
of absentee ownership, avert the threat of expropriation, combat the
hatreds bred by political and business opponents, and deal with different
cultures. The dimensions of international practice and problems are seen
in the far-flung operations of International Telephone & Telegraph Corp.,
Royal Dutch Shell, Unilever, Phillips of the Netherlands, and Standard Oil
of New Jersey. Take I.T.T. for example: it is a diversified worldwide industrial concern with 200 affiliates in 67 countries and 236,000 employees.
It must transact its business in twelve languages and in widely varying cultures and economic climates. I.T.T. employs more than 100 professionals
to carry on this complex task.

International public relations emerged in the 1950s, primarily as a marketing tool in Europe and Latin America, and as a means of fending off expropriation in the developing nations. Most firms emphasized product publicity in these early years; the large extractive companies, understandably, were more concerned with public relations in the broad sense. A survey conducted by the Opinion Research Corporation in 1968 reflects the growth of international practice but indicates that the emphasis is still on product promotion. This survey of 110 major corporations, when compared to a 1964 survey conducted by the National Foreign Trade Council, showed: [1]

1. The number of companies engaging in international public relations activities has increased markedly in recent years. Thirty-two percent of the corporate programs were of five years or less longevity.
2. These companies are carrying out programs on every continent and in every major country.
3. The programs usually are handled by staff members based in the overseas countries.
4. Only one-third of the respondents use either a public relations firm or advertising agency to implement their overseas programs.
5. The principal activities are press releases, product publicity, and exhibits and special events.

Governments, too, employ countless practitioners to win world support for political objectives, to promote tourism, and to establish a nation's identity in the world community. Much of today's international newsflow is provided by governments and their public relations agencies. The short-lived Biafran Government's employment of Markpress, the Swiss-based public relations firm, to publicize its plight is an example. There were some 500 agents of foreign principals registered with the U. S. Department of Justice in the mid-60s. Most of these were public relations agents. Seventy-five percent represented foreign governments. World political struggles and worldwide television have intensified these programs to inform and influence peoples in other lands. The idea is not new—only the channels, the volume, and intensity of competition. Since ancient times, political leaders have supplemented diplomacy and force with communications to weaken an enemy's will, to gain allies or to bring about cooperation and trade. This international practice also is being extended by private organizations in addition to governments and corporations. Davison notes: [2] "Many of

---

[1] Hugh C. Hoffman and Robert C. Worcester, "The International Scene: A Review of Current Practices," *Public Relations Quarterly,* Vol. 13, Spring, 1968, p. 12.

[2] W. Phillips Davison, *International Political Communication* (New York: Praeger, 1965) Chapter 8, "The Structure of International Communication Programs."

these organizations are concerned with economic matters: promoting trade, investment, or tourism. Others are concerned with humanitarian, educational, or religious affairs. A substantial number have political aims."

Robert L. Bliss, an international leader, sees these as the reasons for the swift growth: [3] (1) governmental programs of new nations and nations establishing independent identities out of colonial status; (2) movement of industries overseas, either in joint venture establishment or in their own foreign-based production and sales expansion; (3) tourism; (4) changes in the government or political philosophy of nations, and movement from more traditional, isolated roles toward identification with activities in world interest; (5) broadened transportation programs by air, sea, and land from national to international patterns.

The 1960s saw a perceptible shift in emphasis from marketing to non-marketing problems in public relations practice abroad. Sylvan M. Barnet, Jr., long active in international practice, summarizes: [4]

1. A new emphasis on non-marketing problems
2. Marked impact from the world-wide consumerism movement
3. Development of new government-industry relationships
4. Development of financial public relations as it is known in the United States
5. Centralization in multi-national public relations practice
6. Movement to upgrade the public relations function within the corporate structure.

The non-marketing problems include: Making absentee ownership acceptable in a world of rising nationalism and in which "takeover" and "Americanization" arouse angry political passions; making the mammoth size of multi-national corporations acceptable to the public who fear bigness and cartels; the competition for local capital and labor; and the consumer protest movement circling the world. As a consequence, there is a definite, discernible increase in international practice.

John W. Hill, a pioneer in developing an international practice in the 1950s, has suggested that public relations grows best in a climate characterized by three dominant elements: [5] (1) A stable and democratic government; (2) a political and economic system that allows the develop-

---

[3] In "Public Relations Around the World," *Public Relations Quarterly,* Vol. 10, Winter, 1966, p. 54.

[4] In "New Era Opens for Public Relations Abroad," *Public Relations Journal,* Vol. 24, December, 1968.

[5] In *Handbook on International Public Relations,* Vol. 1 (New York: Praeger, 1967) in Introduction. This guide to public relations in Western Europe was written by staff of Hill & Knowlton.

ment of private enterprise and encourages competition in many fields of endeavor; (3) the existence of prosperous and thoroughly independent media, over which the government has a minimum of control.

World-wide programs require the employment of nationals in the countries where affiliates and subsidiaries are located. United States firms need and, in most cases, retain counsel in countries abroad. Each nation has its own culture, its particular pride and prejudices, its special way of doing things. To communicate effectively with audiences abroad, the communicator must know the culture, the language, and the value systems of the people who comprise the audiences.

Growth of international trade has induced a number of United States counseling agencies to extend their operations abroad. This is done by establishing either a branch office abroad or an affiliation with a local firm in one or more nations. Hill & Knowlton has extended its operations for three kinds of clients—United States firms doing business overseas, foreign companies competing in the United States market, and foreign governments. Bert Goss, H. & K.'s chairman, says, "The practice of public relations extends anywhere in the world where there are publics to inform —and clients who want to attract their attention." The other giant, Carl Byoir & Associates, does not use affiliate firms, although it once did. It has its own offices abroad because, as an executive expressed it, "Our kind of work can only be done by Byoir men. So in Paris—and Europe is one of the really big growth areas—we decided to follow our star, to be advocates." Infoplan, first wholly owned world-wide public relations organization, was established in 1962 by Interpublic, Inc. It has offices in the United States, Canada, United Kingdom, West Germany, France, Italy, Brazil, Mexico, and Japan. There are many patterns in this evolving worldwide operation of public relations agencies. European agencies also are building networks of affiliation. The main thrust in the Western World has been provided by the European Common Market.

THE COMMON MARKET

The European Common Market both demonstrates the value and provides a strong stimulus for extending the practice in member nations and beyond. Nearly 200 persons are employed in the information departments of the several agencies federated under the umbrella term *Common Market*. Embraced in this short-hand term are the European Coal and Steel Community, founded in 1952, the European Atomic Energy Community (Euratom), and the European Economic Community (Common Market). Each of the three communities, as well as the European Parliament, has its own small group of specialists. However, the three community executives have pooled their technical information services into one common service, which is divided into different divisions, each dealing with a medium or a public.

Most of these 200 information officers are stationed in Brussels and Luxemburg, where the Communities have their provisional seat, and occasionally in Strasbourg, where the European Parliament meets in plenary session. In the four capitals of the other member nations—Bonn, The Hague, Paris, and Rome—the Executives have small information offices. Information offices are also maintained in London, Washington, and Geneva. As one information officer observes: "The Community has not generally planned public relations policy, and the actual attitude towards information is either dictated by events or arrived at pragmatically on a non-policy level." [6]

Growth and professionalization has been stimulated by three confederations of practitioners, which serve three major regions of the world —the Centre for European Public Relations serving Western Europe, the Inter-American Public Relations Federation for Latin America, and the Pan Pacific Federation which serves practitioners from Hawaii westward through Pakistan.

GREAT BRITAIN

Public relations practice in Canada and Great Britain is quite comparable to that of the United States in terms of skill, management acceptance, and stage of maturity. Public relations developments in these sister Anglo-Saxon nations have proceeded in parallel courses. The free flow of commerce, executive personnel, and students between the United States and Canada have served to develop this specialty along identical lines in these two nations. In comparing British practice with that of the United States, London's *Financial Times* asserts that "by contrast, the position of public relations is a good deal less secure, and the industry is certainly one of those about which very little is known or understood." In the British Government the function is fully accepted. As of 1970, the British Government employed 1,250 information officers with civil service status. PRO—Public Relations Officer and C.I.O.—Chief Information Officer are common titles in the British government.

Advance of mature public relations has been spearheaded by the Government and by the British Institute of Public Relations, organized in 1948—the same year that PRSA was founded. For its first two decades this Institute required applicants to pass two examinations before gaining

[6] Much of this information comes from a special report prepared by a former student, Miss Clara C. Meyers, a member of the Spokesman Group staff. Opinions expressed are ours.

full membership. This requirement will be phased out in 1971. To be admitted to full membership in BIPR, one must be 28 years of age or older and have had five years' experience; if he has less than five years' experience, the applicant must have also earned the Institute's Diploma of Public Relations in its public relations course. The course is conducted in cooperation with Regent Street Polytechnic. British public relations practice suffers from the lack of university instruction and research. England's traditionally conservative universities do not offer courses in journalism or public relations. As of January, 1970, the British Institute had 2,540 members, of which 1,396 were active members and 326 associate members. There are more than 600 public relations agencies in Britain.

The British association enforces its Code of Ethics. In 1966 it suspended two members because they used a supposedly impartial "front" organization to spread propaganda on behalf of a client. In 1969 the Institute suspended another member for "violating the institute's standards and for bringing the institute and public relations practice into disrepute." The member, who subsequently resigned, was accused of representing to a client—the Greek Government's military junta—that he had a member of Parliament on his payroll as a lobbyist when in fact the MP did no lobbying for the Greek Government. The MP's acceptance of a retainer led to an inquiry by the House of Commons. This committee issued its report December 4, 1969, *Report from the Select Committee of Members' Interests* (Declaration), and declined to recommend to Parliament the registration of practitioners as is required of conventional lobbyists.

Use in British government dates from 1912, paralleling its growth in our federal government. In 1912, after passage of the National Insurance Act, Lloyd George organized a corps of lecturers to explain the new legislation to employers and workers in all parts of the country. The outbreak of war with Germany in 1914 led to a rapid expansion of official information work in Britain and overseas. After 1918, its war-born organizations were abolished, but some of their functions were transferred to other departments—mainly to the Foreign Office. The Air Ministry has had a Press Officer from its inception in 1919, and in the same year the Ministry of Health set up an Information Department. An important stage in British government's public relations development was creating the Empire Marketing Board in 1926 to promote agricultural production and marketing throughout the Commonwealth. This work was directed by the late Sir Stephen Tallents, one of the field's pioneers. He often told his countrymen: "No civilized country can today afford either to neglect the projection of its national personality or to resign its projection to others." [7] He also

---

[7] In *The Projection of England* (London: Published by Olen Press for Film Centre, Ltd., 1955), p. 11.

argued, "Publicity should be recognized as a professional job demanding special training and special capacities." In 1933, Sir Stephen organized the first full-scale government public relations division in the Government Post Office. In 1939, embattled Britain organized the wartime Ministry of Information to carry out the twin functions of "exhortation" and "information." At its peak, the Ministry of Information had a staff of 2,950.[8] At the war's end, the services of the Ministry were reorganized into the Central Office of Information to serve governmental agencies at home and abroad.

Reflecting British political traditions, the function is highly centralized in Britain's government. At the apex of the structure is the Central Office of Information, created April 1, 1946, in a postwar reorganization of public relations. The COI provides the PRO's of the various ministries with all the production, technical, and distribution facilities they need. It has no officers of its own overseas, but supplies material to Information Officers stationed abroad by the Foreign and Commonwealth Office. The British Information Services overseas are made up of three organizations: (1) the Information Services of the Overseas Department; (2) the British Council; and (3) the External Services of the British Broadcasting Corporation.[9] In contrast with former years, the bulk of Britain's overseas information work is devoted to trade and tourist promotion. The three arms of overseas information are loosely coordinated by the Foreign Office, although BBC and British Council operate somewhat independently. A major redirection of the British overseas effort was suggested in 1969 by a Review Committee on Overseas Representation. It recommended: [10] "The future task . . . should be to project Britain as a trading nation with a great culture and democratic traditions, rather than as a world power of the first order."

Broadly speaking, the function is not so mature and secure in British commerce and industry as in government. Still, an Institute official holds, with validity, "it is safe to say that public relations is now recognized as being an important function of management in this country." Such corporate firms as Vickers, British Oxygen, Shell, Unilever, and Wedgewood practice public relations of a high order. The management of Vickers has recognized that: "With the growing tendency towards state intervention in industrial affairs and the increasing complexity of government relations with private industry, it has become more than ever important to provide a "Voice" with which Vickers can speak."

[8] Marjorie Ogilvy-Webb, The Government Explains (London: George Allen and Unwin, Ltd., 1965), p. 58. This Report of the Royal Institute of Public Administration provides essential information on the practice in government.

[9] C.O.I. An Outline of the Functions and Organizations of the Central Office of Information (London: The COI, London SE 1), p. 305.

[10] Report of the Review Committee on Overseas Representation 1968–1969 (London: Her Majesty's Stationery Office, 1969), p. 98.

Yet much of the emphasis in commerce is on publicity getting, because in the view of the *Financial Times,* "too many firms try to measure it (PR) by counting the Press cuttings that result from the P.R. programmes, and putting pressure on the P.R.O. when competitors' names appear in the Press." But the direction is toward maturity. Increasingly, British businessmen recognize its importance. The turn-around of the staid Stock Exchange is typical.[11] American firms operating in England are exerting a strong influence on this trend but the intense competition of Common Market firms in markets long dominated by the British is providing the big push toward adopting the full-range of services.

WEST GERMANY

Public Relations, both as a management concept and as a specialized skill, was virtually unknown in West Germany some 20 years ago. Today there is wide appreciation of its importance in industry and government. The rapid growth of public relations in West Germany reflects a booming industrial economy and adoption of democratic government. There was no satisfactory equivalent in the German language, so the English term *public relations* has been incorporated into the German language. (This is also true of the Scandinavian languages.) Much of the impetus for public relation's growth is born of the need for aggressive marketing programs to sell the consumer goods pouring out of Germany's productive industrial plants in affluent Germany. The shift from the indifference to public opinion that marked the cartel-minded businessman to today's hard-sell marketing tactics is reflected in the spectacular growth of advertising. Advertising has passed the billion-dollar-a-year level in West Germany—a 300 percent increase in one decade. Public relations has had a comparable, if not so spectacular, growth. The new emphasis has brought several United States advertising and public relations agencies to West Germany.

At the end of the 1960s, it was estimated that there were 1,000 public relations counselors in the Federal Republic of Germany. That same year the German Public Relations Society (Deutsche Public Relations-Gesellschaft) had 175 members. Admission requires several years' experience at the management level and that "the principles established by it for the profession are observed." The president of the Federal Republic, the Federal Diet, the Federal Government, almost all Federal ministries, all Land governments, a number of Land ministries, several cities, and the government broadcasting corporation employ a large number of public

<hr>

[11] See John Brooks, "Thaw on Threadneedle Street," *The New Yorker,* Vol. 36, December 31, 1960, pp. 31–39, for full story.

officers. In Germany, as elsewhere, "unfortunately, there are many people who abuse the term 'public relations' to take advantage of the rapid development of this field in Germany." [12]

Typical of the origin and growth of the function in German industry is the department in the giant Bayer-Hoechst firm, which is best described as the duPont of Germany. This chemical giant markets more than 13,000 products around the world. Bayer's public relations department was set up in 1951 on the eve of the company's establishment as an independent firm in the decartelization of I. G. Farben. The staff includes a large number of specialists in a "Department of Social Sciences," which is divided into these sections: Stockholder Information, Commercial Policy, Marketing, Motivation Research and Statistics, Community Relations, and Press Relations. The department gives only technical advice to the employee relations department on employee communications.

The German government employs a large staff to win approval of its policies at home and abroad. This effort is directed by the German Press and Information Agency, headed by a civil servant who has the title, "State Secretary." [13] This agency also directs an extensive overseas information program through its Deutsche Welle radio broadcasts and the corps of able press officers in its consulates and embassies around the world, in many ways emulating the U.S. approach.

In Germany, staff practitioners are much concerned about participation in management's decision making in industry and government. A German practitioner observes: "Those in West Germany who edit house organs, analyze the world's economic and political news for an industrial boss or the governor of a state, work to improve management relations, or prepare an industrial film . . . are nearly all known to be 'specialists' of great skill. But there are few men in public relations who actually help to shape the vital decisions of large corporation. . . ." [14]

A gain came in 1961, when the University of Heidelberg introduced the first course at the university level. Several years prior to this, the Aachen Institute of Technology had been offering a course. A few other non-university institutes teach the subject. The craft was strengthened with the publication of Dr. Albert Oeckl's *Handbuch der Public Relations* in 1964.[15]

---

[12] Dr. Albert Oeckl, "Too Much or Too Little Public Relations Work?", *Frankfurter Allegmeine Zeitung*, December 27, 1962.

[13] Gerry Van der Heuvel, "Free World's Image Makers: They Report & They Censor," *Editor & Publisher*, Vol. 95, November 24, 1962, pp. 11 and 58.

[14] Hanns Dietrich Ahrens, "Western Germany—Public Relations in the Making," PR, Vol. 4, October, 1959.

[15] Published by Suddeutscher Verlag, Munich, Germany. This 400-page book, though it leans heavily on U. S. literature, gives wide view of the practice in West Germany.

FRANCE

Public relations in France is developing at a slower pace than in other Western European countries. Practitioners must fight their way uphill against strong cultural, business, and journalistic traditions. Historically, the French climate has been hostile to both the concept and practice. Barriers to the advance of French public relations include: (1) the Frenchman's traditional caution in the face of innovation; (2) the traditional "it's none of the public's business" attitude of French industrialists; (3) the historic interlocking structure of French newspaper publishing and French advertising space sales; (4) strong opposition from the French advertising agencies; (5) the traditional aloofness of the government in its dealings with the press.

In the early 1950s, as the reconstruction period came to a close, several major industrial firms established departments. As is often the case, the international oil companies led the way. In 1952, ten pioneer practitioners from these firms organized a club, "La Maison de Verre,"—The Glass House—under the leadership of Etienne Bloch. They took their cue, as Frenchmen might, from the words of a French philosopher, Auguste Comte, who wrote, more than a hundred years ago: *"A business enterprise must be open, like a glass house, for all to see. It is the duty of businessmen, who are entrusted with a legitimate power, to enlighten public opinion on their activities and trends."* Not all French businessmen yet accept this view.

Recalling the origins of this club, Claude Chapeau has written: "This first appearance was made 'on tiptoe.' " As the number of practitioners increased, the club was reorganized as the French Public Relations Association. This Association Française des Relations Publiques has established a code of ethics and sponsors a two-year course in the College Libre des Sciences Sociales in Paris. In addition there is a union which functions as a professional corporate group to advance the interests of the small number of French public relations agencies. Public relations instruction was introduced in France in the early 1950s; the first full-scale program was that of the *Institut des Relations Publiques-Cadres Superieurs,* a four year private school operated by M. Francis Dumont, resistance journalist and one of France's leading practitioners. A course was added to the Sorbonne curriculum in 1969. In two decades, a cadre of dedicated practitioners, knowledgeable in the ways of public relations, have set up a few first-rate departments in industrial and service companies and in certain of the government-subsidized establishments. Air France is a notable example.

Yet it was not until 1969 that public relations played a major role in the French corporate sector. That year, in an unprecedented public battle between two giant glass-making companies, public relations was used intensively by both sides. The protagonists were Boussois-Souchon-Neuvesel, number two in the industry, and Saint-Gobain, a towering giant and a tautly conservative firm dating from the seventeenth century. BSN's basic purpose was to buy enough Saint-Gobain shares to force a merger, a move that startled the conservative French business world. BSN set out to woo Saint-Gobain stockholders by U. S. methods—paid advertising, news conferences, booklets. With French newspapers and news magazines blaring fresh headlines, editorials, and cartoons, Saint-Gobain took the giant step of acknowledging public relations' necessity, and this hitherto aloof firm set about vigorously to win public support. *L'Express* observed: "For the first time in French history a financial affair that is not a scandal has become a national event." This spirited public relations battle did much to make the practice known, and its acceptance by Saint-Gobain impressed other executives. The result is roughly analogous to the hiring of Ivy Lee by John D. Rockefeller, Jr. in 1914, and to the public battle in Great Britain in 1961 when Courtaulds turned to public relations to prevent a takeover by ICI.[16]

The French government took official cognizance of the emerging practice in June, 1955, when the Minister of Commerce recommended creation of public relations offices within the organization of the chambers of commerce, which in France are public bodies. In 1957, the Deputy Minister for Civil Service and Administrative Reform issued a memorandum creating civic service positions for "offices of orientation, reception and information." It read, in part: [the creation] "of such offices comes within the framework of a better organization of public relations, the importance of which asserts itself more and more in all productivity research." In 1960, the French minister of Posts, Tele-Communication (PNT), issued an administrative edict to all regional directors of the department, instructing them to appoint part-time public relations men from their local staffs. This large department, which provides the postal and communication services for France, has some 130 men working in public relations, the largest PR staff in France. The basic government attitude in dealing with the press is still generally one of aloofness, though this, too, began to change in the early post-DeGaulle years.

---

[16] This landmark case study in British practice is told in *The Persuasion Industry*, by John Pearson and Graham Turner (London: 1965). See Chapter 18, "PR at Takeover Time."

ITALY

As in many other Western European nations, public relations was little known in Italy at the end of World War II. The birth of democratic government and the rise of a booming industrial economy in northern Italy have provided the impetus for public relation's growth. An increasing number of Italian manufacturers and businessmen realize that public relations is an indispensable means for creating favorable relations with employees, customers, and the public. Similarly, the Italian government is using public relations in winning support for its leaders and their policies. The government is the main employer. Reflecting the north-south cleavage in Italy, there were two associations, one headquartered in Rome, one in Milan. The former, Associazione Italiana Per Le Relazioni Pubbliche, is the second largest in Europe. In 1970, after lengthy discussions, they were incorporated into one federation. The original groups promoted public relations education in institutes. The first university-level course was taught at the University of Torino in 1961. Several now offer courses. A monthly review, *Relazioni Pubbliche,* has promoted understanding of the fundamentals of sound practice. Basic to the literature in Italy is *Le Relazioni Pubbliche,* a comprehensive guide to public relations published in 1968.[17]

Public relations in Italy still lacks acceptance by the media. Two practitioners write: "Mass media are usually suspicious of public relations which they consider disguised advertising or at least a nuisance. Daily papers are often not receptive . . . because of the hostility of publishers. Announcements concerning business reports, appointments, new products, plant openings and the like are, in most cases, carried as paid advertising. The weekly press is somewhat more receptive. The state-owned television network carries news only from state-owned enterprises."[18]

Italian industrialists, once remote and aloof from the public, increasingly take the public into account in their employee, community, and marketing policies. In something of an understatement, the president of Shell Italiana says: "All of us will agree that public relations originates in, and draws its justification from, the profound evolution that we have seen pervade the structure of our society in the last few years." Here, too, the international oil companies have set the pace.

---

[17] This comprehensive guide to public relations practice in Italy was written by Guiseppe A. Roggero with the collaboration of Paolo Baldi and Vittorio Lisanti, and published by Frano Angeli Editore, Milano, in 1968.

[18] G. C. Bertelli and G. Botta, "Italy," in *Handbook on International Public Relations,* Vol. 1, p. 42.

SCANDINAVIA

Indicative of the rapid growth in Scandanavia are the listings in telephone directories. In 1960, the Stockholm directory listed nine consultants under "Public Relations"; by the end of the decade it listed nearly 100. It was not until the mid-1930s that the term began to appear in the trade press, although the Swedish Navy, for example, ran a full-fledged Publicity Department as far back as 1926. The function in the contemporary sense did not emerge until after World War II. In those years, Scandinavian economists and marketing men were influenced by American and other international companies and by studies in schools such as Harvard and Columbia. In 1947, a national society was formed in Finland under the name *Tiedotusmiehet* (The Communicators), consisting of the information specialists who had worked for the Finnish government during and after the war with Russia. Norway and Sweden followed suit only a few years later, but Denmark did not form its national body until 1961.

The Swedish association well exemplifies the significance and diffusion that the function enjoys in Scandinavia. It has nearly 400 members from virtually all career sectors: local authorities, central government, nonprofit organizations, political federations and private enterprise. In recent years the Scandinavian associations have striven to give their craft a professional image. They have drafted new by-laws, imposed stricter criteria for membership, and formulated a code of ethics for the practices. Some associations have set up disciplinary committees to monitor observance of regulations. The concept has been defined in more concrete terms, and efforts have been made to specify the varying duties that may go into the work of the practitioners. Further, the associations have afforded more and better opportunities for internal and external training, encouraged the production of better films and greater disclosure in annual reports, and promoted greater understanding of public relations as a vital function in society.

Another indication of progress can be seen in the public sector, where various administrative agencies have vigorously embarked on influential programs in the past few years. In Norway, for example, the civil service operates a special information center manned by a staff of experts. An official government report was published in Sweden at the end of 1969, which reflected the mature concept, including utilization of mass communications research. A book, *Public Relations—The Company's New Function,* by Nils Tengberg, was published in 1960. Several books reflecting the advance in mass communications have been published since.

Norway has an active professional association, Den Norske Public Relations Klubb with 150 members, and several strong counseling firms. Its major industries utilize public relations in management and marketing. Increasingly, Norway's transportation, shipping, porcelain, and paper industries are employing specialists in their employee and marketing programs. An educational advance was marked when the University of Oslo's faculty of political science introduced a course in public relations. The Norwegian association, founded in October, 1949, has long sponsored seminars and courses in technical institutes.

ELSEWHERE IN EUROPE

In Belgium before 1952, the idea was generally unknown. Late that year a small number of practitioners formed the Centre Belgique des Relations Publiques, and by 1958 they were strong enough to sponsor the first World Congress of Public Relations. Location of the Common Market headquarters in Brussels has given strong impetus to the practice in that nation. Even so, in the opinion of one practitioner: ". . . public relations in Belgium is, with the exception of a few important companies, *not* conceived as a permanent management function . . . the public relations officer is never a member of top management and his role is usually confined to dissemination of information." [19] Belgium has no ministry of information, largely as the result of strong press opposition. Yet the major government departments have press or information officers.

The Holland association, Nederlands Genootschap Voor Public Relations, was organized in 1954 and now has more than 160 members. In cooperation with the Belgian Center, it sponsors a bimonthly journal, published in the Dutch, French, and Flemish languages. Reflecting its lively international commerce, Switzerland has an active association with nearly 300 members. Fewer than 100 of these are full-time practitioners. It publishes *PR Revue* in the three national languages, and another periodical, *Public Relations Practice,* written in English for international circulation. Several Swiss institutes and the University of St. Gall offer courses in public relations. Here, as in most of Europe, practitioners have difficulty in getting journalists to see publicity as news rather than advertising to be paid for at space rates. In Switzerland, there are few public relations agencies. Most business firms use internal staffs. The number of firms is growing, but "in

---

[19] Committee of Free Enterprise, *Public Relations in Belgium* (Brussels: The Committee, 1954). Also see Pierre Jamasen, "Public Relations in Belgium," *Public Relations Journal,* Vol. 14, May, 1958.

95 percent of the cases they handle publicity or do public relations work only as a sideline to advertising." [20]

Held back by Spain's totalitarian regime and backward economy, public relations has had comparatively little development. Nonetheless, firms have been established and awareness is spreading among Spain's businessmen and government officials. There are two large, well-organized agencies, one in Barcelona and one in Madrid, and some 30 individual counselors in Spain. The Associación Técnica Española de Relaciones Públicas has 200 members but still has to develop vitality and direction. The news media view practitioners with reserve and suspicion. Spain is utilizing public relations to promote its rising tourist trade. This textbook, published in Spanish in 1961 and in 1968, has had a wide sale in Spain and Latin America. In 1969, the Spanish Government officially recognized the Escuela Superior de Relaciones Publicas as part of the University of Barcelona.

ELSEWHERE IN THE WORLD

The Pan Pacific Public Relations Federation was formed in 1967, but its roots go back to 1958 when a loosely organized association of consultants was formed to serve those in the Pacific and Near East. In 1960, a biennial meeting was held in Hong Kong, followed by one in Tokyo in 1962 where it was voted to open membership to all practitioners in the vast area. In 1967, members of the then Pan Pacific Public Relations Association approved conversion to the federation. Within seven months, all national practitioner groups had joined: Public Relations Institutes of Australia; Chinese National Association of Public Relations (Republic of China and Taiwan); Public Relations Society of India; Public Relations Society of Japan; Public Relations Institute of New Zealand, Inc.; and Public Relations Society of the Philippines.

In addition, professional members from Australia, Hawaii, Hong Kong, Indonesia, Korea, Japan, New Zealand, Philippines, Republic of China, Singapore and Thailand belong.

INDIA

Public relations in India is emerging from the fluid state of self-definition. Understanding and application as a tool of management is manifesting it-

[20] Charles R. Metzler, "Public Relations in Switzerland," *Public Relations Journal*, Vol. 14, January, 1958.

self in diverse ways in a government confronted by momentous problems in communication and in corporations in an emerging industrial economy. In corporate public relations, press and government relations get the prime emphasis, although employee and stockholder communication programs are beginning to get attention and acquire some maturity. More industrial and business leaders are coming to accept the thought that public relations is not the black art of hoodwinking the public nor a panacea for India's social ills. Though many firms continue to employ the function to put out brush fires along the path of corporate expansion, encouragingly, the more enlightened firms, have embraced the realization that public relations is vital to and an integral part of their managerial stature and success. Market and public opinion research is coming into general use. The Institute of Public Opinion, a Gallup subsidiary, and other research firms are finding an increasing demand for their services, although Indian practice lags in this aspect.

The Government finds the function useful in its efforts to stem the rising tide of births, to combat illiteracy, to promote agricultural production, and to bring unity to a large and diverse sub-continent. Government information is directed from the Ministry of Information and Broadcasting and relies on a staff of 40 information officers in the central government and information officers in the 350 districts of the nation. The state government information efforts vary greatly in numbers employed and in the expertise used. The government's program suffers from lack of sufficient number of professionally qualified practitioners.[21] This deficiency is being met in some degree by the government's Indian Institute of Mass Communications which offers short courses for government officers and undertakes research on its communications problems.

The state enterprises, or "public sector undertakings" as they are commonly called, fully recognize the function's necessity. Such enterprises as Air India, Indian Airlines, and the Life Insurance Corporation have developed programs of strength and sophistication. Strong programs in the growing "public sector" of India's mixed economy have spurred a competing growth in private sector enterprises. There is increasing recognition both within and without government of the need for administrators to effectively communicate with the people and the desirability of matching deeds with words. Development of competing political parties in this decade has given new impetus.

One consequence of these trends has been increased business for consultancy firms, advertising agencies providing publicity services, and an increase in the number of practitioners. The demand for agency service is primarily for publicity. The Public Relations Society of India, head-

[21] Scott M. Cutlip interview with Minister I. K. Gujral, New Delhi, December 23, 1969.

quartered in Bombay, has a growing membership of practitioners, students, and institutions. At the start of this decade it had chapters in Bombay, Calcutta, Madras, and New Delhi, and 250 members. It organized its first All-India convention in New Delhi in 1968 and sponsored its first week-long seminar late in 1969.

India's first university-level course in public relations was taught in the University of Calcutta School of Journalism in 1959. Public relations and communications generally were given strength by the organization of the Indian Institute of Mass Communications in New Delhi in 1966. Short courses also have been organized by the Institutes of Management Studies.

JAPAN

The public relations profession in Japan has paralleled the country's rapid industrial and economic growth beginning in 1950. Before World War II there was no identifiable public relations vocation, although there were many public relations type activities carried out by individuals and groups. Public relations activities by individual firms were handled internally or through various advertising companies.

Public relations emerged several years after World War II. As of 1969 there were close to one hundred public relations counselors in Japan offering their services, mostly in the large cities of Tokyo, Osaka and Nagoya. Japan's industrial prosperity, the growing influence of public opinion, the extensive communication facilities and the high degree of literacy provide fertile soil for the function's growth in this industrial nation of more than 100-million people. In the relatively short time that public relations has existed in Japan, it has made remarkable progress. Capabilities and facilities have expanded swiftly, and the prospects are promising.

The function is being widely utilized to accelerate production and sales. Because of Japan's growth as a market for American goods, more and more American firms are employing the services of Japanese counselors. Likewise, a few United States public relations agencies are establishing offices or affiliates in Japan. The continued expansion of U. S.-Japan trade will serve to spur this development. Advertising is experiencing a similar boom in Japan. The Dentsu Advertising Agency now ranks as the fourth largest agency in the world. In 1961, Dentsu organized a subsidiary firm, Dentsu PR Center Ltd., which by 1968 had 80 clients and 200 employees. A somewhat unique worldwide counseling organization, the International Public Relations Group, a partnership of nearly fifty independent firms, had its genesis in Tokyo in 1959 with the organization of International Public Relations Co., Ltd. Within a few years, its billings totaled more than $2-million. Japan's major industrial firms prefer to contract for worldwide public relations services through Japanese agencies. This led the IPRC to develop arrangements with other firms around the world and ultimately resulted in organization of the international firm as a Delaware corporation in May, 1968, owned by nearly fifty agencies. Its officers hold that this partnership arrangement "appears to overcome many shortcomings of a single corporation attempting to provide worldwide services." The joint ownership assures personal and financial interest in the operation, and a central executive office in Tokyo assures administrative control. In 1969, the IPR Group of Companies claimed to rank first among all international firms. The firm has a Tokyo staff of approximately 150.

Most industrial firms have set up public relations departments, although experts note that public relations in Japan lags far behind that in the United States in reaching the executive level. In fact, many companies have two departments: one to handle corporate affairs and project the corporate image, and another to promote sales of goods through publicity. The latter is the responsibility of the advertising and public relations departments. Basically, Japanese industry is still in "the advertising stage." In Japan there is a sharp cleavage between public relations and advertising as in the United States. For the most part, advertising and public relations counseling are not offered by the same agency although there are a few exceptions.

Growth of an articulate democratic spirit in Japan has compelled industrial firms to pay more attention to public opinion than they once did. For example, an Osaka electric company was forced to apologize publicly for contaminating a river. Industrial firms also have been required to pay costly damages to victims poisoned by stream pollution. The increased power of public opinion again reflected in Japan's Fair Trade Commission, which controls mergers and oversees business practices. However, promotion of the sale of goods is still the primary objective in most industrial programs. Max Factor cosmetics showed the way with product promotion when it launched its Japanese operation in 1948. Osaka's Expo 70 gave fresh impetus to the practice in Japan.

Japan's government utilizes public relations, a reflection of its new democracy. Prior to and during World War II, the government had only a propaganda program, aimed primarily at peoples abroad. The concept and the practice were implanted by the American occupation forces after the war's end. The transition came in May, 1949, when a conference was held for the public relations section chiefs of the ministries under the auspices of the Prime Minister's Office. By the end of the 1960s, the public relations "room" of the Prime Minister's secretariat employed a staff of fifty, headed by a civil servant. Postwar Japan's government fully accepts the principle that people have a right to know public business and that the government must make its policies known. The Secretary of the Cabinet provides policy guidance. Japan's government makes effective use of the public opinion surveys conducted by the Public Relations room of the Prime Minister. These surveys are of three categories: (1) administrative policies survey; (2) public opinion trend surveys; (3) current problems surveys.[22]

SOUTH PACIFIC

Public relations has developed extensively in the Western-oriented nations of Australia and New Zealand, although not on the scale it has in Japan. The Public Relations Institute of Australia had a membership of 500 in 1969, and its president estimated that there were an additional 200 practitioners in the country. The Sydney telephone directory listed just two counseling firms in 1950, ninety in 1969. The Institute runs educational courses at the state level, holds national conventions and publishes *Public Relations Australia* bi-monthly. Universities offer no courses in public relations, although business administration may be taken as a post-graduate course in a few of the larger ones. In Sydney and Melbourne, the two largest cities, part-time diploma courses embracing management and public relations are available at the leading institute of technology.

The PRIA president says, "Roughly one-quarter of the counseling firms and of the internal practitioners in government departments, industrial and commercial associations and major companies are professionals, operating competently by American or European standards in all spheres of public relations. The rest engage mainly in press-agentry, the quality of which varies from excellent to appalling."

In New Zealand, there are now 180 members in the Public Relations Institute of New Zealand, founded in 1953. Public relations has received considerable recognition there in recent years, and most large firms and organizations either employ consultants or have their own departments. There are some fourteen consulting firms mostly operating in the main cities. The Public Relations Institute of New Zealand publishes its own monthly newsletter and holds seminars and arranges public relations courses at educational centers.

Elsewhere in the Pacific: Development of public relations in the Philippines has been slow but was beginning to gain headway at the start of the 1970s. President Ferdinand Marcos's skillful use of public relations has given it impetus in recent years. The practice still suffers from a rather cynical attitude on the part of top government and business leaders. Many

---

[22] Scott M. Cutlip interview with Yoshiharu Matsumoto, Public Relations Officer of the Prime Minister's Office, Tokyo, Japan, in September, 1968.

advertising agencies give free public relations service to attract advertising clients. A few have set up subsidiaries. In Singapore, at least a dozen agencies operate, including offices of two international counseling groups. In Bangkok, there are six firms and some twenty practitioners in addition to those employed in the government. In Hong Kong, there is considerable activity within corporations. There are more than 300 practitioners in Taiwan, where the Chinese Public Relations Association is active in promoting acceptance of the function and in sponsoring courses.

LATIN AMERICA

Generally speaking, public relations is in its embryonic stage in Latin America, but a period of growth appears in the offing. Several active professional associations, introduction of courses in many universities, and the public relations programs of international companies are contributing to awareness of the function's importance. Taking the lead in promoting recognition of this field is the Inter-American Federation of Public Relations Associations, which sponsors annually an Inter-American Conference on Public Relations. This conference, which first met in Mexico City in 1960, provides a forum for the exchange of ideas among Latin American specialists. There are several national associations federated with this overall body. Development of specialized courses at the university level has been encouraged by the International Center for Journalism Education for Latin America (CIESPAL) in Quito, Ecuador. Each year CIESPAL gives a seminar for some forty journalists and teachers.

The main thrust in building awareness in these countries comes from Latin contacts with United States business firms and with various United States agencies in promoting economic development. Public relations has had its strongest growth in Mexico, reflecting that nation's advanced stage of industrialization in comparison with other Hispanic nations. The Mexican association (Asociasión Mexicana de Profesionales en Relaciones Publicas), organized in 1952, has carried on a vigorous program, largely under the direction of Federico Sanchez Fogarty, an international figure in this field. Mexican public relations had its beginnings in the mid-1930s with the advent of commercial air transportation. Wilbur L. Morrison of Pan American Airways is credited with pioneering public relations in Mexico. The first agency was opened in 1944 by Señor Sanchez Fogarty.

Characteristic of the early stages, there is considerable confusion between publicity and public relations and between advertising and public relations in the minds of Latin business and government leaders. To make matters worse, in Spanish *publicidad* means "advertising"; Spanish for "publicity" is *información;* "public relations" is *relaciones públicas.* Howard

Stephenson found, that "there is widespread misconception in Peru as to just what public relations is all about." In Hispanic America, public relations must earn its place, working uphill against a lack of tradition of social responsibility by those in power, an underdeveloped economy, lack of a strong middle class, and widespread illiteracy. The possibilities are there; the faint beginnings can be seen.

John M. Reed, long familiar with the practice in Latin America, summarizes: [23] "Despite the shortcomings evident . . . in Latin America, it is clear that the profession is making gradual progress. National public relations associations exist in most of the countries. . . . Much of the impetus for this development has come from American firms with international operations. . . . As geographic and demographic patterns would indicate, the public relations profession is most highly developed in Mexico, Brazil, and Argentina, probably in that order." Brazil is one of two nations in the world to legally define and thus endeavor to regulate the practice. Generally speaking, Latin American practice continues to suffer from newspapermen's moonlighting as press agents and from professors and lawyers, who lack technical proficiency, working as counselors.

INTERNATIONAL ASSOCIATION ORGANIZED

A developing *esprit* and an exchange of information among the world's practitioners have been furthered by organization of the International Public Relations Association. This Association had its origins in 1949, when a group of Netherlands industries invited some twenty public relations men from Western Europe and the United States to Holland to discuss informally their mutual interests.

Out of three days of spirited shop talk came a provisional committee to study the feasibility of an international association. This committee was organized in 1950 with Odd Medbøe of Norway as chairman and Tim Traverse-Healy of England as secretary. The organizing group found widespread support for the proposed association, but getting international agreement took time. IPRA was finally organized at a meeting in London in 1955, with Tom Fife Clark of Great Britain as its first president.

IPRA's early years were spent in selecting a limited number of members from the various countries and in organizing its committees. This is an association of individual members, not a superstructure over the national public relations associations which now circle the world. In 1961, meeting at the II World Congress of Public Relations, IPRA adopted a Code of

[23] In "Latin America: A Status Report," *Public Relations Quarterly*, Vol. 13, Spring, 1968, pp. 31–33.

Conduct to set the standards for public relations at the international level. This code was written out of nearly five years' conferences and correspondence in IPRA. The association meets annually. At the start of 1970, IPRA had 362 members, nearly a third of them from the United States. Forty-three nations were represented.

The international association provided the impetus for organizing the World Congress of Public Relations, which has stimulated and facilitated exchange of ideas and provided a meeting place for practitioners from all countries. The first Congress, held in Brussels in 1958, attracted 237 delegates from 23 countries, including Russia. The second Congress was held in Venice, Italy, in 1961 and had 700 delegates from 41 nations participating in its deliberations. Russia did not send delegates to Venice. The third World Congress was held in Montreal, Canada, in 1964; the fourth in Rio de Janeiro, Brazil, in October, 1967; the fifth in Israel in June, 1970. The friendships, shop talk and printed proceedings of these world-wide conclaves have done much to spread the practice and promote a sense of professionalism around the world.

CASE PROBLEM

You are a citizen of the United States and have been in the public relations department of Moon Motors, Inc., for five years. As a reward for stellar performance in the home office, you were promoted to public relations director of the French division of Moon Motors, Inc. You took over this post in Paris six months ago. Your firm has found that the French version of the Moon is not competing successfully against the French automobiles in France's industrial resurgence. It decides to consolidate all European production in its new automated Netherlands plant. This requires dropping 3,100 French workers. This is done by divisional management in consultation with the director of employee relations. A terse notice is issued. A storm of protest breaks. The French Minister of Industry heatedly declares: "In the future, new foreign investment programs, particularly from United States firms, must be examined with greatest care." Unions join in demonstrations of protest. French newspapers carry angry editorials. There is much damning of absentee ownership. This violent reaction catches your management flatfooted. Now—

a. What steps do you recommend that management take to end the protests and repair the damage done its reputation in France?

b. What program can you suggest as a means of meeting a similar problem in the future, without creating such bitter reaction on the part of the local citizenry, if you are consulted ahead of time?

ADDITIONAL READING

CANDIDO DE SOUZA ANDRADE, *Entender Relacoes Publicas*. Sao Paulo, Brazil: Rua Miler, 2nd Ed., 1965.

PIERRE BRUNEAU, *Magiciens de la publicité*. Paris: Gallimard, 1956.

PETER COLLINS, "Press Suites—European Style," *Public Relations Journal*, Vol. 24, June, 1968.

FRANCIS DUMONT, *Partage du Quatrieme Pouvoir*. Paris: l'Institut de Relations Publiques, 1969.

FRANK JEFKINS, *Public Relations in World Marketing*. London: Crosby Lockwood & Son, 1966. An appendix gives British Institute's code of ethics.

GEOFFREY KEAN, *The Public Relations Man Abroad*. New York: Frederick A. Praeger, 1968. Superficial treatment of practice's international growth; aimed at U. S. corporations.

OLLE KELLERMAN, "Public Relations in Scandinavia," *Gazette*, Vol. 9, No. 2, 1963.

ERIC LINDSTROM, *PR Fallet, tjugoen exempel pa public relations i praktiken*. Stockholm: Forum, 1959. (The Question of Public Relations. Twenty-one Examples.)

J. P. MALAN and J. A. L'ESTRANGE, *Public Relations Practice in South Africa*. Johannesburg, South Africa: Hansa Press (Pty) Ltd., 1965.

FRANCOIS DE TEYSSIER and JOSETTE DORRA, *Les Milieux Financiers et Les Relations Publiques*. Paris: Editions Denis Huisman, 1966.

CHARLES W. TISDALL, "The Realities of Public Relations in Canada," *Public Relations Quarterly*, Vol. 10, Winter, 1966.

LOET A. VELMANS, "Trends in Europe Today," *Public Relations Quarterly*, Vol. 13, Spring, 1968.

CHAPTER
28

TOWARD
A
PROFESSION

Neither ambition, social snobbery, nor self-assertion will serve to
create a profession or define its area of autonomy; these
will in the long run be determined by the function fulfilled.
—WILLARD HURST

The past three decades have seen a phenomenal growth in public relations. This period has brought increasing signs of professionalism. Public relations, as an organized calling, has come a long way since the days of Theodore Vail, Ivy Lee, and Pendleton Dudley. It still has a considerable distance to go before it matures into a profession.

Events of the post-Depression period awakened widespread interest and increased acceptance of the public relations concept. World War II brought new opportunities, new demonstrations of utility, and new techniques and channels of communication. The tensions and problems of the uneasy postwar years accentuated and extended these developments. National prosperity underwrote the expansion of old programs and the birth of new ones. Expanding world trade and political conflict extended the practice abroad. After a generation of somewhat dizzy expansion, public relations is in the process of settling down.

Contemporary practice has been highlighted by these developments:

1. Steady growth in number of programs in industries, institutions, social agencies, government bureaus, and trade associations. Already established programs have tended to mature and to move beyond straight publicity.

2. An accelerated growth in the number of independent counseling firms, especially in the communication hubs of New York, Washington, Chicago, and Los Angeles.

3. A tremendous spurt in the number of books, articles, and journals devoted to the practice, its philosophy, problems, and techniques. The literature is already voluminous, though somewhat repetitive.

4. Organization of new associations for practitioners and a redirection of those already established. Many of these are now quite mature.

5. An increase in the number of college courses and students, coupled with growth in breadth and depth of the courses. Increased support for collegiate preparation from practitioners and increasing acceptance of young graduates.

6. Internationalization of the practice and its standards.

Reflecting on these and like developments, Pimlott observed: [1] "As is illustrated by the literature, the growth of the associations, and the state of university training, the public relations group has made dramatic progress during and since the war, but its evolution is still in a fluid phase." In the years since Pimlott made his study, the function has gained wider acceptance, become more secure within organizations, and strengthened its competence. The practice is steadily moving toward maturity as it shifts its emphasis to counseling and communication. Today few debate the function's *essentialty* in a society in desperate need of clarifying communication and skillful mediation. Today the questions focus on the *ethics* and *competence* of practitioners.

OUT OF THE SHADOWS

Public relations has come to occupy an important role in society, and, consequently, it is coming under closer public scrutiny. This is proper. Irwin Ross argues, rightly, in his *Image Merchants:* [2] "We should all gain, in sum, if the PR man were edged out of the shadows and subjected to the glare of attention normally reserved for his clients. These days he is important enough to warrant continual scrutiny."

Public concern about the practitioner and his impact on society has been aroused by a number of spectacular cases that made the nation's front pages in recent years. Each of these is laden with issues of concern to the public and the practitioner alike.

THE TRUCKERS VERSUS THE RAILROADS AND CARL BYOIR

A bitter no-holds-barred public relations battle between the trucking industry and the railroads culminated in a lengthy legal battle, which established the practitioner's right to plead a client's case in the court of public opinion, however unethical such pleading might be. In what *Fortune* termed "The Railroad-Truckers Brawl," [3] both parties used dubious and dishonest means to sway public opinion. The railroads had hired Carl Byoir & Associates in August, 1949. Four other agencies seeking the account recommended plans similar to those proposed by the Byoir firm. The

---

[1] J. A. R. Pimlott, *Public Relations and American Democracy* (Princeton, N.J.: Princeton University Press, 1951), p. 21.

[2] This book, published by Doubleday & Co. in 1959, profiled the major agencies and offered illuminating insights on a practitioner's life and role in society. The quote is from page 271.

[3] *Fortune*, Vol. 47, June 1953. Also see Robert Bendiner, "The 'Engineering of Consent'— A Case Study," *The Reporter*, Vol. 13, August 11, 1955.

Pennsylvania Motor Truck Association engaged Allied Public Relations Associates, another New York agency, to present the truckers' case. The battle was on.

The legal battle opened in 1953, when forty-one interstate long-haul trucking firms and their trade association, the Pennsylvania Motor Truck Association, brought suit against thirty-five eastern railroads, the Eastern Railroad Presidents Conference, and Carl Byoir & Associates. The truckers charged the defendants with conspiring to drive them out of business in violation of the Sherman Antitrust Law. The suit had been triggered when a disgruntled Byoir employee took the railroad account files to the truckers.

The trial in the U. S. District Court for Eastern Pennsylvania took a year and resulted in 6,000 pages of testimony. In October, 1957, Judge Thomas J. Clary ruled in favor of the truckers.[4] The Byoir firm and the railroads appealed to the U. S. Court of Appeals which upheld Judge Clary's finding in a 2-to-1 decision in 1959. Chief Judge Wallace Biggs dissented.[5]

Encouraged by Biggs' dissent, Byoir and the railroads carried their case to the United States Supreme Court. They contended that a campaign aimed at influencing public opinion—no matter how untruthful—could not constitute a violation of the Antitrust Law. Moreover, they held that Judge Clary's enjoinment of them from further public relations activity stood as an infringement of their rights of free speech. The United States Supreme Court agreed and reversed the decision of the lower court in a unanimous opinion, handed down February 20, 1961. Justice Hugo Black wrote the opinion, which said, in part: [6]

> In doing so, we have restored what appears to be the true nature of the case—a "no-holds-barred fight" between two industries, both of which are seeking control of a profitable source of income. Inherent in such fights, which are commonplace in the halls of legislative bodies, is the possibility, and in many instances even the probability, that one group or the other will get hurt by the arguments that are made. In this particular instance, each group appears to have utilized all the political powers it could muster in an attempt to bring about the passage of laws that would help it or injure the other. But the contest itself appears to have been conducted along lines normally accepted in our political system, except to the extent that each group has deliberately deceived

[4] For the decision, see "Noerr Motor Freight, Inc. *et al.* v. Eastern Railroad Presidents Conference, *et al.,*" *Federal Supplement,* Vol. 155, Dec. 23, 1957, pp. 768–841. For thoughtful discussion of this case, see: "Pressure Politics in Pennsylvania: The Truckers vs. The Railroads," by Andrew Hacker in *The Uses of Power,* ed. Alan F. Westin (Harcourt, Brace, and World, 1962).

[5] In 273 F. 2d 218 (1959).

[6] 81 *Supreme Court Reporter,* 523, February 20, 1961.

the public and public officials. And that deception, reprehensible as it is, can be of no consequence so far as the Sherman Act is concerned. . . ."

The Court's unanimous opinion "was a rather resounding affirmation of a legal right which has almost never been involved in litigation, the right of petition." A noted authority on Constitutional law further notes "that the right of people to associate together in order to make their activities effective" was closely allied in this case.[7] The legal right of a counselor to plead a cause in public is now clearly defined. The ethical problems posed by the malpractice of both agencies remain for solution. That this battle continues in "no holds barred" fashion was evidenced in 1968 when Senator Lee Metcalf told the U. S. Senate that the railroads were using the *Industrial News Review*—a subsidized canned editorial service—to plant anti-truck articles in the press. The trucking association followed by publishing a bitter pamphlet, "The Manipulators—the Duping of a Free Press by Railroad Propagandists" later that year.[8] The railroads stopped employing the Byoir agency in 1964.

THE S.E.C. INVESTIGATION

A biting indictment of the malpractices of a handful of practitioners was made in 1963 by the United States Securities and Exchange Commission. In a voluminous report, climaxing several years' investigation of the securities market, the S.E.C. indicted financial publicists for using false or misleading information to manipulate the stock market and for trading in the stocks of their clients.[9] Financial editors were found guilty of violating their responsibilities to readers in similar ways. For example, a business editor of *Time* was found to be profiting from his selection and play of business news. He was dismissed by *Time*.

The S.E.C. report said, "Corporate publicity examined ran the gamut from straightforward reporting of corporate affairs to what can only be described as deliberate attempts to falsify a company's financial position and prospects." In citing cases of practitioners greatly profiting from stock trading, the S.E.C. said that these examples "are set forth not to imply manipulative or any other improper intent, but only to demonstrate the conflicts of interest in such situations." [10]

[7] David Fellman, *The Constitutional Right of Association* (Chicago: University of Chicago Press, 1963), pp. 10–12.

[8] Published by American Trucking Associations, Inc., 1616 P St., N.W., Washington, D.C.

[9] Securities and Exchange Commission, *The Report of Special Study of the Securities Markets*, Parts I and III (Washington, D.C.: Government Printing Office, 1963). A summary appeared in *The New York Times*, April 4, 1963.

[10] For examples, see "SEC Runs Up Red Flag on Stock-Selling Publicity," *Editor & Publisher*, Vol. 96, April 13, 1963, pp. 13 and 62.

Reporter Peter Bart places most of the responsibility for correcting "this sorry picture" on the press. He says, "PR men are not going to build an effective self-regulatory code nor are advertisers likely to exercise self-restraint in tampering with the news pages." Bart writes: [11]

> If we are to have better reporting, newspapers must assign their top talent, not their castaways, to the business . . . pages. They must pay them as well as they do their top writers. . . . On the negative side, newspaper and magazine editors must deal sternly with reporters who do favors for friends and help plant dishonest stories. They must also bar junkets for reporters and for financial editors. And they must find a way to keep the PR men out of the newsroom. . . .

The S. E. C.'s prosecution of Texas Gulf Sulphur for issuing a false, misleading press release pertaining to a Canadian ore discovery, and of Great American Industries for making exaggerated claims about planned acquisitions were discussed in Chapter Twenty. Use of publicity to rig the stock market dates back to Jay Gould. It must be strongly emphasized that abuses exposed by the S. E. C. in its 1963 probe and in these prosecutions have involved only a few journalists and practitioners. Yet there are many other unethical acts in the business field which do not violate the law.[12]

THE TIDEROCK CASE

An article, "To Smoke or Not to Smoke—That Is Still the Question," written by Stanley Frank, was published in the January 15, 1968, issue of *True* magazine. The article attempted to debunk evidence linking smoking and lung cancer. Two months later, March 3, 1968, a similar article entitled "Cigarette Cancer Link Is Bunk," bylined by "Charles Golden," was published in the *National Enquirer*. It made the same spurious claims. Shortly after these articles appeared, *The Wall Street Journal* charged that these articles were placed by the Tobacco Institute and that Stanley Frank and "Charles Golden" were the same person.

When the evidence linking cigarettes with lung cancer began to accumulate, the Tobacco Institute, trade association of the tobacco companies, retained Hill & Knowlton, Inc. as counsel in 1955. In late 1967, the Institute also retained Rosser Reeves's Tiderock Corporation as a

---

[11] In "How to Read the Financial Pages Without Going Broke," *Harper's Magazine*, Vol. 227, August, 1963.

[12] For examples, see: "Reporters Allege Pressure by I.T.T.," *New York Times*, April 21, 1967; "Conflicts of Interest, Pressures Still Distort Some Papers' Coverage," *Wall Street Journal*, July 25, 1967; Robert Lewis Shayon, "The duPont Awards: Finis?," *Saturday Review*, March 11, 1967.

second public relations agency. The idea for Frank's article in *True* magazine originated with Douglas Kennedy, then its editor, and Joseph Field, a public relations executive for Brown and Williamson Tobacco Corporation. Frank received $500 from *True* initially, later was paid an additional $1,250 for the article and a $250 bonus because it was featured on the cover. The article was accepted by *True* in April, 1967, and that October, Frank was hired by Hill & Knowlton for its staff. Bert Goss, H. & K. chairman, asserts: "We negotiated with (Frank) and made him an offer before we had any knowledge whatsoever that he had written a tobacco article." [13] Goss repudiates non-attribution or "third party" tactics. Because of the Tiderock affair, Hill & Knowlton resigned the Tobacco Institute account at the end of 1968.

The evidence indicates that publication of the debunking obfuscation of cigarette's link to lung cancer was a Tiderock project. As soon as the article was accepted for *True,* Tiderock made extensive preparations to promote it and to send out reprints. December, 1967, advertisements for the forthcoming article were published in sixty-three newspapers. These ads, carrying such statements as "At the moment all we can say for sure is . . . there is absolutely no proof that smoking causes human cancer," did not disclose who paid for the ads. More than one-million reprints of the article were mailed after its publication, again without the source's being disclosed. The reprints went to the medical and news media personnel, opinion leaders, etc. "Although Tiderock was administering and guiding all phases of the reprint distribution, it had the (Ted) Barash Agency address a letter to the AMA seeking a mailing list ostensibly for the purpose of gaining greater circulation for *True*." The advertising and reprint promotion cost $107,628.77.[14]

OTHER EXAMPLES

The involvement of John F. Fergus, at the time a public relations employee of Eversharp-Schick Company, in the plot to smear then United States Senator Thomas Kuchel of California is another distasteful example of the mis-use of public relations. Patrick J. Frawley Jr., president and chief executive officer of Eversharp and Schick, told a grand jury in 1965 that he hired Fergus in 1962 ". . . to make speeches on free enterprise and against Communism." In the 1960s, Schick spent hundreds of thousands of dollars sponsoring right wing radio and TV programs and ad-

---

[13] Letter to Scott M. Cutlip, dated February 24, 1969.

[14] The details of this malpractice are set forth in the Federal Trade Commission's "Report to Congress Pursuant to the Federal Cigarette Labeling and Advertising Act," dated June 30, 1968, pp. 24–30.

vertising in ultraconservative publications.[15] On July 19, 1965, Fergus was fined $500 and put on three years' probation after pleading no contest to a charge of wrongfully reflecting on a person's moral reputation.[16] He had been indicted earlier in 1965 on charges of conspiracy to commit libel, along with two other men. The plot was aimed at the defeat of Senator Kuchel, a liberal Repulican.

Public relations suffered another black eye when it became known that the First Pennsylvania Banking and Trust Company of Philadelphia had bribed a *Philadelphia Inquirer* reporter through its public relations firm, Ball Associates. Harry J. Karafin was for many years a reporter who, in the words of *Columbia Journalism Review,* "used his power as an investigative reporter . . . to collect from those who might be exposed by his stories." In November, 1967, Karafin and Joseph Ball, a public relations counselor, were indicted by a grand jury on charges of blackmail, unlawful solicitation and conspiracy. They "were accused of collecting fees as public relations men after promising to have laudatory stories published or threatening 'to expose' prospective clients in the newspaper." [17] The bank paid Karafin $61,000 over a five-year period through Ball's agency. Their machinations were first exposed April 4, 1967, by *Philadelphia,* later detailed in a fifteen-column article in the *Inquirer.*[18] Karafin was found guilty of blackmail and corrupt soliciting by a jury October 2, 1968.[19] He appealed his conviction to the Superior Court of Pennsylvania January 9, 1970. As of April, 1970, Ball had not been tried.[20]

Such misdeeds in the guise of public relations are the exception but get wide publicity, thus contributing to the taint that handicaps the practice.

THE FULBRIGHT HEARINGS

Widespread public discussion about the propriety of United States public relations firms' representing foreign governments and the need to label foreign propaganda ensued in the wake of extensive hearings held by the United States Senate Committee on Foreign Relations in 1963. This committee, headed by Senator J. W. Fulbright, conducted an extensive investigation over a two-year period into the "activities of non-diplomatic

[15] Donald Janson, "Right-Wing Groups Gain in Drawing Financial Aid," *New York Times,* June 28, 1965, p. 22.

[16] "Two in Kuchel Case Are Fined $500 Each," *New York Times,* July 20, 1965.

[17] "Jury Indicts 2 in PR Blackmail," *Editor & Publisher,* Dec. 16, 1967, p. 28.

[18] "The Karafin Case," *Columbia Journalism Review,* Spring, 1967, p. 3.

[19] *New York Times,* October 2, 1968, p. L 2.

[20] Letter, Erwin Lodge, Acting Clerk Quarter Sessions Court, County of Philadelphia, dated April 22, 1970.

representatives of foreign principals in the United States." [21] The probe was triggered by the work of lobbyists representing foreign sugar interests. This probe raised anew an old and thorny question for practitioners and the public alike. This question had been debated in the mid-1930s by congressional committees investigating the services rendered Nazi Germany by the Carl Byoir and Ivy Lee-T. J. Ross public relations firms. This led to the passage of a Foreign Agents Registration Act in 1938. This law was not intended to muzzle spokesmen for foreign countries but to make them identify themselves so that officials and the public would not be misled by what they said or did. As of 1970, about 450 such agents were registered. Many of these are practitioners.

The right of a public relations firm to represent a foreign principal was not challenged in this investigation. In Senator Fulbright's view, two serious problems were raised by the findings: [22] (1) Identification of material emanating from foreign governments so that the reader or viewer may know the source of such information. He recognized that disclosure of the source of materials fed from foreign principals through their United States agents must be handled by editors and cannot be legislated. (2) The payment of money or other valuable consideration to newsmen for publication of material from foreign sources. In the latter category are listed press junkets, entertainment, and the presentation of gifts or money.

Fulbright's committee revealed that the 1938 law was being skirted, if not openly violated, and that many practitioners resorted to unscrupulous tactics. One of the flagrant violators was Hearst Columnist Igor Cassini, indicted in 1963 for failure to register as an agent of Rafael Trujillo, despicable dictator of the Dominican Republic. Cassini, who wrote under the name "Cholly Knickerbocker," also operated a public relations firm, the Martial Company, although he never took part in professional activities. His firm had $800,000 in billings in 1962. Cassini pleaded "no contest" in 1964 and was fined $10,000 and placed on probation for six months. The Senate Committee exposed many unhealthy practices on the part of both practitioner and press.[23]

[21] *Activities of Non-diplomatic Representatives of Foreign Principals in the United States.* Hearings Before the Committee on Foreign Relations, 88th Congress, 1963, Parts 1 through 13. Washington, D.C.: U. S. Government Printing Office, 1963. These hearings provide illuminating reading on shortcomings of public relations and the nation's press. For a view of the comparable problem in Britain, see: *Report from the Select Committee on Members' Interests (Declaration),* 4th December, 1969. London: Her Majesty's Stationery Office, 49 High Holborn, London WC 1.

[22] Philip N. Schuyler, "U. S. Seeks Ways to Tell People Who Pays for News," *Editor & Publisher,* Vol. 96, August 24, 1963, pp. 9 and 52.

[23] As a result, the Registration Act was amended in 1966. For provisions, see U. S. Department of Justice, *The Foreign Agents Registration Act of 1938* (Washington, D. C.: Government Printing Office, 1967).

The malpractices brought out in these and similar instances need to be kept in perspective. These infractions are those of a minority, "the tenth-tenth of public relations." L. L. L. Golden observes: "Of course there are charlatans in public relations, as there are in every sphere of human activity. But there are probably no more frauds in public relations than in any other line of work. Most public relations agencies and individuals adhere to ethical standards."

Golden then makes the point that many practitioners fail to see: "One of the great problems in the new business of public relations is the refusal of many practitioners to face the fact that they are special pleaders. But if they themselves recognize the role, and others with whom they deal are not given a false impression, part of the problem is solved." *The practitioner is an advocate*. John W. Hill once said: "Public relations can't cover up mistakes—and shouldn't. However, no one's going to put the worst face on anything. We're primarily advocates and we draw on a deep reservoir of experience in advocating our client's causes."

This underlines what we conceive to be the social justification of the public relations function in a free society: *to ethically, effectively plead the cause of a client or organization in the forum of public debate.* It is a basic democratic right that every idea, individual, or institution shall have a full and fair hearing in the public forum. *To obtain such a hearing today, the individual, idea, or institution needs the expertise of a skilled advocate.* It is our democratic philosophy that the merit of any idea or institution is determined by its ability to get accepted in the public opinion market place.

PUBLIC RELATIONS' IMPACT ON SOCIETY

Of much more importance than these infrequent headline-making incidents is the fundamental question of the function's impact on society. The proponent of public relations can document many values of its work to society. The critic can cite, with equal validity, many harmful effects. These do not damn the function nor vitiate its essentiality; they stand as a challenge to those who would make this a constructive calling. The greatest virtue and sin of public relations is its chameleon nature. Practitioners can adapt easily from fund-raising for a hospital to rousing public opinion against Medicare. In so doing, their "sin" is appearing to have no convictions of their own, of serving the master who pays them. Public relations is not based on a *morality* of its own, but rather on the possession of technical skills in communication and advocacy. The practitioner's position is much like that of the lawyer. Central to this matter is the fact that the practice is shaped by the desires of employers or clients and the opportunism of practitioners. Ivy Lee's one-time partner, William W. Harris, noted this long ago: "If the public relations man is superfluous or useless, that is a matter for the corporation he serves." Raucher thinks public relations lacks "its own goals or social responsibility."

Ultimately, public relations must be judged on the basis of its social utility. Yardsticks for this judgment could be:

1. The social utility of public relations rests in its promotion of free, ethical competition of ideas, individuals, and institutions in the market place of public opinion.
2. Social utility is diminished to the extent that competition of ideas, individuals, and institutions is suppressed in campaigns.
3. Social utility is served to the extent that the goals underlying influence attempts are revealed.
4. Social utility is diminished to the extent that public opinion is not permitted to come to bear on issues once they are made public.
5. Social utility is diminished when the origins of public relations are hidden or ascribed to other than their true source.

Two large minuses can be written against the practice: (1) Public relations has cluttered our already choked channels of communication with the debris of pseudo-events and phony phrases that confuse rather than clarify; (2) Public relations has corroded our channels of communication with cynicism and "credibility gaps." Too often the thrust is to obfuscate and obscure rather than to clarify—and in a day when complex public issues must be made clear.

Robert Heilbroner recognizes public relations as a social force and charges it with a major part "in the general debasement of communications from which we suffer." He wrote: [24]

> No one can quarrel with the essential function that public relations fills as a purveyor of genuine ideas and information. No one denies that many public relations men, working for corporations as well as for colleges or causes, honestly communicate things which are worth communicating. Nor can anyone absolve public relations for loading the communications channels with noise. We read the news and suspect that behind it lies the "news release." We encounter the reputation and ascribe it to publicity. Worst of all, we no longer credit good behavior with good motives, but cheapen it to the level of "good public relations."

Today when a large corporation announces a scholarship program for deserving youths or makes a big gift to the hospital drive, we cynically shrug it off as "smart public relations." Typical is this reaction of a *Mil-*

[24] "Public Relations: The Invisible Sell," *Harper's Magazine,* Vol. 214, June, 1957, pp. 23–31. Reprinted in Christenson and McWilliams, *Voice of the People.*

waukee Journal editorial writer in commenting on an oil company's giving away cardboard bluebird houses: "Perhaps some crafty public relations man is behind the scheme." Awarding a plaque or citation is a standard gimmick. This has reached the point where it is difficult to distinguish the award for achievement from the award for publicity purposes. Eric Sevareid notes wryly:

> For some time now, Gresham's Law has been operating with wild abandon—bad honorary degrees, scrolls, plaques, medals, and gilt-painted zinc trophies have been driving out the good ones, exactly as "celebrity" has been driving out the precious word, "fame," and as the serried rows of Publicity Saints have been taking over the field from Great Men.

Practitioners also stand indicted, with some validity, for loading our channels of communication with noise and clogging them with the clutter of manufactured stories. In his book, *The Image,* Historian Daniel Boorstin introduces a useful term, *pseudo-events,* and argues that these serve to blur, rather than clarify, public issues. Boorstin writes: [25]

> The disproportion between what an informed citizen needs to know and what he can know is ever greater. The disproportion grows with the increase of the officials' power of concealment and contrivance. The news gatherers' need to select, invent, and plan correspondingly increases. Thus inevitably our whole system of public information produces always more "packaged" news, more pseudo-events.

Though Boorstin primarily blames newsmen for this, practitioners are the major producers of pseudo-events. An event planned to promote a cause in the public interest and in keeping with the character of the sponsor has a legitimate place in public relations. This no one will deny. It is the phony event to promote a dubious product or cause that comes under fire. Precious news space or time given to Miss Universe cannot be used in explaining the complex situation in Southeast Asia. *Ethical public relations contributes to clarification of public issues, not to their distortion or obfuscation.*

Even after the practitioners representing competing parties have served their roles as *advocates* by providing the public with a persuasive presentation of each party's position, there remains a nagging doubt about whether the public is adequately informed as a result. One of the epochal public relations battles of modern time was that waged between the advocates of the nation's steel companies and the United Steelworkers' Union

---

[25] The quotation is from page 17. This is a provocative if somewhat thinly-researched and peevish book, but one worth reading. (New York: Atheneum, 1962.)

in 1959 and 1960. Both sides spent millions of dollars presenting their case before and during the long 1959–1960 steel strike but with little noticeable result. A special committee of the National Council of Churches of Christ, which made an exhaustive study of the implications of this dispute, said, "Both sides in this dispute indulged in one of the most spectacular utilizations of mass communications media to be employed in an industrial conflict, involving advertisment, radio, and television programs, and direct mailings."

The Council of Churches committee raises a basic question: [26]

> The methodology for influencing public opinion is full of ethical issues and it is to be noted that during the steel dispute no way was available whereby the public could obtain an objective evaluation of the claims which were being pushed so energetically by both sides.

Similarly, a study of the press's treatment of scientific findings linking cigarette smoking to lung cancer made by editors of the *Columbia Journalism Review* concluded: "Coverage has been sufficiently fragmented, uneven, and affected by publicity efforts on both sides to cause confusion." [27]

Presenting all sides of an issue and providing an objective, balanced appraisal of the merits of conflicting views is a responsibility of the news media, not the practitioner. This the Council of Churches Committee recognized: "When the media of mass communications are used by great power groups to try to win the American public to accept their point of view there is an open necessity for some objective evaluation of the disputed facts. We feel that the newspapers and magazines did not serve the public adequately in this regard and that the radio and television networks did little better. . . ." The editors of the *Columbia Journalism Review* made the same point: "An important place for clarifying confusing news— the editorial page—has been little used."

The large plusses are: (1) By stressing the need for public approval, practitioners improve the conduct of organizations they serve; (2) Practitioners serve the public interest by making all points of view articulate in the public forum; (3) Practitioners serve our segmented, scattered society by using their talents of communication and mediation to replace misinformation with information, and discord with rapport.

Much constructive good can be accurately ascribed to the ethical practice—on behalf of our nation, our colleges and community chests, our corporations and conservation, and mental health and professional

---

[26] "In Search of Maturity in Industrial Relations," The Report of a Special Committee of the National Council of the Churches of Christ in the U.S.A., 1960. See Part IV.

[27] "Smoking and News Coverage of a Decade of Controversy," in Vol. II, Summer, 1963, issue, p. 12.

associations. Opportunities for serving the public have been stressed throughout this book. Public relations' benefits are written in sound economic enterprises providing profit for investors, jobs for employees, and goods for consumers; in the billions raised to build buildings, endow professorships, and provide scholarships in our nation's colleges; in campaigns for eradication of disease; in the lessening of racial and religious discrimination; and in broader understanding of our national and international problems. *The potential good inherent in ethical, effective public relations is as limitless as the potential for enduring world peace that must be won in the minds of men.*

A SEARCH FOR STANDARDS

As public relations has gained stability, and as public debate about its social role has mounted, the search by practitioners for ethical standards has been intensified. There has been a great sensitivity to "public relations for public relations" in this period. This sensitivity has brought some pious platitudes and some self-serving rationalization; it has also brought some honest soul-searching and sincere effort to enforce ethical standards within the craft. This self-searching has resulted in self imposed standards.

One is the serious effort being made by practitioners jointly to surround performance of the function with the status and methods of a profession—in short, *to qualify functionally.* The second is concern for the behavior of individual practitioners—the effort *to qualify morally.* The third aspect is the calibre and kind of training required for recruits and the need for more basic communications research. This represents an effort *to qualify through knowledge and expertness.* These standards tend to fuse with each other in the history of the function in the period of its most rapid growth.

Much of the craft's discussion of ethics and standards is akin to whistling one's way through a graveyard. Counselor David Finn says bluntly: [28] "Unfortunately, it is a subject not being discussed openly and straightforwardly in business circles, which in itself is not a good sign. Rationalizations, self-righteousness, and platitudes do not get rid of discerning challenges—nor do untalked-about skeletons in the closet make for well-adjusted consciences."

It ought to be kept in mind that "no abstract logic has created the concept of the professions." Rather, as a noted legal historian has pointed out, "practice and experience in making society function have led to the

---

[28] In "Struggle for Ethics in Public Relations," *Harvard Business Review,* Vol. 37, January/February 1959, p. 30.

definition of some occupations as professional, and have from time to time determined which ways of earning a living should fit the professional category." [29] Many callings have striven for the status of profession. Few have won it. Much of this effort is self-serving; some of it is public-spirited.

Charles Dollard, while president of the Carnegie Corporation, observed: "While this pressure toward professionalism, might in one sense be labeled selfish, the results are beneficent for society as a whole. Professionalizing any activity tends to institutionalize the best ways of doing the job, and to create standards of quality which serve the public interest. This extension of the professional idea has by and large brought us safer bridges, better houses, higher standards in business, banking, and other fields."

To measure the advance of the contemporary practice toward the much-sought goal of professionalism there must be yardsticks. Professor John Marston lists these characteristics which distinguish professions from merely skilled occupations: [30]

1. A defined area of competence;
2. An organized body of knowledge of some consequence;
3. Self-consciousness;
4. Competence of entrants determined by controlled access;
5. Continuing education;
6. Support of research;
7. Aid in the education of competent replacements;
8. Independence.

Over-all there must be professional competence, recognition of obligations to others in the profession, and a dedication to serve, not injure, the public welfare.

Even though practitioners continue to be "beset with all sorts of complexes and doubts as to their own worthiness," movement in these professional directions is apparent. Many stabilizing influences are at work. Much solid progress has been recorded.

The trend toward professionalism can be seen in these assets: (1) a strong national society supplemented by several strong specialized associations; (2) a code of ethics clearly spelled out; (3) a National Judicial Council created to enforce its standards upon PRSA members and the beginnings of such enforcement in the early 1960s; (4) stiff eligibility standards for membership in PRSA, including an accreditation examination;

---

[29] Willard Hurst, "The Professions of American Life," *Public Relations Journal,* Vol. 13, August, 1957.

[30] "Hallmarks of a Profession," *Public Relations Journal,* Vol. 24, July, 1968.

(5) training, education, and research in many universities and colleges, a small part of which is supported by PRSA; (6) a large and growing body of technical books, papers, and journals; (7) organizational status for the practitioner; (8) increasing contributions to the public service by practitioners.[31]

The 1960s saw most of the foundation stones for a professional structure being put into place. When this foundation is complete, an enduring profession can be built upon something more substantial than self-pleading. Professional recognition cannot be a simple case of practitioners' lifting themselves by telling one another that they are professionals. Public opinion determines what is a profession—a fact that practitioners ought to know better than most. *The task of the practitioner is to earn the status.* Many are doing that.

TOWARD A CODE OF ETHICS

As self-consciousness and a sense of cohesiveness have developed, there has been increasing concern for social responsibility. Most practitioners are demonstrating an earnest effort to qualify morally. These exertions are reflected in a number of codes of professional standards for public relations practice. The principal code is that of the Public Relations Society of America. PRSA's first Code of Professional Standards was adopted in 1954. It was revised in 1959 and further strengthened in 1963. It is included as an appendix. The first penalty for violating these standards was meted out in 1962, when a member was censured for attempting to take away the account of another practitioner. Two members were censured in 1963. Another was suspended in 1964. In a five-year period, 1965 through 1969, twenty-one cases involving apparent unethical practices came before the PRSA Grievance Board. Six of these cases were filed with the judicial panels. In the six cases acted upon, one member was supended, one was reprimanded, one was censured, and three were dismissed. There have been instances when counselors were able to beat the charges filed against them. Yet the fact remains that public relations is the one major segment of mass communications making a serious effort to police its behavior.

Codes of behavior will lack wholly effective means of enforcement until and unless there is legal certification of practitioners. We believe that there must be controlled access, through licensing, to the title of "public relations counselor." This is the only way that the frauds and flacks can be

---

[31] For example a PRSA survey in 1967 showed that its members devote an average of 4.9 hours a week—or the equivalent of 32 working days per year—to voluntary public service activities. See: James E. Pitt, "PR Organizes for Public Service," *Public Relations Journal,* Vol. 25, November, 1969.

separated from legitimate practitioners. Licensing should be done to protect society as well as to advance the cause of professionalism. Codes of ethics are not the whole answer.

Practical men know that adoption of a code of ethics does not automatically bring morality to a calling, but such codes do reflect a concern among the leaders for raising the ethical level. They provide yardsticks of measurement. And, like a New Englander's conscience, a code can make a practitioner "durned uneasy." A distinguished Canadian counselor, Leonard L. Knott, says: [32] "Unfortunately, these codes have little real value unless they are accepted in turn by the employers of practitioners and applied to the conduct of the business itself."

The skill, ethics, and concepts used by the wide variety of practitioners vary greatly. In appraising the ethics, it is well to remember that there is no watertight bulkhead between the practitioners and the society in which they operate. Moreover, they are generally found at the foci of power. And power is not always gained and held by playing according to the rules. When a university scholar can assert that "graft, crime, corruption, 'the fix,' are embedded in the very fabric of our highly competitive society," there is no reason to presume that all practitioners will be immune. When the four horsemen of calumny—"fear, ignorance, bigotry, and smear"—gallop madly about, it is natural to find a few of those skilled in communication and propaganda riding with them. Practitioners will be found to be representative of the institutions and causes they serve.

PROFESSIONAL ORGANIZATIONS

The growth of strong professional associations reflects the serious efforts being made by many practitioners to surround the function with status and to advance its competence. Although these associations include only a minority of those in public relations, they exert considerable influence through their publications, conferences, seminars, awards programs, and central office activities. The largest of these is the Public Relations Society of America, which as of January, 1970 had 7,010 members, 2,000 of whom were accredited. The Society is an amalgam of three older associations organized to win public recognition for this emerging vocation.

The PRSA was formed February 4, 1948, by the merger of the National Association of Public Relations Counsel and the American Council on Public Relations. The former group was first organized in 1936 as the National Association of Accredited Publicity Directors. This organiza-

[32] In his book, *Plain Talk About Public Relations* (Toronto: McClelland and Steward, 1961), p. 3. Book full of good sense by a man who pioneered and shaped the practice in Canada.

tion changed its name in 1944 to reflect the shift in emphasis to public relations. Its membership was composed largely of New York City counselors. The words *national* and *accredited* were used in a very loose sense by this pioneering group. The American Council on Public Relations was started in San Francisco in 1939 as an association for West Coast practitioners.

The goal of forward-looking practitioners and educators for one strong national association, serving all fields of practice, was finally realized July 1, 1961, when the American Public Relations Association merged into PRSA. The American Public Relations Association, headquartered in Washington, D. C., and dominated by trade association practitioners, was organized in 1944 after some seven years' effort among Washington practitioners. At the time of the merger in 1961, PRSA had 3,359 members and APRA 826; 100 practitioners held membership in both organizations.

The APRA made two contributions to advancement of its craft— its Silver Anvil Awards to recognize successful programs and its *Quarterly Review of Public Relations.* Later retitled *Public Relations Quarterly,* it was purchased from Editor Howard Hudson by P.R. Aids, Inc., in 1963. PRSA has continued the Silver Anvil Awards program. The PRSA does much to foster exchange of ideas through its publications and meetings, to promote a sense of professionalism, to provide opportunities for continuing education, and to remind practitioners of the need for more ethical behavior.

The counselors in the Public Relations Society organized a "Counselors' section" in 1960 as a means of dealing more effectively with the problems of special concern to public relations agencies. This section studied counseling fees, issued a booklet defining the role of the counselor, and in 1963 gained PRSA's approval as a voluntary plan of self-accreditation, based on character, experience, and examination. The Counselors' section had 565 members in 1970. PRSA members who were engaged in association work followed suit when they won PRSA's approval for a "Business and Professional Association Section" in 1963. This section had 132 members in 1970. A "Government Section" was formed in 1970. As PRSA continues to expand in size and scope, these sections may well set the pattern for other specialized interest groups. Practitioners for nonprofit agencies complain about the dominance of corporate practitioners in the management of PRSA's affairs.

Several specialized national organizations also have served as spurs for solidarity and professional growth. The broad membership embraced in these vertical groups also indicates the growth in this field. It reflects a sense of common interests and an emerging *esprit de corps* of professionalism.

TITLE	DATE ORGANIZED
Agricultural Relations Council	1953
American College Public Relations Association	1917
American Society for Hospital Public Relations Directors	1964
Chemical Public Relations Association	1952
Bank Marketing Association (Formerly Financial Public Relations Association)	1915
Government Public Relations Association	1949
Library Public Relations Council	1939
National Public Relations Council of Health and Welfare Services	1922
National School Public Relations Association	1935
Railroad Public Relations Association	1952
Religious Public Relations Council	1929

In addition to principal professional groups listed above, a number of informal "inside" groups have developed over the years, with varying degrees of impact in shaping the practice. These include the Wise Men, begun by John W. Hill, Pendleton Dudley, and T. J. Ross, in 1938; the Public Relations Seminar, started in 1951 as an outgrowth of the National Conference of Business Public Relations Executives; Pride and Alarm founded in 1957 by New York-based practitioners who style themselves as "junior Wise Men"; Shop Talk, started in 1965 by twelve New York agencies; and P.R. Counselors Roundtable of Chicago, also established in 1965. These groups function informally and hold their meetings in private. Exclusivity for the "in group" is their hallmark. The Public Relations Seminar annually holds a week-long seminar in some posh resort. Its history has been chronicled by Harold Brayman.[33] Some members of PRSA fear that the proliferation of such groups will drain talent and funds from the field's main general association.

PROFESSIONAL LITERATURE

Related, somewhat, to these associational developments has been the growth in number of journals devoted exclusively to this field, increased space in established periodicals, and a long list of books. PRSA's *Public Relations Journal* emphasizes professionalism, presents case studies, articulates philosophy, and provides a forum for debate on practice and ethics. The *Public Relations Quarterly* is comparable in content, but its articles are often of more depth. *Public Relations News* was started July 17, 1944, by the late Glenn Griswold and his wife, Denny Griswold, as a commercial

---

[33] *Developing a Philosophy for Business Action. A History of the Public Relations Seminar.* Published by the Public Relations Seminar Committee in 1969 in limited edition of 500 copies.

venture. Denny Griswold continues to publish this four-page newsletter. A competitor, *The PR Reporter,* started in 1958 by Charles H. Prout, is now published at Meriden, N. H., by Robert Barbour. More recently, *Jack O'Dwyer's Newsletter* was added to the list. Critical scrutiny of public relations was strengthened by the introduction of a monthly Communications Issue in *Saturday Review.* These specialized publications publicize and promote the maturing practice.

The first comprehensive bibliography of book and periodical literature in this field was published in 1957 under the auspices of PRSA. The second edition, published in 1965, carries nearly 6,000 entries of books and articles about or relevant to the practice.[34] Other publications contribute to the expanding knowledge of public opinion, communication, and public relations:

Advertising Age	Journal of Communication
American City	Journal of Broadcasting
A-V Communication Review	Journal of Personality and
Broadcasting	Social Psychology
Channels	Journal of Marketing
College and University Journal	Journalism Quarterly
Columbia Journalism Review	Marketing/Communications
Editor & Publisher	Nieman Reports
Fortune	Public Opinion Quarterly
Harvard Business Review	Quill
Human Relations	Trends in School Public Relations
It Starts in the Classroom	Television Quarterly
Journal of Applied Psychology	

PROFESSIONAL EDUCATION

University-level instruction in public relations dates from 1920. Concurrent with the beginning of the publicity boom of the 1920s, Jos. F. Wright introduced a publicity course at the University of Illinois. Wright admits that the course was created to bring prestige to his new calling, not in response to student demand. Two years later, in 1922, Frank R. Elliott introduced a publicity course at Indiana University. Both Wright and Elliott organized the first publicity programs for their institutions and taught these courses on a part-time basis. Teaching such courses gave these pioneers faculty status, something they needed in order to earn support among faculty men who looked askance at "propagandists." [35]

---

[34] Compiled by Scott M. Cutlip, *A Public Relations Bibliography,* Second Edition (University of Wisconsin Press, Madison, Wis., 1965).

[35] Scott M. Cutlip, "History of Public Relations Education in the U. S." *Journalism Quarterly,* Vol. 38, Summer, 1961.

The first public relations course with that title was offered in 1923 by Edward L. Bernays, pioneer practitioner, who had just written his *Crystallizing Public Opinion*. Bernays taught the one-semester-credit course in the Department of Journalism of New York University's School of Commerce, Accounts, and Finance for only two years. It was not reinstituted until 1939, when Professor Alfred McClung Lee began teaching it. Typical of the growing demand for skilled publicists to build support was that found in the new fields of social work and philanthropic fund raising. Evart and Mary Swain Routzahn, pioneers of social work public relations, first offered a course in social work publicity in the New York School of Social Work in 1923.

Across the continent, the University of Oregon offered a course in publicity in 1927–1928 taught by George Godfrey, that university's first public relations officer. Godfrey used as a text *Principles of Publicity,* coauthored by Glenn C. Quiett and Ralph D. Casey, one of the best publicity books to appear in that decade. The University of Minnesota made its first offering in 1929 with a course in "Press Relations." In this same period, Professor Byron Christian was pioneering with a course at the University of Washington. In these early years, newspapermen were bitterly critical of giving academic recognition to what they sneeringly derided as "press-agentry." Some still are. For this and other reasons, only a handful of universities added public relations courses to their curricula in the two decades between the two World Wars. By 1945, twenty-one institutions were offering courses.

The years since World War II have brought phenomenal growth in number and depth of public relations courses. In 1946, Professor Lee surveyed fifty-nine major educational institutions and found that at least thirty offered forty-seven courses under public relations titles. Twenty-three of these were being taught in schools or departments of journalism.[36] American journalism schools, which date from the early 1900s, have dominated in the development of public relations education. Some practitioners are dubious about this journalism orientation.

PRSA, under the leadership of Hale Nelson, made a comprehensive survey of public relations education and found that the number of institutions offering courses had tripled between 1946 and 1956. Nelson wrote, evaluating the 1956 research: [37]

> The *extent* of public relations education gives us only one dimension of the whole picture. *What is taught* is a more significant measurement. . . . One very reassuring finding is the practically universal

[36] "Trends in Public Relations Training," *Public Opinion Quarterly*, Vol. 11, Spring, 1947.

[37] "Training for Public Relations," *Public Relations Journal*, Vol. 12, September, 1956.

agreement that all public relations career education should be founded on at least two years of liberal arts. . . . What happens in the junior and senior year varies greatly. The Journalism-oriented PR teaching will bear down heavily on written communications. In the liberal arts-oriented school there is greater emphasis on the social sciences.

In 1970, another survey, financed by PRSA and directed by Professor Ray Hiebert of the University of Maryland, found 303 institutions offered public relations courses. That survey found increased depth in the instruction and much more scholarly research to support it.[38] The majority of the substantial offerings in public relations—sequences or majors—are taught in schools of journalism and communication. Because skill in communications and knowledge constitute the backbone of the practice, this is logical. The dominance of communication-centered education squares with the demands of the practice.[39]

On the surface it would appear that the value of academic instruction has been widely recognized, yet many of America's front-rank institutions still do not offer it. Although we have had more than fifty years of public relations teaching, the pattern of education in this field remains fluid. There continues to be debate by both professional educators and practitioners whether or how to teach public relations. However different their approaches, _public relations teachers are agreed on the need for a specialized program._ They recognize, as do an increasing number of practitioners, that university education and research must play a major role if there is to be progress toward professional status.

Public relations instruction, as it comes to be supported by scholarly research, will grow in scope and in service to this emerging profession. Such education is likely to center on a core of communication skills and public opinion anatomy and analysis. Around this core a serviceable pattern of courses in the social sciences and humanities will be developed to meet the needs. The demand for college training is still not strong. It will grow, however, just as it has in comparable fields.

Education and recruitment have been greatly strengthened by the development of the Public Relations Student Society of America (PRSSA) under the auspices of PRSA. PRSA's interest in organizing student chapters first surfaced in 1950, but it was not until April, 1967, that such an organization was proposed to the PRSA Assembly by Professor Walter

[38] Ray Eldon Hiebert, _Trends in Public Relations Education, 1964–1970._ New York: Foundation for Public Relations Research and Education, 1970. For summary, see: "PR In the Classroom," _Public Relations Journal,_ Vol. 26, September, 1970.

[39] For contrasting views in formative years of public relations education, see: "The University's Role in Public Relations Education," _Journalism Quarterly,_ Vol. 34, Winter, 1957; "Can Public Relations Be Taught in Schools?," _Public Relations Journal,_ Vol. 13, March, 1957.

Seifert of Ohio State University. The proposal won quick approval and the first chapter of PRSSA was chartered in 1968. By January, 1970, thirty-six chapters were functioning. PRSSA's purpose is "to cultivate a favorable and mutually advantageous relationship between students and professional public relations practitioners." To ease the graduating student's way into the field, PRSA in 1969 established a Pre-Associate Membership for PRSSA members.

The advance toward professionalism has been supported by the Foundation for Public Relations Research and Education, a nonprofit organization established by PRSA in 1956 to foster and conduct basic research. In 1959, the Foundation initiated a fellowship program which enables teachers to spend a few weeks working in counseling firms or corporations. A decade later, it set up a graduate scholarship award to a college student working for an advanced degree. In 1961, the foundation began sponsoring a series of annual lectures: the first six of these were by historians and contributed to knowledge of public relations' history. Since 1967, these lectures have been given by practitioners. The foundation also contributed to the literature by subsidizing Morton J. Simon's *Public Relations Law* and Edward J. Robinson's *Public Relations and Survey Research.*

RESEARCH REQUIRED

To earn the title, the practitioner must accept the obligation to work for the advancement of knowledge in the profession. Theodore Roosevelt said: "Every man owes some part of his time to the building up of the industry or profession of which he is a part." *A profession must be built upon a specialized body of knowledge and be devoted to the public interest above the private interest.* Using this yardstick, we should examine this calling's claims to professional status. First, this question: How much specialized knowledge have practitioners contributed to the art of human relations and communication? Are not the scientific methods and procedures borrowed from the social sciences of psychology, sociology, economics, history, and journalism? Can practitioners be hitch-hikers and still lay claim to the title of professional?

One of the sure signs of advancement toward the professional horizon is the increasing demand for research and increasing critical self-examination of old theories. Awareness is growing of the need for re-examination and redirection. Factual foundations will serve to dispel the idea of the practitioner as a sort of witch doctor. In today's world the public relations problems of industry, for example, are every bit as tough and complicated as those of engineering, production, or distribution. Practitioners must approach them as methodically and as thoroughly prepared with facts as engineers, production men, and marketers. Such an approach can come only through extensive research. *Practitioners should strive for certainty in their work.*[40]

Research is not a matter of putting a quarter in the slot, pulling a lever, and then picking up the answers in a tray below. Research takes time and sweat, as well as money. Research in any field is the laborious building of one little brick on another until the structure is finished. It takes lots of bricklayers to build a building. If enough people work at it, the building gets built. *Research, simply put, is the act of searching for information— accurate, reliable, useful information—and organizing this information so that sound conclusions can be drawn.* Research is as much as attitude as it is a method. Research requires an itch and a scratch. The itch is the curiosity to know; the scratch, the will to satisfy the itch.

TOWARD NEW HORIZONS

At mid-century, a practitioner was described this way: [41]

> The public relations counsel is a specialist in verbal symbols. He has been well trained by his home environment and school career in the art of phrase-making. He is prosperous, on the whole, but nevertheless tends to be somewhat more nonconformist, in a political and economic sense, than do his clients. He has been mobile in an upward direction economically, and has often experienced geographic and social mobility as well. He has thus been sensitized to the outlook of people from many social strata. . . . The job of the public relations man is to keep open a two-way channel of communication so that no "misunderstandings" can arise to disturb the true harmony of interests between the publics and management. . . . His is an ideology of defense.

Despite the considerable progress recorded in this generation, public relations still stands short of public acceptance as a true profession. The field lacks maturity, effective self-regulation, full-fledged devotion to the public interest, a generally approved course of training, and a research program of its own. Public relations continues to be plagued with press

[40] The value, uses, and methods of research in public relations are made plain in Edward J. Robinson's *Public Relations and Survey Research,* published in 1969 by Appleton-Century-Crofts. This book, which includes six case studies, was financed by the Foundation for Public Relations Research and Education.

[41] Leila A. Sussman, "The Personnel and Ideology of Public Relations," *Public Opinion Quarterly,* Vol. 12, Winter, 1948–49. Also see Irwin Ross' chapter, "The P.R. Life," in his *Image Merchants* (New York: Doubleday & Company, Inc., 1959).

agents parading as counselors. Then there are those who are more interested in manipulating the opinions of others than in understanding them.
There is still evidence that the function is not fully and widely understood.
The field still has those who cannot qualify *functionally, morally,* or *through
knowledge and expertness.* Many do. *More are needed.*

A start has been made toward deserving the professional status that
practitioners seek. But it is only a start. As public relations practitioners
demonstrate a sense of social responsibility and build a specialized body of
knowledge that they can properly claim as their own, they will surround
the function with the status and prestige its exponents desire. Practitioners
know, better than most, that the way to gain public confidence is to deserve it. This they tell their employers. The practitioner cannot be content
merely to let professional organizations adopt codes of ethics and express
his views.

A newspaper publisher once remarked: "Morality is a highly personal
matter; it is not to be found in the majority vote of the board of directors
of a trade association, or in public expressions of association executives. . . ." Counselor Earl Newsom echoed this when he told his fellow
practitioners: "I suggest that sober self-examination at this point requires
that we come to an understanding of ourselves and what it is we really
want to accomplish. This is not a problem that can be resolved by our
Society or by any committees thereof. It is purely a personal matter. Each
of us lives but once, and each of us wants to spend his life constructively.
. . . I am as certain as can be that if each one of us establishes the highest
of standards for his own conduct, we shall eventually earn the status of
profession." [42]

The future looks promising. The public relations calling has become
an important link in the free communications network upon which this
nation depends for its culture, cohesion, and solidarity. *This profession has
an important role to play in a nation that begs unity, a communion of purpose, and understanding and support among its people—in short, a sense
of community.* In the sustaining of unity and the achievement of it where
it does not now exist, the role of public relations is potentially a vital one.
If practitioners as a group measure up, they will have to practice positive
public relations. They will have to stand for things. Community will not be
achieved in singing hymns of hate.

Hofstadter suggested that conflict may be contained and consensus
reached when "those enlisted in society's contending interests have a basic
minimal regard for each other: one party or interest seeks the defeat of an
opposing interest on matters of policy, but at the same time seeks to avoid

[42] In "Business Does Not Function by Divine Right," *Public Relations Journal,* Vol. 19, January, 1963. In same issue, see Scott M. Cutlip's article, "A Re-Examination of Public
Relations' Platitudes."

crushing the opposition or denying the legitimacy of its existence or values.[43] In achieving and sustaining unity, their role should be carefully weighed by practitioners.

Today's practitioners and the recruits now in training will largely determine the course this calling will take. Public relations can move on to accept John Dewey's challenge of ". . . a responsive art of communication" that will "take possession of the physical machinery of transmission and circulation and breathe life into it."

It can accomplish these things in the best interests of all. Or it can accomplish these things for a greedy minority at the expense of the whole public. Public relations as a technique is a power device. It can be used for good or evil. It can steadily advance toward a mature, responsible profession that contributes to the unity, progress, and public welfare. Or it can decline into what Philosophy Professor William Earnest Hocking has described as a "conscienceless publicity racket" which brings the premiums of advancement to those who have "learned to surround their doings with a cackle of ignorant noise." *Those skilled in its techniques will have to decide which way it will go.*

ADDITIONAL READING

EDWARD L. BERNAYS, *Your Future in Public Relations.* New York: Richards Rosen Press, 1961. A career guide book.

JOHN F. BUDD, JR., "Public Relations Mythology," *Public Relations Journal,* Vol. 24, March, 1968.

JODY DONOHUE, *Your Career in Public Relations.* New York: Julian Messner, 1967. Outlines rewards and requirements of a career in public relations. Contains list of U. S. colleges and universities which offer public relations instruction.

STEPHEN E. FITZGERALD, "How Do You Know?", *Nieman Reports,* Vol. 16, January, 1962.

WILLIAM J. GASKILL, "Accreditation—A Progress Report," *Public Relations Journal,* Vol. 25, September, 1969.

RONALD GOODMAN, "Excellence—An Urgent Need for Public Relations Counselors," *Public Relations Quarterly,* Vol. 11, Winter, 1967.

OTTO LERBINGER and ALBERT J. SULLIVAN, *Information, Influence, and Communication. A Reader.* New York: Basic Books, 1965.

"SEC Reports on Public Relations' Impact on Securities Markets and Public Investors," *Public Relations Journal,* Vol. 19, June, 1963.

[43] Richard Hofstadter, "The Progressive Historians: Turner, Beard, Parrington." (New York: Knopf, 1968).

BERNARD A. SHEPARD, "The Future of PR—A View from the West," *Public Relations Journal*, Vol. 25, November, 1969.

RAYMOND SIMON, ed. *Perspectives in Public Relations.* Norman, Okla.: University of Oklahoma Press, 1966. A book of readings.

ALBERT J. SULLIVAN, "The Value Systems of Public Relations," *Public Relations Quarterly*, Vol. 8, April, July, Oct., 1963. In Three Parts.

PUBLIC RELATIONS SOCIETY OF AMERICA CODE

This Code, adopted in November, 1959, by the 1959 PRSA Board of Directors and ratified by the 1960 PRSA Assembly, was amended in 1963 by the 1963 Board of Directors and 1963 Assembly. It replaces and strengthens a similar Code of Professional Standards for the Practice of Public Relations previously in force since 1954.

Declaration of Principles

Members of the Public Relations Society of America acknowledge and publicly declare that the public relations profession in serving the legitimate interests of clients or employers is dedicated fundamentally to the goals of better mutual understanding and cooperation among the diverse individuals, groups, institutions and elements of our modern society.

In the performance of this mission, we pledge ourselves:

1. To conduct ourselves both privately and professionally in accord with the public welfare.

2. To be guided in all our activities by the generally accepted standards of truth, accuracy, fair dealing and good taste.

3. To support efforts designed to increase the proficiency of the profession by encouraging the continuous development of sound training and resourceful education in the practice of public relations.

4. To adhere faithfully to provisions of the duly adopted Code of Professional Standards for the Practice of Public Relations, a copy of which is in the possession of every member.

Code of Professional Standards for the Practice of Public Relations

This Code of Professional Standards for the Practice of Public Relations is adopted by the Public Relations Society of America to promote and maintain high standards of public service and conduct among its members in order that membership in the Society may be deemed a badge of ethical conduct; that Public Relations justly may be regarded as a profession; that the public may have increasing confidence in its integrity; and that the practice of Public Relations may best serve the public interest.

1. A member has a general duty of fair dealing towards his clients or employers, past and present, his fellow members and the general public.

2. A member shall conduct his professional life in accord with the public welfare.

3. A member has the affirmative duty of adhering to generally accepted standards of accuracy, truth and good taste.

4. A member shall not represent conflicting or competing interests without the express consent of those concerned, given after a full disclosure of the facts; nor shall he place himself in a position where his interest is or may be in conflict with his duty to his client, employer, another member or the public, without a full disclosure of such interests to all concerned.

5. A member shall safeguard the confidences of both present and former clients or employers and shall not accept retainers or employment which may involve the disclosure or use of these confidences to the disadvantage or prejudice of such clients or employers.

6. A member shall not engage in any practice which tends to corrupt the integrity of channels of public communication.

7. A member shall not intentionally disseminate false or misleading infor-

mation and is obligated to use ordinary care to avoid dissemination of false or misleading information.

8. A member shall be prepared to identify to the public the source of any communication for which he is responsible, including the name of the client or employer on whose behalf the communication is made.

9. A member shall not make use of any individual or organization purporting to serve or represent some announced cause, or purporting to be independent or unbiased, but actually serving an undisclosed special or private interest of a member or his client or his employer.

10. A member shall not intentionally injure the professional reputation or practice of another member. However, if a member has evidence that another member has been guilty of unethical, illegal or unfair practices, including practices in violation of this Code, he should present the information to the proper authorities of the Society for action in accordance with the procedure set forth in Article XIII of the Bylaws.

11. A member shall not employ methods tending to be derogatory of another member's client or employer or of the products, business or services of such client or employer.

12. In performing services for a client or employer a member shall not accept fees, commissions or any other valuable consideration in connection with those services from anyone other than his client or employer without the express consent of his client or employer, given after a full disclosure of the facts.

13. A member shall not propose to a prospective client or employer that the amount of his fee or other compensation be contingent on or measured by the achievement of specified results; nor shall he enter into any fee agreement to the same effect.

14. A member shall not encroach upon the professional employment of another member. Where there are two engagements, both must be assured that there is no conflict between them.

15. A member shall, as soon as possible, sever his relations with any or-ganization when he knows or should know that his continued employment would require him to conduct himself contrary to the principles of this Code.

16. A member called as a witness in a proceeding for the enforcement of this Code shall be bound to appear unless, for sufficient reason, he shall be excused by the panel hearing the same.

17. A member shall co-operate with fellow members in upholding and enforcing this Code.

OFFICIAL INTERPRETATIONS OF THE CODE

The following interpretations of Code paragraphs 6, 13 and 14 were adopted by the PRSA Board of Directors on November 6, 1966, and became effective that date.

Interpretation of Code Paragraph 6 which reads, "A member shall not engage in any practice which tends to corrupt the integrity of the channels of public communication."

1. Practices prohibited by this Code paragraph are those which tend to place representatives of media under obligation to the member or his company or his client, such as—

(a.) any form of payment or compensation to a media representative in order to obtain, and in exchange for which, preferential or guaranteed news or editorial coverage in the medium is promised, implied or delivered.

(b.) any retainer of a media employee which involves the use of his position as a media employee for the private purposes of the member or his client or employer where the circumstances of such retainer are not fully disclosed to and accepted by the media employer.

(c.) an agreement between a member and a media employee when such agreement includes a provision that the media employee will secure preferential or guaranteed coverage in the medium for the member, his firm or his client, or utilization by a member of such an agreement between his employer, his firm or his client and a media employee.

(d.) providing vacation trips to media representatives where no news assignment is involved.

(e.) any attempt by a member to lead his employer or client to believe that a member has obtained independent coverage for the employer or client in a medium over which the member has financial or editorial influence or control.

(f.) the use by a member of an investment made by the member, his firm or his client in a medium to obtain preferential or guaranteed coverage in the medium.

(g.) the use by a member of a loan of money made to a medium by the member, his firm or his client to obtain preferential or guaranteed coverage in the medium.

2. This Code paragraph does not prohibit entertaining media representatives for meals or cocktails and hosting press parties, nor does it prohibit the bonafide press junket where media representatives are given an opportunity for on-the-spot viewing of a news event or product or service in which the media representative has a legitimate news interest, provided that independence of action is left to the media representative.

3. This Code paragraph does not prohibit the gift or loan of sample products or services to media representatives whose assignments indicate an interest in such products or services, if the sample products or services are manufactured, sold or rendered by the member's company or client and the sampling is a reasonable method of demonstrating the product or service.

4. This Code paragraph does not prohibit the giving of souvenirs or holiday gifts of nominal value as goodwill gestures to media representatives. Interpretation of Code Paragraph 13

which reads, "A member shall not propose to a prospective client or employer that the amount of his fee or other compensation be contingent on or measured by the achievement of specified results; nor shall he enter into any fee agreement to the same effect."

1. This Code paragraph means that a member may take into consideration the following factors in determining compensation for his services:

(a.) the experience, judgment and skills required to handle the matter properly.

(b.) the characteristics and difficulty of the problems involved.

(c.) the time and labor required.

(d.) the effect on the member's employment by other clients or potential clients.

(e.) the customary or prevailing compensation for similar services.

(f.) the values involved in the matter and the benefits resulting to the client or employer from the services.

(g.) the duration and character of the employment, whether casual or for a continuing period.

(h.) the equipment or personnel investment required in order to perform the function.

2. This Code paragraph prohibits a member from entering into any agreement whereby the member's rate of compensation is determined or conditioned by the amount of newspaper or magazine lineage obtained for the

member's company or client. This applies equally to radio and television coverage, or any form of exposure to a client's message. It applies further to any contingency fee based on increase in sales volume, increase in profit margins, increase in stock value or the attainment of specified political or legislative results. (See also Paragraph 9, "Official Interpretation of the Code as it applies to Financial Public Relations")

3. This Code paragraph means that a member may guarantee to produce certain materials, such as films, feature articles, scripts, news releases, etc., and promise that these will be of high quality or specific type; but any guarantee that such materials, once produced, shall achieve a specified minimum use by media outlets, in other than paid time or space, and failing which use the fee or compensation will be reduced, is a practice prohibited by this Code paragraph.

Interpretation of Code Paragraph 14 which reads, "A member shall not encroach upon the professional employment of another member. Where there are two engagements, both must be assured that there is no conflict between them."

1. This Code paragraph is not designed to curb the freedom of a member to seek employment or business for his counseling firm by all approved and legitimate means. However, it is interpreted to mean that a member shall not invade or infringe upon the counselor-client or employee-employer relationship of another member.

2. A member would not violate this Code paragraph by—

(a.) sending copies of his resume and examples of his work to potential employers even if the employers currently employ members of the Society.

(b.) advertising his or his firm's qualifications in any publication he deems suitable.

(c.) mailing copies of advertisements, circulars or booklets describing his or his firm's services, or copies of speeches or articles to potential clients, provided any such mailing is not one of solicitation and provided the mailing contains no derogatory comment about another member.

(d.) furnishing, upon specific request, factual information about his firm, its principals, personnel and types of services rendered, including names of clients, provided such information contains no proposals to a client of another member.

3. This Code paragraph prohibits a member from seeking individual professional employment by deprecating the character, ability or performance of another member.

4. This Code paragraph requires that a counselor member—

(a.) before soliciting a prospective client, make all reasonable attempts to determine whether the prospective client has an existing relationship with another counselor member who would be replaced, and, if so, make no contact until the incumbent has been notified that his replacement is being considered or the incumbent has been terminated.

(b.) after making an initial contact with a prospective client and subsequently learning that a counselor member-client relationship exists of which he was unaware, shall at that point make no further overtures nor conduct any negotiations with the prospective client until the incumbent has been notified that his replacement is being considered or the incumbent has been terminated.

5. Where a member is solicited by a prospective client to take over the functions currently performed by another member, he shall decline to consider the offer until the incumbent member has been advised that a replacement of his services is being considered. Upon specific request, the member may provide information of a factual nature about his firm and its services but shall make no proposals to the client of another member until he has determined that the incumbent has been notified of a possible change.

6. Where a member is solicited by a prospective client to perform functions separate from those currently performed for the same client by another member, it is the responsibility of the solicited member to determine that the incumbent member has been informed, since both must be assured that there is no conflict between them.

INDEX